Automated Data Collection with R

Automated Data Collection with R

A Practical Guide to Web Scraping and Text Mining

Simon Munzert

Department of Politics and Public Administration, University of Konstanz, Germany

Christian Rubba

Department of Political Science, University of Zurich and National Center of Competence in Research, Switzerland

Peter Meißner

Department of Politics and Public Administration, University of Konstanz, Germany

Dominic Nyhuis

Department of Political Science, University of Mannheim, Germany

WILEY

This edition first published 2015

Registered office
John Wiley & Sons Ltd, The Atrium, Southern Gate, Chichester, West Sussex, PO19 8SQ, United Kingdom

For details of our global editorial offices, for customer services and for information about how to apply for permission to reuse the copyright material in this book please see our website at www.wiley.com.

Library of Congress Cataloging-in-Publication Data

Munzert, Simon.
Automated data collection with R : a practical guide to web scraping and text mining / Simon Munzert, Christian Rubba, Peter Meißner, Dominic Nyhuis.
pages cm
Summary: "This book provides a unified framework of web scraping and information extraction from text data with R for the social sciences"– Provided by publisher.
Includes bibliographical references and index.
ISBN 978-1-118-83481-7 (hardback)
1. Data mining. 2. Automatic data collection systems. 3. Social sciences–Research–Data processing. 4. R (Computer program language) I. Title.
QA76.9.D343M865 2014
006.3′12–dc23

2014032266

A catalogue record for this book is available from the British Library.

ISBN: 9781118834817

Set in 10/12pt Times by Aptara Inc., New Delhi, India.

1 2015

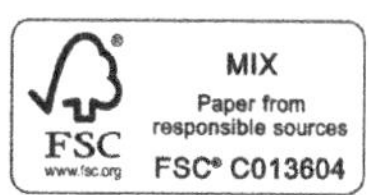

To my parents, for their unending support. Also, to Stefanie.
—Simon

To my parents, for their love and encouragement.
—Christian

To Kristin, Buddy, and Paul for love, regular walks, and a final deadline.
—Peter

Meiner Familie.
—Dominic

Contents

Preface

The rapid growth of the World Wide Web over the past two decades tremendously changed the way we share, collect, and publish data. Firms, public institutions, and private users provide every imaginable type of information and new channels of communication generate vast amounts of data on human behavior. What was once a fundamental problem for the social sciences—the scarcity and inaccessibility of observations—is quickly turning into an abundance of data. This turn of events does not come without problems. For example, traditional techniques for collecting and analyzing data may no longer suffice to overcome the tangled masses of data. One consequence of the need to make sense of such data has been the inception of "data scientists," who sift through data and are greatly sought after by researchers and businesses alike.

Along with the triumphant entry of the World Wide Web, we have witnessed a second trend, the increasing popularity and power of open-source software like R. For quantitative social scientists, R is among the most important statistical software. It is growing rapidly due to an active community that constantly publishes new packages. Yet, R is more than a free statistics suite. It also incorporates interfaces to many other programming languages and software solutions, thus greatly simplifying work with data from various sources.

On a personal note, we can say the following about our work with social scientific data:

- our financial resources are sparse;
- we have little time or desire to collect data by hand;
- we are interested in working with up-to-date, high quality, and data-rich sources; and
- we want to document our research from the beginning (data collection) to the end (publication), so that it can be reproduced.

In the past, we frequently found ourselves being inconvenienced by the need to manually assemble data from various sources, thereby hoping that the inevitable coding and copy-and-paste errors are unsystematic. Eventually we grew weary of collecting research data in a non-reproducible manner that is prone to errors, cumbersome, and subject to heightened risks of death by boredom. Consequently, we have increasingly incorporated the data collection and publication processes into our familiar software environment that already helps with statistical analyses—R. The program offers a great infrastructure to expand the daily workflow to steps before and after the actual data analysis.

Although R is not about to collect survey data on its own or conduct experiments any time soon, we do consider the techniques presented in this book as more than the "the poor man's substitute" for costly surveys, experiments, and student-assistant coders. We believe that they are a powerful supplement to the portfolio of modern data analysts. We value the collection of data from online resources not only as a more cost-sensitive solution compared to traditional data acquisition methods, but increasingly think of it as the exclusive approach to assemble datasets from new and developing sources. Moreover, we cherish program-based solutions because they guarantee reliability, reproducibility, time-efficiency, and assembly of higher quality datasets. Beyond productivity, you might find that you enjoy writing code and drafting algorithmic solutions to otherwise tedious manual labor. In short, we are convinced that if you are willing to make the investment and adopt the techniques proposed in this book, you will benefit from a lasting improvement in the ease and quality with which you conduct your data analyses.

If you have identified online data as an appropriate resource for your project, is web scraping or statistical text processing and therefore an automated or semi-automated data collection procedure really necessary? While we cannot hope to offer any definitive guidelines, here are some useful criteria. If you find yourself answering several of these affirmatively, an automated approach might be the right choice:

- Do you plan to repeat the task from time to time, for example, in order to update your database?
- Do you want others to be able to replicate your data collection process?
- Do you deal with online sources of data frequently?
- Is the task non-trivial in terms of scope and complexity?
- If the task can also be accomplished manually—do you lack the resources to let others do the work?
- Are you willing to automate processes by means of programming?

Ideally, the techniques presented in this book enable you to create powerful collections of existing, but unstructured or unsorted data no one has analyzed before at very reasonable cost. In many cases, you will not get far without rethinking, refining, and combining the proposed techniques due to your subjects' specifics. In any case, we hope you find the topics of this book inspiring and perhaps even eye opening: The streets of the Web are paved with data that cannot wait to be collected.

What you won't learn from reading this book

When you browse the table of contents, you get a first impression of what you can expect to learn from reading this book. As it is hard to identify parts that you might have hoped for but that are in fact not covered in this book, we will name some aspects that you will not find in this volume.

What you will not get in this book is an introduction to the R environment. There are plenty of excellent introductions—both printed and online—and this book won't be just another addition to the pile. In case you have not previously worked with R, there is no reason to set this book aside in disappointment. In the next section we'll suggest some well-written R introductions.

You should also not expect the definitive guide to web scraping or text mining. First, we focus on a software environment that was not specifically tailored to these purposes. There might be applications where R is not the ideal solution for your task and other software solutions might be more suited. We will not bother you with alternative environments such as PHP, Python, Ruby, or Perl. To find out if this book is helpful for you, you should ask yourself whether you are already using or planning to use R for your daily work. If the answer to both questions is no, you should probably consider your alternatives. But if you already use R or intend to use it, you can spare yourself the effort to learn yet another language and stay within a familiar environment.

This book is not strictly speaking about data science either. There are excellent introductions to the topic like the recently published books by O'Neil and Schutt (2013), Torgo (2010), Zhao (2012), and Zumel and Mount (2014). What is occasionally missing in these introductions is how data for data science applications are actually acquired. In this sense, our book serves as a preparatory step for data analyses but also provides guidance on how to manage available information and keep it up to date.

Finally, what you most certainly will not get is the perfect solution to your specific problem. It is almost inherent in the data collection process that the fields where the data are harvested are never exactly alike, and sometimes rapidly change shape. Our goal is to enable you to adapt the pieces of code provided in the examples and case studies to create new pieces of code to help you succeed in collecting the data you need.

Why R?

There are many reasons why we think that R is a good solution for the problems that are covered in this book. To us, the most important points are:

1. R is freely and easily accessible. You can download, install, and use it wherever and whenever you want. There are huge benefits to not being a specialist in expensive proprietary programs, as you do not depend on the willingness of employers to pay licensing fees.

2. For a software environment with a primarily statistical focus, R has a large community that continues to flourish. R is used by various disciplines, such as social scientists, medical scientists, psychologists, biologists, geographers, linguists, and also in business. This range allows you to share code with many developers and profit from well-documented applications in diverse settings.

3. R is open source. This means that you can easily retrace how functions work and modify them with little effort. It also means that program modifications are not controlled by an exclusive team of programmers that takes care of the product. Even if you are not interested in contributing to the development of R, you will still reap the benefits from having access to a wide variety of optional extensions—packages. The number of packages is continuously growing and many existing packages are frequently updated. You can find nice overviews of popular themes in R usage on http://cran.r-project.org/web/views/.

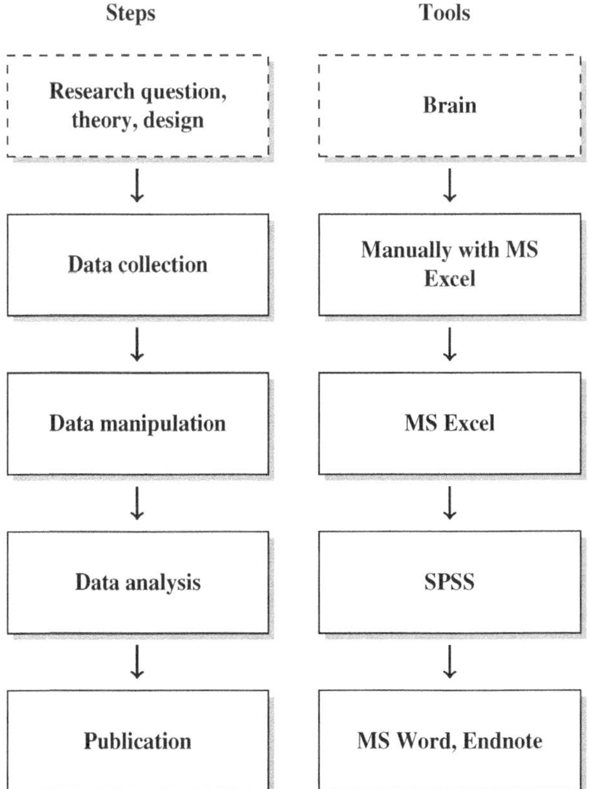

Figure 1 The research process **not** using R—stylized example

4. R is reasonably fast in ordinary tasks. You will likely agree with this impression if you have used other statistical software like SPSS or Stata and have gotten into the habit of going on holiday when running more complex models—not to mention the pain that is caused by the "one session, one data frame" logic. There are even extensions to speed up R, for example, by making C code available from within R, like the Rcpp package.

5. R is powerful in creating data visualizations. Although this not an obvious plus for data collection, you would not want to miss R's graphics facilities in your daily workflow. We will demonstrate how a visual inspection of collected data can and should be a first step in data validation, and how graphics provide an intuitive way of summarizing large amounts of data.

6. Work in R is mainly command line based. This might sound like a disadvantage to R rookies, but it is the only way to allow for the production of reproducible results compared to point-and-click programs.

7. R is not picky about operating systems. It can generally be run under Windows, Mac OS, and Linux.

8. Finally, R is the entire package from start to finish. If you read this book, you are likely not a dedicated programmer, but hold a substantive interest in a topic or specific

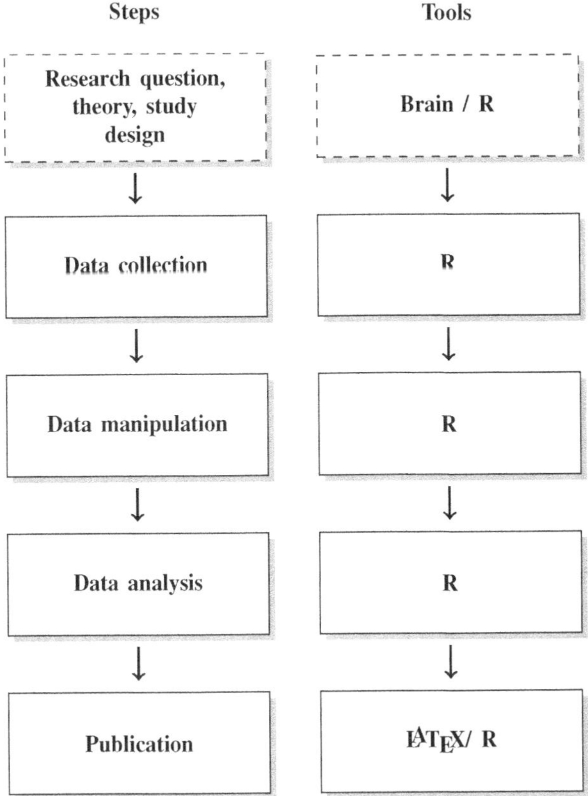

Figure 2 The research process using R—stylized example

data source that you want to work with. In that case, learning another language will not pay off, but rather prevent you from working on your research. An example of a common research process is displayed in Figure 1. It is characterized by a permanent switching between programs. If you need to make corrections to the data collection process, you have to climb back down the entire ladder. The research process using R, as it is presented in this book, takes place within a single software environment (Figure 2). In the context of web scraping and text processing, this means that you do not have to learn another programming language for the task. What you will need to learn are some basics in the markup languages HTML and XML and the logic of regular expressions and XPath, but the operations are executed from within R.

Recommended reading to get started with R

There are many well-written books on the market that provide great introductions to R. Among these, we find the following especially helpful:

Crawley, Michael J. 2012. *The R Book*, 2nd edition. Hoboken, NJ: John Wiley & Sons.

Adler, Joseph. 2009. *R in a Nutshell. A Desktop Quick Reference.* Sebastopol, CA: O'Reilly.

Teetor, Paul. 2011. *R Cookbook.* Sebastopol, CA: O'Reilly.

Besides these commercial sources, there is also a lot of free information on the Web. A truly amazing online tutorial for absolute beginners by the *Code School* is made available at http://tryr.codeschool.com/. Additionally, *Quick-R* (http://www.statmethods.net/) is a good reference site for many basic commands. Lastly, you can also find a lot of free resources and examples at http://www.ats.ucla.edu/stat/r/.

R is an ever-growing software, and in order to keep track of the developments you might periodically like to visit some of the following websites: *Planet R* (http://planetr.stderr.org/) provides the history of existing packages and occasionally some interesting applications. *R-Bloggers* (http://www.r-bloggers.com/) is a blog aggregator that collects entries from many R-related blog sites in various fields. It offers a broad view on hundreds of R applications from economics to biology to geography that is mostly accompanied by the necessary code to replicate the posts. *R-Bloggers* even features some basic examples that deal with automated data collection.

When running into problems, R help files are sometimes not too helpful. It is often more enlightening to look for help in online forums like *Stack Overflow* (http://stackoverflow.com) or other sites from the *Stack Exchange* network. For complex problems, consider the R experts on *GitHub* (http://github.com). Also note that there are many Special Interest Group (SIG) mailing lists (http://www.r-project.org/mail.html) on a variety of topics and even local R User Groups all around the world (http://blog.revolutionanalytics.com/local-r-groups.html). Finally, a CRAN Task View has been set up, which gives a nice overview over recent advances in web technologies and services in the R framework: http://cran.r-project.org/web/views/WebTechnologies.html

Typographic conventions

This is a practical book about coding, and we expect you to often have it sitting somewhere next to the keyboard. We want to facilitate the orientation throughout the book with the following conventions: There are three indices—one for general topics, one for R packages, and one for R functions. Within the text, variables and R (and other) code and functions are set in typewriter typeface, as in `summary()`. Actual R code is also typewriter style and indented. Note that code input is indicated with "R" and a prompt symbol ("`R>`"); R output is printed without the prompt sign, as in

```
R> hello <- "hello, world"
R> hello
[1] "hello, world"
```

The book's website

The website that accompanies this book can be found at http://www.r-datacollection.com

Among other things, the site provides code from examples and case studies. This means that you do not have to manually copy the code from the book, but can directly access and modify the corresponding R files. You will also find solutions to some of the exercises, as well as a list of errata. If you find any errors, please do not hesitate to let us know.

Disclaimer

This is not a book about spidering the Web. Spiders are programs that graze the Web for information, rapidly jumping from one page to another, often grabbing the entire page content. If you want to follow in Google's Googlebot's footsteps, you probably hold the wrong book in your hand. The techniques we introduce in this book are meant to serve more specific and more gentle purposes, that is, scraping specific information from specific websites. In the end, you are responsible for what you do with what you learn. It is frequently not a big leap from the code that is presented in this book to programs that might quickly annoy website administrators. So here is some fundamental advice on how to behave as a practitioner of web data collection:

1. Always keep in mind where your data comes from and, whenever possible, give credit to those who originally collected and published it.[1]
2. Do not violate copyrights if you plan to republish data you found on the Web. If the information was not collected by yourself, chances are that you need permission from the owners to reproduce them.
3. Do not do anything illegal! To get an idea of what you can and cannot do in your data collection, check out the Justia BlawgSearch (http://blawgsearch.justia.com/), which is a search site for legal blogs. Looking for entries marked 'web scraping' might help to keep up to date regarding legal developments and recent verdicts. The Electronic Frontier Foundation (http://www.eff.org/) was founded as early as 1990 to defend the digital rights of consumers and the public. We hope, however, that you will never have to rely on their help.

We offer some more detailed recommendations on how to behave when scraping content from the Web in Section 9.3.3.

Acknowledgments

Many people helped to make this project possible. We would like to take the opportunity to express our gratitude to them. First of all, we would like to say thanks to Peter Selb to whom we owe the idea of creating a course on alternative data collection. It is due to his impulse that we started to assemble our somewhat haphazard experiences in a comprehensive volume. We are also grateful to several people who have provided invaluable feedback on parts of the book. Most importantly we thank Christian Breunig, Holger Döring, Daniel Eckert, Johannes

[1]To lead by example, we owe some of the suggestions to Hemenway and Calishain (2003)'s *Spidering Hacks* (Hack #6).

Kleibl, Philip Leifeld, and Nils Weidmann, whose advice has greatly improved the material. We also thank Kathryn Uhrig for proofreading the manuscript.

Early versions of the book were used in two courses on "Alternative data collection methods" and "Data collection in the World Wide Web" that took place in the summer terms of 2012 and 2013 at the University of Konstanz. We are grateful to students for their comments—and their patience with the topic, with R, and outrageous regular expressions. We would also like to thank the participants of the workshops on "Facilitating empirical research on political reforms: Automating data collection in R" held in Mannheim in December 2012 and the workshop "Automating online data collection in R," which took place in Zurich in April 2013. We thank Bruno Wüest in particular for his assistance in making the Zurich workshop possible, and Fabrizio Gilardi for his support.

It turns out that writing a volume on automating data collection is a surprisingly time-consuming endeavor. We all embarked on this project during our doctoral studies and devoted a lot of time to learning the intricacies of web scraping that could have been spent on the tasks we signed up for. We would like to thank our supervisors Peter Selb, Daniel Bochsler, Ulrich Sieberer, and Thomas Gschwend for their patience and support for our various detours. Christian Rubba is grateful for generous funding by the Swiss National Science Foundation (Grant Number 137805).

We would like to acknowledge that we are heavily indebted to the creators and maintainers of the numerous packages that are applied throughout this volume. Their continuous efforts have opened the door for new ways of scholarly research—and have provided access to vast sources of data to individual researchers. While we cannot possibly hope to mention all the package developers in these paragraphs, we would like to express our gratitude to Duncan Temple Lang and Hadley Wickham for their exceptional work. We would also like to acknowledge the work of Yihui Xie, whose package was crucial in typesetting this book.

We are grateful for the help that was extended from our publisher, particularly from Heather Kay, Debbie Jupe, Jo Taylor, Richard Davies, Baljinder Kaur and others who were responsible for proofreading and formatting and who provided support at various stages of the writing process.

Finally, we happily acknowledge the great support we received from our friends and families. We owe special and heartfelt thanks to: Karima Bousbah, Johanna Flock, Hans-Holger Friedrich, Dirk Heinecke, Stefanie Klingler, Kristin Lindemann, Verena Mack, and Alice Mohr.

Simon Munzert
Christian Rubba
Peter Meißner
Dominic Nyhuis

1

Introduction

Are you ready for your first encounter with web scraping? Let us start with a small example that you can recreate directly on your machine, provided you have R installed. The case study gives a first impression of the book's central themes.

1.1 Case study: World Heritage Sites in Danger

The *United Nations Educational, Scientific and Cultural Organization (UNESCO)* is an organization of the United Nations which, among other things, fights for the preservation of the world's natural and cultural heritage. As of today (November 2013), there are 981 heritage sites, most of which of are man-made like the Pyramids of Giza, but also natural phenomena like the Great Barrier Reef are listed. Unfortunately, some of the awarded places are threatened by human intervention. Which sites are threatened and where are they located? Are there regions in the world where sites are more endangered than in others? What are the reasons that put a site at risk? These are the questions that we want to examine in this first case study.

Wikipedia—information source of choice

What do scientists always do first when they want to get up to speed on a topic? They look it up on Wikipedia! Checking out the page of the world heritage sites, we stumble across a list of currently and previously endangered sites at http://en.wikipedia.org/wiki/List_of_World_Heritage_in_Danger. You find a table with the current sites listed when accessing the link. It contains the name, location (city, country, and geographic coordinates), type of danger that is facing the site, the year the site was added to the world heritage list, and the year it was put on the list of endangered sites. Let us investigate how the sites are distributed around the world.

While the table holds information on the places, it is not immediately clear where they are located and whether they are regionally clustered. Rather than trying to eyeball the table, it could be very useful to plot the locations of the places on a map. As humans deal well with

Automated Data Collection with R: A Practical Guide to Web Scraping and Text Mining, First Edition.
Simon Munzert, Christian Rubba, Peter Meißner and Dominic Nyhuis.

visual information, we will try to visualize results whenever possible throughout this book. But how to get the information from the table to a map? This sounds like a difficult task, but with the techniques that we are going to discuss extensively in the next pages, it is in fact not. For now, we simply provide you with a first impression of how to tackle such a task with R. Detailed explanations of the commands in the code snippets are provided later and more systematically throughout the book.

To start, we have to load a couple of packages. While R only comes with a set of basic, mostly math- and statistics-related functions, it can easily be extended by user-written packages. For this example, we load the following packages using the `library()` function:[1]

```
R> library(stringr)
R> library(XML)
R> library(maps)
```

In the next step, we load the data from the webpage into R. This can be done easily using the `readHTMLTable()` function from the XML package:

```
R> heritage_parsed <- htmlParse("http://en.wikipedia.org/wiki/
List_of_World_Heritage_in_Danger",
    encoding = "UTF-8")
R> tables <- readHTMLTable(heritage_parsed, stringsAsFactors = FALSE)
```

We are going to explain the mechanics of this step and all other major web scraping techniques in more detail in Chapter 9. For now, all you need to know is that we are telling R that the imported data come in the form of an HTML document. R is capable of interpreting HTML, that is, it knows how tables, headlines, or other objects are structured in this file format. This works via a so-called parser, which is called with the function `htmlParse()`. In the next step, we tell R to extract all HTML tables it can find in the parsed object `heritage_parsed` and store them in a new object `tables`. If you are not already familiar with HTML, you will learn that HTML tables are constructed from the same code components in Chapter 2. The `readHTMLTable()` function helps in identifying and reading out these tables.

All the information we need is now contained in the `tables` object. This object is a list of all the tables the function could find in the HTML document. After eyeballing all the tables, we identify and select the table we are interested in (the second one) and write it into a new one, named `danger_table`. Some of the variables in our table are of no further interest, so we select only those that contain information about the site's name, location, criterion of heritage (cultural or natural), year of inscription, and year of endangerment. The variables in our table have been assigned unhandy names, so we relabel them. Finally, we have a look at the names of the first few sites:

```
R> danger_table <- danger_table <- tables[[2]]
R> names(danger_table)
[1] "NULL.Name"          "NULL.Image"          "NULL.Location"
[4] "NULL.Criteria"      "NULL.Area.ha..acre." "NULL.Year..WHS."
```

[1]This assumes that the packages are already installed. If they are not, type the following into your console: `install.packages(c("stringr", "XML", "maps"))`

```
[7] "NULL.Endangered"      "NULL.Reason"          "NULL.Refs"
R> danger_table <- danger_table[, c(1, 3, 4, 6, 7)]
R> colnames(danger_table) <- c("name", "locn", "crit", "yins", "yend")

R> danger_table$name[1:3]
[1] "Abu Mena"                          "Air and Ténéré Natural Reserves"
[3] "Ancient City of Aleppo"
```

This seems to have worked. Additionally, we perform some simple data cleaning, a step often necessary when importing web-based content into R. The variable `crit`, which contains the information whether the site is of cultural or natural character, is recoded, and the two variables `y_ins` and `y_end` are turned into numeric ones.[2] Some of the entries in the `y_end` variable are ambiguous as they contain several years. We select the last given year in the cell. To do so, we specify a so-called regular expression, which goes `[[:digit:]]4$`—we explain what this means in the next paragraph:

```
R> danger_table$crit <- ifelse(str_detect(danger_table$crit, "Natural") ==
TRUE, "nat", "cult")
R> danger_table$crit[1:3]
[1] "cult" "nat"  "cult"

R> danger_table$yins <- as.numeric(danger_table$yins)
R> danger_table$yins[1:3]
[1] 1979 1991 1986

R> yend_clean <- unlist(str_extract_all(danger_table$yend, "[[:digit:]]4$"))
R> danger_table$yend <- as.numeric(yend_clean)
R> danger_table$yend[1:3]
2001 1992 2013
```

The `locn` variable is a bit of a mess, exemplified by three cases drawn from the data-set:

```
R> danger_table$locn[c(1, 3, 5)]
[1] "EgyAbusir, Egypt30°50'30<U+2033>N 29°39'50<U+2033>E<U+FEFF> /
<U+FEFF>30.84167°N 29.66389°E<U+FEFF> / 30.84167; 29.66389<U+FEFF>
(Abu Mena)"
[2] "Syria !Aleppo Governorate,  Syria36°14'0<U+2033>N 37°10'0<U+2033
>E<U+FEFF> / <U+FEFF>36.23333°N 37.16667°E<U+FEFF> / 36.23333; 37.16667
<U+FEFF> (Ancient City of Aleppo)"
[3] "Syria !Damascus Governorate,  Syria33°30'41<U+2033>N 36°18'23
<U+2033>E<U+FEFF> / <U+FEFF>33.51139°N 36.30639°E<U+FEFF> / 33.51139;
36.30639<U+FEFF> (Ancient City of Damascus)"
```

The first regular expression

The variable contains the name of the site's location, the country, and the geographic coordinates in several varieties. What we need for the map are the coordinates, given by the latitude (e.g., 30.84167N) and longitude (e.g., 29.66389E) values. To extract this information, we have to use some more advanced text manipulation tools called "regular expressions",

---

[2] We assume that you are familiar with the basic object classes in R. If not, check out the recommended readings in the Preface.

which are discussed extensively in Chapter 8. In short, we have to give R an exact description of what the information we are interested in looks like, and then let R search for and extract it. To do so, we use functions from the stringr package, which we will also discuss in detail in Chapter 8. In order to get the latitude and longitude values, we write the following:

```
R> reg_y <- "[/][ -]*[[:digit:]]*[.]*[[:digit:]]*[;]"
R> reg_x <- "[;][ -]*[[:digit:]]*[.]*[[:digit:]]*"
R> y_coords <- str_extract(danger_table$locn, reg_y)
R> y_coords <- as.numeric(str_sub(y_coords, 3, -2))
R> danger_table$y_coords <- y_coords
R> x_coords <- str_extract(danger_table$locn, reg_x)
R> x_coords <- as.numeric(str_sub(x_coords, 3, -1))
R> danger_table$x_coords <- x_coords
R> danger_table$locn <- NULL
```

Do not be confused by the first two lines of code. What looks like the result of a monkey typing on a keyboard is in fact a precise description of the coordinates in the `locn` variable. The information is contained in the `locn` variable as decimal degrees as well as in degrees, minutes, and seconds. As the decimal degrees are easier to describe with a regular expression, we try to extract those. Writing regular expressions means finding a general pattern for strings that we want to extract. We observe that latitudes and longitudes always appear after a slash and are a sequence of several digits, separated by a dot. Some values start with a minus sign. Both values are separated by a semicolon, which is cut off along with the empty spaces and the slash. When we apply this pattern to the `locn` variable with the `str_extract()` command and extract the numeric information with `str_sub()`, we get the following:

```
R> round(danger_table$y_coords, 2)[1:3]
[1] 30.84 18.28 36.23

R> round(danger_table$x_coords, 2)[1:3]
[1] 29.66  8.00 37.17
```

This seems to have worked nicely. We have retrieved a set of 44 coordinates, corresponding to 44 World Heritage Sites in Danger. Let us have a first look at the data. `dim()` returns the number of rows and columns of the data frame; `head()` returns the first few observations:

```
R> dim(danger_table)
[1] 44  6
R> head(danger_table)
                               name crit yins yend y_coords x_coords
1                          Abu Mena cult 1979 2001    30.84    29.66
2    Air and Ténéré Natural Reserves  nat 1991 1992    18.28     8.00
3           Ancient City of Aleppo cult 1986 2013    36.23    37.17
4            Ancient City of Bosra cult 1980 2013    32.52    36.48
5         Ancient City of Damascus cult 1979 2013    33.51    36.31
6 Ancient Villages of Northern Syria cult 2011 2013    36.33    36.84
```

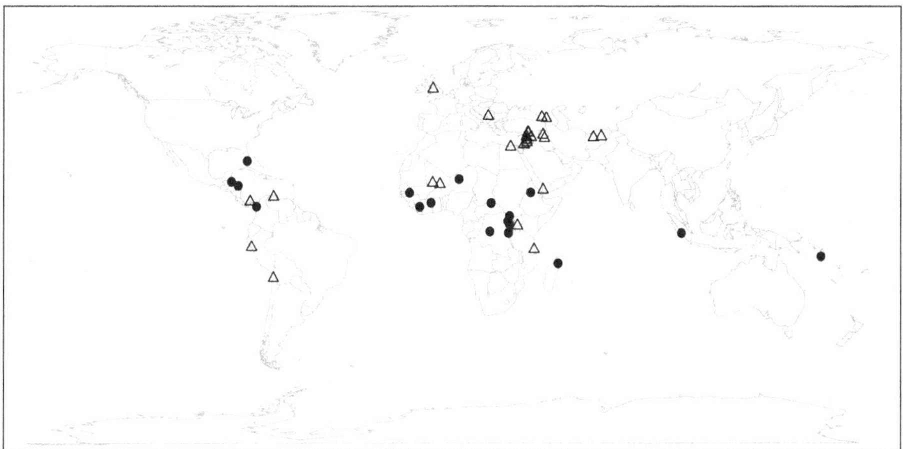

Figure 1.1 Location of UNESCO World Heritage Sites in danger (as of March 2014). Cultural sites are marked with triangles, natural sites with dots

A first look at the data

The data frame consists of 44 observations and 6 variables. The data are now set up in a way that we can proceed with mapping the sites. To do so, we use another package named "maps." In it we find a map of the world that we use to pinpoint the sites' locations with the extracted y and x coordinates. The result is displayed in Figure 1.1. It was generated as follows:

```
R> pch <- ifelse(danger_table$crit == "nat", 19, 2)
R> map("world", col = "darkgrey", lwd = 0.5, mar = c(0.1, 0.1, 0.1, 0.1))
R> points(danger_table$x_coords, danger_table$y_coords, pch = pch)
R> box()
```

We find that many of the endangered sites are located in Africa, the Middle East, and Southwest Asia, and a few others in South and Central America. The endangered cultural heritage sites are visualized as the triangle. They tend to be clustered in the Middle East and Southwest Asia. Conversely, the natural heritage sites in danger, here visualized as the dots, are more prominent in Africa. We find that there are more cultural than natural sites in danger.

```
R> table(danger_table$crit)

cult  nat
  26   18
```

The UNESCO behaves politically

We can speculate about the political, economic, or environmental conditions in the affected countries that may have led to the endangerment of the sites. While the information in the table might be too sparse for firm inferences, we can at least consider some time trends and potential motives of the UNESCO itself. For that purpose, we can make use of the two variables `y_ins` and `y_end`, which contain the year a site was designated a world heritage and the year it was put on the list of endangered World Heritage Sites. Consider Figure 1.2, which displays the distribution of the second variable that we generated using the `hist()`

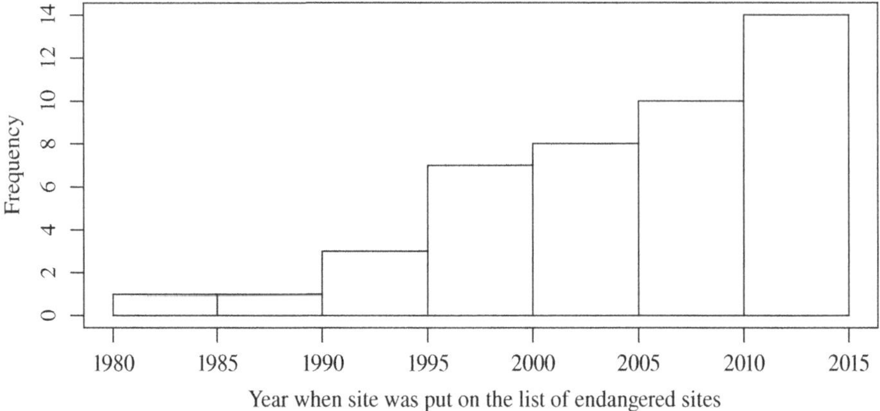

Figure 1.2 Distribution of years when World Heritage Sites were put on the list of endangered sites

command. We find that the frequency with which sites were put on the "red list" has risen in recent decades—but so has the number of World Heritage Sites:

```
R> hist(danger_table$yend,
R>      freq = TRUE,
R>      xlab = "Year when site was put on the list of endangered sites",
R>      main = "")
```

Even more interesting is the distribution of time spans between the year of inscription and the year of endangerment, that is, the time it took until a site was put on the "red list" after it had achieved World Heritage Site status. We calculate this value by subtracting the endangerment year from the inscription year. The result is plotted in Figure 1.3.

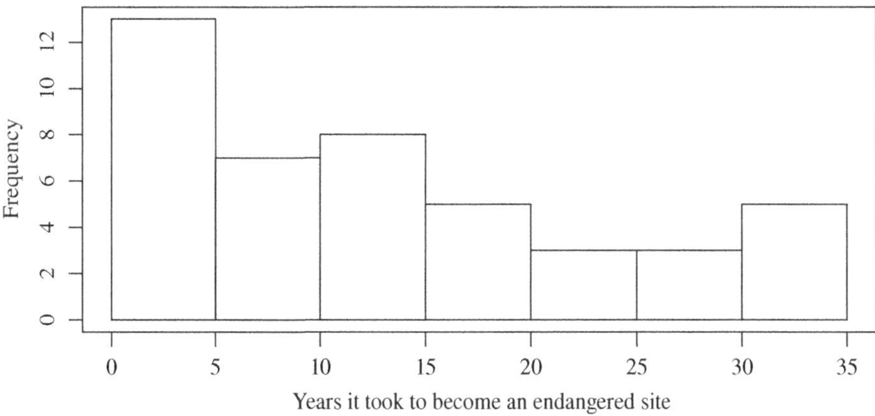

Figure 1.3 Distribution of time spans between year of inscription and year of endangerment of World Heritage Sites in danger

```
R> duration <- danger_table$yend - danger_table$yins
R> hist(duration,
R>      freq = TRUE,
R>      xlab = "Years it took to become an endangered site",
R>      main = "")
```

Many of the sites were put on the red list only shortly after their designation as world heritage. According to the official selection criteria for becoming a cultural or natural heritage, it is not a necessary condition to be endangered. In contrast, endangered sites run the risk of losing their status as world heritage. So why do they become part of the List of World Heritage Sites when it is likely that the site may soon run the risk of losing it again? One could speculate that the committee may be well aware of these facts and might use the list as a political means to enforce protection of the sites.

Now take a few minutes and experiment with the gathered data for yourself! Which is the country with the most endangered sites? How effective is the List of World Heritage Sites in Danger? There is another table on the Wikipedia page that has information about previously listed sites. You might want to scrape these data as well and incorporate them into the map.

Using only few lines of code, we have enriched the data and gathered new insights, which might not have been obvious from examining the table alone.[3] This is a variant of the more general *mantra*, which will occur throughout the book: **Data are abundant—retrieve them, prepare them, use them.**

1.2 Some remarks on web data quality

The introductory example has elegantly sidestepped some of the more serious questions that are likely to arise when approaching a research problem. What type of data is most suited to answer your question? Is the quality of the data sufficiently high to answer your question? Is the information systematically flawed? Although this is not a book on research design or advanced statistical methods to tackle noise in data, we want to emphasize these questions before we start harvesting gigabytes of information.

What is the primary source of secondary data?

When you look at online data, you have to keep its origins in mind. Information can be firsthand, like posts on Twitter or secondhand data that have been copied from an offline source, or even scraped from elsewhere. There may be situations where you are unable to retrace the source of your data. If so, does it make sense to use data from the Web? We think the answer is yes.

Regarding the transparency of the data generation, web data do not differ much from other secondary sources. Consider Wikipedia as a popular example. It has often been debated whether it is legitimate to quote the online encyclopedia for scientific and journalistic purposes. The same concerns are equally valid if one cares to use data from Wikipedia tables or texts for analysis. It has been shown that Wikipedia's accuracy varies. While some studies find that Wikipedia is comparable to established encyclopedias (Chesney 2006; Giles 2005; Reavley et al. 2012), others suggest that the quality might, at times, be inferior (Clauson et al. 2008; Leithner et al. 2010; Rector 2008). But how do you know when relying on one specific article? It is always recommended to find a second source and to compare the content.

[3] The watchful eye has already noticed a link on the site that leads to a map visualizing the locations as we did in Figure 1.1. We acknowledge the work, but want to be able to generate such output ourselves.

If you are unsure whether the two sources share a common source, you should repeat the process. Such cross-validations should be standard for the use of any secondary data source, as reputation does not prevent random or systematic errors.

Data quality depends on the user's purposes

Besides, data quality is nothing that is stuck to the data like a badge, but rather depends on the application. A sample of tweets on a random day might be sufficient to analyze the use of hash tags or gender-specific use of words, but is less useful for predicting electoral outcomes when the sample happens to have been collected on the day of the Republican National Convention. In the latter case, the data are likely to suffer from a bias due to the collection day, that is, they lack quality in terms of "representativeness." Therefore, the only standard is the one you establish yourself. As a matter of fact, quality standards are more alike when dealing with factual data—the African elephant population most likely has not tripled in the past 6 months and Washington D.C., not New York, is the capital of the United States.

Why web data can be of higher quality for the user

To be sure, while it is not the case that demands on data quality should be lower when working with online data, the concerns might be different. Imagine you want to know what people think about a new phone. There are several standard approaches to deal with this problem in market research. For example, you could conduct a telephone survey and ask hundreds of people if they could imagine buying a particular phone and the features in which they are most interested. There are plenty of books that have been written about the pitfalls of data quality that are likely to arise in such scenarios. For example, are the people "representative" of the people I want to know something about? Are the questions that I pose suited to solicit the answers to my problem?

Another way to answer this question with data could be to look for "proxies," that is, indicators that do not directly measure the product's popularity itself, but which are strongly related. If the meaning of popularity entails that people prefer one product over a competing one, an indirect measurement of popularity could be the sales statistics on commercial websites. These statistics usually contain rankings of all phones currently on sale. Again, questions of representativeness arise—both with regard to the listed phones (are some phones not on the list because the commercial website does not sell them?) and the customers (who buy phones from the Web and from a particular site?). Nevertheless, the ranking does provide a more comprehensive image of the phone market—possibly more comprehensive than any reasonably priced customer survey could ever hope to be. The availability of entirely new information is probably the most important argument for the use of online data, as it allows us to answer new questions or to get a deeper understanding of existing questions. Certainly, hand in hand with this added value arise new questions of data quality—can phones of different generations be compared at all, and can we say anything about the stability of such a ranking? In many situations, choosing a data source is a trade-off between advantages and disadvantages, accuracy versus completeness, coverage versus validity, and so forth.

To sum up, deciding which data to collect for your application can be difficult. We propose five steps that might help to guide your data collection process:

1. **Make sure you know exactly what kind of information you need.** This can be specific ("the gross domestic product of all OECD countries for the last 10 years") or vague ("peoples' opinion on company X's new phone," "collaboration among members of the US senate").

2. **Find out whether there are any data sources on the Web that might provide direct or indirect information on your problem.** If you are looking for hard facts, this is probably easy. If you are interested in rather vague concepts, this is more difficult.

A country's embassy homepage might be a valuable source for foreign policy action that is often hidden behind the curtain of diplomacy. Tweets might contain opinion trends on pretty much everything, commercial platforms can inform about customers' satisfaction with products, rental rates on property websites might hold information on current attractiveness of city quarters....

3. **Develop a theory of the data generation process when looking into potential sources.** When were the data generated, when were they uploaded to the Web, and by whom? Are there any potential areas that are not covered, consistent or accurate, and are you able to identify and correct them?

4. **Balance advantages and disadvantages of potential data sources.** Relevant aspects might be availability (and legality!), costs of collection, compatibility of new sources with existing research, but also very subjective factors like acceptance of the data source by others. Also think about possible ways to validate the quality of your data. Are there other, independent sources that provide similar information so that random cross-checks are possible? In case of secondary data, can you identify the original source and check for transfer errors?

5. **Make a decision!** Choose the data source that seems most suitable, document your reasons for the decision, and start with the preparations for the collection. If it is feasible, collect data from several sources to validate data sources. Many problems and benefits of various data collection strategies come to light only after the actual collection.

1.3 Technologies for disseminating, extracting, and storing web data

Collecting data from the Web is not always as easy as depicted in the introductory example. Difficulties arise when data are stored in more complex structures than HTML tables, when web pages are dynamic or when information has to be retrieved from plain text. There are some costs involved in automated data collection with R, which essentially means that you have to gain basic knowledge of a set of web and web-related technologies. However, in our introduction to these fundamental tools we stick to the necessary basics to perform web scraping and text mining and leave out the less relevant details where possible. It is definitely not necessary to become an expert in all web technologies in order to be able to write good web scrapers.

There are three areas that are important for data collection on the Web with R. Figure 1.4 provides an overview of the three areas. In the remainder of this section, we will motivate each of the subfields and illustrate their various linkages. This might help you to stay on top of things when you study the fundamentals in the first part of the book before moving on to the actual web scraping tasks in the book's second part.

1.3.1 Technologies for disseminating content on the Web

In the first pillar we encounter technologies that allow the distribution of content on the Web. There are multiple ways of how data are disseminated, but the most relevant technologies in this pillar are XML/HTML, AJAX, and JSON (left column of Figure 1.4).

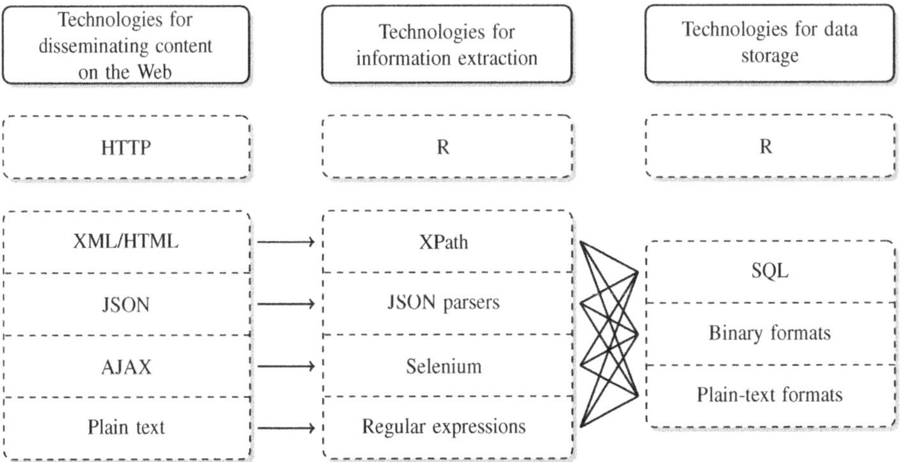

Figure 1.4 Technologies for disseminating, extracting, and storing web data

HTML For browsing the Web, there is a hidden standard behind the scenes that structures how information is displayed—the Hypertext Markup Language or HTML. Whether we look for information on Wikipedia, search for sites on Google, check our bank account, or *become social* on Twitter, Facebook, or YouTube—using a browser means using HTML. Although HTML is not a dedicated data storage format, it frequently contains the information that we are interested in. We find data in texts, tables, lists, links, or other structures. Unfortunately, there is a difference between the way data are presented in a browser on the one side and how they are stored within the HTML code on the other. In order to automatically collect data from the Web and process them with R, a basic understanding of HTML and the way it stores information is indispensable. We provide an introduction to HTML from a web scraper's perspective in Chapter 2.

XML The Extensible Markup Language or XML is one of the most popular formats for exchanging data over the Web. It is related to HTML in that both are markup languages. However, while HTML is used to shape the display of information, the main purpose of XML is to store data. Thus, HTML documents are interpreted and transformed into pretty-looking output by browsers, whereas XML is "just" data wrapped in user-defined tags. The user-defined tags make XML much more flexible for storing data than HTML. In recent years, XML and its derivatives—so-called schemes—have proliferated in various data exchanges between web applications. It is therefore important to be familiar with the basics of XML when gathering data from the Web (Chapter 3). Both HTML and XML-style documents offer natural, often hierarchical, structures for data storage. In order to recognize and interpret such structures, we need software that is able to "understand" these languages and handle them adequately. The necessary tools—parsers—are introduced in Chapters 2 and 3.

JSON Another standard data storage and exchange format that is frequently encountered on the Web is the JavaScript Object Notation or JSON. Like XML, JSON is used by many web applications to provide data for web developers. Imagine both XML and JSON as standards that define containers for plain text data. For example, if developers want to analyze trends on Twitter, they can collect the necessary data from an interface that was set up by Twitter to distribute the information in the JSON format. The main reason why data are preferably distributed in the XML or JSON formats is that both are compatible with many programming languages and software, including R. As data providers cannot know the software that is being used to postprocess the information, it is preferable for all parties involved to distribute the data in formats with universally accepted standards. The logic of JSON is introduced in the second part of Chapter 3.

AJAX is a group of technologies that is now firmly integrated into the toolkit of modern web developing. AJAX plays a tremendously important role in enabling websites to request data asynchronously in the background of the browser session and update its visual appearance in a dynamic fashion. Although we owe much of the sophistication in modern web apps to AJAX, these technologies constitute a nuisance for web scrapers and we quickly run into a dead end with standard R tools. In Chapter 6 we focus on JavaScript and the XMLHttpRequest, two key technologies, and illustrate how an AJAX-enriched website departs from the classical HTML/HTTP logic. We also discuss a solution to this problem using browser-integrated Web Developer Tools that provide deep access to the browser internals. **AJAX**

We frequently deal with plain text data when scraping information from the Web. In a way, plain text is part of every HTML, XML, and JSON document. The crucial property we want to stress is that plain text is unstructured data, at least for computer programs that simply read a text file line by line. There is no introductory chapter to plain text data, but we offer a guide on how to extract information from such data in Chapter 8. **Plain text**

To retrieve data from the Web, we have to enable our machine to communicate with servers and web services. The *lingua franca* of communication on the Web is the Hypertext Transfer Protocol (HTTP). It is the most common standard for communication between web clients and servers. Virtually every HTML page we open, every image we view in the browser, every video we watch is delivered by HTTP. Despite our continuous usage of the protocol we are mostly unaware of it as HTTP exchanges are typically performed by our machines. We will learn that for many of the basic web scraping applications we do not have to care much about the particulars of HTTP, as R can take over most of the necessary tasks just fine. In some instances, however, we have to dig deeper into the protocol and formulate advanced requests in order to obtain the information we are looking for. Therefore, the basics of HTTP are the subject of Chapter 5. **HTTP**

1.3.2 Technologies for information extraction from web documents

The second pillar of technologies for web data collection is needed to retrieve the information from the files we gather. Depending on the technique that has been used to collect files, there are specific tools that are suited to extract data from these sources (middle column of Figure 1.4). This section provides a first glance at the available tools. An advantage of using R for information extraction is that we can use all of the technologies from within R, even though some of them are not R-specific, but rather implementations via a set of packages.

The first tool at our disposal is the XPath query language. It is used to select specific pieces of information from marked up documents such as HTML, XML or any variant of it, for example SVG or RSS. In a typical data web scraping task, calling the webpages is an important, but usually only intermediate step on the way toward well-structured and cleaned datasets. In order to take full advantage of the Web as a nearly endless data source, we have to perform a series of filtering and extraction steps once the relevant web documents have been identified and downloaded. The main purpose of these steps is to recast information that **XPath** is stored in marked up documents into formats that are suitable for further processing and analysis with statistical software. This task consists of specifying the data we are interested in and locating it in a specific document and then tailoring a query to the document that extracts the desired information. XPath is introduced in Chatper 4 as one option to perform these tasks.

JSON parsers In contrast to HTML or XML documents, JSON documents are more lightweight and easier to parse. To extract data from JSON, we do not draw upon a specific query language, but rely on high-level R functionality, which does a good job in decoding JSON data. We explain how it is done in Chapter 3.

Selenium Extracting information from AJAX-enriched webpages is a more advanced and complex scenario. As a powerful alternative to initiating web requests from the R console, we present the Selenium framework as a hands-on approach to getting a grip on web data. Selenium allows us to direct commands to a browser window, such as mouse clicks or keyboard inputs, via R. By working directly in the browser, Selenium is capable of circumventing some of the problems discussed with AJAX-enriched webpages. We introduce Selenium in one of our scraping scenarios of Chapter 9 in Section 9.1.9. This section discusses the Selenium framework as well as the RWebdriver package for R by means of a practical application.

Regular expressions A central task in web scraping is to collect the relevant information for our research problem from heaps of textual data. We usually care for the systematic elements in textual data—especially if we want to apply quantitative methods to the resulting data. Systematic structures can be numbers or names like countries or addresses. One technique that we can apply to extract the systematic components of the information are regular expressions. Essentially, regular expressions are abstract sequences of strings that match concrete, recurring patterns in text. Besides using them to extract content from plain text documents we can also apply them to HTML and XML documents to identify and extract parts of the documents that we are interested in. While it is often preferable to use XPath queries on markup documents, regular expressions can be useful if the information is hidden within atomic values. Moreover, if the relevant information is scattered across an HTML document, some of the approaches that exploit the document's structure and markup might be rendered useless. How regular expressions work in R is explained in detail in Chapter 8.

Text mining Besides extracting meaningful information from textual data in the form of numbers or names we have a second technique at our disposal—text mining. Applying procedures in this class of techniques allows researchers to classify unstructured texts based on the similarity of their word usages. To understand the concept of text mining it is useful to think about the difference between manifest and latent information. While the former describes information that is specifically linked to individual terms, like an address or a temperature measurement, the latter refers to text labels that are not explicitly contained in the text. For example, when analyzing a selection of news reports, human readers are able to classify them as belonging to particular topical categories, say politics, media, or sport. Text mining procedures provide solutions for the automatic categorization of text. This is particularly useful when analyzing web data, which frequently comes in the form of unlabeled and unstructured text. We elaborate several of the available techniques in Chapter 10.

1.3.3 Technologies for data storage

Finally, the third pillar of technologies for the collection of web data deals with facilities for data storage (right column of Figure 1.4). R is mostly well suited for managing data storage technologies like databases. Generally speaking, the connection between technologies for information extraction and those for data storage is less obvious. The best way to store data does not necessarily depend on its origin.

Simple and everyday processes like online shopping, browsing through library catalogues, wiring money, or even buying a couple of sweets at the supermarket all involve databases. We hardly ever realize that databases play such an important role because we do not interact with them directly—databases like to work behind the scenes. Whenever data are key to a project, web administrators will rely on databases because of their reliability, efficiency, multiuser access, virtually unlimited data size, and remote access capabilities. Regarding automated data collection, databases are of interest for two reasons: One, we might occasionally be granted access to a database directly and should be able to cope with it. Two, although, R has a lot of data management facilities, it might be preferable to store data in a database rather than in one of the native formats. For example, if you work on a project where data need to be made available online or if you have various parties gathering specific parts of your data, a database can provide the necessary infrastructure. Moreover, if the data you need to collect are extensive and you have to frequently subset and manipulate the data, it also makes sense to set up a database for the speed with which they can be queried. For the many advantages of databases, we introduce databases in Chapter 7 and discuss SQL as the main language for database access and communication. **SQL**

Nevertheless, in many instances the ordinary data storage facilities of R suffice, for example, by importing and exporting data in binary or plain text formats. In Chapter 11, we provide some details on the general workflow of web scraping, including data management tasks.

1.4 Structure of the book

We wrote this book with the needs of a diverse readership in mind. Depending on your ambition and previous exposure to R, you may read this book from cover to cover or choose a section that helps you accomplish your task.

- If you have some basic knowledge of R but are not familiar with any of the scripting languages frequently used on the Web, you may just follow the structure as is.
- If you already have some text data and need to extract information from it, you might start with Chapter 8 (Regular expressions and string functions) and continue with Chapter 10 (Statistical text processing).
- If you are primarily interested in web scraping techniques, but not necessarily in scraping textual data, you might want to skip Chapter 10 altogether. We recommend reading Chapter 8 in either case, as text manipulation basics are also a fundamental technique for web scraping purposes.
- If you are a teacher, you might want to use the book as basic or supplementary literature. We provide a set of exercises after most of the chapters in Parts I and II for this purpose. Solutions are available on the book's website www.r-datacollection.com for about half the exercises, so you can assign them as homework or use them for test questions.

For all others, we hope you will find the structure useful as well. The following is a short outline of the book's three parts.

Part I: A primer on web and data technologies In the first part, we introduce the fundamental technologies that underlie the communication, exchange, storage, and display of information on the World Wide Web (HTTP, HTML, XML, JSON, AJAX, SQL), and provide basic techniques to query web documents and datasets (XPath and regular expressions). These fundamentals are especially useful for readers who are unfamiliar with the architecture of the Web, but can also serve as a refresher if you have some prior knowledge. The first part of the book is explicitly focused on introducing the basic concepts for extracting the data as performed in the rest of the book, and on providing an extensive set of exercises to get accustomed quickly with the techniques.

Part II: A practical toolbox for web scraping and text mining The book's second part consists of three core chapters: The first covers several scraping techniques, namely the use of regular expressions, XPath, various forms of APIs, other data types and source-specific techniques. We present a set of frequently occurring scenarios and apply popular R packages for these tasks. We also address legal aspects of web scraping and give advice on how to behave nicely on the Web. The second core chapter deals with techniques for statistical text processing. Data are frequently available in the form of text that has to be further analyzed to make it fit for subsequent analyses. We present several techniques of the two major methods for statistically processing text—supervised and unsupervised text classification—and show how latent information can be extracted. In the third chapter, we provide insights into frequently occurring topics in the management of data projects with R. We discuss how to work with the file system, how to use loops for more efficient coding, how to organize scraping procedures, and how to schedule scraping tasks that have to be executed on a regular basis.

Part III: A bag of case studies In the third part of the book, we provide a set of applications that make use of the techniques introduced in the previous parts. Each of the case studies starts out with a short motivation and the goal of the analysis. The case studies go into more detail than the short examples in the technical chapters and address a wide range of problems. Moreover, they provide a practical insight into the daily workflow of data scraping and text processing, the pitfalls of real-life data, and how to avoid them. Additionally, this part comes with a tabular overview of the case studies' contents' with a view of the main techniques to retrieve the data from the Web or from texts and the main packages and functions used for these tasks.

Part One

A PRIMER ON WEB AND DATA TECHNOLOGIES

2

HTML

There is a hidden standard behind almost everything that we see and do when surfing the web, the **H**yper**T**ext **M**arkup **L**anguage, short: **HTML**. Whether we look for information on Wikipedia, search for sites on Google, check our bank account, or *become social* on Twitter, Facebook, and YouTube—when we use a browser—we use HTML.

HTML is a language for presenting content on the Web that was first proposed by Tim Berners-Lee (1989). The standard has continuously evolved since the initial introduction, the most recent incarnation is HTML5 that is being developed by the World Wide Web Consortium (W3C) and the Web Hypertext Application Technology Working Group (WHATWG).[1] Although each revision of HTML has established new features and restructured old ones, the basic grammar of HTML documents has not changed much over the years and is likely to remain fairly stable in the foreseeable future, making it one of the most important standards for working with and on the Web.

This chapter introduces the fundamentals of HTML from the perspective of a web data collector. We will learn how to use browsers to display the source code of webpages and inspect specific HTML elements (Section 2.1). Section 2.2 develops the logic of markup languages in general and the syntax of HTML as a specific instance of a markup language. We go on to present the most important vocabulary in HTML (Section 2.3). Finally, we consider parsing—the process of reconstructing the structure and semantics of HTML documents—and how it helps to retrieve information from web documents in Section 2.4.

[1] The W3C develops standards for web technologies. It was founded by Tim Berners-Lee and currently comprises a staff of a couple dozen employees as well as hundreds of member organizations (see www.w3.org). In the course of this book we will mainly get in touch with W3C because of their recommended techniques. For example, HTML, XML, HTTP, and other technologies we are discussing in this volume are W3C recommendations. Endorsements by the W3C are a strong signal to web developers that they can and should rely on these techniques.

Automated Data Collection with R: A Practical Guide to Web Scraping and Text Mining, First Edition.
Simon Munzert, Christian Rubba, Peter Meißner and Dominic Nyhuis.

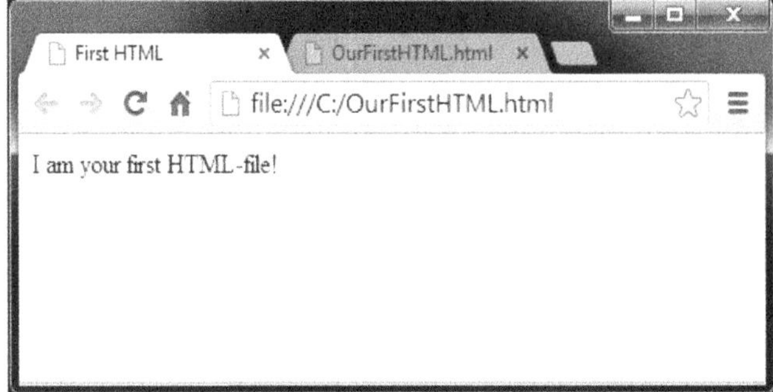

Figure 2.1 Browser view of a simple HTML document

2.1 Browser presentation and source code

An HTML file is basically nothing but plain text—it can be opened and edited with any text editor. What makes HTML so powerful is its marked up structure. HTML markup allows defining the parts of a document that need to be displayed as headlines, the parts that contain links, the parts that should be organized as tables, and numerous other forms. The markup definitions rely on predefined character sequences—the tags—that enclose parts of the text. Markup tells browsers (more specifically, parsers; see Section 2.4) how the document is structured and the function of its various parts.

What you see in your browser is therefore not the HTML document itself but an interpretation of it. Let us elaborate this idea with a small example. Figures 2.1 and 2.2 show the same HTML document—*OurFirstHTML.html*. Figure 2.1 displays an interpreted version of the file like we are used to; Figure 2.2 shows the *source code* of the document. Try it yourself. Use your browser and go to http://www.r-datacollection.com/materials/html/OurFirstHTML.html. Right-click on the window and select *view source code* from the context menu. Now check out other websites and inspect their source code. Under ordinary circumstances there is little reason to inspect the source code, but in online data collection it is often crucial. Incidentally, as we introduce the specifics of the HTML format over the course of this chapter

First HTML OurFirstHTML.html
view-source:file:///C:/OurFirstHTML.htr

```
<!DOCTYPE html>
<html>
  <head>
    <title>First HTML</title>
  </head>
  <body>
    I am your first HTML-file!
  </body>
</html>
```

Figure 2.2 Source view of a simple HTML document

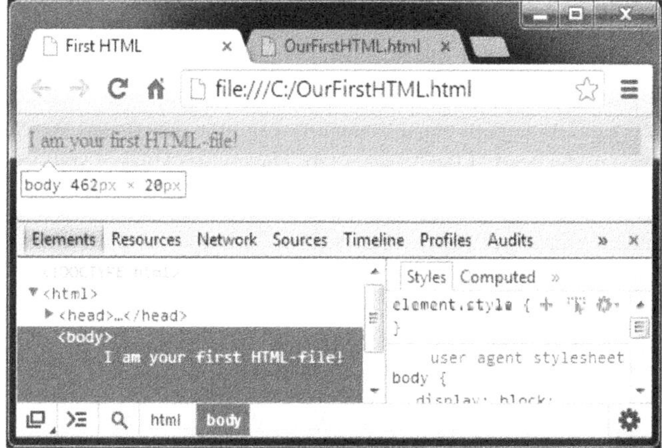

Figure 2.3 Inspect elements view of a simple HTML document

we will make reference to several supplementary files that are available at http://www.r-datacollection.com/materials/html/.

Markup in action

It might seem that a lot of information from the source code gets lost in the interpretation of the document. After all, there is considerably more text in the source code than just the single sentence we see in Figure 2.1. In fact, the scale of structuring information and actual content is clearly tipped in favor of the former. There is a fair amount of text in the source code that contains instructions for the browser that is not printed to the screen. Nevertheless, part of the information is in fact displayed, but in more subtle ways. Have a look at the browser tab headings in Figure 2.1. The page title is *First HTML*, which was defined in the source code: `<title>First HTML</title>`. This is HTML markup in action: `First HTML` was marked up by `<title>` and `</title>` to define it as the title of the document.

To identify which parts of the source code correspond to which elements in the browser window and vice versa, we can use an *element inspector*, which is implemented in most browsers. Again, try it yourself. Highlight the sentence in the browser window that we opened above, right-click on the window, and select *inspect element* from the context menu. The browser will display the part of the HTML document that is responsible for the selected element (Figure 2.3). We can also reverse the process by clicking on parts of the source code to highlight the corresponding parts in the interpreted version of the document. Try to do the same with other websites and start inspecting elements.

2.2 Syntax rules

Now that we have checked out our first HTML document and learned about the difference between the interpreted version of a document and its source code, let us dive deeper into the rules and concepts that underlie HTML.[2]

[2] Note that although there are several versions of HTML and you might encounter websites that adhere to older standards, we present documents that follow HTML5 rules. Either way, for the purposes of data collection the differences are negligible.

2.2.1 Tags, elements, and attributes

Elements Plain text is turned into an HTML document by tags that can be interpreted by a browser. They can be thought of as named braces that enclose content and define its structural function. For instance, the <title> tags in our introductory example designated the enclosed text as title to be displayed in the head of the browser tab. The combination of start tag, content, and end tag is called *element*, as in:

```
<title>First HTML</title>
```

Start tags and end tags are also known as opening and closing tags. Tags are always enclosed by < and > to distinguish them from the content. Start and end tags carry the same name, but the end tag is preceded by a slash /. When referring to an element, it is common to leave out the angle brackets and just use the name within the tags, as in body tag, title tag and so on. We sometimes find that elements and tags are actually used synonymously. Throughout the book, we will refer to the start tag—for example, <name>—to address the entire element.

Although it is recommended that each element has a start and an end tag, this is not common practice for all types of elements. For example, the <br> tag indicates a line break and is not closed by a </br> counterpart. Tags can also be closed within the start tag by adding a slash at the end, as in <body/>. We call such elements *empty* because they do not hold any content. Otherwise they would have to be written as <body></body>. It is possible to write a tag as <tagname>, <TAGNAME>, <TagName> or any other combination of capital and small letters, as standard HTML is not case sensitive. It is nevertheless recommended to always use small letters as in <tagname>.

Attributes Another feature of tags are attributes. A widely used attribute is the following:

```
<a href="http://www.r-datacollection.com/">Link to Homepage</a>
```

The anchor tag <a> allows the association of text—here, 'Link to Homepage'—with a hyperlink—http://www.r-datacollection.com/—that points to another address. The href="http://www.r-datacollection.com/" attribute specifies the anchor. Browsers automatically format such elements by underlining the content and making it clickable. In general, attributes enable the specification of options for how the content of a tag should be handled. Which attributes are permitted depends on the specific tag.

Attributes are always placed within the start tag right after the tag name. A tag can hold multiple attributes that are simply separated by a space character. Attributes are expressed as name–value pairs, as in name="value". The value can either be enclosed by single or double quotation marks. However, if the attribute value itself contains one type of quotation mark, the other type has to be used to enclose the value:

```
<example quote='He sat down and spoke: "What?", he said.'>
<example quote="He sat down and spoke: 'What?', he said.">
```

```
<!DOCTYPE html>
<html>
  <head>
   <title>First HTML</title>
  </head>
  <body>
   I am your first HTML file!
  </body>
</html>
```

Figure 2.4 Source code of *OurFirstHTML.html*

2.2.2 Tree structure

Have another look at the source code of *OurFirstHTML.html* in Figure 2.4. Ignoring <!DOCTYPE html> for now, the first element in the example is the <html> element. Between the tags of this element, several tags are opened and closed again: <head>, <title>, and <body>. The <head> and <body> tags are directly enclosed by the <html> element; the <title> element is enclosed by the <head> tag. A good way to describe the multiple layers of an HTML document is the tree analogy. Figure 2.5 illustrates the simple tree structure of *OurFirstHTML.html*. The <html> element is the root element that splits into two branches, <head> and <body>. <head> is followed by another branch called <title>.

Elements need to be strictly nested within each other in a well-formed and valid HTML file. A pair of start and end tags has to be completely enclosed by another pair of tags. An obvious violation of this rule would be:

```
<head>
 <title>Do not
</head>
 do this</title>
```

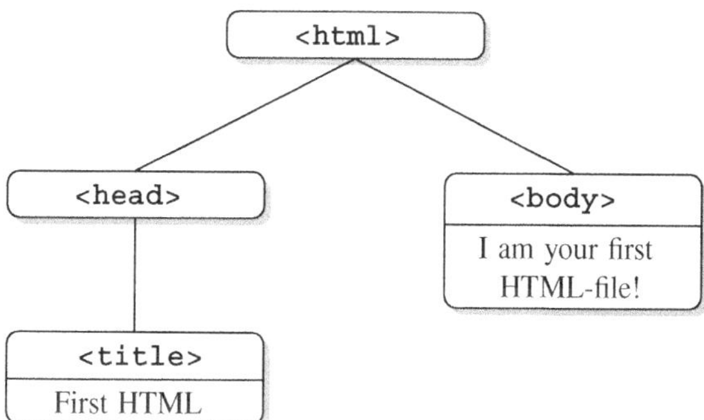

Figure 2.5 A tree perspective on *OurFirstHTML.html* (see Figure 2.4)

2.2.3 Comments

HTML offers the possibility to insert comments into the code that are not evaluated and therefore not displayed in the browser. Comments are marked by <!-- at the beginning and --> at the end. All text between these character sequences will be ignored. In practice, a comment could look like this:

```
<!-- Hi, I am a comment.
I can span several lines and I am able to store additional
  content that is not displayed by the browser. -->
```

Note that comments are still part of the document and can be read by anyone who inspects the source code of a page.

2.2.4 Reserved and special characters

Reserved characters are used for control purposes in a language. We have learned that HTML content is written in plain text, which is true both for the markup and the content part of the document. As some characters are needed for the markup, they cannot be used literally in the content. For example, we have learned that < and > are used to form tags in HTML. They are markup characters. Imagine we want to display something like this in the browser: 5 < 6 but 7 > 3. It is impossible to include them plainly into an HTML file, like…

```
<p>5 < 6 but 7 > 3 </p>
```

Character entities

… as the parser would interpret the < and > signs as enclosing a tag name. In order to display the characters literally in a browser window, HTML relies on specific sequences of characters called *character entities* or simply *entities*. All the entities start with an ampersand & and end with a semicolon ;. Thus, < and > can be included in the content of a file with their entity expressions < and >. When interpreting the HTML file, the browser will now display the character that these entities represent. The above example therefore needs to be rewritten as follows:

```
<p>5 &lt; 6 but 7 &gt; 3 </p>
```

Since HTML documents can be written in numerous languages that often contain non-simple latin characters like *Ö*, *É*, or *Ø*, there is an extensive list of entities, all starting with an ampersand (&) and ending with a semicolon (;). Table 2.1 provides a couple of examples of characters and their entity representation—note that entities can be written either by number or name.

Table 2.1 HTML entities

Character	Entity number	Entity name	Explanation
"	"	"	quotation mark
'	'	'	apostrophe
&	&	&	ampersand
<	<	<	less than
>	>	>	greater than
			non-breaking space
§	§	§	section
Á	À	À	A with grave accent
É	È	È	E with grave accent
á	à	à	a with grave accent
é	è	è	e with grave accent
♡	♥	♥	heart
𐇑	𐇑		plumed head (Phaistos Disc)

Note: For a more comprehensive list of HTML entities, visit http://unicode-table.com

2.2.5 Document type definition

Recall the example from the beginning of the chapter? The first line of the HTML read <!DOCTYPE html>. It contains the so-called document type definition (DTD) that informs the browser about the version of the HTML standard the document adheres to. HTML emerged more than 20 years ago and has since seen some reformulation of the rules that might lead to misinterpretations if the HTML version of the document was not made explicit. As the DTD plays a more crucial role in XML, we postpone an extensive elaboration of the concept to Section 3.3. For now, it suffices to know that DTDs are found—if included—in the first line of the HTML document. Below you find a list of various DTDs.

- HTML5:

```
<!DOCTYPE HTML>
```

- Strict HTML version 4.01:

```
<!DOCTYPE HTML PUBLIC "-//W3C//DTD HTML 4.01//EN"
 "http://www.w3.org/TR/html4/strict.dtd">
```

2.2.6 Spaces and line breaks

Spaces and line breaks in HTML source code do not translate directly into spaces and line breaks in the browser presentation. While line breaks are ignored altogether, any number of consecutive spaces are presented as a single space. To force spaces into the interpreted version of the document, we use the non-breaking space entity ` ` and the line break tag `<br>` for line breaks:

```
<p>Writing<br>   code<br>    
 is<br> poetry</p>
```

For a more extensive treatment of the subject, you may want to look into *SpacesAndLineBreaks.html* from the book's materials.

2.3 Tags and attributes

HTML has plenty of legal tags and attributes, and it would go far beyond the scope of this book to talk about each and every one. Instead, we will focus on a subset of tags that are of special interest in the context of web data collection. Note that if not specified otherwise working examples of the tags introduced in the following can be found in the *TagExample.html* from the book's materials.

2.3.1 The anchor tag <a>

The H in HTML

The anchor tag `<a>` is what turns HTML from just a markup language into a hypertext markup language by enabling HTML documents to link to other documents. Much of the site-to-site navigation in browsers works via anchor elements.

We often find ourselves in situations where we want to extract information not from a single page but from a whole series of pages. If we are lucky, the pages are listed on an index page. More frequently, however, we have to collect links from one page that points to the next page, which points to the next page, and so on. In both cases the information we are looking for—the location of another page—is stored in an `<a>` element.

The flexibility of `<a>` and `href`

In fact, `<a>` elements are even more flexible as they can not only link to other files, but also link to specific parts of a document. It is possible to link to anchors in a document to make navigation on a site more convenient.

Have a look at *TagExample.html*. The parts of the HTML that are most interesting to us at the moment are the blue underlined text snippets—the hyperlinks. There should be three links. One refers to another webpage and two other point to the top and bottom, respectively, of the current page. Have a look at the source code or the following list to see how this was achieved.

- Linking to another document:

```
<a href="en.wikipedia.org/wiki/List_of_lists_of_lists">Link with
    absolute path</a>
```

- Setting a reference point:

```
<a id="top">Reference Point</a>
```

- Linking to a reference point:

```
<a href="#top">Link to Reference Point</a>
```

- Linking to reference point in another document:

```
<a href="http://en.wikipedia.org/wiki/List_of_pharaohs#New_Kingdom">
    Link to Reference Point</a>
```

2.3.2 The metadata tag <meta>

The <meta> tag is an empty tag written in the head element of an HTML document. <meta> elements do not have to be closed and thus differ from the general rule that empty elements have to be closed with a dash /. As the name already suggests, <meta> provides meta information on the HTML document and answers questions like: Who is the author of the document? Which encoding scheme is used? Are there any keywords characterizing the page? What is the language of the document?

In general, two attributes are specified in a meta element. The first attribute can be either name or http-equiv; the second is always content. <meta> elements with name as first attribute refer to information on the document while meta elements with http-equiv define how the document needs to be handled by HTTP (see Chapter 5). Below you find several examples showing the diverse usage of meta. To see <meta> in a real HTML document, check out *TagExample.html* again. Some popular <meta> tags are used for:

- specifying keywords:

```
<meta name="keywords" content="Automation, Data, R">
```

- asking robots not to index the page or to follow its links (on robots see Section 9.3.2):

```
<meta name="robots" content="noindex, nofollow">
```

- declaring character encodings (since HTML5):

```
<meta charset="ISO-8859-1"/>
```

- defining character encodings (prior to HTML5):

```
<meta http-equiv="content-type" content="text/html; charset=ISO-8859-1">
```

2.3.3 The external reference tag <link>

The link tag is used to link to and include information and external files. External information linked to the the HTML document might be license information for the website, a document listing authors, a help page for the website, an icon that appears in the browser tab or one or more style sheets that are used for layouts. The <link> element is empty and used within the <head> element. All information is provided with attributes. Below you find two examples of the most common use.

- specifying style sheets to use:

```
<link rel="stylesheet" href="htmlresources/awesomestyle.css"
type="text/css"/>
```

- specifying the icon associated with the website:

```
<link rel="shortcut icon" href="htmlresources/favicon.ico"
type="image/x-icon"/>
```

Again, you might also like to check the source code of *TagExample.html*. Note that the rel attribute describes the type of relationship between the current and the linked document. The href attribute specifies the location of the external file. The type attribute describes the file type according to the MIME scheme[3].

2.3.4 Emphasizing tags <b>, <i>, <strong>

Tags like <b>, <i>, <strong> are layout tags that refer to bold, italics, and strong emphasis. We can make use of the information in emphasis tags to locate content with a specific layout. Imagine a document that contains a list of addresses where the name is set in italics. Looking for the <i> tag makes it easy to identify the useful information. The examples below exemplify the usage of these various *layout* tags. *TagExample.html* shows how they work in a full-fledged HTML document.

- Text with bold type setting:

```
<b>some text set in bold</b>
```

- Text set in italics:

```
<i>some text set in italics</i>
```

[3] The MIME scheme is a standardized two-part identifier for file formats. For a more extensive discussion of the subject, see Chapter 5.

- Text defined as important:

```
<strong>some text so important to be emphasized</strong>
```

2.3.5 The paragraphs tag <p>

<p>

The <p> tag labels its content as being a paragraph and ensures that line breaks are inserted before and after its content:

```
<p>This text is going to be a paragraph one day and separated from other
    text by line breaks.</p>
```

2.3.6 Heading tags <h1>, <h2>, <h3>, ...

<h1>, <h2>,...

In order to define different levels of headlines—level 1 to level 6—HTML provides a series of tags <h1>, <h2>, ... down to <h6>. See below for some examples:

```
<h1>heading of level 1 -- this will be BIG</h1>
<h2>heading of level 2 -- this will be big</h2>
...
<h6>heading of level 6 -- the smallest heading</h6>
```

2.3.7 Listing content with <ul>, <ol>, and <dl>

Several tags exist to list content. They are used depending on whether they wrap around an ordered list (<ol>), an unordered list (ul), or a description list (<dl>). The former two tags make use of nested <li> elements to define list items, while the latter needs two further elements: <dt> for keyword and <dd> for its description. An example for an unordered list would be:

```
<ul>
  <li>Dogs</li>
  <li>Cats</li>
  <li>Fish</li>
</ul>
```

2.3.8 The organizational tags <div> and <span>

Another way of defining the appearance of parts of the HTML document are the <div> and <span> tags. While <div> and <span> themselves do not change the appearance of the content they enclose, these tags are used to group parts of the document—the former is used to define groups across lines, tags, and paragraphs, while the latter is used for in-line grouping.

CSS Grouping parts of an HTML document is handy when combined with Cascading Style Sheets (CSS), a language for describing the layout of HTML and other markup documents like XML, SVG, and XHTML. Below you find example definitions of two styles. The first style definition applies to all `<div>` elements of class `happy`, while the second does the same for `<span>` elements:

```
div.happy { color:pink;
          font-family:"Comic Sans MS";
          font-size:120% }
span.happy { color:pink;
          font-family:"Comic Sans MS";
          font-size:120% }
```

Style definitions are commonly stored in separate CSS files, for example, *awesomestyle .css*, and are later included via `<link>` tags in the header:

```
<link href="htmlresources/awesomestyle.css"
    rel="stylesheet" type="text/css"/>
```

Later in the document they are passed to an element using an additional `class` attribute:

```
<div class="happy"><p>I am a happy styled paragraph</p></div>
non-happy text with <span class="happy">some happiness</span>
```

Alternatively, the style can be directly defined within the `style` attribute of an element:

```
<div
  style="color:pink; font-family:"Comic Sans MS"; font-size:120%">
<p>I am a happy styled paragraph</p></div>
```

The purpose of CSS is to separate content from layout to improve the document's accessibility. Defining styles outside of an HTML and assigning them via the `class` attribute enables the web designer to reuse styles across elements and documents. This enables developers to change a style in one single place—within the CSS file—with effects on all elements and documents using this style.

So why should we care about style? First of all, one should always care about style. But second, as CSS is so handy for developers, `<div>`, `<span>`, and `class` tags are used frequently. They thus provide structure to the HTML document that we can make use of to identify where our desired information is stored.

2.3.9 The <form> tag and its companions

An advanced feature of HTML are forms. HTML forms do more than just layout content. They enable users to interact with servers by sending data to them instead of only receiving data from them. Forms are introduced by the `<form>` tag and supported by other tags like `<fieldset>`, `<input>`, `<textarea>`, `<select>`, and `<option>` and their respective attributes. This two-way exchange of information between user and server allows for a more dynamic browsing experience. Instances where we use forms on a daily basis are search engines like Google. We type in a query in the text field and a new site is called based on our request. Let us proceed with an example to explain various concepts of HTML forms. The code snippet below is part of *FormExample.html* from the book's materials:

```
<form name="submitPW" action="Passed.html" method="get">
 password:
 <input name="pw" type="text" value="">
 <input type="submit" value="SubmitButtonText">
 </form>
```

How HTML forms work

The form in the example consists of one `<form>` element and two `<input>` elements nested within the former. The `<form>` tag has a `name` attribute, an `action` attribute, and a specific `method`. The `name` of the form serves as an internal identifier. The `action` and `method` attributes define what the browser is supposed to do once the *submit button* is pressed. `action` defines the location of the response.

The most common protocol for requesting and receiving resources on the Web is HTTP (Hypertext Transfer Protocol). The `method` attribute refers to the HTTP method that is used to send the information to the server. Most likely it will be *POST* or *GET*. For now it suffices to say that when *GET* is used, the information that is sent to the server is appended to the URL. Conversely, when *POST* is used the information is not transmitted via the requested URL. For details on HTTP methods, see Chapter 5.

Regarding the `<input>` elements we can distinguish between several *flavors*. There are normal inputs, hidden inputs, reset inputs, and those that are used to define the submit button. Normal inputs collect the data to be sent to the server and come in various forms like text fields, color selectors, check boxes, date selectors, and sliders. Hidden inputs define data that is sent to the server but the user has no option to manipulate the input. Reset inputs simply reset all inputs and selections made so far. Inputs that form submit buttons result in sending the supplied data. The input *flavor* is defined by the value of the `type` attribute. For hidden inputs the type is `hidden`, for reset inputs `reset`, and for submit buttons `submit`. The types for normal inputs depend on the type of information that is collected, for example, `text`, `color`, `checkbox`, `date`, and `range`.

Inputs require two attributes. First, the `name` attribute unambiguously associates the information with a specific input; the `type` attribute is required to tell the browser how to gather the information. An optional attribute, `value`, supplies a default value that is sent to the server if no information is supplied by the user.

Three other tags can be used to gather information in a form—`<textarea>` and `<select>` in combination with `<option>`. `<textarea>` elements are used to gather text that spans multiple lines. To select one or multiple items from a list, HTML documents use

`<select>`. While the `<select>` element serves to set attribute values, the nested `option` elements define the list of items the user can select from. Similar to the `<input>` elements, a name attribute is needed for sending the data from `<textarea>` and `<select>` elements. For an overview of the various types of inputs, check out *InputTypes.html*.

To see forms in action, go to: http://www.r-datacollection.com/materials/html/FormExample.html. The page pretends to be a gate keeper and asks for a password. As we are about halfway through the HTML chapter we trust that you are able to guess the password with three tries at most. Go ahead and give it a try! In the example the `action` attribute is set to *Passed.html*, meaning that the password gathered on the first page gets submitted to this new page. Try it out once more and select another password. Again, we get to the new document and the page contains the information that we typed into the text field. HTML forms turn the static HTML dinosaur into a flexible and mighty tool.[4] The takeaway point is that the information gets sent and the response changes according to our inputs.

Let us consider the example form from above again. We notice that `pw` is the `name` of the first `<input>` element. We already know that the `name` attribute of `<input>` serves as a label for transporting the information. If you inspect the URL of the response you notice that the password has been appended to the URL, which now looks something like `.../Passed.html?pw=xxxxxxx`. From this we conclude that the form uses a `GET` method rather than a `POST` method—otherwise the pasword would not show up in the URL. The part of the URL that contains our password is called *query string*. Query strings always appear at the end of the URL and start with `?`. The information in query strings is written as `parameter=value` pairs—just like HTML tag attributes—and are separated by `&` if more than one pair is specified.

Now that you know about HTML forms and query strings, take a moment and use your browser to check out forms in actions. Find pages that use forms and look carefully if and how they use query strings. You might also want to go back to *Passed.html* in your browser and manipulate the `pw` value directly within the address bar to see what happens.

2.3.10 The foreign script tag <script>

HTML itself is not a programming language. HTML is a markup language that describes content and defines its presentation. Once an HTML file is loaded in the browser, it remains stable and does not change by events or user interaction. Nevertheless, we all know examples of highly dynamic websites. Most of them probably make heavy use of the `<script>` element.[5]

A first stab at JavaScript

The `<script>` element is a container for scripts that enable HTML to include functionality from other programming languages. This other language will frequently be JavaScript. JavaScript allows the browser to change the content and structure of the document after it has been loaded from the server, enabling user interaction and event handling.

In *FormExample.html* and *Passed.html* we already made use of the `<script>` element. There are two `<script>` elements in the *Passed.html* document. The first is placed within the header and defines the function that extracts the value of a specific parameter from the URL. The second is placed directly within the body and executes the function that searches

[4]To be fair, *Passed.html* is not pure HTML but includes some JavaScript, which we will touch upon in Chapter 6.

[5]See Chapter 6 for a more elaborate discussion of the topic.

for the value of the pw parameter. After storing the value in a variable, it writes the value into the HTML document.

Once again, go ahead and try it yourself: Open *Passed.html* and manipulate the URL so it looks something like this: .../Passed.html?pw=xxxx. Save the page on your hard disk (*right click*, *save as*) and reopen the saved page in your browser. Now check out the source code of the page before and after saving. While the original page contained the original source code, the second includes the changes your browser made after loading the page.

Let us get back to HTML and how we can recognize that JavaScript has been used. JavaScript can appear broadly in three forms: explicitly in a <script> element, implicitly by referring to an external JavaScript within a <script> element, and implicitly as an event in an HTML element. Below you find examples of all three types of JavaScript usage.

- Explicit JavaScript (printing the current time and date):

```
<script> document.write( Date() ); </script>
```

  This snippet adds the current date and time to the document.

- Reference to an external JavaScript and using its functions within another script element (printing the browser used to view the document):

```
<script src="htmlresources/browserdetect.js"></script>
<script> document.write(BrowserDetect.browser); </script>
```

  This snippet loads an external JavaScript file (browserdetect.js) and uses the functions it contains (BrowserDetect) to add information about the browser of the document.

- Triggering JavaScript with events (changing the style class when hovering over the element)

```
<p onmouseover="this.className='over'"
onmouseout="this.className='out'">
Hover Me!</p>
```

  This snippet triggers two events, one when the mouse cursor hovers over the element and one when the mouse cursor leaves the area of the element—onmouseover and onmouseout—and assigns two JavaScript functions that are executed whenever the events take place. The functions change the class of the element to *over* or *out* and the styles associated with these two classes take effect.

Now open http://www.r-datacollection.com/materials/html/JavaScript.html in your browser and have a look at the examples. The document displays the time you opened the document, shows the current time, indicates which browser you are using (the version number as well as the platform it is running on), changes colors from white to black as long

Table 2.2 Nominal GDP per capita

Rank	Nominal GDP (per capita, USD)	Name
1	170,373	Lichtenstein
2	167,021	Monaco
3	115,377	Luxembourg
4	98,565	Norway
5	92,682	Qatar

as you hover over the `Hover Me!` text, and adds text to the document when you fill out the text field and press enter.

Have a look at the source code and try to map which parts of the document are plain HTML and which are the work of JavaScript.

2.3.11 Table tags <table>, <tr>, <td>, and <th>

The next group of elements enables HTML to display tables. Check out Table 2.2 and compare it to its HTML code representation below. To begin a table we make use of `<table>`. We start new lines with `<tr>`. Within `<tr>`, we can either use `<td>` for defining cells or `<th>` for header cells.

Table 2.2 as HTML code—the full HTML document is *HTMLTable.html* from the book's materials:

```
<table>
  <tr> <th>Rank</th> <th>Nominal GDP</th> <th>Name</th>  </tr>
  <tr> <th></th>  <th>(per capita, USD)</th> <th></th>   </tr>
  <tr> <td>1</td> <td>170,373</td> <td>Lichtenstein</td> </tr>
  <tr> <td>2</td> <td>167,021</td> <td>Monaco</td>       </tr>
  <tr> <td>3</td> <td>115,377</td> <td>Luxembourg</td>   </tr>
  <tr> <td>4</td> <td>98,565</td>  <td>Norway</td>       </tr>
  <tr> <td>5</td> <td>92,682</td>  <td>Qatar</td>        </tr>
</table>
```

2.4 Parsing

After having learned the key features of HTML documents, we now turn to loading and representing the contents of HTML/XML files in an R session.[6] This step is crucial if we care to extract information from web documents in a principled and robust fashion from within R.[7]

[6] Although different in many respects, HTML and XML are similar regarding their grammar and thus, the discussion on HTML parsing is very relevant for XML parsing, too. XML is subject of the next chapter (Chapter 3).

[7] See Chapter 4 on how to exploit the parsed representation of parsed documents for data extraction.

While performing web scraping, we usually get in touch with HTML in two steps: First, we inspect content on the Web and examine whether it is attractive for further analyses. Second, we import HTML files into R and extract information from them. Parsing HTML occurs at both steps—by the browser to display HTML content nicely, and also by parsers in R to construct useful representations of HTML documents in our programming environment. In the remainder of this chapter we begin by motivating the use of parsers and then discuss some of the problems inherent in the process as well as their solutions.

2.4.1 What is parsing?

Before showing the application of a parser, let us think about why we need to *parse* the contents of marked up web documents such as HTML compared to merely *reading* them into an R session. The difference between reading and parsing is not just a semantic one. Instead, reading functions differ from parsing functions in that the former do not care to *understand* the formal grammar that underlies HTML but merely recognize the sequence of symbols included in the HTML file. To see that, let us employ base R's `readLines()` function, which loads the content of an HTML file. As a stylized, running example in this part, we consider *fortunes.html* (see the chapter's materials)—a simple HTML file that consists of several nuggets of R wisdoms. We apply `readLines()` on the document, store the output in an object called `fortunes`, and print its content to the screen:

```
R> url <- "http://www.r-datacollection.com/materials/html/fortunes.html"
R> fortunes <- readLines(con = url)
R> fortunes
```

`readLines()` maps every line of the input file to a separate value in a character vector. Although easy to use, `readLines()` creates a flat representation of the document, which is of limited use for extracting information from it. The main problem is that `readLines()` is agnostic about the different tag elements (name, attribute, values, etc.) and produces results that do not reflect the document's internal hierarchy as implied by the nested tags in any sensible way.

Document Object Model (DOM)

To achieve a useful representation of HTML files, we need to employ a program that *understands* the special meaning of the markup structures and reconstructs the implied hierarchy of an HTML file within some R-specific data structure. This representation is also referred to as the Document Object Model (DOM). It is a queryable data object that we can build from any HTML file and is useful for further processing of document parts. This transformation from HTML code to the DOM is the task of a DOM-style parser. Parsers belong to a general class of domain-specific programs that traverse over symbol sequences and reconstruct the semantic structure of the document within a data object of the programming environment. In the remainder of this book, we will use functionality from the XML package to parse web documents (Temple Lang 2013c). XML provides an interface to *libxml2*, a powerful parsing library written in C that is able to cope with many parsing-specific problems. To get started, let us parse *fortunes.html* and store it in a new object called `parsed_fortunes` using XML's `htmlParse()` function:

```
R> library(XML)
R> parsed_fortunes <- htmlParse(file = url)
R> print(parsed_fortunes)
<!DOCTYPE HTML PUBLIC "-//IETF//DTD HTML//EN">
```

```
<html>
<head><title>Collected R wisdoms</title></head>
<body>
<div id="R Inventor" lang="english" date="June/2003">
  <h1>Robert Gentleman</h1>
  <p><i>'What we have is nice, but we need something very different'</i></p>
  <p><b>Source: </b>Statistical Computing 2003, Reisensburg</p>
</div>

<div lang="english" date="October/2011">
  <h1>Rolf Turner</h1>
  <p><i>'R is wonderful, but it cannot work magic'</i> <br><emph>answering
  a request for automatic generation of 'data from a known mean and 95% CI'
</emph></p>
  <p><b>Source: </b><a href="https://stat.ethz.ch/mailman/listinfo/r-help">
R-help</a></p>
</div>

<address>
<a href="http://www.r-datacollectionbook.com"><i>The book homepage</i></a>
<a></a>
</address>

</body>
</html>
```

Printing the object to the screen, we receive a visual feedback that we created a copy of the file inside the R session. For conventional parsing tasks, `htmlParse()` will be all that is necessary to create a properly parsed document object. At a minimum, the function needs to be handed the file path via its `file` argument. This may either be an HTML file (or compressed archive of HTML files) that already exists on the hard drive or an URL pointing to a web document.

DOM parsing: A two-step process

`htmlParse()` and other DOM-style parsers effectively conduct the following steps.

1. `htmlParse()` first parses the entire target document and creates the DOM in a tree-like data structure of the C language. In this data structure every element that occurs in the HTML is now represented as its own entity, or as an individual node. All nodes taken together are referred to as the node set. The parsing process also includes an automatic validation step for malformation. From its source code (see object `fortunes`) we learn that *fortunes.html* contains two structural errors. Not only have some of the attribute values been left unquoted but also a closing tag for the second paragraph tag (`<p>`) is missing. Yet, as we see from the parsed output, these two flaws have both been remedied. This is due to *libxml2* which is capable to work on non-well-formed HTML documents because it recognizes errors and corrects them in order to create a valid DOM.

2. In the next step the C-level node structure is converted into an object of the R language. This is necessary because further processing of the DOM, for example, modifying and extracting information from it, is tremendously more convenient in a higher-level language such as R. Internally, R uses lists to reflect the hierarchical order of nodes. More specifically, the transformation between C and R is managed through so-called

handler functions. These handler functions regulate the translation of a C-level node into an R list element and can be intercepted by the user to determine whether and how a node should be reflected in the R object.

For most parsing tasks, you will find that `htmlParse()`'s default options are sufficiently powerful to create the DOM. Nevertheless, some control over the parsing process can be beneficial in cases where the target document is of considerable size, carries unnecessary information, or needs to be altered in some predefined way. To deal with these situations, the next section looks at ways to affect the building process of the DOM, for example, by formulating rules that structure the mapping of specific elements into an R object.

2.4.2 Discarding nodes

Discarding unnecessary parts of web documents in the parsing stage can help mitigate memory issues and enhance extraction speed. Handlers provide a comfortable way to manipulate (i.e., delete, add, modify) nodes in the tree construction stage. As we have already noted, handler functions regulate the conversion of the C-level node structure into the R-object. By default, that is, when the handlers are left unchanged, all nodes will be mapped into the R list structure, but we are free to manipulate this process.

Specifying handler functions

We specify handlers as a list of named functions, where the name corresponds to a node name and the function specifies what should happen with the node. The function is executed on encountering a node with a specific name. To exemplify, consider the problem of deleting the `<body>` node in our example HTML file. In the parsing stage, we can easily get rid of this node including all of its children, that is, nodes that are nested deeper in the tree as follows:

```
R> h1 <- list("body" = function(x){NULL})

R> parsed_fortunes <- htmlTreeParse(url, handlers = h1, asTree = TRUE)
R> parsed_fortunes$children
$html
<html>
 <head>
  <title>Collected R wisdoms</title>
 </head>
</html>
```

We first create an object `h1` containing a list of a function named after the node we want to delete. We then pass this object to the `htmlTreeParse()` function via its `handlers` argument. Printing `parsed_doc` to the screen shows that the `<body>` node is not part of the DOM tree anymore. Internally, the handler has replaced all instances of the `<body>` node with the `NULL` object, which is equivalent to deleting these nodes. When using handler functions, one needs to set the `asTree` argument to `TRUE` to indicate that the DOM should be returned and not the handler function itself.

Generic handlers

Via the XML package we can pass generic handler functions to operate on specific XML elements such as the processing instructions, XML comments, CDATA, or the general node set.[8] A complete overview over these generic handlers is presented in Table 2.3. To illustrate

[8]For an explanation of XML comments and CDATA see Chapter 3.

Table 2.3 Generic handlers for DOM-style parsing

Function name	Node type
`startElement()`	XML element
`text()`	Text node
`comment()`	Comment node
`cdata()`	<CDATA> node
`processingInstruction()`	Processing instruction
`namespace()`	XML namespace
`entity()`	Entity reference

Source: Adapted from Nolan and Temple Lang (2014, p. 153).

their use, consider the problem of deleting all nodes with name `div` or `title` as well as comments that appear in the document. We start again by creating a list of handler functions. Inside this list, the first handler element specifies a function for all XML nodes in the document (`startElement`). Handlers of that name allow describing functions that are executed on all nodes in the document. The function specifies a request for a node's name (`xmlName`) and implements a control structure that returns the `NULL` object if the node's name is either `div` or `title` (meaning we discard this node) or else includes the full node in the DOM tree. The second handler element (`comment`) specifies a function for discarding any HTML comment:

```
R> h2 <- list(
          startElement = function(node, ...){
            name <- xmlName(node)
            if(name %in% c("div", "title")){NULL}else{node}
          },
          comment = function(node){NULL}
)
```

Let us pass the handler function to `htmlTreeParse()`:

```
R> parsed_fortunes <- htmlTreeParse(file = url, handlers = h2, asTree = TRUE)
```

If we print `parsed_fortunes` to the screen, we find that we rid ourselves of the nodes specified in the handlers:

```
R> parsed_fortunes$children
$html
<html>
 <head/>
 <body>
  <address>
   <a href="http://www.r-datacollectionbook.com">
    <i>The book homepage</i>
   </a>
   <a/>
  </address>
 </body>
</html>
```

2.4.3 Extracting information in the building process

We motivated the parsing of HTML files as a necessary intermediate step to extracting information from web documents. In this process, we usually want the parser to traverse the entire C-level node set and then build the document tree in an R data structure from which we extract a particular information. Conceptually, there is an alternative strategy where we conduct the extraction directly during the parsing process. Under some circumstances, this strategy can provide considerable advantages since multiple loadings of a document can be avoided, although it is also a little bit more challenging compared to the DOM-style parsing approach presented before. Once again, handler functions play a key role in this process. But rather than using the handler to describe how a C-level node should be converted into an element of the R DOM tree, we now want to specify the handlers to route specific nodes into an R object of our own choosing. Ultimately, this saves us an additional traversal step and thus constitutes a more efficient way to pull out target information. Before we dive deeper into this section, we would like to point out that the contents of this section are fairly advanced. If you are not too familiar with R scoping issues, you might like to skip ahead to the summary of this chapter. You can continue with the book just fine without having read this part.

Scope issues

For an example, consider the problem of extracting the information from *fortunes.html* that is written in italics, that is, encapsulated with `<i>` tags. Underlying this task is a tricky problem of functional scope that we need to address. Ultimately, we want to create a data object containing the information in our current workspace or global environment. But functions in R—and our handler functions are no different—operate on local variables and have no writing access to the global environment, which is a necessary requirement for this problem.

Using closure handler functions

The solution is to define the handler function for the `<i>` nodes in the document as a so-called closure—a function that is capable of referencing objects that are not local to it. A closure function not only contains a function's arguments and body, but also an environment. Here, the environment is needed to define container variables to which we route the handler's output, as well as a return function for the variables' contents.

We start by defining a nesting function `getItalics()`. `i_container` is our local container variable that will hold all information set in italics. Next, we define the handler function for the `<i>` nodes. On the right side of the first line of this function, we concatenate the contents of the container variable with a new instance of the `<i>` node value. The resulting vector then overwrites the existing container object by using the super assignment operator `<<-`, which allows making an assignment to nonlocal variables. Lastly, we create a function called `returnI()` with the purpose of returning the container object just created:

```
R> getItalics = function() {
     i_container = character()
     list(i = function(node, ...) {
         i_container <<- c(i_container, xmlValue(node))
     }, returnI = function() i_container)
}
```

Next, we execute `getItalics()` and route its return values into a new object `h3`. Essentially, `h3` now contains our handler function, but additionally, the function can access `i_container` and `returnI()` as these two objects were created in the same environment as the handler function:

```
R> h3 <- getItalics()
```

Now we can pass this function to `htmlTreeParse()`'s handlers argument:

```
R> invisible(htmlTreeParse(url, handlers = h3))
```

For clarity, we employ the `invisible()` function to suppress printing of the DOM to the screen. To take a look at the fetched information we can make a call to `h3()`'s `returnI()` function to print all the occurrences of `<i>` nodes in the document to the screen:

```
R> h3$returnI()
[1] "'What we have is nice, but we need something very different'"
[2] "'R is wonderful, but it cannot work magic'"
[3] "The book homepage"
```

Summary

In this chapter we focused on getting a basic understanding of HTML. We learned that what we get presented when surfing the web is an interpreted version of the marked up source code that holds the content. Tags form the core of the markup used in HTML and can be used to define structure, appearance, and content. Furthermore, elements not only contain information but can also be used to transmit information from user to server or to incorporate functionality from other computer languages, most notably JavaScript. We should be able at this point to locate information we seek in the source code and to connect source code to browser interpretation and vice versa. Along with knowledge about the structure of HTML elements we are ready to learn how to exploit structure and layout of HTML files to collect the information we need.

Parsing is an important step in processing information from web documents. The native structure of HTML does not naturally map into R objects. We can import HTML files as raw text, but this deprives us of the most useful features of these documents. We have learned in this chapter how to parse the tree structure of HTML documents, giving them a representation in the R environment. We will learn powerful tools to locate and extract nodes within these objects and the information they hold in Chapter 4. But first we turn to XML, a more generic counterpart to HTML and a frequently used format to exchange data on the Web.

Further reading

As HTML is a W3C standard, we recommend a look at the W3 pages and the accompanied W3schools pages (http://www.w3schools.com) if you want to dive deeper into HTML and JavaScript. As HTML is also a WHATWG standard, you might like to check out their web pages for further information on HTML and related technologies (http://www.whatwg.org/). For example, the history section explains why W3C and WHATWG develop HTML5 parallelly. Further helpful web sources are the following.

- A complete list of tags with description and example:
  http://www.w3schools.com/tags
- A long list of special characters, symbols, and their entity representation:
  http://www.w3schools.com/charsets/ref_html_8859.asp

- A much much longer list of characters and their entity representation: http://unicode-table.com
- An HTML validator: http://validator.w3.org

For those who like it short but also like to hold a real book in their hands there is Niederst Robbins's (2013) less than 200 pages *HTML5 Pocket Reference*. You can find more thorough treatments of the subjects in Castro and Hyslop (2014) for HTML and CSS and Flanagan (2011) for JavaScript.

Problems

1. Why is it important that HTML is a web standard?
2. Write down the HTML tags for (a) the primary heading, (b) starting a new paragraph, (c) inserting foreign code, (d) constructing ordered lists, (e) creating a hyperlink, and (f) creating an email link!
3. HTML source code inspection.
   (a) Open three webpages you frequently use in your browser.
   (b) Have a look at the source code of all three.
   (c) Inspect various elements with the *Inspect Elements* tool of your browser.
   (d) Save each of them to your hard drive.
4. Building a basic HTML document, part I.
   (a) Write a minimal HTML file.
   (b) Add your name as a comment.
   (c) Add a level one and a level two headline.
   (d) Add some further content, for example, a sentence about the current weather.
   (e) Add a paragraph with some further content, for example, a sentence about tomorrow's weather.
5. Building a basic HTML document, part II.
   (a) Write a minimal HTML document.
   (b) Include a paragraph that contains 10 special characters—only five of them may be mentioned in Table 2.1.
   (c) Use http://www.r-datacollection.com/materials/html/simple.css as your default style file.
   (d) Check the validity of your document at http://validator.w3.org.
6. Building a basic HTML document, part III.
   (a) Write a minimal HTML document.
   (b) Include a table with two columns and three rows.
   (c) The first column should contain *first*, *second*, and *third*. The second column should contain links to your top three web pages.
   (d) Have a look at the list of tags at http://www.w3schools.com/tags. Try to use some of the tags you are not yet familiar with in your HTML document.

7. The base R function `download.file()` is a standard tool to gather data from the Web with R. Investigate the function's syntax and try to use it to save the front pages of your three most favorite websites to your local disk.

8. The base R functions `readLines()` and `writeLines()` can be used to import and export character data to and from R Try to use them to import the webpages you have gathered in the previous exercise and save them in different objects. Next, combine the three objects into a list object. Finally, use `writeLines()` to store the pages again in external files.

9. An encounter with JavaScript.
   (a) Check out http://www.r-datacollection.com/materials/html/fortunes3.html in your browser.
   (b) View the page's source code.
   (c) Download both JavaScript files linked to the document using the `download.file()` function.

10. Building a basic HTML document, part IV.
    (a) Write a minimal HTML document.
    (b) Include a form that has two inputs—`name` and `age`.
    (c) Define the form in a way that it sends data to http://www.r-datacollection.com/materials/http/GETexample.php via the GET method.
    (d) Make sure it works—the server should respond with *Hello YourName! You are YourAge years old.*
    (e) Try to send high age values. At what point does the response message change?

3

XML and JSON

XML, the e**X**tensible **M**arkup **L**anguage, is one of the most popular formats for exchanging data over the Web. But it is more than that. It is ubiquitous in our daily life. As Harold and Means (2004, xiii) note:

> XML has become the syntax of choice for newly designed document formats across almost all computer applications. It's used on Linux, Windows, Macintosh, and many other computer platforms. Mainframes on Wall Street trade stocks with one another by exchanging XML documents. Children playing games on their home PCs save their documents in XML. Sports fans receive real-time game scores on their cell phones in XML. XML is simply the most robust, reliable, and flexible document syntax ever invented.

XML looks familiar to someone with basic knowledge about HTML, as it shares the same features of a markup language. Nevertheless, HTML and XML both serve their own specific purposes. While HTML is used to shape the display of information, the main purpose of XML is to store data. Therefore, the content of an XML document does not get much nicer when it is opened with a browser—XML is data wrapped in user-defined tags. The user-defined tags make XML much more flexible for storing data than HTML. The main goal of this chapter is not to turn you into an XML coding expert, but to get you used to the key components of XML documents.

We start with a look at a running XML example (Section 3.1) and continue with an inspection of the XML syntax (Section 3.2). There are several ways to limit the endless flexibility in XML markup. We cover technologies that allow extending XML as well as defining new standards that simplify exchanging specific data on the Web efficiently in Sections 3.3 and 3.4. Section 3.5 shows how to handle XML data with R. If your web scraping task does not specifically involve XML data you might be fine to just scan this part

---

Automated Data Collection with R: A Practical Guide to Web Scraping and Text Mining, First Edition.
Simon Munzert, Christian Rubba, Peter Meißner and Dominic Nyhuis.

of the chapter as you are already familiar with the most important concepts of the XML language from the previous chapter.

Another standard for data storage and interchange we frequently find on the Web is the **J**avaScript **O**bject **N**otation, abbreviated JSON. JSON is an increasingly popular alternative to XML for data exchange purposes that comes with some preferable features. The second part of this chapter therefore turns to JSON. We introduce the format with a small example (Section 3.6), talk about the syntax (Section 3.7), and learn how to import JSON content into R and process the information (Section 3.8).

3.1 A short example XML document

We start with a short example of an XML file. The XML code in Figure 3.1 provides a sample of three James Bond movies, along with some basic information. Probably the most distinctive feature of XML code is that human readers have no problem in interpreting the data. Values and names are wrapped in meaningful tags. Each of the three movies is attributed with a name, a year, two actors, the budget, and the box office results. Indentation further facilitates reading but is not a necessary component of XML. It highlights the hierarchical structure of the document. The document starts with the root element <bond_movies>, which also closes the document. The elements are repeated for each movie entry—the content varies.

```
<?xml version="1.0" encoding="ISO-8859-1"?>
<bond_movies>
  <movie id="1">
    <name>Dr. No</name>
    <year>1962</year>
    <actors bond="Sean Connery" villain="Joseph Wiseman"/>
    <budget>1.1M</budget>
    <boxoffice>59.5M</boxoffice>
  </movie>
  <movie id="2">
    <name>Live and Let Die</name>
    <year>1973</year>
    <actors bond="Roger Moore" villain="Yaphet Kotto"/>
    <budget>7M</budget>
    <boxoffice>126.4M</boxoffice>
  </movie>
  <movie id="3">
    <name>Skyfall</name>
    <year>2012</year>
    <actors bond="Daniel Craig" villain="Javier Bardem"/>
    <budget>175M</budget>
    <boxoffice>1108.6M</boxoffice>
  </movie>
</bond_movies>
```

Figure 3.1 An XML code example: James Bond movies

Some elements are special. The element in the first line (`<?xml...>`) is not repeated, and this and the `<actors>` element hold some additional information between the `<...>` signs.

The XML language works quite intuitively. You should have no problems to expand and refine the dataset before even knowing every rule of the syntax. In fact, why not try it? Copy the file, go to Wikipedia, look for other details on the movies, and try to add them to the file! You can check later if you have written correct XML code. This is because information is stored as plain text and the tags that allow arranging the data in meaningful ways are entirely user-defined and should be comprehensible. While the tags might not even be necessary to interpret the data, they make XML a computer language and as such useful for communication on and between computers.

Why XML is so popular

The fact that XML is a plain text format is what makes it ultimately compatible. This means that whatever browser, operating system, or PC hardware we use, we can process it. No further information or decoder is needed to interpret the data and their structure. The tags are delivered along with the data and fully describe the document—this is commonly called *self-describing*. Further, as tags can be nested within each other, XML documents can be used to represent complex data structures (Murrell 2009, p. 116). We will discuss these structures in the following section. To be sure, although XML is so flexible, it possesses a clear set of rules that defines the basic layout of a document. We can use simple tools to check if these rules are obeyed.[1] There are also tools to further restrict structure and content in an XML document. Many developers have used the syntax of XML to create new XML-based languages that basically restrict XML to a fixed set of elements, structure, and content, which we will look deeper into in Sections 3.4.3 and 3.4.4. Still, these derived languages remain valid XML. XML has gained a considerable amount of its popularity through these extensions.

The downside of storing information in XML files is a lack of efficiency. Plain text XML documents often hold a lot of redundant information. Note that in standard XML, the starting and closing tags are repeated for every entry. This can consume more space in the document than the actual data. Especially when we deal with large datasets or data that provide highly hierarchical structure, it may take up a lot of memory to try to import and manipulate the data.

How to view XML files

The preferred program to open XML files are programs that are capable of highlighting the syntax of the documents and automatically indent the elements according to their level in the hierarchical structure. Current versions of all mainstream browsers are able to layout XML files adequately, and it is quite likely that your favorite code editor is capable of XML highlighting as well. Note, however, that XML files can be very large and contain millions of lines of data, so it may take a while to open them.

In the following sections we will talk more about the syntax of XML. We will learn how to import XML data into R and how to transform it into other data formats that are more convenient for analysis. We will also look at other XML "flavors" that are used to store a variety of data types. You might be surprised about the numerous applications that rely on XML and how one can make use of this knowledge for data scraping purposes.

3.2 XML syntax rules

As any other computer language, XML has a set of syntax rules and key elements we have to know in order to find our way in any document. But fear not: XML rules are very simple.

---

[1] However, as mostly passive users of XML, this is rarely of interest to us.

3.2.1 Elements and attributes

XML declaration

Take another look at Figure 3.1. It helps explain large parts of what we have to know about XML. An XML document always starts with a line that makes declarations for the XML document:

```
<?xml version="1.0" encoding="ISO-8859-1"?>
```

`version="1.0"` indicates the version of XML that is being used. There are currently two versions: XML 1.0 and XML 1.1.[2] Additionally, the declaration can, but need not hold the character encoding of the document, which in our case is `encoding="ISO-8859-1"`.[3] Another attribute the declaration can contain—but does not in our example—is the `standalone` attribute, which take values of `yes` or `no` and indicates whether there are external markup declarations that may affect the content of the document.[4]

Root element

An XML file must contain one and only one root element that embraces the whole document. In our case, it is:

```
<bond_movies>
  ...
<\bond_movies>
```

Element syntax

Information is usually stored in elements. An XML element is defined by its start tag and the content. An element frequently has an end tag, but can also be closed in the start tag with a slash `/`. It can contain

- *other elements*.
- *attributes*, bits of information that describe the element in more detail. Attributes, like elements, are slots for information, but they cannot contain further elements or attributes.
- *data* of any form and length, for example, text, numbers or symbols.
- *a mixture of everything*, which sounds complicated but is a rather ordinary case when elements contain other elements that contain data. For example, the `<movie>` elements in Figure 3.1 all contain an attribute, other elements, and data within the children elements.
- *nothing*, which means really nothing—no data, no other element, not even white spaces.

---

[2]The differences between the two existing versions are marginal and relate to encoding issues that are usually of no interest to us.

[3]To learn more about encodings, see Section 8.3.

[4]For more information, see the elucidations by W3C on http://www.w3.org/TR/xml/#sec-rmd

Consider the first <title> element from above:

```
<title>Dr. No</title>
```

Its constituent parts are

the element title	title
the start tag	<title>
the end tag	</title>
the data value	Dr. No

We are already familiar with the start tag–end tag logic from HTML. The benefit of this syntax is that we can easily locate data of a certain element in the document, regardless of where, that is, on which line or hierarchical level it is located. The element <title> occurs three times in the example. We could retrieve all of these elements by building a query like "give me the content of all elements named <title>." This is what we will learn in Chapter 4 when we learn how to use the query language XPath. A more compact way of writing elements is

```
<actors bond="Sean Connery" villain="Joseph Wiseman"/>
```

This element contains

the element name	actors
the start tag	<actors.../>
first attribute's name	bond
first attribute's value	Sean Connery
second attribute's name	villain
second attribute's value	Joseph Wiseman

Attributes

In this case there is no end tag but only a start tag. This is a so-called *empty* element because the element contains no data. Empty elements are closed with a slash /. The element in the example is of course not literally empty. Just like in HTML, XML elements can contain attributes that provide further information. There is no limit to the number of attributes an element can contain. The example element has two attributes. They are separated by a white space. Attributes are always part of a start tag and hold their values in quotes after an equal sign. The information stored in attributes is called *attribute value*. Attribute values always have to be put in quotes, either using single quotes like bond='Sean Connery' or double quotes like bond="Daniel Craig". However, if the attribute value itself contains quotes, you should use the opposed pair of quotes for the attribute value:

```
<actors henchman="Richard 'Jaws' Kiel"/>
```

Elements vs. attributes

As the structure of an XML document is inherently flexible, there are many ways to store the same content. Note how the actors were stored in the running example in Figure 3.1. Another way would have been the following:

```
<actors>
  <bond>Sean Connery</bond>
  <villain>Jospeh Wiseman</villain>
</actors>
```

All information is retained, but the actors' names are now stored in elements, not attributes. Both ways are equally valid. The problem with attributes is that they do not allow further branching—attributes cannot be expanded and can only contain one value. Besides, we find them more difficult to read and more inconvenient to extract compared to elements. They are, however, not altogether useless. Take a look at the code in Figure 3.1. Attributes named `id` are used to make elements with the same name uniquely identifiable. This can be of help when we need to manipulate information in a particular element of the XML tree.

3.2.2 XML structure

Each XML document can be represented as a hierarchical tree. The fact that data are stored in a hierarchical manner is well suited for many data structures we are confronted with: Survey participants are nested within countries. Survey participants' responses are nested within survey participants. Votes are nested within polling stations that are nested within electoral districts that are nested within countries, and so on. Figure 3.2 gives a graphical representation of the XML data from the XML code in Figure 3.1. At the very top stands the root element <bond_movies>. All other elements have one and only one *parent*. In fact, we can apply a family tree analogy to the entire document, describing each element as a *node*:

- the `movie` nodes are *children* of the root node `bond_movies`;
- the `movie` nodes are *siblings*;
- the `bond_movie` node is the *parent* of the `movie` nodes, which are *parents* of the `title, ..., boxoffice` nodes;
- the `title, ..., boxoffice` nodes are *grandchildren* of `bond_movies`.

Note that the attributes and their values are presented in the element value boxes in Figure 3.2, even though they could be viewed as further leaves in the XML tree. However, as attributes cannot be parents to other elements or attributes, they are rather *element-describing* content than autonomous nodes. Nevertheless, they are strictly speaking attribute nodes.

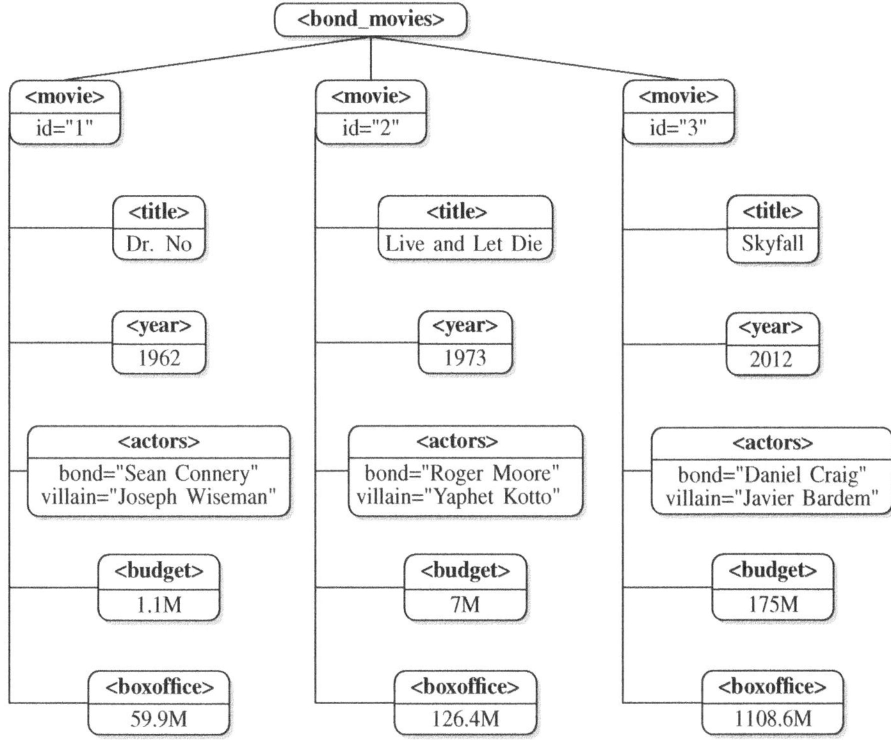

Figure 3.2 Tree perspective on an XML document

Elements must be strictly nested, which means that no cross-nesting is allowed. An illegal document structure would be:

```
<family>
  <father>Jack</father>
  <mother>Josephine</mother>
  <child>Jonathan
     <family>
     <mother>Julia</mother>
     <child>Jeff</child>
</family>
     </family>
  </child>
```

While it is theoretically sensible that the element `<child>` with the value `Jonathan` opens a new `<family>` branch containing `Jonathan`'s wife `Julia` and their child `Jeff`, `Jonathan`'s `<child>` element has to be closed before the `<family>` element.

3.2.3 Naming and special characters

Element names One of the strengths of XML is that we are basically free to chose the names of elements. However, there are some naming rules:

- Element names can be composed of letters, numbers, and other characters, like in `<name1>…</name1>`. Special characters like ä, ö, ü, é, è, or à are allowed, but not recommended—they might limit the compatibility of XML files across systems.
- Names must not start with a number, like in `<123name>…</123name>`.
- Names must not start with a punctuation character, like in `<.name>…</.name>`.
- Names must not start with the letters xml (or XML, or Xml, etc.), like in `<xml.rootname>…</xml.rootname>`.
- Element names and attribute names are case sensitive. `<movie>` is not the same as `<MOVIE>` or `<Movie>`.
- Names must not contain spaces, like in `<my family>…</my family>`.

As in HTML, there are some characters that cannot be used literally in the content as they are needed for markup. To represent these characters in the content, they have to be replaced by escape sequences. These entities are listed in Table 3.1 and used as follows

```
<actor protagonist="Scarlett O&apos;Hara"/>
<math_wisdom>pi&gt;3</math_wisdom>
```

You do not always need to escape special characters. For example, apostrophes are sometimes left unescaped, like in `"Richard 'Jaws' Kiel"` in the example above. In this case, the apostrophes are unambiguous because the attribute value is enclosed by double quotes. Using apostrophes in XML element values is usually no problem either, because they have no special meaning in the value slot of the element, only inside tags as limiters to attribute values.

Table 3.1 Predefined entities in XML

Character	Entity reference	Description
<	`<`	Less than
>	`>`	Greater than
&	`&`	Ampersand
"	`"`	Double quotation mark
'	`'`	Single quotation mark

3.2.4 Comments and character data

Comments

XML provides a way to comment content with the syntax

```
<!-- an arbitrary comment -->
```

Everything in between <!-- and --> is not treated as part of the XML code and therefore ignored by parsers. Comments may be used between tags or within element content, but not within element or attribute names.

The use of escape sequences can be cumbersome when the elements to be escaped are common in the data values. For example, imagine the following character sequence needs to be stored in an XML file

```
1 < 3 < pi < 9 <= sqrt(81) < 1'081 > -2 > -999
```

In XML code, this would translate to

```
1 &lt; 3 &lt; pi &lt; 9 &lt;= sqrt(81) &lt; 1&apos;081 &gt; -2 &gt; -999
```

CDATA

To avoid this mess, XML provides an environment that prevents the content from being interpreted. It is called *CDATA* and works as follows

```
<![CDATA[
1 < 3 < pi < 9 <= sqrt(81) < 1'081 > -2 > -999
]]>
```

All characters in the *CDATA* section are taken as is. The difference between comments and a *CDATA* section is that a comment is not part of the document ...

```
<?xml version="1.0" encoding="ISO-8859-1"?>
<bond_movies>
  <movie id="1">
    <title>Dr. No</title>
    <year>1962</year>
    <actors bond="Sean Connery" villain="Joseph Wiseman"/>
    <budget>1.1M</budget>
    <boxoffice>59.5M</boxoffice>
  </movie>
<!-- more movies & details to follow here!  -->
</bond_movies>
```

… whereas a *CDATA* section is:

```
<?xml version="1.0" encoding="ISO-8859-1"?>
<bond_movies>
  <movie id="1">
    <title>Dr. No</title>
    <year>1962</year>
    <actors bond="Sean Connery" villain="Joseph Wiseman"/>
    <budget>1.1M</budget>
    <boxoffice>59.5M</boxoffice>
    <deadpeople>
    <![CDATA[
           "John Strangways" & "Chauffeur" & "Prof R.J. Dent"
           & "Quarrel" & "Dr. No"
       ]]>
       </deadpeople>
  </movie>
</bond_movies>
```

If we write both snippets in an XML file and open it with a browser, the comments are not displayed or explicitly highlighted as part of the XML tree. In contrast, the *CDATA* section is displayed in the tree. If we delete the *CDATA* tags, this will produce an error because the browser fails to interpret the ampersands and quotation marks.

You may want to try this out yourself. Save the last code snippet with your text editor as an XML file and open it with your browser. Modify the content of the XML file, save it, and reload the content with the browser. Experiment with allowed and disallowed changes. Try special characters, cross-nested tags, and forbidden element names.

3.2.5 XML syntax summary

To sum up, the XML syntax comprises the following set of rules:

1. An XML document must have a root element.
2. All elements must have a start tag and be closed, except for the declaration, which is not part of the actual XML document.
3. XML elements must be properly nested.
4. XML attribute values must be quoted.
5. Tags are named with characters and numbers, but may not start with a number or “xml.”
6. Tag names may not contain spaces and are case sensitive.
7. Space characters are preserved.
8. Some characters are illegal and have to be replaced by meta characters.

9. Comments can be included as follows: `<!-- comment -->`.
10. Content can be excluded from parsing using: `<![CDATA[...]]>`.

3.3 When is an XML document well formed or valid?

Well-formed and valid XML

In short, an XML document is *well formed* when it follows all of the syntax rules from the previous section. Techniques to extract information from XML documents rely on properly written syntax. If we are in doubt that an XML document is well formed, there are ways to check. For instance, the XML Validator on http://www.xmlvalidation.com/ checks for mismatches between start and end tags, whether attribute values are quoted, whether illegal characters have been used, in short: whether any of the rules are violated.

The Document Type Definition (DTD)

We can distinguish between *well formed* and *valid* XML. An XML document is valid when it

1. is well formed and
2. conforms to the rules of a Document Type Definition.

As we have seen, the structure of an XML document is arbitrary—tag names and levels of hierarchy are defined by the user. However, there is a way to restrict this arbitrariness by using Document Type Definitions, DTDs. A DTD is a set of declarations that defines the XML structure, how elements are named, and what kind of data they should contain. A DTD for our running example in Figure 3.1 could look like this

```
<?xml version="1.0" encoding="ISO-8859-1"?>
<!DOCTYPE bond_movies [
<!ELEMENT bond_movies (movie)>
<!ELEMENT movie (title,year,actors,budget,boxoffice)>
<!ELEMENT title (#PCDATA)>
<!ELEMENT year (#PCDATA)>
<!ELEMENT actors (#PCDATA)>
<!ELEMENT budget (#PCDATA)>
<!ELEMENT boxoffice (#PCDATA)>
<!ATTLIST actors
 bond CDATA #IMPLIED
 villain CDATA #IMPLIED>
<!ATTLIST movie id CDATA #IMPLIED>
]>
<bond_movies>
  ...
<\bond_movies>
```

In this variant, the DTD is included in the XML document and wrapped in a DOCTYPE definition, `<!DOCTYPE bond_movies [...]>`. This is called an internal DTD. For the purpose of web scraping we normally do not need to be able to write DTDs, so we will not explain every detail of the declaration syntax but just provide some fundamentals on the appearance of DTDs. Elements can be declared like

```
<!ELEMENT element (#PCDATA)> <!-- element contains only parsed
    character data -->
<!ELEMENT element ANY> <!-- element contains any data that can be
    parsed -->
```

Children of elements are declared as follows

```
<!ELEMENT element (child1,child2,child3,...)>
<!ELEMENT element (child1)>  <!-- child occurs only once -->
<!ELEMENT element (child1+)> <!-- child occurs 1 or more times -->
<!ELEMENT element (child1*)> <!-- child occurs 0 or more times -->
<!ELEMENT element (child1?)> <!-- child occurs at most once -->
```

It gets a bit more complicated with the declaration of mixed content. If, for example, an element contains one or more occurrences of the <child1> to <child3> elements or simply parsed character data, the declaration would look like

```
<!ELEMENT element (child1|child2|child3|#PCDATA)+>
```

Declaring attributes can look as follows

```
<!ATTLIST element attribute CDATA #IMPLIED>
```

The IMPLIED attribute value means that the corresponding attribute is optional; REQUIRED would mean that the attribute is required. There are multiple online tools that allow validating XML files against a DTD. Just type "dtd validation" into a search engine and pick one of the first results.

Why should we care whether an XML document is well formed or valid? Above all, it is important to know that many files come with an internal DTD at the beginning of the document. In general, DTDs serve several purposes. Data exchanges can be standardized as senders and receivers know in advance what they are supposed to send and get. As a sender, you can check if your own XML files are valid. As a receiver it is possible to check whether the XML you retrieve is of the kind you or your program expects.

XML schemas DTD itself is only one of several XML schema languages. Such languages help to describe and constrain the structure and content of an XML document. Another schema language is XML Schema (XSD), developed by W3C. It allows defining a schema in XML syntax and has some merits that are of little interest for our purposes. One area where XML schemas play an important role is XML extensions, which are the topic of the next section.

3.4 XML extensions and technologies

We have seen that XML has advantages compared to HTML for exchanging data on the Web as it is extensible—and thus flexible. However, flexibility also carries the potential for uncertainty or inconsistency, for example, when the same element names are used for different content. Several extensions and technologies exist that improve the usability of XML by suggesting standards or providing techniques to set such standards. Some of the most important of these techniques are described in this section.

3.4.1 Namespaces

Consider the following two pieces of HTML and XML:

```
<head>
      <title>Basic HTML Sample Page</title>
</head>
```

```
<book id="1">
      <author>Douglas Crockford</author>
      <title>JavaScript: The Good Parts</title>
</book>
```

Both pieces store information in the element <title>. If the XML code were embedded in HTML code, this might create confusion. As we will see, there are many XML extensions to store specific data, for example, geographic, graphical, or financial data. All of these languages are basically XML with limited vocabulary. When several of these XML-based languages are used in one document, element or attribute names can become ambiguous if they are multiply assigned. XML namespaces are used to circumvent such problems. The idea is very simple: Ambiguous elements become distinguishable if some unique identifier is added. Just like zip codes allow distinguishing between many different Springfields and area codes make phone numbers unambiguous, namespaces help make elements and attributes uniquely identifiable.

The implementation of namespaces is straightforward:

```
<root xmlns:h="http://www.w3.org/1999/xhtml"
xmlns:t="http://funnybooknames.com/crockford">

      <h:head>
            <h:title>Basic HTML Sample Page</h:title>
      </h:head>
```

```
    <t:book id="1">
        <t:author>Douglas Crockford</t:author>
        <t:title>JavaScript: The Good Parts</t:title>
    </t:book>

</root>
```

In this example, namespaces are declared in the root element using the `xmlns` attribute and two prefixes, `h` and `t`. The namespace name, that is, the namespace attribute value, usually carries a Uniform Resource Identifier (URI) that points to some Internet address. The URIs in the example are two URLs that refer to an existing Internet resource on the W3C homepage and the fictional domain `funnybooknames.com`. When dealing with namespaces, note the following rules:

(i) Namespaces can be declared in the root element or in the start tag of any other element. In the latter case, all children of this element are considered part of this namespace.

(ii) The namespace name does not necessarily have to be a working URL. Parsers will never try to follow the link, not even a URI. Any other string is fine. However, it is common practice to use URIs for two reasons: First, as they are a long, unique string of characters, duplicates are unlikely, and second, actual URLs can point the human reader to pages where more information about the namespace is given.[5]

(iii) Prefixes do not have to be explicitly stated, so the declaration can either be `xmlns` or `xmlns:`*`prefix`*. If the prefix is dropped, the xmlns is assumed to be the default namespace and any element without a prefix is considered to be in that namespace. When prefixes are used, it is bound to a namespace in the declaration. Attributes, however, never belong to the default namespace.

3.4.2 Extensions of XML

Thus far, we have praised XML for its flexibility and extensibility. However, standardization also has its benefits in data exchange scenarios. Recall how browsers deal with HTML. They "know" what a table looks like, how headings should be formatted, and so on. In general, many data exchange processes can be standardized because sender and recipient agree on the content and structure of the data to be exchanged.

Following this logic, a multitude of extensions of the XML language has been developed that combine the classical XML features of openness with the benefits of standardization. In that sense, XML has become an important metalanguage—it provides the general architecture for other XML markup languages. Varieties of XML rely on XML schemas that specify

[5]When the same URL is used again and again—such as http://www.w3.org/1999/xhtml—this reduces the usefulness of namespaces. Therefore, one should think of references to locations one has full control over, like an owned web domain where a DTD or XML schema is stored.

Table 3.2 List of popular XML markup languages

Name	Purpose	Common filename extensions
Atom	web feeds	*.atom*
RSS	web feeds	*.rss*
EPUB	open e-book	*.epub*
SVG	vector graphics	*.svg*
KML	geographic visualization	*.kml, .kmz*
GPX	GPS data (waypoint, tracks, routes)	*.gpx*
Office Open XML	Microsoft Office documents	*.docx, .pptx, .xlsx*
OpenDocument	Apache OpenOffice documents	*.odt, .odp, .ods, .odg*
XHTML	HTML extension and standardization	*.xhtml*

For a more comprehensive list, see http://en.wikipedia.org/wiki/List_of_XML_markup_languages.

allowed structure, elements, attributes, and content. Table 3.2 lists some of the most popular XML derivations. Among them are languages for geographic applications like KML or GPX as well as for web feeds and widely used office document formats. You might be surprised to find that MS Word makes heavy use of XML. To gain basic insight into XML extensions that are ubiquitous on the Web, we focus on two popular XML markup languages—RSS and SVG.

3.4.3 Example: Really Simple Syndication

Web users commonly cultivate a list of bookmarks of their favorite webpages. It can be rather tiresome to regularly check for new content on the sites. Really Simple Syndication (RSS)[6] was built to solve this problem—both for the user and the content providers. The basic idea is that news sites, blog owners, etc., convert their content into a standardized format that can be syndicated to any user.

The logic of RSS

We illustrate the logic of RSS in Figure 3.3. Authors of a blog or news site set up an RSS file that contains some information on the news provider, which is stored on a web server. The file is updated whenever new content is published on the blog. Both are usually done by an RSS creation program like RSS builder. The list of entries or notifications is often called *RSS feed* or *RSS channel* and might be located at http://www.example.net/feed.rss. It is written in XML that follows the rules of the RSS format. Common elements that are allowed in this XML flavor are listed in Table 3.3. There are elements that describe the channel and others that describe single entries. Users collect channels by subscribing to an RSS reader or aggregator like Feedly, which automatically locates the RSS feed on a given website and lays out the content. These readers automatically update subscribed feeds and offer further management functionalities. This way, users are able to assemble their own online news.

There are several versions of RSS, the current one being RSS 2.0. RSS syntax has remained fairly simple, especially for users who are familiar with XML. The rules are strict, that is,

[6]Originally, RSS was an abbreviation of RDF Site Summary and was later redefined as Rich Site Summary. In 2002, it was redubbed again to Really Simple Syndication.

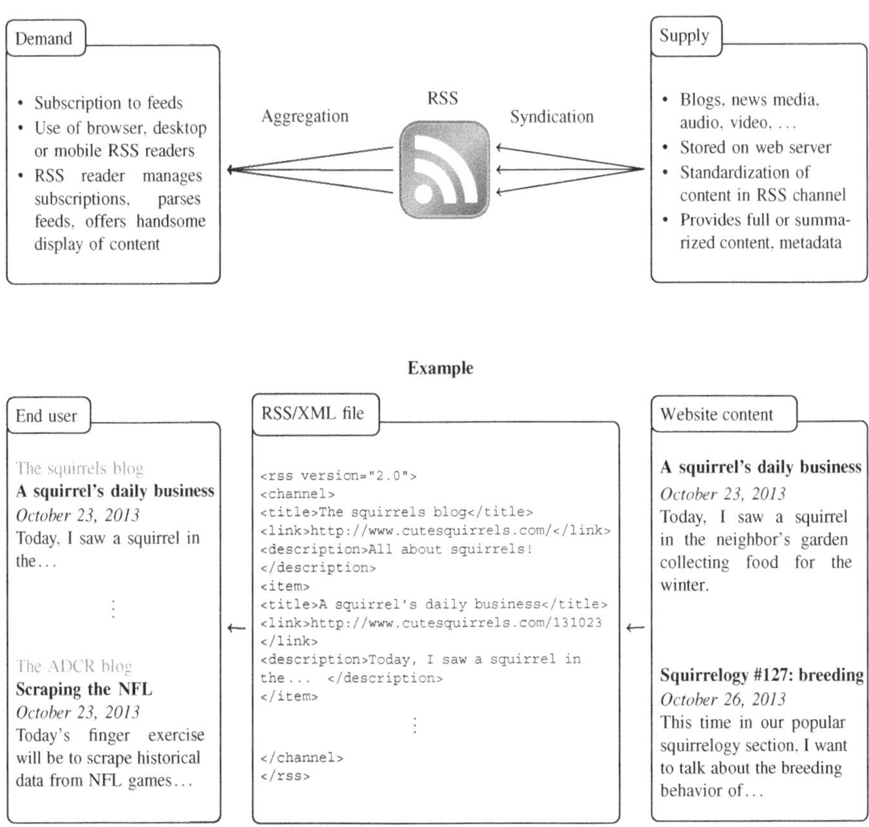

Figure 3.3 How RSS works

there is a very limited set of allowed elements and a clear document structure. Consider the following example of a fictional RSS channel accompanying this book:

```
<?xml version="1.0" encoding="UTF-8" ?>
<rss version="2.0">
<channel>
 <title>The ADCR blog</title>
 <description>Blog to the ADCR book; Wiley 2014</description>
 <link>http://www.r-datacollection.com/blog</link>
 <lastBuildDate>Tue, 22 Oct 2013 00:01:00 +0000 </lastBuildDate>
  <item>
  <title>Why R is useful for web scraping</title>
  <description>R is becoming the most popular statistical
      software and is growing fast due to an active community
      publishing several additional packages every day. Yet,
      R is more than [...]</description>
```

```
    <link>http://www.r-datacollection.com/blog/why-r-is-useful</link>
    <pubDate>Tue, 22 Oct 2013 00:01:00 +0000 </pubDate>
   </item>
   </channel>
  </rss>
```

RSS documents start with an XML and RSS declaration in the first two lines. The <channel> element wraps around both meta information and the actual entries. The channel's *meta* block has three required elements <title>, <description>, and <link>. In the example, there is another optional element, <lastBuildDate>, that indicates the last time content was changed on the channel. The *content* block consists of a set of <item> elements. Whenever a new story, blog entry, etc., is published, a new <item> element is added to the feed. <item> elements have three obligatory children—again, they are called <title>, <description>, and <link>. The main content is usually stored in the <description> element. Sometimes the whole entry is stored here, sometimes just the first few lines or a summary. In general, RSS syntax obeys the same set of rules as XML syntax.

Table 3.3 List of common RSS 2.0 elements and their meaning

Element name	Meaning
root elements	
`rss`	The feed's root element
`channel`	A channel's root element
channel elements	
`description*`	Short statement describing the feed
`link*`	URL of the feed's website
`title*`	Name of the feed
`item`	The core information element: each item contains an entry of the feed
item elements	
`link*`	URL of the item
`title*`	Title of the item
`description*`	Short description of the item
`author`	Email address of the item's author
`category`	Classification of item's content
`enclosure`	Additional content, for example, audio
`guid`	Unique identifier of the item
`image`	Display of image (with children <url>, <title>, and <link>)
`language`	Language of the feed
`pubDate`	Publishing date of item
`source`	RSS source of the item
`ttl`	"Time-to-live," number of minutes until the feed is refreshed from the RSS

Elements marked with "*" are mandatory. For more information on RSS 2.0 specification, see http://www.rssboard.org/rss-specification

```
<?xml version="1.0" standalone="no"?>
<!DOCTYPE svg PUBLIC "-//W3C//DTD SVG 1.1//EN"
"http://www.w3.org/Graphics/SVG/1.1/DTD/svg11.dtd">

<svg xmlns="http://www.w3.org/2000/svg" version="1.1">
 <ellipse cx="100" cy="70" rx="100" ry="70" style="fill:grey"/>
 <ellipse cx="110" cy="75" rx="80" ry="50" style="fill:white"/>
 <text x="65" y="160" fill="blue" style="font-size:160; font-stretch:
     ultraexpanded;font-family:sans;font-weight:bold">R</text>
</svg>
```

Figure 3.4 SVG code example: R logo

Take a moment to look at actual RSS feeds. They are all around the Web and indicated with the RSS icon ( ). There are several popular news and blogging platforms about R. For example, have a look at http://planetr.stderr.org/ where new R packages are posted (via Dirk Eddelbuettel's CRANberries blog http://dirk.eddelbuettel.com/cranberries/), and at http://www.r-bloggers.com/, a meta-blogging platform that collects content from the R blogosphere.

RSS 2.0 is not the only content syndication format. Besides various predecessors, another popular standard is Atom, which is also XML-based and has a very similar syntax. In order to grab RSS feeds into R, we can use the same XML extraction tools that are presented in Section 3.5.

3.4.4 Example: scalable vector graphics

A more peculiar but incredibly popular extension of XML is scalable vector graphics (SVG). SVG is used to represent two-dimensional vector graphics. It has been developed at the W3C since 1999 and was initially released in 2001 (Dailey 2010). The idea was to create a vector graphic format that stores graphic information in lightweight, flexible form for exchange over the Web.

Vector graphics versus raster graphics

Vector graphic formats consist of basic geometric forms such as points, curves, circles, lines, or polygons, all of which can be expressed mathematically. In contrast, raster graphic formats store graphic information as a raster of pixels, that is, rectangular cells of a certain color. In contrast to raster graphics, vector graphics can be resized without any loss of quality and are usually smaller. As the SVG format is based on XML, SVG graphics can be manipulated with an ordinary text editor. There are, however, SVG editors that simplify this task. For example, Inkscape is an open-source graphics editor that implements SVG by default and runs on all common operating systems.[7] In order to view SVG files, we can use current versions of the common browsers.

An SVG example

To get a first impression of how SVG works, Figure 3.4 provides code of a small SVG file. This code generates a stylized representation of the R icon just like the one displayed in Figure 3.5. In fact, if we open an SVG file with the content of the sample code with our browser, we see the graphic shown in Figure 3.5. The syntax does not only resemble XML, it

[7] See http://inkscape.org/ for further information and download.

Figure 3.5 The R logo as SVG image from code in Figure 3.4

is XML with a limited set of legal elements and attributes. An SVG file starts with the usual XML declaration. The `standalone` attribute indicates that the document refers to an external file, in this case an external DTD in lines 2 and 3. This DTD is stored at the www.w3.org webpage and describes which elements and attributes are legal in the current SVG version 1.1 (as of March 2014). The actual SVG code that describes the graphic is enclosed in the `<svg>` element. It contains a namespace and a version attribute.

SVG basics

SVG uses a predefined set of elements and attributes to represent parts of a graphic ('SVG shapes'). Among the basic shapes of SVG are lines (`<line>`), rectangles (`<rect>`), circles (`<circle>`), ellipses (`<ellipse>`), polygons (`<polygon>`), (`<text>`), and, the most general of all, paths (`<path>`). Each of these elements comes with a specific set of attributes to tune the object's properties, for example, the position of the corners, the size and radius of a circle, and so on. Elements are placed on a virtual coordinate system, with the origin (0,0) in the upper-left corner. Formatted text can also be placed into the graphic. The order of elements is important. A later-listed element covers a previous element—elements can therefore be thought of as layers. Further, there is a palette of special effects like blurs or color gradients. Elements can even be animated. A complex SVG graphic is often generated by quite complex SVG code. The complexity usually does not stem from a highly hierarchical structure—most of the elements are often just children of the root element—but from the mass of elements and their attributes. Our basic graphic in Figure 3.5 is composed of only three elements—two ellipses and one text element. By default, elements come in the compact form of XML element syntax: Elements are usually empty and contain no further information than those given in the attributes.

Back to the example, the locations of the ellipses are defined by their attributes `cx` and `cy`, their shape by the horizontal and vertical radius in `rx` and `ry`. Colors and other effects can be passed via arguments in the `style` attribute. The white ellipse is plotted on the top of the grey ellipse simply because it appears second in the code, creating the donut effect. Finally, shape, color, font, and location of the "R" is defined in the `<text>` element.

SVG and the Web

Beyond the principle advantages of vector over raster graphics, SVG, in particular, has some features that make it attractive as a graphic standard on the Web: It can be edited with any text editor, opened with the common browsers, follows a familiar syntax as it is basically just XML, and has been developed for a wide range of applications. We have learned that XML is flexible but because of the flexibility cannot be interpreted further by a browser. This is not true for XML extensions such as SVG. As the set of elements and attributes is clearly defined, browsers can be programmed to display SVG content as meaningful graphic, not as code—just as they interpret and display HTML code. In HTML5, SVG graphics can even be embedded as simply as this

```
<html>
<body>
<svg> <rect width="300" height="100"/> </svg>
</body>
</html>
```

SVG is useful for data gatherers

Why could SVG be useful in the context of automated data collection? At first glance, SVG is a flexible and widely used vector graphics format. From the data collection perspective, however, it is more than that. The information in these graphs—and often more than just the visible parts—are stored in text form and can therefore be searched, subsetted, etc. SVG is becoming more and more popular on the Web and is used for increasingly complex tasks, for example, to store geographic information, create interactive maps, or visualize massive amounts of data.[8]

The takeaway message of these two examples is that XML is present in many different areas, and many of these applications hold potentially useful information. And the neat thing is: We will learn how easy it is to retrieve and process this information with R, regardless of whether the information is stored in "pure" XML or any of its extensions.

3.5 XML and R in practice

Let us now turn to practice. How can XML files be viewed, how can they be imported and accessed in an R session, and how can we convert information from an XML document into data structures that are more convenient for further graphical or statistical analysis, like ordinary data frames, for example?

As we said before, XML files can be opened and viewed in all text editors and browsers. However, while text editors usually take the XML file as is, modern web browsers automatically parse the XML and try to represent its structure. This fails when the XML document is not valid. In this case, the browser might tell you why it thinks the parsing failed, for example, because of an opening and ending tag mismatch on a certain line. From this perspective, the web browser is a decent tool to check if your XML is well formed. In standard web scraping tasks, we usually do not view XML documents file by file but download them in a first step and import them into our R workspace in a second (see Chapter 9).

3.5.1 Parsing XML

We parse XML for the same reason that we parse HTML documents (see Section 2.4.1), to create a structure-aware representation of XML files that allows a simple information

[8]To learn more about SVG check out Eisenberg (2002) and the elucidations on the W3C pages: http://www.w3.org/Graphics/SVG/. For a quick access to the language, the SVG primer by Dailey (2010) should prove useful.

```
<?xml version="1.0"?>
<!DOCTYPE document SYSTEM "technologystocks.dtd">
<document>
  <Apple>
    <date>2013/11/13</date>
    <close>520.634</close>
    <volume>7022001.0000</volume>
    <open>518</open>
    <high>522.25</high>
    <low>516.96</low>
    <company>Apple</company>
    <year>2013</year>
  </Apple>
  <Apple>
    <date>2013/11/12</date>
    <close>520.01</close>
    <volume>7295400.0000</volume>
    <open>517.67</open>
    <high>523.92</high>
    <low>517</low>
    <company>Apple</company>
    <year>2013</year>
  </Apple>
  (...)
</document>
```

Figure 3.6 XML example document: stock data

extraction from these files. Similar to what was outlined in the HTML parsing section, the process of parsing XML essentially includes two steps. First, the symbol sequence that constitutes the XML file is read in and used to build a hierarchical tree-like data structure from its elements in the C language, and second, this data structure is translated into an R data structure via the use of handlers.

The package we use to import and parse XML documents is, appropriately enough, called XML (Temple Lang 2013c). Using the XML package we can read, search, and create XML documents—although we only care about the former two tasks. Let us see how to load XML files into R. For DOM-style parsing of XML files one can use `xmlParse()`. The arguments of the function coincide with those of `htmlParse()` for the most part. We illustrate the process with the help of *technology.xml*, an XML file that holds stock information for three technology companies. The first few lines of the document are presented in Figure 3.6. As we see, the file contains stock information like the closing value, lowest and highest value for a day, and the traded volume. To obtain the XML tree with R, we pass the path of the file to `xmlParse()`'s `file` argument:

```
R> library(XML)
R> parsed_stocks <- xmlParse(file = "stocks/technology.xml")
```

```
<!ELEMENT document (Apple,IBM,Google)>
<!ELEMENT Apple (date,close,volume,open,high,low,company,year)>
<!ELEMENT Google (date,close,volume,open,high,low,company,year)>
<!ELEMENT IBM (date,close,volume,open,high,low,company,year)>
<!ELEMENT close (#PCDATA)>
<!ELEMENT company (#PCDATA)>
<!ELEMENT date (#PCDATA)>
<!ELEMENT high (#PCDATA)>
<!ELEMENT low (#PCDATA)>
<!ELEMENT open (#PCDATA)>
<!ELEMENT volume (#PCDATA)>
<!ELEMENT year (#PCDATA)>
```

Figure 3.7 DTD of stock data XML file (see Figure 3.6)

The `xmlParse()` function is used to parse the XML document.[9] The parsing function offer a set of options that can be ignored in most settings but are still worth knowing. It is possible to treat the input as XML and not as a file name (option `asText`), to decide whether both namespace URI and prefix should be provided on each node or just the prefix (option `fullNamespaceInfo`), to determine whether an XML schema is parsed (option `isSchema`), or to validate the XML against a DTD (option `validate`). Let us consider this last option in more detail.

XML validation

Although HTML and XML are very similar in most respects, a noteworthy difference exists in that XML is confined to much stricter specification rules. As we have seen in Section 3.3, valid XML not only has to be well formed, that is, tags must be closed, attributes names must be in quotes, etc., but also has to adhere to the specifications in its DTD. To check whether the document conforms to the specification, a validation step can be included after the DOM has been created by setting the `validate` argument to TRUE. We try to validate *technology.xml* with the corresponding external *technologystocks.dtd* (see Figure 3.7), which is deposited in our folder and referred to in line 2 of the XML file (see Figure 3.6):

```
R> library(XML)
R> parsed_stocks <- xmlParse(file = "stocks/technology.xml", validate = TRUE)
```

There is no complaint; the validation has succeeded. To demonstrate what happens if an XML does not conform to a given DTD, we manipulate the DTD such that the document node is no longer defined. As a consequence, the XML file does not conform to the (corrupted) DTD anymore and the function raises a complaint:

```
R> library(XML)
R> stocks <- xmlParse(file = "stocks/technology-manip.xml", validate = TRUE)
No declaration for element document
Error: XML document is invalid
```

[9]The XML package provides a set of other XML parsing functions, namely `xmlTreeParse()`, `xmlInternalTreeParse()`, `xmlNativeTreeParse()`, and `xmlEventParse()`. As their names suggest, they differ in the way how the XML tree is parsed. `xmlInternalTreeParse()` and `xmlNativeTreeParse()` are equivalent to `xmlParse()`. Further, all are almost equivalent to `xmlTreeParse()`, except that the parser automatically relies on the internal nodes (the `useInternalNodes` parameter is set `TRUE`).

In general, the rather bulky logic of XML validation with DTD, XSD, or other schemas should not discourage you from making use of the full power of the XML DOM structure. In most web scraping scenarios, there is no need to validate the files and we can simply process them as they are.

3.5.2 Basic operations on XML documents

Once an XML document is parsed we can access its content using a set of functions in the XML package. While we recommend using the more general and robust XPath for searching and pulling out information from XML documents, here we present some basic operations that might suffice for less complex XML documents. To see how they work, let us go back to our running example: We start by parsing the *bond.xml* file:

```
R> bond <- xmlParse("bond.xml")
R> class(bond)
[1] "XMLInternalDocument" "XMLAbstractDocument"
```

When we type bond into our console, the output looks pretty much like the original XML file. We know, however, that the object is anything but pure character data. For instance, we can perform some basic operations on the root element. The top-level node is extracted with the `xmlRoot()` function; `xmlName()` and `xmlSize()` return the root element's name and the number of children:

```
R> root <- xmlRoot(bond)
R> xmlName(root)
[1] "bond_movies"
R> xmlSize(root)
[1] 3
```

Within the node sets, basic navigation or subsetting works in analogy to indexing ordinary lists in R. That is, we can use numerical or named indices to select certain nodes. This is not possible with objects of class `XMLInternalDocument` that are generated by `xmlParse()`. We therefore work with the `root` object, which belongs to the class `XMLInternalElementNode`. Indexing with predicate "`1`" yields the first child: **Navigation**

```
R> root[[1]]
<movie id="1">
  <name>Dr. No</name>
  <year>1962</year>
  <actors bond="Sean Connery" villain="Joseph Wiseman"/>
  <budget>1.1M</budget>
  <boxoffice>59.5M</boxoffice>
</movie>
```

We have to use double brackets to access the internal node. By adding another index, we can move further down the tree and extract the first child of the first child:

```
R> root[[1]][[1]]
<name>Dr. No</name>
```

Element names can be used as predicates, too. Using double brackets yields the first element in the tree, single brackets return objects of class `XMLInternalNodeList`. To see the difference, compare

```
R> root[["movie"]]
<movie id="1">
  <name>Dr. No</name>
  <year>1962</year>
  <actors bond="Sean Connery" villain="Joseph Wiseman"/>
  <budget>1.1M</budget>
  <boxoffice>59.5M</boxoffice>
</movie>
```

with

```
R> root["movie"]
$movie
<movie id="1">
  <name>Dr. No</name>
  <year>1962</year>
  <actors bond="Sean Connery" villain="Joseph Wiseman"/>
  <budget>1.1M</budget>
  <boxoffice>59.5M</boxoffice>
</movie>

$movie
<movie id="2">
  <name>Live and Let Die</name>
  <year>1973</year>
  <actors bond="Roger Moore" villain="Yaphet Kotto"/>
  <budget>7M</budget>
  <boxoffice>126.4M</boxoffice>
</movie>

$movie
<movie id="3">
  <name>Skyfall</name>
  <year>2012</year>
  <actors bond="Daniel Craig" villain="Javier Bardem"/>
  <budget>175M</budget>
  <boxoffice>1108.6M</boxoffice>
</movie>

attr(,"class")
[1] "XMLInternalNodeList" "XMLNodeList"
```

Names and numbers can also be combined. To return the atomic value of the first `<name>` element, we could write

```
R> root[["movie"]][[1]][[1]]
Dr. No
```

The structure of the object is retained and can be used to locate elements and values. However, content retrieval from XML files via ordinary predicates is quite complex, error prone, and anything but convenient. Further, this method does not capitalize on node relations—a core feature of parsed XML documents. For anybody who is seriously working with XML data, there are good reasons to learn the very powerful query language XPath. We will show how this is done in the next chapter.

Accessing documents of the XML family

In general, all methods and all those to follow are applicable to other XML-based languages as well. The parser does not care about naming and structure of documents as long as the code is valid. Therefore, documents like the RSS sample code from above can be imported just as easy as

```
R> xmlParse("rsscode.rss")
<?xml version="1.0" encoding="UTF-8"?>
<rss version="2.0">
  <channel>
    <title>The ADCR blog</title>
    <description>Blog to the ADCR book; Wiley 2014</description>
    <link>http://www.r-datacollection.com/blog</link>
    <lastBuildDate>Tue, 22 Oct 2013 00:01:00 +0000 </lastBuildDate>
    <item>
      <title>Why R is useful for web scraping</title>
      <description>R is becoming the most popular statistical software
and is growing fast due to an active community publishing several
additional packages every day. Yet, R is more than [...]</description>
      <link>http://www.r-datacollection.com/blog/why-r-is-useful</link>
      <pubDate>Tue, 22 Oct 2013 00:01:00 +0000 </pubDate>
    </item>
  </channel>
</rss>
```

3.5.3 From XML to data frames or lists

Sometimes it suffices to transform an entire XML object into common R data structures like vectors, data frames, or lists. The XML package provides some appropriate functions that make such operations straightforward if the original structure is not too complex.

Single vectors can be extracted with `xmlSApply()`, a wrapper function for `lapply()` and `sapply()` that is built to deal with children of a given XML node. The function operates on an XML node (provided as first argument), applies any given function on its children (given as the second argument), and commonly returns a vector. We can use the function in combination with `xmlValue()` and `xmlGetAttr()` (and other functions; see Table 4.4) to extract element or attribute values:

```
R> xmlSApply(root[[1]], xmlValue)
     name      year    actors    budget boxoffice
 "Dr. No"    "1962"        ""    "1.1M"   "59.5M"
R> xmlSApply(root, xmlAttrs)
movie.id movie.id movie.id
     "1"      "2"      "3"
R> xmlSApply(root, xmlGetAttr, "id")
movie movie movie
  "1"   "2"   "3"
```

As long as XML documents are flat in the hierarchical sense, that is, the root node's most distant relatives are grandchildren or children, they can usually be transformed easily into a data frame with `xmlToDataFrame()`

```
R> (movie.df <- xmlToDataFrame(root))
               name year actors budget boxoffice
1            Dr. No 1962          1.1M     59.5M
2 Live and Let Die 1973            7M    126.4M
3           Skyfall 2012          175M   1108.6M
```

Note, however, that this function already runs into trouble with the `<actor>` element, which is itself empty except for two attributes. The corresponding variable in the `data.frame` object is left empty with a shrug.

Similarly, a conversion into a list is possible with `xmlToList()`:

```
R> movie.list <- xmlToList(bond)
```

XML and other data exchange formats like JSON can store much more complicated data structures. This is what makes them so powerful for data exchange over the Web. Forcing such structures into one common data frame comes at a certain cost—complicated data transformation tasks or the loss of information. `xmlToDataFrame()` is not an almighty function to achieve the task for which it is named. Rather, we are typically forced to develop and apply own extraction functions.

3.5.4 Event-driven parsing

While parsing the XML example files in Section 3.5.1 was processed quickly by R, files of larger size can lead to overloaded working memory and concomitant data management problems. As a format primarily designed for carrying data across services, XML files are oftentimes of substantially greater size than HTML files. In many instances, file sizes can exceed the memory capacity of ordinary desktop PCs and laptops. This problem is aggravated when data streams are concerned, where XML data arrives iteratively. These applications obstruct the DOM-based parsing approach we have been applying in this and the previous chapter and demand for a more iterative parsing style.

Event-driven/ SAX parser

The root of the problem stems from the way the DOM-style parsers process and store information. The parser creates two copies of a given XML file—one as the C-level node set and the second as the data structure in the R language. To detect certain elements in an XML file, we can deal with this problem by employing a parsing technique called event-driven parsing or SAX parsing (Simple API for XML). Event-driven parsing differs from DOM-style parsing in that it skips the construction of the complete DOM at the C level. Instead, event-driven parsers sequentially traverse over an XML file, and once they find a specified element of interest they prompt an instant, user-defined reaction to this event. This procedure provides a huge advantage over DOM-style parsers because the machine's memory never has to hold the complete document.

Let us reconsider *technology.xml* and the problem of extracting information about the Apple stock. Assume we are interested in obtaining Apple's daily closing value along with the date. Once again, we make use of a handler function to specify how to handle a node of interest. Similar to the extraction problem considered in Section 2.4.3, we define the handler as a nested function to combine it with a reference environment and container

```
1  branchFun <- function(){
2        container_close <- numeric()
3        container_date <- numeric()

5        "Apple" = function(node,...) {
6              date <- xmlValue(xmlChildren(node)[[c("date")]])
7              container_date <<- c(container_date, date)
8              close <- xmlValue(xmlChildren(node)[[c("close")]])
9              container_close <<- c(container_close, close)
10             #print(c(close, date));Sys.sleep(0.5)
11    }
12    getContainer <- function() data.frame(date=container_date,
      close=container_close)
13    list(Apple=Apple, getStore=getContainer)
14 }
```

Figure 3.8 R code for event-driven parsing

variables (see Figure 3.8). `branchFun()` defines two local variables `container_close` and `container_date`, serving as the container variables. Since we are interested in Apple stock information, we suggest the following approach: We start by defining a handler function for the `<Apple>` nodes (lines 6 and 8). Conditional on these elements, we look for their children called `date` and `close` and return their values (lines 7 and 9). A return function `getContainer()` is defined (line 12) that assembles the container variable's contents into a data frame and returns this object.

To generate a usable instance of the handler function, we execute the function and pass its return value into a new object called `h5`:

```
R> (h5 <- branchFun())
$Apple
function (node, ...)
{
    date <- xmlValue(xmlChildren(node)[[c("date")]])
    container_date <<- c(container_date, date)
    close <- xmlValue(xmlChildren(node)[[c("close")]])
    container_close <<- c(container_close, close)
}
<environment: 0x0000000008c4afa8>

$getStore
function ()
data.frame(date = container_date, close = container_close)
<environment: 0x0000000008c4afa8>
```

We are now ready to run the SAX parser over our *technology.xml* file using XML's `xmlEventParse()` function. Instead of the `handlers` argument we will pass the handler function to the `branches` argument. The `branches` is a more general version of the `handlers` argument, which allows to specify functions over the entire node content, including its children. This is exactly what we need for this task since in our handler function `h5` we have been making use of the `xmlChildren` function for retrieving child information. Additionally, for the `handlers` argument we need to pass an empty list:

```
R> invisible(xmlEventParse(file = "stocks/technology.xml",
branches = h5, handlers = list()))
```

To get an idea about the iterative traversal through the document, remove the commented line in the handler and rerun the SAX parser. Finally, to fetch the information from the local environment we employ the `getStore()` function and route the contents into a new object:

```
R> apple.stock <- h5$getStore()
```

To verify parsing success, we display the first five rows of the returned data frame:

```
R> head(apple.stock, 5)
R> # date close 1 2013/11/13 520.634 2 2013/11/12 520.01 3 2013/11/
11 519.048 4
R> # 2013/11/08 520.56 5 2013/11/07 512.492
```

As we have seen, the event-driving parsing works and returns the correct information. Nonetheless, we do not recommend users to resort to this style of parsing as their preferred means to obtain data from XML documents. Although event-style parsing exceeds the DOM-style parsing approach with respect to speed and may, in case of really large XML files, be the only practical method, it necessitates a lot of code overhead as well as background knowledge on R functions and environments. Therefore, for the small- to medium-sized documents that we deal with in this book, in the coming chapters we will focus on the DOM-style parsing and extraction methods provided through the XPath query language (Chapter 4).

3.6 A short example JSON document

In this section, we will become acquainted with the benefits of the data exchange standard JSON. The acronym (pronounced "Jason") stands for **J**avaScript **O**bject **N**otation. JSON was designed for the same tasks that XML is often used for—the storage and exchange of human-readable data. Many APIs by popular web applications provide data in the JSON format.

As its name suggests, JSON is a data format that has its origins in the JavaScript programming language. However, JSON itself is language independent and can be parsed with many existing programming languages, including R. JSON has turned into one of the most popular formats for web data provision. It is therefore worth studying for our purposes. We start again with a synthetic example and continue with a more systematic look at the syntax. In the final part of the chapter, we will learn the JSON syntax and how to access JSON data with R.

Indiana Jones and the first JSON example

The JSON code in Figure 3.9 holds some basic information on the first three Indiana Jones movies. We observe that JSON has a more slender appearance than XML. Data are stored in key/value pairs, for example, `"name" : "Raiders of the Lost Ark"`, which obviates the need for end tags. Different types of brackets (curly and square ones) allow describing hierarchical structures and to differentiate between unordered and ordered data. Just as in XML, JSON data structures can become arbitrarily complex regarding nestedness. Apart from differences in the syntax, JSON is as intuitive as XML, particularly when indented like in the example code, although this is no necessary requirement for valid JSON data.

```
{"indy movies" :[
      {
      "name" : "Raiders of the Lost Ark",
      "year" : 1981,
      "actors" : {
            "Indiana Jones": "Harrison Ford",
            "Dr. René Belloq": "Paul Freeman"
            },
      "producers": ["Frank Marshall", "George Lucas", "Howard Kazanjian"],
      "budget" : 18000000,
      "academy_award_ve": true
      },
      {
      "name" : "Indiana Jones and the Temple of Doom",
      "year" : 1984,
      "actors" : {
            "Indiana Jones": "Harrison Ford",
            "Mola Ram": "Amish Puri"
            },
      "producers": ["Robert Watts"],
      "budget" : 28170000,
      "academy_award_ve": true
      },
      {
      "name" : "Indiana Jones and the Last Crusade",
      "year" : 1989,
      "actors" : {
            "Indiana Jones": "Harrison Ford",
            "Walter Donovan": "Julian Glover"
            },
      "producers": ["Robert Watts", "George Lucas"],
      "budget" : 48000000,
      "academy_award_ve": false
      }]
}
```

Figure 3.9 JSON code example: Indiana Jones movies

3.7 JSON syntax rules

JSON syntax is easy to learn. We only have to know (a) how brackets are used to structure the data, (b) how keys and values are identified and separated, and (c) which data types exist and how they are used.

Brackets play a crucial role in structuring the document. As we see in the example data in Figure 3.9, the whole document is enclosed in curly brackets. This is because `indy movies` is the first object that holds the three movie records in an array, that is, an ordered sequence. Arrays are framed by square brackets. The movies, in turn, are also objects and therefore enclosed by curly brackets. In general, brackets work as follows:

1. Curly brackets, "{" and "}," embrace objects. Objects work much like elements in XML and can contain collections of key/value pairs, other objects, or arrays.

2. Square brackets, "[" and "]," enclose arrays. An array is an ordered sequence of objects or values.

Actual data are stored in key/value pairs. The rules for keys and values are

1. Keys are placed in double quotes, data are only placed in double quotes if they are string data

```
"name" : "Indiana Jones and the Temple of Doom"
"year" : 1984
```

2. Keys and values are always separated by a colon

```
"year" : 1981
```

3. Key/value pairs are separated by commas

```
{"Indiana Jones": "Harrison Ford",
"Dr. Rene Belloq": "Paul Freeman"}
```

4. Values in an array are separated by commas

```
["Frank Marshall", "George Lucas", "Howard Kazanjian"]
```

JSON allows a set of different data types for the value part of key/value pairs. They are listed in Table 3.4.

Table 3.4 Data types in JSON

Data type	Meaning
Number	integer, real, or floating point (e.g., 1.3E10)
String	white space, zero, or more Unicode characters (except `"` or `\`; `\` introduces some escape sequences)
Boolean	`true` or `false`
Null	`null`, an unknown value
Object	content in curly brackets
Array	ordered content in square brackets

And that is it.[10] From the perspective of an XML user, note what is not possible in JSON: We cannot add comments, we do not distinguish between missing values and null values, there are no namespaces and no internal validation syntax like XML's DTD. But this does not make JSON inferior to XML in absolute terms. They are rather based on different concepts. JSON is not a markup language and not even a document format. It is anticipated to be versionless—there is no JSON 1.0—and no change in the grammar is expected. It is just a data interchange standard that is so general that it can be parsed by many languages without effort.

JSON pocketknife tools

Although there is not much to highlight in JSON data, there are some tools that facilitate accessing JSON documents for human readers. The JSON Formatter & Validator at http://jsonformatter.curiousconcept.com/ is just one of several tools on the Web that automatically indent JSON input. This makes it much easier to read because JSON data frequently come without indentation or line breaks. The tool also helps check for bugs in the data. If you want to convert XML to JSON data, take a look at http://www.freeformatter.com/xml-to-json-converter.html or similar tools. However, such conversions are never isomorphic and rules have to be set to deal with, for example, attributes and namespaces.

The importance of JSON for the Web

Why is JSON so important for the Web even though XML already provides a popular data exchange format? First of all, there are some technical properties that make JSON preferable to XML. Generally, it is more lightweight due to its less verbose syntax and only allows a limited set of data types that are compatible with many if not most existing programming languages. Regarding compatibility, JSON has another crucial feature: We cover only basics of JavaScript in this book (see Chapter 6), but JavaScript is a major player on the Web to generate dynamic content and user–browser interactions. JSON is ultimately compatible with JavaScript and can be directly parsed into JavaScript objects. From a practical point of view, JSON seems to become the most widely used data exchange format for web APIs; Twitter as well as YouTube and many bigger and smaller web services have begun using JSON-only APIs.

3.8 JSON and R in practice

While R has one standard set of tools to handle XML-type data—the XML package—there are several packages that allow importing, exporting, and manipulating JSON data. The first published package was rjson (Couture-Beil 2013) and is still used in some R-based API wrappers. The package that is currently more established, however, is RJSONIO (Temple Lang 2013b), which we will use in this section. Finally, we also discuss the recently published package jsonlite (Ooms and Temple Lang 2014), which builds on RJSONIO and improves mapping between R objects and JSON strings.

We begin the discussion with an inspection of the RJSONIO package. In its current version (1.0.3), the package offers 24 functions, most of which we usually do not apply directly. We now return to the running example, the data in the *indy.json* file. Using the `isValidJSON()` function, we first check whether the document consists of valid JSON data:

```
R> isValidJSON("indy.json")
[1] TRUE
```

[10]There are some encoding details we do not dwell on here—if you want to go a little bit more into details, http://www.json.org/ provides further information.

This seems to be the case. The two core functions are `fromJSON()` and `toJSON()`. `fromJSON()` reads content in JSON format and converts it to R objects, `toJSON()` does the opposite:

```
R> indy <- fromJSON(content = "indy.json")
```

`fromJSON()`

`content` is the function's main argument. In our case, *indy.json* is a file in the working directory, but it could also be a character string possibly from the Web via `getURL()` or imported with `readLines()`. The `fromJSON()` function offers several other useful arguments, and as the package is well maintained, the documentation—accessible with `?fromJSON`—is worth a look. A very useful argument is `simplify`, controlling whether the function tries to combine identical elements to vectors. Otherwise the individual elements remain separate list elements. The `nullValue` argument allows specifying how to deal with JSON `null`s. In general, JSON data types (see Table 3.4) match R data types nicely (numeric, integer, character, logical). The `null` value is a little more differentiated in R, however. There is `NULL` for empty objects and `NA` for indicating a missing value. Therefore, the `nullValue` argument helps to specify how to deal with these cases, like turning them into `NA`s. The function maps the JSON data structure into an R list object:

```
R> class(indy)
[1] "list"
```

There is no ultimate `XML/JSON-to-R` function

From this point on we can deal with the data the *standard* R way, that is, decompose or subset the list or force (parts of) it into vectors, data frames, or other structures. We have already observed that seemingly powerful functions like `xmlToDataFrame()` can be of limited use when we face *real* data. Data frames are useful to represent a simple "observations by variables" structure, but become very complex if they are used to represent highly hierarchical data. In contrast, JSON and XML can represent far more complex data structures. When loading JSON or XML data into R, one often has to decide which subsets of information are necessary and need to be inserted into a data frame. Consequently, there cannot be a global and universal function for JSON/XML to R data format conversion. We have to build our own tools case by case. In our example, we might want to try to map the list to a data frame, consisting of three observations and several variables. The problem is that `actors` and `producers` have several values. One option is to extract the information variable by variable and merge in the end. This could work as follows:

```
R> library(stringr)
R> indy.vec <- unlist(indy, recursive = TRUE, use.names = TRUE)
R> indy.vec[str_detect(names(indy.vec), "name")]
                      indy movies.name
             "Raiders of the Lost Ark"
                      indy movies.name
"Indiana Jones and the Temple of Doom"
                      indy movies.name
  "Indiana Jones and the Last Crusade"
```

This strategy first flattens the complex list structure into one vector. The `recursive` argument ensures that all components of the list are unlisted. Since the key names are retained in the vector by setting `use.names` to `TRUE`, we can identify all original key/value pairs with the name `name` using a simple regular expression and the `str_detect()` function from the stringr package (see also Chapter 8). This strategy has its drawbacks. First, all list elements are coerced to a common mode, resulting in character vectors in most cases. This is useful for the `names` variable, but less appropriate for the `years` variable. Further, this step-by-step approach is tedious when many variables have to be extracted. An only slightly more comfortable option uses `sapply()` and feeds it with the `[[` operators and the variable name for element subsetting, calling `indy[[1]][[1]][['name']]`, `indy[[1]][[2]][['name']]`, and so on:

```
R> sapply(indy[[1]], "[[", "year")
[1] 1981 1984 1989
```

The benefit of this approach over the first is that data types are retained. Finally, to pull all variables and directly assemble them into a data frame, we have to take into account that some variables do not exist or vary in structure from observation to observation in the sample data. For example, the number of producers varies. We do the conversion as follows:

```
R> library(plyr)
R> indy.unlist <- sapply(indy[[1]], unlist)
R> indy.df <- do.call("rbind.fill", lapply(lapply(indy.unlist, t),
data.frame, stringsAsFactors = FALSE))
```

We first unlist the elements within the list. The second command is more complex. First, we transpose each list element, turn them into data frames, and finally make use of the `rbind.fill()` function of the plyr package to combine the data frames into one single data frame, taking care of the fact that some variables do not exist in some data frames. The result reveals that we would have to continue with some data cleansing—note for example the split-up producer variables:

```
R> names(indy.df)
 [1] "name"                     "year"
 [3] "actors.Indiana.Jones"     "actors.Dr..René.Belloq"
 [5] "producers1"               "producers2"
 [7] "producers3"               "budget"
 [9] "academy_award_ve"         "actors.Mola.Ram"
[11] "producers"                "actors.Walter.Donovan"
```

It is clear that importing JSON data, or working with lists in general, can be painful. Even if data structures are simpler, we need to use apply functions. Consider this last example of a JSON data import with a simple Peanuts dataset:

```
[
  {
    "name":"van Pelt, Lucy",
    "sex":"female",
    "age":32
  },
  {
    "name":"Peppermint, Patty",
    "sex":"female",
    "age":null
  },
```

```
  {
    "name":"Brown, Charlie",
    "sex":"male",
    "age":27
  }
]
```

We turn the data into an ordinary data frame with the following expression:

```
R> peanuts.json <- fromJSON("peanuts.json", nullValue = NA,
simplify = FALSE )
R> peanuts.df <- do.call("rbind", lapply(peanuts.json, data.frame,
stringsAsFactors = FALSE))
```

We parse the JSON snippet with the `fromJSON` function and tell the parser to set `null` values to zero. We also set `simplify` to `FALSE` in order to retain the list structure in all elements. Otherwise, the parser would convert the second entry to a character vector, rendering the `data.frame()` apply function useless. We use the `lapply()` function to turn the lists into data frames and keep strings as strings with the `stringsAsFactors = FALSE` argument. Finally, we join the data frames with a `do.call()` on `rbind()`. The result looks acceptable:

```
R> peanuts.df
                 name    sex age
1     van Pelt, Lucy female  32
2 Peppermint, Patty female  NA
3     Brown, Charlie   male  27
```

`toJSON()`

To do the conversion the other way round, that is from R to JSON data, the function we need is `toJSON()`:

```
R> peanuts.json <- toJSON(peanuts.df, pretty = TRUE)
R> file.output <- file("peanuts_out.json")
R> writeLines(peanuts.json, file.output)
R> close(file.output)
```

More consistent mapping with jsonlite

While transforming JSON data into appropriate R objects cannot always be done with preexisting functions, but require some postprocessing of the resulting objects, the recently developed jsonlite package offers more consistency between both data structures. It builds upon the parser of the RJSONIO package and provides the main functions `fromJSON()` and `toJSON` as well, but implements a different mapping scheme (see Ooms 2013). A set of rules ensures that data from an external source like an API are transformed in a way that guarantees consistent transformations. Some important conventions for JSON-to-R conversions for arrays are

- arrays are encoded as character data if at least one value is of type character;
- `null` values are encoded as `NA`;
- `true` and `false` values are encoded as 1 and 0 in numerical vectors and `TRUE` and `FALSE` in character and logical vectors.

There are more conventions for the transformation of vectors, matrices, lists, and data frames. They are documented in Ooms (2013). For our purposes, the rules concerning JSON-to-R conversion are most important, as this is part of the regular scraping workflow. Consider the following set of transformations from JSON arrays into R objects to see how the conventions cited above work in practice:

```
R> library(jsonlite)
R> x <- '[1, 2, true, false]'
R> fromJSON(x)
[1] 1 2 1 0
R> x <- '["foo", true, false]'
R> fromJSON(x)
[1] "foo"   "TRUE"  "FALSE"
R> x <- '[1, "foo", null, false]'
R> fromJSON(x)
[1] "1"     "foo"   NA      "FALSE"
```

The consistent mapping rules of jsonlite not only ensure that data are transformed adequately on the vector level, but also make mapping of JSON data into R data frames a lot easier. Reconsidering the Peanuts example with jsonlite, it turns out that the JSON data are conveniently mapped into the desired R object of type `data.frame` right away:

```
R> (peanuts.json <- fromJSON("peanuts.json"))
                 name    sex age
1    van Pelt, Lucy female  32
2 Peppermint, Patty female  NA
3    Brown, Charlie   male  27
```

In the Indiana Jones example, the Indy JSON is also mapped into a list. However, the only element in the list is a data frame of the desired content. We simply pull the data frame from the list to access the variables

```
R> (indy <- fromJSON("indy.json"))
$'indy movies'
                                  name year actors.Indiana Jones
1              Raiders of the Lost Ark 1981        Harrison Ford
2 Indiana Jones and the Temple of Doom 1984        Harrison Ford
3   Indiana Jones and the Last Crusade 1989        Harrison Ford
  actors.Dr. René Belloq actors.Mola Ram actors.Walter Donovan
1           Paul Freeman            <NA>                 <NA>
2                   <NA>      Amish Puri                 <NA>
3                   <NA>            <NA>        Julian Glover
                                   producers   budget academy_award_ve
1 Frank Marshall, George Lucas, Howard Kazanjian 18000000             TRUE
2                                  Robert Watts 28170000             TRUE
3                    Robert Watts, George Lucas 48000000            FALSE
R> indy.df <- indy$'indy movies'
R> indy.df$name
[1] "Raiders of the Lost Ark"
[2] "Indiana Jones and the Temple of Doom"
[3] "Indiana Jones and the Last Crusade"
```

In short, whenever RJSONIO returns a list when you would expect a data frame, jsonlite manages to generate tabular data from JSON data structures as long as it is appropriate, because the mapping scheme acknowledges the way in which tabular data are stored in R, which is column based, and JSON—and many other formats, languages, or databases—which is row based (see Ooms 2013).

To be sure, the functionality of jsonlite does not solve all problems of JSON-to-R transfer. However, the choice of rules implemented in jsonlite makes the import of JSON data into R more consistent. We therefore suggest to make this package the standard tool when working with JSON data even though it is still in an early version.

Summary

Both XML and JSON are very important standards for data exchange on the Web, and as such will occur several times in the course of this book (for example in Chapter 4 and the case study on Twitter, Chapter 14). Knowing how to handle both data types is helpful in many web data collection tasks.

We have seen that XML serves as a basic standard for many other formats, such as GPX, KML, RSS, SVG, XHTML. Whenever we encounter such data on the Web we are able to import and process them in Rtoo. JSON is an increasingly popular alternative to XML for the exchange of data on the Web, especially when working with web services/web APIs. JSON is derived from JavaScript and can be parsed in many languages, including R.

Further reading

There are many books that go far beyond this basic introduction to XML and JSON. If you have acquired a taste for the languages of the Web and plan to go deeper into web developing, you could have a look at *XML in a Nutshell* by Harold and Means (2004) or at Ray (2003). For the web scraping tasks presented in this book, however, deeper knowledge of XML should not be necessary.

If you want to dig deeper into JSON and JavaScript, the book *JavaScript: The Good Parts* by JSON developer Douglas Crockford (2008) might be a good start. For a quick overview, the excellent website http://www.json.org/ is highly recommended.

Problems

1. Describe the relationship between XML and HTML.
2. What are possible ways to import XML data into R? What are the advantages and disadvantages of each approach?
3. What is the purpose of namespaces in XML-style documents?
4. What are the main elements of the JSON syntax?
5. Write the smallest well-formed XML document you can think of.
6. Why do we need an escape sequence for the ampersand in XML?
7. Take a look at the invalid XML code snippet in Section 3.2.2. How could the family structure be represented in a valid XML document so that it is possible to identify Jonathan both as a child and as a father?

8. Go to your vinyl record, CD, DVD, or Blu-ray Disc shelf and randomly pick three titles. Create an XML document that holds useful information about your sample of discs.

9. Inform yourself about the Election Markup Language (EML).
   (a) Find out the purpose of EML.
   (b) Look for the current specification of the language and identify the key concepts.
   (c) Search for a real EML document, load it into R and turn parts of it into native data structures.

10. Working with SVG files.
   (a) Manipulate the *ricon.svg* file such that the icon is framed with a black box. Redefine the color, size, and font of the image.
   (b) Rebuild the RSS icon as an SVG document.

11. Find the formatting errors in the following JSON piece.[11]

```
{
   "text": "@slowpoketweeter @yaaawn123: Just saw a cat on
       the road. Awesome! #YOLO",
   "truncated": false,
   "favorited": "true",
   "source": "<a href= \"http://twitter.com/ \" rel= \"
       nofollow \">Twitter for iPhone</a>",
   "id_str": "61723550048377463",
"user_mentions": ["slowpoketweeter" "yaaawn123"],
"screen_name": "SlowpokeTweeter",
      "id",
   "retweet_count": 4,
   "geo": NULL,
   "created_at": "Sun Apr 03 23:48:36 +0000 2011";
      user: {
   "statuses_count": 3,511,
   "profile_background_color": "C0DEED",
   "followers_count": "48",
   "description": "watcha doin in my waters?",
   "screen_name": "OldGREG85",
   "time_zone": "Hawaii",
   'lang': "en",
   "friends_count": 81,
   "geo_enabled": false,
      }
```

12. Convert the James Bond XML example from Figure 3.1 into valid JSON.

13. Convert the Indiana Jones example from Figure 3.9 into valid XML.

14. Import the *indy.json* file into R and extract the values of all `budget` keys.

[11] The example is a shortened fragment of the content that is being returned by the Twitter Streaming API.

15. The XML file *potus.xml* (available in the book's materials) contains biographical information on US presidents.

(a) Use the DOM-style XML parser and parse the document into an R object called `potus`. Inspect the source code. The `<occupation>` nodes contain additional white space at the end of the text string. Find the appropriate argument to remove them in the parsing stage.

(b) The XML file contains `<salary>` nodes. Discard them while parsing the file. Remove the additional white space in the `<occupation>` nodes by using a custom handler function and a string manipulation function (see Section 8.2).

(c) Write a handler for extracting the `<hometown>` nodes' value and pass it to the DOM-style parser. Repeat the process with an event-driven parser. Inspect the results.

4

XPath

In Chapters 2 and 3 we introduced and illustrated how HTML/XML documents use markup to store information and create the visual appearance of the webpage when opened in the browser. We also explained how to use a scripting language like R to transform the source code underlying web documents into modifiable data objects called the DOM with the use of dedicated parsing functions (Sections 2.4 and 3.5.1). In a typical data analysis workflow, these are important, but only intermediate steps in the process of assembling well-structured and cleaned datasets from webpages. Before we can take full advantage of the Web as a nearly endless data source, a series of filtering and extraction steps follow once the relevant web documents have been identified and downloaded. The main purpose of these steps is to recast information that is encoded in formats using markup language into formats that are suitable for further processing and analysis with statistical software. Initially, this task comprises asking what information we are interested in and identifying where the information is located in a specific document. Once we know this, we can tailor a query to the document and obtain the desired information. Additionally, some data reshaping and exception handling is often necessary to cast the extracted values into a format that facilitates further analysis.

This chapter walks you through each of these steps and helps you to build an intuition for querying tree-based data structures like HTML/XML documents. We will see that accessing particular information from HTML/XML documents is straightforward using the concise, yet powerful path statements provided by the XML Path language (short **XPath**), a very popular web technology and W3C standard (W3C 1999). After introducing the basic logic underlying XPath, we show how to leverage the full power of its vocabulary using predicates, operators, and custom extractor functions in an application to real documents. We further explore how to work with namespace properties (Section 4.3.2). The chapter concludes with a pointer to helpful tools (Section 4.3.3) and a more high-level discussion about general problems in constructing efficient and robust extraction code for HTML/XML documents (Section 4.3.3).

Automated Data Collection with R: A Practical Guide to Web Scraping and Text Mining, First Edition.
Simon Munzert, Christian Rubba, Peter Meißner and Dominic Nyhuis.

4.1 XPath—a query language for web documents

XPath is a query language that is useful for addressing and extracting parts from HTML/XML documents. XPath is best categorized as a domain-specific language, which indicates that its field of application is a rather narrow one—it is simply a very helpful tool for selecting information from marked up documents such as HTML, XML, or any variant of it such as SVG or RSS (see Sections 3.4.3 and 3.4.3). XPath is also a W3C standard, which means that the language is subjected to constant maintenance and widely employed in modern web applications. Among the two versions of XPath that are in current use, we apply XPath 1.0 as it provides sufficiently powerful statements and is implemented in the XML package for R.

First stop: Parsing

As a stylized, running example, we revisit *fortunes.html*—a simple HTML file that includes short quotes of R wisdoms. A first, necessary step prior to applying XPath is to parse the document and make its content available in the workspace of the R session, since XPath only works on the DOM representation of a document and cannot be applied on the native code. We begin by loading the XML package and use `htmlParse()` to parse the file into the object `parsed_doc`:

```
R> library(XML)
R> parsed_doc <- htmlParse(file = "fortunes.html")
```

The document is now available in the workspace and we can examine its content using XML's `print()` method on the object:

```
R> print(parsed_doc)
<!DOCTYPE HTML PUBLIC "-//IETF//DTD HTML//EN">
<html>
<head><title>Collected R wisdoms</title></head>
<body>
<div id="R Inventor" lang="english" date="June/2003">
  <h1>Robert Gentleman</h1>
  <p><i>'What we have is nice, but we need something very different'</i></p>
  <p><b>Source: </b>Statistical Computing 2003, Reisensburg</p>
</div>

<div lang="english" date="October/2011">
  <h1>Rolf Turner</h1>
  <p><i>'R is wonderful, but it cannot work magic'</i> <br><emph>answering a
request for automatic generation of 'data from a known mean and 95% CI'
</emph></p>
  <p><b>Source: </b><a href="https://stat.ethz.ch/mailman/listinfo/r-help">
R-help</a></p>
</div>

<address>
<a href="http://www.r-datacollection.com"><i>The book homepage</i>
</a><a></a>
</address>

</body>
</html>
```

Before proceeding, we would like to restate a crucial idea from Chapter 2 that will be helpful in understanding the basic logic of XPath statements. HTML/XML documents use tags to markup information and the nestedness of the tags describe a hierarchical order.

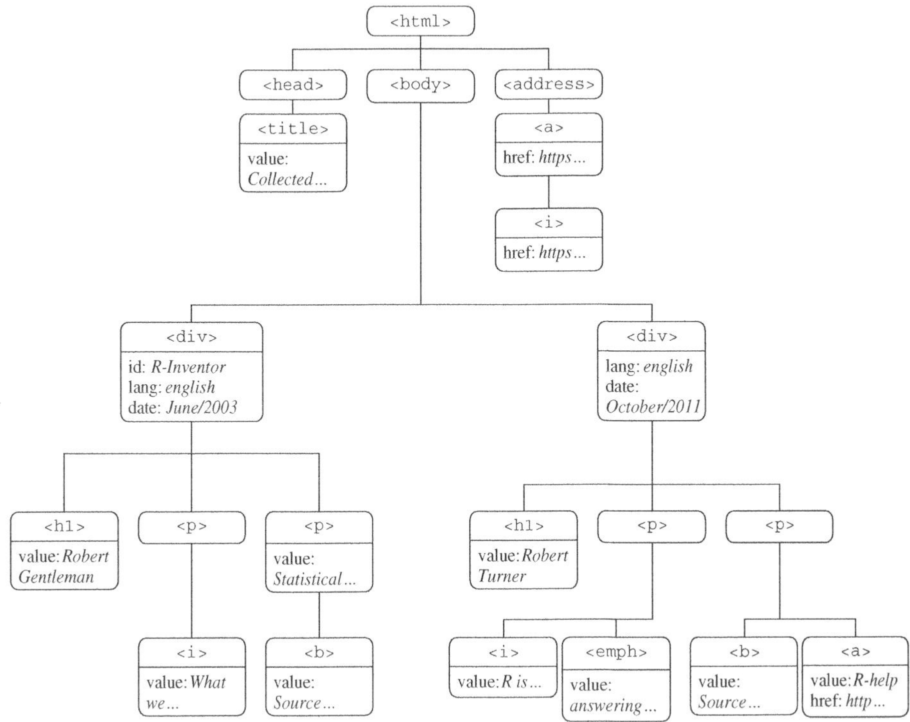

Figure 4.1 A tree perspective on `parsed_doc`

One way to depict this hierarchical order of tags is by means of a tree as it is portrayed in Figure 4.1. In the tree, edges represent the nestedness of a lower-level node inside a higher-level node. Throughout this chapter we will not only refer to this image but also adopt graph language to describe the location of the tags in the document as well as their relations. Therefore, if we refer to the `<div>` node, we mean the entire information that is encapsulated within the `div` tags, that is, the value of the node, its set of attributes as well as their values, and its children nodes. When we use the word node set, we refer to a selection of multiple nodes.

4.2 Identifying node sets with XPath

4.2.1 Basic structure of an XPath query

Hierarchical addressing mechanism

To get started, let us put ourselves to the task of extracting information from the `<i>` nodes, that is, text that is written in italics, which contain the actual quotes. A look at either HTML code or the document tree in Figure 4.1 reveals that there are two nodes of interest and they are both located at the lowest level of the document. In XPath, we can express this hierarchical order by constructing a sequence of nodes separated by the / (forward slash). This is called a hierarchical addressing mechanism and it is similar to a location path on a local file system. The resemblance is not accidental but results from a similar hierarchical organization of the underlying document/file system. Just like folders can be nested inside other folders on a local hard drive, the DOM treats an XML document as a tree of nodes, where the nestedness of nodes within other nodes creates a node hierarchy.

Absolute paths For our HTML file we can describe the position of the `<i>` nodes by describing the sequence of nodes that lead to it. The XPath that represents this position is "`/html/body/div/p/i`." This statement reads from left to right: Start at the root node `<html>`—the top node in a tree is also referred to as the root note—proceed to the `<body>` node, the `<div>` node, the `<p>` node, and finally the `<i>` node. To apply this XPath we use XML's `xpathSApply()` function. Essentially, `xpathSApply()` allows us to conduct two tasks in one step. First, the function returns the complete node set that matches the XPath expression. Second, if intended, we can pass an extractor function to obtain a node's value, attribute, or attribute value.[1] In our case, we set `xpathSApply()`'s first argument `doc` to the parsed document and the second argument `path` to the XPath statement that we wish to apply:

```
R> xpathSApply(doc = parsed_doc, path = "/html/body/div/p/i")
[[1]]
<i>'What we have is nice, but we need something very different'</i>

[[2]]
<i>'R is wonderful, but it cannot work magic'</i>
```

Relative paths In the present case, the specified path is valid for two `<i>` nodes. Thus, the XPath query extracts more than one node at once if it describes a valid path for multiple nodes. The path that we just applied is called an absolute path. The distinctive feature about absolute paths is that they always emanate from the root node and describe a sequence of consecutive nodes to the target node. As an alternative we can construct shorter, relative paths to the target node. Relative paths tolerate "jumps" between nodes, which we can indicate with `//`. To exemplify, consider the following path:

```
R> xpathSApply(parsed_doc, "//body//p/i")
[[1]]
<i>'What we have is nice, but we need something very different'</i>

[[2]]
<i>'R is wonderful, but it cannot work magic'</i>
```

This statement reads as follows: Find the `<body>` node at some level of the document's hierarchy—it does not have to be the root—then find one or more levels lower in the hierarchy a `<p>` node, immediately followed by an `<i>` node. We obtain the same set of `<i>` nodes as previously. An even more concise path for the `<i>` nodes would be the following:

```
R> xpathSApply(parsed_doc, "//p/i")
[[1]]
<i>'What we have is nice, but we need something very different'</i>

[[2]]
<i>'R is wonderful, but it cannot work magic'</i>
```

---

[1] These two steps may be conducted separately from one another. You can use `getNodeSet()` to apply the XPath. Using a looping structure or functionality from the `apply()` family, the received node set can be postprocessed and the information recast.

These three examples help to stress an important point in XPath's design. There are virtually always several ways to describe the same node set by means of different XPath statements. So why do we construct a long absolute path if a valid relative path exists that returns the same information? `xpathSApply()` traverses through the complete document and resolves node jumps of any width and at any depth within the document tree. The appeal of relative paths derives from their shortness, but there are reasons for favoring absolute paths in some instances. Relative path statements result in complete traversals of the document tree, which is rather expensive computationally and decreases the efficiency of the query. For the small HTML file we consider here, computational efficiency is of no concern. Nonetheless, the additional strain will become noticeable in the speed of code execution when larger file sizes or extraction tasks for multiple documents are concerned. Hence, if speed is an issue to your code execution, it is advisable to express node locations by absolute paths.

Deciding between relative and absolute paths

Beyond pure path logic, XPath allows the incorporation of symbols with special meaning in the expressions. One such symbol is the wildcard operator `*`. The wildcard operator matches any (single) node with arbitrary name at its position. To return all <i> nodes from the HTML file we can use the operator between the <div> and <i> node to match the <p> nodes:

Wildcard operator

```
R> xpathSApply(parsed_doc, "/html/body/div/*/i")
[[1]]
<i>'What we have is nice, but we need something very different'</i>

[[2]]
<i>'R is wonderful, but it cannot work magic'</i>
```

Two further elements that we repeatedly make use of are the `.` and the `..` operator. The `.` operator selects the current nodes (or self-axis) in a selected node set. This operation is occasionally useful when using predicates. We postpone a detailed exploration of the `.` operator to Section 4.2.3, where we discuss predicates. The `..` operator selects the node one level up the hierarchy from the current node. Thus, if we wish to select the <head> node we could first locate its child <title> and then go one level up the hierarchy:

Selection expressions

```
R> xpathSApply(parsed_doc, "//title/..")
[[1]]
<head>
  <title>Collected R wisdoms</title>
</head>
```

Lastly, we sometimes want to conduct multiple queries at once to extract elements that lie at different paths. There are two principal methods to do this. The first method is to use the pipe operator | to indicate several paths, which are evaluated individually and returned together. For example, to select the <address> and the <title> nodes, we can use the following statement:

Multiple paths

```
R> xpathSApply(parsed_doc, "//address | //title")
[[1]]
<title>Collected R wisdoms</title>
```

```
[[2]]
<address>
  <a href="http://www.r-datacollectionbook.com">
    <i>The book homepage</i>
  </a>
  <a/>
</address>
```

Another option is to store the XPath queries in a vector and pass this vector to `xpathSApply()`. Here, we first generate a named vector `twoQueries` where the elements represent the distinct XPath queries. Passing `twoQueries` to `xpathSApply()` we get

```
R> twoQueries <- c(address = "//address", title = "//title")
R> xpathSApply(parsed_doc, twoQueries)
[[1]]
<title>Collected R wisdoms</title>

[[2]]
<address>
  <a href="http://www.r-datacollectionbook.com">
    <i>The book homepage</i>
  </a>
  <a/>
</address>
```

4.2.2 Node relations

The XPath syntax introduced so far is sufficiently powerful to select some of the nodes in the document, but it is of limited use when the extraction tasks become increasingly complex. Connected node sequences simply lack expressiveness, which is required for singling out specific nodes from smaller node subsets. This issue is nicely illustrated by the queries that we used to identify the `<i>` nodes in the document. Assume we would like to identify the `<i>` node that appears within the second section element `<div>`. With the syntax introduced so far, no path can be constructed to return this single node since the node sequence to this node is equally valid for the `<i>` nodes within the first section of the document.

The family tree analogy

In this type of situation, we can make use of XPath's capability to exploit other features of the document tree. One such feature is the position of a node relative to other nodes in the document tree. These relationships between nodes are apparent in Figure 4.1. Most nodes have nodes that precede or follow their path, an information that is often unique and thus differentiates between nodes. As is usual in describing tree-structured data formats, we employ notation based on family relationships (child, parent, grandparent, ...) to describe the between-node relations. This feature allows analysts to extract information from a specific target node with an unknown name solely based on the relationship to another node with a known name. The construction of a proper XPath statement that employ this feature follows the pattern `node1/`*`relation`*`::node2`, where `node2` has a specific *relation* to `node1`. Let us try to apply this technique on the problem discussed above, selecting the second `<div>` node in the document. We learn from Figure 4.1 that only the second `<div>` node has an `<a>`

node as one of its grandchildren. This constitutes a unique feature of the second `<div>` node that we can extract as follows:

```
R> xpathSApply(parsed_doc, "//a/ancestor::div")
[[1]]
<div lang="english" date="October/2011">
  <h1>Rolf Turner</h1>
  <p><i>'R is wonderful, but it cannot work magic'</i> <br/><emph>answering a
request for automatic generation of 'data from a known mean and 95% CI'
</emph></p>
  <p><b>Source: </b><a href="https://stat.ethz.ch/mailman/listinfo/r-help">
R-help</a></p>
</div>
```

Here, we first select the `<a>` nodes in the document and then subselect among this set all ancestor nodes with name `div`. Comparing the resulting node set to the results from above, we find that a smaller set is returned. If we were interested on extracting only the text in italics from this node set, we can make a straightforward extension to this expression. To proceed from the thus selected `<div>` node to all the `<i>` that come one or more levels lower in the hierarchy, we add `//i` to the expression:

```
R> xpathSApply(parsed_doc, "//a/ancestor::div//i")
[[1]]
<i>'R is wonderful, but it cannot work magic'</i>
```

As a testament to XPath's capability to reflect complex relationships between nodes, consider the following statement:

```
R> xpathSApply(parsed_doc, "//p/preceding-sibling::h1")
[[1]]
<h1>Robert Gentleman</h1>

[[2]]
<h1>Rolf Turner</h1>
```

Here, we first select all the `<p>` nodes in the document and then all the `<h1>` siblings that precede these nodes.[2]

Generally, XPath statements are limitless with respect to their length and the number of special symbols used in it. To illustrate the combination of the wildcard operator with another node relation, consider the following statement:

```
R> xpathSApply(parsed_doc, "//title/parent::*")
[[1]]
<head>
  <title>Collected R wisdoms</title>
</head>
```

[2]When we apply XPath in real scraping scenarios, we usually cannot draw on visual representations of node relations like the one in Figure 4.1. Such information must be read directly from the page's source code. This often is the most demanding part in information extraction tasks that use XPath.

Table 4.1 XPath axes

Axis name	Result
ancestor	Selects all ancestors (parent, grandparent, etc.) of the current node
ancestor-or-self	Selects all ancestors (parent, grandparent, etc.) of the current node and the current node itself
attribute	Selects all attributes of the current node
child	Selects all children of the current node
descendant	Selects all descendants (children, grandchildren, etc.) of the current node
descendant-or-self	Selects all descendants (children, grandchildren, etc.) of the current node and the current node itself
following	Selects everything in the document after the closing tag of the current node
following-sibling	Selects all siblings after the current node
namespace	Selects all namespace nodes of the current node
parent	Selects the parent of the current node
preceding	Selects all nodes that appear before the current node in the document except ancestors, attribute nodes, and namespace nodes
preceding-sibling	Selects all siblings before the current node
self	Selects the current node

Source: http://www.w3schools.com/xpath/xpath_axes.asp

The parent selects nodes in the tree that appear one level higher with respect to the reference node `<title`. The wildcard operator is used to express indifference regarding the node names. In combination, this statement returns every parent node for every `<title>` node in the document. For a full list of available relations, take a look at Table 4.1. A visual impression of all available node relationships is displayed in Figure 4.2.

4.2.3 XPath predicates

Beside exploiting relationship properties of the tree, we can use predicates to obtain and process numerical and textual properties of the document. Applying these features in a conditioning statement for the node selection adds another level of expressiveness to XPath statements. Put simply, predicates are nothing but simple functions that are applied to a node's name, value, or attribute, and which evaluate whether a condition (or set of conditions) is true or false. Internally, a predicate returns a logical response. Nodes where the response is true are selected. Their general use is as follows: After a node (or node set) we specify the predicate in square brackets, for example, `node1[`*`predicate`*`]`. We select all `<node1>` nodes in the document that comply with the condition formulated by the *predicate*. As a complete coverage of all predicates is neither possible nor helpful for this introduction, we restrict our attention to the most frequent—and in our view most helpful—predicates in XPath. We have

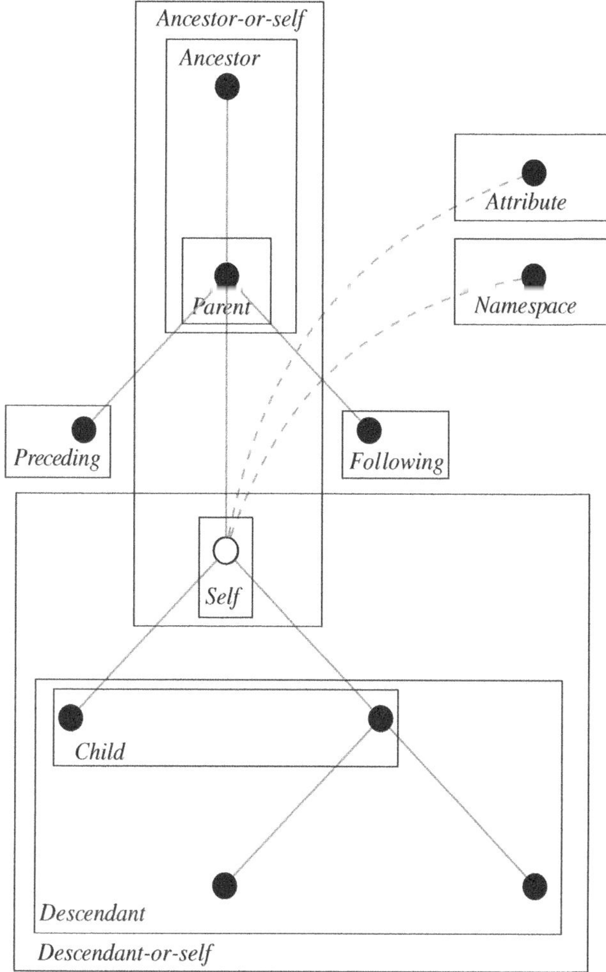

Figure 4.2 Visualizing node relations. Descriptions are presented in relation to the white node

listed some of the available predicates in Table 4.2. Our goal is not to provide an exhaustive examination of this topic, but to convey the inherent logic in applying predicates. We will see that some predicates work in combination with so-called operators. A complete overview of available operators is presented in Table 4.3.

4.2.3.1 Numerical predicates

Implicit numerical properties

XPath offers the possibility to take advantage of implied numerical properties of documents, such as counts or positions. There are several predicates that return numerical properties, which can be used to create conditional statements. The position of a node is an important

Table 4.2 Overview of some important XPath functions

Function	Description	Example
name(<node>)	Returns the name of <node> or the first node in a node set	//*[name()='title']; Returns: <title>
text(<node>)	Returns the value of <node> or the first node in a node set	//*[text()='The book homepage']; Returns: <i> with value *The book homepage*
@*attribute*	Returns the value of a node's *attribute* or of the first node in a node set	//div[@id='R Inventor']; Returns: <div> with attribute *id* value *R Inventor*
string-length(str1)	Returns the length of str1. If there is no string argument, it returns the length of the string value of the current node	//h1[string-length()>11]; Returns: <h1> with value *Robert Gentleman*
translate(str1, str2, str3)	Converts str1 by replacing the characters in str2 with the characters in str3	//div[translate(./@date, '2003', '2005')='June/2005']; Returns: first <div> node with date attribute value *June/2003*
contains(str1,str2)	Returns TRUE if str1 contains str2, otherwise FALSE	//div[contains(@id, 'Inventor')]; Returns: first <div> node with id attribute value *R Inventor*
starts-with(str1,str2)	Returns TRUE if str1 starts with str2, otherwise FALSE	//i[starts-with(text(), 'The')]; Returns: <i> with value *The book homepage*
substring-before (str1,str2)	Returns the start of str1 before str2 occurs in it	//div[substring-before(@date, '/')='June']; Returns: <div> with date attribute value *June/2003*
substring-after (str1,str2)	Returns the remainder of str1 after str2 occurs in it	//div[substring-after(@date, '/')=2003]; Returns: <div> with date attribute value *June/2003*
not(arg)	Returns TRUE if the boolean value is FALSE, and FALSE if the boolean value is TRUE	//div[not(contains(@id, 'Inventor'))]; Returns: the <div> node that does not contain the string *Inventor* in its id attribute value
local-name(<node>)	Returns the name of the current <node> or the first node in a node set—without the namespace prefix	//*[local-name()='address']; Returns: <address>
count(<node>)	Returns the count of a nodeset <node>	//div[count(.//a)=0]; Result: The second <div> with one <a> child
position(<node>)	Returns the index position of <node> that is currently being processed	//div/p[position()=1]; Result: The first <p> node in each <div> node
last()	Returns the number of items in the processed node list <node>	//div/p[last()]; Result: The last <p> node in each <div> node

Table 4.3 XPath operators

Operators	Description	Example
|	Computes two node sets	`//i	//b`
+	Addition	`5 + 3`
-	Subtraction	`8 - 2`
*	Multiplication	`8 * 5`
div	Division	`8 div 5`
=	Equal	`count = 27`
!=	Not equal	`count != 27`
<	Less than	`count < 27`
≤	Less than or equal to	`count <= 27`
>	Greater than	`count > 27`
≥	Greater than or equal to	`count >= 27`
or	Or	`count = 27 or count = 28`
and	And	`count > 26 and count < 30`
mod	Modulo (division remainder)	`7 mod 2`

Source: Adapted from http://www.w3schools.com/xpath/xpath_operators.asp

numerical characteristic that we can easily implement. Let us collect the `<p>` nodes that appear on first position:

```
R> xpathSApply(parsed_doc, "//div/p[position()=1]")
[[1]]
<p>
  <i>'What we have is nice, but we need something very different'</i>
</p>

[[2]]
<p><i>'R is wonderful, but it cannot work magic'</i> <br/><emph>answering a
request for automatic generation of 'data from a known mean and 95% CI'
</emph></p>
```

The predicate we use is `position()` in combination with the equal operator `=`.[3] The statement returns two nodes. The position predicate does not evaluate which `<p>` node is on first position among all `<p>` nodes in the document but on first position in each node subset relative to its parent. If we wish to select the last element of a node set without knowing the number of nodes in a subset in advance, we can use the `last()` operator:

```
R> xpathSApply(parsed_doc, "//div/p[last()]")
[[1]]
<p><b>Source: </b>Statistical Computing 2003, Reisensburg</p>

[[2]]
<p>
  <b>Source: </b>
  <a href="https://stat.ethz.ch/mailman/listinfo/r-help">R-help</a>
</p>
```

[3]Please note that an even more concise way of expressing the same query is `//div/p[1]`.

Output from numerical predicates may be further processed with mathematical operations. To select the next to last <p> nodes, we extend the previous statement:

```
R> xpathSApply(parsed_doc, "//div/p[last()-1]")
[[1]]
<p>
  <i>'What we have is nice, but we need something very different'</i>
</p>

[[2]]
<p><i>'R is wonderful, but it cannot work magic'</i> <br/><emph>answering a
request for automatic generation of 'data from a known mean and 95% CI'
</emph></p>
```

A count is another numerical property we can use as a condition for node selection. One of the most frequent uses of counts is selecting nodes based on their number of children nodes. An implementation of this logic is the following:

```
R> xpathSApply(parsed_doc, "//div[count(.//a)>0]")
[[1]]
<div lang="english" date="October/2011">
  <h1>Rolf Turner</h1>
  <p><i>'R is wonderful, but it cannot work magic'</i> <br/><emph>answering a
request for automatic generation of 'data from a known mean and 95% CI'
</emph></p>
  <p><b>Source: </b><a href="https://stat.ethz.ch/mailman/listinfo/r-help">
R-help</a></p>
</div>
```

Piece by piece, the statement reads as follows. We start by selecting all the <div> nodes in the document (`//div`). We refine the selection by using the `count()` predicate, which takes as argument the *thing* we need to count. In this case we count the number of <a> nodes that precede the selected <div> nodes (`.//a`). The `.` element is used to condition on the previous selection. Internally, this results in another node set, which we then pass to the `count()` function. Combining the operator with a value >`0`, we ask for those <div> nodes in the document that have more than zero <a> nodes as children. Besides nodes, we can also condition on the number of attributes in a node:

```
R> xpathSApply(parsed_doc, "//div[count(./@*)>2]")
[[1]]
<div id="R Inventor" lang="english" date="June/2003">
  <h1>Robert Gentleman</h1>
  <p><i>'What we have is nice, but we need something very different'</i></p>
  <p><b>Source: </b>Statistical Computing 2003, Reisensburg</p>
</div>
```

The `@` element retrieves the attributes from a selected node. Here, the `./@*` expression returns all the attributes—regardless of their name—from the currently selected nodes. We pass these attributes to the count function and evaluate whether the number of attributes is greater than 2. Only the nodes returning `TRUE` for this function are selected.

The number of characters in the content of an element is another kind of count we can obtain and use to condition node selection. This is particularly useful if all we know about our extraction target is that the node contains some greater amount of text. It is implemented as follows:

```
R> xpathSApply(parsed_doc, "//*[string-length(text())>50]")
[[1]]
<i>'What we have is nice, but we need something very different'</i>

[[2]]
<emph>answering a request for automatic generation of 'data from a
known mean and 95% CI'</emph>
```

We first obtain a node set of all the nodes in the document (`//*`). On this set, we impose the condition that the content of these nodes (as returned by `text()`) must contain more than 50 characters.

Boolean functions

It is sometimes useful to invert the node selection and return all nodes for which the predicate does not return `TRUE`. XPath includes a couple of functions that allow employing Boolean logic in the query. To express an inversion of a node set, one can use the Boolean `not` function to select all nodes that are not selected by the query. To select all `<div>` with two or fewer attributes, we can write

```
R> xpathSApply(parsed_doc, "//div[not(count(./@*)>2)]")
[[1]]
<div lang="english" date="October/2011">
  <h1>Rolf Turner</h1>
  <p><i>'R is wonderful, but it cannot work magic'</i> <br/><emph>answering a
request for automatic generation of 'data from a known mean and 95% CI'
</emph></p>
  <p><b>Source: </b><a href="https://stat.ethz.ch/mailman/listinfo/r-help">
R-help</a></p>
</div>
```

4.2.3.2 Textual predicates

Since HTML/XML files or any of their variants are plain text files, textual properties of the document are useful predicates for node selection. This might come in handy if we need to pick nodes on the basis of text in their names, content, attributes, or attributes' values. Besides exact matching, working with strings often requires tools for partial matching of substrings. While XPath 1.0 is sufficiently powerful in this respect, version 2.0 has seen huge improvements with the implementation of a complete library of regular expression predicates (for an introduction to string manipulation techniques see Chapter 8). Nonetheless, XPath 1.0 fares well enough in most situations, so that switching to other XPath implementations is not necessary. To begin, let us explore methods to perform exact matches for strings. We already introduced the = operator for equalizing numerical values, but it works just as well for exact string matching. To select all `<div>` nodes in the document, which contain quotes written in October 2011, that is, contain an attribute `date` with the value `October/2011`, we can write

```
R> xpathSApply(parsed_doc, "//div[@date='October/2011']")
[[1]]
<div lang="english" date="October/2011">
  <h1>Rolf Turner</h1>
  <p><i>'R is wonderful, but it cannot work magic'</i> <br/><emph>answering a
request for automatic generation of 'data from a known mean and 95% CI'
</emph></p>
```

```
  <p><b>Source: </b><a href="https://stat.ethz.ch/mailman/listinfo/r-help">
R-help</a></p>
</div>
```

We first select all the `<div>` nodes in the document and then subselect those that have an attribute `date` with the value `October/2011`. In many instances, exact matching for strings as implied by the equal sign is an exceedingly strict operation. One way to be more liberal is to conduct partial matching for strings. The general use of these methods is as follows: `string_method(text1, 'text2')`, where `text1` refers to a text element in the document and `text2` to a string we want to match it to. To select all nodes in a document that contain the word `magic` in their value, we can construct the following statement:

```
R> xpathSApply(parsed_doc, "//*[contains(text(), 'magic')]")
[[1]]
<i>'R is wonderful, but it cannot work magic'</i>
```

In this statement we first select all the nodes in the document and condition this set using the `contains()` function on whether the value contains the word `magic` as returned by `text()`. Please note that all partial matching functions are case sensitive, so capitalized versions of the term would not be matched. To match a pattern to the beginning of a string, the `starts_with()` function can be used. The following code snippet illustrates the application of this function by selecting all the `<div>` nodes with an attribute `id`, where the value starts with the letter `R`:

```
R> xpathSApply(parsed_doc, "//div[starts-with(./@id, 'R')]")
[[1]]
<div id="R Inventor" lang="english" date="June/2003">
  <h1>Robert Gentleman</h1>
  <p><i>'What we have is nice, but we need something very different'</i></p>
  <p><b>Source: </b>Statistical Computing 2003, Reisensburg</p>
</div>
```

Preprocessing node strings

`ends_with()` is used to match a string to the end of a string. It is frequently useful to preprocess node strings before conducting matching operations. The purpose of this step is to normalize node values, attributes, and attribute values, for example, by removing capitalization or replacing substrings. Let us try to extract only those quotes that have been published in 2003. As we see in the source code, the `<div>` nodes contain a date attribute, which holds information about the year of the quote. To condition our selection on this value, we can issue the following expression:

```
R> xpathSApply(parsed_doc, "//div[substring-after(./@date, '/')='2003']//i")
[[1]]
<i>'What we have is nice, but we need something very different'</i>
```

Let us consider the statement piece by piece. We first select all the `<div>` nodes in the document (`//div`). The selection is further conditioned on the returned attribute value from the predicate. In the predicate we first obtain the `date` value for all the selected nodes (`./@date`). This yields the following vector: `June/2003, October/2011`. The values are passed to the `substring-after()` function where they are split according to the `/`, specified as the second argument. Internally, the function outputs `2003, 2011`. We then conduct exact matching against the value `2003`, which selects the `<div>` node we are looking for. Finally, we move down to the `<i>` node by attaching `//i` to the expression.

4.3 Extracting node elements

So far, we have used `xpathSApply()` to return nodes that match specified XPath statements. We learned that the function returns a list object that contains the nodes' name, value, and attribute values (if specified). We usually do not care for the node in its entirety, but need to extract a specific information from the node, for example, its value. Fortunately, this task is fairly straightforward to implement. We simply pass an extractor function to the `fun` argument in the function call. The XML package offers an extensive set of these functions to select the pieces of information we are interested in. A complete overview of all extractor functions is presented in Table 4.4. For example, in order to extract the value of the `<title>` node we can simply write

```
R> xpathSApply(parsed_doc, "//title", fun = xmlValue)
[1] "Collected R wisdoms"
```

Extractor functions

Instead of a list with complete node information, `xpathSApply()` now returns a vector object, which only contains the value of the node set that matches the XPath statement. For nodes without value information, the functions would return an `NA` value. Beside the value, we can also extract information from the attributes. Passing `xmlAttrs()` to the `fun` argument will select all attributes that are in the selected nodes:

```
R> xpathSApply(parsed_doc, "//div", xmlAttrs)
[[1]]
          id          lang          date
"R Inventor"    "english"   "June/2003"

[[2]]
          lang            date
     "english" "October/2011"
```

In most applications we are interested in specific rather than all node attributes. To select a specific attribute from a node, we use `xmlGetAttr()` and add the attribute name:

```
R> xpathSApply(parsed_doc, "//div", xmlGetAttr, "lang")
[1] "english" "english"
```

Table 4.4 XML extractor functions

Function	Argument	Return value
`xmlName`		Node name
`xmlValue`		Node value
`xmlGetAttr`	`name`	Node attribute
`xmlAttrs`		(All) node attributes
`xmlChildren`		Node children
`xmlSize`		Node size

4.3.1 Extending the fun argument

Processing returned node sets from XPath can easily extend beyond mere feature extraction as introduced in the last section. Rather than extracting information from the node, we can adapt the fun argument to perform any available numerical or textual operation on the node element. We can build novel functions for particular purposes or modify existing extractor functions for our specific needs and pass them to xpathSApply(). The goal of further processing can either lie in cleansing the numeric or textual content of the node, or some kind of exception handling in order to deal with extraction failures.

Custom functions for xpathSApply()

To illustrate the concept in a first application, let us attempt to extract all quotes from the document and convert the symbols to lowercase during the extraction process. We can use base R's tolower() function, which transforms strings to lowercase. We begin by writing a function called lowerCaseFun(). In the function, we simply feed the information from the node value to the tolower() function and return the transformed text:

```
R> lowerCaseFun <- function(x) {
        x <- tolower(xmlValue(x))
        x
}
```

Adding the function to xpathSApply()'s fun argument, yields:

```
R> xpathSApply(parsed_doc, "//div//i", fun = lowerCaseFun)
[1] "'what we have is nice, but we need something very different'"
[2] "'r is wonderful, but it cannot work magic'"
```

The returned vector now consists of all the transformed node values and spares us an additional postprocessing step after the extraction. A second and a little more complex postprocessing function might include some basic string operations that employ functionality from the stringr package. Again, we begin by writing a function that loads the stringr package, collects the date and extracts the year information[4]:

```
R> dateFun <- function(x) {
     require(stringr)
     date <- xmlGetAttr(node = x, name = "date")
     year <- str_extract(date, "[0-9]{4}")
     year
}
```

Passing this function to the fun argument in xpathSApply() yields:

```
R> xpathSApply(parsed_doc, "//div", dateFun)
[1] "2003" "2011"
```

We can also use the fun argument to cope with situations where an XPath statement returns an empty node set. In XML's DOM the NULL object is used to indicate a node that

[4]See Chapter 8 for an introduction to string manipulation. In particular, the function str_extract() in the custom extractor function collects four consecutive digits using a so-called regular expression. The concept and details of regular expressions will also be explained in Chapter 8.

does not exist. We can employ a custom function that includes a test for the NULL object and makes further processing dependent on positive or negative evaluation of this test:

```
R> idFun <- function(x) {
     id <- xmlGetAttr(x, "id")
     id <- ifelse(is.null(id), "not specified", id)
     return(id)
}
```

The first line in this custom function saves the node's id value into a new object id. Conditional on this value being NULL, we either return not specified or the id value in the second line. To see the results, let us pass the function to xpathSApply():

```
R> xpathSApply(parsed_doc, "//div", idFun)
[1] "R Inventor"    "not specified"
```

4.3.1.1 Using variables in XPath expressions

The previous examples were simple enough to allow querying all information with a single, fixed XPath expression. Occasionally, though, it becomes inevitable to treat XPath expressions themselves as variable parts of the extraction program. Data analysts often find that a specific type of information is encoded heterogeneously across documents, and hence, constructing a valid XPath expression for all documents may be impossible, especially when future versions of a site are expected to change. To illustrate this, consider extracting information from the XML file *technology.xml*, which we introduced in Section 3.5.1. Previously, we extracted the Apple stock from this file, but now we tackle the problem of pulling out all companies' stock information. The problem is that the target closing stock information (<close>) is encapsulated in parent nodes with different names (Apple, Google, IBM). Instead of creating separate query functions for each company, we can help ourselves by using the sprintf() function to create flexible XPath expressions. We start by parsing the document again and building a character vector with the relevant company names:

```
R> parsed_stocks <- xmlParse(file = "technology.xml")
R> companies <- c("Apple", "IBM", "Google")
```

Next, we use sprintf() to create the queries. Inside the function, we set the basic template of the XPath expression. The string %s is used to indicate the variable part, where s stands for a string variable. The object companies indicates the elements we want to substitute for %s:

```
R> (expQuery <- sprintf("//%s/close", companies))
[1] "//Apple/close"  "//IBM/close"    "//Google/close"
```

We can proceed as usual by first laying out an extractor function…

```
R> getClose <- function(node) {
     value <- xmlValue(node)
     company <- xmlName(xmlParent(node))
     mat <- c(company = company, value = value)
}
```

...and then passing this extractor function to `xpathSApply()`. Here, we additionally convert the output to a more convenient data frame format and change the vector type:

```
R> stocks <- as.data.frame(t(xpathSApply(parsed_stocks, expQuery, getClose)))
R> stocks$value <- as.numeric(as.character(stocks$value))
R> head(stocks, 3)
  company value
1   Apple 520.6
2   Apple 520.0
3   Apple 519.0
```

4.3.2 XML namespaces

In our introduction to XML technologies in Chapter 3, we introduced namespaces as a feature to create uniquely identified nodes in a web document. Namespaces become an indispensable part of XML when different markup vocabularies are used inside a single document. Such may be the result of merging two different XML files into a single document. When the constituent XML files employ similar vocabulary, namespaces help to resolve ambiguities and prevent name collisions.

Separate namespaces pose a problem to the kinds of XPath statements we have been considering so far, since XPath ordinarily considers the default namespace. In this section we learn how to specify the namespace under which a specific node set is defined and thus extract the elements of interest. Let us return to the example we used in our introduction to XML namespaces (Section 3.4). The file *books.xml* not only contains an HTML title but also information on a book enclosed in XML nodes. We start by parsing the document with `xmlParse()` and print its contents to the screen:

```
R> parsed_xml <- xmlParse("titles.xml")
R> parsed_xml
<?xml version="1.0" encoding="UTF-8"?>
<!DOCTYPE presidents SYSTEM "presidents.dtd">
<root xmlns:h="http://www.w3.org/1999/xhtml" xmlns:t="http://
funnybooknames.com/crockford">
  <h:head>
     <h:title>Basic HTML Sample Page</h:title>
  </h:head>
  <t:book id="1">
    <t:author>Douglas Crockford</t:author>
    <t:title>JavaScript: The Good Parts</t:title>
  </t:book>
</root>
```

For the sake of the example, let us assume we are interested in extracting information from the `<title>` node, which holds the text string `JavaScript: The Good Parts`. We can start by issuing a call to all `<title>` nodes in the document and retrieve their values:

```
R> xpathSApply(parsed_xml, "//title", fun = xmlValue)
list()
```

Bypassing namespaces Evidently, the call returns an empty list. The key problem is that neither of the two `<title>` nodes in the document has been defined under the default namespace on which standard XPath operates. The specific namespaces can be inspected in the xmlns statements in the attributes of the <root> node. Here, two separate namespaces are declared, which are referred to by the letters h and t. One way to bypass the unique namespaces is to make a query directly to the local name of interest:

```
R> xpathSApply(parsed_xml, "//*[local-name()='title']", xmlValue)
[1] "Basic HTML Sample Page"      "JavaScript: The Good Parts"
```

Here, we first select all the nodes in the document and then subselect all the nodes with local name title. To conduct namespace-aware XPath queries on the document, we can extend the function and use the namespaces argument in the xpathSApply() function to refer to the particular namespace under which the second <title> node has been defined. We know that the namespace information appears in the <root> node. We can pass the second namespace string to the namespaces argument of the xpathSApply() function:

```
R> xpathSApply(parsed_xml, "//x:title", namespaces = c(x = "http://
funnybooknames.com/crockford"),
    fun = xmlValue)
[1] "JavaScript: The Good Parts"
```

Similarly, if we were interested in extracting information from the <title> node under the first namespace, we would simply change the URI:

```
R> xpathSApply(parsed_xml, "//x:title", namespaces = c(x = "http://
www.w3.org/1999/xhtml"),
    fun = xmlValue)
[1] "Basic HTML Sample Page"
```

These methods require the namespaces under which the nodes of interest have been declared to be known in advance. The literal specification of the URI can be circumvented if we know where in the document the namespace definition occurs. Namespaces are always declared as attribute values of an XML element. For the sample file, the information appears in the <root> node's xmlns attribute. We capitalize on this knowledge by extracting the namespace URI for the second namespace using the xmlNamespaceDefinitions() function:

```
R> nsDefs <- xmlNamespaceDefinitions(parsed_xml)[[2]]
R> ns <- nsDefs$uri
R> ns
[1] "http://funnybooknames.com/crockford"
```

Having stored the information in a new object, the namespace URI can be passed to the XPath query in order to extract information from the <title> node under that namespace:

```
R> xpathSApply(parsed_xml, "//x:title", namespaces = c(x = ns), xmlValue)
[1] "JavaScript: The Good Parts"
```

4.3.3 Little XPath helper tools

XPath's versatility comes at the cost of a steep learning curve. Beginners and experienced XPath users may find the following tools helpful in verifying and constructing valid statements for their extraction tasks:

SelectorGadget SelectorGadget (http://selectorgadget.com) is an open-source bookmarklet that simplifies the generation of suitable XPath statements through a point-and-click approach. To make use of its functionality, visit the SelectorGadget website and create a bookmark for the page. On the website of interest, activate SelectorGadget by clicking on the bookmark. Once a tool bar on the bottom left appears, SelectorGadget is activated and highlights the page's DOM elements when the cursor moves across the page. Clicking an element adds it to the list of nodes to be scraped. From this selection, SelectorGadget creates a generalized statement that we can obtain by clicking on the *XPath* button. The XPath expression can then be passed to `xpathSApply()`'s `path` argument. Please note that in order to use the generated XPath expressions in `xpathSApply()`, you need to be aware that the type of quotation mark that embrace the XPath expression may not be used inside the expression (e.g., for the attribute names). Replace them either with double (" ") or single (‘’) quotation marks.

Web Developer Tools Many modern browsers contain a suite of developer tools to help inspect elements in the webpage and create valid XPath statements that can be passed to XML's node retrieval functions. Beyond information on the current DOM, developer tools also allow tracing changes to DOM elements in dynamic webpages. We will make use of these tools in Section 6.3.

Summary

In this chapter we made a broad introduction to the XPath language for querying XML documents. We hope to have shown that XPath constitutes an indispensable investment for data analysts who want to work with data from webpages in a productive and efficient manner. With the tools introduced at the end of this chapter, many extraction problems may even be solved through simply clicking elements and pasting the returned expression. Despite their helpfulness, these tools may fail for rather intricate extraction problems, and, thus, knowing how to build expressions from scratch remains a necessary skill. We also would like to assert that the construction of an applicable XPath statement is rarely a one-shot affair but requires an iterative learning process. This process can be described as a cycle of three steps. In the construction stage, we assemble an XPath statement that is believed to return the correct information. In the testing stage, we apply the XPath, observe the returned node set or error message, and find that perhaps the returned node set is too broad or too narrow. The learning stage is a necessary stage when the XPath query has failed. Learning from this failure, we might infer a more suitable XPath expression, for example, by making it more strict or more lax in order to obtain only the desired information. Going back to step number one, we apply the refined XPath to check whether it now yields the correct set of nodes. For many extraction problems we find that multiple traverses through this cycle are necessary to build confidence in the robustness of the programmed extraction routine. We are going to elaborate on the XPath scraping strategy again in Section 9.2.2.

The issue of XPath robustness is exacerbated when the code is to work on unseen instances of a webpage, for example, when the extraction code is automatically executed daily (see Section 11.2). Inevitably, websites undergo changes to their structure; elements are removed or shifted, new features are implemented, visual appearances are modified, which ultimately affect the page's contents as well. This is especially true for popular websites. But we will see that certain dispositions can be made in the XPath statements and auxiliary code design to increase robustness and warn the analyst when the extraction fails. One possibility is to rely on textual predicates when textual information should be extracted from the document. Adding information to the query on the substantive interest can add necessary robustness to the code.

Further reading

A full exploration of XPath and the XML package is beyond the scope of this chapter. For an extensive overview of the XML package, interested readers are referred to Nolan and Temple Lang (2014). A more concise introduction to the package is provided by Temple Lang (2013c). Tennison provides a comprehensive overview of XPath 1.0 (Tennison 2001). Another helpful overview of XPath 1.0 and 2.0 methods can be found in Holzner (2003). For an excellent online documentation on web technologies, including XPath, consult Mozilla Developer Network (2013).

Problems

1. What makes XPath a domain-specific language?
2. XPath is the XML Path language, but it also works for HTML documents. Explain why.
3. Return to the *fortunes1.html* file and consider the following XPath expression: `//a[text()[contains(., 'R-help')]]§`. Replace § to get the `<h1>` node with value "Robert Gentleman."
4. Construct a predicate with the appropriate string functions to test whether the month of a quote is October.
5. Consider the following two XPath statements for extracting paragraph nodes from a HTML file. 1. `//div//p`, 2. `//p`. Decide which of the two statements makes a more narrow request. Explain why.
6. Verify that for extracting the quotes from *fortunes.html* the XPath expression `//i` does not return the correct results. Explain why not.
7. The XML file *potus.xml* contains biographical information on US presidents. Parse the file into an object of the R session.
   (a) Extract the names of all the presidents.
   (b) Extract the names of all presidents, beginning with the 40th term.
   (c) Extract the value of the `<occupation>` node for all Republican presidents.
   (d) Extract the `<occupation>` node for all Republican presidents that are also Baptists.
   (e) The `<occupation>` node contains a string with additional white space at the beginning and the end of the string. Remove the white space by extending the extractor function.
   (f) Extract information from the `<education>` nodes. Replace all instances of "No formal education" with `NA`.
   (g) Extract the `<name>` node for all presidents whose terms started in or after the year 1960.

8. The State of Delaware maintains a repository of datasets published by the Delaware Government Information Center and other Delaware agencies. Take a look at *Naturalizations.xml* (included in the chapter's materials at http://www.r-datacollection.com). The file contains information about naturalization records from the Superior Court. Convert the data into an R data frame.

9. The Commonwealth War Graves Commission database contains geographical information on burial plots and memorials across the globe for those who lost their lives as a result of World War I. The data have been recast as a KML document, an XML-type data structure. Take a look at *cwgc-uk.kml* (included in the chapter's materials). Parse the data and create a data frame from the information on name and coordinates. Plot the distribution on a map.

10. Inspect the SelectorGadget (see Section 4.3.3). Go to http://planning.maryland.gov/Redistricting/2010/legiDist.shtml and identify the XPath expression suited to extract the links in the bottom right table named *Maryland 2012 Legislative District Maps (with Precincts)* using SelectorGadget.

5

HTTP

To retrieve data from the Web, we have to enable our software to communicate with servers and web services. The *lingua franca* of communication on the Web is HTTP, the **H**yper**t**ext **T**ransfer **P**rotocol. HTTP dates back to the late 1980s when it was invented by Tim Berners-Lee, Roy Fielding and others at the CERN near Geneva, Switzerland (Berners-Lee 2000; Berners-Lee et al. 1996). It is the most common protocol for communication between web clients (e.g., browsers) and servers, that is, computers that respond to requests from the network. Virtually every HTML page we open, every image we view in a browser, every video we watch is delivered by HTTP. When we type a URL into the address bar, we usually do not even start with `http://` anymore, but with the hostname directly (e.g., r-datacollection.com) as a request via HTTP is taken for granted and automatically processed by the browser. HTTP's current official version 1.1 dates back to 1999 (Fielding et al. 1999), a fact that nicely illustrates its reliability over the years—in the same time period, other web standards such as HTML have changed a lot more often.

We hardly ever come into direct contact with HTTP. Constructing and sending HTTP requests and processing servers' HTTP responses are tasks that are automatically processed by our browsers and email clients. Imagine how exhausting it would be if we had to formulate requests like "Hand me a document called index.html from the host www.nytimes.com/ in the directory pages/science/ using the HTTP protocol" every time we wanted to search for articles. But have you ever tried to use R for that purpose? To maintain our heroic claim that R is a convenient tool for gathering data from the Web, we need to prove that it is in fact suited to mimic browser-to-web communication. As we will see, for many of the basic web scraping tasks we still do not have to care much about the HTTP particulars in the background, as R handles this for us by default. In some instances, however, we have to dig deeper into protocol file transfers and formulate precise requests in order to get the information we want. This chapter serves as an introduction to those parts of HTTP that are most important to us to become successful web scrapers.

Automated Data Collection with R: A Practical Guide to Web Scraping and Text Mining, First Edition.
Simon Munzert, Christian Rubba, Peter Meißner and Dominic Nyhuis.

The chapter starts with an introduction to client–server conversation (Section 5.1.1). Before we turn to the technical details of HTTP, we briefly digress to talk about URLs, standardized names of resources on the Internet (Section 5.1.2). Our presentation of HTTP is then subdivided into a fundamental look at the logic of HTTP messages (Section 5.1.3), request methods (Section 5.1.4), status codes (Section 5.1.5), and headers (Section 5.1.6). In the second part, we inspect more advanced features of HTTP for identification and authentication purposes (Sections 5.2.1 and 5.2.2) and talk about the use of proxies (Section 5.2.3). Although HTTP is by far the most widespread protocol on the Web, we also take a look at HTTPS and FTP (Section 5.3). We conclude with the practical implementation of HTTP-based communication using R (Section 5.4). All in all, we have tried to keep this introduction to HTTP as nontechnical as possible, while still enabling you to use R as a web client in situations that are not explicitly covered in this book.

5.1 HTTP fundamentals

5.1.1 A short conversation with a web server

To access content on the Web, we are used to typing URLs into our browser or to simply clicking on links to get from one place to another, to check our mails, to read news, or to download files. Behind this program layer that is designed for user interaction there are several more layers—techniques, standards, and protocols—that make the whole thing work. Together they are called the Internet Protocol Suite (IPS). Two of the most prominent players of this Protocol Suite are TCP (Transmission Control Protocol) and IP (Internet Protocol). They represent the *Internet layer* (IP) and the *transportation layer* (TCP). The inner workings of these techniques are beyond the scope of this book, but fortunately there is no need to manually manipulate contents of either of these protocols to conduct successful web scraping. What is worth mentioning, however, is that TCP and IP take care of reliable data transfer between computers in the network.[1]

On top of these *transportation* standards there are specialized message exchange protocols like HTTP (Hyper Text Transfer Protocol), FTP (File Transfer Protocol), Post Office Protocol (POP) for email retrieval, SMTP (Simple Mail Transfer Protocol) or IMAP (Internet Message Access Protocol) for email storage and retrieval. All of these protocols define standard vocabulary and procedures for clients and servers to *talk* about specific tasks—retrieving or storing documents, files, messages, and so forth. They are subsumed under the label *application layer.*

Other than the name suggests, HTTP is not only a standard for hypertext document retrieval. Although HTTP is quite simple, it is flexible enough to ask for nearly any kind of resource from a server and can also be used to send data to the server instead of retrieving it.

Client-server communication

Figure 5.1 presents a stylized version of ordinary user–client interactions. Simply put, when we access a website like www.r-datacollection.com/index.html, our browser serves as the HTTP client. The client first asks a DNS server (**D**omain **N**ame **S**ystem) which IP

[1] If you care to learn more about the Transmission Control Protocol or the Internet Protocol, both Fall and Stevens (2011) and Forouzan (2010) provide extensive introductions to the topic. For a more accessible introduction, check out https://www.netbsd.org/docs/guide/en/chap-net-intro.html

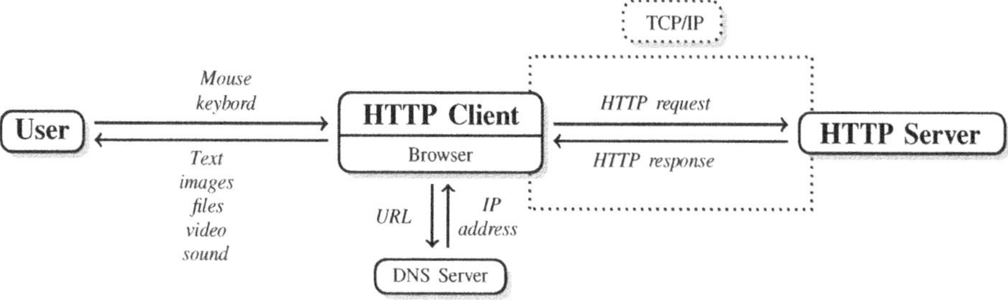

Figure 5.1 User–server communication via HTTP

address is associated with the domain part of the URL we typed in.[2] In our example, the domain part is www.r-datacollection.com.[3] After the browser has received the IP address as response from the DNS server, it establishes a connection to the requested HTTP server via TCP/IP. Once the connection is established, client and server can exchange information—in our case by exchanging HTTP messages. The most basic HTTP conversation consists of one client request and one server response. For example, our browser asks for a specific HTML document, an image, or some other file, and the server responds by delivering the document or giving back an error code if something went wrong. In our example, the browser would ask for *index.html* and start parsing the content of the response to provide the representation of the website. If the received document contains further linked resources like images, the browser continues sending HTTP requests to the server until all necessary resources are transmitted. In the early days of the Internet, one could literally observe how the browser loaded webpages piece by piece. By now, it almost seems like webpages are received all at once due to the availability of higher bandwidths, keeping HTTP connections alive or posing numerous requests in parallel.

There are two important facts about HTTP that should be kept in mind. First, HTTP is not only a protocol to transport hypertext documents but is used for all kinds of resources. Second, HTTP is a stateless protocol. This means that without further effort each pair of request and response between client and server is handled by default as though the two were talking to each other for the first time no matter how often they previously exchanged information.

HTTP messages

Let us take a look at one of these standardized messages. For the sake of the example we establish a connection to www.r-datacollection.com and ask the server to send us *index.html*. The HTTP client first translates the host URL into an IP address and then establishes a connection to the server on the default HTTP port (port 80). The port can be imagined as a door at the server's house where the HTTP client knocks. Consider the following summary of the client-side of the conversation:[4]

[2]Note that we only scratch the surface of the technologies of client–server communication. If you want to learn more about the technologies behind it, for example, how DNS servers are contacted, we point you to the "Further reading" section of this chapter.

[3]We consider the structure of URLs in the next section.

[4]We will elaborate further below how to monitor the HTTP exchanges.

```
About to connect() to www.r-datacollection.com port 80 (#0)
  Trying 173.236.186.125... connected
Connected to www.r-datacollection.com (173.236.186.125) port 80 (#0)
Connection #0 to host www.r-datacollection.com left intact
```

After having established the connection the server expects a request and our client sends the following HTTP request to the server:

```
GET /index.html HTTP/1.1
Host: www.r-datacollection.com
Accept: */*
```

Now it is the client's turn to expect a response from the server. The server responds with some general information followed by the content of our requested document.[5] The HTTP response reads as follows:

```
HTTP/1.1 200 OK
Date: Thu, 27 Feb 2014 09:40:35 GMT
Server: Apache
Vary: Accept-Encoding
Content-Length: 131
...

<!DOCTYPE HTML PUBLIC "-//IETF//DTD HTML//EN">
<html> <head>
<title></title>
</head>
...
```

After having received all the data, the connection is closed again by the client ...

```
Closing connection #0
```

... and the transaction is completed.

5.1.2 URL syntax

The location of websites and other web content are identified by **U**niform **R**esource **L**ocators (URLs). They are not part of HTTP but make communication via HTTP and

[5]Several lines of the server response have been omitted for purposes of presentation.

other protocols straightforward for users.[6] The general URL format can be expressed as follows:

```
scheme://hostname:port/path?querystring#fragment
```

A corresponding real-life example would be

```
http://www.w3.org:80/People/Berners-Lee/#Bio
```

Each URL starts with a **scheme** that defines the protocol that is used to communicate between client/application and server. In the example, the scheme is `http`, separated by a colon. There are other schemes like `ftp` (File Transfer Protocol) or `mailto`, which corresponds to email addresses that rely on the SMTP (Simple Mail Transfer Protocol) standard. Most enable communication in networks, but you will also find the `file` scheme familiar, which addresses files on local or network drives.

The **hostname** provides the name of the server where the resource of interest is stored. It is a unique identifier of a server. The hostname along with the **port** component tell the client at which door it has to knock in order to get access to the requested resource. The information is provided in the example as `www.w3.org:80`. Port 80 is the default port in the Transmission Control Protocol (TCP). If the client is fine with using the default port, this part of the URL can be dropped. Hostnames are usually human readable, but every hostname also has a machine-readable IP address. In the example, www.w3.org belongs to the IP address `128.30.52.37`, making the following an equivalent URL:[7]

```
http://128.30.52.37/People/Berners-Lee/#Bio
```

As we usually provide the human-friendly versions of URLs, the Domain Name System (DNS) translates hostnames into numerical IP addresses. Therefore, the DNS is frequently compared to a worldwide phone book that redirects users who provide hostnames to services or devices.

The **path** determines the location of the requested resource on the server. It works like paths on any conventional file system where files are nested in folders that may again be nested in folders and so on. Path segments are separated by slashes (/).

In some cases, URLs provide supplementary information in the path that helps the server to process the request correctly. The additional information is delivered in **query strings** that hold one or more `name=value` pairs. The query string is separated from the rest of the URL by a question mark. It encodes data using a '*field = value*' format and uses the ampersand symbol (&) to separate multiple name–value pairs.

```
https://www.google.com/search?q=RCurl+filetype%3Apdf
```

A comparable URL is constructed when we search for "RCurl" documents on Google that are of type PDF. The name–value pair `q=RCurl+filetype%3Apdf` is the transformed

---

[6]We will learn in Section 9.1.3 that one of the easiest ways to collect data from websites is often to inspect and manipulate the URLs that refer to content of interest. Sometimes the URLs follow a simple logic, for example, when they contain a running index. It is simple to generate a set of URLs, automatically access them, and store their content.

[7]We can use services like the one at http://whatismyipaddress.com/ip-lookup to look up the corresponding IP addresses of hostnames.

actual request written in the search form as "RCurl filetype:pdf," a compact syntax to search for PDF files that include the term "RCurl." One could easily extend the request with further search parameters such as `tbs=qdr:y`. This would limit the results to hits that are younger than one year.[8]

Finally, **fragments** help point to a specific part of a document. This works well if the requested resource is HTML and the fragment identifier refers to a section, image, or similar. In the example above, the fragment `#Bio` requests a direct jump to the biography section of the document. Note that fragments are handled by the browser, that is, on the client side. After the server has returned the whole document, the fragment is used to display the specified part.

URL encoding

There are some encoding rules for URLs. URLs are transmitted using the ASCII character set, which is limited to a set of 128 characters. All characters not included in this set and most special characters need to be escaped, that is, they are replaced by a standardized representation. Consider once again the example. The expression "RCurl filetype:pdf" is converted to `q=RCurl+filetype%3Apdf`. Both white space and the colon character seem to be "unsafe" and have been replaced with a + sign and the URL encoding `%3A`, respectively. URL encodings are also called percent-encoding because the percent character `%` initializes each of these encodings. Note that the plus character is a special case of a URL escape sequence that is only valid in the query part. In other parts, the valid URL encoding of space is `%20`. A complete list of URL encodings can be found at http://www.w3schools.com/tags/ref_urlencode.asp.

We can encode or decode characters in URLs with the base functions `URLencode()` and `URLdecode()` in R. The `reserved` argument in the former function ensures that non-alphanumeric characters are encoded with their percent-encoding representation:

```
R> t <- "I'm Eddie! How are you & you? 1 + 1 = 2"
R> (url <- URLencode(t, reserve = TRUE))
[1] "I'm%20Eddie!%20How%20are%20you%20%26%20you%3f%201%20+%201%20%3d%202"

R> URLdecode(url)
[1] "I'm Eddie! How are you & you? 1 + 1 = 2"
```

These functions can be useful when we want to construct URLs manually, for example, to specify a *GET* form (see below), without having to insert the percent-encodings by hand.

5.1.3 HTTP messages

HTTP messages, whether client requests or server response messages, consist of three parts: **start line**, **headers**, and **body**—see Figures 5.2 and 5.3. While start lines differ for request and response, the messages' header and body sections are structured identically.

To separate start line from headers and headers from body, carriage return and line feed characters (CRLF) are used.[9] Note that start line and headers are separated by one sequence of CRLF while the last header before the body is followed by two CRLF. In R, these characters are represented as escaped characters `\r` for carriage **r**eturn and `\n` for **n**ew line feed.

The start line is the first and indispensable line of each HTTP message. In requests, the start line defines the method used for the request, followed by the path to the resource

[8]We can identify additional parameters by specifying advanced searches and observing the changes in the URL. For a comprehensive overview, see http://jwebnet.net/advancedgooglesearch.html

[9]Carriage return and line feed are control characters that are inherited from typewriters. Using a typewriter, starting a new line required returning the carriage to the left and moving the plate one line further down.

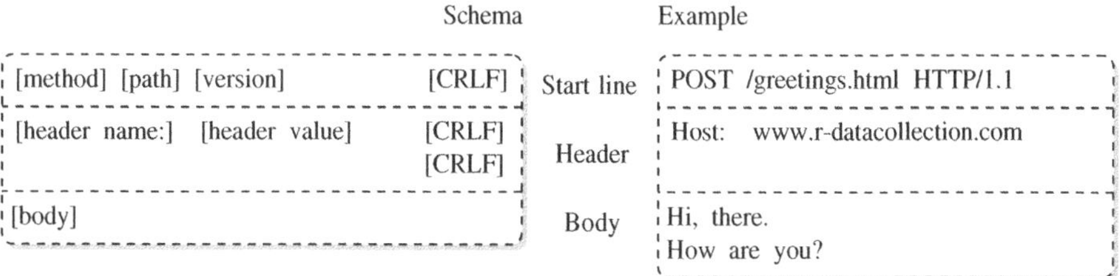

Figure 5.2 HTTP request schema

Schema		Example
[version] [status] [phrase] [CRLF]	Start line	HTTP/1.1 200 OK
[header name:] [header value] [CRLF] [CRLF]	Header	Content-type: text/plain
[body]	Body	I am fine, thank you very much. What else might I help you with?

Figure 5.3 HTTP response schema

requested, followed by the highest HTTP version the client can handle. In our example we use the *POST* method requesting *greetings.html* and indicate that our client understands HTTP up to version 1.1.

The server response start line begins with a statement on the highest HTTP version the server can handle, followed by a status code, followed by a human-readable explanation of the status. Here, www.r-datacollection.com tells us that it understands HTTP up to version 1.1, that everything went fine by returning 200 as status code, and that this status code means something like *OK*.

The header section below the start line provides client and server with meta information about the other sides' preferences or the content sent along with the message. Headers contain a set of header fields in the form of name–value pairs. Ordinarily, each header field is placed on a new line and header field name and value are separated by colon. If a header line becomes very long, it can be divided into several lines by beginning the additional line with an empty space character to indicate that they belong to the previous header line.

MIME types

The body of an HTTP message contains the data. This might be plain text or binary data. Which type of data the body is composed of is specified in the `content-type` header, following the MIME type specification (**M**ultipurpose **I**nternet **M**ail **E**xtensions). MIME types tell the client or server which type of data it should expect. They follow a scheme of *main-type/sub-type*. Main types are, for example, application, audio, image, text, and video with subtypes like application/pdf, audio/mpg, audio/ogg, image/gif, image/jpeg, image/png, text/plain, text/html, text/xml, video/mp4, video/quicktime, and many more.[10]

[10] For the full set, see the list provided by IANA (**I**nternet **A**ssigned **N**umbers **A**uthority) at http://www.iana.org/assignments/media-types/media-types.xhtml.

Table 5.1 Common HTTP request methods

Method	Description
GET	Retrieves resource from server
POST	Retrieves resource from server using the message body to send data or files to the server
HEAD	Works like *GET*, but server responds only with start line and header, no body
PUT	Stores the body of the request message on the server
DELETE	Deletes a resource from the server
TRACE	Traces the route of the message along its way to the server
OPTIONS	Returns list of supported HTTP methods
CONNECT	Establishes a network connection

Source: Fielding et al. (1999).

5.1.4 Request methods

When initiating HTTP client requests, we can choose among several request methods—see Table 5.1 for an overview. The two most important HTTP methods are *GET* and *POST*. Both methods request a resource from the server, but differ in the usage of the body. Whereas *GET* does not send anything in the body of the request, *POST* uses the body to send data. In practice, simple requests for HTML documents and other files are usually executed with the *GET* method. Conversely, *POST* is used to send data to the server, like a file or inputs from an HTML form.

If we are not interested in content from the server we can use the *HEAD* method. *HEAD* tells the server to only send the start line and the headers but not transfer the requested resource, which might be convenient to test if our requests are accepted. Two more handy methods for testing are *OPTIONS*, which asks the server to send back the methods it supports and *TRACE*, which requests the list of proxy servers (see Section 5.2.3) the request message has passed on its way to the server.

Last but not least there are two methods for uploading files to and deleting files from a server—*PUT* and *DELETE*—as well as *CONNECT*, a method for establishing an HTTP connection that might be used, for example, for SSL tunneling (see Section 5.3.1).

We will elaborate the methods *GET* and *POST*, the two most important methods for web scraping, when we discuss HTTP in action (see Section 5.4).

5.1.5 Status codes

When a server responds to a request, it will always send back a status code in the start line of the response. The most famous response that nearly everybody knows from browsing the Web is 404, stating that the server could not find the requested document. Status codes can range from 100 up to 599 and follow a specific scheme: the leading digit signifies the status category—1xx for informations, 2xx for success, 3xx for redirection, 4xx for client errors and 5xx for server errors—see Table 5.2 for a list of common status codes.

Table 5.2 Common HTTP status codes

Code	Phrase	Description
200	OK	Everything is fine
202	Accepted	The request was understood and accepted but no further actions have yet taken place
204	No Content	The request was understood and accepted but no further data needs to be returned except for potentially updated header information
300	Multiple Choices	The request was understood and accepted but the request applies to more than one resource
301	Moved Permanently	The requested resource has moved, the new location is included in the response header *Location*
302	Found	Similar to *Moved Permanently* but temporarily
303	See Other	Redirection to the location of the requested resource
304	Not Modified	Response to a conditional request stating that the requested resource has not been changed
305	Use Proxy	To access the requested resource a specific proxy server found in the *Location* header should be used
400	Bad Request	The request has syntax errors
401	Unauthorized	The client should authenticate itself before progressing
403	Forbidden	The server refuses to provide the requested resource and does not give any further reasons
404	Not Found	The server could not find the resource
405	Method Not Allowed	The method in the request is not allowed for the specific resource
406	Not Acceptable	The server has found no resource that conforms to the resources accepted by the client
500	Internal Server Error	The server has encountered some internal error and cannot provide the requested resource
501	Not Implemented	The server does not support the request method
502	Bad Gateway	The server acting as intermediate proxy or gateway got a negative response forwarding the request
503	Service Unavailable	The server can temporarily not fulfill the request
504	Gateway Timeout	The server acting as intermediate proxy or gateway got no response to its forwarded request
505	HTTP Version Not Supported	The server cannot or refuses to support the HTTP version used in the request

Source: Fielding et al. (1999).

5.1.6 Header fields

Headers define the actions to take upon reception of a request or response. Headers can be general or belong to one specialized group: header fields for requests, header fields for responses, and header fields regarding the body of the message. For example, request header fields can inform the server about the type of resources the client accepts as response, like restricting the responses to plain HTML documents or give details on the technical specification of the client, like the software that was used to request the document. They can also describe the content of the message, which might be plain text or binary, an image or audio file and might also have gone through encoding steps like compression. Header fields always follow the same, simple syntax. The name comes first and is separated with a colon from the value. Some header fields contain multiple values that are separated by comma.

Let us go through a sample of common and important header fields to see what they can do and how they are used. The paragraphs in the following overview provide the name of the header in bold and the field type in parentheses, that is, whether the header is used for request, response, or body.

Accept (request)

```
Accept: text/html,image/gif,image/*,*/*;q=0.8
```

Accept is a request header field that tells the server about the type of resources the client is willing to accept as response. If no resource fits the restrictions made in `Accept`, the server *should* send a 406 status code. The specification of accepted content follows the MIME type scheme. Types are separated by commas; semicolons are used to specify so-called accept parameters `type/subtype;acceptparameter=value,type/...`. The asterisk (`*`) can be used to specify ranges of type and subtypes. The rules of content-type preferences are as follows: (1) more specific types are preferred over less specific ones and (2) types are preferred in decreasing order of the `q` parameter while (3) all type specifications have a default preference of q = 1 if not specified otherwise.

The above example can be read as follows: The client accepts HTML and GIF but if neither is available will accept any other image type. If no other image type is available, the client will also accept any other type of content.

Accept-Encoding (request)

```
Accept-Encoding: gzip,deflate,sdch;q=0.9,identity;q=0.8;*;q=0
```

`Accept-Encoding` tells the server which encodings or compression methods are accepted by the client. If the server cannot send the content in the specified encoding, it *should* return a 406 status code.

The example reads as follows: The client accepts `gzip` and `deflate` for encoding. If neither are available it also accepts `sdch` and otherwise content that was not encoded at all. It will not accept any other encodings as the value of the acceptance parameter is 0, which equals nonacceptance.

Allow (response; body)

```
Allow: GET, PUT
```

Allow informs the client about the HTTP methods that are allowed for a particular resource and will be part of responses with a status code of 405.

Authorization (request)

```
Authorization: Basic cm9va2llOjEyM0lzTm90QVNlY3VyZVBX
```

Authorization is a simple way of passing username and password to the server. Username and password are first merged to username:password and encoded according to the *Base64* scheme. The result of this encoding can be seen in the header field line above. Note that the encoding procedure does not provide encryption, but simply ensures that all characters are contained in the ASCII character set. We discuss HTTP authorization methods in more detail in Section 5.2.2.

The Authorization header field in the example indicates that the authorization method is Basic and the *Base64*-encoded username–password combination is cm9va2...

Content-Encoding (response; body)

```
Content-Encoding: gzip
```

Content-Encoding specifies the transformations, for example, compression methods, that have been applied to the content—see Accept-Encoding for further details.

Content-Length (response; body)

```
Content-Length: 108
```

Content-Length provides the receiver of the message with information on the size of the content in decimal number of OCTETs (bytes).

Content-Type (response; body)

```
Content-Type: text/plain; charset=UTF-8
```

Content-Type provides information on the type of content in the body. Content types are described as MIME types—see Accept for further details.

Cookie (request)

```
Cookie: sessionid=2783321; path=/; domain=r-datacollection.com;
    expires=Mon, 31-Dec-2035 23:00:01 GMT
```

Cookies are information sent from server to client with the `Set-Cookie` header field. They allow identifying clients—without cookies servers would not know that they have had contact with a client before. The `Cookie` header field returns the previously received information. The syntax of the header field is simple: Cookies consist of `name=value` pairs that are separated from each other by semicolon. Names like `expires`, `domain`, `path`, and `secure` are reserved parameters that define how the cookie should be handled by the client. `expires` defines a date after which the cookie is no longer valid. If no expiration date is given the cookie is only valid for one session. `domain` and `path` specify for which resource requests the cookie is needed. `secure` is used to indicate that the cookie should only be sent over secured connections (SSL; see Section 5.3.1). We introduce cookies in greater detail in Section 5.2.1.

The example reads as follows: The cookie `sessionid=2783321` is valid until 31st of December 2035 for the domain www.r-datacollection.com and all its subdirectories (declared with /).

From (response)

```
From: eddie@r-datacollection.com
```

`From` provides programmers of web crawlers or scraping programs with the option to send their email address. This helps webmasters to contact those who are in control of automated robots and web crawlers if they observe unauthorized behavior. This header field is useful for web scraping purposes, and we discuss it in Section 5.2.1.

Host (request)

```
Host: www.r-datacollection.com:80
```

`Host` is a header field required in HTTP/1.1 requests and helps servers to decide upon ambiguous URLs when more than one host name redirects to the same IP address.

If-Modified-Since (request)

```
If-Modified-Since: Thu, 27 Feb 2014 13:05:34 GMT
```

`If-Modified-Since` can be used to make requests conditional on the time stamp associated with the requested resource. If the server finds that the resource has not been modified since the date provided in the header field, it *should* return a 304 (Not Modified) status code. We can make use of this header to write more efficient and friendly web scrapers (see Section 9.3.3).

Connection (request, response)

```
Connection: Keep-Alive
```

```
Connection: Close
```

`Connection` is an ambiguous header field in the sense that it has two completely different purposes in HTTP/1.0 and HTTP/1.1. In HTTP/1.1, connections are persistent by default. This means that client and server keep their connection alive after the request–response procedure has finished. In contrast, it is standard in HTTP/1.0 to close connections after the client has got its response. Since establishing connections for each request, the value `Keep-Alive` can be specified in HTTP/1.0, while this is the default procedure in HTTP/1.1 and thus does not have to be explicitly stated. Instead, the server or client can force the connection to be shut down after the request–response exchange with the `Close` value.

Last-Modified (response; body)

```
Last-Modified: Tue, 25 Mar 2014 19:24:50 GMT
```

`Last-Modified` provides the date and time stamp of the last modification of the resource.

Location (response; body)

```
Location: redirected.html
```

`Location` serves to redirect the receiver of a message to the location where the requested resource can be found. This header is used in combination with status code 3xx when content has moved to another place or in combination with status code 201 when content was created as result of the request.

Proxy-Authorization (request)

```
Proxy-Authentication: Basic bWFnaWNpYW5zYXlzOmFicmFrYWRhYnI=
```

The same as `Authorization`, only for proxy servers. For more information on proxies, see Section 5.2.3.

Proxy-Connection (request)

```
Proxy-Connection: keep-alive
```

The same as `Connection`, only for proxy servers. For more information on proxies, see Section 5.2.3.

Referer (request)

```
Referer: www.r-datacollection.com/index.html
```

`Referer` is a header field that informs the server *what referred* to the requested resource. In the example, www.r-datacollection.com/index.html might provide a link to a picture (e.g., `/pictures/eddie.jpg`). In a request for this picture the referer header field can be added to signal that the user has already been on the site and does not want to access the image from elsewhere, like another website.

Server (response)

```
Server: Apache/2.4.7 (Unix) mod_wsgi/3.4 Python/2.7.5 OpenSSL/1.0.1e
```

```
Server: Microsoft-IIS/8.0
```

`Server` provides information about the server addressed in the request. The first server above is based on Apache software using a Unix platform (httpd.apache.org/), while the second one is based on Microsoft's Internet Information Service (www.microsoft.com/).

Set-Cookie (response)

```
Set-Cookie: sessionid=2783321; path=/; domain=r-datacollection.com;
 expires=Mon, 31-Dec-2035 23:00:01 GMT
```

`Set-Cookie` asks the client to store the information contained in the `Set-Cookie` header field and send them along in subsequent requests as part of the `Cookie` header. See `Cookie` and Section 5.2.1 for further explanation.

User-Agent (request)

```
User-Agent: Mozilla/4.0 (compatible; MSIE 7.0; Windows NT 6.0)
```

The `User-Agent` header field indicates the type of client that makes a request to the server. These more or less cryptic descriptions can indicate the use of a certain browser on a certain operating system. This information can be helpful for the server to adapt the content of the response to the system of the client. Nevertheless, the `User-Agent` can contain arbitrary user-defined information, such as `User-Agent: My fabulous web crawler` or `User-Agent: All your base are belong to us`. Web scrapers can and should use User-Agents responsibly. We discuss how this is done in Sections 5.2.1 and 9.3.3.

Vary (response)

```
Vary: User-Agent, Cookie, Accept-Encoding
```

```
Vary: *
```

The server response sometimes depends on certain parameters, for example, on the browser or device of the client (e.g., a desktop PC or a mobile phone), on whether the user has previously visited a site and has received a cookie, and on the encoding format the client accepts. Servers can indicate that content changes according to these parameters with the `Vary` header field.

The first example above indicates that the content might vary with changes in `User-Agent`, `Cookie`, or `Accept-Encoding`. The second example is rather unspecific. It states that changes on an unspecified set of parameters lead to changes in the response. This header field is important for the behavior of browser caches that try to load only new content and retrieve old and unchanged content from a local source.

Via (request, response)

```
Via: 1.1 varnish
```

```
Via: 1.1 www.spiegel.de, 1.0 lnxp-3960.srv.mediaways.net (squid/3.1.4)
```

`Via` is like `Server` but for proxy servers and gateways that HTTP messages pass on their way to the server or client. Each proxy or gateway can add its ID to this header, which is usually a protocol version and a platform type or a name.

WWW-Authenticate (response)

```
WWW-Authenticate: Basic realm="r-datacollection"
```

```
WWW-Authenticate: Digest realm="r-datacollection" qop="auth"
 nonce="ecf88f261853fe08d58e2e903220da14"
```

`WWW-Authenticate` asks the client to identify itself and is sent along a 401 *Unauthorized* status code. It is the counterpart to the `Authorization` request header field. The `WWW-Authenticate` header field describes the method of identification as well the "realm" this identification is valid for, as well as further parameters needed for authorization. The first example requests basic authentication while the second asks for digest authentication, which ensures that passwords cannot be read out by proxies. We explain both types of authentication in Section 5.2.2.

5.2 Advanced features of HTTP

What we have learned so far are just the basics of HTTP-based communication. There are more complex tasks that go beyond the default configuration of standard HTTP methods. Both web users and server maintainers may ask questions like the following:

- How can servers identify revisiting users?
- How can users avoid being identified?
- How can communication between servers and clients be more than "stateless," that is, how can they memorize and rely on previous conversations?
- How can users transfer and access confidential content securely?
- How can users check if content on the server has changed—without requesting the full body of content?

Many of these tasks can be handled with means that are directly implemented in HTTP. We will now highlight three areas that extend the basic functionality of HTTP. The first comprises issues of identification, which are useful to personalize web experiences. The second area deals with different forms of authentication that serve to make server–client exchanges more secure. The third area covers a certain type of web intermediaries, that is, middlemen between clients and servers, namely proxy servers. These are implemented for a variety of reasons like safety or efficiency. As the availability of content may depend on the use of such advanced features, basic knowledge about them is often useful for web data collection tasks.

Using httpbin.org to test HTTP requests

To showcase some advanced HTTP requests, we use the server at http://httpbin.org. This server, set up by Kenneth Reitz, offers a testing environment for HTTP requests and returns JSON-encoded content. It is a useful service to test HTTP calls before actually implementing them in real-life scenarios. We use it to formulate calls to the server via RCurl commands and evaluate the returned message within R.

Further, we will gently introduce the RCurl package to demonstrate some advanced HTTP features by example. RCurl provides means to use R as a web client software. The package is introduced in greater detail in Section 5.4.

5.2.1 Identification

The communication between client and server via the HTTP protocol is an amnesic matter. Connections are established and closed for each session; the server does not keep track of earlier requests from the same user by default. It is sometimes desirable that server responses are built upon results from previous conversations. For example, users might prefer that sites are automatically displayed in their language or adapted to fit a specific device or operating system. Moreover, customers of an online shop want to place items into a virtual shopping cart and continue browsing other products, while the website keeps track of these operations. Apart from scenarios like these that enhance user experience, some basic knowledge about clients is interesting for web administrators who want to know, for example, from which other sites their pages are visited most frequently.

HTTP offers a set of procedures that are used for such purposes. We discuss the most popular and relevant ones in the context of web scraping—basic identification header fields and cookies.

5.2.1.1 HTTP header fields for client identification

By default, modern web browsers deliver basic client identification in the HTTP header when sending a request to a server. This information is usually not sufficient to uniquely identify users but may improve surfing experience. As we will see, it can also make sense to pass these fields to servers when the request does not come from a browser but, for example, from a program like R that processes a scraping script.

User-Agent

The `User-Agent` header field contains information about the software that is used on the client side. Ordinary browsers deliver `User-Agent` header fields like the following:

```
GET /headers HTTP/1.1
Host: httpbin.org
User-Agent: Mozilla/5.0 (Windows NT 6.3) AppleWebKit/537.36
    (KHTML, like Gecko) Chrome/31.0.1650.57 Safari/537.36
```

What is hidden behind this cryptic string is that the request was performed by a Chrome browser, version 31.0.1650.57. The browser is 'Mozilla-compatible' (this is of no further interest), operates on a Windows system, and draws upon the web kit.[11] This information does not suffice to uniquely identify the user. But they still serve an important purpose: They allow web designers to deliver content that is adapted to the clients' software.

While an adequate layout is hardly relevant for web scraping purposes, we can deliver information on the software we use for scraping in the User-Agent field to keep our work as transparent as possible. Technically, we could put any string in this header. A both useful and convenient approach is to provide the current R version number along with the platform that R is run on. This way, the webmaster at the other end of the interaction is told what kind of program puts a series of requests to the server. The following command returns the current R version number and the corresponding platform:

```
R> R.version$version.string
[1] "R version 3.0.2 (2013-09-25)"

R> R.version$platform
[1] "x86_64-w64-mingw32"
```

We can use this string to configure a *GET* request that we conduct with the `getURL()` function of the RCurl package:

```
R> cat(getURL("http://httpbin.org/headers",
              useragent = str_c(R.version$platform,
                                R.version$version.string,
                                sep=", ")))
```

[11] If you care to see the User-Agent of your default browser, copy the string that is given back when you request the site http://httpbin.org/user-agent and paste it into the 'Analyze' form at http://useragentstring.com.

```
{
 "headers": {
   "X-Request-Id": "0726a0cf-a26a-43b9-b5a4-9578d0be712b",
   "User-Agent": "x86_64-w64-mingw32, R version 3.0.2 (2013-09-25)",
   "Connection": "close",
   "Accept": "*/*",
   "Host": "httpbin.org"
 }
}
```


`cat()` is used to concatenate and print the results over several lines. The `useragent` argument allows specifying a `User-Agent` header field string. RCurl takes care of writing this string into a header field and passes it to the server. http://httpbin.org/headers returns the sent header information in JSON format.[12] Beside the set of header fields that are used by default, we find that a `User-Agent` header field has been added.[13]

We will later learn that the basis of the RCurl package is the C library *libcurl*. Many of the options that *libcurl* offers can also be used in RCurl's high-level functions (for more details, see Section 5.4.1). We will return to the use of User-Agents in practical web scraping in Section 9.3.3.

Referer

The second header field that is informative about the client is the `Referer`. It stores the URL of the page that referred the user to the current page. Referrers can be used for traffic evaluation to asses where visitors of a site come from. Another purpose is to be able to limit access to specific server content like image files. A webmaster could modify the settings of the server such that access to images is only possible from another resource on the server in order to prevent other people from using images on their own webpage by referring to the location on the original server. This causes unwanted traffic and is therefore unwelcome behavior. The default browser setting is that the `Referer` header is delivered automatically. This may look as follows:

```
GET /headers HTTP/1.1
Host: httpbin.org
Referer: http://www.r-datacollection.com/
```

We can provide the `Referer` header field with R using `getURL()`'s `referer` argument. We test the request to http://httpbin.org/headers with:[14]

```
R> getURL("http://httpbin.org/headers", referer = "http://www.r-
datacollection.com/")
```

---

[12]Note that we use the `cat()` function to concatenate and print the returned JSON string.

[13]We do not have to care about the `X-Request-Id` and `Heroku-Request-Id` header fields, they are added by the service at http://httpbin.org for debugging purposes.

[14]We do not print the JSON output from now on—you can easily see the returned content by loading RCurl and pasting the command in your R console.

Note that adding information on the `Referer` from within R is misleading when R has not actually been referred from the site provided. We suggest that if it is necessary to provide a valid referrer in order to get access to certain resources, stay identifiable, for example, by properly specifying the `From` header field as described below, and contact the webmaster if in doubt. Providing wrong information in the Referer header field in order to disguise the source of the access request is called referrer spoofing. This may have its legitimacy for data privacy purposes but is not encouraged by scraping etiquette (see Section 9.3.3).

From

The `From` header field for client identification is not delivered by browsers but a convenient header for well-behaved web spiders and robots. It carries the user's email address to make her identifiable for web administrators. In web scraping, it is good practice to specify the `From` header field with a valid email address, as in

```
GET /headers HTTP/1.1
Host: httpbin.org
From: eddie@r-datacollection.com
```

Providing contact details signals good intentions and enables webmasters who note unusual traffic patterns on their sites to get in touch. We thus reformulate our request:

```
R> getURL("http://httpbin.org/headers", httpheader = c(From =
"eddie@r-collection.com"))
```

Note that we have to use the `httpheader` option here to add the `From` header field, as `from` is not a valid option—in contrast to "`referer`," for example. `httpheader` allows us to specify additional other header fields.

5.2.1.2 Cookies

Cookies help to keep users identifiable for a server. They are a tool to turn stateless HTTP communication into a stateful conversation where future responses depend on past conversations. Cookies work as follows: Web servers store a unique session ID in a cookie that is placed on the client's local drive, usually in a text file. The next time a browser sends an HTTP request to the same web server, it looks for stored cookies that belong to the server and—if successful—adds the cookie information to the request. The server then processes this "we already met" information and adapts its response. Usually, further information on the user has been stored on the server over the course of several conversations and can be "reactivated" using cookies. In other words, cookies enable browsers and servers to continue conversations from the past.

Cookies are shared via the HTTP header fields "`Set-Cookie`" (in the response header) and "`Cookie`" (in the request header). A typical conversation via HTTP that results in a cookie exchange looks as follows. First, the client makes a request to a web server:

```
GET /headers HTTP/1.1
Host: httpbin.org
```

If the request is successful, the server responds and passes the cookie with the `Set-Cookie` response header field. The field provides a set of name–value pairs:

```
HTTP/1.1 200 OK
Set-cookie: id="12345"; domain="httpbin.org"
...
```

The `id` attribute allows the server to identify the user in a subsequent request and the `domain` attribute indicates which domain the cookie is associated with. The client stores the cookie and attaches it in future requests to the same domain, using the `Cookie` request header field:

```
GET /headers HTTP/1.1
Host: httpbin.org
Cookie: id="12345"
```

Different types of cookies

There are several types of cookies that differ in terms of persistence and range. *Session cookies* are kept in memory only as long as the user visits a website and are deleted as soon as the browser is closed. *Persistent cookies*, or tracking cookies, last longer—their lifetime is defined by the value of the `max-age` attribute or the `expires` attribute (not shown in the examples above). The browser delivers the cookie with every request during a cookie's lifetime, which makes the user traceable for the server across several sessions. *Third-party cookies* are used to personalize content across different sites. They do not belong to the domain the client visits but to another domain. If you have ever wondered how personalized ads are placed on pages you visit—this is most likely done with third-party cookies that are placed by advertising companies on domains you visit and which can be used by advertisers to tailor ads to your interests. The use of cookies for such purposes surely has contributed to the fact that cookies have a bad reputation regarding privacy. In general, however, cookies are only sent to the server that created them. Further, the user can decide how to handle locally stored cookies. And in the end, cookies are useful as they often enhance the web experience considerably.

If cookies influence the content a server returns in response to a request, they can be relevant for web scraping purposes as well. Imagine we care to scrape data from our crammed shopping cart in an online store. During our visit we have added several products to the cart. In order to track our spending spree, the server has stored a session ID in a cookie that keeps us identifiable. If we want to request the webpage that lists the shopped items, we have to deliver the cookie with our request.

In order to deliver existing cookies with R, we can draw upon the `cookie` argument:

```
R> getURL("http://httpbin.org/headers", cookie = "id=12345;domain=
httpbin.org")
```

It is usually not desirable to manage cookies manually, that is, retrieve them, store them, and send them. This is why browsers automatically take care of such operations by default.

In order to achieve similar convenience in R, we can rely on *libcurl*'s `cookiefile` and `cookiejar` options that, if specified correctly, manage cookies for us. We show in detail how this can be done in Section 9.1.8.

5.2.2 Authentication

While techniques for client identification are useful to personalize web content and enable stateful communication, they are not suited to protect content that only the user should see. A set of authentication techniques exist that allow qualified access to confidential content. Some of these techniques are part of the HTTP protocol. Others, like *OpenID* or *OAuth* (see Section 9.1.11), have been developed more recently to extend authentication functionality on the Web.

Basic authentication

The simplest form of authentication via the HTTP protocol is basic authentication (Franks et al. 1999). If a client requests a resource that is protected by basic authentication, the server sends back a response that includes the `WWW-Authenticate` header. The client has to repeat its request with a username and password in order to be granted access to the requested resource. Both are stored in the response's `Authorization` header. If the server can verify that the username/password combination is correct, it returns the requested resource in a HTTP 200 message. Technically, basic authentication looks as follows.

1. The client requests a protected resource:

```
GET /basic-auth/user/passwd HTTP/1.1
```

2. The server asks the client for a user name and password:

```
HTTP/1.1 401 Authorization required
WWW-Authenticate: Basic realm="Protected area"
```

3. The client/user provides the requested username and password in Base64 encoding:

```
GET /basic-auth/user/passwd HTTP/1.1
Authorization: Basic dXNlcm5hbWU6cGFzc3dvcmQ=
```

4. The server returns the requested resource:

```
HTTP/1.1 200 OK
...
```

Note that in the third step, the username/password combination has been automatically "encrypted" into the string sequence "`dXNlcm5hbWU6cGFzc3dvcmQ=`." This transformation is done via Base64 encoding. Base64 encoding is not actually an encrypting technique but follows a rather trivial and static scheme (see Gourley and Totty 2002, Appendix E). We can perform Base64 encoding and decoding with R; the necessary functions are implemented in the RCurl package:

```
R> (secret <- base64("This is a secret message"))
[1] "VGhpcyBpcyBhIHNlY3JldCBtZXNzYWdl"
attr(,"class")
[1] "base64"

R> base64Decode(secret)
[1] "This is a secret message"
```

The example reveals the insecurity of basic HTTP authentication: As long as it is done via standard HTTP, the sensitive information is sent practically unencrypted across the network. Therefore, basic authentication should only be used in combination with HTTPS (see Section 5.3.1).

Digest authentication

A more sophisticated authentication technique is digest authentication (Franks et al. 1999). The idea behind digest authentication is that passwords are never sent across the Web in order to verify a user, but only a "digest" of it. The server attaches a little random string sequence to its response, called *nonce*. The browser transforms username, password, and the nonce into a hash code, following one of several algorithms that are known to both server and browser. This hash code is then sent back, compared to the hash calculations of the server, and if both match the server grants access to the client. The crucial point is that the hash alone does not suffice to learn anything about the password; it is just a "digest" of it. This makes digest authentication an improvement relative to basic authentication, as the encrypted client message is incomprehensible for an eavesdropper.

Steps 2 and 3 in the authentication procedure sketched above are slightly different. The server returns something like the following:[15]

2a. The server asks the client for a username and password and delivers a nonce, reports a "quality of protection" value (`qop`) and describes the realm as `Protected area`:

```
HTTP/1.1 401 Authorization required
WWW-Authenticate: Digest realm="Protected area",
qop="auth",nonce="f7hf4xu8n2kxuujnszrctx4fexqnahopjdrn4zbi"
```

3a. The client provides the encrypted username and password in the `response` attribute, as well as the unencrypted username, the `qop` and `nonce` parameters and a client nonce (`cnonce`):

```
GET /basic-auth/user/passwd HTTP/1.1
Authorization: Digest username="user", nonce="
    f7hf4xu8n2kxuujnszrctx4fexqnahopjdrn4zbi", qop="auth",
    cnonce="1g443t8b", response="
    ylh5uafdsda8r2wsxdylvxzhqnht5ngry2m5argc"
```

[15]Note that this is a simplified example. We have left out some intermediate steps, but the fundamental logic remains the same.

Figure 5.4 The principle of web proxies

In Section 9.1.6 we give a short demonstration of HTTP authentication in practice with RCurl.

5.2.3 Proxies

Web proxy servers, or simply proxies, are servers that act as intermediaries between clients and other servers. HTTP requests from clients are first sent to a proxy, which evaluates the request and passes it to the desired server. The server response takes the way back via the proxy. In that sense, the proxy serves as a server to clients and as a client to other servers (see Figure 5.4).

The use of proxies

Proxies are useful for several purposes. They are deployed for performance, economic, and security reasons. For users, proxies can help to

- speed up network use;
- stay anonymous on the Web;
- get access to sites that restrict access to IPs from certain locations;
- get access to sites that are normally blocked in the country from where the request is put; or
- keep on querying resources from a server that blocks requests from IPs we have used before.

Especially when proxies are used for any of the last three reasons, web scrapers might get into troubles with the law. Recent verdicts point in the direction that it is illegal to use proxy servers in order to get access to public websites that one has been disallowed to visit (see Kerr 2013). We therefore do not recommend the use of proxies for any of these purposes.

Types of proxies

In order to establish connections via a proxy server, we have to know the proxy's IP address and port. Some proxies require authentication as well, that is, a username and a password. There are many services on the Web that provide large databases of open and free proxies, including their location and specification. Open proxies can be used by anyone who knows their IP address and port. Note that proxies vary in the degree to which they provide anonymity to the user. **Transparent proxies** specify a `Via` header field in their request to the server, filling it with their IP. Further, they offer an `X-Forwarded-For` header field with your IP. **Simple anonymous proxies** replace both the `Via` and the `X-Forwarded-For` header field with their IP. As both fields are delivered only when a proxy is used, the server knows that the requests comes from a server, but does not easily see the client's IP address behind it. **Distorting proxies** are similar but replace the value of the `X-Forwarded-For` header field with a random IP address. Finally, **High anonymity proxies** or **elite proxies** behave like normal clients, that is, they neither provide the `Via` nor the `X-Forwarded-For` header field but only their IP and are not immediately identifiable as proxy servers.

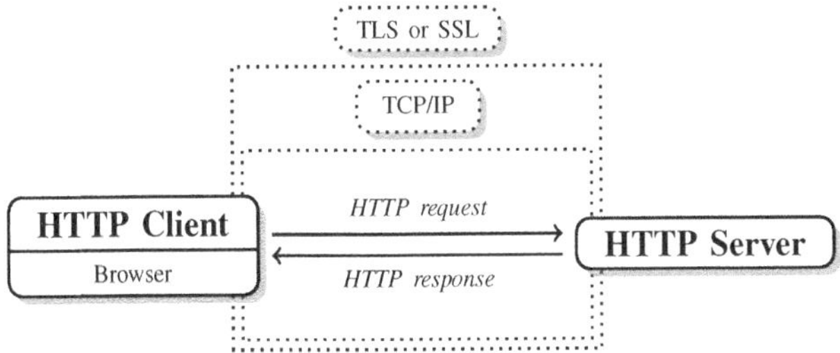

Figure 5.5 The principle of HTTPS

To send a request to a server detouring via a proxy with R, we can add the `proxy` argument to the request command. In the following, we choose a fictional proxy from Poland that has the IP address `109.205.54.112` and is on call on port 8080:

```
R> getURL("http://httpbin.org/headers",
R>        proxy = "109.205.54.112:8080",
R>        followlocation = TRUE)
```

IP address and port of the proxy are specified in the `proxy` option. Further, we set the `followlocation` argument to `TRUE` to ensure that we are redirected to the desired resource.

5.3 Protocols beyond HTTP

HTTP is far from the only protocol for data transfer over the Internet. To get an overview of the protocols that are currently supported by the RCurl package, we call

```
R> library(RCurl)
R> curlVersion()$protocols
 [1] "tftp"   "ftp"    "telnet" "dict"   "ldap"   "ldaps"  "http"
 [8] "file"   "https"  "ftps"   "scp"    "sftp"
```

Not all of them are relevant for web scraping purposes. In the following, we will highlight two protocols that we often encounter when browsing and scraping the Web: HTTPS and FTP.

5.3.1 HTTP Secure

Strictly speaking, the **H**ypertext **T**ransfer **P**rotocol **S**ecure (HTTPS) is not a protocol of its own, but the result of a combination of HTTP with the SSL/TLS (**S**ecure **S**ockets **L**ayer/**T**ransport **S**ecurity **L**ayer) protocol. HTTPS is indispensable when it comes to the transfer of sensitive data, as is the case in banking or online shopping. To transfer money or credit card information we need to ensure that the information is inaccessible to third parties. HTTPS encrypts all the client–server communication (see Figure 5.5). HTTPS URLs have the scheme `https` and use the port 443 by default.[16]

[16] Recall that the default HTTP port is 80.

HTTPS serves two purposes: First, it helps the client to ensure that the server it talks to is trustworthy (server authentication). Second, it provides encryption of client–server communication so that users can be reasonably sure that nobody else reads what is exchanged during communication.

SSL/TLS The SSL/TLS security layer runs as a sublayer of the application layer where HTTP operates. This means that HTTP messages are encrypted before they get transmitted. The SSL protocol was first defined in 1994 by Netscape (see Freier et al. 2011) and was updated as TLS 1.0 in 1999 (see Dierks and Allen 1999). When using the term "SSL" in the following, we refer to both SSL and TLS as their differences are of no importance to us.

A crucial feature of SSL that allows secure communication in an insecure network is public key, or asymmetric, cryptography. As the name already indicates, encryption keys are in fact not kept secret but publicly available to everyone. In order to encrypt a message for a specific receiver, the receiver's public key is used. In order to decrypt the message, both the public and a private key is needed, and the private key is only known to the receiver. The basic idea is that if a client wants to send a secret message to a server, it knows how to encrypt it because the server's public key is known. After encryption, however, nobody—not even the sender—is able to decipher the message except for the receiver, who possesses both the public and the private key.

SSL handshake We do not have to delve deeply into the details of public key encryption, how the secret codes (ciphers) work, and why it is so hard to crack them in order to understand HTTPS's purpose. For the details of cryptography behind SSL, we refer to the excellent introductions by Gourley and Totty (2002) and Garfinkel (2002). If you want to get a more profound understanding of digital cryptography, the books by Ferguson et al. (2010) and Paar and Pelzl (2011) are a good choice. What is worth knowing though is how secure channels between client and server are actually established and how we can achieve this from within R. A very simplified scheme of the "SSL handshake," that is, the negotiation between client and server about the establishment of an HTTPS connection before actually exchanging encrypted HTTP messages, works as follows (see Gourley and Totty 2002, pp. 322–328).

1. The client establishes a TCP connection to the server via port 443 and sends information about the SSL version and cipher settings.
2. The server sends back information about the SSL and cipher settings. The server also proves his identity by sending a certificate. This certificate includes information about the authority that issued the certificate, for whom it was issued and its period of validity. As anybody can create his or her own certificates without much effort, the signature of a trusted certificate authority (CA) is of great importance. There are many commercial CAs, but some providers also issue certificates for free.
3. The client checks if it trusts the certificate. Browsers and operating systems are shipped with lists of certificate authorities that are automatically trusted. If one of these authorities has signed the server's certificate, the client trusts the server. If this is not the case, the browser asks the user whether she finds the server trustworthy and wants to continue, or if communication should be stopped.
4. By using the public key of the HTTPS server, the client generates a session key that only the server can read, and sends it to the server.
5. The server decrypts the session key.

6. Both client and server now possess a session key. Thus, knowledge about the key is not asymmetric anymore but symmetric. This reduces computational costs that are needed for encryption. Future data transfers from server to client and vice versa are encrypted and decrypted through this symmetric SSL tunnel.

It is important to note that what is protected is the content of communication. This includes HTTP headers, cookies, and the message body. What is not protected, however, are IP addresses, that is, websites a client communicates with.

We will address how connections via HTTPS are established in R and how much of the technical details are hidden deeply in the respective functions in Section 9.1.7—using HTTPS with R is not difficult at all.

5.3.2 FTP

FTP vs. HTTP The **F**ile **T**ransfer **P**rotocol (FTP) was developed to transfer files from client to server (upload), from server to client (download), and to manage directories. FTP was first specified in 1971 by Abhay Bhushan (1971); its current specification (see Postel and Reynolds 1985) is almost 30 years old. In principle, HTTP has several advantages over FTP. It allows persistent, keep-alive connections, that is, connections between client and server that are maintained for several transfers. This is not possible with FTP, where the connection has to be reestablished after each transfer. Further, FTP does not natively support proxies and pipelining, that is, several simultaneous requests before receiving an answer. On the upside, FTP may be faster under certain circumstances, as it does not come with a bunch of header fields like HTTP—just the binary or ASCII files are transferred.

Active and passive modes FTP uses two ports on each side, one for data exchange ("data port," the default is port 20) and one for command exchange ("control port," the default is port 21). Just like HTTP, FTP comes with a set of commands that specify which files to transfer, what directories to create, and many other operations.[17] FTP connections can be established in two different modes: the active mode and the passive mode. In active FTP, the client connects with the server's command port and then requests a data transfer to another port. The problem with this mode is that the actual data connection is established by the server. As the client's firewall has not been told that the client expects data to come in on a certain port, it usually blocks the server's attempt to deliver the data. This issue is tackled with the passive mode in which the client initiates both the command and the data connection. We are going to demonstrate accessing FTP servers with R in Section 9.1.2.

5.4 HTTP in action

We now learn to use R as an HTTP client. We will have a closer look at two available packages: the powerful RCurl package (Temple Lang 2013a), and the more lightweight but sometimes also more convenient httr package (Wickham 2012) that rests on the voluminous RCurl package.

---

[17] For an overview over existing commands, see http://www.nsftools.com/tips/RawFTP.htm

Base R already comes with basic functionality for downloading web resources. The `download.file()` function handles many download procedures where we do not need complex modifications of the HTTP request. Further, there is a set of basic functions to set up and manipulate connections. For an overview, type `?connections` in R. However, using these functions is anything but convenient. Regarding `download.file()`, there are two major drawbacks for sophisticated web scraping. First, it is not very flexible. We cannot use it to connect with a server via HTTPS, for example, or to specify additional headers. Second, it is difficult to adhere to our standards of friendly web scraping with `download.file()`, as it lacks basic identification facilities. However, if we just want to download single files, `download.file()` works perfectly fine. For more complex tasks, we can apply the functionality of the RCurl and the httr package.

5.4.1 The *libcurl* library

Much of what we need to do with R on the web is dramatically facilitated by *libcurl* (Stenberg 2013). *libcurl* is an external library programmed in C. Development began in 1996 by Daniel Stenberg and the *cURL* project and has since been under continuous development. The purpose of *libcurl* is to provide an easy interface to various Internet protocols for programs on many platforms. Over time, the list of features has grown and now comprises a multitude of possible actions and options to configure, among others, HTTP communication. We can think of it as a tool that knows how to

- specify HTTP headers;
- interpret URL encoding;
- process incoming streams of data from web servers;
- establish SSL connections;
- connect with proxies;
- handle authentication;

and much more. In contrast, R's `url()` and `download.file()` are precious little help when it comes to complex tasks like filling forms, authentication, or establishing a stateful conversation. Therefore, *libcurl* has been tapped to enable users to work with the *libcurl* library in their ordinary programming environment. In his manifest of RCurl and *libcurl*'s philosophy, Temple Lang points out the benefits of *libcurl*: Being the most widely used file transfer library, *libcurl* is extraordinarily well tested and flexible (Temple Lang 2012a). Further, being programmed in C makes it fast. To get a first impression about the flexibility of *libcurl*, you might want to start by taking a look at the available options of *libcurl*'s interface at http://curl.haxx.se/libcurl/c/curl_easy_setopt.html. Alternatively, you can type the following into R to get the comprehensive list of *libcurl*'s "easy" interface options that can be specified with RCurl:

```
R> names(getCurlOptionsConstants())
```

Currently, there are 174 available options. Among them are some that we have already relied on above, like `useragent` or `proxy`. We sometimes speak of *curl* options instead of *libcurl* options for reasons of convenience. *curl* is a command line tool also developed by the *cURL* software project. With R we draw on the *libcurl* library.[18]

5.4.2 Basic request methods

5.4.2.1 The *GET* method

High-level functions

In order to perform a basic *GET* request to retrieve a resource from a web server, the RCurl package provides some high-level functions—`getURL()`, `getBinaryURL()`, and `getURLContent()`. The basic function is `getURL()`; `getBinaryURL()` is convenient when the expected content is binary, and `getURLContent()` tries to identify the type of content in advance by inspecting the `Content-Type` field in the response header and proceeding adequately. While this seems preferable, the configuration of `getURLContent()` is sometimes more sophisticated, so we continue to use `getURL()` by default except when we expect binary content.

The function automatically identifies the host, port, and requested resource. If the call succeeds, that is, if the server gives a 2XX response along with the body, the function returns the content of the response. Note that if everything works fine, all of the negotiation between R/*libcurl* and the server is hidden from us. We just have to pass the desired URL to the high-level function. For example, if we try to fetch *helloworld.html* from www.r-datacollection.com/materials/http, we type

```
R> getURL("http://www.r-datacollection.com/materials/http/helloworld.html")
[1] "<html>\n<head><title>Hello World</title></head>\n<body><h3>Hello World
</h3>\n</body>\n</html>"
```

The body is returned as character data. For binary content, we use `getBinaryURL()` and get back raw content. For example, if we request the PNG image file *sky.png* from www.r-datacollection.com/materials/http, we write

```
R> pngfile <- getBinaryURL("http://www.r-datacollection.com/materials/http/
sky.png")
```

It depends on the format how we can actually process it; in our case we use the `writeBin()` function to locally store the file:

```
R> writeBin(pngfile, "sky.png")
```

GET forms

Sometimes content is not embedded in a static HTML page but returned after we submit an HTML form. The little example at http://www.r-datacollection.com/materials/http/GETexample.html lets you specify a name and age as input fields. The HTML source code looks as follows:

```
<!DOCTYPE HTML>
<html>
<head>
<title>HTTP GET Example</title></head> <body>
<h3>HTTP GET Example</h3>
```

[18] See also http://daniel.haxx.se/docs/curl-vs-libcurl.html for the differences between *cURL*, *curl*, and *libcurl*.

```
<form action="GETexample.php" method="get">
   Name: <input type="text" name="name" value="Anny Omous"><br>
   Age:  <input type="number" name="age" value="23"><br><br>
   <input type="submit" value="Send Form and Evaluate"><br><br>
   <input type="submit" value="Send Form and Return Request" name="return">
</form>
</body>
</html>
```

The <form> element indicates that data put into the form is sent to a file called *GETexample.php*.[19] After having received the data from the *GET* request, the PHP script evaluates the input and returns "Hello <name>! You are <age> years old." In the browser, we see an URL of form http://www.rdatacollection.com/materials/http/GETexample.php?name=<name>&age=<age>, which indicates that a PHP script has generated the output.

How can we process this and similar requests from within R? There are several ways to specify the arguments of an HTML form. The first is to construct the URL manually using paste() and to pass it to the getURL() function:

```
R> url <- "http://www.r-datacollection.com/materials/http/GETexample.php"
R> namepar <- "Eddie"
R> agepar <- "32"
R> url_get <- str_c(url, "?", "name=", namepar, "&", "age=", agepar)

R> cat(getURL(url_get))
Hello Eddie!
You are 32 years old.
```

An easier way than using getURL() and constructing the *GET* form request manually is to use getForm(), which allows specifying the parameters as separate values in the function. This is our preferred procedure as it simplifies modifying the call and does not require manual URL encoding (see Section 5.1.2). In order to get the same result as above, we write

```
R> url <- "http://www.r-datacollection.com/materials/http/GETexample.php"
R> cat(getForm(url, name = "Eddie", age = 32))
Hello Eddie!
You are 32 years old.
```

5.4.2.2 The *POST* method

POST forms

When using HTML forms we often have to use the *POST* method instead of *GET*. In general, *POST* allows more sophisticated requests, as the request parameters do not have do be inserted into the URL, which may be limited in length. The *POST* method implies that parameters and their values are sent in the request body, not in the URL itself. We replicate the example from above, except that now a *POST* request is required. The form is located at

[19]PHP, Hypertext Preprocessor or previously Personal Home Page Tools is a scripting language which is frequently implemented on the server side to create dynamic webpages. The ending *.php* indicates that the content is generated by a PHP script.

http://www.r-datacollection.com/materials/http/POSTexample.html. The HTML source code reads as follows:

```
<!DOCTYPE HTML>
<html>
<head>
<title>HTTP POST Example</title></head>
<body>
<h3>HTTP POST Example</h3>
<form action="POSTexample.php" method="post">
   Name: <input type="text" name="name" value="Anny Omous"><br>
   Age:  <input type="number" name="age" value="23"><br><br>
   <input type="submit" value="Send Form and Evaluate" name="send"><br><br>
   <input type="submit" value="Send Form and Return Request" name="return">
</form>
</body>
</html>
```

We find that the <form> element has remained almost identical, except for the required method, which is now *POST*. When we submit the *POST* form in the browser we see that the URL changes to *../POSTexample.php* and no query parameters have been added as in the *GET* query. In order to replicate the *POST* query with R, we do not have to construct the request manually but can use the postForm() function:

```
R> url <- "http://www.r-datacollection.com/materials/http/POSTexample.php"
R> cat(postForm(url, name = "Eddie", age = 32, style = "post"))
Hello Eddie!
You are 32 years old.
```

postForm() automatically constructs the body and fills it with the pre-specified parameter pairs. Unfortunately, there are several ways to format these pairs, and we sometimes have to explicitly specify the one that is accepted in advance using the style argument (see Nolan and Temple Lang 2014, p. 270–272 and http://www.w3.org/TR/html401/interact/forms.html for details on the form content types). For the application/x-www-form-urlencoded form content type, we have to specify style = "post" and for the multipart/form-data form content type, style = "httppost". This formats the parameter pairs in the body correctly and adds the request header "Content-Type" = "application/x-www-form-urlencoded" or "Content-Type" = "multipart/form-data". To find the adequate *POST* format, we can look for an attribute named enctype in the <form> element. If it is specified as enctype='application/x-www-form-urlencoded', we use style = "post". If it is missing (as above), leaving out the style parameter should also work.

5.4.2.3 Other methods

RCurl offers functions to deal with other HTTP methods as well. We can change methods in calls to getURL(), getBinaryURL(), getURLContent() by making use of the customrequest option, for example,

```
R> url <- "r-datacollection.com/materials/http/helloworld.html"
R> res <- getURL(url = url, customrequest = "HEAD", header = TRUE)
R> cat(str_split(res, "\r")[[1]])
HTTP/1.1 200 OK
Date: Wed, 26 Mar 2014 00:20:07 GMT
Server: Apache
Vary: Accept-Encoding
Content-Type: text/html
```

As we hardly encounter situations where we need these methods, we refrain from going into more detail.

5.4.3 A low-level function of RCurl

RCurl builds on the powerful *libcurl* library, making it a mighty weapon in the hands of the initiated and an unmanageable beast in the hands of others. The low-level function `curlPerform()` is the workhorse of the package. The function gathers options specified in R on how to perform web requests—which protocol or methods to use, which headers to set—and patches them through to *libcurl* to execute the request. Everything in this function has to be specified explicitly so later on we will come back to more high-level functions. Nevertheless, it is useful to demonstrate how the high-level functions work under the hood.

We start with a call to `curlPerform()` to request an HTML document:

```
R> url <- "www.r-datacollection.com/materials/http/helloworld.html"
R> (pres <- curlPerform(url = url))
OK
 0
```

Instead of getting the content of the URL we only get the information that everything seems to have worked as expected by the function. This is because we have to specify everything explicitly when using `curlPerform()`. The function did retrieve the document but did not know what to do with the content. We need to define a handler for the content. Let us create one ourselves. First, we create an object `pres` to store the document and a function that takes the content as argument and writes it into `pres`. As the list of options can get extensive we save them in a separate object `performOptions` and pass it to `curlPerform()`:

```
R> pres <- NULL
R> performOptions <- curlOptions(url = url,
                                 writefunc = function(con) pres <<- con )
R> curlPerform(.opts = performOptions)
OK
 0
R> pres
[1] "<html>\n<head><title>Hello World</title></head>\n<body><h3>Hello
World</h3>\n</body>\n</html>"
```

That looks more like what we would have expected. In addition to the content handler, there are other handlers that can be supplied to `curlPerform()`: a debug handler via `debugfunc`, and a HTTP header handler via `headerfunc`. There are sophisticated functions in RCurl for each of these types that spare us the need to specify our own handler functions. For content and headers, `basicTextGatherer()` turns an object into a list of functions that handles updates, resets, and value retrieval. In the following example we make use of all three. Note that in order for `debugfunc` to work we need to set the `verbose` option to `TRUE`:

```
R> content <- basicTextGatherer()
R> header  <- basicTextGatherer()
R> debug   <- debugGatherer()
R> performOptions <- curlOptions(url = url,
                                 writefunc = content$update,
                                 headerfunc = header$update,
                                 debugfunc = debug$update,
                                 verbose = T)
R> curlPerform(.opts=performOptions)
OK
 0
```

Using the `value()` function of content we can extract the content that was sent from the server.

```
R> str_sub(content$value(), 1, 100)
[1] "<html>\n<head><title>Hello World</title></head>\n<body><h3>Hello
World</h3>\n</body>\n</html>"
```

`header$value()` contains the headers sent back from the server:

```
R> header$value()
[1] "HTTP/1.1 200 OK\r\nDate: Wed, 26 Mar 2014 00:20:10 GMT\r\nServer:
Apache\r\nVary: Accept-Encoding\r\nContent-Length: 89\r\nContent-Type:
text/html\r\n\r\n"
```

`debug$value()` stores various pieces of information on the HTTP request. See Section 5.4.6 for more information on this topic:

```
R> names(debug$value())
[1] "text"       "headerIn"    "headerOut"   "dataIn"      "dataOut"
[6] "sslDataIn"  "sslDataOut"
R> debug$value()["headerOut"]

                     headerOut
"GET /materials/http/helloworld.html HTTP/1.1\r\nHost: www.r-datacollection.
com\r\nAccept: */*\r\n\r\n"
```

5.4.4 Maintaining connections across multiple requests

It is a common scenario to make multiple requests to a server, especially if we are interested in accessing a set of resources like multiple HTML pages. The default setting in HTTP/1.0 is to establish a new connection with each request, which is slow and inefficient. Connections in HTTP/1.1 are persistent by default, meaning that we can use the same connection for multiple requests. RCurl provides the functionality to reuse established connections, which we can exploit to create faster scrapers.

Reusing connections works with the so-called "curl handles." They serve as containers for the connection itself and additional features/options. We establish a handle as follows: **Curl handles**

```
R> handle <- getCurlHandle()
```

The handle in the `handle` object is of class `CURLHandle` and currently an empty container. We can add useful curl options from the list `listCurlOptions()`, for example:

```
R> handle <- getCurlHandle(useragent = str_c(R.version$platform,
R>                                            R.version$version.string,
R>                                            sep=", "),
R>                         httpheader = c(from = "ed@datacollection.com"),
R>                         followlocation = TRUE,
R>                         cookiefile = "")
```

In the example, we specify a `User-Agent` header field that contains the current R version and a `From` header field containing an email address, set the `followlocation` argument to `TRUE`, and activate cookie management (see Section 5.4.5). The curl handle can now be used for multiple requests using the `curl` argument. For instance, if we have a vector of URLs in the object `url`, we can retrieve them with `getURL()` fed with the settings in the curl handle from above.

```
R> lapply(urls, getURL, curl = handle)
```

Note that the curl handle container is not fixed across multiple requests, but can be modified. As soon as we specify new options in a request, these are added—or old ones overridden—in the curl handle, for example, with `getURL(urls, curl = handle, httpheader = c(from = "max@datacollection.com"))`. To retain the status of the handle but use a modified handle for another request, we can duplicate it and use the "cloned" version with `dupCurlHandle()`: **Cloning handles**

```
R> handle2 <- dupCurlHandle(curlhandle,
R>                          httpheader = c(from = "ed@datacollection.com"))
```

Cloning handles can be especially useful if we want to reuse the settings specified in a handle in requests to different servers. Not all settings may be useful for every request (e.g., protocol settings or referrer information), and some of the information should probably be communicated only to one specific server, like authentication details.

When should we use curl handles? First, they are generally convenient for specifying and using curl options across an entire session with RCurl, simplifying our code and making it more reliable. Second, fetching a bunch of resources from the same server is faster when we reuse the same connection.

5.4.5 Options

We have seen that we can use curl handles to specify options in RCurl function calls. However, there are also other means. Generally, RCurl options can be divided into those that define the behavior of the underlying *libcurl* library and those that define how information is handled in R. The list of possible options is vast, so we selected the ones we frequently use and listed them in Table 5.3. Some of these options were already introduced above, the others will be explained below. Let us begin by showing the various ways to declare options.

Table 5.3 List of useful *libcurl* options that can be specified in RCurl functions

Option	Description	Example
	HTTP	
`connecttimeout`	Set maximum number of seconds waiting to connect to server	`connecttimeout = 10`
`customrequest`	Define HTTP method to use in `RCurl`'s high-level functions	`customrequest = "HEAD"`
`.encoding`	Specifies the encoding scheme we expect	`.encoding = "UTF-8"`
`followlocation`	Follow the redirection to another URL if suggested by the server	`followlocation = TRUE`
`header`	Retrieve response header information as well	`header = TRUE`
`httpheader`	Specifies additional HTTP request headers	`httpheader = c('Accept-Charset' = "utf-8")`
`maxredirs`	Limit the number of redirections to avoid infinite loop error with `followlocation = TRUE`	`maxredirs = 5L`
`range`	Retrieve a certain byte range from a file, that is, only parts of a document (does not work with every server; see p. 264)	`range = "1-250"`
`referer`	Convenience option to specify a `Referer` header field	`referer = "www.example.com"`
`timeout`	Set maximum number of seconds waiting for curl request to execute	`timeout = 20`
`useragent`	Convenience option to specify a `User-agent` header field	`useragent = "RCurl"`

	FTP (see Sections 5.3.2 and 9.1.2)	
dirlistonly	Set if only the file names and no further information should be downloaded from FTP servers	dirlistonly = TRUE
ftp.use.epsv	Set extended or regular passive mode when accessing FTP servers	ftp.use.epsv = FALSE
	Cookies (see Sections 5.2.1.1 and 9.1.8)	
cookiefile	Specifies a file that contains cookies to read from it or, if argument remains empty, activates cookie management	cookiefile = ""
cookiejar	Writes cookies that have been gathered over several requests to a file	cookiejar = "/files/cookies"
	SSL (see Sections 5.3.1 and 9.1.7)	
cainfo	Specify file with digital signatures for SSL certificate verification	cainfo = system.file("CurlSSL", "cacert.pem", package = "RCurl")
ssl.verifyhost	Set validation of the certificate-host match true or false	ssl.verifyhost = FALSE
ssl.verifypeer	Set validation of server certificate true or false—useful if a server lacks a certificate but is still trustworthy	ssl.verifypeer = FALSE

Options as arguments We can declare options for single calls to the high-level functions (e.g., getURL, getURLContent, and getBinaryURL). In this case the options will only affect that single function call. In the following example we add header = TRUE in order to not only retrieve the content but also the response header:[20]

```
R> url <- "www.r-datacollection.com/materials/http/helloworld.html"
R> res <- getURL(url = url, header = TRUE)
R> cat(str_split(res, "\r")[[1]])
HTTP/1.1 200 OK
Date: Wed, 26 Mar 2014 00:20:11 GMT
Server: Apache
Vary: Accept-Encoding
Content-Length: 89
Content-Type: text/html

<html>
<head><title>Hello World</title></head>
<body><h3>Hello World</h3>
</body>
</html>
```

Options in handles Another, more persistent way of specifying options is to bind them to a curl handle as described in the previous section. Every function using this handle via the curl option will use the same options. If a function uses the handle and redefines some options or adds others, these changes will stick to the handle. In the following example we create a new handle and specify that the HTTP method *HEAD* should be used for the request:

```
R> handle <- getCurlHandle(customrequest = "HEAD")
R> res <- getURL(url = url, curl = handle)
R> cat(str_split(res, "\r")[[1]])
```

The first function call using the handle results in an empty vector because *HEAD* provides no response body and the header option was not specified. In the second call we add the header argument to retrieve header information:

```
R> res <- getURL(url = url, curl = handle, header = TRUE)
R> cat(str_split(res, "\r")[[1]])
HTTP/1.1 200 OK
Date: Wed, 26 Mar 2014 00:20:14 GMT
Server: Apache
Vary: Accept-Encoding
Content-Type: text/html
```

The added header specification has become part of the handle. When we reuse it, we do not need to specify header = TRUE anymore:

```
R> res <- getURL(url = url, curl = handle)
R> cat(str_split(res, "\r")[[1]])
```

[20]Note that unfortunately not all options work the same way for each of the high-level functions. The header argument, for example, does not expect Boolean input in getURLContent(). We will point to exceptions when we come across them.

```
HTTP/1.1 200 OK
Date: Wed, 26 Mar 2014 00:20:16 GMT
Server: Apache
Vary: Accept-Encoding
Content-Type: text/html
```

With dupCurlHandle() we can also copy the options set in one handle to another handle:

```
R> handle2 <- dupCurlHandle(handle)
R> res <- getURL(url = url, curl = handle2)
```

Global options

Two more global approaches exist. First, we can define a list of options, save it in an object, and pass it to .opts when initializing a handle or calling a function. The curlOptions() function helps to expand and match option names:

```
R> curl_options <- curlOptions(header = TRUE, customrequest = "HEAD")
R> res <- getURL(url = url, .opts = curl_options)
```

To specify further curl options when using getForm() and postForm(), we have to use the .opts argument. Otherwise the function cannot distinguish between form parameters and curl options. Further, instead of specifying the parameters of *POST* directly after the URL, they can also be processed in a list passed to the .params option:

```
R> cat(postForm(url, .params = c(name = "Eddie", age = "32"),
               style = "post",
               .opts = list(useragent = "Eddie's R scraper",
                            referer = "www.r-datacollection.com")))
<html>
<head><title>Hello World</title></head>
<body><h3>Hello World</h3>
</body>
</html>
```

Second, we can even use R's global option system to specify standard values that will be part of each curl handle or function call unless specified otherwise:

```
R> options(RCurlOptions = list(header = TRUE, customrequest = "HEAD"))
R> res <- getURL(url = url)
R> options(RCurlOptions = list())
```

Now that we know how to set options, we should inspect two options a little closer because they can control HTTP methods and HTTP headers: customrequest and httpheader. The customrequest option was already used throughout the examples above and tells *libcurl* to use whatever method specified—for example, *POST*, *HEAD*, or *PUT* instead of the default *GET*. For instance, we can transform getURL() into a function that posts form information:

```
R> res <- getURL("www.r-datacollection.com/materials/http/POSTexample.php",
               customrequest = "POST",
               postfields = "name=Eddie&age=32")
R> cat(str_split(res, "\r")[[1]])
Hello Eddie!
You are 32 years old.
```

Adding request header fields Individual HTTP headers can be added using the `httpheaders` option. We add them as a list where names of the list items identify the header name and their values correspond to header values. Let us specify some helpful standard headers and pass them to a call to `getURL()`. To check which headers are sent along the HTTP request, we send our request to a page that simply returns the HTTP request that was received. First we send a request without any further specifications:

```
R> url <- "r-datacollection.com/materials/http/ReturnHTTP.php"
R> res <- getURL(url = url)
R> cat(str_split(res, "\r")[[1]])
GET /materials/http/ReturnHTTP.php HTTP/1.1
Authorization:
Host: r-datacollection.com
Accept: */*
Connection: close
```

The results from above show that only few headers are sent along our HTTP request. Now we want to add a `from` and `user-agent` header specification to the list:[21]

```
R> standardHeader <- list(
   from         = "eddie@r-datacollection.com",
  'user-agent' = str_c(R.version$platform,
                        R.version$version.string,
                        sep=", "))
R> res <- getURL(url = url, httpheader = standardHeader)
R> cat(str_split(res, "\r")[[1]])
GET /materials/http/ReturnHTTP.php HTTP/1.1
Authorization:
Host: r-datacollection.com
Accept: */*
From: eddie@r-datacollection.com
User-Agent: x86_64-w64-mingw32, R version 3.0.2 (2013-09-25)
Connection: close
```

A set of default options To conclude this section we provide an example of a list of default options. We recommend setting these options via `options()` directly at the start of a session after loading RCurl. This way it is transparent which options are set as default values for all functions and handles with the convenience of having to type the options only once. First, we include the `from` and `user-agent` options from above to always identify ourselves. Next we set `followlocation` to `TRUE` to tell *libcurl* to automatically follow redirections—`maxredirs` restricts these redirections to avoid infinite loops. Next, we specify a default connection timeout as well as a completion timeout (`connecttimeout` and `timeout`). The former tells *libcurl* to stop trying to connect to a server after 10 seconds while the latter timeout is for the maximum time we give *libcurl* to complete a request altogether. The standard *libcurl* connection timeout is 300 seconds. Setting the `cookiefile` option enables *libcurl* to receive,

[21]For a list of other conventional header fields, see Section 5.1.6 or the comprehensive list at http://www.w3.org/Protocols/rfc2616/rfc2616-sec14.html

save, and send back cookies. The last option specifies the location for files that contain digital signatures for SSL certificate verification:

```
R> defaultOptions <-  curlOptions(
  httpheader = list(
  from = "Eddie@r-datacollection.com",
  'user-agent'   = str_c(R.version$platform,
                         R.version$version.string,
                         sep=", ")),
  followlocation = TRUE,
  maxredirs      = 10,
  connecttimeout = 10,
  timeout        = 300,
  cookiefile     = "RCurlCookies.txt",
  cainfo = system.file("CurlSSL","cacert.pem", package = "RCurl"))
R> options(RCurlOptions = defaultOptions)
```

The list of default options can be emptied using

```
R> options(RCurlOptions = list())
```

5.4.6 Debugging

What happens in case of an error in an HTTP call? We have documented in Section 5.1.5 that many things can go wrong and the server communicates the presumed type of error. In the simplest of cases, we might have gotten the URL wrong:

```
R> getURL("http://www.stata-datacollection.com")
Error: Could not resolve host: www.stata-datacollection.com; Host
not found
```

Some errors might be less obvious but still prevent us from receiving content from a server. In this section we will show some tools that help identify reasons why things do not work as expected. We know already that we can ask RCurl functions to capture the response headers in addition to the content by setting the `header` option to `TRUE`. Often, however, we want to have more information, for example the information that arrives at the server after we put a request to it.

A generally useful tool for HTTP debugging is the service at http://httpbin.org, which provides a set of endpoints for specific HTTP requests. To check whether a *GET* request is specified correctly and what information arrives at the server, we write

```
R> url <- "httpbin.org/get"
R> res <- getURL(url = url)
R> cat(res)
{
  "args": {},
  "origin": "134.34.221.149",
  "headers": {
    "Accept": "*/*",
    "X-Request-Id": "348467d6-6641-4863-abb3-a79a602f17e5",
```

```
    "Host": "httpbin.org",
    "Connection": "close"
  },
  "url": "http://httpbin.org/get"
}
```

RCurl debugging functions

Moreover, RCurl provides its own way of checking HTTP calls by specifying a debug gatherer within the function call. The procedure is powerful and does not rely on external resources. It works as follows. First, we create an object that contains three functions (`update()`, `value()`, `reset()`) by calling the `debugGatherer()`:

```
R> debugInfo <- debugGatherer()
R> names(debugInfo)
[1] "update" "value"  "reset"
R> class(debugInfo[[1]])
[1] "function"
```

In a second step, we request a document using the ordinary `getURL()` function and use the `debugfunction` option. With this option we specify a function that gathers debug information as is supplied by *libcurl*—the `update()` function we stored in `debugInfo`. To make the necessary debugging information available, we have to set the `verbose` option to `TRUE`:

```
R> url <- "r-datacollection.com/materials/http/helloworld.html"
R> res <- getURL(url = url, debugfunction = debugInfo$update,
verbose = T)
```

In a third and last step, we access the debugging information gathered during the execution of `getURL()` by calling the `value()` function stored in the `debugInfo` object. The value function provides seven items:

```
R> names(debugInfo$value())
[1] "text"       "headerIn"    "headerOut"  "dataIn"      "dataOut"
[6] "sslDataIn"  "sslDataOut"
```

The first item of the resulting vector—`text`—captures information *libcurl* provides about the procedure:

```
R> cat(debugInfo$value()["text"])
About to connect() to r-datacollection.com port 80 (#0)
  Trying 173.236.186.125... connected
Connected to r-datacollection.com (173.236.186.125) port 80 (#0)
Connection #0 to host r-datacollection.com left intact
Closing connection #0
```

`headerIn` stores the HTTP response header:

```
R> cat(str_split(debugInfo$value()["headerIn"], "\r")[[1]])
HTTP/1.1 200 OK
Date: Wed, 26 Mar 2014 00:20:25 GMT
Server: Apache
```

```
Vary: Accept-Encoding
Content-Length: 89
Content-Type: text/html
```

The HTTP request header is stored in `headerOut`:

```
R> cat(str_split(debugInfo$value()["headerOut"], "\r")[[1]])
GET /materials/http/helloworld.html HTTP/1.1
Host: r-datacollection.com
Accept: */*
```

The body of the response is contained in `dataIn`:

```
R> cat(str_split(debugInfo$value()["dataIn"], "\r")[[1]])
<html>
<head><title>Hello World</title></head>
<body><h3>Hello World</h3>
</body>
</html>
```

The body of the sent data—for example, if we use the *POST* method—is found in `dataOut`:

```
R> cat(str_split(debugInfo$value()["dataOut"], "\r")[[1]])
```

In this example it is empty as we used the *GET* method, which, by definition, does not send any data along with the request body.

The remaining two items `sslDataIn` and `sslDataOut` are analogous to `dataIn` and `dataOut` but for encrypted connections. They are also empty in our request:

```
R> cat(str_split(debugInfo$value()["sslDataIn"], "\r")[[1]])
R> cat(str_split(debugInfo$value()["sslDataOut"], "\r")[[1]])
```

Another source of valuable information might be the `getCurlInfo()` function, which provides additional information on the present state of a curl handle. To get the information we first specify a handle, use it in a function call, and then apply `getCurlInfo()` to the handle:

```
R> handle <- getCurlHandle()
R> url <- "r-datacollection.com/materials/http/helloworld.html"
R> res <- getURL(url = url, curl = handle)
R> handleInfo <- getCurlInfo(handle)
```

The information provided is manifold:

```
R> names(handleInfo)
 [1] "effective.url"          "response.code"
 [3] "total.time"             "namelookup.time"
 [5] "connect.time"           "pretransfer.time"
 [7] "size.upload"            "size.download"
 [9] "speed.download"         "speed.upload"
[11] "header.size"            "request.size"
[13] "ssl.verifyresult"       "filetime"
```

```
[15] "content.length.download" "content.length.upload"
[17] "starttransfer.time"      "content.type"
[19] "redirect.time"           "redirect.count"
[21] "private"                 "http.connectcode"
[23] "httpauth.avail"          "proxyauth.avail"
[25] "os.errno"                "num.connects"
[27] "ssl.engines"             "cookielist"
[29] "lastsocket"              "ftp.entry.path"
[31] "redirect.url"            "primary.ip"
[33] "appconnect.time"         "certinfo"
[35] "condition.unmet"
```

A useful operation might be to consider the total time it took to complete the request and the time it took to do all the things necessary to start the transfer—that is, resolve the host name, establish the connection to the host, and send the request—to get an idea where possible bottlenecks occur:

```
R> handleInfo[c("total.time", "pretransfer.time")]
$total.time
[1] 0.219

$pretransfer.time
[1] 0.11
```

If the time before the actual download takes up a substantial part of the overall time it takes to complete a request, we should—for multiple requests to the same server—ensure that connections are reused. Let us gather the ratio of pre-transfer time to total time ten times in succession with and without reusing the same handle:

```
R> preTransTimeNoReuse <- rep(NA, 10)
R> preTransTimeReuse <- rep(NA, 10)
R> url <- "r-datacollection.com/materials/http/helloworld.html"

R> # no reuse
R> for (i in 1:10) {
    handle <- getCurlHandle()
    res <- getURL(url = url, curl = handle)
    handleInfo <- getCurlInfo(handle)
    preTransTimeNoReuse[i] <- handleInfo$pretransfer.time
}

R> # reuse
R> handle <- getCurlHandle()
R> for (i in 1:10) {
    res <- getURL(url = url, curl = handle)
    handleInfo <- getCurlInfo(handle)
    preTransTimeReuse[i] <- handleInfo$pretransfer.time
}
```

The gathered times show quite nicely how connection times can accumulate when establishing connections for each request and how this can be prevented by reusing curl handles that establish a connection once and reuse this connection to send multiple requests:

```
R> preTransTimeNoReuse
 [1] 0.110 0.094 0.109 0.109 0.094 0.109 0.110 0.109 0.125 0.110
R> preTransTimeReuse
 [1] 0.125 0.000 0.000 0.000 0.000 0.000 0.000 0.000 0.000 0.000
```

5.4.7 Error handling

After discussing tools for discovering why things might not work, this section presents an RCurl specific way to handle errors. We can experience various types of errors—those that we generated ourselves (e.g., by specifying a wrong host name or asking for a nonexisting resource), those that are due to a broken connection, and those generated on the server side. The set of functions provided by RCurl to retrieve content know a lot of different error types. We get a list by calling the `getCurlErrorClassNames()` function. We selected a couple of the most common ones:

```
R> getCurlErrorClassNames()[c(2:4, 7, 8, 10, 23, 29, 35, 64)]
 [1] "UNSUPPORTED_PROTOCOL" "FAILED_INIT"          "URL_MALFORMAT"
 [4] "COULDNT_RESOLVE_HOST" "COULDNT_CONNECT"      "REMOTE_ACCESS_DENIED"
 [7] "HTTP_RETURNED_ERROR"  "OPERATION_TIMEDOUT"   "HTTP_POST_ERROR"
[10] "FILESIZE_EXCEEDED"
```

Using `tryCatch()`[22] we can specify individual actions to react to different types of errors. As an example we choose a user-generated error. We have a set of two URLs. We begin by trying to collect the first one. This operation fails because the host does not exist. The second URL serves as a replacement in case the first URL produces an error of class *COULDNT_RESOLVE_HOST*:

```
R> url1 <- "wwww.r-datacollection.com/materials/http/helloworld.html"
R> res <- getURL(url1)
Error: Could not resolve host: wwww.r-datacollection.com; Host not
found
```

The call produces an error and `res` is not created. This can cause further errors in the program if we try to process the `res` object.

Now let us try to react to the error. In the following snippet, the object `res` stores the results from a call to `tryCatch()`. Within the function we first state the default—retrieving the URL. The next two statements are of the form *errorType = errorFunction*. For each error `tryCatch` checks whether the class of the error matches one of the error names provided—in our case *COULDNT_RESOLVE_HOST* and `error`—and executes the matching function. In the example the default statement produces a resolve host error and the second URL will be retrieved. Any other error would have produced an `NA` that would have been assigned to `res` and the default error message would have been printed.

```
R> url2 <-  "www.r-datacollection.com/materials/http/helloworld.html"
R> res <- tryCatch(
  getURL(url = url1),
  COULDNT_RESOLVE_HOST = function(error) {
      getURL(url = url2)
    },
```

[22]See Section 11.3.2 for a more general elaboration of this function.

```
  error = function(error) {
    print(error$message)
    NA
  }
)
R> cat(str_split(res,"\r")[[1]])
<html>
<head><title>Hello World</title></head>
<body><h3>Hello World</h3>
</body>
</html>
```

5.4.8 RCurl or httr—what to use?

RCurl is a quite powerful package that helps to make the most sophisticated requests and to receive and process the incoming response. At times, it is a bit bulky, however. Fortunately, there is a package that offers a more slender interface: the httr package (Wickham 2012). It builds upon RCurl by wrapping the functions we have discussed so far.

In Table 5.4 we contrast functions of both packages to perform selected HTTP and authentication tasks. Some of the functions have quite a different syntax and do not always provide the same functionality. Although we do not want to go into more details of the httr package at this point, there is no reason to be dogmatic and work with only one of the two packages. In fact, httr offers several features that considerably ease some data collection tasks, for example, authentication via *OAuth* (see Section 9.1.11).

Summary

A basic knowledge of HTTP is fundamental to specify advanced requests to web servers with R. In this chapter, we gave a brief overview of the basic concepts of HTTP and some more intricate features that prove useful in web scraping. We also introduced RCurl, which provides excellent facilities to use R as an HTTP client and for other protocols.

There may be R users who have performed some rudimentary web scarping tasks with `download.file()` and have thus largely disregarded most of the features of RCurl and *libcurl* to specify advanced HTTP requests. We have argued that the RCurl toolbox offers a number of handy features that should pay off even for basic scraping tasks. And after all, even though the package is not too easily accessible for users who are not yet experienced with HTTP, the fundamentals can be learned and implemented quickly. For those who are deterred by the vast range of functions in the manual, the httr package offers convenient wrappers for the most useful RCurl features and a couple more handy functions. In Section 9.1 we will come back to some scenarios of HTTP communication with R. We will show, among other things, how to efficiently deal with forms, use HTTP authentication, and collect data via HTTP Secure.

Further reading

Gourley and Totty (2002) offer an encyclopedic introduction to HTTP. The shorter—and a little less useful—version is the "HTTP Pocket Reference" by Wong (2000). A very thorough

Table 5.4 Selected HTTP and authentication tasks and how to realize them with RCurl or httr

Task	RCurl function/option	httr function
	HTTP methods (verbs)	
Specify *GET* request	`getURL()`, `getURLContent()`, `getForm()`	`GET()`
Specify *POST* request	`postForm()`	`POST()`
Specify *HEAD* request	`httpHEAD()`	`HEAD()`
Specify *PUT* request	`httpPUT()`	`PUT()`
	Content extraction	
Extract raw or character content from response	`content <- getURLContent()`	`content()`
	Curl handle specification	
Specify curl handle	`getCurlHandle()`, `curl`	`handle()`
	Request configuration	
Specify curl options	`.opts`	`config()`
Specify glocal curl options	`options(RCUrlOptions = list()), .opts`	`set_config()`
Execute code with curl options		`with_config()`
Add headers to request	`httpheaders`	`add_headers()`
Authenticate via one type of HTTP authentication	*`userpwd`*	`authenticate()`
Specify proxy connection	`proxy`	`use_proxy()`
Specify User-Agent header field	`useragent`	`user_agent()`
Specify cookies	`cookiefile`	`set_cookies()`
	Error and exception handling	
Display HTTP status code	`getCurlInfo(handle)$response.code`	`http_status()`
Display R error if request fails		`stop_for_status()`
Display R warning if request fails		`warn_for_status()`
Return TRUE if returned status code is exactly 200		`url_ok()`
Return TRUE if returned status code is in the 200s	`url.exists()`	`url_success()`
Set maximum request time	`timeout`	`timeout()`
Provide more information about client–server communication	*`verbose`*	`verbose()`

(*continued*)

Table 5.4 (*Continued*)

Task	RCurl function/option	httr function
	URL modification	
Parse URL into constituent components		`parse_url()`
Replace components in parsed URL		`modify_url()`
Build URL string from parsed URL		`build_url()`
	OAuth registration	
Retrieve OAuth 1.0 access token		`oauth1.0_token()`
Retrieve OAuth 2.0 access token		`oauth2.0_token()`
Register OAuth application		`oauth_app()`
Describe Oauth endpoint		`oauth_endpoint()`
Sign Oauth 1.0 request		`sign_oauth1.0()`
Sign Oauth 2.0 request		`sign_oauth2.0()`

Functions are indicated as `function()`, arguments within RCurl high-level functions, as `argument`.

treatment of the subject can be found in "DNS and BIND" (Liu and Albitz 2006), although we doubt that this will add much to your practical web scraping skills. While *libcurl* is generally well documented on the Web at http://curl.haxx.se/libcurl/, RCurl and httr are less so. Fortunately, the recently published "XML and Web Technologies for Data Sciences with R" (Nolan and Temple Lang 2014) provides an extensive overview of RCurl's functionality.

Problems

1. What are the common methods defined in HTTP/1.1? Describe what they are used for. Which are most important for web scraping?
2. Describe the basic makeup of an HTTP message!
3. What are the five basic status types a server can respond with?
4. What headers can be used for identification purposes?
5. Why can cookies be necessary or even useful when we scrape information from websites?
6. Browse to http://curl.haxx.se/libcurl/c/curl_easy_setopt.html and read about the `autoreferer`, `followlocation`, and `customrequest` options. Are these options part of the RCurl package?
7. Create a handle called `problemsH` that defines options to identify yourself and provide information about your software.

8. Using the `problemsH` handle, download http://www.r-datacollection.com/materials/http/simple.html with …
   (a) …`getURL()` and save it as *simple1.html*.
   (b) …`getBinaryURL()` and save it as *simple2.html*.
   (c) …`getURLContent()` and save it as *simple3.html*.
   (d) Add cookie management to the handler and download all verses from http://www.r-datacollection.com/materials/http/SessionCookie.php

9. Create a debug gatherer object called `info` and a new handle called `problemsD` with the following features:
   (a) Cookie management is enabled.
   (b) `info` is used as debugfunction.
   (c) You should identify yourself and your software.

10. Using `problemsD` as handle, replicate the previous problem and save all request headers (outgoing headers) in *hout.txt* and response headers (incoming headers) in *hin.txt*. Inspect both files with a text editor and answer the following questions.
    (a) How many times did the server ask for a specific cookie in subsequent requests?
    (b) Which parameters did the server send in the request(s) for sending a specific cookie in subsequent requests?
    (c) How many times was the cookie sent to the server?
    (d) Which parameters/values where sent to the server as cookies?
    (e) Learn about the details of the last request executed by `problemsD`, specifically: response code, time it took to complete the request, download size, download speed, list of cookies, number of times the request was redirected, and content type of the response.

11. Declare the following options as default values for all RCurl functions:
    (a) Server redirections should be followed.
    (b) The maximum number of redirects should be 10.
    (c) Identify yourself and your software.
    (d) Enable cookie management.

    Create a new handle called `problemsG`. Check whether your specifications work by downloading http://httpbin.org/cookies/set?myname=Eddie, http://httpbin.org/redirect/20, and http://httpbin.org/headers using `getURL()` and `problemsG`.

12. Write a function called `presentHTTP()` that prints header and content information to the screen in a readable format. Use `str_split()` and `cat()` to solve the problem.

13. Create a debug gatherer object `info` or reset the one you created in a previous problem. Create a new handle called `problemsM` that uses `info`'s update function as debug function parameter.
    (a) Use `readLines()` to read http://www.r-datacollection.com/materials/http/bunchoffiles.html into a vector called `urls`.
    (b) Use the following functions to download the files and save them to disk: `getURL()`, `getURLContent()`, `download.file()`—names should be of form: *geturl1.html, geturl2.html, …; geturlcontent1.html, geturlcontent2.html, …; downloadfile1.html, downloadfile2.html*.
    (c) Which of the functions accept a vector of urls as argument?

14. Use `getForm()` and `postForm()` to send five query parameters to http://www.r-datacollection.com/materials/http/return.php and capture the returned document in objects `getParameters` and `postParameters`.

15. Replicate the following RCurl commands with httr functions:

(a) `getURL("www.r-datacollection.com/index.html", useragent = "R", httpheader = c(From = your@email.address))`

(b) `getForm("www.r-datacollection.com/materials/http/GETexample.php", name = "Eddie", age = 32)`

(c) `postForm("www.r-datacollection.com/materials/http/POSTexample.php", name = "Eddie", age = 32, style = "post")`

(d) `getCurlHandle(useragent ="R", httpheader = c(from = "your@email.address"), followlocation = TRUE, cookiefile = "")`

6

AJAX

At this point in the book you are familiar with HTML's versatile markup vocabulary for structuring content (Chapter 2) and HTTP, the primary protocol for requesting information from web servers (Chapter 5). In combination, these two technologies not only provide the foundation for virtually all web services, but they also define a reliable infrastructure for disseminating information throughout the Web.

Despite their popularity, HTML/HTTP impose strict constraints on the way users access information. If you abstract from the examples we have previously introduced, you find that the HTML/HTTP infrastructure implies a rather *static* display of content in a page layout, which is retrieved through sequential, iterative requests initiated by the user. The inherent inflexibility of HTML/HTTP is most apparent in its inability to create more dynamic displays of information, such as we are used to from standard desktop applications. After receiving an HTML document from the server the visual appearance of the screen will not change since HTTP provides no mechanism to update a page after it has been downloaded. What impedes HTML/HTTP from providing content more dynamically is its lack of three critical elements:

1. a mechanism to register user behavior in the browser (and not just on the server);
2. a scripting engine to formulate responses to those events;
3. a more versatile data requesting mechanism for fetching information asynchronously.

Because HTML/HTTP is technically unable to provide any of the above features, a series of additional web technologies have found their way into the toolkit of modern web developers over the last 15 years. A prominent role in this transformation is assumed by a group of technologies that are subsumed under the term AJAX, short for "**A**synchronous **J**avaScript **a**nd **X**ML." AJAX has become a staple web technology to which we owe much of the sophistication of modern web applications such as Facebook, Twitter, the Google services, or any kind of shopping platform.

Automated Data Collection with R: A Practical Guide to Web Scraping and Text Mining, First Edition.
Simon Munzert, Christian Rubba, Peter Meißner and Dominic Nyhuis.

Although AJAX-enriched websites provide tremendous advantages from a user perspective, they create difficulties for our efforts to automatically gather web data. This is so because AJAX-enriched webpages constitute a significant departure from the static HTML/HTTP site model in which a HTTP-requested webpage is displayed equally for all users and all information that is displayed on screen is delivered upfront. This presents a serious obstacle to analysts who care to collect web data since a simple HTTP *GET* request (see Section 5.1.4) may not suffice if information is loaded iteratively only after the site has been requested. We will see that the key to circumventing this problem is to understand at which point the data of interest is loaded and apply this knowledge to trace the origin of the data.

The remainder of this chapter introduces AJAX technologies that turn static into dynamic HTML. We will focus on the conceptual ideas behind AJAX that will inform solutions for data retrieval. In Section 6.1 we start by introducing JavaScript, the most popular programming language for web content and show how it turns HTML websites into dynamic documents via DOM manipulation. In Section 6.2 we discuss the XMLHttpRequest, an Application Programming Interface (API) for browser–server communication and important data retrieval mechanism for dynamic web applications. Finally, to solve problems caused by AJAX, Section 6.3 explicates how browser-implemented Developer Tools can be helpful for gathering insight into a page's underlying structure as well as tracing the source of dynamic data requests.

6.1 JavaScript

The JavaScript programming language has a prominent role in the group of AJAX technologies. Developed by Brendan Eich at Netscape in 1995, JavaScript is a *complete*, high-level programming language (Crockford 2008). What sets JavaScript apart from other languages is its seamless integration with other web technologies (e.g., HTML, CSS, DOM) as well as its support by all modern browsers, which contain powerful engines to interpret JavaScript code. Because JavaScript has become such an important part in the architecture of web applications, the language has been raised to a W3C web standard. Similar to R's packaging system, extra functionality in JavaScript is incorporated through the use of libraries. In fact, most web development tasks are not executed in native JavaScript code anymore, but are carried out using special purpose JavaScript libraries. We follow this practice for the examples in this chapter and use functionality from jQuery—the self-ascribed *"write less, do more"* library—with a particular focus on easing DOM manipulation.

6.1.1 How JavaScript is used

To recognize JavaScript in the wild, it is important to know that there are three methods for enhancing HTML with JavaScript functionality. A dedicated place for *in-line code* to appear is between the HTML `<script>` tags (see also Section 2.3.10). These tags are typically located before the `<head>` section of the document but they may as well be placed at any other position of the document. Another way is to make *reference* to an externally stored JavaScript code file via a path passed to the `scr` attribute of the `<script>` element. This method helps to organize HTML and JavaScript at two separate locations and thus eases maintainability. Lastly, JavaScript code can appear directly in an attribute of a specific HTML element in so-called event handlers. Regardless of the method, a JavaScript-enhanced HTML file requires the browser to not only parse the HTML content and construct the DOM, but also to read the

JavaScript code and carry out its commands. Let us illustrate this process with JavaScript's DOM manipulation functionality.

6.1.2 DOM manipulation

A popular application for JavaScript code is to create some kind of alteration of the information or appearance of the current browser display. These modifications are called DOM manipulations and they constitute the basic procedures for generating dynamic browser behavior. The possible alterations allowed in JavaScript are manifold: HTML elements may either be removed, added or shifted, attributes to any HTML element can be added or changed, or CSS styles can be modified. To show how such scripts may be employed, consider *fortunes1.html* for a lightly JavaScript-enriched webpage.

```
1  <!DOCTYPE HTML PUBLIC "-//IETF//DTD HTML//EN">
2  <html>

4  <script type="text/javascript" src="jquery-1.8.0.min.js"></script>
5  <script type="text/javascript" src="script1.js"></script>

7  <head>
8  <title>Collected R wisdoms</title>
9  </head>

11 <body>
12 <div id="R Inventor" lang="english" date="June/2003">
13   <h1>Robert Gentleman</h1>
14   <p><i>'What we have is nice, but we need something very different'</i></p>
15   <p><b>Source: </b>Statistical Computing 2003, Reisensburg</p>
16 </div>

18 <div lang="english" date="October/2011">
19   <h1>Rolf Turner</h1>
20   <p><i>'R is wonderful, but it cannot work magic'</i> <br><emph>answering a
       request for automatic generation of 'data from a known mean and 95% CI'
       </emph></p>
21   <p><b>Source: </b><a href="https://stat.ethz.ch/mailman/listinfo/r-help">R-
       help</a></p>
22 </div>

24 <address><a href="http://www.r-datacollection.com"><i>The book homepage</i></a>
     </address>
25 </body>
26 </html>
```

For the most part, the code is identical to the *fortunes* example we introduced in Section 2.4.1. The only modification of the file concerns the extra code appearing in lines 4 and 5. The HTML `<script>` element offers a way to integrate HTML with functionality drawn from other scripting languages. The type of scripting language to be used is set via the `type` attribute. Since browsers expect that incorporated code is written in JavaScript by default, we can leave this attribute unspecified. Here, we include JavaScript using the reference method as it helps emphasize the conceptual difference between the two documents and enhances clarity. In line 4 we make a reference to the jQuery library for which there exists a copy in the folder of the HTML document. By referencing the file *jquery-1.8.0.min.js*, jQuery can be accessed throughout the program. The next line makes a reference to the file *script1.js*, which includes the code responsible for the DOM alterations. To view the file's content, you can open the file in any text processor:

```
$(document).ready(function() {
   $("p").hide();
   $("h1").click(function(){
      $(this).nextAll().slideToggle(300);
   });
});
```

Before explaining the script, take the time to download the *fortunes1.html* file from the materials section at http://www.r-datacollection.com and open it in a browser to discover differences to the example file in Section 2.4.1. Opening the file you should see two named headers and a hyperlink to the book's homepage (see Figure 6.1, panel (a)). Apparently, some information that is contained in the HTML code, such as the quotes and their contexts, has been concealed in the browser display of the webpage. Assuming that JavaScript is enabled in your browser, a click on one of the headers should initiate a rolling transition and further content relating to the quote should become visible (see Figure 6.1, panel (b)). Another click on the header results in the content being hidden again. The dynamic behavior just observed is the result of the code in *script1.js*. To get an understanding of how these behaviors are produced, let us parse this code line by line and discuss what it does.

The first line starts with the `$()` operator, jQuery's method for selecting elements in the DOM. Inside the parentheses we write `document` to indicate that all elements that are defined

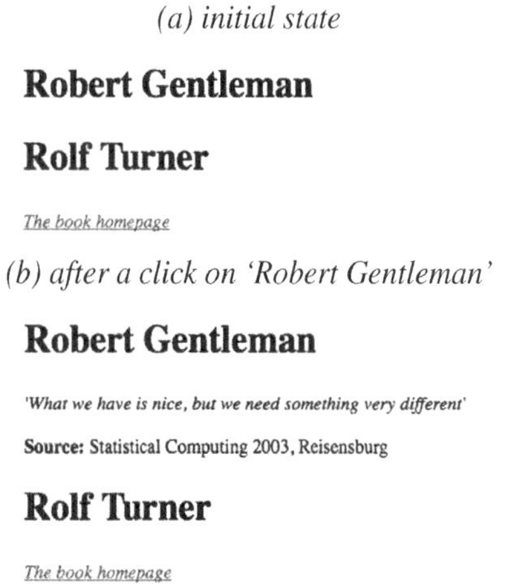

(a) initial state

Robert Gentleman

Rolf Turner

The book homepage

(b) after a click on 'Robert Gentleman'

Robert Gentleman

'What we have is nice, but we need something very different'

Source: Statistical Computing 2003, Reisensburg

Rolf Turner

The book homepage

Figure 6.1 Javascript-enriched *fortunes1.html (a) Initial state (b) After a click on "Robert Gentleman"*

in the DOM are to be selected. The returned selection of the `$()` operator is passed to the `ready()` method. Essentially, the document ready handler `ready()` instructs the script to pause all JavaScript code execution until the entire DOM has been built inside the browser, meaning that all the HTML elements are in existence. This is necessary for any reasonably sized HTML file since the browser will take some time to build the DOM. Not instructing the script to pause until all HTML information is loaded could lead to a situation where the script acts on elements that do not yet exist in the DOM. The essential part starts in line 2, which defines the dynamic behaviors. Once again we employ the `$()` operator but only to select all the `<p>` nodes in the document. As you can see in *fortunes1.html*, these are the elements that contain more information on the quote and its source. The selection of all paragraph nodes is passed to the `hide()` method, which accounts for the behavior that in the initial state of the page all paragraph elements are hidden. The third line initiates a selection of all `<h1>` header nodes in the document, which are used to mark up the names of the quoted. We bind an event handler to this selection for the "*click*" JavaScript event. The `click()` handler allows recognizing whenever a mouse click on a `<h1>` element in the browser occurs and to trigger an action. What we want the action to be is defined in the parentheses from lines 3 to 5. On line 4, we first return the element on which the click has occurred via `$(this)`. The `nextAll()` method selects all the nodes following after the node on which the click has occurred (see Section 4.1 for the DOM relations) and binds the `slideToggle()` method to this selection, which defines a rather slow (300 ms) toggle effect for fading the elements in and out again.

Implications of JavaScript for scraping, 1

On a conceptual level, this example illustrates that the underlying HTML code and the information displayed in the browser do not necessarily coincide in a JavaScript-enriched website. This is due to the flexibility of the DOM and JavaScript that allow HTML elements to be manipulated, for example, by fading them in and out. But what are the implications of this technology for scraping information from this page? Does DOM manipulation complicate the scraping process with the tools introduced earlier? To address this question, we parse *fortunes1.html* into an R object and display its content:

```
R> library(XML)
R> (fortunes1 <- htmlParse("fortunes1.html"))
<!DOCTYPE HTML PUBLIC "-//IETF//DTD HTML//EN">
<html>
<head>
<script type="text/javascript" src="jquery-1.8.0.min.js"></script><script
type="text/javascript" src="script1.js"></script><title>Collected R wisdoms
</title>
</head>
<body>
<div id="R Inventor" lang="english" date="June/2003">
  <h1>Robert Gentleman</h1>
  <p><i>'What we have is nice, but we need something very different'</i></p>
  <p><b>Source: </b>Statistical Computing 2003, Reisensburg</p>
</div>

<div lang="english" date="October/2011">
  <h1>Rolf Turner</h1>
  <p><i>'R is wonderful, but it cannot work magic'</i> <br><emph>answering a
  request for automatic generation of 'data from a known mean and 95% CI'
</emph></p>
```

```
  <p><b>Source: </b><a href="https://stat.ethz.ch/mailman/listinfo/r-help">R-
help</a></p>
  </div>

<address><a href="http://www.r-datacollection.com"><i>The book homepage</i></a>
  </address>
</body>
</html>
```

Evidently, all the information is included in the HTML file and can be accessed via the HTTP request, parsing, and extraction routines we previously presented. As we will see further below, this is unfortunately not always the case.

6.2 XHR

A limitation of the HTTP protocol is that communication between client and server necessarily follows a synchronous request–response pattern. Synchronous communication means that the user's interaction with the browser is being disabled while a request is received, processed, and a new page is delivered by the web server.

A more flexible data exchange mechanism is required to enable a continuous user experience that resembles the behavior of desktop applications. A popular method to allow for a continuous exchange of information between the browser and the web server is the so-called XMLHttpRequest (XHR), an interface that is implemented in nearly all modern web browsers. It allows initiating HTTP or HTTPS requests to a web server in an asynchronous fashion. XHR's principal purpose is to allow the browser to fetch additional information in the background without interfering with the user's behavior on the page.

User–server communication with XHR

To illustrate this process, take a look at the graphical illustration of the XHR-enriched communication model in Figure 6.2. As in the traditional HTTP communication process (see Section 5.1.1), XHR provides a mechanism to exchange data between a client and a server. A typical communication proceeds as follows.

1. Commonly, but not necessarily, the user of a webpage is also the initiator of the AJAX request. The initiating event can be any kind of event that is recognizable by the browser, for example, a click on a button. JavaScript then instantiates an XHR object

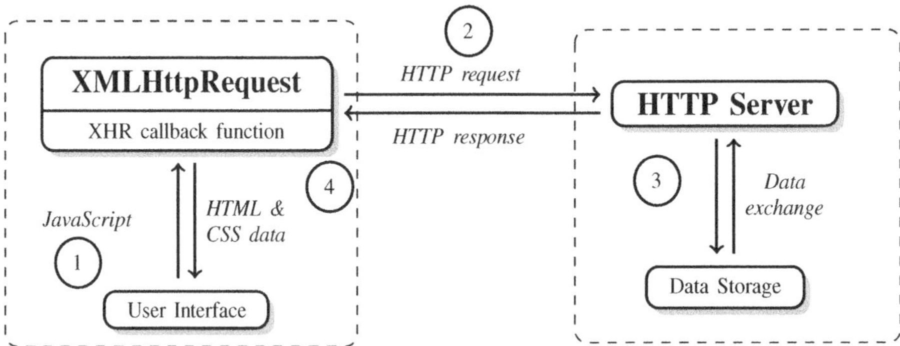

Figure 6.2 The user–server communication process using the XMLHttpRequest. Adapted from Stepp et al. (2012)

that serves as the object that makes the request and may also define how the retrieved data is used via a callback function.

2. The XHR object initiates a request to the server for a specified file. This request may either be sent through HTTP or HTTPS. Due to JavaScript's Same Origin Policy, cross-domain requests are forbidden in native AJAX applications, meaning that the file to be requested must be in the domain of the current webpage. While the request is taking place in the background, the user is free to continue interacting with the site.

3. On the server side, the request is received, processed, and the response including data is sent back to the browser client via the XHR object.

4. Back in the browser client, the data are received and an event is triggered that is caught by an event handler. If the content of the file needs to be displayed on the page, the file may be relayed through a previously defined callback event handler. Via this handler the content can be manipulated to present it in the browser. Once the process handler has processed the information, it can be fed back into the current DOM and displayed on the screen.

To see XHR in action, we now discuss two applications.

6.2.1 Loading external HTML/XML documents

The simplest type of data to be fetched from the server via an XHR request is a document containing HTML code. The task we illustrate here is to gather an HTML code and feed it back into the current webpage. The proper method to carry out this task in jQuery is its `load()` method. The `load()` method instantiates an XHR object that sends an HTTP *GET* request to the server and retrieves the data. Consider the following empty HTML file named *fortunes2.html*, which will serve as a placeholder document:

```
1  <!DOCTYPE HTML PUBLIC "-//IETF//DTD HTML//EN">
2  <html>

4  <script type="text/javascript" src="jquery-1.8.0.min.js"></script>
5  <script type="text/javascript" src="script2.js"></script>

7  <head>
8  <title>Collected R wisdoms</title>
9  </head>

11 <body>

13 <address><a href="http://www.r-datacollection.com"><i>The book homepage</i></a>
       </address>
14 </body>
15 </html>
```

The task is to insert substantially interesting information from another HTML document into *fortunes2.html*. Key to this task is once again a JavaScript code to which we refer in line 5.

```
1 $(document).ready(function() {
2    $("body").load("quotes/quotes.html", function() {
3       alert("Quotes.html was fetched.");
4    });
5 });
```

Like the previous script, *script2.js* starts with the document ready handler `ready()` to ensure the DOM is completely loaded before executing the script. In line 2 we initiate a selection for the `<body>` node. The `<body>` node serves as an anchor to which we link the data returned from the XHR data request. The essential part of the script uses jQuery's `load()` method to fetch information that is accessible in "*quotes/quotes.html*." The `load()` method creates the XHR object, which is not only responsible for requesting information from the server but also for feeding it back into the HTML document. The file *quotes.html* contains the marked up quotes.

```
<div id="R Inventor" lang="english" date="June/2003">
  <h1>Robert Gentleman</h1>
  <p><i>'What we have is nice, but we need something very different'</i></p>
  <p><b>Source: </b>Statistical Computing 2003, Reisensburg</p>
</div>

<div lang="english" date="October/2011">
  <h1>Rolf Turner</h1>
  <p><i>'R is wonderful, but it cannot work magic'</i> <br><emph>answering a
      request for automatic generation of 'data from a known mean and 95% CI'
      </emph></p>
  <p><b>Source: </b><a href="https://stat.ethz.ch/mailman/listinfo/r-help">R-
      help</a></p>
</div>
```

As part of the `load()` method, we also assign a callback function that is executed in case the XHR request is successful. In line 3, we use JavaScript to open an alert box with the text in quotation marks. This is purely for illustrative purpose and could be omitted without causing any problems. To check the success of the method, open *fortunes2.html* in a browser and compare the displayed information with the HTML code outlined above.

Implications of JavaScript for scraping, 2

How does the XHR object interfere with attempts to obtain information from the quotes? Once again we compare the information displayed in the browser with what we get by parsing the document in R:

```
R> library(XML)
R> (fortunes2 <- htmlParse("fortunes2.html"))
<!DOCTYPE HTML PUBLIC "-//IETF//DTD HTML//EN">
<html>
<head>
<script type="text/javascript" src="jquery-1.8.0.min.js"></script><script
type="text/javascript" src="script2.js"></script><title>Collected R wisdoms</title>
</head>
<body>
<address><a href="http://www.r-datacollection.com"><i>The book homepage</i></a>
</address>
</body>
</html>
```

Unlike in the previous example, we observe that information shown in the browser is not included in the parsed document. As you might have guessed, the reason for this is the XHR object, which loads the quote information only after the placeholder HTML file has been requested.

6.2.2 Loading JSON

Although the X in AJAX stands for the XML format, XHR requests are not limited to retrieving data formatted this way. We have introduced the JSON format in Chapter 3, which has become a viable alternative, preferred by many web developers for its brevity and wide support. jQuery not only provides methods for retrieving JSON via XHR request but it also includes parsing functions that facilitate further processing of JSON files. Compared to the example before, we need to remind ourselves that JSON content is displayed unformatted in the browser. In this example, we therefore show first how to instruct jQuery to access a JSON file and second, how to convert JSON information into HTML tags, to obtain a clearer and more attractive display of the information. Take a look at *fortunes3.html* for our generic placeholder HTML document.

```
<!DOCTYPE HTML PUBLIC "-//IETF//DTD HTML//EN">
<html> <head>
<title>Collected R wisdoms (JavaScript Extension)</title>
</head>
<body>

<button id="quoteButton">Click for quotes!</button>

</body>

<script type="text/javascript" src="jquery-1.8.0.min.js"></script>
<script type="text/javascript" src="script3.js"></script>

<address><a href="http://www.r-datacollection.com"><i>The book homepage</i></a>
</address>
</body> </html>
```

The new element here is an HTML button element to which we assign the id `quoteButton`. Inside the HTML code there is a reference to *script3.js*.

```
$("#quoteButton").click(function(){
    $.getJSON("quotes/all_quotes.json", function(data){
        $.each(data, function(key, value){
            $("body").prepend("<div date='"+value.date+"'><h1>"+value.author+"
                </h1><p><i>'"+value.quote+"'</i></p><p><b>Source: </b>'"+value.
                source+"'</p></div>");
        });
    });
});
```

Once again, go ahead and open *fortunes3.html* to check out the behavior of the document. What you should observe is that upon clicking on the button, new quote information appears that is visually similar to what we have seen in *fortunes.html*.

Let us dismantle the script into its constituent parts. In the top line, the scripts initiates a query for a node with id `quoteButton`. This node is being bound to the click event handler. The next lines detail the click's functionality. If a click occurs a data request is sent via jQuery's `getJSON()` method. This method does two things. First, the request for the file is initiated and the data fetched using a HTTP *GET* request. Second, the data are parsed by a JSON parser, which disassembles the file's key and value pairs into usable JavaScript objects. The file to be requested is specified as *all_quotes.json*, which contains the complete set of R wisdoms and is located in the folder named *quotes*. The first couple of lines of this file are printed below:

```
1  [
2  {
3  "quote": "What we have is nice, but we need something very different.",
4  "author": "Robert Gentleman",
5  "context": null,
6  "source": "Statistical Computing 2003, Reisensburg",
7  "date": "June 2003"
8  },
9  {
10 "quote": "R is wonderful, but it cannot work magic.",
11 "author": "Rolf Turner",
12 "context": "answering a request for automatic generation of 'data from a
       known mean and 95% CI'",
13 "source": "R-help",
14 "date": "October 2011"
15 },
```

Line 3 initiates a looping construct that iterates over the objects of the retrieved JSON file and defines a function for the *key* and *value* variables. The function first performs a selection of the HTML document's `<body>` node to which it prepends the expression in parentheses. As you can see, this expression is a mixture of HTML markup and some sort of variable objects (encapsulated by + signs) through we can inject JSON information. Effectively, this statement produces familiar HTML code that includes data, author, quote, and source information from each object of the JSON file.

6.3 Exploring AJAX with Web Developer Tools

When sites employ more sophisticated request methods, a cursory look at the source code will usually not suffice to inform our R scraping routine. To obtain a sufficient understanding of the underlying structure and functionality we need to dig a little deeper. Despite our praise for the R environment, using R would render this task unnecessarily cumbersome and, at least for AJAX-enriched sites, it simply does not provide the necessary functionality. Instead, we examine the page directly in the browser. The majority of browsers comes with functionality that has turned them into powerful environments for developing web projects—and helpful companions for web scrapers. These tools are not only helpful for on-the-fly engagement with a site's DOM, but they may also be used for inspecting network performance and activities that are triggered through JavaScript code. In this section, we make use of Google Chrome's suite of Web Developer Tools (WDT), but tools of comparable scope are available in all the major browser clients.

6.3.1 Getting started with Chrome's Web Developer Tools

We return to the previously introduced *fortunes2.html* file, which caused some headache due to its application of XHR-based data retrieval. Open the file in Google Chrome to accustom yourself once again with the site's structure. By default, WDT are not visible. To bring them to the forefront, you can right-click on any HTML element and select the *Inspect Element* option. Chrome will split the screen horizontally, with the lower panel showing the WDT and the upper panel the classical page view of *fortunes2.html*. IInside the WDT (Chrome version 33.0.1750.146), the top-aligned bar shows eight panels named Elements, Network, Sources, Timeline, Profiles, Resources, Audits, and Console and which correspond to the different aspects of a site's behavior that we can analyze. Not all of these panels will be important for our purposes, so the next sections only discuss the *Elements* and the *Network* panels in the context of investigating a site's structure and creating an R scraping routine.

6.3.2 The Elements panel

Perspective on the DOM tree

From the *Elements* panel, we can learn useful information about the HTML structure of the page. It reveals the live DOM tree, that is, all the HTML elements that are displayed at any given moment. Figure 6.3 illustrates the situation upon opening the WDT on *fortunes2.html*. The *Elements* panel is particularly useful for learning about the links between specific HTML code and its corresponding graphical representation in the page view. By hovering your cursor over a node in the WDT, the respective element in the HTML page view is highlighted. To do the reverse and identify the code piece that produces an element in the page view, click on the magnifying glass symbol at the top right of the panel bar. Now, once you click on an element in the page view, the WDT highlights the respective HTML element in the DOM tree. The *Elements* panel is also helpful for generating an XPath expression that can be passed directly to R's extractor functions (see Chapter 4). Simply right-click on an element and choose "*Copy XPath*" from the menu.

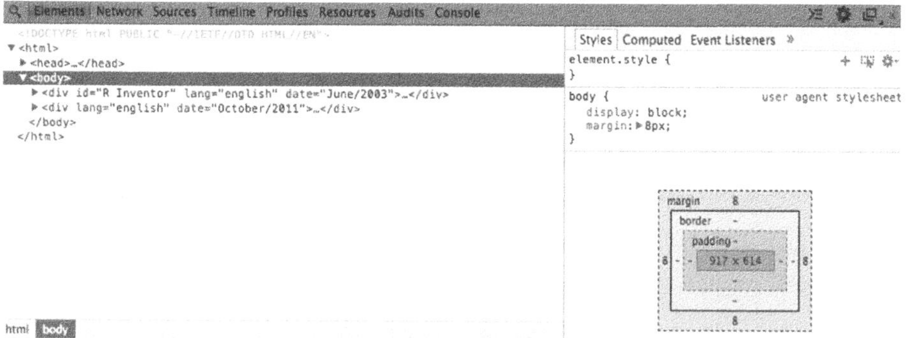

Figure 6.3 View on *fortunes2.html* from the Elements panel

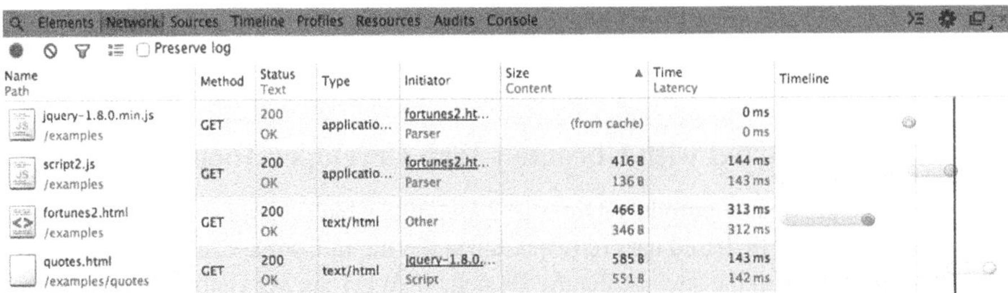

Figure 6.4 View on *fortunes2.html* from the Network panel

6.3.3 The Network panel

Tracing resources The *Network* panel provides insights into resources that are requested and downloaded over the network in real time. It is thus an ideal tool to investigate resource requests that have been initiated by JavaScript-triggered XHR objects. Make sure to open the *Network* panel tab before loading a webpage, otherwise the request will not be captured. Figure 6.4 shows the *Network* panel after loading *fortunes2.html*. The panel shows that altogether four resources have been requested since the *fortunes2.html* has been opened. The first column of the panel displays the file names, that is, *fortunes2.html*, *jquery-1.8.0.min.js*, *script2.js*, and *quotes.html*. The second column provides information on the HTTP request method that provided the file. Here, all four files have been requested via HTTP GET. The next column displays the HTTP status code that was returned from the server (see Section 5.1.5). This can be of interest when an error occurs in the data request. The type column depicts the files' type such as HTML or JavaScript. From the initiator column we learn about the file that triggered the request. Lastly, the size, time, and timeline columns provide auxiliary information on the requested resources.

We are interested in collecting the quote information. Since the information is not part of the source HTML, we can refrain from further inspecting *fortunes2.html*. From the other three files, we can also ignore *jquery-1.8.0.min.js* as this is a library of methods. While *script2.js* could include the required quote information in principle, good web development practice usually separates data from scripts. By the principle of exclusion, we have thus identified *quotes.html* as the most likely candidate for containing the quotes. To take a closer look, click on the file, like in Figure 6.5. From the *Preview* tab we observe that *quotes.html* indeed contains the information. In the next step we need to identify the request URL for this specific file so we can pass it to R. This information is easily obtained from the *Headers* tab, which provides us with the header information that requested *quotes.html*. For our purpose, we only need the URL next to the **Request URL** field, which is http://r-datacollection.com/materials/ajax/quotes/quotes.html. With this information, we can return to our R session and pass the URL to RCurl's `getURL()` command:

```
R> (fortunes_xhr <- getURL("r-datacollection.com/materials/ajax/quotes/
quotes.html"))
[1] "<div id=\"R Inventor\" lang=\"english\" date=\"June/2003\">\n <h1>
Robert Gentleman</h1>\n  <p><i>'What we have is nice, but we need something
very different'</i></p>\n  <p><b>Source: </b>Statistical Computing 2003,
Reisensburg</p>\n</div>\n\n<div lang=\"english\" date=\"October/2011\">\n
```

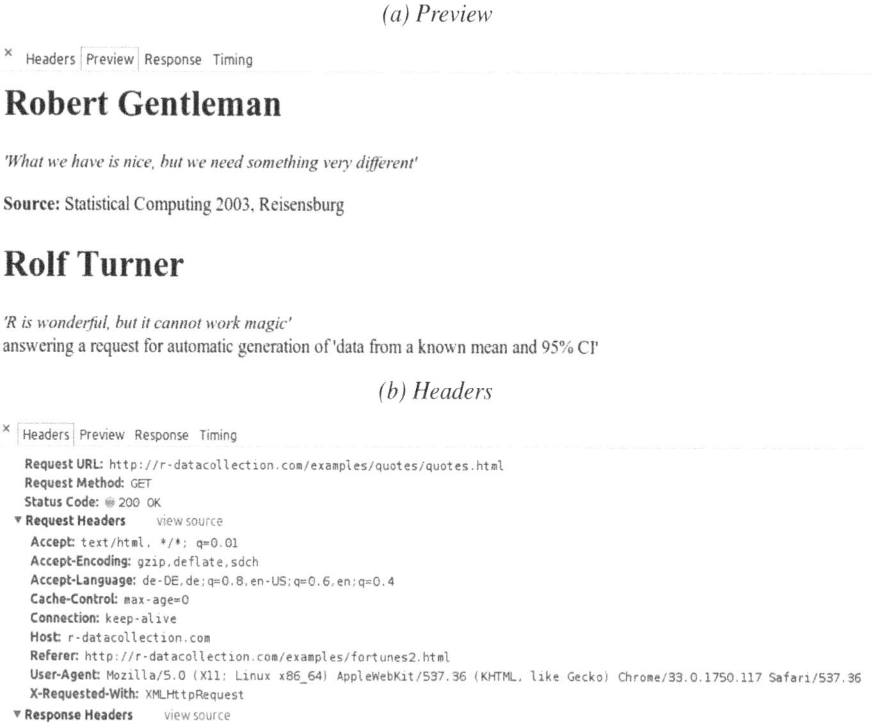

(a) Preview

× Headers Preview Response Timing

Robert Gentleman

'What we have is nice, but we need something very different'

Source: Statistical Computing 2003, Reisensburg

Rolf Turner

'R is wonderful, but it cannot work magic'
answering a request for automatic generation of 'data from a known mean and 95% CI'

(b) Headers

× Headers Preview Response Timing

Request URL: http://r-datacollection.com/examples/quotes/quotes.html
Request Method: GET
Status Code: 200 OK
▾ **Request Headers** view source
Accept: text/html, */*; q=0.01
Accept-Encoding: gzip,deflate,sdch
Accept-Language: de-DE,de;q=0.8,en-US;q=0.6,en;q=0.4
Cache-Control: max-age=0
Connection: keep-alive
Host: r-datacollection.com
Referer: http://r-datacollection.com/examples/fortunes2.html
User-Agent: Mozilla/5.0 (X11; Linux x86_64) AppleWebKit/537.36 (KHTML, like Gecko) Chrome/33.0.1750.117 Safari/537.36
X-Requested-With: XMLHttpRequest
▾ **Response Headers** view source

Figure 6.5 Information on *quotes.html* from the Network panel *(a) Preview (b) Headers*

```
<h1>Rolf Turner</h1>\n  <p><i>'R is wonderful, but it cannot work magic'</i>
<br><emph>answering a request for automatic generation of 'data from a known
mean and 95% CI'</emph></p>\n  <p><b>Source: </b><a href=\"https://stat.
ethz.ch/mailman/listinfo/r-help\">R-help</a></p>\n</div>"
```

The results do in fact contain the target information, which we can now process with all the functions that were previously introduced.

Summary

AJAX has made a lasting impact on the user friendliness of services provided on the Web. This chapter gave a short introduction to the principles of AJAX and it sought to convey the conceptual differences between AJAX and classical HTTP-transmitted contents. From the perspective of a web scraper, AJAX constitutes a challenge since it encourages a separation of the stylistic structure of the page (HTML, CSS) and the information that is displayed (e.g., XML, JSON). Therefore, to retrieve data from a page it might not suffice to download and parse the front-end HTML code. Fortunately, this does not prevent our data scraping efforts. As we have seen, the AJAX-requested information was located in a file on the domain of the main page that is accessible to anyone who takes an interest in the data. With Web Developer Tools such as provided in Chrome, we can trace the file's origin and obtain a URL that oftentimes leads us directly to the source of interest. We will come back to problems created by dynamically rendered pages when we discuss the Selenium/Webdriver framework as an alternative solution to these kinds of scraping problems (see Section 9.1.9).

Further reading

To learn more about AJAX consult Holdener III (2008) or Stepp et al. (2012). A good way to learn and discover useful features of the Chrome Web Developer Tools is on the tool's reference pages Google (2014) or for a book reference Zakas (2010).

Problems

1. Why are AJAX-enriched webpages often valuable for web users, but an obstacle to web scrapers?
2. What are the three methods to embed JavaScript in HTML?
3. Why are Web Developer Tools particularly useful for web scraping when the goal is to gather information from websites using dynamic HTML?
4. Return to *fortunes3.html*. Implement the JavaScript `alert()` function at two points of the document. First, put the function in the `<node>` section of the document with text "*fortunes3.html successfully loaded!*" Second, open *script3.js* and include the `alert()` function here as well with text "*quotes.html successfully loaded!*" Watch the page's behavior in the browser.
5. Use the appropriate parsing function for *fortunes3.html* and verify that it does not contain the quotes of interest.
6. Use the Web Developer Tools to identify the source of the quote information in *fortunes3.html*. Obtain the request URL for the file and create an R routine that parses it.
7. Write a script for *fortunes2.html* that extracts the source of the quote. Conduct the following steps:
   - **(a)** Parse *fortunes2.html* into an R object called `fortunes2`.
   - **(b)** Write an XPath statement to extract the names of the JavaScript files and create a regular expression for extracting the name of the JavaScript script (and not the library).
   - **(c)** Import the JavaScript code using `readLines()` and extract the file path of the requested HTML document *quotes.html*.
   - **(d)** Parse *quotes.html* into an R object called *quotes* and query the document for the names.
8. Repeat exercise two for *fortunes3.html*. Extract the sources of the quotes.
9. The website http://www.parl.gc.ca/About/Parliament/FederalRidingsHistory/hfer.asp?Language=E&Search=C provides information on candidates in Canadian federal elections via a request to a database.
   - **(a)** Request information for all candidates with the name "Smith." Inspect the live DOM tree with Web Developer Tools and find out the HTML tags of the returned information.

(b) Which mechanism is used to request the information from the server? Can you manipulate the request manually to obtain information for different candidates?

10. The city of Seattle maintains an open data platform, providing ample information on city services. Take a look at the violations database at https://data.seattle.gov/Community/Seattle-code-violations-database/8agr-hifc
    (a) Use the Web Developer Tools to learn about how the database information is stored in HTML code.
    (b) Assess the data requesting mechanism. Can you access the underlying database directly?

7

SQL and relational databases

Handling and analyzing data are key functions of R. It is capable of handling vectors, matrices, arrays, lists, data frames as well as their import and export, aggregation, transformation, subsetting, merging, appending, plotting, and, not least, analysis. If one of the standard data formats does not suffice there is always the possibility of defining new ones and incorporating them into the R data family. For example, the sp package defines a special purpose data object to handle spatial data (see Bivand and Lewin-Koh 2013; Pebesma and Bivand 2005). So, why should we care about databases and yet another language called SQL?

Simple and everyday processes like shopping online, browsing through library catalogs, wiring money, or even buying sweets in the supermarket all involve databases. We hardly ever realize that databases play an important role because we neither see nor interact with them directly—databases like to work behind the scenes. Whenever data are key to a project, web administrators will rely on databases because of their reliability, efficiency, multiuser access, virtually unlimited data size, and remote access capabilities.

When databases become useful

Regarding automated data collection, databases are of interest for two reasons: First, we might occasionally get direct access to a database and should be able to cope with it. Second, and more importantly, we can use databases as a tool for storing and managing data. Although R has a lot of useful data management facilities, it is after all a tool designed to analyze data, not to store it. Databases on the other hand are specifically designed for data storage and therefore offer some features that base R cannot provide. Consider the following scenarios.

- You work on a project where data needs to be presented or made accessible on a website—using a database, you only need one tool to achieve this.
- In a data collection project, you do not gather all the data yourself but have other parties gathering specific parts of it—with a database you have a common, current, always accessible, and reliable infrastructure at hand that several users can access at the same time.

Automated Data Collection with R: A Practical Guide to Web Scraping and Text Mining, First Edition.
Simon Munzert, Christian Rubba, Peter Meißner and Dominic Nyhuis.

- When several parties are involved, most databases allow for defining different users with different rights—one party might only be able to read, others have access only to parts of the data, and yet others are equipped with administrative rights but cannot create new users.
- You have loads of data that exceed the RAM available on your computer—databases are only limited by the available disk size. In fact, databases can even be distributed across multiple disks or several machines altogether.
- If your data are complex it might be difficult to write into one data table—databases are best at storing such kind of data. Not only do they allow storing but also retrieving and subsetting data with complex data structures.
- Your data are large and you have to subset and manipulate them frequently—querying databases is fast.
- Your data are complex and you use them for various purposes—for example, the information is distributed across several tables but depending on the context you need to combine information from specific tables in a task-specific way. Databases allow the definition of virtual tables to have data always up to date, organized in a specific way without using much disk space.
- You care about data quality and have several rules when data are valid and when they are not. Using databases you can define specific rules for extending or updating your database.

Section 7.1 provides a brief overview of how R and databases are related to one another and defines some of the vocabulary indispensable for talking about databases. Subsequently, Section 7.2 dives into the conceptual basics of relational databases, followed by an introduction to SQL fundamentals, the language to handle relational databases in Section 7.3. In the last part (Section 7.4) we learn how to deal with databases using R—establishing connections, passing through SQL queries, and using convenient functions of the numerous R packages that provide database connectivity.

7.1 Overview and terminology

For a start let us consider a schematic overview of how R, SQL, the database and the database management system are related (see Figure 7.1). As you can see, we do not access the database directly. Instead, R provides facilities to connect to the database management system—DBMS—which then executes the user requests written as SQL queries. The tasks are defined by the user, but how the tasks are achieved is up to the DBMS. SQL is the tool for speaking to a whole range of DBMS. It is the workhorse of relational database management.

Some definitions

Let us define some of the terms that we have used up to this point to have a common basis to build upon throughout the remainder of the chapter.

Data are basically a collection of information such as numbers, logical values, text, or some other format. Sometimes collections of information might be data for one purpose but a useless bunch of bits and bytes for another. Imagine that we have collected names of people that have participated in the Olympic Games. If we only care to know who has participated, it might suffice if our data has the format of: `"Carlo Pedersoli"`. If, however, we want to

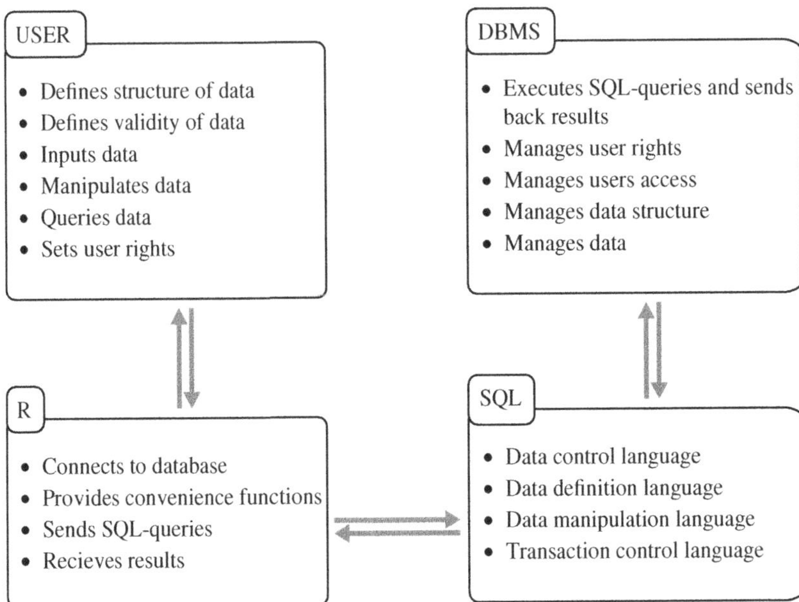

Figure 7.1 How users, R, SQL, DBMS, and databases are related to each other

sort the data by last name, a format like `"Pedersoli, Carlo"` is more appropriate. To be on the safe side, we might even consider splitting the names into first name (`"Carlo"`) and last name (`"Pedersoli"`). *Being on the safe side* plays a crucial role in database design and we will come back to it.

In general a **database** is simply a collection of data. Within most database systems and relational database systems, the data are related to each other. Consider for example a table that contains the bodyweights of various people. We have at least two types of data in the table: bodyweights and names. What is more, not only does the table store the two variables, but additionally it provides information on how these two pieces of information are related to each other. The most basic rule is this: Every piece of information in a single row is related to each other. We are familiar with handling tables that are structured in this way. In relational databases, these relations between data can be far more complex and will typically be spread across multiple tables.

A **database management system (DBMS)** is an implementation of a specific database concept bundled together with software. The software is responsible for managing the user rights and access, the way data and meta information are stored physically, or how SQL statements are interpreted and executed. DBMS are numerous and exist as open source as well as commercial products for all kinds of purposes, operation systems, data sizes, and hardware architectures.

Relational database management systems (RDBMS) are a specific type of DBMS based on the relational model and the most common form of database management systems. Relational databases have been around for a while. The concept goes back to the 1970s when Edgar F. Codd proposed to store data in tables that would be related and the relations again stored in tables (Codd 1970). Relational databases, although simple in their conceptual basics, are general and flexible enough to store all kinds of different data structures, while the specific parts of the database remain easy to understand. Popular relational DBMS are Oracle, MySQL, Microsoft SQL Server, PostgreSQL, DB2, Microsoft Access, Sybase, SQLite, Teradata, and File-Maker.[1] In this book we exclusively talk about RDBMS and use DBMS and RDBMS interchangeably.

SQL[2] is a language to communicate with relational database management systems. When Codd proposed the relational model for databases in 1970, he also proposed to use a language to communicate with database systems that should be general and work only on a meta level. The idea was to be able to express exactly what a DBMS should do—the same statement on different DBMS should always lead to the same result—but leave it completely up to the DBMS how to achieve it computationally (Codd 1970). Such a language would be user friendly and would allow using a common framework for different implementations of the relational model. Based on these conceptual ideas, SQL was later developed by Donald D. Chamberlin and Raymond F. Boyce (1974) and, although occasionally revised throughout the decades, still lives on today as the one common language for relational database communication.

A **query** is strictly speaking a request sent to a DBMS to retrieve data. In a broader and more frequently used sense it refers to any request made to a DBMS. Such requests might define or manipulate the structure of the data, insert new data, or retrieve data from the database.

7.2 Relational Databases

7.2.1 Storing data in tables

Tables and relations

The main concept of relational databases is that any kind of information can be represented in a table. We already know that tables are devices to store data as well as relations—each piece of information within the same row is related to the same entity. To achieve more complex relations—for example, a persons' weight is measured twice, or the weight is measured for a persons' children as well—we can relate data from one table to another.

Let us take a look at an example to make this point clear. Imagine that we have collected data on some of our friends—Peter, Paul, and Mary. We collected information on their birthdays, their telephone numbers, and their favorite foods—see Tables 7.1 and 7.2. We had trouble putting the data into one table and ended up separating the data into two tables. Because we do not like to duplicate information, we did not add the full names to the telephone table(Table 7.2), but specified IDs referring to the names in a column called `nameid`. Now how do we find Peter's telephone number? First, we look up Peter's ID in the birthdays table (Table 7.1) because we know that data on the same line is related—Peter's ID is `1`. Second, we check which row in the telephone table has a `1` on `nameid`—rows one and three. Third, we look up the telephone numbers for these rows—`001665443` and `001878345`—and realize

[1] See also http://db-engines.com/en/ranking/relational+dbms

[2] There is an ongoing debate about whether or not SQL is an acronym and how to pronounce it correctly—well, *no* and *S-Q-L* are the correct answers. SQL is the successor name of SEQUEL, which was the name of an airplane and thus had to be changed (McJones et al. 1997, p. 22). SEQUEL (not SQL) was an acronym for: **S**tructured **E**nglish **QU**ery **L**anguage (McJones et al. 1997, p. 14). The pronunciation of SQL was officially declared as S-Q-L (Gillespie 2012).

Table 7.1 Our friends' birthdays and favorite foods

nameid	name	birthday	favoritefood1	favoritefood2	favoritefood3
1	Peter Pascal	01/02/1991	spaghetti	hamburger	
2	Paul Panini	02/03/1992	fruit salad		
3	Mary Meyer	03/04/1993	chocolate	fish fingers	hamburger

that Peter has two telephone numbers. We can also reverse the process and ask which name of the birthdays table belongs to a specific telephone number or what number we need to call to speak to a fruit salad or spaghetti lover.

The relation in our example is called *1:m* or *one-to-many*, as one person can be related to zero, one, or more telephone numbers. There are of course also *1:1*, *n:1*, and *n:m* relations (*one-to-one*, *many-to-one*, *many-to-many*), which work just the same way except that the number of data that might show up on one or the other side of the relation differs.

Keys This connection of tables to express relations between data is one of the most important concepts in relational database models. But note that to make it work we had to include identifiers in both tables. These so-called keys ensure that we know which entity the data belongs to and how to combine information from different tables.

Redundancy and exclusiveness Including keys makes some parts of the data redundant—the `nameid` column exists in Table 7.1 and in Table 7.2—but it also reduces redundancy. Let us consider the example again to make this point clear. Have another look at Table 7.1. There are three columns to store the same type of data. We have to store the data somewhere and what can we do about the fact that some of our friends did name more than one preference? Imagine what it would look like if we recorded more than just these 3 preferences, maybe 5 or 7 or even 10. We would have to add another column for each preference and if somebody only had one preference all the other columns would remain empty. Clearly there has to be another way to cope with this kind of data rather than adding column after column to store some more preferences. Indeed there is.

We divide the data contained in the birthdays table into two separate tables that are related to each other via a key. Have a look at Tables 7.3 and 7.4 for the result. Now we do not have to care how many favorite foods somebody names, because we always have the option of adding another row whenever necessary and still all preferences are unambiguously related to one person.

Even though the data are stored in a cleaner way, we still have some redundancy in our food preference table. Is it necessary to have hamburgers in the table twice? In our example it does not change much, but if the example was just a little more complex, for example, with

Table 7.2 Our friends' telephone numbers

telephoneid	nameid	telephonenumber
1	1	001665443
2	2	00255555
3	1	001878345

Table 7.3 Our friends' birthdays—revised

name id	first name	last name	birthday
1	Peter	Pascal	01/02/1991
2	Paul	Panini	02/03/1992
3	Mary	Meyer	03/04/1993

Table 7.4 Our friends' food preferences

nameid	foodname	rank
1	spaghetti	1
1	hamburger	2
2	fruit salad	1
3	chocolate	1
3	fish fingers	2
3	hamburger	3

10 instead of 3 friends and 80% of them being fans of hamburgers, the table would grow quickly. What if we would like to add further information on the food types? Do we store it in the same table—repeating the information for hamburger over and over again? No, we would do something similar to what we did when putting telephone numbers in a separate table (Table 7.2). In the new food preference table (Table 7.5) all information on the preferences itself remains untouched, because this will be the table on preferences. Furthermore, the key relating it to the birthdays table (Table 7.3)—`nameid`—and the key relating it to the new table on food (Table 7.6)—`foodid`—are kept.

After restructuring our data, we now have a decent database. Take a look at Figure 7.2 to see how the data are structured. In the schema each table is represented by a square. As we can see, there are four tables. Let us call them *birthdays*, *telephone*, *foodranking*, and *foodtypes*. The upper part of the square gives the name of the table, the column names are listed in the lower part. The double-headed arrows show which tables are related by pointing to the columns that serve as keys—the columns set in bold and the columns set in italics.

Table 7.5 Our friend's food preferences—revised

rankid	nameid	foodid	rank
1	1	1	1
2	1	2	2
3	2	3	1
4	3	4	1
5	3	5	2
6	3	2	3

Table 7.6 Food types

foodid	food name	healthy	kcalp100g
1	spaghetti	no	0.158
2	hamburger	no	0.295
3	fruit salad	yes	0.043
4	chocolate	no	0.546
5	fish fingers	no	0.290

Primary keys and foreign keys

The reason why some keys are set in bold and some are set in italics is because there are two types of keys: primary keys and foreign keys. Primary keys are keys that unambiguously identify each row in a table—`nameid` in our birthdays table (Table 7.3) is an example where each person is associated with exactly one unique `nameid`. `nameid` is not a primary key in our telephone table (Table 7.2), as subjects might well have more than one telephone number, making the ID value non-unique. Thus, while `nameid` in the telephone table is still a key, it is now called a foreign key. Foreign keys are keys that unambiguously identify rows in another table. In other words, each `nameid` found in the telephone table refers to one and only one row in the birthdays table. There cannot be a `nameid` in the telephone table that matches more than one `nameid` in the birthdays table.

Combined keys

Note that it does not matter whether keys consist of one single value per row or a combination of values. Nor does it matter whether the identifier is a number, a string, something else, or a combination of those. A key can span across several columns as long as the value combinations fulfill the requirements for primary or foreign keys. Primary keys in our example are restricted to one single column and are always running integers, but they could look different.

Let us consider an example of an alternative primary key to make this point clear. In our food preference table (Table 7.5) neither `nameid` nor `foodid` are sufficient as primary keys, because individuals appear multiple times depending on their stated preferences and the same food might be preferred by several subjects. However, as no one prefers the same food twice, the combination of name identifier and food identifier would be valid as primary key for the food preference table.

7.2.2 Normalization

In the previous paragraphs we decomposed our data step by step. We did so because it saves unnecessary work in the long run and keeps redundancy at bay. Normalization is the process

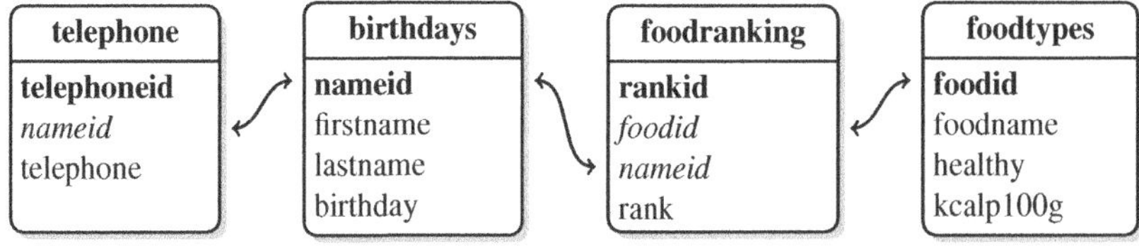

Figure 7.2 Database scheme

of getting rid of redundancies and possible inconsistencies. In the following section, we will learn about this procedure, which is quite helpful to cope with complex data. If you do not plan to use databases to store data—for example, you only want to store large amounts of data that otherwise fit nicely into a single table, or you only need it for its user management capabilities—you can simply skip this section or come back to it later on.

Let us go through the formal rules for normalization to ensure we understand why databases often look the way they do and how we might do it ourselves. While there are numerous ways of decomposing data stored in tables—called normal forms—we will only cover the first three, as they are the most important and most common.

First normal form

1. *One column shall refer to one thing and to one thing only and any column row intersection should contain only one piece of data (the atomacy of data requirement).*

   This rule requires that different types of information are not mixed within one column. One could argue that we violated this rule by storing both first and last names in the `name` column of our first birthdays table (Table 7.1). We corrected this in the updated birthdays table (Table 7.3), where first name and last name were split up into two columns. Furthermore, it requires that the same data are saved in only one column.

   This rule was violated in the first version of our birthdays table, where we had three columns to store a person's favorite food. By exporting the information to the favorite food table (Tables 7.4 and 7.5) and food type table (Table 7.6), this problem was taken care of—a person's favorite food is now stored in a single column. In addition it is not allowed to store more than one piece of the same information in an intersection of row and column. For example, it is not allowed to store two telephone numbers in a single cell of a table. Take a look at Tables 7.7, 7.8, and 7.9 for three examples that violate the first normal form.

2. *Each table shall have a primary key.*

   This rule is easy to understand as keys were covered at length in the previous section. It ensures that data can be related across tables and that data in one row is related to the same entity.

Table 7.7 First normal form error—1

zip code and city
789222 Big Blossom
43211 Little Hamstaedt
123456 Bloomington
...

This table fails the first rule of the first normal form because two different types of information are saved in one column—a city's zip code and a city's name.

Table 7.8 First normal form error—2

telephone
0897729344, 0666556322
123123454
675345334
...

This table fails the first rule of the first normal form because two telephone numbers are saved within the first row.

Table 7.9 First normal form error—3

telephone1	telephone2
0897729344	0666556322
123123454	
675345334	
...	

This table fails the first rule of the first normal form because it uses two columns to store the same kind of information.

Second normal Form

1. *All requirements for the first normal form shall be met.*
2. *Each column of a table shall relate to the complete primary key.*

   We have learned that a primary key can be a combination of the values of more than one column. This rule requires that all data in a table describe one thing only: only people, only telephone numbers, only food preferences or only food types. One can think of this rule as a topical division of data among tables.

   Consider Table 7.10 for a violation of this rule. The primary key of the table is a combination of `nameid` and `foodid`. The problem is that `firstname` and `birthday` relate to `nameid` only while `favoritefood` relates to `foodid` only. The only column that depends on the whole primary key—the combination of `nameid` and `foodid`—is `rank`, which stores the rank of a specific food in a specific person's food preference order.

   A solution to this violation of the second normal form is to split the table into several tables. One table to capture information on persons, one on food and yet another on food preferences. Take a look at Tables 7.3, 7.5, and 7.6 from the previous section for tables that are compliant with the second normal form.

Third normal form

1. *All requirements for the second normal form shall be met.*

Table 7.10 A second normal form error

nameid	firstname	birthday	favoritefood	foodid	rank
1	Peter	01/02/1991	spaghetti	1	1
1	Peter	01/02/1991	hamburger	2	2
2	Paul	02/03/1992	fruit salad	3	1
3	Mary	03/04/1993	chocolate	4	1
3	Mary	03/04/1993	fish fingers	5	2
3	Mary	03/04/1993	hamburger	1	3

This table does not comply to second normal form because all columns except `rank` either relate to one part of the combined primary key (`nameid` and `foodid`) or to other part but not to both.

2. *Each column of a table shall relate only and directly to the primary key.*

   The third normal form is actually a more strict version of the second normal form. Simply stated, it excludes that data on different things are kept in one table.

   Consider Table 7.11. The table only contains three entries, so we could easily use `nameid` as primary key. Because the primary key only consists of one column, every piece of information depends on the whole primary key. But the table remains odd, because it contains two kinds of information—information related to individuals and information related to food. As the primary key is based on subjects, all information on them relates directly to the primary key. Things look different for information that relates to food. Food-specific information is only related to the primary key insofar as subjects have food preferences. Therefore, including information on food in the table violates the third normal form. Again, the information should be stored in separate tables like in Tables 7.3, 7.5, and 7.6 from the previous subsection.

Keep in mind that there are several other normal forms, but for our purposes these three should suffice. Recall that normalization is primarily done to ensure data consistency—meaning that any given piece of information is stored only once in a database. If the same piece of information is stored twice, changes would have to be made in multiple places and might contradict each other if forgotten.

There are, however, no technical restrictions that prevent us from putting redundant or inconsistent data structures into a database. Whether this benefits our goal strongly depends on questions like: What purpose does the database serve? What do we describe in our database? How are the elements in our database related to each other? Will information be added in the future? Will the database serve other purposes in the future? How much effort is it

Table 7.11 A third normal form error

nameid	firstname	birthday	favoritefood	healthy	kcalp100g
1	Peter	01/02/1991	spaghetti	no	0.158
2	Paul	02/03/1992	fruit salad	yes	0.043
3	Mary	03/04/1993	chocolate	no	0.546

This table does not comply to third normal form because `favoritefood`, `healthy` and `kcalp100g` do not relate directly to persons which the primary key (`nameid`) is based on.

to completely normalize our database? The higher the complexity of the data, the higher the number of different purposes a database might serve and the higher the probability that information might be added in the future, the greater the effort that should be put into planning and rigorously designing the database structure. Generally speaking, when you try to extract data from an unknown database, you should always check the structure of the database to make sure you get the right information.

7.2.3 Advanced features of relational databases and DBMS

Understanding how to store data in tables, how to decompose the data, and how relations work in databases is enough for a basic understanding of the nature of databases. But often DBMS have implemented further features like data type definitions, data constraints, virtual tables or views, procedures, triggers, and events that make DBMS powerful tools but go far beyond what can be captured in this short introduction. Nonetheless, we will briefly describe these concepts to provide an idea of what is possible when working with DBMS.

Data types One aspect we usually have to take care of when building up a database is to specify each column's data type. The data type definition tells the DBMS how to handle and store the data; it affects the required disk space and also impacts efficiency. There are several broad data types that are implemented in one way or another in every DBMS: boolean data, that is, true and false values, numeric data (integer and float), character or text data, data referring to dates, times, and time spans as well as data types for files (so-called BLOBs—binary large objects). Which types are available and how they are implemented depends on the specific DBMS, so we will not go into details here. The manual section of each DBMS should list and describe the supported data types, how they are implemented, and further features that are associated with it. To get an idea, consider Table 7.11 once more. Column by column the data types can be specified as: integer, character, date, character, boolean, and float.

Constraints Beyond fixing columns to specific types of data, some DBMS even implement the possibility to constrain data. Constraining data enables the user to define under which circumstances—for which values and value ranges—data should be accepted and in which cases the DBMS should reject to store the data. In general, there are two ways to constrain data validity: Specifying columns as primary or foreign keys and explicitly specifying which values or value ranges are valid and which are not. Setting a column as primary key results in the rejection of duplicated values because primary keys must identify each row unambiguously. Defining a column as foreign key will lead to the rejection of values that are not already part of the primary key it relates to. Explicit constraining of data instead is user-defined and might be as simple as forbidding negative values or more complex involving several clauses and references to other tables. No matter which type of constraint is used the general behavior of the DBMS is to reject values that do not fulfill the constraint.

Transactions DBMS are designed for consistent handling of data. This entails that queries to the database should not break it, for example, if an invalid change is requested or a data import suddenly breaks up—for example, when our system crashes. This is ensured by enforcing that a manipulation is completely carried out or not at all. Furthermore, DBMS usually provide a way to define transactional blocks. This feature is useful whenever we have a manipulation that takes several steps and we want all steps to take effect or none—that is, we do not want the process to stop halfway through because one statement causes an error, leaving us with data that is partially manipulated.

User management Nearly all DBMS provide a way to secure access to the database. The simplest possibility is to ask for a password before granting access to the whole database but more elaborate frameworks are common like having several users with their own passwords. Furthermore, each user account can be accompanied with different user rights. One user might only be allowed to read a single table, while another can read all tables and even add new data. Yet other users might be allowed to create new tables and grant user rights to other users.

Multi-user access

DBMS can easily handle accesses of more than one user to the same database at the same time. That is, DBMS will always give you the present state of the database as response to a query including changes made by other users but only those that were completely executed. How a DBMS precisely solves problems of concurrent access is DBMS specific.

Views

As the normalization of data and complex structures makes it more cumbersome to assemble the data needed for a specific purpose, most DBMS have the possibility to define virtual tables called views. Imagine that we want to retrieve and compose data from different data tables frequently. We can define a query each time we need the specific combination of data. Alternatively, we can define the query once and save it in a separate table. The downside of this operation is that it takes up additional disk space. Further, we have to recreate the table each time to make sure it is up to date, which is identical to defining the query anew each time we need the specific combination of data.

Another, more elegant solution is to store the query that provides the data we need as a virtual table. This table is virtual because instead of the data only the query that provides the data is stored. This virtual table behaves exactly as if the data was stored in the table, but potentially saves a lot of rewriting and rethinking. Compared to executing the query once and saving the results in the database, the data in the virtual table will always be up to date.

Functions

All DBMS provide functions for data manipulation and aggregation in addition to the simple data storage capacities. These functions might provide us with the current date, the absolute value of a number, a substring, the mean for a set of values, and so on. Note that while R functions can return all kinds of data formats, database functions are restricted to scalars. Which functions are provided and how they are named is DBMS dependent. Furthermore, most DBMS allow user-defined functions as well but, again, the syntax for function definition might vary.

Procedures and triggers

Another DBMS-dependent feature is procedures and triggers. Procedures and triggers help extending the functionality of SQL. Imagine a database with a lot of tables, where adding a new entry involves changes to many tables. Procedures are stored sequences of queries that can be recalled whenever needed, thus making repeating tasks much easier. While procedures are executed upon user request, triggers are procedures that are executed automatically when certain events, like changes in a table, take place.

7.3 SQL: a language to communicate with Databases

7.3.1 General remarks on SQL, syntax, and our running example

SQL, a multi-purpose language

Now that we have learned how databases and DBMS work and which features they provide, we can turn our attention to SQL, the language to communicate with DBMS. SQL is a multipurpose language that incorporates vocabulary and syntax for various tasks:

- **DCL (data control language)**
  The DCL part of SQL helps us to define who is allowed to do what and where in our database and allows for fine-grained user rights definitions.

- **DDL (data definition language)**
  DDL is the part of SQL that defines the structure of the data and its relations. This means that the vocabulary enables us to create tables and columns, define data types, primary keys and foreign keys, or to set constraints.
- **DML (data manipulation language)**
  The DML part of SQL takes care of actually filling our database with data or retrieving information from it.
- **TCL (transaction control language)**
  The last part of SQL is TCL, which enables us to commit or rollback previous queries. This is similar to save and undo buttons in ordinary desktop programs.

General syntax

The syntax and vocabulary of SQL is rather simple. Let us first consider the general syntax before moving on to specific vocabularies and syntaxes of the different language branches of SQL.

SQL statements generally start with a command describing which action should be executed—for example, `CREATE`, `SELECT`, `UPDATE`, or `INSERT INTO`—followed by the unit on which it should be executed—for example, `FROM table1`—and one or more clauses—for example, `WHERE column1 = 1`. Below you find four SQL statement examples.

```
> CREATE DATABASE database1 ;
> SELECT column1 FROM table1 WHERE column2 = 1 ;
> UPDATE table1 SET column1 = 1 WHERE column2 > 3 ;
> INSERT INTO table1 (column1, column2)
  VALUES ('rc11', 'rc12'), ('rc21', 'rc22') ;
```

Although it is customary to write all SQL statements in capital letters, SQL is actually case insensitive towards its key words. Using capital or small case does not change the interpretation of the statements. Note however, that depending on the DBMS, the DBMS might be case sensitive to table and column names. For purposes of readability we will stick to the capitalized key words and lower case table and column names.

Each SQL statement ends with a semicolon—therefore, SQL statements might span across multiple lines.

```
> CREATE TABLE table (
> column1 INTEGER NOT NULL AUTO_INCREMENT ,
> column2 VARCHAR(100) NOT NULL ,
> PRIMARY KEY (column1)
> ) ;
```

Comments either start with `--` or have to be put in between `/*` and `*/`.

```
> -- One line comment.
> /*
> Comment spanning
> several lines
> */
```

Running example and SQL execution

For the remainder of this section we will use the birthdays, foodranking, and foodtypes tables (Tables 7.3, 7.5, and 7.6) from the database that we built up in the previous sections. As SQL is the common standard for a broad range of DBMS, the examples should work with most DBMS that speak SQL. However, there might always be slight differences—for example, SQLite does not support user management.

To access the database, you can either use R as client—you will find a description of the possible ways in the next section—or install and use another client software. Before you can access the database, you have to create your own server—except when using SQLite, which works with the R package RSQLite out of the box. We recommend using a MySQL community server in combination with MySQL Workbench CE for a start. Both the MySQL server and MySQL Workbench are easy to install, easy to use, and can be downloaded free of charge. Furthermore, MySQL ODBC drivers are reliable, are available for a large range of platforms, and it is easy to connect to the server from within R by making use of RODBC.[3]

7.3.2 Data control language—DCL

To control access and privileges to our database, we first ask the DBMS to create a database called `db1`:

```
> CREATE DATABASE db1 ;
```

Next, we create and delete several users identifying themselves by password:

```
> CREATE USER 'tester'  IDENTIFIED BY '123456' ;
> CREATE USER 'tester2' IDENTIFIED BY '123456' ;
> CREATE USER 'tester3' IDENTIFIED BY '123456' ;
> DROP   USER 'tester3' ;
```

Now we can use two powerful SQL commands to define what a user is allowed to do. `GRANT` for granting privileges and `REVOKE` to remove privileges. A full SQL statement granting user `tester` all privileges; all privileges for a certain database, and all privileges for a certain table in a database looks as follows:

```
> GRANT ALL ON *.* TO 'tester2' ;
> GRANT ALL ON db1.* TO 'tester2' ;
> GRANT ALL ON db1.table1 TO 'tester2' ;
```

[3]The examples were checked with MySQL 5.5.34 and MySQL Workbench CE 5.2.47 to establish the connection. You can download the MySQL Community Server and MySQL Workbench from http://www.mysql.com. When asked for an account login or sign up, look for the *No thanks, just start my download* button—or create an account if you like.

We can also grant specific privileges only, for example, for selecting and inserting information:

```
> GRANT SELECT, INSERT ON *.* TO 'tester2' ;
```

We can add the right to grant privileges to other users as well:

```
> GRANT SELECT, INSERT ON *.* TO 'tester2' WITH GRANT OPTION ;
```

To remove all privileges from our test user, we can use REVOKE or delete the user altogether.

```
> REVOKE ALL ON *.* FROM 'tester2' ;
> DROP USER 'tester2' ;
```

7.3.3 Data definition language—DDL

CREATE TABLE

After having created a database and a user and having set up the user rights, we can turn to those statements that define the structure of our data. The commands for data definition are CREATE TABLE for the definition of tables, ALTER TABLE for changing aspects of an existing table, and DROP TABLE to delete a table from the database. Let us start by defining Table 7.3, the revised birthdays table.

```
> CREATE TABLE birthdays (
>   nameid INTEGER NOT NULL AUTO_INCREMENT ,
>   firstname VARCHAR(100) NOT NULL ,
>   lastname VARCHAR(100) NOT NULL ,
>   birthday DATE ,
>   PRIMARY KEY (nameid)
> ) ;
```

Let us go through this line by line. The first line starts the statement by using CREATE TABLE to indicate that we want to define a new table and also specifies the name 'birthdays' for this new table. The details of the columns follow in parentheses. Each column definition is separated by a colon and always starts with the name of the column. After the name we specify the data type and may add further options. While the data types of nameid and birthday—INTEGER and DATETIME—are self-explaining, the name variables were defined as characters with a maximum length of 100 characters—VARCHAR(100).

Using the options NOT NULL and AUTO_INCREMENT we define some basic constraints. NOT NULL specifies that this column cannot be left empty—we demand that each person included in birthdays has to have a name identifier, a first name and a last name. Should we try to add an observation to the table without all of these pieces of information, the DBMS will refuse to include it in birthdays. The AUTO_INCREMENT parameter for the nameid column adds the option that whenever no name identifier is manually specified when inserting data, the DBMS takes care of that by assigning a unique number. The last line before we close the parentheses and terminate the statement with a semicolon adds a further constraint to the table. With `PRIMARY KEY (nameid)` we define that `nameid` should serve as primary key. The DBMS will prevent the insertion of duplicated values into this column.

Let us add two more tables to our database to add some complexity and to showcase some further concepts. We define the structure of Tables 7.5 and 7.6, where we recorded food preferences and food attributes.

```
> CREATE TABLE foodtypes (
>   foodid INT NOT NULL AUTO_INCREMENT,
>   foodname VARCHAR(100) NOT NULL,
>   healthy INT,
>   kcalp100g float,
>   PRIMARY KEY (foodid)
> );
```

```
> CREATE TABLE foodranking (
> rankid INT NOT NULL AUTO_INCREMENT ,
> foodid INT ,
> nameid INT ,
> rank INT NULL ,
> PRIMARY KEY (rankid) ,
> FOREIGN KEY (foodid) REFERENCES foodtypes (foodid) ON UPDATE CASCADE,
> FOREIGN KEY (nameid) REFERENCES birthdays (nameid) ON UPDATE CASCADE ) ;
```

The creation of `foodtypes` is quite similar to that of `birthdays`. More interesting is the creation of the food preference table, because it relates to data about subjects as well as to information about food—captured in `birthdays` and `foodtypes`. Take a look at the lines starting with `FOREIGN KEY`. First, we choose the column that serves as foreign key, then we define which primary key this column refers to, followed by further options. By specifying `ON UPDATE CASCADE` we choose that whenever the primary key changes, this change is cascaded down to our foreign key column that is changed accordingly.

To change the definition of a table later on, we can make use of the `ALTER TABLE` command. Below you find several examples for adding a column, changing the data type of this column, and dropping it again. **ALTER TABLE**

```
> ALTER TABLE foodtypes ADD COLUMN dummy INT ;
> ALTER TABLE foodtypes MODIFY COLUMN dummy FLOAT ;
> ALTER TABLE foodtypes DROP COLUMN dummy ;
```

To get rid of a table, we can use `DROP TABLE`. **DROP TABLE**

```
> CREATE TABLE dummy (dcolumn INT) ;
> DROP TABLE dummy ;
```

Figure 7.3 SQL example database scheme

7.3.4 Data manipulation language—DML

Now that we have defined some tables in our database, we need to learn how to insert, manipulate, and retrieve data from it. Figure 7.3 provides an overview of the structure of our database—bold column names refer to primary keys while italics denote foreign keys; the arrows show which foreign keys relate to which primary keys.

`INSERT INTO`

The following three SQL statements use the `INSERT INTO` command to fill our tables with data. After selecting the name of the table to fill, we also specify column names—enclosed in parentheses—to specify for which columns data are provided and in which order. If we had not specifed column names, data for all columns would be provided in the same order as in the definition of the table. As each table contains one column that is automatically filled with identification numbers—`nameid`, `foodid`, `rankid`—we do not want to specify this information manually but let the DBMS take care of it. Note that every non-numeric value—text and dates—is enclosed in single quotes`'`.

```
> INSERT INTO birthdays (firstname, lastname, birthday)
> VALUES  ('Peter', 'Pascal', '1991-02-01'),
>         ('Paul',  'Panini', '1992-03-02'),
>         ('Mary',  'Meyer',  '1993-04-03') ;
>
> INSERT INTO foodtypes (foodname, healthy,kcalp100g)
> VALUES ('spaghetti',     0, 0.158),
>        ('hamburger',     0, 0.295),
>        ('fruit salad',   1, 0.043),
>        ('chocolate',     0, 0.546),
>        ('fish fingers',  0, 0.290) ;
>
> INSERT INTO foodranking (nameid, foodid, rank)
> VALUES (1, 1, 1),
>        (1, 2, 2),
>        (2, 3, 1),
>        (3, 4, 1),
>        (3, 5, 2),
>        (3, 2, 3) ;
```

`UPDATE`

To update and delete rows of data, we have to specify for which rows the update or deletion takes place. For this we can make use of the `WHERE` clause. Let us create a new column that captures whether or not the energy of a food type is above 0.2 kcal per 100 g. To achieve this, we tell the DBMS to create a new column and to update the column.[4] In a last step, we delete the column again:

```
> SET SQL_SAFE_UPDATES = 0 ;
> ALTER TABLE foodtypes ADD COLUMN highenergy INT ;
> UPDATE foodtypes SET highenergy=1 WHERE kcalp100g > 0.2 ;
> UPDATE foodtypes SET highenergy=0 WHERE kcalp100g <= 0.2 ;
> ALTER TABLE foodtypes DROP COLUMN highenergy ;
```

DELETE

Let us have another example of deleting data. We first create a row with false data and then drop the row:

```
> INSERT INTO foodtypes (foodname, healthy, kcalp100g)
> VALUES ("Dominic's incredible pancakes", NULL, NULL) ;
> DELETE FROM foodtypes WHERE foodname = "Dominic's incredible pancakes" ;
```

SELECT

Data retrieval works similar to insertion of data and is achieved using the `SELECT` command. After the `SELECT` command we specify the columns we want to retrieve, followed by the keyword `FROM` and the name of the table from which we want to get the data. The following query retrieves all columns of the birthday table:

```
> SELECT * FROM birthdays ;
+--------+-----------+----------+------------+
| nameid | firstname | lastname | birthday   |
+--------+-----------+----------+------------+
|      1 | Peter     | Pascal   | 1991-02-01 |
|      2 | Paul      | Panini   | 1992-03-02 |
|      3 | Mary      | Meyer    | 1993-04-03 |
+--------+-----------+----------+------------+
```

This retrieves only the birthdays:

```
> SELECT birthday FROM birthdays ;
+------------+
| birthday   |
+------------+
| 1991-02-01 |
| 1992-03-02 |
| 1993-04-03 |
+------------+
```

[4]The first line is only relevant for MySQL. By default, MySQL prevents updates that have a `WHERE` clause not referring to a primary key.

Retrieving birthdays and first names:

```
> SELECT firstname, birthday FROM birthdays ;
+-----------+------------+
| firstname | birthday   |
+-----------+------------+
| Peter     | 1991-02-01 |
| Paul      | 1992-03-02 |
| Mary      | 1993-04-03 |
+-----------+------------+
```

JOIN

So far we only retrieved data from a single table but often we need to combine data from multiple tables. Combining data is done with the `JOIN` command—similar to the `merge()` function in R. There are four possible joins:[5]

1. `INNER JOIN` will return a row whenever there is a match in both tables.
2. `LEFT JOIN` will return a row whenever there is a match in the first table.
3. `RIGHT JOIN` will return a row whenever there is a match in the second table.
4. `FULL JOIN` will return a row whenever there is a match in one of the tables.

To show how joins work, let us consider three examples in which data from the birthdays table and the foodranking table are combined. Both tables are related by `nameid`. We will match rows on this identifier, meaning that information from both tables is merged by identical values on `nameid`.

To show the differences in the join statements, let us add a row to the birthdays table with a `nameid` value that is not included in the foodranking table:

```
> INSERT INTO birthdays (nameid,firstname,lastname,birthday)
> VALUES (10,"Donald","Docker","1934-06-09") ;
```

The birthdays table now has one additional row:

```
> SELECT * FROM birthdays ;
+--------+-----------+----------+------------+
| nameid | firstname | lastname | birthday   |
+--------+-----------+----------+------------+
|      1 | Peter     | Pascal   | 1991-02-01 |
|      2 | Paul      | Panini   | 1992-03-02 |
|      3 | Mary      | Meyer    | 1993-04-03 |
|     10 | Donald    | Docker   | 1934-06-09 |
+--------+-----------+----------+------------+
```

[5]Note that support of the different join commands is DBMS dependent. For example, SQLite only supports `INNER JOIN` and `LEFT JOIN` while MySQL has no implementation of `FULL JOIN`.

Recall the food ranking table (Table 7.5). The first JOIN command is an inner join, which needs matching keys in both tables. Therefore, only information related to Peter, Paul, and Mary should show up in the resulting table, because Donald does not have a nameid in both tables:

```
> SELECT birthdays.nameid, firstname, lastname, birthday, foodid, rank
> FROM birthdays
> INNER JOIN foodranking
> ON birthdays.nameid=foodranking.nameid ;
+--------+-----------+----------+------------+--------+------+
| nameid | firstname | lastname | birthday   | foodid | rank |
+--------+-----------+----------+------------+--------+------+
|      1 | Peter     | Pascal   | 1991-02-01 |      1 |    1 |
|      1 | Peter     | Pascal   | 1991-02-01 |      2 |    2 |
|      2 | Paul      | Panini   | 1992-03-02 |      3 |    1 |
|      3 | Mary      | Meyer    | 1993-04-03 |      4 |    1 |
|      3 | Mary      | Meyer    | 1993-04-03 |      5 |    2 |
|      3 | Mary      | Meyer    | 1993-04-03 |      2 |    3 |
+--------+-----------+----------+------------+--------+------+
```

Joins are *de facto* extended SELECT statements. As in an ordinary SELECT statement we first specify the command followed by the names of the columns to be retrieved. Note that the columns to be retrieved can be from both tables. If columns with the same name exist in both tables they should be preceded by the table name to clarify which column we are referring to—for example, birthdays.nameid refers to the name identification column in the birthdays table. The column specification is followed by FROM and the name of the first table. In contrast to ordinary SELECT statements we now specify the join keywords—in this case INNER JOIN—followed by the name of the second table. Using the keyword ON we specify which columns serve as keys for the match.

As expected, Donald does not show up in the resulting table because his id is not included in the foodranking table. Furthermore, the resulting table has a row for each food preference so that information from the birthdays table like name and birthday is duplicated as needed.

```
> SELECT birthdays.nameid, firstname, lastname, birthday, foodid, rank
> FROM birthdays
> LEFT JOIN foodranking
> ON birthdays.nameid=foodranking.nameid ;
+--------+-----------+----------+------------+--------+------+
| nameid | firstname | lastname | birthday   | foodid | rank |
+--------+-----------+----------+------------+--------+------+
|      1 | Peter     | Pascal   | 1991-02-01 |      1 |    1 |
|      1 | Peter     | Pascal   | 1991-02-01 |      2 |    2 |
|      2 | Paul      | Panini   | 1992-03-02 |      3 |    1 |
|      3 | Mary      | Meyer    | 1993-04-03 |      4 |    1 |
|      3 | Mary      | Meyer    | 1993-04-03 |      5 |    2 |
|      3 | Mary      | Meyer    | 1993-04-03 |      2 |    3 |
|     10 | Donald    | Docker   | 1934-06-09 |   NULL | NULL |
+--------+-----------+----------+------------+--------+------+
```

Because `LEFT JOIN` only requires that a key appears in the first—or left—table, Donald Docker is now included in the resulting table, but there is no information on food preference—both columns show `NULL` values for Donald Docker. If we had specified the join the other way around with `foodranking` being the first table and `birthdays` second, Donald would not have been included as his id is not part of `foodranking`.

More than one table can be combined with join statements. To get the individuals' preferences as well as the actual name of the food—we need columns from three tables. We gather this information by extending the `INNER JOIN` of our previous example with another join that specifies that tables `foodranking` and `foodtypes` are related via their `foodid` columns and a request for the `foodname` column:

```
> SELECT firstname, rank, foodname FROM birthdays
> INNER JOIN foodranking
> ON birthdays.nameid = foodranking.nameid
> INNER JOIN foodtypes
> ON foodranking.foodid = foodtypes.foodid ;
+-----------+------+--------------+
| firstname | rank | foodname     |
+-----------+------+--------------+
| Peter     |    1 | spaghetti    |
| Peter     |    2 | hamburger    |
| Mary      |    3 | hamburger    |
| Paul      |    1 | fruit salad  |
| Mary      |    1 | chocolate    |
| Mary      |    2 | fish fingers |
+-----------+------+--------------+
```

Let us clean up before moving to the next section by dropping the data on Donald from the database:

```
> DELETE FROM birthdays WHERE firstname = 'Donald' ;
```

7.3.5 Clauses

We have already used the `WHERE` clause in SQL statements to restrict data manipulations to certain rows, but we have neither treated the clause thoroughly nor have we mentioned that SQL also has other clauses.

WHERE and operators

Let us begin by extending our knowledge of the `WHERE` clause. We already know that it restricts data manipulations and retrievals to specific rows. Restrictions are specified in the form of `column_name operator value`, where operator defines the type of comparison and value, the content of the comparison. Possible operators are `=` and `!=` for equality/inequality, `<`, `<=`, `>`, `>=` for smaller (or equal) and greater (or equal) values, `LIKE` for basic matching of text patterns and `IN` to specify a set of acceptable values.

We can also use `AND` and `OR` to build more complex restrictions and even nest restrictions by using parentheses. Let us start with a composite `WHERE` clause with two conditions—see the code snippet below. This statement retrieves data from all three tables but the resulting set of rows is restricted by the `WHERE` clause to those lines that have a food preference rank equal or larger than `2` and where the `firstname` matches `'Mary'`.

```
> SELECT firstname, foodname, rank FROM birthdays
> INNER JOIN foodranking ON birthdays.nameid = foodranking.nameid
> INNER JOIN foodtypes ON foodranking.foodid = foodtypes.foodid
> WHERE rank >= 2 AND firstname = 'Mary' ;
+-----------+--------------+------+
| firstname | foodname     | rank |
+-----------+--------------+------+
| Mary      | hamburger    |    3 |
| Mary      | fish fingers |    2 |
+-----------+--------------+------+
```

The next statement has a nested composite `WHERE` clause and uses alphabetical sorting of text (`firstname < 'Peter'`). While `firstname` should never match `'Mary'`, the other part of the clause states that either `healthy` should equal to `1` or `firstname` should be a string that precedes Peter alphabetically.

```
> SELECT firstname, foodname, healthy FROM birthdays
> INNER JOIN foodranking ON birthdays.nameid = foodranking.nameid
> INNER JOIN foodtypes ON foodranking.foodid = foodtypes.foodid
> WHERE (healthy = 1 OR firstname < 'Peter') AND firstname != 'Mary' ;
+-----------+-------------+---------+
| firstname | foodname    | healthy |
+-----------+-------------+---------+
| Paul      | fruit salad |       1 |
+-----------+-------------+---------+
```

The following statement is an example of using `IN`—the value of `firstname` should match one of three names:

```
> SELECT firstname, lastname FROM birthdays
> WHERE firstname IN ('Peter','Paul','Karl') ;
+-----------+----------+
| firstname | lastname |
+-----------+----------+
| Peter     | Pascal   |
| Paul      | Panini   |
+-----------+----------+
```

The last statement showcases the usage of `LIKE`—`%` is a wildcard for any number of any character and _ is a wildcard for any one character. The statement requires that a row is part of the resulting table if either `firstname` contains `er` at the end of the string preceded by any number of characters or that `lastname` contains an `e` that is preceded by any number of characters and followed by exactly one character.

```
> SELECT firstname, lastname FROM birthdays
> WHERE firstname LIKE '%er' OR lastname LIKE '%e_';
+-----------+----------+
| firstname | lastname |
+-----------+----------+
| Peter     | Pascal   |
| Mary      | Meyer    |
+-----------+----------+
```

ORDER BY

A second clause is the `ORDER BY` clause, which enables us to order results by column values. Below you find several examples that order the results of a data retrieval. The standard for sorting is to do it in ascending order.

```
> SELECT firstname FROM birthdays ORDER BY firstname ;
+-----------+
| firstname |
+-----------+
| Mary      |
| Paul      |
| Peter     |
+-----------+
```

To revert this behavior, we can add the keyword `DESC`. We can also specify more than one column to define the sort order and choose for every column whether it should be used in ascending or descending order.

```
> SELECT firstname FROM birthdays
> ORDER BY birthday DESC, firstname ASC ;
+-----------+
| firstname |
+-----------+
| Mary      |
| Paul      |
| Peter     |
+-----------+
```

GROUP BY

The `GROUP BY` clause allows aggregating values. The type of aggregation depends on the specific aggregation function that we use.[6] In the following example the use of `GROUP`

[6] Aggregation functions are, for example, averages (`AVG`), counts (`COUNT`), first values (`FIRST`), maxima (`MAX`), and sums (`SUM`).

BY is exemplified with the COUNT aggregation function, which returns a count of how many food preferences each person has—the result is a table with a row for each unique nameid from the birthdays table and a count of how many times a food preference was recorded.

```
> SELECT firstname, COUNT(rank) FROM birthdays
> INNER JOIN foodranking ON birthdays.nameid = foodranking.nameid
> INNER JOIN foodtypes ON foodranking.foodid = foodtypes.foodid
> GROUP BY birthdays.nameid ;
+-----------+-------------+
| firstname | COUNT(rank) |
+-----------+-------------+
| Peter     |           2 |
| Paul      |           1 |
| Mary      |           3 |
+-----------+-------------+
```

HAVING

To filter the aggregation table resulting from a GROUP BY clause, a special clause is needed—a WHERE clause can be used in combination with GROUP BY, but this excludes rows only before aggregation not after. Using HAVING we can filter the aggregation results.

```
> SELECT firstname, COUNT(rank) FROM birthdays
> INNER JOIN foodranking ON birthdays.nameid = foodranking.nameid
> INNER JOIN foodtypes ON foodranking.foodid = foodtypes.foodid
> GROUP BY birthdays.nameid
> HAVING COUNT(rank) > 1 ;
+-----------+-------------+
| firstname | COUNT(rank) |
+-----------+-------------+
| Peter     |           2 |
| Mary      |           3 |
+-----------+-------------+
```

7.3.6 Transaction control language—TCL

START TRANSACTION and COMMIT

SQL statements are usually executed after a statement is sent to the DBMS and made permanent unless some error occurs. This standard behavior can be modified by explicitly starting a transacting with START TRANSACTION. Using this statement a save point is created. Instead of executing each SQL statement immediately and making them permanent, each statement is executed temporarily until it is explicitly committed by the user with the COMMIT command. If an error occurs before COMMIT was specified all changes until the last save point are reversed.

ROLLBACK

We can achieve the same behavior by asking the DBMS to ROLLBACK until the last save point. Below you find an example where some data are added and then the database is reversed to the status when the save point was set.

```
> START TRANSACTION ;
> INSERT INTO birthdays (firstname, lastname)
> VALUES ('Simon', 'Sorcerer') ;
> SELECT firstname, lastname FROM birthdays ;
+-----------+-----------+
| firstname | lastname  |
+-----------+-----------+
| Peter     | Pascal    |
| Paul      | Panini    |
| Mary      | Meyer     |
| Simon     | Sorcerer |
+-----------+-----------+
> ROLLBACK ;
> SELECT firstname, lastname FROM birthdays ;
+-----------+----------+
| firstname | lastname |
+-----------+----------+
| Peter     | Pascal   |
| Paul      | Panini   |
| Mary      | Meyer    |
+-----------+----------+
```

7.4 Databases in action

7.4.1 R packages to manage databases

R has several packages to connect to DBMS: One way is to use packages that rely on the DBI package (R Special Interest Group on Databases 2013) like RMySQL (James and DebRoy 2013), ROracle (Denis Mukhin and Luciani 2013), RPostgreSQL (Conway et al. 2013) and RSQLite (James and DebRoy 2013) to establish a "native" connection to a specific DBMS. While the DBI package defines virtual functions, the database-specific packages implement these functions in database-specific ways. The added value of this approach is that while there is a common set of functions that are expected to work the same way, different package authors can concentrate on developing and maintaining solutions for one type of database only.

Another approach to work with DBMS via R is to rely on RODBC (Ripley and Lapsley 2013). This package uses open database connectivity (ODBC) drivers as an indirect way to connect to DBMS and requires that the user installs and configures the necessary driver before using it in R. ODBC drivers are available across platforms and for a wide variety of DBMS. They even exist for data storage formats that are no databases at all, like CSV or XLS/XLSX. The package also delivers a general approach to manage different types of databases with the same set of functions. On the downside, this approach depends on whether ODBC drivers are available for the DBMS type to be used in combination with the platform R is working on.

Which package to use is essentially a matter of taste and how difficult it is to get the package or driver running—at the moment and to the authors' best knowledge RSQLite is the only package that works completely out of the box across multiple platforms. All other packages need driver installation and/or package compilation.

7.4.2 Speaking R-SQL via DBI-based packages

As the DBI package defines a common framework for working with databases from within R, all database packages that rely on this framework work the same way, regardless of which particular DBMS we establish a connection to. To show how things work for DBI-based packages, we will make use of RSQLite. Let us load the birthdays database, which has been bundled as an SQLite file and execute a simple `SELECT` statement:

```
R> # loading package
R> library(RSQLite)

R> # establish connection
R> sqlite <- dbDriver("SQLite")
R> con <- dbConnect(sqlite, "birthdays.db")

R> # 'plain' SQL
R> sql <- "SELECT * FROM birthdays"
R> res <- dbGetQuery(con, sql)
R> res
  nameid firstname lastname   birthday
1      1     Peter   Pascal 1991-02-01
2      2      Paul   Panini 1992-03-02
3      3      Mary    Meyer 1993-04-03

R> res <- dbSendQuery(con, sql)
R> fetch(res)
  nameid firstname lastname   birthday
1      1     Peter   Pascal 1991-02-01
2      2      Paul   Panini 1992-03-02
3      3      Mary    Meyer 1993-04-03
```

Using these functions we are able to perform basic database operations from within R. Let us go through the code line by line. First we load the RSQLite package so that R knows how to handle SQLite databases. Next, we build up a connection to the database by first defining the driver and then using the driver in the actual connection. Because our SQLite database has no password, we do not have to specify much except the database driver and the location of the database. Now we can query our database. We have two functions to do so: `dbGetQuery()` and `dbSendQuery()`. Both functions ask the DBMS to execute a single query, but differ in how they handle the results returned by the DBMS. The first one fetches all results and converts them to a data frame, while the second one will not fetch any results unless we explicitly ask R to do so with the `fetch()` function.

Because we can send any SQL query that is supported by the specific DBMS, these four functions suffice to fully control databases from within R. Nonetheless, there are several other functions provided by DBI-based packages. These functions do not add further features but help to make communication between R and DBMS more convenient. There are, for example, functions for getting an overview of the database properties—`dbGetInfo()`—and the tables that are provided—`dbListTables()`:

```
R> # general information
R> dbGetInfo(con)[2]
$serverVersion
[1] "3.7.17"

R> # listing tables
R> dbListTables(con)
[1] "birthdays"        "foodranking"      "foodtypes"        "sqlite_sequence"
```

There are also functions for reading, writing, and removing tables, which are as convenient as they are self-explanatory: `dbReadTable()`, `dbWriteTable()`, `dbExistsTable()`, and `dbRemoveTable()`.

```
R> # reading tables
R> res <- dbReadTable(con, "birthdays")
R> res
 nameid firstname lastname   birthday
1      1     Peter   Pascal 1991-02-01
2      2      Paul   Panini 1992-03-02
3      3      Mary    Meyer 1993-04-03

R> # writing tables
R> dbWriteTable(con, "test", res)
[1] TRUE

R> # table exists?
R> dbExistsTable(con, "test")
[1] TRUE

R> # remove table
R> dbRemoveTable(con, "test")
[1] TRUE
```

To check the data type an R object would be assigned if stored in a database, we use `dbDataType()`:

```
R> # checking data type
R> dbDataType(con, res$nameid)
[1] "INTEGER"
R> dbDataType(con, res$firstname)
[1] "TEXT"
R> dbDataType(con, res$birthday)
[1] "TEXT"
```

We can also start, revert, and commit transactions as well as close a connection to a DBMS:

```
R> # transaction management
R> dbBeginTransaction(con)
[1] TRUE
R> dbRollback(con)
```

```
[1] TRUE
R> dbBeginTransaction(con)
[1] TRUE
R> dbCommit(con)
[1] TRUE
R> # closing connection
R> dbDisconnect(con)
[1] TRUE
```

7.4.3 Speaking R-SQL via RODBC

Communicating with databases by relying on the RODBC package is quite similar to the DBI-based packages. There are functions that forward SQL statements to the DBMS and convenience functions that do not require the user to specify SQL statements.[7]

Let us start by establishing a connection to our database and passing a simple `SELECT *` statement to read all lines of the birthdays table:

```
R> # reading package
R> require(RODBC)

R> # establishing connection
R> con <- odbcConnect("db1")

R> # 'plain' SQL
R> sql <- "SELECT * FROM birthdays ;"
R> res <- sqlQuery(con, sql)
R> res
 nameid firstname lastname   birthday
1      1     Peter   Pascal 1991-02-01
2      2      Paul   Panini 1992-03-02
3      3      Mary    Meyer 1993-04-03
```

The code to establish a connection and pass the SQL statement to the DBMS is quite similar to what we have seen before. One difference is that we do not have to specify any driver as the driver and all other connection information have already been specified in the ODBC manager so that we only have to refer to the name we gave this particular connection in the ODBC manager.

Besides the direct execution of SQL statements, there are numerous convenience functions similar to those found in the DBI-based packages. To get general information on the connection and the drivers used or to list all tables in the database, we can use `odbcGetInfo()` and `sqlTables()`:

```
R> # general information
R> odbcGetInfo(con)[3]
Driver_ODBC_Ver
      "03.51"
```

[7]The example works with MySQL drivers. They are available at http://dev.mysql.com/downloads/connector/odbc/. MySQL ODBC drivers are reliable and available for a whole range of platforms. If you have followed the examples in the last section with your own MySQL database, you can now connect to it to follow the example.

```
R> # listing tables
R> sqlTables(con)[, 3:5]
   TABLE_NAME TABLE_TYPE REMARKS
1   birthdays      TABLE
2 foodranking      TABLE
3   foodtypes      TABLE
```

To get an overview of the ODBC driver connections that are currently specified in our ODBC manager, we can use `odbcDataSources()`. The function reveals that `db1` to which we are connected is based on MySQL drivers version 5.2:

```
R> odbcDataSources()
                          db1
"MySQL ODBC 5.2 ANSI Driver"
```

We can also ask for whole tables without specifying the SQL statement by a simple call to `sqlFetch()`:

```
R> # 'plain' SQL
R> res <- sqlFetch(con, "birthdays")
R> res
  nameid firstname lastname   birthday
1      1     Peter   Pascal 1991-02-01
2      2      Paul   Panini 1992-03-02
3      3      Mary    Meyer 1993-04-03
```

Similarly, we can write R data frames to SQL tables with convenience functions. We can also empty tables or delete them altogether:

```
R> # writing tables
R> test <- data.frame(x = 1:3, y = letters[7:9])
R> sqlSave(con, test, "test")
R> sqlFetch(con, "test")
  x y
1 1 g
2 2 h
3 3 i

R> # empty table
R> sqlClear(con, "test")
R> sqlFetch(con, "test")
[1] x y
<0 rows> (or 0-length row.names)

R> # drop table
R> sqlDrop(con, "test")
```

Summary

In this chapter we learned about databases, SQL, and several R packages that enable us to connect to databases and to access the data stored in them. Simply put, relational databases are collections of tables that are related to one another by keys. Although R is capable of handling data, databases offer solutions to certain data management problems that are best dealt with in a specific environment. SQL is the *lingua franca* for communication between the user and a wide range of database management systems. While SQL allows us to define what should be done, it is in fact the DBMS that manages how this is achieved in a reliable manner. As a multipurpose language we can use SQL to manage user rights, define data structures, import, manipulate, and retrieve data as well as to control transactions. We have seen that R is capable of communicating with a variety of databases and provides additional convenience functions. As DBMS were designed for reliable and efficient handling of data they might be solutions to limited RAM size, multipurpose usages of data, multiuser access to data, complex data storage, and remote access to data.

Further reading

Relational databases and SQL are part of the web technology community and are therefore treated in hundreds of forums, blogs, and manuals. Therefore, you can easily find a solution to most problems by typing your question into any ordinary search engine. To learn the full spectrum of options for a specific DBMS, you might be better advised to turn to a comprehensive treatment of the subject. For an introduction to MySQL we recommend Beaulieu (2009). Those who like it a little bit more fundamental might find the *SQL Bible* (Kriegel and Trukhnov 2008) or *Relational Database Design and Implementation* (Harrington 2009) helpful sources. Last but not least the *SQL Pocket Guide* (Gennick 2011) is a gentle pocket reference that fits in every bookshelf.

Problems

The following problems are built around two—more or less—real-life databases, one on Pokemon characters, the other on data about elections, governments, and parties. The Pokemon data was gathered and provided by Francisco S. Velazquez. We extracted some of the tables and provide them as CSV files along with supplementary material for this chapter. The complete database is available at https://github.com/kikin81/pokemon-sqlite. The *ParlGov* database is provided by Döring (2013). It combines data on "elections, parties, and governments for all EU and most OECD members from 1945 until today" gathered from multiple sources. More information is available at http://parlgov.org. Downloading the whole database will be part of the exercise.

Pokemon problems

1. Load the RSQLite package and create a new RSQLite database called *pokemon.sqlite*.

2. Use `read.csv2()` to read *pokemon.csv*, *pokemon_species.csv*, *pokemon_stats.csv*, *pokemon_types.csv*, *stats.csv*, *type_efficacy.csv*, and *types.csv* into R and write the tables to *pokemon.sqlite*. Have a look at *PokemonReadme.txt* to learn about the tables you imported.

3. Use functions from DBI/RSQLite to read the tables that you stored in the database back into R and save them in objects named: `pokemon`, `pokemon_species`, `pokemon_stats`, `pokemon_types`, `stats`, `type_efficacy`, and `types`.

4. Build a query that `SELECT`s those pokemon from table *pokemon* that are heavier than 4000. Next, build a `SELECT` query that `JOIN`s tables *pokemon* and *pokemon_species*.

5. Combining the previous SQL queries, build a query that `JOIN`s both tables and restricts the results to Pokemon that are heavier than 4000.

6. Build a query that `SELECT`s all Pokemon names from table *pokemon_species* that have *Nido* as part of their name.

7. Fetching names.
   (a) Build a query that `SELECT`s Pokemon names.
   (b) Send the query to the database using `dbSendQuery()` and save the result in an object.
   (c) Use `fetch()` three times in a row, each time retrieving another set of five names.
   (d) Use `dbClearResult()` to clean up afterwards.

8. Creating views.
   (a) Create a `VIEW` called *pokeview* …
   (b) … that `JOIN`s table *pokemon* with table *pokemon_species*,
   (c) … and contains the following information: height and weight, species identifier, Pokemon id from which the Pokemon evolves, the id of the evolution chain, and ids for Pokemon and species.
   (d) Create a `VIEW` called *typeview* …
   (e) … that `JOIN`s *pokemon_types* and *types* …
   (f) … and contains the following information: slot of the type, identifier of the type, and ids for Pokemon, damage class, and type.
   (g) Create a `VIEW` called *statsview* …
   (h) … that `JOIN`s *pokemon_stats* and *stats* …
   (i) … and contains the following information: identifier of the statistic, base value of the statistics, and ids for Pokemon, statistics, and damage class.

9. Using the views you created, which Pokemon are of type dragon? Which Pokemon has most health points, which has the best attack, defense, and speed?

ParlGov problems

10. Use `download.file()` with `mode="wb"` to save the following resource http://parlgov.org/stable/static/data/parlgov-stable.db as *parlgov.sqlite* and establish a connection.

11. Get a list of all tables in the database. According to *info_data_source*, which external data sources were used for the database?

12. Figure out for which countries the database offers data.

13. Which time span is covered by the election table?

14. How many early elections were there in Spain, the United Kingdom, and Switzerland?

15. Creating views.
    (a) `CREATE` a `VIEW` named *edata* …
    (b) … that `JOIN`s table *election_result* …
    (c) … with tables *election*, *country*, and *party* …

(d) ... so that the view contains the following information: country name, date of the election, the abbreviated party name, party name in English, seats to be won in total, seats won by party, vote share won by the party, as well as ids for country, election, election results, and party.
(e) Make sure the `VIEW` is restricted to elections of type 13 (elections to parliament).
(f) Read the data of the view into R and save it in an object.
(g) Add a variable storing the seat share.
(h) Plot vote shares versus seat shares. Use `text()` to add the name of the country if vote share and seat share differ by more than 20 percentage points.

16. Find answers to the following questions in the database.
(a) Which country had a cabinet lead by Lojze Peterle?
(b) Which parties were part of that government?
(c) What were their vote shares in the election?

17. More `SELECT` queries.
(a) Build a query that `SELECT`s column *tbl_name* and *type* from table *sqlite_master*.
(b) Build a query that `SELECT`s column *sql* from table *sqlite_master* `WHERE` column *tbl_name* equals *edata*. Save the result in an object and use `cat()` to display the contents of the object.
(c) Do the same for *tbl_name* equal to *view_election*.

8

Regular expressions and essential string functions

The Web consists predominantly of unstructured text. One of the central tasks in web scraping is to collect the relevant information for our research problem from heaps of textual data. Within the unstructured text we are often interested in systematic information—especially when we want to analyze the data using quantitative methods. Systematic structures can be numbers or recurrent names like countries or addresses. We usually proceed in three steps. First we gather the unstructured text, second we determine the recurring patterns behind the information we are looking for, and third we apply these patterns to the unstructured text to extract the information. This chapter will focus on the last two steps. Consider HTML documents from the previous chapters as an example. In principle, they are nothing but collections of text. Our goal is always to identify and extract those parts of the document that contain the relevant information. Ideally we can do so using XPath—but sometimes the crucial information is hidden within atomic values. In some settings, relevant information might be scattered across an HTML document, rendering approaches that exploit the document structure useless. In this chapter we introduce a powerful tool that helps retrieve data in such settings—regular expressions. Regular expressions provide us with a syntax for systematically accessing patterns in text.

A short example Consider the following short example. Imagine we have collected a string of names and corresponding phone numbers from fictional characters of the "*The Simpsons*" TV series. Our task is to extract the names and numbers and to put them into a data frame.

```
R> raw.data <- "555-1239Moe Szyslak(636) 555-0113Burns, C. Montgomery555
-6542Rev. Timothy Lovejoy555 8904Ned Flanders636-555-3226Simpson,
Homer5553642Dr. Julius Hibbert"
```

Automated Data Collection with R: A Practical Guide to Web Scraping and Text Mining, First Edition.
Simon Munzert, Christian Rubba, Peter Meißner and Dominic Nyhuis.

The first thing we notice is how the names and numbers come in all sorts of formats. Some numbers include area codes, some contain dashes, others even parentheses. Yet, despite these differences we also notice the similarities between all the phone numbers and the names. Most importantly, the numbers all contain digits while all the names contain alphabetic characters. We can make use of this knowledge by writing two regular expressions that will extract only the information that we are interested in. Do not worry about the details of the functions at this point. They simply serve to illustrate the task that we tackle in this chapter. We will learn the various elements the queries are made up of and also how they can be applied in different contexts to extract information and get it into a structured format. We will return to the example in Section 8.1.3.

```
R> library(stringr)

R> name <- unlist(str_extract_all(raw.data, "[[:alpha:]., ]{2,}"))
R> name
[1] "Moe Szyslak"       "Burns, C. Montgomery" "Rev. Timothy Lovejoy"
[4] "Ned Flanders"      "Simpson, Homer"       "Dr. Julius Hibbert"

R> phone <- unlist(str_extract_all(raw.data, "\\(?(\\d{3})?\\)?
(-| )?\\d{3}(-| )?\\d{4}"))
R> phone
[1] "555-1239"       "(636) 555-0113" "555-6542"       "555 8904"
[5] "636-555-3226"   "5553642"
```

We can input the results into a data frame:

```
R> data.frame(name = name, phone = phone)
                  name          phone
1          Moe Szyslak       555-1239
2 Burns, C. Montgomery (636) 555-0113
3 Rev. Timothy Lovejoy       555-6542
4         Ned Flanders       555 8904
5       Simpson, Homer   636-555-3226
6   Dr. Julius Hibbert        5553642
```

Although R offers the main functions necessary to accomplish such tasks, R was not designed with a focus on string manipulation. Therefore, relevant functions sometimes lack coherence. As the importance of text mining and natural language processing in particular has increased in recent years, several packages have been developed to facilitate text manipulation in R. In the following sections—and throughout the remainder of this volume—we rely predominantly on the stringr package, as it provides most of the string manipulation capability we require and it enforces a more consistent coding behavior (Wickham 2010).

The following section introduces regular expressions as implemented in R. Section 8.2 provides an overview on how string manipulation can be used in practice. This is done by presenting commands that are available in the stringr package. If you have previously worked with regular expressions, you can skip Section 8.1 without much loss. Section 8.3 concludes with some aspects of character encodings—an important concept in web scraping.

8.1 Regular expressions

Regular expressions are generalizable text patterns for searching and manipulating text data. Strictly speaking, they are not so much a tool as they are a convention on how to query strings across a wide range of functions. In this section, we will introduce the basic building blocks of extended regular expressions as implemented in R. The following string will serve as a running example:

```
R> example.obj <- "1. A small sentence. - 2. Another tiny sentence."
```

8.1.1 Exact character matching

At the most basic level characters match characters—even in regular expressions. Thus, extracting a substring of a string will yield itself if present:

```
R> str_extract(example.obj, "small")
[1] "small"
```

Otherwise, the function would return a missing value:

```
R> str_extract(example.obj, "banana")
[1] NA
```

The function we use here and in the remainder of this section is `str_extract()` from the stringr package, which we assume is loaded in all subsequent examples. It is defined as `str_extract(string, pattern)` such that we first input the string that is to be operated upon and second the expression we are looking for. Note that this differs from most base functions, like `grep()` or `grepl()`, where the regular expression is typically input first.[1] The function will return the first instance of a match to the regular expression in a given string. We can also ask R to extract *every* match by calling the function `str_extract_all()`:

```
R> unlist(str_extract_all(example.obj, "sentence"))
[1] "sentence" "sentence"
```

The stringr package offers both `str_`*`whatever`*`()` and `str_`*`whatever`*`_all()` in many instances. The former addresses the first instance of a matching string while the latter accesses all instances. The syntax of all these functions is such that the character vector in question is the first element, the regular expression the second, and all possible additional values come after that. The functions' consistency is the main reason why we prefer to use the stringr package by Hadley Wickham (2010). We introduce the package in more detail in Section 8.2. See Table 8.5 for an overview of the counterparts of the stringr functions in base R.

As `str_extract_all()` is ordinarily called on multiple strings, the results are returned as a list, with each list element providing the results for one string. Our input string in the call above is a character vector of length one; hence, the function returns a list of length one, which we `unlist()` for convenience of exposition. Compare this to the behavior of the function when we call it upon multiple strings at the same time. We create a vector containing

[1]See also Table 8.5 for a comparison between base R and stringr string manipulation functions.

the strings `text`, `manipulation`, and `basics`. We use the function `str_extract_all()` to extract all instances of the pattern `a`:

```
R> out <- str_extract_all(c("text", "manipulation", "basics"), "a")
R> out
[[1]]
character(0)

[[2]]
[1] "a" "a"

[[3]]
[1] "a"
```

The function returns a list of the same length as our input vector—three—where each element in the list contains the result for one string. As there is no `a` in the first string, the first element is an empty character vector. String two contains two `a`s, string three one occurrence.

By default, character matching is case sensitive. Thus, capital letters in regular expressions are different from lowercase letters.

```
R> str_extract(example.obj, "small")
[1] "small"
```

`small` is contained in the example string while `SMALL` is not.

```
R> str_extract(example.obj, "SMALL")
[1] NA
```

Consequently, the function extracts no matching value. We can change this behavior by enclosing a string with `ignore.case()`.[2]

```
R> str_extract(example.obj, ignore.case("SMALL"))
[1] "small"
```

We are not limited to using regular expressions on words. A string is simply a sequence of characters. Hence, we can just as well match particles of words ...

```
R> unlist(str_extract_all(example.obj, "en"))
[1] "en" "en" "en" "en"
```

... or mixtures of alphabetic characters and blank spaces.

```
R> str_extract(example.obj, "mall sent")
[1] "mall sent"
```

Matching beginnings and ends

Searching for the pattern `en` in the example string returns every instance of the pattern, that is, both occurrences in the word `sentence`, which is contained twice in the example object. Sometimes we do not simply care about finding a match anywhere in a string but are

[2] This behavior is a property of the stringr package. For case-insensitive matching in base functions, set the `ignore.case` argument to `TRUE`. Incidentally, if you have never worked with strings before, `tolower()` and `toupper()` will convert your string to lower/upper case.

concerned about the specific location within a string. There are two simple additions we can make to our regular expression to specify locations. The caret symbol (^) at the beginning of a regular expression marks the beginning of a string—$ at the end marks the end.[3] Thus, extracting 2 from our running example will return a 2.

```
R> str_extract(example.obj, "2")
[1] "2"
```

Extracting a 2 from the beginning of the string, however, fails.

```
R> str_extract(example.obj, "^2")
[1] NA
```

Similarly, the $ sign signals the end of a string, such that …

```
R> unlist(str_extract_all(example.obj, "sentence$"))
character(0)
```

The pipe operator

… returns no matches as our example string ends in a period character and not in the word sentence. Another powerful addition to our regular expressions toolkit is the pipe, displayed as |. This character is treated as an OR operator such that the function returns all matches to the expressions before and after the pipe.

```
R> unlist(str_extract_all(example.obj, "tiny|sentence"))
[1] "sentence" "tiny"     "sentence"
```

8.1.2 Generalizing regular expressions

Up to this point, we have only matched fixed expressions. But the power of regular expressions stems from the possibility to write more flexible, generalized search queries. The most general among them is the period character. It matches any character.

```
R> str_extract(example.obj, "sm.ll")
[1] "small"
```

Another powerful generalization in regular expressions are character classes, which are enclosed in brackets—[]. A character class means that *any* of the characters within the brackets will be matched.

```
R> str_extract(example.obj, "sm[abc]ll")
[1] "small"
```

The above code extracts the word small as the character a is part of the character class [abc]. A different way to specify the elements of a character class is to employ ranges of characters, using a dash -.

```
R> str_extract(example.obj, "sm[a-p]ll")
[1] "small"
```

[3]Note that inside a character class a caret has a different meaning (see p. 202).

Table 8.1 Selected predefined character classes in R regular expressions

`[:digit:]`	Digits: 0 1 2 3 4 5 6 7 8 9
`[:lower:]`	Lowercase characters: a–z
`[:upper:]`	Uppercase characters: A–Z
`[:alpha:]`	Alphabetic characters: a–z and A–Z
`[:alnum:]`	Digits and alphabetic characters
`[:punct:]`	Punctuation characters: . , ; etc.
`[:graph:]`	Graphical characters: `[:alnum:]` and `[:punct:]`
`[:blank:]`	Blank characters: Space and tab
`[:space:]`	Space characters: Space, tab, newline, and other space characters
`[:print:]`	Printable characters: `[:alnum:]`, `[:punct:]` and `[:space:]`

Source: Adapted from http://stat.ethz.ch/R-manual/R-patched/library/base/html/regex.html

In this case, any characters from `a` to `p` are valid matches. Apart from alphabetic characters and digits, we can also include punctuation and spaces in regular expressions. Accordingly, they can be part of a character class. For example, the character class `[uvw. ]` matches the letters `u`, `v` and `w` as well as a period and a blank space. Applying this to our running example (Recall: `"1. A small sentence. - 2. Another tiny sentence."`) yields all of its constituent periods and spaces but neither `u`, `v`, or `w` as there are none in the object. Note that the period character in the character class loses its special meaning. Inside a character class, a dot only matches a literal dot.

```
R> unlist(str_extract_all(example.obj, "[uvw. ]"))
[1] "." " " " " " " " " "." " " " " " " "." " " " " " " " " "."
```

Character classes

So far, we have manually specified character classes. However, there are some typical collections of characters that we need to match in a body of text. For example, we are often interested in finding all alphabetic characters in a given text. This can be accomplished with the character class `[a-zA-Z]`, that is, all letters from `a` to `z` as well as all letters from `A` to `Z`. For convenience, a number of common character classes have been predefined in R. Table 8.1 provides an overview of selected predefined classes.

In order to use the predefined classes, we have to enclose them in brackets. Otherwise, R assumes that we are specifying a character class consisting of the constituent characters. Say we are interested in extracting all the punctuation characters in our example. The correct expression is

```
R> unlist(str_extract_all(example.obj, "[[:punct:]]"))
[1] "." "." "-" "." "."
```

Notice how this differs from

```
R> unlist(str_extract_all(example.obj, "[:punct:]"))
[1] "n" "t" "n" "c" "n" "t" "t" "n" "n" "t" "n" "c"
```

Not enclosing the character class returns all the `:`, `p`, `u`, `n`, `c`, and `t` in our running example. Note that the duplicate `:` does not throw off R. A redundant inclusion of a character in a character class will only match each instance once.

```
R> unlist(str_extract_all(example.obj, "[AAAAAA]"))
[1] "A" "A"
```

Furthermore, while `[A-Za-z]` is almost identical to `[:alpha:]`, the former disregards special characters, such that …

```
R> str_extract("François Hollande", "Fran[a-z]ois")
[1] NA
```

… returns no matches, while …

```
R> str_extract("François Hollande", "Fran[[:alpha:]]ois")
[1] "François"
```

… does. The predefined character classes will cover many requests we might like to make but in case they do not, we can even extend a predefined character class by adding elements to it.

```
R> unlist(str_extract_all(example.obj, "[[:punct:]ABC]"))
[1] "." "A" "." "-" "." "A" "."
```

In this case, we extract all punctuation characters along with the capital letters `A`, `B`, and `C`. Incidentally, making use of the range operator we introduced above, this extended character class could be rewritten as `[[:punct:]A-C]`. Another nifty use of character classes is to *invert* their meanings by adding a caret (^) at the beginning of a character class. Doing so, the function will match everything *except* the contents of the character class.

```
R> unlist(str_extract_all(example.obj, "[^[:alnum:]]"))
[1] "." " " " " " " "." " " "-" " " "." " " " " " " "."
```

Quantifiers

Accordingly, in our case every non-alphanumeric character yields every blank space and punctuation character. To recap, we have learned that every digit and character matches itself in a regular expression, a period matches any character, and a character class will match any of its constituent characters. However, we are still missing the option to use quantification in our expressions. Say, we would like to extract a sequence starting with an `s`, ending with a `l`, and any three alphabetic characters in between from our running example. With the tools we have learned so far, our only option is to write an expression like `s[[:alpha:]][[:alpha:]][[:alpha:]]l`. Recall that we cannot use the `.` character as this would match any character, including blank spaces and punctuation.

```
R> str_extract(example.obj, "s[[:alpha:]][[:alpha:]][[:alpha:]]l")
[1] "small"
```

Writing our regular expressions in this manner not only quickly becomes difficult to read and understand, but it is also inefficient to write and more prone to errors. To avoid this we can add quantifiers to characters. For example, a number in {} after a character signals a fixed number of repetitions of this character. Using this quantifier, a sequence such as `aaaa` could be shortened to read `a{4}`. In our case, we thus write …

```
R> str_extract(example.obj, "s[[:alpha:]]{3}l")
[1] "small"
```

Table 8.2 Quantifiers in R regular expressions

`?`	The preceding item is optional and will be matched at most once
`*`	The preceding item will be matched zero or more times
`+`	The preceding item will be matched one or more times
`{n}`	The preceding item is matched exactly *n* times
`{n,}`	The preceding item is matched *n* or more times
`{n,m}`	The preceding item is matched at least *n* times, but not more than *m* times

Source: Adapted from http://stat.ethz.ch/R-manual/R-patched/library/base/html/regex.html

... where `[[:alpha:]]{3}` matches any three alphabetic characters. Table 8.2 provides an overview of the available quantifiers in R. A common quantification operator is the + sign, which signals that the preceding item has to be matched one or more times. Using the `.` as any character we could thus write the following in order to extract a sequence that runs from an `A` to `sentence` with any number—greater than zero—of any characters in between.

```
R> str_extract(example.obj, "A.+sentence")
[1] "A small sentence. - 2. Another tiny sentence"
```

Greedy quantification and how to avoid it

R applies greedy quantification. This means that the program tries to extract the greatest possible sequence of the preceding character. As the `.` matches any character, the function returns the greatest possible sequence of any characters before a sequence of `sentence`. We can change this behavior by adding a `?` to the expression in order to signal that we are only looking for the shortest possible sequence of any characters before a sequence of `sentence`. The `?` means that the preceding item is optional and will be matched at most once (see again Table 8.2).

```
R> str_extract(example.obj, "A.+?sentence")
[1] "A small sentence"
```

We are not restricted to applying quantifiers to single characters. In order to apply a quantifier to a group of characters, we enclose them in parentheses.

```
R> unlist(str_extract_all(example.obj, "(.en){1,5}"))
[1] "senten" "senten"
```

In this case, we are asking the function to return a sequence of characters where the first character can be any character and the second and third characters have to be an `e` and an `n`. We are asking the function for all instances where this sequence appears at least once, but at most five times. The longest possible sequence that could conform to this request would thus be $3 \times 5 = 15$ characters long, where every second and third character would be an `e` and an `n`. In the next code snippet we drop the parentheses. The function will thus match all sequences that run from any character over `e` to `n` where the `n` has to appear at least once but at most five times. Consider how the previous result differs from the following:

```
R> unlist(str_extract_all(example.obj, ".en{1,5}"))
[1] "sen" "ten" "sen" "ten"
```

Table 8.3 Selected symbols with special meaning

`\w`	Word characters: `[[:alnum:]_]`
`\W`	No word characters: `[^[:alnum:]_]`
`\s`	Space characters: `[[:blank:]]`
`\S`	No space characters: `[^[:blank:]]`
`\d`	Digits: `[[:digit:]]`
`\D`	No digits: `[^[:digit:]]`
`\b`	Word edge
`\B`	No word edge
`\<`	Word beginning
`\>`	Word end

Metacharacters So far, we have encountered a number of characters that have a special meaning in regular expressions.[4] They are called metacharacters. In order to match them literally, we precede them with two backslashes. In order to literally extract all period characters from our running example, we write

```
R> unlist(str_extract_all(example.obj, "\\."))
[1] "." "." "." "."
```

The double backslash before the period character is interpreted as a single literal backslash. Inputting a single backslash in a regular expression will be interpreted as introducing an escape sequence. Several of these escape sequences are quite common in web scraping tasks and should be familiar to you. The most common are `\n` and `\t` which mean new line and tab. For example, "`a\n\n\na`" is interpreted as `a`, three new lines, and another `a`. If we want the entire regular expression to be interpreted literally, we have a better alternative than preceding every metacharacter with a backslash. We can enclose the expression with `fixed()` in order for metacharacters to be interpreted literally.

```
R> unlist(str_extract_all(example.obj, fixed(".")))
[1] "." "." "." "."
```

Most metacharacters lose their special meaning inside a character class. For example, a period character inside a character class will only match a literal period character. The only two exceptions to this rule are the caret (`^`) and the `-`. Putting the former at the beginning of a character class matches the inverse of the character class' contents. The latter can be applied to describe ranges inside a character class. This behavior can be altered by putting the `-` at the beginning or the end of a character class. In this case it will be interpreted literally.

Further shortcuts One last aspect of regular expressions that we want to introduce here are a number of shortcuts that have been assigned to several specific character classes. Table 8.3 provides an overview of available shortcuts.

[4]We have encountered `.`, `|`, `(`, `)`, `[`, `]`, `{`, `}`, `^`, `$`, `*`, `+`, `?` and `-`.

Consider the `\w` character. This symbol matches any word character in our running example, such that …

```
R> unlist(str_extract_all(example.obj, "\\w+"))
[1] "1"        "A"        "small"    "sentence" "2"        "Another"
[7] "tiny"     "sentence"
```

… extracts every word separated by blank spaces or punctuation. Note that `\w` is equivalent to `[[:alnum:]_]` and thus the leading digits are interpreted as whole words. Consider further the useful shortcuts for word edges `\>`, `\<`, and `\b`. Using them, we can be more specific in the location of matches. Imagine we would like to extract all `e` from our running example that are at the end of a word. To do so, we could apply one of the following two expressions:

```
R> unlist(str_extract_all(example.obj, "e\\>"))
[1] "e" "e"
R> unlist(str_extract_all(example.obj, "e\\b"))
[1] "e" "e"
```

Backreferencing

This query extracts the two `e` from the edges of the word `sentence`. Finally, it is even possible to match a sequence that has been previously matched in a regular expression. This is called backreferencing. Say, we are looking for the first letter in our running example and—whatever it may be—want to match further instances of that particular letter. To do so, we enclose the element in question in parentheses—for example, `([[:alpha:]])` and reference it using `\1`.[5]

```
R> str_extract(example.obj, "([[:alpha:]]).+?\\1")
[1] "A small sentence. - 2. A"
```

In our example, the letter is an `A`. The function returns this match and the subsequent characters up to the next instance of an `A`. To make matters a little more complicated, we now look for a lowercase word without the letter `a` up to and including the second occurrence of this word.

```
R> str_extract(example.obj, "(\\<[b-z]+\\>).+?\\1")
[1] "sentence. - 2. Another tiny sentence"
```

The expression we use is `(\\<[b-z]+\\>).+?\\1`. First, consider the `[b-z]+` part. The expression matches all sequences of lowercase letters of length one or more that do not contain the letter `a`. In our running example, neither the `1` nor the `A` fulfill this requirement. The first substring that would match this expression is the double `l` in the word `small`. Recall that the `+` quantifier is greedy. Hence, it tries to capture the longest possible sequence which would be `ll` instead of `l`. This is not what we want. Instead, we are looking for a whole word of lowercase letters that do not contain the letter `a`. Thus, to exclude this finding we add the `\\<` and `\\>` to the expression to signal a word's beginning and end. This entire expression is enclosed in parentheses in order to reference it further down in the expression. The first part of the string that this expression matches is the word `sentence`. Next, we are looking for the subsequent occurrence of this substring in our string using the `\\1`—regardless of what comes in between (`.+?`). Not so easy, is it?

[5]There can be up to nine backreferences, which would be labeled `\1`, `\2`, etc.

8.1.3 The introductory example reconsidered

Now that we have encountered the main ingredients of regular expressions, we can come back to our introductory example of sorting out the *Simpsons* phone directory. Take another look at the raw data.

```
R> raw.data
[1] "555-1239Moe Szyslak(636) 555-0113Burns, C. Montgomery555-6542Rev.
Timothy Lovejoy555 8904Ned Flanders636-555-3226Simpson, Homer5553642Dr.
Julius Hibbert"
```

In order to extract the names, we used the regular expression `[[:alpha:]., ]{2,}`. Let us have a look at it step by step. At its core, we used the character class `[:alpha:]`, which signals that we are looking for alphabetic characters. Apart from these characters, names can also contain periods, commas and empty spaces, which we want to add to the character class to read `[[:alpha:]., ]`. Finally, we add a quantifier to impose the restriction that the contents of the character class have to be matched at least twice to be considered a match. Failing to add a quantifier would extract every single character that matches the character class. Moreover, we have to specify that we only want matches of at least length two; otherwise the expression would return the empty spaces between some of the phone numbers.

```
R> name <- unlist(str_extract_all(raw.data, "[[:alpha:]., ]{2,}"))
R> name
[1] "Moe Szyslak"          "Burns, C. Montgomery" "Rev. Timothy Lovejoy"
[4] "Ned Flanders"         "Simpson, Homer"       "Dr. Julius Hibbert"
```

We also wanted to extract all the phone numbers from the string. The regular expression we used for the task was a little more complicated to conform to the different formats of the phone numbers. Let us consider the elements that phone numbers consist of, mostly digits (`\\d`). The primary source of difficulty stems from the fact that the phone numbers were not formatted identically. Instead, some contained empty spaces, dashes, parentheses, or did not have an area code attached to them.

Applying our knowledge of regular expressions, we are now able to dismantle the regular expression. In its entirety it reads `\\(?(\\d{3})?\\)?(-| )?\\d{3}(-| )?\\d{4}`. Let us go through the expression. The first part of the expression reads `\\(?(\\d{3})?\\)?`. In the center we find `\\d{3}`, which we use to collect the three-digit area code. As this is not contained in every phone number we enclose the expression with two parentheses and add a question mark, signaling that this part of the expression can be dropped. Before and after this core element we add `\\(` and `\\)` to incorporate two literal parentheses surrounding the three-digit area code. These too can be dropped, if the phone number does not contain them, using the `?`. Next, our regular expression contains the expression `(-| )?`. This means that either a dash or an empty space will be matched, but again, we enclose the entire expression with parentheses and add a question mark in order to signal that this part of the expression might be missing. These elements are then simply repeated. Specifically, we are looking for three digits, another dash or empty space that might or might not be part of the phone number, and four more digits. Applying this to our mock example yields

```
R> phone <- unlist(str_extract_all(raw.data, "\\(?(\\d{3})?\\)?(-| )?\\d
{3}(-| )?\\d{4}"))
```

```
R> phone
[1] "555-1239"       "(636) 555-0113" "555-6542"       "555 8904"
[5] "636-555-3226"   "5553642"
```

Regular expression flavors

Before moving on to discuss how regular expressions can be used in practice in the subsequent section, we would like to conclude this part with some general observations on regular expressions. First, even though we have provided a fairly comprehensive picture on how we can go about generalizing regular expressions to meet our string manipulation needs, there are still several aspects that we have not covered in this section. In particular, there are two flavors of regular expressions implemented in R—extended basic and *Perl* regular expressions. In the above example we have exclusively relied on the former. While *Perl* regular expressions provide some additional features, most tasks can be accomplished by relying on the default flavor—the extended basic variant.[6]

Although there is no harm in learning *Perl* regular expressions we advise you to stick to the default for several reasons. One, it is generally confusing to keep two flavors in mind—especially if this is your first time approaching regular expressions. Two, most tasks can be accomplished with the default implementation. Sometimes this means solving a task in two steps rather than one but in many instances this behavior is even preferable. We believe that it is poor practice to try and come up with a "golden expression" that accomplishes all your string manipulation needs in just one line. For the sake of readability one should try to restrict the number of steps that are taken in any given line of code. This simplifies error detection and furthermore helps grasp what is going on in your code when revisiting it at a later stage. Keeping this rule in mind, the use of such intricate concepts as backreferences becomes dubious. While there may be instances when they cannot be avoided, they also tend to make code confusing. Splitting all the steps that are taken inside a backreference expression into several smaller steps is often preferable.

Now we have the building blocks ready to take a look at what can be accomplished with regular expressions in practice.

8.2 String processing

8.2.1 The stringr package

In this section we present some of the available functions that rely on regular expressions. To do so we look at functions that are implemented in the stringr package. Two functions we have used throughout the last section were `str_extract()` and `str_extract_all()`. They extract the first/all instance/s of a match between the regular expression and the string. To reiterate, `str_extract()` extracts the first matching instance to a regular expression ...

```
R> str_extract(example.obj, "tiny")
[1] "tiny"
```

... while `str_extract_all()` extracts all of the matches.

```
R> str_extract_all(example.obj, "[[:digit:]]")
[[1]]
[1] "1" "2"
```

[6]If you care to use *Perl* regular expressions, simply enclose the expression with `perl()`. This behavior is a convention of the stringr package. For *Perl* regular expressions in base functions, set the `perl` switch to `TRUE`. For information on additional functionality in *Perl* regular expressions, check out http://www.pcre.org/.

Table 8.4 Functions of package stringr in this chapter

Function	Description	Output
Functions using regular expressions		
`str_extract()`	Extracts first string that matches pattern	Character vector
`str_extract_all()`	Extracts all strings that match pattern	List of character vectors
`str_locate()`	Returns position of first pattern match	Matrix of start/end positions
`str_locate_all()`	Returns positions of all pattern matches	List of matrices
`str_replace()`	Replaces first pattern match	Character vector
`str_replace_all()`	Replaces all pattern matches	Character vector
`str_split()`	Splits string at pattern	List of character vectors
`str_split_fixed()`	Splits string at pattern into fixed number of pieces	Matrix of character vectors
`str_detect()`	Detects patterns in string	Boolean vector
`str_count()`	Counts number of pattern occurrences in string	Numeric vector
Further functions		
`str_sub()`	Extracts strings by position	Character vector
`str_dup()`	Duplicates strings	Character vector
`str_length()`	Returns length of string	Numeric vector
`str_pad()`	Pads a string	Character vector
`str_trim()`	Discards string padding	Character vector
`str_c()`	Concatenates strings	Character vector

We have pointed out that the function outputs differ. In the former case a character vector is returned, while a list is returned in the latter case. Table 8.4 gives an overview of the different functions that will be introduced in the present chapter. Column two presents a short description of the function's purpose, column three specifies the format of the return value. If instead of extracting the result we are interested in the location of a match in a given string, we use the functions `str_locate()` or `str_locate_all()`.

```
R> str_locate(example.obj, "tiny")
     start end
[1,]    35  38
```

Substring extraction

The function outputs a matrix with the start and end position of the first instance of a match, in this case the 35th to 38th characters in our example string. We can make use of positional information in a string to extract a substring using the function `str_sub()`.

```
R> str_sub(example.obj, start = 35, end = 38)
[1] "tiny"
```

Here we extract the 35th to 38th characters that we know to be the word `tiny`. Possibly, a more common task is to replace a given substring. As usual, this can be done using the assignment operator.

```
R> str_sub(example.obj, 35, 38) <- "huge"
R> example.obj
[1] "1. A small sentence. - 2. Another huge sentence."
```

`str_replace()` and `str_replace_all()` are used for replacements more generally.

```
R> str_replace(example.obj, pattern = "huge", replacement = "giant")
[1] "1. A small sentence. - 2. Another giant sentence."
```

We might care to split a string into several smaller strings. In the easiest of cases we simply define a split, say at each dash. **String splitting**

```
R> unlist(str_split(example.obj, "-"))
[1] "1. A small sentence. "        " 2. Another huge sentence."
```

We can also fix the number of particles we want the string to be split into. If we wanted to split the string at each blank space, but did not want more than five resulting strings, we would write

```
R> as.character(str_split_fixed(example.obj, "[[:blank:]]", 5))
[1] "1."                          "A"
[3] "small"                       "sentence."
[5] "- 2. Another huge sentence."
```

So far, all the examples we looked at have assumed a single string object. Recall our little running example that consists of two sentences—but only one string.

```
R> example.obj
[1] "1. A small sentence. - 2. Another huge sentence."
```

We can apply the functions to several strings at the same time. Consider a character vector that consists of several strings as a second running example:

```
R> char.vec <- c("this", "and this", "and that")
```

The first thing we can do is to check the occurrence of particular pattern inside a character vector. Assume we are interested in knowing whether the pattern `this` appears in the elements of a given vector. The function we use to do this is `str_detect()`. **String detection**

```
R> str_detect(char.vec, "this")
[1]  TRUE  TRUE FALSE
```

Moreover, we could be interested in how often this particular word appears in the elements of a given vector ... **String counting**

```
R> str_count(char.vec, "this")
[1] 1 1 0
```

… or how many words there are in total in each of the different elements.

```
R> str_count(char.vec, "\\w+")
[1] 1 2 2
```

String duplication We can duplicate strings …

```
R> dup.obj <- str_dup(char.vec, 3)
R> dup.obj
[1] "thisthisthis"               "and thisand thisand this"
[3] "and thatand thatand that"
```

… or count the number of characters in a given string.

```
R> length.char.vec <- str_length(char.vec)
R> length.char.vec
[1] 4 8 8
```

String padding Two important functions in web data manipulation are `str_pad()` and `str_trim()`. They are used to add characters to the edges of strings or trim blank spaces.

```
R> char.vec <- str_pad(char.vec, width = max(length.char.vec),
side = "both", pad = " ")
R> char.vec
[1] "  this  " "and this" "and that"
```

String trimming In this case we add white spaces to the shorter string equally on both sides such that each string has the same length. The opposite operation is performed using `str_trim()`, which strips excess white spaces from the edges of strings.

```
R> char.vec <- str_trim(char.vec)
R> char.vec
[1] "this"     "and this" "and that"
```

String joining Finally, we can join strings using the `str_c()` function.

```
R> cat(str_c(char.vec, collapse = "\n"))
this
and this
and that
```

Here, we join the three strings of our character vector into a single string. We add a new line character (\n) and produce the result using the `cat()` function, which interprets the new line character as a new line. Beyond joining the contents of one vector, we can use the function to join two different vectors.

```
R> str_c("text", "manipulation", sep = " ")
[1] "text manipulation"
```

If the length of one vector is the multiple of the other, the function automatically recycles the shorter one.

```
R> str_c("text", c("manipulation", "basics"), sep = " ")
[1] "text manipulation" "text basics"
```

Table 8.5 Equivalents of the functions in the stringr package in base R

stringr function	Base function
Functions using regular expressions	
`str_extract()`	`regmatches()`
`str_extract_all()`	`regmatches()`
`str_locate()`	`regexpr()`
`str_locate_all()`	`gregexpr()`
`str_replace()`	`sub()`
`str_replace_all()`	`gsub()`
`str_split()`	`strsplit()`
`str_split_fixed()`	–
`str_detect()`	`grepl()`
`str_count()`	–
Further functions	
`str_sub()`	`regmatches()`
`str_dup()`	–
`str_length()`	`nchar()`
`str_pad()`	–
`str_trim()`	–
`str_c()`	`paste()`, `paste0()`

Throughout this book we frequently rely on the stringr package for strings processing. However, base R provides string processing functionality as well. We find the base functions less consistent and thus more difficult to learn. If you still want to learn them or want to switch from base R functionality to the stringr package, have a look at Table 8.5. It provides an overview of the analogue functions from the stringr package as implemented in base R.

8.2.2 A couple more handy functions

Approximate matching

Many string manipulation tasks can be accomplished using the stringr package we introduced in the previous section. However, there are a couple of additional functions in base R we would like to introduce in this section. Text data, especially data scraped from web sources, is often messy. Data that should be matched come in different formats, names are spelled differently—problems come from all sorts of places. Throughout this volume we stress the need to cleanse data after it is collected. One way to deal with messy text data is the `agrep()` function, which provides approximate matching via the Levenshtein distance. Without going into too much detail, the function calculates the number of insertions, deletions, and substitutions necessary to transform one string into another. Specifying a cutoff, we can provide a criterion on whether a pattern should be considered as present in a string.

```
R> agrep("Barack Obama", "Barack H. Obama", max.distance = list(all = 3))
[1] 1
```

In this case, we are looking for the pattern `Barack Obama` in the string `Barack H. Obama` and we allow three alterations in the string.[7] See how this compares to a search for the pattern in the string `Michelle Obama`.

```
R> agrep("Barack Obama", "Michelle Obama", max.distance = list(all = 3))
integer(0)
```

Too many changes are needed in order to find the pattern in the string; hence there is no result. You can change the maximum distance between pattern and string by adjusting both the `max.distance` and the `costs` parameter. The higher the `max.distance` parameter (default = 0.1), the more approximate matches it will find. Using the `costs` parameter you can adjust the costs for the different operations necessary to liken to strings.

Detecting positions Another handy function is `pmatch()`. The function returns the positions of the strings in the first vector in the second vector. Consider the character vector from above, `c("this", "and this", "and that")`.

```
R> pmatch(c("and this", "and that", "and these", "and those"), char.vec)
[1]  2  3 NA NA
```

We are looking for the positions of the elements in the first vector (`c("and this", "and that", "and these", "and those")` in the character vector. The output signals that the first element is at the second position, the second at the third. The third and fourth elements in the first vector are not contained in the character vector. A final useful function is `make.unique()`. Using this function you can transform a collection of nonunique strings by adding digits where necessary.

```
R> make.unique(c("a", "b", "a", "c", "b", "a"))
[1] "a"   "b"   "a.1" "c"   "b.1" "a.2"
```

Extending base functionality Although there are a lot of handy functions already available, there will always be problems and situations when the one special function desperately needed is missing. One of those problems might be the following. Imagine we have to check for more than one pattern within a character vector and want to get a logical vector indicating compliant rows or an index listing all the compliant row numbers. For checking patterns, we know that `grep()`, `grepl()`, or `str_detect()` might be good candidates. Because `grep()` offers a switch for returning the matched text or a row index vector, we try to build a solution starting with `grep()`. We begin by downloading a test dataset of *Simpsons* episodes and store it in the local file *episodes.Rdata*.

```
R> library(XML)
R> # download file
R> if(!file.exists("listOfSimpsonsEpisodes.html")){
   link <- "http://en.wikipedia.org/wiki/List_of_The_Simpsons_episodes"
   download.file(link, "listOfSimpsonsEpisodes.html", mode="wb")
   }
R> # getting the table
```

[7] An alternative way to specify the maximum distance between two strings is to input a fraction of changes over the entire length of a string.

```
R> tables <- readHTMLTable("listOfSimpsonsEpisodes.html",
                          header=T, stringsAsFactors=F)
R> tmpcols <- names(tables[[3]])
R> for(i in 3:20){
   tmpcols <- intersect(tmpcols, names(tables[[i]]))
   }
R> episodes <- NULL
R> for(i in 3:20){
   episodes <- rbind(episodes[,tmpcols],tables[[i]][,tmpcols])
   }
R> for(i in 1:dim(episodes)[2]){
   Encoding(episodes[,i]) <- "UTF-8"
   }
R> names(episodes) <- c("pnr", "nr", "title", "directedby",
                        "Writtenby", "airdate", "productioncode")
R> save(episodes,file="episodes.Rdata")
```

Let us load the table containing all the *Simpsons* episodes.

```
R> load("episodes.Rdata")
```

As you can see below, it is easy to switch between different answers to the same question—which episodes mention Homer in the title—using `grep()`, `grepl()` and using the `value = TRUE` option. The easy switch makes these functions particularly valuable when we start developing regular expressions, as we might need an index or logical vector at the end, but we can use the value option to check if the used pattern actually works.

```
R> grep("Homer",episodes$title[1:10], value=T)
[1] "Homer's Odyssey"   "Homer's Night Out"
R> grepl("Homer",episodes$title[1:10])
[1] FALSE FALSE  TRUE FALSE FALSE FALSE FALSE FALSE FALSE  TRUE
```

What is missing, however, is the option to ask for a whole bunch of patterns to be matched at the same time. Imagine we would like to know whether there are episodes where Homer and Lisa are mentioned in the title. The standard solution would be to make a logical vector for each separate pattern to be matched and later combine them to a logical vector that equals `TRUE` when all patterns are found.

```
R> iffer1 <- grepl("Homer",episodes$title)
R> iffer2 <- grepl("Lisa",episodes$title)
R> iffer  <- iffer1 & iffer2
R> episodes$title[iffer]
[1] "Homer vs. Lisa and the 8th Commandment"
```

Although this solution might seem acceptable in the case of two patterns, it becomes more and more inconvenient if the number of patterns grows or if the task has to be repeated. We will therefore create a new function built upon `grep()`.

```
R> grepall <- function(pattern, x,
                       ignore.case = FALSE, perl = FALSE,
                       fixed = FALSE, useBytes = FALSE,
                       value=FALSE, logic=FALSE){
```

```
    # error and exception handling
      if(length(pattern)==0 | length(x)==0){
         warning("Length of pattern or data equals zero.")
         return(NULL)
    }
    # apply grepl() and all()
      indicies <- sapply(pattern, grepl, x,
                         ignore.case, perl, fixed, useBytes)
      index    <- apply(indicies, 1, all)
    # indexation and return of results
      if(logic==T) return(index)
      if(value==F) return((1:length(x))[index])
      if(value==T) return(x[index])
    }
R> grepall(c("Lisa","Homer"), episodes$title)
[1]  26
R> grepall(c("Lisa","Homer"), episodes$title, value=T)
[1] "Homer vs. Lisa and the 8th Commandment"
```

The idea of the `grepall()` function is that we need to repeat the pattern search for a series of patterns—as we did in the previous code snippet when doing two separate pattern searches. Going through a series of things can be done by using a loop or more efficiently by using apply functions. Therefore, we first apply the `grepl()` function to get the logical vectors indicating which patterns were found in which row. We use `sapply()` because we have a vector as input and would like to have a matrix like object as output. What we get is a matrix with columns referring to the different search patterns and rows referring to the individual strings. To make sure all patterns were found in a certain row we use a second apply—this time we use `apply()` because we have a matrix as input—where the `all()` function returns `TRUE` when all values in a row are true and `FALSE` if any one value in a row is false. Depending on whether or not we want to return a vector containing the row numbers or a vector containing the text for which all the patterns were found the `value` option switches between two different uses of the internal logical vector to return row numbers or text accordingly. To get the full logical vector we can use the `logic` option. Besides providing functionality that works like `grep()` and `grepl()` for multiple search terms, all other options like `ignore.case`, `perl`, `fixed`, or `useBytes` are forwarded to the first apply step, so that this functionality is also part of the new function.

8.3 A word on character encodings

When working with web-based text data—particularly non-English data—one quickly runs into encoding issues. While there are no simple rules to deal with these problems, it is important to keep the difficulties that arise from them in mind. Generally speaking, character encodings refer to how the digital binary signals are translated into human-readable characters, for example, making a "d" from "`01100100`." As there are many languages around the world, there are also many special characters, like ä, ø, ç, and so forth. The issues arise since there are different translation tables such that without knowing which particular table is used to encode a binary signal it is difficult to draw inferences on the correct content of a signal. If you have not changed the defaults, R works with the system encoding scheme to present the output. You can query this standard with the following function:

```
R> Sys.getlocale()
[1] "LC_COLLATE=German_Germany.1252;LC_CTYPE=German_Germany.1252;
LC_MONETARY=German_Germany.1252;LC_NUMERIC=C;LC_TIME=German_Germany.1252"
```

If you have not figured it out already from the names on the cover, this book was written by four guys from Germany on a computer with a German operating system. The name of the character encoding, hidden behind the number `1252`, is `Windows-1252` and it is the default character encoding on systems that run Microsoft Windows in English and some other languages. Your output is likely to be a different one. For example, if you are working on a Windows PC and are located in the United States, R will give you a feedback like `English_United States.1252`. If you are operating on a Mac, the encoding standard is UTF-8.[8] Let us input a string with some special characters. Consider this fragment from a popular Swedish song, called "small frogs" (små grodorna):

```
R> small.frogs <- "Små grodorna, små grodorna är lustiga att se."
R> small.frogs
[1] "Små grodorna, små grodorna är lustiga att se."
```

There are several special characters in this fragment. By default, our inputs and outputs are assumed to be of Windows-1252 standard; thus the output is correct. Using the function `iconv()`, we can translate a string from one encoding scheme to another:

Convert encodings

```
R> small.frogs.utf8 <- iconv(small.frogs, from = "windows-1252",
to = "UTF-8")
R> Encoding(small.frogs.utf8)
[1] "UTF-8"
R> small.frogs.utf8
[1] "Små grodorna, små grodorna är lustiga att se."
```

In this case, the function applies a translation table from the Windows-1252 encoding to the UTF-8 standard. Thus, the binary sequence is recast as a UTF-8-encoded string. Consider how this behavior differs from the one we encounter when applying the `Encoding()` function to the string.

Declare encodings

```
R> Encoding(small.frogs.utf8) <- "windows-1252"
R> small.frogs.utf8
[1] "SmÃ¥ grodorna, smÃ¥ grodorna Ã¤r lustiga att se."
```

Doing so, we force the system to treat the UTF-8-encoded binary sequence as though it were generated by a different encoding scheme (our system default Windows-1252), resulting in the well-known garbled output we get, for example, when visiting a website with malspecified encodings. There are currently 350 conversion schemes available, which can be accessed using the `iconvlist()` function.

[8] This is quite convenient for working with data from the Web, as UTF-8 is probably the most popular scheme and therefore used on many websites.

```
R> sample(iconvlist(), 10)
[1] "PT154"          "latin7"         "UTF-16BE"       "CP51932"
[5] "IBM860"         "CP50221"        "IBM424"         "CP1257"
[9] "WINDOWS-50221" "IBM864"
```

Having established the importance of keeping track of the encodings of text and web-based text, in particular, we now turn to the question of how to figure out the encoding of an unknown text. Luckily, in many instances a website gives a pointer in its header. Consider the <meta> tag with the http-equiv attribute from the website of the Science Journal, which is located at http://www.sciencemag.org/.

```
R> library(RCurl)
R> enc.test <- getURL("http://www.sciencemag.org/")

R> unlist(str_extract_all(enc.test, "<meta.+?>"))
[1] "<meta http-equiv=\"Content-Type\" content=\"text/html;
charset=UTF-8\" />"
[2] "<meta name=\"googlebot\" content=\"NOODP\" />"
[3] "<meta name=\"HW.ad-path\" content=\"/\" />"
```

Testing for encodings

The first tag provides some structured information on the type of content we can expect on the site as well as how the characters are encoded—in this case UTF-8. But what if such a tag is not available? While it is difficult to guess the encoding of a particular text, a couple of handy functions toward this end have been implemented in the tau package. There are three functions available to test the encoding of a particular string, is.ascii(), is.locale(), and is.utf8(). What these functions do is to test whether the binary sequences are "legal" in a particular encoding scheme. Recall that the letter "å" is stored as a particular binary sequence in the local encoding scheme. This binary sequence is not valid in the ASCII scheme—hence, the string cannot have been encoded in ASCII. And in fact, this is what we find:

```
R> library(tau)
R> is.locale(small.frogs)
[1] TRUE
R> is.ascii(small.frogs)
[1] FALSE
```

Summary

Many aspects of automated data collection deal with textual data. Every step of a typical web scraping exercise might involve some form of string manipulation. Be it that you need to format a URL request according to your needs, collect information from an HTML page, (re-)arrange results that come in the form of strings, or general data cleansing. All of these tasks could require some form of string manipulation. This chapter has introduced the most important tool for any of these tasks—regular expressions. These expressions allow you to search for information using highly flexible queries.

The chapter has also outlined the main elements of string manipulation. First, we considered the ingredients of regular expressions as implemented in R. Starting with the simplest of all cases where a character represents itself in a regular expression, we subsequently treated more elaborate concepts to generalize searches, such as quantifiers and character classes. In the second step, we considered how regular expressions and string manipulation is generally performed. To do so, we principally looked at the function range that is provided by the stringr package and several functions that go beyond the package. The chapter concluded with a discussion on how to deal with character encodings.

Further reading

In this chapter, we introduced extended basic regular expressions as implemented in R. Check out http://stat.ethz.ch/R-manual/R-patched/library/base/html/regex.html for an overview of the available concepts. We restricted our exposition to extended regular expressions, as these suffice to accomplish most common tasks in string manipulation. There is, however, a second flavor of regular expressions that is implemented in R—*Perl* regular expressions. These introduce several aspects that allow string manipulations that were not discussed in this chapter.[9] Should you be interested in finding out more about Perl regular expressions, check out http://www.pcre.org/.

Problems

1. Describe regular expressions and why they can be used for web scraping purposes.

2. Find a regular expression that matches any text.

3. Copy the introductory example. The vector `name` stores the extracted names.

```
R> name
[1] "Moe Szyslak"          "Burns, C. Montgomery" "Rev. Timothy Lovejoy"
[4] "Ned Flanders"         "Simpson, Homer"       "Dr. Julius Hibbert"
```

(a) Use the tools of this chapter to rearrange the vector so that all elements conform to the standard `first_name last_name`.

(b) Construct a logical vector indicating whether a character has a title (i.e., `Rev.` and `Dr.`).

(c) Construct a logical vector indicating whether a character has a second name.

4. Describe the types of strings that conform to the following regular expressions and construct an example that is matched by the regular expression.

(a) `[0-9]+\\$`

(b) `\\b[a-z]{1,4}\\b`

(c) `.*?\\.txt$`

(d) `\\d{2}/\\d{2}/\\d{4}`

(e) `<(.+?)>.+?</\\1>`

[9] In almost all cases, however, one can break up search queries into several smaller queries that can easily be handled by the extended regular expressions.

5. Rewrite the expression `[0-9]+\\$` in a way that all elements are altered but the expression performs the same task.

6. Consider the mail address chunkylover53[at]aol[dot]com.
   (a) Transform the string to a standard mail format using regular expressions.
   (b) Imagine we are trying to extract the digits in the mail address. To do so we write the expression `[:digit:]`. Explain why this fails and correct the expression.
   (c) Instead of using the predefined character classes, we would like to use the predefined symbols to extract the digits in the mail address. To do so we write the expression `\\D`. Explain why this fails and correct the expression.

7. Consider the string `<title>+++BREAKING NEWS+++</title>`. We would like to extract the first HTML tag. To do so we write the regular expression `<.+>`. Explain why this fails and correct the expression.

8. Consider the string `(5-3)^2=5^2-2*5*3+3^2 conforms to the binomial theorem`. We would like to extract the formula in the string. To do so we write the regular expression `[^0-9=+*()]+`. Explain why this fails and correct the expression.

9. The following code hides a secret message. Crack it with R and regular expressions. *Hint: Some of the characters are more revealing than others! The code snippet is also available in the materials at www.r-datacollection.com.*

```
clcopCow1zmstc0d87wnkig7OvdicpNuggvhryn92Gjuwczi8hqrfpRxs5Aj5dwpn0Tanwo
Uwisdij7Lj8kpf03AT5Idr3coc0bt7yczjatOaootj55t3Nj3ne6c4Sfek.r1w1YwwojigO
d6vrfUrbz2.2bkAnbhzgv4R9i05zEcrop.wAgnb.SqoU65fPa1otfb7wEm24k6t3sR9zqe5
fy89n6Nd5t9kc4fE905gmc4Rgxo5nhDk!gr
```

10. Why it is important to be familiar with character encodings when working with string data?

Part Two

A PRACTICAL TOOLBOX FOR WEB SCRAPING AND TEXT MINING

9

Scraping the Web

Having learned much about the basics of the architecture of the Web, we now turn to data collection in practice. In this chapter, we address three main aspects of web scraping with R. The first is how to retrieve data from the Web in different scenarios (Section 9.1). Recall Figure 1.4. The first part of the chapter looks at the stage where we try to get resources from servers into R. The principal technology to deal with in this step is HTTP. We offer a set of real-life scenarios that demonstrate how to use *libcurl* to gather data in various settings. In addition to examples based on HTTP or FTP communication, we introduce the use of web services (web application programming interfaces [APIs]) and a related authentication standard, *OAuth*. We also offer a solution for the problem of scraping dynamic content that we described in Chapter 6. Section 9.1.9 provides an introduction to Selenium, a browser automation tool that can be used to gather content from JavaScript-enriched pages.

The second part of the chapter turns to strategies for extracting information from gathered resources (Section 9.2). We are already familiar with the necessary technologies: regular expressions (Chapter 8) and XPath (Chapter 4). From a technology-based perspective, this corresponds to the second column of Figure 1.4. In this part we shed light on these techniques from a more practical perspective, providing a stylized sketch of the strategies and discuss their advantages and disadvantages. We also consider APIs once more. They are an ideal case of automated web data collection as they offer a seamless integration of the retrieval and extracting stages.

On the art of web scraping

Whatever the level of difficulty for scraping information from the web, the circle of scraping remains almost always identical. The followings tasks are part of most scraping exercises:

1. Information identification
2. Choice of strategy
3. Data retrieval

Automated Data Collection with R: A Practical Guide to Web Scraping and Text Mining, First Edition.
Simon Munzert, Christian Rubba, Peter Meißner and Dominic Nyhuis.

4. Information extraction
5. Data preparation
6. Data validation
7. Debugging and maintenance
8. Generalization

The art of scraping lies in cleverly combining and redefining these tasks, and we can only sketch out some basic principles, either theoretically (as in Section 9.2) or by examples in the set of retrieval scenarios and case studies. In the end, questions such as "Is automation efficient?," "Is R the right tool for my web data collection work?," and "Is my data source of choice reliable in the long run?" are project-specific and lack a generally helpful answer.

The third part of this chapter addresses an important, but sometimes disregarded aspect of web scraping. It deals with the question of how to behave nicely on the Web as a web scraper. We are convinced that the abundance of online data is something positive and opens up new ways for understanding human interactions. Whether collecting these data is inherently positive depends in no small part on (a) the behavior of data gatherers and (b) on the purpose for which data are collected. The latter point is entirely up to you. For the former point, we offer some basic advice in Section 9.3. We discuss legal implications of web scraping, show how to take *robots.txt*, an informal standard for web crawler behavior, into account, and offer a practical guideline for friendly web-scraping practice.

We conclude the chapter with a glimpse of ongoing efforts for giving R more interfaces with web data and on lighthouses of web scraping more generally (Section 9.4).

Spiders versus scrapers

A final remark before we get started: This chapter is mostly about how to build special-purpose web *scrapers*. In our definition scrapers are programs that grab specific content from web pages. Such information could be telephone data (see Chapter 15), data on products (see Chapter 16), or political behavior (see Chapter 12). *Spiders* (or crawlers or web robots), in contrast, are programs that grab and index entire pages and move around the Web following every link they can find. Most scraping work involves a spidering component. In order to extract content from webpages, we usually first download them as a whole and then continue with the extraction part. In general, however, we disregard scenarios in which the goal is to wander through the Web without a specific data collection target.

9.1 Retrieval scenarios

For the following scenarios of web data retrieval, we rely on the following set of R packages which were introduced in the first part of the book. We assume that you have loaded them for the exercises. We will indicate throughout the chapter whenever we make use of additional packages.

```
R> library(RCurl)
R> library(XML)
R> library(stringr)
```

9.1.1 Downloading ready-made files

The first way to get data from the Web is almost too banal to be considered here and actually not a case of web scraping in the narrower sense. In some situations, you will find data of interest ready for download in TXT, CSV, or any other plain-text/spreadsheet or binary format like PDF, XLS, or JPEG. R can still prove useful for such simple tasks, as (a) the data acquisition process remains reproducible in principle and (b) it may save a considerable amount of time. We picked two common examples to illustrate the benefits of using R in scenarios like these.

9.1.1.1 CSV election results data

The Maryland State Board of Elections at http://www.elections.state.md.us/ provides a rich data resource on past elections. We identified a set of comma-separated value spreadsheets that comprise information on state-, county-, and precinct-level election results for the 2012 Presidential election in Maryland in one of the page's subdirectories at http://www.elections.state.md.us/elections/2012/election_data/index.html. The targeted files are accessible via "General" hyperlinks. Suppose we want to download these files for analyses.

The links to the CSV files are scattered across several tables on the page. We are only interested in some of the documents, namely those that contain the raw election results for the general election. The page provides data on the primaries and on ballot questions, too. In order to retrieve the desired files, we want to proceed in three steps.

1. We identify the links to the desired files.
2. We construct a download function.
3. We execute the downloads.

The XML package provides a neat function to identify links in an HTML document—`getHTMLLinks()`. We introduce this and other convenience functions from the package in greater detail in Section 9.1.4.

We use `getHTMLLinks()` to extract all the URLs and external file names in the HTML document that we first assign to the object `url`. The list of links in `links` comprises more entries than we are interested in, so we apply the regular expression `_General.csv` to retrieve the subset of external file names that point to the general election result CSVs. Finally, we store the file names in a list to be able to apply a download function to this list in the next step. **Identifying locations**

```
R> url <- "http://www.elections.state.md.us/elections/2012/election_
data/index.html"

R> links <- getHTMLLinks(url)

R> filenames <- links[str_detect(links, "_General.csv")]

R> filenames_list <- as.list(filenames)
R> filenames_list[1:3]
[[1]]
```

```
[1] "http://www.elections.state.md.us/elections/2012/election_data/
State_Legislative_Districts_2012_General.csv"

[[2]]
[1] "http://www.elections.state.md.us/elections/2012/election_data/
Allegany_County_2012_General.csv"

[[3]]
[1] "http://www.elections.state.md.us/elections/2012/election_data/
Allegany_By_Precinct_2012_General.csv"
```

Constructing a download function

Next, we set up a function to download all the files and call the function `downloadCSV()`. The function wraps around the base R function `download.file()`, which is perfectly sufficient to download URLs or other files in standard scenarios. Our function has three arguments. `filename` refers to each of the entries in the `filenames_list` object. `baseurl` specifies the source path of the files to be downloaded. Along with the file names, we can thus construct the full URL of each file. We do this using `str_c()` and feed the result to the `download.file()` function. The second argument of the function is the destination on our local drive. We determine a folder where we want to store the CSV files and add the file name parameter. We tweak the download by adding (1) a condition which ensures that the file download is only performed if the file does not already exist in the folder using the `file.exists()` function and (2) a pause of 1 second between each file download. We will motivate these tweaks later in Section 9.3.3.

```
R> downloadCSV <- function(filename, baseurl, folder) {
R>      dir.create(folder, showWarnings = FALSE)
R>      fileurl <- str_c(baseurl, filename)
R>      if (!file.exists(str_c(folder, "/", filename))) {
R>              download.file(fileurl,
R>                      destfile = str_c(folder, "/", filename))
R>              Sys.sleep(1)
R>      }
R> }
```

Executing the download

We apply the function to the list of CSV file names `filenames_list` using `l_ply()` from the plyr package. The function takes a list as main argument and passes each list element as argument to the specified function, in our case `downloadCSV()`. We can pass further arguments to the function. For `baseurl` we identify the path where all CSVs are located. With `folder` we select the local folder where want to store the files.

```
R> library(plyr)
R> l_ply(filenames_list, downloadCSV,
R>     baseurl = "www.elections.state.md.us/elections/2012/election_data/",
R>     folder = "elec12_maryland")
```

To check the results, we consider the number of downloaded files and the first couple of entries.

```
R> length(list.files("./elec12_maryland"))
[1] 68
```

```
R> list.files("./elec12_maryland")[1:3]
[1] "Allegany_By_Precinct_2012_General.csv"
[2] "Allegany_County_2012_General.csv"
[3] "Anne_Arundel_By_Precinct_2012_General.csv"
```

Sixty-eight CSV files have been added to the folder. We could now proceed with an analysis by importing the files into R using `read.csv()`. The web scraping task is thus completed and could easily be replicated with data on other elections stored on the website.

9.1.1.2 PDF legislative district maps

`download.file()` frequently does not provide the functionality we need to download files from certain sites. In particular, `download.file()` does not support data retrieval via HTTPS by default and is not capable of dealing with cookies or many other advanced features of HTTP. In such situations, we can switch to RCurl's high-level functions which can easily handle problems like these—and offer further useful options.

As a showcase we try to retrieve PDF files of the 2012 Maryland legislative district maps, complementing the voting data from above. The maps are available at the Maryland Department of Planning's website: http://planning.maryland.gov/Redistricting/2010/legiDist.shtml.[1] The targeted PDFs are accessible in a three-column table at the bottom right of the screen and named "1A," "1B," and so on. We reuse the download procedure from above, but specify a different base URL and regular expression to detect the desired files.

```
R> url <- "http://planning.maryland.gov/Redistricting/2010/legiDist.shtml"
R> links <- getHTMLLinks(url)
R> filenames <- links[str_detect(links, "2010maps/Leg/Districts_")]
R> filenames_list <- str_extract_all(filenames, "Districts.+pdf")
```

The download function `downloadPDF()` now relies on `getBinaryURL()`. We allow for the use of a curl handle. We cannot specify a destination file in the `getBinaryURL()` function, so we store the raw data in a `pdffile` object first and then pass it to `writeBin()`. This function writes the PDF files to the specified folder. The other components of the function remain the same.

Download with RCurl

```
R> downloadPDF <- function(filename, baseurl, folder, handle) {
R>     dir.create(folder, showWarnings = FALSE)
R>     fileurl <- str_c(baseurl, filename)
R>     if (!file.exists(str_c(folder, "/", filename))) {
R>         content <- getBinaryURL(fileurl, curl = handle)
R>         writeBin(content,  str_c(folder, "/", filename))
R>         Sys.sleep(1)
R>     }
R> }
```

We execute the function with a handle that adds a `User-Agent` and a `From` header field to every call and keeps the connection alive. We could specify further options if we had to deal with cookies or other HTTP specifics.

[1] Note that the "2010" in the URL is misleading—it is the 2012 election maps that are offered at this address.

```
R> handle <- getCurlHandle(useragent = str_c(R.version$platform,
R.version$version.string, sep=", "), httpheader = c(from =
"eddie@datacollection.com"))

R> l_ply(filenames_list, downloadPDF,
R>       baseurl = "planning.maryland.gov/PDF/Redistricting/2010maps/Leg/",
R>       folder = "elec12_maryland_maps",
R>       handle = handle)
```

Again, we examine the results by checking the number of files in the folder and the first couple of results.

```
R> length(list.files("./elec12_maryland_maps"))
[1] 68

R> list.files("./elec12_maryland_maps")[1:3]
[1] "Districts_10.pdf" "Districts_11.pdf" "Districts_12.pdf"
```

Everything seems to have worked out fine—68 PDF files have been downloaded. The bottom line of this exercise is that downloading plain-text or binary files from a website is one of the easiest tasks. The core tools are `download.file()` and RCurl's high-level functions. `getHTMLLinks()` from the XML package often does a good job of identifying the links to single files, especially when they are scattered across a document.

9.1.2 Downloading multiple files from an FTP index

We have introduced an alternative network protocol to HTTP for pure file transfer, the File Transfer Protocol (FTP) in Section 5.3.2. Downloading files from FTP servers is a rewarding task for data wranglers because FTP servers host files, nothing else. We do not have to care about getting rid of HTML layout or other unwanted information. Again, RCurl is well-suited to fetch files via FTP.

Let us have a look at the CRAN FTP server to see how this works. The server has the URL ftp://cran.r-project.org/. It stores a lot of R-related data, including older R versions, CRAN task views, and all CRAN packages. Say we want to download all CRAN task view HTML files for closer inspection. They are stored at ftp://cran.r-project.org/pub/R/web/views/. Our downloading strategy is similar to the one in the last scenario.

1. We identify the desired files.
2. We construct a download function.
3. We execute the downloads.

Fetch FTP directory

In order to load the FTP directory list into R, we assign the URL to `ftp`. Next, we save the list of file names to the object `ftp_files` with `getURL()`.[2] By setting the *libcurl* option `dirlistonly` to `TRUE`, we ensure that only the file names are fetched, but no further information about file size or creation date.

---

[2]For FTP servers the `getHTMLLinks()` command is not an option, because the documents are not structured as HTML.

```
R> ftp <- "ftp://cran.r-project.org/pub/R/web/views/"
R> ftp_files <- getURL(ftp, dirlistonly = TRUE)
```

It is sometimes the case that the default FTP mode in *libcurl*, extended passive (EPSV), does not work with some FTP servers. In this case, we have to add the `ftp.use.epsv = FALSE` option. In our example, we have successfully downloaded the list of files and stored it in a character vector, `ftp_files`. The information is corrupted with line feeds and carriage returns representations `\r` `\n`, however, and still contains CTV files.

```
R> ftp_files

[1] "Bayesian.ctv\r\nBayesian.html\r\nChemPhys.ctv\r\nChemPhys.html\r..."
```

To get rid of them we use them as splitting patterns for `str_split()`. We also apply a regular expression to select only the HTML files with `str_extract_all()`:

Extract file names

```
R> filenames <- str_split(ftp_files, "\r\n")[[1]]
R> filenames_html <- unlist(str_extract_all(filenames, ".+(.html)"))

R> filenames_html[1:3]
[1] "Bayesian.html"       "ChemPhys.html"       "ClinicalTrials.html"
```

An equivalent, but more elegant way to get only the HTML files would be

```
R> filenames_html <- getURL(ftp, customrequest = "NLST *.html")
R> filenames_html = str_split(filenames_html, "\\\r\\\n")[[1]]
```

This way we pass the FTP command `NLST *.html` to our function. This returns a list of file names in the FTP directory that end in *.html*. We thus exploit the *libcurl* option `customrequest` that allows changing the request method and do not have to extract the HTML files ex post.[3]

In the last step, we construct a function `downloadFTP()` that fetches the desired files from the FTP server and stores them in a specified folder. It basically follows the syntax of the `downloadPDF()` function from the previous section.

Download files

```
R> downloadFTP <- function(filename, folder, handle) {
R>      dir.create(folder, showWarnings = FALSE)
R>      fileurl <- str_c(ftp, filename)
R>      if (!file.exists(str_c(folder, "/", filename))) {
R>              content <- try(getURL(fileurl, curl = handle))
R>              write(content, str_c(folder, "/", filename))
R>              Sys.sleep(1)
R>      }
R> }
```

[3]Recall that FTP has a list of commands of its own, just as there are HTTP commands like *GET* and *POST*. A list of FTP commands—some of which can easily be implemented with curl's `customrequest` option—can be found at http://www.nsftools.com/tips/RawFTP.htm.

We set up a handle that disables FTP-extended passive mode and download the CRAN task HTML documents to the *cran_tasks* folder:

```
R> handle <- getCurlHandle(ftp.use.epsv = FALSE)

R> l_ply(filenames_list, downloadFTP,
R>       folder = "cran_tasks",
R>       handle = handle)
```

A quick inspection of our newly created folder reveals that the files were successfully downloaded.

```
R> length(list.files("./cran_tasks"))
[1] 34
R> list.files("./cran_tasks")[1:3]
[1] "Bayesian.html"       "ChemPhys.html"       "ClinicalTrials.html"
```

It is also possible to upload data to an FTP server. As we do not have any rights to upload content to the CRAN server, we offer a fictional example.

```
R> ftpUpload(what = "example.txt", to = "ftp://example.com/",
userpwd = "username:password")
```

Where to find FTP archives

To get a taste of the good old FTP times where there was no more than just data and directories, visit http://www.search-ftps.com/ or http://www.filesearching.com/ to search for existing archives. What you will find might occasionally be content of dubious quality, however.

9.1.3 Manipulating URLs to access multiple pages

We usually care little about the web addresses of the sites we visit. Sometimes we might access a web page by entering a URL into our browser, but more frequently we come to a site through a search engine. Either way, once we have accessed a particular site we move around by clicking on links, but do not take note of the fact that the URL changes when accessing the various sites on the same server. We already know that directories on a web server are comparable to the folders on our local hard drive. Once we realize that the directories of the website follow specific systematics, we can make use of this fact and apply it in web scraping by manipulating the URL of a site. Compared with other retrieval strategies, URL manipulation is a "quick and dirty" approach, as we usually do not care about the internal mechanisms that create URLs (e.g., *GET* forms).

Navigating through pages by URL manipulation

Imagine we would like to collect all press releases from the organization Transparency International. Check out the organization's press releases under the heading "News" at http://www.transparency.org/news/pressreleases/. Now select the year 2011 from the drop-down menu. Notice how the statement `year/2011` is appended to the URL. We can apply this observation and call up the press releases from 2010 by changing the figure in the URL. As expected, the browser now displays all press releases from 2010, starting with releases in late December. Notice how the webpage displays 10 hits for each search. Click on "Next" at the bottom of the page. We find that the URL is appended with the statement `P10`. Apparently, we are able to select specific results pages by using multiples of 10. Let us try this by choosing the fourth site of the 2010 press releases by selecting the directory http://www.transparency.org/news/pressreleases/year/2010/P30. In fact, we can wander through the pages by manipulating the URL instead of clicking on HTML buttons.

Now let us capitalize on these insights and implement them in small scraper. We proceed in five steps.

1. We identify the running mechanism in the URL syntax.
2. We retrieve links to the running pages.
3. We download the running pages.
4. We retrieve links to the entries on the running pages.
5. We download the single entries.

URL manipulation

We begin by constructing a function that returns a list of URLs for every page in the index. We have already identified the running mechanism in the URL syntax—a `P` and a multiple of 10 is attached to the base URL for every page other than the first one. To know how many of these pages exist, we retrieve the total number of pages from the bottom line on the base page, which reads "Page x of X". "X" is the total number of pages. We fetch the number with the XPath command `//div[@id='Page']/strong[2]` and use the result (`total_pages`) to construct a vector `add_url` with string additions to the base URL. The first entries are stored on the base URL page which does not need an addition. Therefore, we construct X – 1 snippets to be added to the base URL. We store this number 10 times, as the index runs from 10 to X * 10, rather than from 1 to X in `max_url` and merge it with `/P10` and store it in the object `add_url`.

```
R> baseurl <- htmlParse("http://www.transparency.org/news/
pressreleases/year/2010")
R> xpath <- "//div[@id='Page']/strong[2]"
R> total_pages <- as.numeric(xpathSApply(baseurl, xpath, xmlValue))
R> total_pages
[1] 16

R> max_url <- (total_pages - 1) * 10
R> add_url <- str_c("/P", seq(10, max_url, 10))
R> add_url
 [1] "/P10"  "/P20"  "/P30"  "/P40"  "/P50"  "/P60"  "/P70"  "/P80"
 [9] "/P90"  "/P100" "/P110" "/P120" "/P130" "/P140" "/P150"
```

Next, we construct the full URLs and put them in a list. To fetch entries from the first page as well, we add the base URL to the list. Everything is wrapped into a function `getPageURLs()` that returns the URLs of single index pages as a list.

```
R> getPageURLs <- function(url) {
       baseurl <- htmlParse(url)
       xpath <- "//div[@id='Page']/strong[2]"
       total_pages <- as.numeric(xpathSApply(baseurl, xpath, xmlValue))
       max_url <- (total_pages - 1) * 10
       add_url <- str_c("/P", seq(10, max_url, 10))
```

```
        urls_list <- as.list(str_c(url, add_url))
        urls_list[length(urls_list) + 1] <- url
        return(urls_list)
}
```

Applying the function yields

```
R> url <- "http://www.transparency.org/news/pressreleases/year/2010"
R> urls_list <- getPageURLs(url)
R> urls_list[1:3]
[[1]]
[1] "http://www.transparency.org/news/pressreleases/year/2010/P10"

[[2]]
[1] "http://www.transparency.org/news/pressreleases/year/2010/P20"

[[3]]
[1] "http://www.transparency.org/news/pressreleases/year/2010/P30"
```

Downloading index pages In the third step, we construct a function to download each index page. The function takes the returned list from `getPageURLs()`, extracts the file names, and writes the HTML pages to a local folder.

Notice that we have to add a file name for the base URL index manually because the regular expression `"/P.+"` which identifies the file names does not apply here. This is done in the fourth line of the function. As usual, the download is conducted with `getURL`:

```
R> dlPages <- function(pageurl, folder ,handle) {
       dir.create(folder, showWarnings = FALSE)
       page_name <- str_c(str_extract(pageurl, "/P.+"), ".html")
       if (page_name == "NA.html") { page_name <- "/base.html" }
       if (!file.exists(str_c(folder, "/", page_name))) {
              content <- try(getURL(pageurl, curl = handle))
              write(content, str_c(folder, "/", page_name))
              Sys.sleep(1)
       }
}
```

We perform the download with `l_ply` to download the files stored in the `baselinks_list` list elements.

```
R> handle <- getCurlHandle()
R> l_ply(urls_list, dlPages,
         folder = "tp_index_2010",
         handle = handle)
R> list.files("tp_index_2010")[1:3]
[1] "base.html" "P10.html"  "P100.html"
```

Sixteen files have been downloaded. Now we parse the downloaded index files to identify the links to the individual press releases. The `getPressURLs()` function works as follows. First, we parse the documents into a list. We retrieve all links in the documents using `getHTMLLinks()`. Finally, we extract only those links that refer to one of the press releases.

To do so, we apply the regular expression "http.+/pressrelease/" which uniquely identifies the releases and stores them in a list.

```
R> getPressURLs <- function(folder) {
        pages_parsed <- lapply(str_c(folder, "/", dir(folder)), htmlParse)
        urls <- unlist(llply(pages_parsed, getHTMLLinks))
        press_urls <- urls[str_detect(urls, "http.+/pressrelease/")]
        press_urls_list <- as.list(press_urls)
        return(press_urls_list)
}
```

Applying the function we retrieve a list of links to roughly 150 press releases.

```
R> press_urls_list <- getPressURLs(folder = "tp_index_2010")
R> length(press_urls_list)
[1] 152
```

Downloading press releases

The press releases are downloaded in the last step. The function works similarly to the one that downloaded the index pages. Again, we first retrieve the file names of the press releases based on the full URLs. We apply the rather nasty regular expression `[^//][[:alnum:]_.]+$`. We download the press release files with `getURL()` and store them in the created folder.

```
R> dlPress <- function(press_url, folder, handle) {
        dir.create(folder, showWarnings = FALSE)
        press_filename <- str_c(str_extract(press_url,
                        "[^//][[:alnum:]_.]+$") , ".html")
        if (!file.exists(str_c(folder, "/", press_filename))) {
                content <- try(getURL(press_url, curl = handle))
                write(content, str_c(folder, "/", press_filename))
                Sys.sleep(1)
        }
}
```

We apply this function using

```
R> handle <- getCurlHandle()
R> l_ply(press_urls_list, dlPress,
         folder = "tp_press_2010",
         handle = handle)
R> length(list.files("tp_press_2010"))
[1] 152
```

All 152 files have been downloaded successfully. To process the press releases, we would have to parse them similar to the `getPressURLs()` function and extract the text. Moreover, to accomplish the task that was specified at the beginning of the section we would also have to generalize the functions to loop over the years on the website but the underlying ideas do not change.

In scenarios where the range of URLs is not as clear as in the example described above, we can make use of the `url.exists()` function from the RCurl package. It works analogously to `file.exists()` and indicates whether a given URL exists, that is, whether the server responds without an error.

In many web scraping exercises, we can apply URL manipulation to easily access all the sites that we are interested in. The downside of this type of access to a website is that we need a fairly intimate knowledge of the website and of the websites' directories in order to perform URL manipulations. This is to say that URL manipulation cannot be used to write a crawler for multiple websites as the specific manipulations must be developed for each website.

9.1.4 Convenient functions to gather links, lists, and tables from HTML documents

The XML package provides powerful tools for parsing XML-style documents. Yet it offers more commands that considerably ease information extraction tasks in the web-scraping workflow. The functions `readHTMLTable()`, `readHTMLList()`, and `getHTMLLinks()` help extract data from HTML tables, lists, and internal as well as external links. We illustrate their functionality with a Wikipedia article on Niccolò Machiavelli, an "Italian historian, politician, diplomat, philosopher, humanist, and writer" (Wikipedia 2014).

Extracting links The first function we will inspect is `getHTMLlinks()` which serves to extract links from HTML documents. To illustrate the flexibility of the convenience functions, we prepare several objects. The first object stores the URL for the article (`mac_url`), the second stores the source code (`mac_source`), the third stores the parsed document (`mac_parsed`), and the fourth and last object (`mac_node`) holds only one node of the parsed document, namely the `<p>` node that includes the introductory text.

```
R> mac_url    <- "http://en.wikipedia.org/wiki/Machiavelli"
R> mac_source <- readLines(mac_url, encoding = "UTF-8")
R> mac_parsed <- htmlParse(mac_source, encoding = "UTF-8")
R> mac_node   <- mac_parsed["//p"][[1]]
```

All of these representations of an HTML document (URL, source code, parsed document, and a single node) can be used as input for `getHTMLLinks()` and the other convenience functions introduced in this section.

```
R> getHTMLLinks(mac_url)[1:3]
[1] "/w/index.php?title=Machiavelli&redirect=no"
[2] "/wiki/Machiavelli_(disambiguation)"
[3] "/wiki/File:Portrait_of_Niccol%C3%B2_Machiavelli_by_Santi_di_Tito.jpg"

R> getHTMLLinks(mac_source)[1:3]
[1] "/w/index.php?title=Machiavelli&redirect=no"
[2] "/wiki/Machiavelli_(disambiguation)"
[3] "/wiki/File:Portrait_of_Niccol%C3%B2_Machiavelli_by_Santi_di_Tito.jpg"

R> getHTMLLinks(mac_parsed)[1:3]
[1] "/w/index.php?title=Machiavelli&redirect=no"
[2] "/wiki/Machiavelli_(disambiguation)"
[3] "/wiki/File:Portrait_of_Niccol%C3%B2_Machiavelli_by_Santi_di_Tito.jpg"

R> getHTMLLinks(mac_node)[1:3]
[1] "/wiki/Help:IPA_for_Italian" "/wiki/Renaissance_humanism"
[3] "/wiki/Renaissance"
```

We can also supply XPath expressions to restrict the returned documents to specific subsets, for example, only those links of class `extiw`.

```
R> getHTMLLinks(mac_source,
                xpQuery="//a[@class='extiw']/@href")[1:3]
[1] "//en.wiktionary.org/wiki/chancery"
[2] "//en.wikisource.org/wiki/Catholic_Encyclopedia_(1913)/Niccol%
C3%B2_Machiavelli"
[3] "//commons.wikimedia.org/wiki/Niccol%C3%B2_Machiavelli"
```

`getHTMLLinks()` retrieves links from HTML as well as names of external files. We already made use of the latter feature in Section 9.1.1. An extension of `getHTMLLinks()` is `getHTMLExternalFiles()`, designed to extract only links that point to external files which are part of the document. Let us use the function along with its `xpQuery` parameter. We restrict the set of returned links to those mentioning *Machiavelli* to hopefully find a URL that links to a picture.

```
R> xpath <- "//img[contains(@src, 'Machiavelli')]/@src"
R> getHTMLExternalFiles(mac_source,
                        xpQuery = xpath)[1:3]
[1] "//upload.wikimedia.org/wikipedia/commons/thumb/e/e2/Portrait
_of_Niccol%C3%B2_Machiavelli_by_Santi_di_Tito.jpg/220px-Portrait_
of_Niccol%C3%B2_Machiavelli_by_Santi_di_Tito.jpg"
[2] "//upload.wikimedia.org/wikipedia/commons/thumb/a/a4/
Machiavelli_Signature.svg/128px-Machiavelli_Signature.svg.png"
[3] "//upload.wikimedia.org/wikipedia/commons/thumb/f/f3/
Cesare_borgia-Machiavelli-Corella.jpg/220px-Cesare_borgia-
Machiavelli-Corella.jpg"
```

The first three results look promising; they all point to image files stored on the Wikimedia servers.

Extracting lists

The next convenient function is `readHTMLList()` and as the name already suggests, it extracts list elements (see Section 2.3.7). Browsing through the article we find that under *Discourses on Livy* several citations from the work are pooled as an unordered list that we can easily extract. Note that the function returns a list object where each element corresponds to a list in the HTML. As the citations are the tenth list within the HTML, we figured this out by eyeballing the output of `readHTMLList()` and we use the index operator `[[10]]`.

```
R> readHTMLList(mac_source)[[10]][1:3]
[1] "\"In fact, when there is combined under the same constitution
a prince, a nobility, and the power of the people, then these three
powers will watch and keep each other reciprocally in check.\" Book
I, Chapter II"
[2] "\"Doubtless these means [of attaining power] are cruel and
destructive of all civilized life, and neither Christian, nor even
human, and should be avoided by every one. In fact, the life of a
private citizen would be preferable to that of a king at the expense
of the ruin of so many human beings.\" Bk I, Ch XXVI"
[3] "\"Now, in a well-ordered republic, it should never be necessary
to resort to extra-constitutional measures. ...\" Bk I, Ch XXXIV"
```

Extracting tables The last function of the XML package we would like to introduce at this point is `readHTMLTable()`, a function to extract HTML tables. Not only does the function locate tables within the HTML document, but also transforms them into data frames. As before, the function extracts all tables and stores them in a list. Whenever the extracted HTML tables have information that can be used as name, they are stored as named list item. Let us first get an overview of the tables by listing the table names.

```
R> names(readHTMLTable(mac_source))
 [1] "Niccolò Machiavelli" "NULL"                "NULL"
 [4] "NULL"                "NULL"                "NULL"
 [7] "NULL"                "NULL"                "NULL"
[10] "persondata"
```

There are ten tables; two of them are labeled. Let us extract the last one to retrieve personal information on Machiavelli.

```
R> readHTMLTable(mac_source)$persondata
                 V1                                           V2
1              Name                         Machiavelli, Niccolò
2 Alternative names                         Machiavelli, Niccolò
3 Short description Italian politician and political theorist
4     Date of birth                                  May 3, 1469
5    Place of birth                                     Florence
6     Date of death                                June 21, 1527
7    Place of death                                     Florence
```

Applying element functions A powerful feature of `readHTMLList()` and `readHTMLTable()` is that we can define individual element functions using the `elFun` argument. By default, the function applied to each list item (`<li>`) and each cell of the table (`<td>`), respectively, is `xmlValue()`, but we can specify other functions that take XML nodes as arguments. Let us use another HTML table to demonstrate this feature. The first table of the article gives an overview of Machiavelli's personal information and, in the seventh and eighth rows, lists persons and schools of thought that have influenced him in his thinking as well as those that were influenced by him.

```
R> readHTMLTable(mac_source, stringsAsFactors = F)[[1]][7:8, 1]
[1] "Influenced by\nXenophon, Plutarch, Tacitus, Polybius, Cicero,
Sallust, Livy, Thucydides"
[2] "Influenced\nPolitical Realism, Bacon, Hobbes, Harrington,
Rousseau, Vico, Edward Gibbon, David Hume, John Adams, Cuoco,
Nietzsche, Pareto, Gramsci, Althusser, T. Schelling, Negri, Waltz,
Baruch de Spinoza, Denis Diderot, Carl Schmitt"
```

In the HTML file, the names of philosophers and schools of thought are also linked to the corresponding Wikipedia articles, but this information gets lost by relying on the default element function. Let us replace the default function by one that is designed to extract links—`getHTMLLinks()`. This allows us to extract all links for influential and influenced thinkers.

```
R> influential <- readHTMLTable(mac_source,
                                elFun = getHTMLLinks,
                                stringsAsFactors = FALSE)[[1]][7,]
R> as.character(influential)[1:3]
[1] "/wiki/Xenophon" "/wiki/Plutarch" "/wiki/Tacitus"
```

```
R> influenced <- readHTMLTable(mac_source,
                              elFun = getHTMLLinks,
                              stringsAsFactors = FALSE)[[1]][8,]
R> as.character(influenced)[1:3]
[1] "/wiki/Political_Realism" "/wiki/Francis_Bacon"
[3] "/wiki/Thomas_Hobbes"
```

Extracting links, tables, and lists from HTML documents are ordinary tasks in web scraping practice. These functions save a lot of time or otherwise we would have to spend on constructing suited XPath expressions and keeping our code tidy.

9.1.5 Dealing with HTML forms

Forms are a classical feature of user–server interaction via HTTP on static websites. They vary in size, layout, input type, and other parameters—just think about all the search bars you have used, the radio buttons you have slided, the check marks you have set, the user names and passwords typed in, and so on. Forms are easy to handle with a graphical user interface like a browser, but a little more difficult when they have to be disentangled in the source code. In this section, we will cover the general approach to master forms with R. In the end you should be able to recognize forms, determine the method used to pass the inputs, the location where the information is sent, and how to specify options and parameters for sending data to the servers and capture the result.

We will consider three different examples throughout this section to learn how to prepare your R session, approach forms in general, use the HTTP *GET* method to send forms to the server, use *POST* with *url-encoded* or *multipart* body, and let R automatically generate functions that use *GET* or *POST* with adequate options to send form data.

Filling out forms in the browser and handling them from within R differs in many respects, because much of the work that is usually done by the browser in the background has to be specified explicitly. Using a browser, we

1. fill out the form,
2. push the *submit*, *ok*, *start*, or the *like!* button.
3. let the browser execute the action specified in the source code of the form and send the data to the server,
4. and let the browser receive the returned resources after the server has evaluated the inputs.

In scraping practice, things get a little more complicated. We have to

1. recognize the forms that are involved,
2. determine the method used to transfer the data,
3. determine the address to send the data to,
4. determine the inputs to be sent along,
5. build a valid request and send it out, and
6. process the returned resources.

Preparations In this section, we use functions from the RCurl, XML, stringr, and the plyr packages. Furthermore, we specify an object that captures debug information along the way so that we can check for details if something goes awry (see Section 5.4.3 for details). Additionally, we specify a curl handle with a set of default options—`cookiejar` to enable cookie management, `followlocation` to follow page redirections which may be triggered by the *POST* command, and `autoreferer` to automatically set the `Referer` request header when we have to follow a location redirect. Finally, we specify the `From` and `User-Agent` header manually to stay identifiable:

```
R> info   <- debugGatherer()
R> handle <- getCurlHandle(cookiejar      = "",
                           followlocation = TRUE,
                           autoreferer    = TRUE,
                           debugfunc      = info$update,
                           verbose        = TRUE,
                           httpheader     = list(
                             from         = "eddie@r-datacollection.com",
                             'user-agent' = str_c(R.version$version.string,
                                              ", ", R.version$platform)
                           ))
```

Another preparatory step is to define a function that translates lists of XML attributes into data frames. This will come in handy when we are going to evaluate the attributes of HTML form elements of parsed HTML documents. The function we construct is called `xmlAttrsToDF()` and takes two arguments. The first argument supplies a parsed HTML document and the second an XPath expression specifying the nodes from which we want to collect the attributes. The function extracts the nodes' attributes via `xpathApply()` and `xmlAttrs()` and transforms the resulting list into a data frame while ensuring that attribute names do not get lost and that each attribute value is stored in a separate column:

```
R> xmlAttrsToDF <- function(parsedHTML, xpath) {
    x <- xpathApply(parsedHTML, xpath, xmlAttrs)
    x <- lapply(x, function(x) as.data.frame(t(x)))
    do.call(rbind.fill, x)
}
```

9.1.5.1 GETting to grips with forms

To presenting how to generally approach forms and specifically how to handle forms that demand HTTP *GET*, we use *WordNet*. *WordNet* is a service provided by Princeton University at http://wordnetweb.princeton.edu/perl/webwn. Researchers at Princeton have built up a database of synonyms for English nouns, verbs, and adjectives. They offer their data as an online service. The website relies on an HTML form to gather the parameters and send a request for synonyms—see Princeton University (2010a) for further details and Princeton University (2010b) for the license.

Let us browse to the page and type in a word, for example, *data*. Hitting the *Search WordNet* button results in a change to the URL which now contains 13 parameters.

```
http://wordnetweb.princeton.edu/perl/webwn?s=data&sub=Search+
    WordNet&o2=&o0=1&o8=1&o1=1&o7=&o5=&o9=&o6=&o3=&o4=&h=
```

We have been redirected to another page, which informs us that *data* is a noun and that it has two semantic meanings.

From the fact that the URL is extended with a query string when submitting our search term we can infer that the form uses the HTTP *GET* method to send the data to the server. But let us verify this conclusion. To briefly recap the relevant facts from Chapter 2: HTML forms are specified with the help of `<form>` nodes and their attributes. The `<form>` nodes' attributes define the specifics of the data transfer from client to server. `<input>` nodes are nested in `<form>` nodes and define the kind of data that needs to be supplied to the form.

Inspecting forms with R

We can either use *view source code* feature of a browser to check out the attributes of the form nodes, or we use R to get the information. This time we do the latter. First, we load the page into R and parse it.

```
R> url         <- "http://wordnetweb.princeton.edu/perl/webwn"
R> html_form   <- getURL(url, curl = handle)
R> parsed_form <- htmlParse(html_form)
```

Let us have a look at the form node attributes to learn the specifics of sending data to the server. We use the `xmlAttrsToDF()` that we have set up above for this task.

```
R> xmlAttrsToDF(parsed_form, "//form")
  method action             enctype   name
1    get  webwn multipart/form-data      f
2    get  webwn multipart/form-data change
```

There are two HTML forms on the page, one called `f` and the other `change`. The first form submits the search terms to the server while the second takes care of submitting further options on the type and range of data being returned. For the sake of simplicity, we will ignore the second form.

With regard to the specifics of sending the data, the attribute values tell us that we should use the HTTP method *GET* (`method`) and send it to `webwn` (`action`) which is the location of the form we just downloaded and parsed. The `enctype` parameter with value `multipart/form-data` comes as a bit of a surprise. It refers to how content is encoded in the body of the request. As *GET* explicitly does not use the body to transport data, we disregard this option.

The next task is to get the list of input parameters. When *GET* is used to send data, we can easily spot the parameters sent to the server by inspecting the query string added to the URL. But those parameters might only be a subset of all possible parameters. We therefore use `xmlAttrsToDF()` again to get the full set of inputs and their attributes.

```
R> xmlAttrsToDF(parsed_form, "//form[1]/input")
     type name maxlength           value
1    text    s       500            <NA>
2  submit  sub      <NA> Search WordNet
3  hidden   o2      <NA>
4  hidden   o0      <NA>               1
5  hidden   o8      <NA>               1
6  hidden   o1      <NA>               1
7  hidden   o7      <NA>
8  hidden   o5      <NA>
9  hidden   o9      <NA>
10 hidden   o6      <NA>
```

```
11 hidden   o3       <NA>
12 hidden   o4       <NA>
13 hidden    h       <NA>
```

As suggested by the long query string added to the URL after searching for our first search term, we get a list of 13 input nodes. Recall that there was only one input field on the page—the text field where we specified the search term. Inspecting the inputs reveals that 11 of the input fields are of type `hidden`, that is, input fields which cannot be manipulated by the user. Moreover, input fields of type `submit` are hidden from user manipulation as well, so there is only one parameter left for us to take care of. It turns out that the other parameters are used for submitting options to the server and have nothing to do with the actual search. To make simple search requests, the `s` parameter is sufficient.

Specifying *GET* requests with R

Combining the informations on HTTP method, request location, and parameters, we can now build an adequate request by using one of RCurl's form functions. As the HTTP method to send data to the server is *GET*, we use `getForm()`. Since the location to which we send the request remains the same, we can reuse the URL we used before. As parameter we only supply the `s` parameter with a value equal to the search term that we want to get synonyms for.

```
R> html_form_res <- getForm(uri = url, curl = handle, s = "data")
R> parsed_form_res <- htmlParse(html_form_res)
R> xpathApply(parsed_form_res, "//li", xmlValue)
[[1]]
[1] "S: (n) data, information (a collection of facts from which
conclusions may be drawn) \"statistical data\""

[[2]]
[1] "S: (n) datum, data point (an item of factual information
derived from measurement or research) "
```

Let us also have a look at the header information we supply by inspecting the information stored in the `info` object with the `debugGatherer()` function and reset it afterwards.

```
R> cat(str_split(info$value()["headerOut"], "\r")[[1]])
GET /perl/webwn HTTP/1.1
Host: wordnetweb.princeton.edu
Accept: */*
from: eddie@r-datacollection.com
user-agent: R version 3.0.2 (2013-09-25), x86_64-w64-mingw32

GET /perl/webwn?s=data HTTP/1.1
Host: wordnetweb.princeton.edu
Accept: */*
from: eddie@r-datacollection.com
user-agent: R version 3.0.2 (2013-09-25), x86_64-w64-mingw32
R> info$reset()
```

We find that the requests for fetching the form information and sending the form data are nearly identical, except that in the latter case the query string `?s=data` is appended to the requested resource.

The same could have been achieved by supplying a URL with appended query string and a call to `getURL()`:

```
R> url <- "http://wordnetweb.princeton.edu/perl/webwn?s=data"
R> html_form_res <- getURL(url = url, curl = handle)
```

9.1.5.2 POSTing forms

Forms that use the HTTP method *POST* are in many respects identical to forms that use *GET*. They key difference between the two methods is that with *POST*, the information is transferred in the body of the request. There are two common styles for transporting data in the body, either as *url-encoded* or as *multipart*. While the former is efficient for text data, the latter is better suited for sending files. Thus, depending on the purpose of the form, one or the other *POST* style is expected. The next two sections will show how to handle *POST* forms in practice. The first example deals with a *url-encoded* body and the second one showcases sending *multipart* data.

POST with url-encoded body In the first example, we use a form from http://www.read-able.com. The website offers a service that evaluates the readability of webpages and texts. As before, we use the precomposed handle to retrieve the page and directly parse and save it.

```
R> url  <- "http://read-able.com/"
R> form <- htmlParse(getURL(url = url, curl = handle))
```

Inspecting *POST* forms

Looking for `<form>` nodes reveals that there are two forms in the document. An examination of the site reveals that the first is used to supply a URL to evaluating a webpage's readability, and the second form allows inputting text directly.

```
R> xmlAttrsToDF(form, "//form")
  method    action
1    get check.php
2   post check.php
```

There is no `enctype` specified in the attributes of the second form, so we expect the server to accept both encoding styles. Because *url-encoded* bodies are more efficient for text data, we will use this style to send the data.

An inspection of the second form's input fields indicates that there seem to be no inputs other than the submit button.

```
R> xmlAttrsToDF(form, "//form[2]//input")
```

Looking at the entire source code of the form, we find that there is a `textarea` node that gathers text to be sent to the server.

```
R> xpathApply(form, "//form[2]")
[[1]]
<form method="post" action="check.php">

                                             <p class="instructions">
```

```
                                                    <label title="Paste
a complete (HTML) Document here" for="directInput">Enter text to
check the readability:</label><br /><textarea id="directInput"
name="directInput" rows="10" cols="60"></textarea>

                                                    HTML is allowed - it
will be stripped from the text.
                                            </p>

                                            <p>
                                                    <input type="submit"
value="Calculate Readability" /></p>

                                    </form>

attr(,"class")
[1] "XMLNodeSet"
```

Its `name` attribute is `directInput` which serves as parameter name for sending the text. Let us use a famous quote about data found at http://www.goodreads.com/ to check its readability.

```
R> sentence <- "\"It is a capital mistake to theorize before one has
data. Insensibly one begins to twist facts to suit theories, instead
of theories to suit facts.\" -- Arthur Conan Doyle, Sherlock Holmes"
```

Specifying *POST* requests with R

We send it to the *read-able* server for evaluation. Within the call to `postForm()` we set `style` to `"POST"` for an *url-encoded* transmission of the data.

```
R> res <- postForm(uri = str_c(url, "check.php"),
                   curl = handle,
                   style = "POST",
                   directInput = sentence)
```

Most of the results are presented as HTML tables as shown below.

```
R> readHTMLTable(res)
$'NULL'
  Flesch Kincaid Reading Ease 66.5
1  Flesch Kincaid Grade Level  6.6
2           Gunning Fog Score  6.8
3                  SMOG Index    5
4          Coleman Liau Index 11.4
5 Automated Readability Index  5.7

$'NULL'
             No. of sentences     3
1                No. of words    32
2        No. of complex words     2
3    Percent of complex words 6.25%
4 Average words  per sentence 10.67
5  Average syllables per word  1.53
```

All in all, with a *Grade Level* of 6.6, 12- to 13-year-old children should be able to understand Sherlock Holmes' dictum. Let us check out the header information that was sent to the server.

```
R> cat(str_split(info$value()["headerOut"], "\r")[[1]])
GET / HTTP/1.1
Host: read-able.com
Accept: */*
from: eddie@r-datacollection.com
user-agent: R version 3.0.2 (2013-09-25), x86_64-w64-mingw32

POST /check.php HTTP/1.1
Host: read-able.com
Accept: */*
from: eddie@r-datacollection.com
user-agent: R version 3.0.2 (2013-09-25), x86_64-w64-mingw32
Content-Length: 277
Content-Type: application/x-www-form-urlencoded
```

The second header confirms that the data have been sent via *POST*, using the following *url-encoded* body.[4]

```
R> cat(str_split(info$value()["dataOut"], "\r")[[1]])
directInput=%22It%20is%20a%20capital%20mistake%20to%20theorize%20
before%20one%20has%20data%2E%20Insensibly%20one%20begins%20to%20
twist%20facts%20to%20suit%20theories%2C%20instead%20of%20theories%20
to%20suit%20facts%2E%22%20%2D%2D%20Arthur%20Conan%20Doyle%2C%20
Sherlock%20Holmes

R> info$reset()
```

POST with multipart-encoded body The second example considers a *POST* with a *multipart*-encoded body. *Fix Picture* (http://www.fixpicture.org/) is a web service to transform image files from one format to another. In our example we will transform a picture from PNG format to PDF.

Let us begin by retrieving a picture in PNG format and save it to our disk.

```
R> url <- "r-datacollection.com/materials/http/sky.png"
R> sky <- getBinaryURL(url = url, curl = handle)
R> writeBin(sky, "sky.png")
```

Next, we collect the main page of *Fix Picture* including the HTML form.

```
R> url   <- "http://www.fixpicture.org/"
R> form  <- htmlParse(getURL(url = url, curl = handle))
```

[4]Recall that URL encoding refers to the process of replacing special characters with their percent-escaped representations. For more information on the topic see Section 5.1.2.

We check out the attributes of the form nodes.

```
R> xmlAttrsToDF(form, "//form")
  name   id               action method                enctype
1 form form resize.php?LANG=en   post multipart/form-data
```

We find that there is only one form on the page. The form expects data to be sent with *POST* and a *multipart*-encoded body. The list of possible inputs is extensive, as we can not only transform the picture from one format to another but also flip and rotate it, restrict it to grayscale, or choose the quality of the new format. For the sake of simplicity, we restrict ourselves to a simple transformation from one format to another.

```
R> xmlAttrsToDF(form, "//input")[1:2, c("name", "type", "class", "value")]
   name  type       class value
1 image  file upload-file  <NA>
2  <NA> image  btn_submit  <NA>
```

The important input is the image. The `upload-file` value for the `class` attribute in one of the `<input>` nodes suggests that we supply the file's content under this name.

There is no `input` node for selecting the format of the output file. Inspecting the source code reveals that a `select` node is enclosed in the form. Select elements allow choosing between several options which are supplied as `option` nodes:

```
R> xmlAttrsToDF(form, "//select")
        onchange     id   name
1 changeSelect() format format
```

The name attribute of the `select` node indicates under which name (`format`) the value—listed within the *option* nodes should be sent to the server.

```
R> xmlAttrsToDF(form, "//select/option")
  value
1  jpeg
2   png
3  tiff
4   pdf
5   bmp
6   gif
```

Disregarding all other possible options, we are ready to send the data along with parameters to the server. For RCurl to read the file and send it to the server, we have to use RCurl's `fileUpload()` function that takes care of providing the correct information for the underlying *libcurl* library. The following code snippet sends the data to the server.

```
R> res <- postForm(uri = "http://www.fixpicture.org/resize.php?LANG=en",
                   image = fileUpload(filename = "sky.png",
                                      contentType = "image/png"),
                   format = "pdf",
                   curl = handle)
```

The result is not the transformed file itself but another HTML document from which we extract the link to the file.

```
R> doc <- htmlParse(res)
R> link <- str_c(url, xpathApply(doc, "//a/@href", as.character)[[1]])
```

We download the transformed file and write it to our local drive.

```
R> resImage <- getBinaryURL(link, curl = handle)
R> writeBin(resImage, "sky.pdf", useBytes = TRUE)
```

The result is the PNG picture transformed to PDF format. Last but not least let us have a look at the *multipart* body with the data that have been sent via *POST*:

```
R> cat(str_split(info$value()["dataOut"], "\r")[[1]])
----------------------------30059d14e820
Content-Disposition: form-data; name="image"; filename="sky.png"
Content-Type: image/png

[[BINARY DATA]]
----------------------------30059d14e820
Content-Disposition: form-data; name="format"

pdf
----------------------------30059d14e820--
```

The `[[BINARY DATA]]` snippet indicates binary data that cannot be properly displayed with text. Finally, we reset the info slot again.

```
R> info$reset()
```

9.1.5.3 Automating form handling—the RHTMLForms package

The tools we have introduced in the previous paragraphs can be adapted to specific cases to handle form interactions. One shortcoming is that the interaction requires a lot of manual labor and inspection of the source code. One attempt to automate some of the necessary steps is the RHTMLForms package (Temple Lang et al. 2012). It was designed to automatically create functions that fill out forms, select the appropriate HTTP method to send data to the server, and retrieve the result. The RHTMLForms package is not hosted on CRAN. You can install it by supplying the location of the repository.

```
R> install.packages("RHTMLForms", repos = "http://www.omegahat.org/R",
type = "source")
R> library(RHTMLForms)
```

The basic procedure of RHTMLForms works as follows:

1. We use `getHTMLFormDescription()` on the URL where the HTML form is located and save its results in an object—let us call it `forms`.
2. We use `createFunction()` on the first item of the `forms` object and save the results in another object, say `form_function`.
3. `formFunction()` takes input fields as options to send them to the server and return the result.

Purpose-built form functions

Let us go through this process using *WordNet* again. We start by gathering the form description information and creating the form function.

```
R> url          <- "http://wordnetweb.princeton.edu/perl/webwn"
R> forms        <- getHTMLFormDescription(url)
R> formFunction <- createFunction(forms[[1]])
```

Having created `formFunction()`, we use it to send form data to the server and retrieve the results.

```
R> html_form_res   <- formFunction(s = "data", .curl = handle)
R> parsed_form_res <- htmlParse(html_form_res)
R> xpathApply(parsed_form_res,"//li", xmlValue)
[[1]]
[1] "S: (n) data, information (a collection of facts from which
conclusions may be drawn) \"statistical data\""

[[2]]
[1] "S: (n) datum, data point (an item of factual information
derived from measurement or research) "
```

Let us have a look at the function we just created.

```
R> args(formFunction)

function ( s = "",
          .url = "http://wordnetweb.princeton.edu/perl/webwn",
           ...,
          .reader = NULL,
          .formDescription = list(formAttributes = c(
            "get",
            "http://wordnetweb.princeton.edu/perl/webwn",
            "multipart/form-data",
            "f"),
          elements = list(
            s = list(name = "s",
                    nodeAttributes = c("text", "s", "500"),
                    defaultValue = ""),
            o2 = list(name = "o2", value = "" ),
            o0 = list(name = "o0", value = "1"),
            o8 = list(name = "o8", value = "1"),
            o1 = list(name = "o1", value = "1"),
            o7 = list(name = "o7", value = "" ),
            o5 = list(name = "o5", value = "" ),
            o9 = list(name = "o9", value = "" ),
            o6 = list(name = "o6", value = "" ),
            o3 = list(name = "o3", value = "" ),
            o4 = list(name = "o4", value = "" ),
            h  = list(name = "h" , value = "" )),
          url = "http://wordnetweb.princeton.edu/perl/webwn"),
          .opts = structure(list(
                  referer = "http://wordnetweb.princeton.edu/perl/webwn"),
                  .Names = "referer"),
          .curl = getCurlHandle(),
          .cleanArgs = NULL)
```

Although it might look intimidating at first, it is easier than it looks because most of the options are for internal use. The options are set automatically and we can disregard them—`.reader`, `.formDescription`, `elements`, `.url`, `url`, and `.cleanArgs`. We are already familiar with some of the options like `.curl` and `.opts`. In fact, when looking at the call to `formFunction()` above you will notice that the same handler was used as before and the updation of `info` was successful. That is because under the hood of these functions all requests are made with the RCurl functions `getForm()` and `postForm()` so that we can expect `.opts` and `.curl` to work in the same way as when using pure RCurl functions.

The last set of options are the names of the inputs we fill in and send to the server. In our case, `createFunction()` correctly recognized `o0` to `o8` and `h` as inputs that need not be manipulated by users. The `elements` argument stores the default values, but in contrast to the input that stores the search term—`s`—which got an option with the same name, `createFunction()` did not create arguments for `formFunction()` that allow specifying values for `o0`, `o1`, and so on, as they are not necessary for the *POST* command.

The RHTMLForms packages might sound like they simplify interactions with HTML forms to a great extent. While it is true that we save some of the actual coding, the interactions still require a fairly intimate knowledge of the form in order to be able to interact with it. This is to say that it is difficult to interact sensibly with a form if you do not know the type of input and output for a form.

9.1.6 HTTP authentication

Not all places on the Web are accessible to everyone. We have learned in Section 5.2.2 that HTTP offers authentication techniques which restrict content from unauthorized users, namely basic and digest authentication. Performing basic authentication with R is straightforward with the RCurl package.

As a short example, we try to access the "solutions" section at www.r-datacollection.com/materials/solutions. When trying to access the resources with our browser, we are confronted with a login form (see Figure 9.1). In R we can pass username and password to the server with *libcurl*'s `userpwd` option. Base64 encoding is performed automatically.

```
R> url <- "www.r-datacollection.com/materials/solutions"
R> cat(getURL(url, userpwd = "teacher:sesame", followlocation = TRUE))
solutions coming soon
```

The `userpwd` option also works for digest authentication, and we do not have to manually deal with nonces, algorithms, and hash codes—*libcurl* takes care for these things on its own.

Storing passwords

To avoid storing passwords in the code, it can be convenient to put them in the *.Rprofile* file, as R reads it automatically with every start (see Nolan and Temple Lang 2014, p. 295).

```
R> options(RDataCollectionLogin = "teacher:sesame")
```

We can retrieve and use the password using `getOption()`.

```
R> getURL(url, userpwd = getOption("RDataCollectionLogin"),
followlocation = TRUE)
```

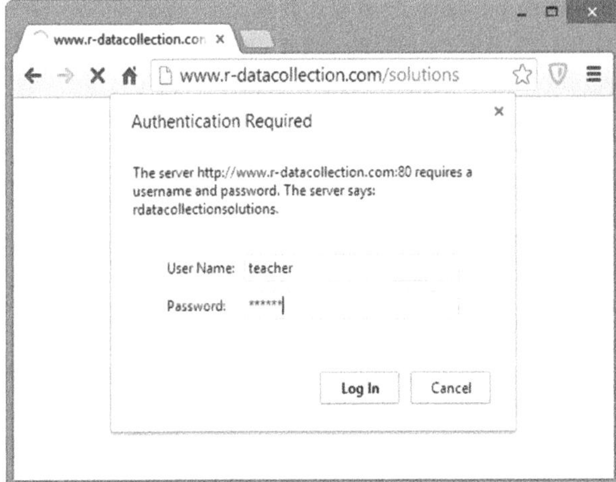

Figure 9.1 Screenshot of HTTP authentication mask at http://www.r-datacollection.com/materials/solutions

9.1.7 Connections via HTTPS

The secure transfer protocol HTTPS (see Section 5.3.1) becomes increasingly common. In order to retrieve content from servers via HTTPS, we can draw on *libcurl*/RCurl which support SSL connections. In fact, we do not have to care much about the encryption and SSL negotiation details, as they are handled by *libcurl* in the background by default.

Let us consider an example. The Inter-university Consortium for Political and Social Research (ICPSR) at the University of Michigan provides access to a huge archive of social science data. We are interested in just a tiny fraction of it—some meta-information on survey variables. At https://www.icpsr.umich.edu/icpsrweb/ICPSR/ssvd/search, the ICPSR offers a fielded search for variables. The search mask allows us to specify variable label, question text or category label, and returns a list of results with some snippets of information. What makes this page a good exercise is that it has to be accessed via HTTPS, as the URL in the browser reveals. In principle, connecting to websites via HTTPS can be just as easy as this

```
R> url <- "https://www.icpsr.umich.edu/icpsrweb/ICPSR/ssvd/search"
R> getURL(url)
Error: SSL certificate problem, verify that the CA cert is OK.
Details:
error:14090086:SSL routines:SSL3_GET_SERVER_CERTIFICATE:certificate
verify failed
```

Setting up a successful connection does not seem to always be straightforward. The error message states that the server certificate signed by a trusted certificate authority (CA)—necessary to prove the server's identity—could not be verified. This error could indicate that the server should not be trusted because it is not able to provide a valid proof of its identity. In this case, however, the reason for this error is different and we can easily remedy the problem. What *libcurl* tries to do when connecting to a server via HTTPS is to access the locally stored library of CA signatures to validate the server's first response. On some systems—ours included—*libcurl* has difficulties finding the relevant file (*cacert.pem*) on the local drive. We therefore have to specify the path to the file manually and hand it to our gathering function with the argument `cainfo`. We can either supply the directory where our browser stores its library of certificates or use the file that comes with the installation of RCurl.

```
R> signatures = system.file("CurlSSL", cainfo = "cacert.pem",
                           package = "RCurl")
R> res <- getURL(url, cainfo = signatures)
```

Alternatively, we can update the bundle of CA root certificates. A current version can be accessed at http://curl.haxx.se/ca/cacert.pem. In cases where validation of the server certificate still fails, we can prevent *libcurl* from trying to validate the server altogether. This is done with the `ssl.verifypeer` argument (see Nolan and Temple Lang 2014, p. 300).

```
R> res <- getURL(url, ssl.verifypeer = FALSE)
```

This might be a potentially risky choice if the server is in fact not trustworthy. After all, it is the primary purpose of HTTPS to provide means to establish secure connections to a verified server.

Returning to the example, we examine the *GET* form with which we can query the ICPSR database. The `action` parameter reveals that the *GET* refers to /icpsrweb/ICPSR/ssvd/variables. The `<input>` elements are `variableLabel`, `questionText`, and `categoryLabel`. We re-specify the target URL in `u_action` and set up a curl handle. It stores the CA signatures and can be used across multiple requests. Finally, we formulate a `getForm()` call searching for questions that contain 'climate change' in their label, and extract the number of results from the query.

```
R> url_action <- "https://www.icpsr.umich.edu/icpsrweb/ICPSR/ssvd/
variables?"
R> handle <- getCurlHandle(cainfo = signatures)
R> res <- getForm(url_action,
                 variableLabel = "climate+change",
                 questionText = "",
                 categoryLabel = "",
                 curl = handle)
R> str_extract(res, "Your query returned [[:digit:]]+ variables")
[1] "Your query returned 263 variables"
```

This is a minimal evaluation of our search results. We could easily extract more information on the single questions and query other question specifics, too.

9.1.8 Using cookies

Cookies are used to allow HTTP servers to *re*-recognize clients, because HTTP itself is a stateless protocol that treats each exchange of request and response as though it were the first (see Section 5.2.1). With RCurl and its underlying *libcurl* library, cookie management with R is quite easy. All we have to do is to turn it on and keep it running across several requests with the use of a curl handle—setting and sending the right cookie at the right time is managed in the background.

Preparations

In this section, we draw on functions from the packages RCurl, XML, and stringr for HTTP client support, HTML parsing, and XPath queries as well as convenient text manipulation. Furthermore, we create an object `info` that logs information on exchanged information between our client and the servers we connect to. We also create a handle that is used throughout this section.

```
R> info   <- debugGatherer()
R> handle <- getCurlHandle(cookiejar      = "",
                           followlocation = TRUE,
                           autoreferer    = TRUE,
                           debugfunc      = info$update,
                           verbose        = TRUE,
                           httpheader     = list(
                             from         = "eddie@r-datacollection.com",
                             'user-agent' = str_c(R.version$version.string,
                                 ", ", R.version$platform)
                           ))
```

The most important option for this section is the first argument in the handle—`cookiejar = ""`. Specifying the `cookiejar` option even without supplying a file name for the jar—a place to store cookie information in—activates cookie management by the handle. The two options to follow (`followlocation` and `autoreferer`) are nice-to-have options that preempt problems which might occur due to redirections to other resources. The remaining options are known from above.

The general approach for using cookies with R is to rely on RCurl's cookie management by reusing a handle with activated cookie management, like the one specified above, in subsequent requests.

9.1.8.1 Filling an online shopping cart

Although cookie support is most likely needed for accessing webpages that require logins in practice, the following example illustrates cookies with a bookshop shopping cart at *Biblio*, a page that specializes in finding and ordering *used, rare, and out-of-print books*.

Let us browse to http://www.biblio.com/search.php?keyisbn=data and put some books into our cart. For the sake of simplicity, the query string appended to the URL already issues a search for books with `data` as keyword. Each time we select a book for our cart by clicking on the *add to cart* button, we are redirected to the cart (http://www.biblio.com/cart.php). We can go back to the search page, select another book and add it to the cart.

To replicate this from within R, we first define the URL leading to the search results page (`search_url`) as well as the URL leading to the shopping cart (`cart_url`) for later use.

```
R> search_url <- "www.biblio.com/search.php?keyisbn=data"
R> cart_url   <- "www.biblio.com/cart.php"
```

Next, we download the search results page and directly parse and save it in `searchPage`.

```
R> search_page <- htmlParse(getURL(url = search_url, curl = handle))
```

Adding items to the shopping cart is done via HTML forms.

```
R> xpathApply(search_page, "//div[@class='order-box'][position()<2]/
form")
[[1]]
<form class="ob-add-form" action="http://www.biblio.com/cart.php"
method="get">
```

```
  <input type="hidden" name="bid" value="652559100" />
  <input type="hidden" name="add" value="1" />
  <input type="hidden" name="int" value="keyword_search" />
  <input type="submit" value="Add to cart" class="add-cart-button"
title="Add this item to your cart" onclick="_gaq.push(['_trackEvent',
'cart_search_add', 'relevance', '1']);" />
</form>

attr(,"class")
[1] "XMLNodeSet"
```

We extract the book IDs to later add items to the cart.

```
R> xpath <- "//div[@class='order-box'][position()<4]/form/input
[@name='bid']/@value"
R> bids <- unlist(xpathApply(search_page, xpath, as.numeric))
R> bids
[1] 652559100 453475278 468759385
```

Requests with cookies

Now we add the first three items from the search results page to the shopping cart by sending the necessary information (`bid`, `add`, and `int`) to the server. Notice that by passing the same handle to the request via the `curl` option, we automatically add received cookies to our requests.

```
R> for (i in seq_along(bids)) {
    res <- getForm(uri = cart_url, curl = handle, bid = bids[i],
add = 1, int = "keyword_search")
}
```

Finally, we retrieve the shopping cart and check out the items that have been stored.

```
R> cart <- htmlParse(getURL(url = cart_url, curl = handle))
R> clean <- function(x) str_replace_all(xmlValue(x), "(\t)|(\n\n)", "")
R> cat(xpathSApply(cart, "//div[@class='title-block']", clean))

DATA
by Hill, Anthony (ed)
Developing Language Through Design and Technology
by DATA
Guide to Design and technology Resources
by DATA
```

Reconsidering the headers

As expected, there are three items stored in the cart. Let us consider again the headers sent with our requests and received from the server. We first issued a request that did not contain any cookies.

```
R> cat(str_split(info$value()["headerOut"], "\r")[[1]][1:13])

GET /search.php?keyisbn=data HTTP/1.1
Host: www.biblio.com
Accept: */*
from: eddie@r-datacollection.com
user-agent: R version 3.0.2 (2013-09-25), x86_64-w64-mingw32
```

The server responded with the prompt to set two cookies—one called `vis`, the other `variation`.

```
R> cat(str_split(info$value()["headerIn"], "\r")[[1]][1:14])

HTTP/1.1 200 OK
Server: nginx
Date: Thu, 06 Mar 2014 10:27:23 GMT
Content-Type: text/html; charset=UTF-8
Transfer-Encoding: chunked
Connection: keep-alive
Keep-Alive: timeout=60
Set-Cookie: vis=language%3Ade%7Ccountry%3A6%7Ccurrency%3A9%7Cvisitor
%3AVrCZ...; expires=Tue, 05-Mar-2019 10:27:21 GMT; path=/;
domain=.biblio.com; httponly
Set-Cookie: variation=res_a; expires=Fri, 07-Mar-2014 10:27:21 GMT;
path=/; domain=.biblio.com; httponly
Vary: User-Agent,Accept-Encoding
Expires: Fri, 07 Mar 2014 10:27:23 GMT
Cache-Control: max-age=86400
Cache-Control: no-cache
```

Our client responded with a new request, now containing the two cookies.

```
R> cat(str_split(info$value()["headerOut"], "\r")[[1]][1:13])

GET /cart.php?bid=652559100&add=1&int=keyword%5Fsearch HTTP/1.1
Host: www.biblio.com
Accept: */*
Cookie: variation=res_a; vis=language%3Ade%7Ccountry%3A6%7Ccurrency
%3A9%7Cvisitor%3AVrCZz...
from: eddie@r-datacollection.com
user-agent: R version 3.0.2 (2013-09-25), x86_64-w64-mingw32
```

If we had failed to supply the cookies, our shopping cart would have remained empty. The following request is identical to the request made above—we use the same handler and code—except that we use `cookielist = "ALL"` to reset all cookies collected so far.

```
R> cart <- htmlParse(getURL(url = cart_url, curl = handle,
cookielist = "ALL"))
R> clean <- function(x) str_replace_all(xmlValue(x), "(\t)|(\n\n)", "")
R> cat(xpathSApply(cart, "//div[@class='title-block']", clean))
```

Consequently, the cart is returned empty because without cookies the server has no way of knowing which actions, like adding items to the shopping cart, have been taken so far.

9.1.8.2 Further tricks of the trade

The approach from above—define and use a handle with enabled cookie management and let RCurl and *libcurl* take care of further details of HTTP communication—will be sufficient in most cases. Nevertheless, sometimes more control of the specifics is needed. In the following we will go through some further features in handling cookies with RCurl.

Adding cookies manually

We have specified `cookiejar = ""` in the previous section to activate automatic cookie management. If a file name is supplied to this option, for example, `cookiejar = "cookies.txt"`, all cookies are stored in this file whenever `cookielist = "FLUSH"` is specified as option to an RCurl function using the handle or via `curlSetOpt()`.

```
R> handle <- getCurlHandle(cookiejar = "cookies.txt")
R> res <- getURL("http://httpbin.org/cookies/set?k1=v1&k2=v2",
curl = handle)
R> handle <- curlSetOpt(cookielist = "FLUSH", curl = handle)
```

An example of a cookie file looks as follows:

```
R> readLines("cookies.txt")
[1] "# Netscape HTTP Cookie File"
[2] "# http://curl.haxx.se/rfc/cookie_spec.html"
[3] "# This file was generated by libcurl! Edit at your own risk."
[4] ""
[5] "httpbin.org\tFALSE\t/\tFALSE\t0\tk2\tv2"
[6] "httpbin.org\tFALSE\t/\tFALSE\t0\tk1\tv1"
```

We can use the information in the file to get a set of initial cookies using the `cookiefile` option.

```
R> new_handle <- getCurlHandle(cookiefile = "cookies.txt")
```

Besides writing collected cookies to a file, we can also clear the list of cookies collected so far with `cookielist="ALL"`.

```
R> getURL("http://httpbin.org/cookies", curl = new_handle,
cookielist = "ALL")
[1] "{\n  \"cookies\": {\n    \"k2\": \"v2\",\n    \"k1\": \"v1\" n
}\n}"
```

Last but not least, although RCurl and *libcurl* will handle cookies set via HTTP reliably if cookies are set by other technologies, for example, by JavaScript—it is necessary to provide some cookies manually. We can do this by providing the `cookie` option with the exact specification of the contents of cookies.

```
R> getURL("http://httpbin.org/cookies", cookie = "name=Eddie;age=32")
[1] "{\n  \"cookies\": {\n    \"name\": \"Eddie\",\n    \"age\":
\"32\"\n  }\n}"
```

9.1.9 Scraping data from AJAX-enriched webpages with Selenium/Rwebdriver

We learned in Chapter 6 that accessing particular information in webpages may be impeded when a site employs methods for dynamic data requests, especially through XHR objects. We illustrated that in certain situations this problem can be circumvented through the use of Web Developer Tools which can reveal the target source from which AJAX-enriched webpages query their information. Unfortunately, this approach does not constitute a universal solution to all extraction problems where dynamic data requests are involved. For one reason, the source may not be so easily spotted as in the stylized examples that we introduced but requires time-consuming investigation of the respective code and considerably more knowledge about JavaScript and the XHR object. Another problem that renders this approach infeasible is that AJAX is frequently not directly responsible for accessing a specific data source but only interacts with an intermediate server-side scripting language like PHP. PHP allows evaluating queries and sending requests to a database, for example, a MySQL database (see Chapter 7), and then feeds the returned data back to the AJAX callback function and into the DOM tree. Effectively, such an approach would conceal the target source and eliminate the option of directly accessing it.

In this section, we introduce a generalized approach to cope with dynamically rendered webpages by means of browser control. The idea is the following: Instead of bypassing web browsers, we leverage their capabilities of interpreting JavaScript and formulating changes to the live DOM tree by directly including them into the scraping process. Essentially, this means that all communication with a webpage is routed through a web browser session to which we send and from which we receive information. There are numerous programs which allow such an approach. Here, we introduce the Selenium/Webdriver framework for browser automation (Selenium Project 2014a,b) and its implementation in R via the Rwebdriver package. We start by presenting the problems caused by a running example. We then turn to illustrating the basic idea behind Selenium/Webdriver, explain how to install the Rwebdriver package, and show how to direct commands to the browser directly from the R command line. Using the running example, we discuss the implemented methods and how we can leverage them for web scraping.

9.1.9.1 Case study: Federal Contributions Database

As a running example we try to obtain data from a database on financial contributions to US parties and candidates. The data have originally been collected and published by OpenSecrets.org under a non-restrictive license (Center for Responsive Politics 2014). A sample of the data has been fed to a database that can be accessed at http://r-datacollection.com/materials/selenium/dbQuery.html. As always, we start by trying to learn the structure of the page and the way it requests and handles information of interest. The tool of choice for this task are browser-implemented Web Developer Tools which were introduced in Section 6.3. Let us go through the following steps:

1. Open a new browser window and go to http://r-datacollection.com/materials/selenium/dbQuery.html. In the *Network* tab of your Web Developer Tools you should spot that opening the page has triggered requests of three additional files: *dbQuery.html* which includes the front end HTML code as well as the auxiliary JavaScript code, *jquery-1.8.0.min.js* which is the *jQuery* library, and *bootstrap.css*, a style sheet. The visual display of the page should be more or less similar to the one shown in Figure 9.2.

2. Choose input values from the scroll-down menus and click the submit button. Upon clicking, your *Network* tab should indicate the request of a file named *getEntry.php?y=2013&m=01&r=&p=&t=T* or similar, depending on the values you have picked.

3. Take a look again at the page view to ensure that an HTML table has been created at the lower end of the page. While it is not directly obvious where this information

Federal Contributions Database

DB Query

Year: 2013

Month: January

Recipient:

Party:
Republican
Democrat

Type:
Table
Visualization

Submit

Results

No results

Figure 9.2 The Federal Contributions database

comes from, usually a request to a PHP file is employed to fetch information from an underlying MySQL database using the parameter value pairs transmitted in the URL to construct the query to the database. This complicates extraction matters, since working directly with the database is usually not possible because we do not have the required access information and are thus restricted to working with the retrieved output from the PHP file.

9.1.9.2 Selenium and the Rwebdriver package

Selenium/Webdriver is an open-source suite of software with the primary purpose of providing a coherent, cross-platform framework for testing applications that run natively in the browser. In the development of web applications, testing is a necessary step to establish expected functionality of the application, minimize potential security and accessibility issues, and guarantee reliability under increased user traffic. Before the creation of Selenium this kind of testing had been carried out manually—a tedious and error-prone undertaking. Selenium solves this problem by providing drivers to control browser behavior such as clicks, scrolls, swipes, and text inputs. This enables programmatic approaches to the problem by using a scripting language to characterize sequences of user behaviors and report if the application fails.

Installing the Rwebdriver package

Selenium's capability to drive interactions with the webpage through the browser is of more general use besides testing purposes. Since it allows to remote-control the browser, we can work with and request information directly from the live DOM tree, that is, how the visual display is presented in the browser window. Accessing Selenium functionality from within R is possible via the Rwebdriver package. It is available from a GitHub repository and can be

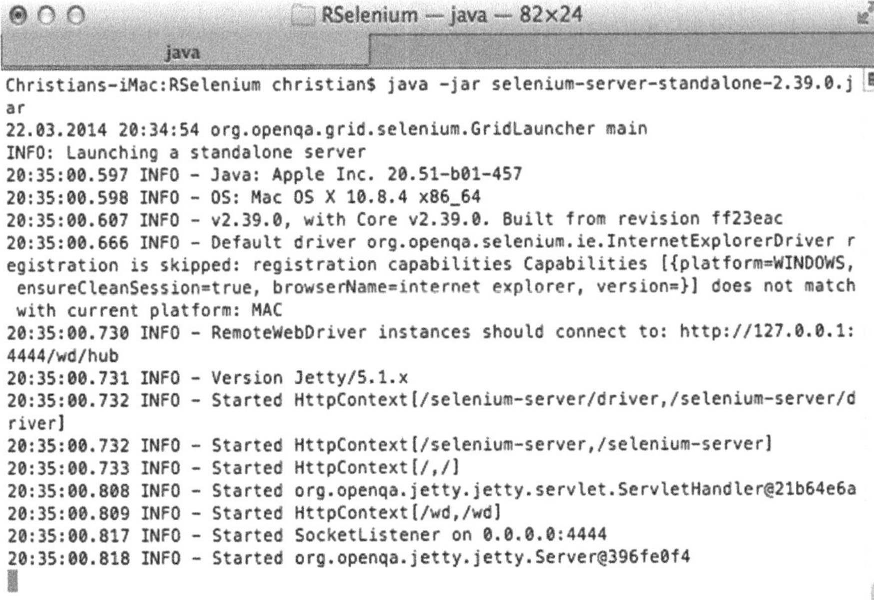

Figure 9.3 Initializing the Selenium Java Server

installed with the `install_github()` function from the devtools package (Wickham and Chang 2013).

```
R> library(devtools)
R> install_github(repo = "Rwebdriver", username = "crubba")
```

Getting started with Selenium Webdriver Using Selenium requires initiating the Selenium Java Server. The server is responsible for launching and killing browsers as well as receiving and interpreting the browser commands. The communication with the server from inside the programming environment works via simple HTTP messages. To get the server up and running, the Selenium server file needs to be downloaded from http://docs.seleniumhq.org/download/ to the local file system. The server file follows the naming convention (*selenium-server-standalone-<version-number>.jar*).[5] In order to initiate the server, open the system prompt, change the directory to the jar-file location, and execute the file.

```
cd Rwebdriver/
java -jar selenium-server-standalone-2.39.0.jar
```

The console output should resemble the one printed in Figure 9.3. The server is now initiated and waits for commands. The system prompt may be minimized and we can turn

[5] At the time of writing, the latest server version is 2.39.0.

our attention back to the R console. Here, we first load the Rwebdriver as well as the XML package.

```
R> library(Rwebdriver)
R> library(XML)
```

The first step is to create a new browser window. This can be accomplished through the `start_session()` function which requires passing the address of the Java server—by default http://localhost:4444/wd/hub/. Additionally, we pass `firefox` to the `browser` argument to instruct the server to produce a Firefox browser window.

```
R> start_session(root = "http://localhost:4444/wd/hub/", browser =
"firefox")
```

Once the command is executed, the Selenium API opens a new Firefox window to which we can now direct browser requests.

Using Selenium for web scraping We now return to the running example and explore some of Selenium's capabilities. Note that we are not introducing all functionality of the package but focus our attention to functions most commonly used in the web scraping process. For a full list of implemented methods, see Table 9.1.

Accessing a webpage

Let us assume we wish to access the database through its introductory page at http://www.r-datacollection.com/materials/selenium/intro.html. To direct the browser to a specific webpage, we can use `post.url()` with specified `url` parameter.

```
R> post.url(url = "http://www.r-datacollection.com/materials/
selenium/intro.html")
```

Retrieving the current URL

The browser should respond and display the *intro* webpage. When a page forwards the browser to another page, it can be helpful to retrieve the current browser URL, since this may differ from the one that was specified in the query. We can obtain the information through the `get.url()` command.

```
R> get.url()

[1]"http://r-datacollection.com/materials/selenium/intro.html"
```

Retrieving the page title

The returned output is a standard character vector. To pull the page title of the browser window, use `page_title()`.

```
R> page_title()

[1]"The Federal Contributions Database"
```

Performing clicks

To arrive at the form for querying the database, we need to perform a click on the *enter* button at the bottom right. Performing clicks with Selenium requires a two-step process. First, we need to create an identifier for the button element. Selenium allows specifying such an identifier through multiple ways. Since we already know how to work with XPath expressions (see Chapter 4), we will employ this method. By using the Web Developer Tools, we can obtain the following XPath expression for the button element, `/html/body/div/div[2]/form/input`. When we pass the XPath expression as a string

Table 9.1 Overview of Selenium methods (v.0.1)

Command	Arguments	Output
`start_session()`	`root, browser`	Creates a new session
`quit_session()`		Closes session
`status()`		Queries the server's current status
`active_sessions()`		Retrieves information on active sessions
`post.url()`	`url`	Opens new *url*
`get.url()`		Receives URL from current webpage
`element_find()`	`by, value`	Finds elements *by* method and the *value*
`element_xpath_find()`	`value`	Finds elements corresponding to XPath string *value*
`element_ptext_find()`	`value`	Finds elements corresponding to text string *value*
`element_css_find()`	`value`	Finds elements corresponding to CSS selector string *value*
`element_click()`	`ID, times, button`	Clicks on element *ID*
`element_clear()`	`ID`	Clears input value from element *ID*'s text field
`page_back()`	`times`	One page backward
`page_forward()`	`times`	One page forward
`page_refresh()`		Refreshes current webpage
`page_source()`		Receives HTML source string
`page_title()`		Receives webpage title string
`window_handle()`		Returns handle of the activated window
`window_handles()`		Returns all window handles in current session
`window_change()`	`handle`	Changes focus to window with *handle*
`window_close()`	`handle`	Closes window with *handle*
`get_window_size()`	`handle`	Returns vector of current window size
`post_window_size()`	`size, handle`	Posts a new window *size* for window *handle*
`get.window_position()`	`handle`	Returns *x,y* coordinates of window *handle*
`post_window_position()`	`position, handle`	Changes coordinates of window *handle*
`key`	`terms`	Post keyboard *term* values

to the `element_xpath_find()` function, we are returned the corresponding element ID from the live DOM. Let us go ahead and save the ID in a new object called `buttonID`.

```
R> buttonID <- element_xpath_find(value = "/html/body/div/div[2]/
form/input")
```

The second step is to actually perform the left-mouse click on the identified element. For this task, we make use of `element_click()`, and pass `buttonID` as the `ID` argument.

```
R> element_click(ID = buttonID)
```

Window handles

This causes the browser to change the page to the one displayed in Figure 9.2. Additionally, you might have observed a pop-up window opening upon clicking the button. The occurrence of pop-ups generates a little complication, since they cause Selenium to switch the focus of its activate window to the newly opened pop-up. To return focus to the database page, we need to first obtain all active window handles using `window_handles()`.

```
R> allHandles <- window_handles()
```

To change the focus back on the database window, you can use the `window_change()` function and pass the window handle that corresponds to the correct window. In this case, it is the first element in `allHandles`.[6]

```
R> window_change(allHandles[1])
```

Identifying elements

Now that we have accessed the database page, we can start to query information from it. Let us try to fetch contribution records for Barack Obama from January 2013. To accomplish this task, we change the value in the *Month* field. Again, this requires obtaining the ID for the *Month* input field. From the Web Developer Tools we learn that the following XPath expression is appropriate: `'//*[@id="yearSelect"]'`. At the same time, we save the IDs for the month and the recipient text field.

```
R> yearID <- element_xpath_find(value = '//*[@id="yearSelect"]')
R> monthID <- element_xpath_find(value = '//*[@id="monthSelect"]')
R> recipID <- element_xpath_find(value = '//*[@id="recipientSelect"]')
```

In order to change the year, we perform a mouse click on the year field by executing `element_click()` with the appropriate `ID` argument.

```
R> element_click(yearID)
```

Passing keyboard input

Next, we need to pass the keyboard input that we wish to enter into the database field. Since we are interested in records from the year 2013, we use the `keys()` function with the first argument set to the correct term.

```
R> keys("2013")
```

[6]Another option would be to close the window using `close_window()`. This automatically returns the focus to the previous window.

In a similar fashion, we do the same for the other fields.[7]

```
R> element_click(monthID)
R> keys("January")
R> element_click(recipID)
R> keys("Barack Obama")
```

We can now send the query to the database with a click on the *submit* button. Again, we first identify the button using XPath and pass the corresponding ID element to the clicking function.

```
R> submitID <- element_xpath_find(value = '//*[@id="yearForm"]
/div/button')
R> element_click(submitID)
```

Accessing source code This action should have resulted in a new HTML table being displayed at the bottom of the page. To obtain this information, we can extract the underlying HTML code from the live DOM tree and search the code for a table.

```
R> pageSource <- page_source()
R> moneyTab <- readHTMLTable(pageSource, which = 1)
```

With a few last processing steps, we can bring the information into a displayable format.

```
R> colnames(moneyTab) <- c("year", "name", "party", "contributor",
"state", "amount")
R> moneyTab <- moneyTab[-1, ]
R> head(moneyTab)

  year         name party              contributor state amount
2 2013 Barack Obama     D           ROBERTS, GARY    TX     -50
3 2013 Barack Obama     D    TOENNIES, MICHAEL MR    CO     -55
4 2013 Barack Obama     D            PENTA, NEELAM    NY    -100
5 2013 Barack Obama     D        VALENSTEIN, JILL    NY     -15
6 2013 Barack Obama     D SPRECHER KEATING, KAREN    DC    -100
7 2013 Barack Obama     D          FISCHER, DAMIEN    CA    -100
```

Concluding remarks The web scraping process laid out in this section departs markedly from the techniques and tools we have previously outlined. As we have seen, Selenium provides a powerful framework and a way for working with dynamically rendered webpages when simple HTTP-based approaches fail. It helps keep in mind that this flexibility comes with a cost, since the browser itself takes some time to receive the request, process it, and render the page. This has the potential to slow down the extraction process drastically, and we therefore advise users to use Selenium only for tasks where other tools are unfit. We oftentimes find using Selenium most helpful for describing transitions between multiple webpages and posting clicks and keyboard commands to a browser window, but once we encounter solid URLs, we switch back to the R-based HTTP methods outlined previously for speed purposes.

[7] If necessary, we can also remove any input from a text field with the `element_clear()` function on the respective element.

Besides the Rwebdriver package there is a package called Relenium which resembles the package introduced in this chapter (Ramon and de Villa 2013). Although Relenium provides a more straightforward initiation process of the Selenium server, it has, at the time of writing, a more limited functionality.

9.1.10 Retrieving data from APIs

We have mentioned APIs in passing when introducing XML, JSON, and other fundamentals. Generally, APIs encompass tools which enable programmers to connect their software with "something else." They are useful in programming software that relies on external soft- or hardware because the developers do not have to go into the details of external soft- or hardware mechanics.

The rise of web APIs

When we talk about APIs in this book, we refer to web services or (web) APIs, that is, interfaces with web applications. We treat the terms "API" and "web service" synonymously, although the term API encompasses a much larger body of software. The reason why APIs are of importance for web data collection tasks is that more and more web applications offer APIs which allow retrieving and processing data. With the rise of Web 2.0, where web APIs provided the basis for many applications, application providers recognized that data on the Web are interesting for many web developers. As APIs help make products more popular and might, in the end, generate more advertising revenues, the availability of APIs has rapidly increased.

Basic logic

The general logic of retrieving data from web APIs is simple. We illustrate it in Figure 9.4. The API provider sets up a service that grants access to data from the application or to the application itself. The API user accesses the API to gather data or communicate with the application. It may be necessary to write wrapper software for convenient data exchange with the web service. Wrappers are functions that handle details of API access and data transformation, for example, from JSON to R objects. The modus operandi of APIs varies—we shortly discuss the popular standards *REST* and *SOAP* further below. APIs provide data in various formats. JSON has probably become the most popular data exchange format of

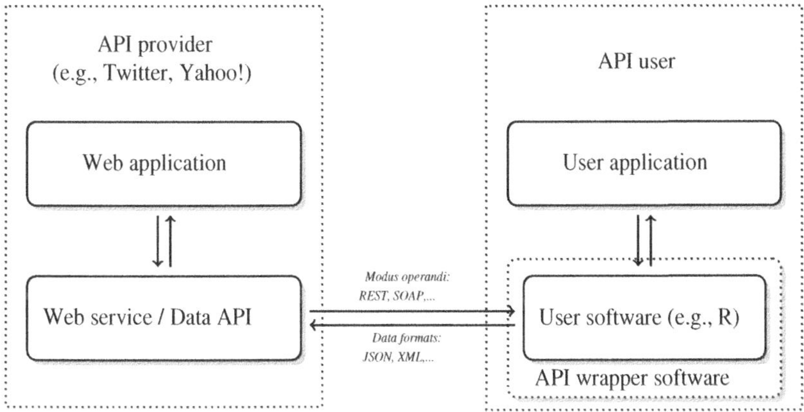

Figure 9.4 The mechanics of web APIs

modern web APIs, but XML is still frequently used, and any other formats such as HTML, images, CSVs, and binary data files are possible.

Documentation APIs are implemented for developers and thus must be understandable to humans. Therefore, an extensive documentation of features, functions, and parameters is often part of an API. It gives programmers an overview of the content and form of information an API provides, and what information it expects, for example, via queries.

Standards Standardization of APIs helps programmers familiarize themselves with the mechanics of an API quickly. There are several API standards or styles, the more popular ones being *REST* and *SOAP*. It is important to note that in order to tap web services with R, we often do not have to have any deeper knowledge of these techniques—either because others have already programmed a handy interface to these APIs or because our knowledge about HTTP, XML, and JSON suffices to understand the documentation of an API and to retrieve the information we are looking for. We therefore consider them just briefly.

REST *REST* stands for Representational State Transfer (Fielding 2000). The core idea behind *REST* is that resources are referenced (e.g., via URLs) and representations of these resources are exchanged. Representations are actual documents like an HTML, XML, or JSON file. One might think of a conversation on Twitter as a resource, and this resource could be represented with JSON code or equally valid representations in other formats. This sounds just like what the World Wide Web is supposed to be—and in fact one could say that the World Wide Web itself conforms to the idea of *REST*. The development of *REST* is closely linked to the design of HTTP, as the standard HTTP methods *GET*, *POST*, *PUT*, and *DELETE* are used for the transfer of representations. *GET* is the usual method when the goal is to retrieve data. To simplify matters, the difference between a *GET* request of a *REST* API and a *GET* request our browser puts to a server when asking for web content is that (a) parameters are often well-documented and (b) the response is simply the content, not any layout information. *POST*, *PUT*, and *DELETE* are methods that are implemented when the user needs to create, update, and delete content, respectively. This is useful for APIs that are connected to personal accounts, such as APIs from social media platforms like Facebook or Twitter. Finally, a *REST*ful API is an API that confirms to the *REST* constraints. The constraints include the existence of a base URL to which query parameters can be added, a certain representation (JSON, XML,...), and the use of standard HTTP methods.

SOAP Another web service standard we sometimes encounter is SOAP, originally an acronym for Simple Object Access Protocol. As the technology is rather difficult to understand and implement, it is currently being gradually superseded by *REST*. SOAP-based services are frequently offered in combination with a WSDL (Web Service Description Language) document that fully describes all the possible methods as well as the data structures that are expected and returned by the service. WSDL documents themselves are based on XML and can therefore be interpreted by XML parsers. The resulting advantage of *SOAP*-based web services is that users can automatically construct API call functions for their software environment based on the WSDL, as the API's functionality is fully described in the document. For more information on working with SOAP in R, see Nolan and Temple Lang (2014, Chapter 12). The authors provide the SSOAP package that helps work with *SOAP* and R (Temple Lang 2012b) by transforming the rules documented in a WSDL document into R functions and classes.[8] Generating wrapper functions on-the-fly has the advantage that programs can easily react to

[8] At the time of writing, the package is not yet listed on CRAN.

API changes. However, as the *SOAP* technology is becoming increasingly uncommon, we focus on *REST*-based services in this section.

Example: Yahoo Weather RSS Feed

Using a *REST*ful API with R can be very simple and not very different from what we have learned so far regarding ordinary *GET* requests. As a toy example we consider Yahoo's Weather RSS Feed, which is documented at http://developer.yahoo.com/weather/. It provides information on current weather conditions at any given place on Earth as well as a five-day forecast in the form of an RSS file, that is, an XML-style document (see Section 3.4.3). The feed basically delivers the data part of what is offered at http://weather.yahoo.com/. We could use the API to generate our own forecasts or to build an R-based weather gadget. According to the Terms of Use in the documentation, the feeds are provided free of charge for personal, non-commercial uses.

Making requests to the feed is pretty straightforward when studying the documentation. All we have to specify is the location for which we want to get a feedback from the API (the w parameter) and the preferred degrees unit (Fahrenheit or Celsius; the u parameter). The location parameter requires a WOEID code, the Where On Earth Identifier. It is a 32-bit identifier that is unique for every geographic entity (see http://developer.yahoo.com/geo/geoplanet/guide/concepts.html). From a manual search on the Yahoo Weather application, we find that the WOEID of Hoboken, New Jersey, is 2422673. Calling the feed is simply done using the HTTP *GET* syntax. We already know how to do this in R. We specify the API's base URL and make a *GET* request to the feed, providing the w parameter with the WOEID and the u parameter for degrees in Celsius.

```
R> feed_url <- "http://weather.yahooapis.com/forecastrss"
R> feed <- getForm(feed_url, .params = list(w = "2422673", u = "c"))
```

As the retrieved RSS feed is basically just XML content, we can parse it with XML's parsing function.

```
R> parsed_feed <- xmlParse(feed)
```

The original RSS file is quite spacious, so we only provide the first and last couple of lines.

```
<?xml version="1.0" encoding="UTF-8" standalone="yes"?>
<rss xmlns:yweather="http://xml.weather.yahoo.com/ns/rss/1.0"
    xmlns:geo="http://www.w3.org/2003/01/geo/wgs84_pos}" version="2.0">
  <channel>
    <title>Yahoo! Weather - Hoboken, NJ</title>
    <link>http://us.rd.yahoo.com/dailynews/rss/weather/Hoboken__NJ/*
        http://weather.yahoo.com/forecast/USNJ0221_c.html</link>
    <description>Yahoo! Weather for Hoboken, NJ</description>
    <language>en-us</language>
    <lastBuildDate>Tue, 18 Feb 2014 7:35 am EST</lastBuildDate>
    <ttl>60</ttl>
    <yweather:location city="Hoboken" region="NJ" country="United
        States"/>
    <yweather:units temperature="C" distance="km" pressure="mb"
        speed="km/h"/>
    <yweather:wind chill="-3" direction="40" speed="11.27"/>
```

```
    <yweather:atmosphere humidity="93" visibility="1.21"
        pressure="1015.92" rising="2"/>
    ...
    <item>
        ...
      <yweather:condition text="Cloudy" code="26" temp="0" date="Tue,
          18 Feb 2014 7:35 am EST"/>
      <yweather:forecast day="Tue" date="18 Feb 2014" low="-2"
          high="4" text="Rain/Snow" code="5"/>
      <yweather:forecast day="Wed" date="19 Feb 2014" low="-2"
          high="7" text="Showers" code="11"/>
      <yweather:forecast day="Thu" date="20 Feb 2014" low="3" high="7"
          text="Partly Cloudy" code="30"/>
      <yweather:forecast day="Fri" date="21 Feb 2014" low="1"
          high="12" text="Rain/Thunder" code="12"/>
      <yweather:forecast day="Sat" date="22 Feb 2014" low="-1"
          high="9" text="Partly Cloudy" code="30"/>
    </item>
  </channel>
</rss>
```

We can process the parsed XML object using standard XPath expressions and convenience functions from the XML package. As an example, we extract the values of current weather parameters which are stored in a set of attributes.

```
R> xpath <- "//yweather:location|//yweather:wind|//yweather:condition"
R> conditions <- unlist(xpathSApply(parsed_feed, xpath, xmlAttrs))
R> data.frame(conditions)
                               conditions
city                              Hoboken
region                                 NJ
country                     United States
chill                                  -3
direction                              40
speed                               11.27
text                               Cloudy
code                                   26
temp                                    0
date         Tue, 18 Feb 2014 7:35 am EST
```

We also build a small data frame that contains the forecast statistics for the next 5 days.

```
R> location <- t(xpathSApply(parsed_feed, "//yweather:location", xmlAttrs))
R> forecasts <- t(xpathSApply(parsed_feed, "//yweather:forecast", xmlAttrs))
R> forecast <- merge(location, forecasts)
R> forecast
     city region       country day        date low high          text code
1 Hoboken     NJ United States Tue 18 Feb 2014  -2    4     Rain/Snow    5
2 Hoboken     NJ United States Wed 19 Feb 2014  -2    7       Showers   11
3 Hoboken     NJ United States Thu 20 Feb 2014   3    7 Partly Cloudy   30
4 Hoboken     NJ United States Fri 21 Feb 2014   1   12  Rain/Thunder   12
5 Hoboken     NJ United States Sat 22 Feb 2014  -1    9 Partly Cloudy   30
```

Web service interfaces for R

Processing the result from a *REST* API query is entirely up to us if no R interface to a web service exists. We could also construct convenient wrapper functions for the API calls. Packages exist for some web services which offer convenience functions to pass R objects to the API and get back R objects. Such functions are not too difficult to create once you are familiar with an API's logic and the data technology that is returned. Let us try to construct such a wrapper function for the Yahoo Weather Feed example.

Building a wrapper function

There are always many ways to specify wrapper functions for existing web services. We want to construct a command that takes a place's name as main argument and gives back the current weather conditions or a forecast for the next few days. We have seen above that the Yahoo Weather Feed needs a WOEID as input. To manually search for the corresponding WOEID of a place and then feed it to the function seems rather inconvenient, so we want to automate this part of the work as well. Indeed, there is another API that does this work for us. At http://developer.yahoo.com/geo/geoplanet/ we find a set of *REST*ful APIs subsumed under the label *Yahoo! GeoPlanet* which offer a range of services. One of these services returns the WOEID of a specific place.

http://where.yahooapis.com/v1/places.q('northfield%20mn%20usa')?appid=[yourappidhere]

The URL contains the query parameter `appid`. We have to obtain an app ID to be able to use this service. Many web services require registration and sometimes even involve a sophisticated authentication process (see next section). In our case we just have to register for the Yahoo Developer Network to obtain an ID. We register our application named *RWeather* at Yahoo. After providing the information, we get the ID and can add it to our API query. In order to be able to reuse the ID without having to store it in the code, we save it in the R options:[9]

```
R> options(yahooid = "t.2cnduc0BqpWb7qmlc14vEk8sbL7LijbHoKS.utZ0")
```

The call to the WOEID API is as follows. We start with the base URL and add the place we are looking for in the URL's placeholder between the parentheses. The `sprintf()` function is useful because it allows pasting text within another string. We just have to mark the string placeholder with `%s`.

```
R> baseurl <- "http://where.yahooapis.com/v1/places.q('%s')"
R> woeid_url <- sprintf(baseurl, URLencode("Hoboken, NJ, USA"))
```

Notice also that we have to encode the place name with URL encoding (see Section 5.1.2).

http://where.yahooapis.com/v1/places.q('Hoboken,%20NJ,%20USA')

Next we formulate a *GET* call to the API. We add our Yahoo app ID which we retrieve from the options. The service returns an XML document which we directly parse into an object named `parsed_woeid`.

```
R> parsed_woeid <- xmlParse((getForm(woeid_url, appid = getOption
("yahooid"))))
```

[9]See Section 9.1.6. Needless to say that the printed ID is fictional.

The XML document itself looks as follows.

```
<?xml version="1.0" encoding="UTF-8"?>
<places xmlns="http://where.yahooapis.com/v1/schema.rng" xmlns:
    yahoo="http://www.yahooapis.com/v1/base.rng" yahoo:start="0"
    yahoo:count="1" yahoo:total="1">
  <place yahoo:uri="http://where.yahooapis.com/v1/place/2422673"
      xml:lang="en-US">
    <woeid>2422673</woeid>
    <placeTypeName code="7">Town</placeTypeName>
    <name>Hoboken</name>
    <country type="Country" code="US" woeid="23424977">United
        States</country>
    <admin1 type="State" code="US-NJ" woeid="2347589">New Jersey
        </admin1>
    <admin2 type="County" code="" woeid="12589266">Hudson</admin2>
    <admin3/>
    <locality1 type="Town" woeid="2422673">Hoboken</locality1>
    ...
    <timezone type="Time Zone" woeid="56043648">America/New_York
        </timezone>
  </place>
</places>
```

There are several WOEIDs stored in the document, one for the country, one for the state, and one for the town itself. We can extract the town WOEID with an XPath query on the retrieved XML file. Note that the document comes with namespaces. We access the `<locality1>` element where the WOEID is stored with the XPath expression `//*[local-name()='locality1']` which addresses the document's local names.

```
R> woeid <- xpathSApply(parsed_woeid, "//*[local-name()='locality1']",
xmlAttrs)[2,]
R> woeid
    woeid
"2422673"
```

Voilà, we have retrieved the corresponding WOEID. Recall that our goal was to construct one function which returns the results of a query to Yahoo's Weather Feed in a useful R format. We have seen that such a function has to wrap around not only one, but two APIs—the WOEID returner and the actual Weather Feed. The result of our efforts, a function named `getWeather()`, are displayed in Figure 9.5.

The wrapper function The wrapper function splits into five parts. The first reports errors if the function's arguments `ask`—to determine if current weather conditions or a forecast should be reported—and `temp`—to set the reported degrees Celsius or Fahrenheit—are wrongly specified. The second part (`get woeid`) replicates the call to the WOEID API which we have considered in detail above. The third part (`get weather feed`) uses the WOEID and makes a call to Yahoo's Weather Feed. The fourth part (`get current conditions`) is evaluated if the user asks for the current weather conditions at a given place. We have stored some condition

```
getWeather <- function(place = "New York", ask = "current", temp = "c") {
      if (!ask %in% c("current","forecast")) {
            stop("Wrong ask parameter. Choose either 'current' or
             'forecast'.")
      }
      if (!temp %in%  c("c", "f")) {
            stop("Wrong temp parameter. Choose either 'c' for Celsius or
             'f' for Fahrenheit.")
      }
## get woeid
      base_url <- "http://where.yahooapis.com/v1/places.q('%s')"
      woeid_url <- sprintf(base_url, URLencode(place))
      parsed_woeid <- xmlParse((getForm(woeid_url, appid = getOption("
      yahooid"))))
      woeid <- xpathSApply(parsed_woeid, "//*[local-name()='locality1']",
      xmlAttrs)[2,]
## get weather feed
      feed_url <- "http://weather.yahooapis.com/forecastrss"
      parsed_feed <- xmlParse(getForm(feed_url, .params = list(w = woeid,
      u = temp)))
## get current conditions
      if (ask == "current") {
            xpath <- "//yweather:location|//yweather:condition"
            conds <- data.frame(t(unlist(xpathSApply(parsed_feed, xpath,
            xmlAttrs))))
            message(sprintf("The weather in %s, %s, %s is %s. Current
            temperature is %s degrees %s.", conds$city, conds$region,
            conds$country, tolower(conds$text), conds$temp, toupper(temp)))
      }
## get forecast
      if (ask == "forecast") {
            location <-
data.frame(t(xpathSApply(parsed_feed, "//yweather:
            location", xmlAttrs)))
            forecasts <- data.frame(t(xpathSApply(parsed_feed,
            "//yweather:forecast", xmlAttrs)))
            message(sprintf("Weather forecast for %s, %s, %s:",
            location$city, location$region, location$country))
            return(forecasts)
      }
}
```

Figure 9.5 An R wrapper function for Yahoo's Weather Feed

parameters in a data frame conds and input the results into a single sentence—not very useful if we want to post-process the data, but handy if we just want to know what the weather is like at the moment.[10] If a forecast is requested, the function's fifth part is activated. It constructs a data frame from the forecasts in the XML document and returns it, along with a short message.

[10]Seasoned programmers will appreciate the possibility of getting a weather update without having to leave the basement, not even the familiar programming environment.

Let us try out the function. First, we ask for the current weather conditions in San Francisco.

```
R> getWeather(place = "San Francisco", ask = "current", temp = "c")
The weather in San Francisco, CA, United States is cloudy. Current
temperature is 9 degrees C.
```

This call was successful. Note that Yahoo's Weather API is tolerant concerning the definition of the place. If place names are unique, we do not have to specify the state or country. If the place is not unique (e.g., "Springfield"), the API automatically picks a default option. Next, we want to retrieve a forecast for the weather in San Francisco.

```
R> getWeather(place = "San Francisco", ask = "forecast", temp = "c")
Weather forecast for San Francisco, CA, United States:
  day        date low high          text code
1 Tue 18 Feb 2014  10   18 Partly Cloudy   30
2 Wed 19 Feb 2014  13   19 Partly Cloudy   30
3 Thu 20 Feb 2014  12   18        Cloudy   26
4 Fri 21 Feb 2014  11   17   Few Showers   11
5 Sat 22 Feb 2014  10   19 Partly Cloudy   30
```

Where to find APIs on the Web

We could easily expand the function by adding further parameters or returning more useful R objects. This example served to demonstrate how *REST*-based web services work in general and how easy it is to tap them from within R. There are many more useful APIs on the Web. At http://www.programmableweb.com/apis we get an overview of thousands of web APIs. Currently, there are more than 11,000 web APIs listed as well as over 7,000 mashups, that is, applications which make use and combine existing content from APIs. We provide some additional advice on finding useful data sources, including APIs, in Section 9.4.

9.1.11 Authentication with OAuth

Authentication and authorization

Many web services are open to anybody. In some cases, however, APIs require the user to register and provide an individual key when making a request to the web service. Authentication is used to trace data usage and to restrict access. Related to authentication is authorization. Authorization means granting an application access to authentication details. For example, if you use a third-party twitter client on your mobile device, you have authorized the app to use your authentication details to connect to your Twitter account. We have learned about HTTP authentication methods in Section 5.2.2. APIs often require more complex authentication via a standard called *OAuth*.

OAuth is an important authorization standard serving a specific scenario. Imagine you have an account on Twitter and regularly use it to inform your friends about what is currently on your mind and to stay up to date about what is going on in your network. To stay tuned when you are on the road, you use Twitter on your mobile phone. As you are not satisfied with the standard functions the official Twitter application offers, you rely on a third-party client app (e.g., *Tweetbot*), an application that has been programmed by another company and that offers additional functionality. In order to let the app display the tweets of people you follow and give yourself the opportunity to tweet, you have to grant it some of your rights on Twitter. What you should never want to do is to hand out your access information, that is, login name and password, to anybody—not even the Twitter client. This is where *OAuth* comes into play. *OAuth* differs from other authentication techniques in that it distinguishes between the following three parties:

- The service or API provider. The provider implements *OAuth* for his service and is responsible for the website/server which the other parties access.
- The data owners. They own the data and control which consumer (see next party) is granted access to the data, and to what extent.
- The data consumer or client. This is the application which wants to make use of the owner's data.

When we are working with R, we usually take two of the roles. First, we are data owners when we want to authorize access to data from our own accounts of whatever web service. Second, we are data consumers because we program a piece of R software that should be authorized to access data from the API.

OAuth versions

OAuth currently exists in two flavors, *OAuth 1.0* and *OAuth 2.0* (Hammer-Lahav 2010; Hardt 2012). They differ in terms of complexity, comfort, and security.[11] However, there have been controversies on the question whether OAuth is indeed more secure and useful than its predecessor.[12] As users, we usually do not have to make the choices between the two standards; hence, we do not go into more into detail here. *OAuth*'s official website can be found at http://oauth.net/. More information, including a beginner's guide and tutorials, are available at http://hueniverse.com/oauth/.

The _OAuth_ workflow

How does authorization work in the *OAuth* framework? First of all, *OAuth* distinguishes between three types of credentials: *client credentials* (or consumer key and secret), *temporary credentials* (or request token and secret), and *token credentials* (or access token and secret). Credentials serve as a proof for legitimate access to the data owner's information at various stages of the authorization process. Client credentials are used to register the application with the provider. Client credentials authenticate the client. When we use R to tap APIs, we usually have to start with registering an application at the provider's homepage which we could call "My R-based program" or similar. In the process of registration, we retrieve client credentials, that is, a consumer key and secret that is linked with our (and only our) application. Temporary credentials prove that an application's request for access tokens is executed by an authorized client. If we set up our application to access data from a resource owner (e.g., our own Twitter account), we have to obtain those temporary credentials, that is, a request token and secret, first. If the resource owner agrees that the application may access his/her data (or parts of it), the application's temporary credentials are authorized. They now can be exchanged for token credentials, that is, an access token and secret. For future requests to the API, the application now can use these access credentials and the user does not have to provide his/her original authentication information, that is, username and password, for this task.

OAuth use with R

The fact that several different types of credentials are involved in *OAuth* authorization practice makes it clear that this is a more complicated process that encompasses several

---

[11] See "Introducing OAuth 2.0" by Eran Hammer-Lahav at http://hueniverse.com/2010/05/introducing-oauth-2-0/.

[12] See "OAuth 2.0 and the Road to Hell" by Eran Hammer-Lahav at http://hueniverse.com/2012/07/oauth-2-0-and-the-road-to-hell/.

steps. Fortunately, we can rely on R software that facilitates *OAuth* registration. The ROAuth package (Gentry and Lang 2013) provides a set of functions that help specify registration requests from within R. A simplified *OAuth* registration interface is provided by the httr package (Wickham 2012). We illustrate *OAuth* authentication in R with the commands from the httr package.

`oauth_endpoint()` is used to define *OAuth* endpoints at the provider side. Endpoints are URLs that can be requested by the application to gain tokens for various steps of the authorization process. These include an endpoint for the request token—the first, unauthenticated token—and the access token to exchange the unauthenticated for the authenticated token.

`oauth_app()` is used to create an application. We usually register an application manually at the API provider's website. After registration we obtain a consumer key and secret. We copy and paste both into R. The `oauth_app()` function simple bundles the consumer key and secret to a list that can be used to request the access credentials. While the consumer key has to be specified in the function, we can let the function fetch the consumer secret automatically from the R environment by placing it there in the *`APPNAME`*`_CONSUMER_SECRET` option. The benefit of this approach is that we do not have to store the secret in our R code.

`oauth1.0_token()` and `oauth2.0_token()` are used to exchange the consumer key and secret (stored in an object created with the `oauth_app()` function) for the access key and secret. The function tries to retrieve these credentials from the access endpoint specified with `oauth_endpoint()`.

Finally, `sign_oauth1.0()` and `sign_oauth2.0()` are used to create a signature from the received access token. This signature can be added to API requests from the registered application—we do not have to pass our username and password.

Tapping the Facebook Graph API

We demonstrate by example how *OAuth* registration is done using Facebook's Graph API. The API grants access to publicly available user information and—if granted by the user—selected private information. The use of the API requires that we have a Facebook account. We first have to register an application which we want to grant access to our profile. We go to https://developers.facebook.com and sign in using our Facebook authentication information. Next, we create a new application by clicking on *Apps* and *Create a new app*. We have to provide some basic information and pass a check to prove that we are no robot. Now, our application *RDataCollectionApp* is registered. We go to the app's dashboard to retrieve information on the app, that is, the App ID and the App secret. In *OAuth* terms, these are consumer key and consumer secret.

Next, we switch to R to obtain the access key. Using httr's functionality, we start by defining Facebook's *OAuth* endpoints. This works with the `oauth_endpoint()` function.

```
R> facebook <- oauth_endpoint(
R>   authorize = "https://www.facebook.com/dialog/oauth",
R>   access = "https://graph.facebook.com/oauth/access_token")
```

We bundle the consumer key and secret of our app in one object with the `oauth_app()` function. Note that we have previously dumped the consumer secret in the R environment with `Sys.setenv(FACEBOOK_CONSUMER_SECRET = "3983746230hg8745389234...")` to keep this confidential information out of the R code. `oauth_app()` automatically retrieves it from the environment and writes it to the new `fb_app` object.

```
R> fb_app <- oauth_app("facebook", "485980054864321")
```

Now we have to exchange the consumer credentials with the access credentials. Facebook's Graph API uses *OAuth 2.0*, so we have to use the `oauth2.0_token()` function. However, before we execute it, we have to do some preparations. First, we add a website URL to our app account in the browser. We do this in the *Settings* section by adding a website and specifying a site URL. Usually this should work with the URL http://localhost:1410/ but you can also call `oauth_callback()` to retrieve the callback URL the for the *OAuth* listener, a web server that listens for the provider's *OAuth* feedback.[13] Second, we define the scope of permissions to apply for. A list of possible permissions can be found at https://developers.facebook.com/docs/facebook-login/permissions/. We pick some of those and write them into the `permissions` object.

```
R> permissions <- "user_birthday, user_hometown, user_location,
user_status, user_checkins, friends_birthday, friends_hometown,
friends_location, friends_relationships, friends_status, friends_
checkins, publish_actions, read_stream, export_stream"
```

Now we can ask for the access credentials. Again, we use httr's `oauth2.0_token()` command to perform *OAuth 2.0* negotiations.

```
R> fb_token <- oauth2.0_token(facebook, fb_app, scope = permissions,
type = "application/x-www-form-urlencoded")

starting httpd help server ... done
Waiting for authentication in browser...
Authentication complete.
```

During the function call we approve the access in the browser. The authentication process is successful. We use the received access credentials to generate a signature object.

```
R> fb_sig <- sign_oauth2.0(fb_token)
```

We are now ready to access the API from within R. Facebook's web service provides a large range of functions. Fortunately, there is an R package named Rfacebook that makes the API easily accessible (Barberá 2014). For example, we can access publicly available data from Facebook users with

```
R> getUsers("hadleywickham", fb_sig, private_info = FALSE)
  id       name           username       first_name last_name ...
1 16910108 Hadley Wickham hadleywickham Hadley     Wickham   ...
```

The package also allows us to access information about our personal network.

```
R> friends <- getFriends(fb_sig, simplify = TRUE)
R> nrow(friends)
[1] 143
R> table(friends_info$gender)
female   male
    71     72
```

[13]This step departs from the simplified *OAuth* workflow from above. Unfortunately, we often face departures from the norm when working with *OAuth* and have to adapt the procedure.

It provides a lot more useful functions. For a more detailed tutorial, check out http://pablobarbera.com/blog/archives/3.html.

9.2 Extraction strategies

We have learned several methods to gather data from the Web. There are three standard procedures. Scraping with HTTP and extracting information with regular expressions, information extraction via XPath queries, and data gathering using APIs. They should usually be preferred over each other in ascending order (i.e., scraping with regular expressions is least preferable and gathering data via an API is most preferable), but there will be situations where one of the approaches is not applicable or some of the techniques have to be combined. It thus makes sense to become familiar with all of them.

In the following, we offer a general comparison between the different approaches. Each scraping scenario is different, so some of the advantages or disadvantages of a method may not apply for your task. Besides, as always, there is more than one way to skin a cat.

If data on a site are not provided for download in ready-made files or via an API, scraping them off the screen is often the only alternative. With regular expressions and XPath queries we have introduced two strategies to extract information from HTML or XML code. We continue discussing both techniques according to some practical criteria which become relevant in the process of web scraping, like robustness, complexity, flexibility, or general power. Note that these elaborations primarily target static HTML/XML content.

9.2.1 Regular expressions

Figure 9.6 provides a schema of the scraping procedure with regular expressions. In step ①, we identify information on-site that follows a general pattern. The decision to use regular expressions to scrape data or another approach depends on our intuition whether the information is actually generalizable to a regular expression. In some cases, the data can be described by means of a regular expression, but the pattern cannot distinguish from other irrelevant content on the page. For example, if we identify important information wrapped in `<b>` tags, this can be difficult to distinguish from other information marked with `<b>` tags. If data need to be retained in their context, regular expressions also have a rough ride.

Step ② is to download the websites. Many of the methods described in Section 9.1 might prove useful here. Additionally, regular expressions can already be of help in this step. They could be used to assemble a list of URLs to be downloaded, or for URL manipulation (see Section 9.1.3).

In step ③, the downloaded content is imported into R. When pursuing a purely regex-based scraping strategy, this is done by simply reading the content as character data with the `readLines()` or similar functions. When importing the textual data, we have to be exceptionally careful with the encoding scheme used for the original document, as we want to avoid applying regular expressions to get rid of encoding errors. If you start using `str_replace()` in order to get ä, ó, or ç, you are likely to have forgotten specifying the encoding argument in the `readLines()` or the parsing function (see Section 8.3). Incidentally, regular expressions do not make use of an HTML or XML DOM, so we do not need to parse the documents. In fact, documents parsed with `htmlParse()` or `xmlParse()` cannot be accessed with regular expressions directly. If we use regular expressions in combination with an XPath approach,

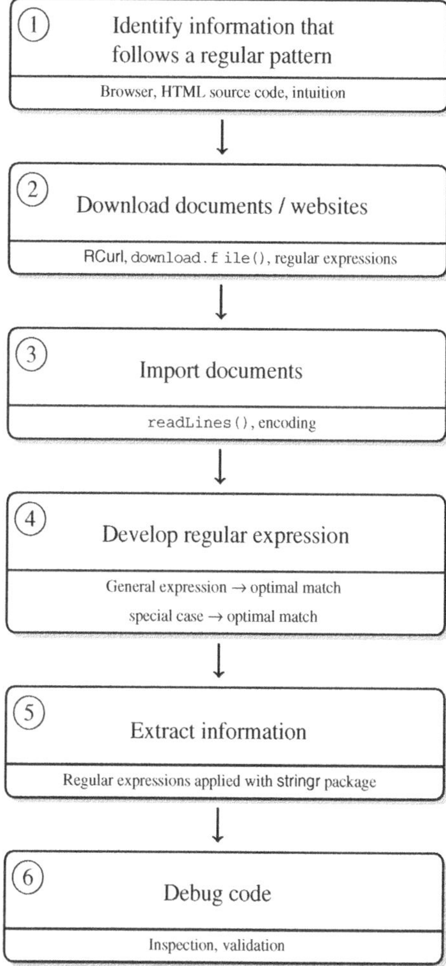

Figure 9.6 Scraping with regular expressions

we first parse the document, extract information with XPath queries and finally modify the retrieved content with regular expressions.

Step ④ is the crucial one for successful web scraping with regular expressions. One has to develop one or more regular expressions which extract the relevant information. The syntax of regular expressions as implemented in R often allows a set of different solutions. The problem is that these solutions may not differ in the outcome they produce for a certain sample of text to be regexed, but they can make a difference for new data. This makes debugging very complex. There are some useful tools which help make regex development more convenient, for example, http://regex101.com/ or http://www.regexplanet.com/.[14] These

[14]For a more complete overview, see http://scraping.pro/10-best-online-regex-testers/

pages offer instant feedback to given regular expressions on sample text input, which makes the process of regex programming more interactive. In general, we follow one of two strategies in regular expression programming. The first is to start with a special case and to work toward a more general solution that captures every piece. For example, only one bit of information is matched with a regular expression—this is the information itself, as characters match themselves. The second strategy is to start with a general expression and introduce restrictions or exceptions that limit the number of matched strings to the desired sample. One could label the first approach the "inductive" and the second one "deductive." The "deductive" approach is probably more efficient because it starts at an abstract level—and regular expressions are often meant to be abstract—, but usually requires more knowledge about regular expressions. Another feasible strategy which could be located between the two is to start with several rather different pieces of information to be matched and find the pick lock that fits for all of them.

As soon as the regular expression is programmed, extracting the information is the next step (⑤). As shown in Chapter 8, the stringr package (Wickham 2010) is enormously useful for this purpose, possibly in combination with apply-like functions (the native R functions or those provided by the plyr package (Wickham 2011)) for efficient looping over documents.

In the last step ⑥, the code has to be debugged. It is likely that applying regular expressions on the full sample of strings reveals further problems, like false positives, that is, information that has been matched should not be matched, or false negatives, that is, some information to be matched is not matched. It is sometimes necessary to split documents or delete certain parts before regexing them to exclude a bunch of false positives a priori.

9.2.1.1 Advantages of regular expressions for web scraping

What are the advantages of scraping with regular expressions? In the opinion of many seasoned web scrapers, there are not too many. Nevertheless, we think that there are circumstances under which a purely regex-based approach may be superior to any other strategy.

Robustness to malformed XML Regular expressions do not operate on context-defining parts of a document. This can be an advantage over an XPath strategy when the XML or HTML document is malformed. When DOM parsers fail, regular expressions, ignorant as they are of DOM structure, continue to search for information. Moreover, to retrieve information from a heterogeneous set of documents, regular expressions can deal with them as long as they can be converted to a plain-text format. Generally, regular expressions are powerful for parsing unstructured text.

Efficiency String patterns can be the most efficient way to identify and extract content in a document. Imagine a situation where you want to scrape a list of URLs which are scattered across a document and which share a common string feature like a running index. It is possible to identify these URLs by searching for anchor tags, but you would have to sort out the URLs you are looking for in a second step by means of a regular expression.

Speed Regular expression scraping can be faster than XPath-based scraping, especially when documents are large and parsing the whole DOM consumes a lot of time. However, the speed argument cannot be generalized, and the construction of regular expressions or XPath queries is also an aspect of speed. And after all, there are usually more important arguments than speed.

Power for data cleansing Finally, regular expressions are a useful instrument for data-cleansing purposes as they enable us to get extracted information in the desired shape.

9.2.1.2 Disadvantages of regular expressions for web scraping

As soon as information in a document are connected, and should remain so after harvesting, regular expressions are stretched to their limits. Data without context are often rather uninteresting. Think back to the introductory example from Chapter 8. It was already a complex task to extract telephone numbers from an unstructured document, but to match the corresponding names is often hardly possible if a document does not follow a specific structure. When scraping information from web pages, sticking to regular expressions as a standard scraping tool means ignoring the virtue that sites are hierarchically or sometimes even semantically structured by construction. Markup is structure, and while it is possible to exploit markup with regular expressions, elements which are anchored in the DOM can usually be extracted more efficiently by means of XPath queries. **Lack of context sensitivity**

Besides, regular expressions are difficult to master. Building regular expressions is a brain-teaser. It is sometimes very challenging to identify and then formulate the patterns of information we need to extract. In addition, due to their complexity it is hard to read what is going on in a regular expression. This makes it hard to debug regex scraping code when one has not looked at the scraper for a while. **Difficult to develop and debug**

Many scraping tasks cannot be solved with regular expressions because the content to be scraped is simply too heterogeneous. This means that it cannot be abstracted and formulated as a generalized string pattern. The structure of XML/HTML documents is inherently hierarchical. Sometimes this hierarchy implies different levels of observations in your final dataset. It can be a very complex task to disentangle these information with regular expressions alone. If regular expressions make use of nodes that structure the document, the regex strategy soon becomes very fragile. Incremental changes in the document structure can break. We have observed that such errors can be fixed more easily when working with XPath. **Lack of flexibility**

The usefulness of regular expressions depends not least on the kind of information one is looking for. If content on websites can be abstracted by means of a general string pattern, regular expressions probably should be used, as they are rather robust toward changes in the page layout. And even if you prefer to work with XPath, regular expressions are still an important tool in the process. First, when parsing fails, regular expressions can constitute a "last line of defense." Second, when content has been scraped, the desired information is often not available in atomic pieces but is still raw text. Regular expressions are extraordinarily useful for data-cleaning tasks, such as string replacements, string deletions, and string splits.

In the third part of the book, we provide an application that relies mainly on regular expressions to scrape data from web resources. In Chapter 13, we try to convert an unstructured table—a "format" we sometimes encounter on the Web—into an appropriate R data structure.

9.2.2 XPath

Although the specifics of scraping with XPath are different from regex scraping, the road maps are quite similar. We have sketched the path of XPath scraping in Figure 9.7. First, we identify the relevant information that is stored in an XML/HTML document and is therefore accessible with XPath queries (step ①). In order to identify the source of information, we can inspect the source code in our browser and rely on Web Developer Tools.

Step ② is equivalent to the regular expressions scraping approach. We download the required resources to our local drive. In principle, we could bypass this step and instantly parse the document "from the webpage." Either way, the content has to be fetched from the

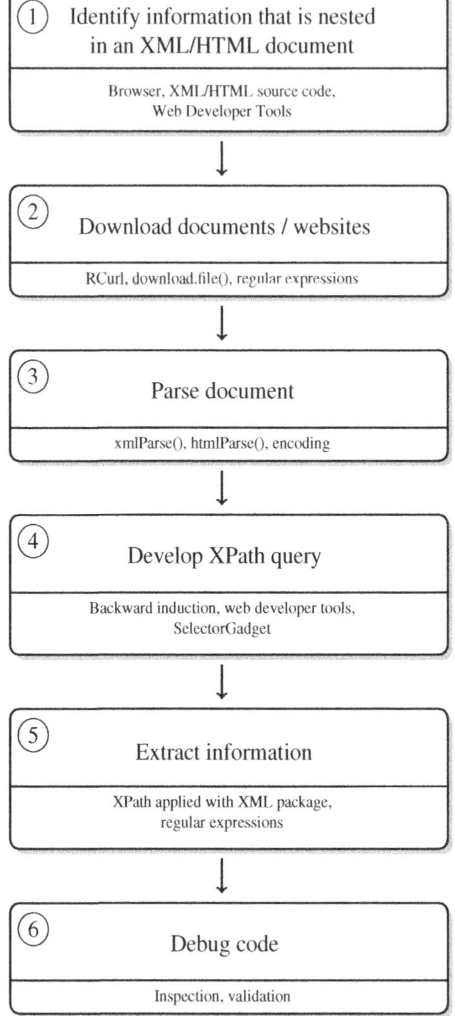

Figure 9.7 Scraping with XPath

server, and by first storing it locally, we can repeat the parsing process without having to scrape documents multiple times.

In step ③, we parse the downloaded documents using the parsers from the XML package. We suggest addressing character-encoding issues in this step—the later we resolve potential encoding problems, the more difficult it gets. We have learned about different techniques of document subsetting and parsing (e.g., SAX parsing methods)—which method we chose depends upon the requirements or restrictions of the data resources.

Next, we extract the actual information in step ④ by developing one or more XPath queries. The more often you work with XPath, the more intuitive this step becomes. For a start, we recommend two basic procedures. The first is to construct XPath expressions with SelectorGadget (see Section 4.3.3). It returns an expression that usually works, but is likely not the most efficient way to express what you want. The other strategy is the do-it-yourself method. We find it most intuitive to pursue a "backwards induction" approach here. This means that we start by defining where the actual information is located and develop the expression from there on, usually up the tree, until the expression uniquely identifies the information we are looking for. One could also label this a bottom-up search procedure—regardless of how we name it, it helps construct expressions that are slim and potentially more robust to major changes in the document structure.

Once we have constructed suitable XPath expressions, extracting the information from the documents (step ⑤) is easy. We apply the expression with adequate functions from the XML package. The most promising procedure is to use `xpathSApply()` in combination with one of the XML extractor functions (see Table 4.4). In practice, steps ④ and ⑤ are not distinct. Finding adequate XPath expressions is a continuous trial-and-error process and we frequently jump between expression construction and information extraction. Additionally, XML extractor functions often produce not as clear-cut results as we wish them to be, and bringing the pieces of information into shape takes more than one iteration. Imagine, for example, that we want to extract reviews from a shopping website. While each of these reviews could be stored in a leaf in the DOM, we may want to extract more information that is part of the text, either in a manifest (words, word counts) or latent (sentiments, classes) manner. We can draw upon regular expressions or more advanced text mining algorithms to gather information at this level.

In the final step ⑥, we have to debug and maintain the code. Again, this is not literally the last step, but part of an iterative process.

9.2.2.1 Advantages of XPath

We have stressed that we prefer XPath over regular expressions for scraping content from static HTML/XML. XPath is the ideal counterpart for working with XML-style files, as it was explicitly designed for that purpose. This makes it the most powerful, flexible, easy to learn and write, and robust instrument to access content in XML/HTML files. **Naturally fits XML/HTML**

More specifically, the fact that XPath was designed for XML documents makes queries intuitive to write and read. This is all the more true when you compare it with regular expressions, which are defined on the basis of content, not context. As context follows a clearly defined structure, XPath queries are easier, especially for common cases. **Easy to read and write**

XPath is an expressive language, as it allows the scraping task to be substantially informed about a node of interest using a diverse set of characteristics. We can use a node's name, numeric or character features, its relation to other nodes, or content-like attributes. Single nodes can be uniquely defined. Additionally, working with XPath is efficient because it allows returning node sets with comparatively minimal code input. **Powerful and flexible**

As this strategy mainly relies on structural features of documents, XPath queries are robust to content changes. Certain content is fundamentally heterogeneous, such as press releases, customer reviews, and Wikipedia entries. As long as the fundamental architecture of a page remains the same, an XPath scraping strategy remains valid. **Robust toward changes in content**

9.2.2.2 Disadvantages of XPath

Although XPath is generally superior for scraping tasks compared with regular expressions, there are situations where XPath scraping fails.

Restriction to valid XML content When the parser fails, that is, when it does not produce a valid representation of the document, XPath queries are essentially useless. While our browser may be tolerant toward broken HTML documents and still interpret them correctly, our R XML parser might not. If we work on non-XML-style data, XPath expressions are of no help either.

Fragile in fragile contexts Complementary to the advantages of regular expression scraping for clearly defined patterns in a fragile environment, using XPath expressions to extract information is difficult when the context is highly variable, for example when the layout of a webpage is constantly altered.

9.2.3 Application Programming Interfaces

There is little doubt that gathering data from APIs/web services is the gold standard for web data collection. Scraping data from HTML websites is often a difficult endeavor. We first have to identify in which slots of the HTML tree the relevant data are stored and how to get rid of everything else that is not needed. APIs provide exactly the information we need, without any redundant information. They standardize the process of data dissemination, but also retain control for the provider over who accesses what data. Developers use different programming languages and use data for many different purposes. Web services allow providing standardized formats that most programming languages can deal with.

We illustrate the data collection procedure with APIs and R in Figure 9.8. In step ①, we have to find an API and become familiar with the terms of use or limits and the available methods. Commercial APIs can be very restrictive or offer no data at all if you do not pay a monthly fee, so you should find out early what you get for which payment. And do not invest time for nothing—not all web services are well-maintained. Before you start to program wrappers around an existing API, check whether the API is regularly updated. The API directory at http://www.programmableweb.com/apis also indicates when services are deprecated or moved to another place.

Steps ② and ③ are optional. Some web services require the users to register. Authentication or authorization methods can be quite different. Sometimes it suffices to register by email to obtain an individual key that has to be delivered with every request. Other ways of authentication are based on user/password combinations. Authentication via *OAuth* as described in Section 9.1.11 can be even more complex.

In step ④, we formulate a call to the API to request the resources. If we are lucky, we can draw upon an existing set of R functions that provide an interface to the API. We suggest some possible repositories which may offer the desired piece of R software that helps work with an API in Section 9.4. However, as the number of available web services increases quickly, chances are that we have to program our own R wrapper. Wrappers are pieces of software which wrap around existing software—in our case to be able to use R functions to call an API and to make the data we retrieve from an API accessible for further work in R.

In step ⑤, we process the incoming data. How we do this depends upon the data format delivered by the web service. In Chapter 3, we have learned how to use tools from the XML and jsonlite packages to parse XML and JSON data and eventually convert them to R objects. R packages which provide ready-made interfaces to web services (see Section 9.4) usually take care of this step and are therefore exceptionally handy to use.

As always, we should regularly check and debug our code (step ⑥). Be aware of the fact that API features and guidelines can change over time.

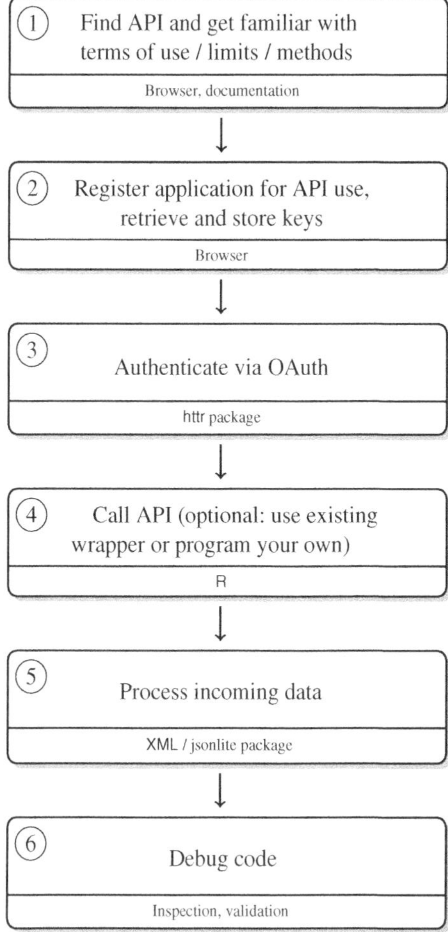

Figure 9.8 Data collection with APIs

9.2.3.1 Advantages of working with APIs

'Pure' data collection

The advantages of web services over the other techniques stem from the fact that tapping APIs is in fact not web scraping. Many of the disadvantages of screen scraping, malformed HTML, other robustness to legal issues, do not apply to data collection with web services. As a result, we can draw upon clean data structures and have higher trust in the collection outcomes.

Standardized data access procedures

Further, by registering an application for an API we make an agreement between provider and user. In terms of stability, chances are higher that databases from maintained APIs are updated regularly. When scraping data from HTML, we are often less sure about this. Some APIs provide exclusive access to content which we could not otherwise access. In terms of transparency, as data access procedures are standardized across many computer languages, the data collection process of projects based on data from web services can be replicated in other software environments as well.

Robustness As the focus of web services is on the delivery of data, not layout, our code is generally more robust. Web services usually satisfy a certain demand and we are often not the only ones interested in the data. If many people create interfaces to the API from various programming environments, we can benefit from this "wisdom of the crowds" and adding robustness to our code.

To sum up, APIs provide important advantages which make them—if available—the source of choice for any project that involves automated online data collection.

9.2.3.2 Disadvantages of working with APIs

The fact that the overwhelming majority of resources on the Web are still not accessed by web APIs motivates large parts of this book. This is no drawback of web services as a tool for data collection *per se* but merely reflects the fact that there are more data sources on the Web people like to work with than data providers who are willing to offer neat access to their databases.

Dependency on API providers Although there are not many general disadvantages of using APIs for automated data collection, relying on web service infrastructure can have its own drawbacks. Data providers can decide to limit their API's functionality from one day to the other, as has happened with popular social media APIs.

Lack of natural connection to R From the R perspective, we have to acknowledge that we work in a software environment that is not naturally connected to the data formats which plop out of ordinary web services.

However, the advantages of web services often easily outweigh the disadvantages, and even more so because the potential disadvantages do not necessarily apply to every web service and some of the drawbacks can partly be attributed to the other approaches as well.

9.3 Web scraping: Good practice

9.3.1 Is web scraping legal?

In the disclaimer of the book (see p. xix), we noted a caveat concerning the unauthorized use or reproduction of somebody else's intellectual work. As Dreyer and Stockton (2013) put it: "Scraping inherently involves copying, and therefore one of the most obvious claims against scrapers is copyright infringement." Our advice is to work as transparently as possible and document the sources of your data at any time. But even if one follows these rules, where is the line between legal scraping of public content and violations of copyright or other infringements of the law? Even for lawyers who are devoted to Internet issues the case of web crawling seems to be a difficult matter. Additionally, as the prevailing law varies across countries, we are unfortunately not able to give a comprehensive overview of what is legal in which context. To get an impression of what currently seems to be regarded as illegal, we offer some anecdotal evidence on past decisions. It should be clear, however, that you should not rely on any of these cases to justify your doings.

eBay v. Bidder's Edge Most of the prominent legal cases involve commercial interests. The usual scenario is that one company crawls information from another company, processes, and resells it. In the classical case eBay v. Bidder's Edge,[15] eBay successfully defended itself against the use of

[15] http://en.wikipedia.org/wiki/EBay_v._Bidder%27s_Edge, https://www.law.upenn.edu/fac/pwagner/law619/f2001/week11/bidders_edge.pdf

bots on their website. Bidder's Edge (BE), a company that aggregated auction listings, had used automated programs to crawl information from different auction sites. Users could then search listings on their webpage instead of posing many requests to each of the auction sites. According to the verdict,[16]

> BE accessed the eBay site approximate 100,000 times a day. (...) eBay allege[d] that BE activity constituted up to 1.53% of the number of requests received by eBay, and up to 1.10% of the total data transferred by eBay during certain periods in October and November of 1999.

Further,

> eBay allege[d] damages due to BE's activity totaling between $ 45,323 and $ 61,804 for a ten month period including seven months in 1999 and the first three months in 2000.

The defendant did not steal information that was not public to anyone, but harmed the plaintiff by causing a considerable amount of traffic on its servers. eBay also complained about the use of deep links, that is, links that directly refer to content that is stored somewhere "deeply" on the page. By using such links clients are able to circumvent the usual process of a website visit.

AP v. Meltwater

In another case, Associated Press v. Meltwater, scraper's rights were also curtailed.[17] Meltwater is a company that offers software which scrapes news information based on specific keywords. Clients can order summaries on topics which contain excerpts of news articles. Associated Press (AP) argued that their content was stolen by Meltwater and that they need to license before distributing it. The judge's argument in favor of the AP was that Meltwater is rather a competitor of AP than an ordinary search engine like Google News. From a more distant perspective, it is hard to see the difference to other news-aggregating services like Google News (Essaid 2013b; McSherry and Opsahl 2013).

Facebook v. Pete Warden

A case which was settled out of court was that of programmer Pete Warden who scraped basic information from Facebook users' profiles (Warden 2010). His idea was to use the data to offer services that help manage communication and networks across services. He described the process of scraping as "very easy" and in line with the *robots.txt* (see next section), an informal web bot guideline Facebook had put on its pages. After he had put a first visualization of the data on his blog, Facebook contacted and pushed him to delete the data. According to Warden, "Their contention was *robots.txt* had no legal force and they could sue anyone for accessing their site even if they scrupulously obeyed the instructions it contained. The only legal way to access any web site with a crawler was to obtain prior written permission" (Warden 2010).

United States v. Aaron Swartz

In the tragic case of Aaron Swartz, the core of contention was scientific work, not commercial reuse. Swartz, who co-created RSS (see Section 3.4.3), Markdown, and Infogami (a predecessor of Reddit), was arrested in 2011 for having illegally downloaded millions of articles from the article archive JSTOR. The case was dismissed after Swartz' suicide in January 2013 (United States District Court District of Massachusetts 2013).

---

[16] https://www.law.upenn.edu/fac/pwagner/law619/f2001/week11/bidders_edge.pdf

[17] https://www.eff.org/sites/default/files/ap_v._meltwater_sdny_copy.pdf

In an interesting, thoughtful comment, Essaid (2013a) points out that the jurisdiction on the issue of web scraping has changed direction several times over the last years, and there seem to be no clear criteria about what is allowed and what is not, not even in a single judicial system like the United States. Snell and Care (2013) deliver further anecdotal evidence and put court decisions in the context of legal theories.

The lesson to be learned from these disconcerting stories is that it is not clear which actions that can be subsumed under the "web scraping" label are actually illegal and which are not. In this book we focus on very targeted examples, and republishing content for a commercial purpose is a much more severe issue than just downloading pages and using them for research or analysis. Most of the litigations we came across involved commercial intentions. The Facebook v. Warden case has shown, however, that even following informal rules like those documented in the *robots.txt* does not guard against prosecution. But after all, as Frances Irwing from ScraperWiki puts it, "Google and Facebook effectively grew up scraping," and if there were significant restrictions on what data can be scraped then the Web would look very different today.[18]

In the next sections, we describe how to identify unofficial web scraping rules and how to behave in general to minimize the risk of being put in a difficult position.

9.3.2 What is robots.txt?

When you start harvesting websites for your own purposes, you are most likely only a small fish in the gigantic data ocean. Besides you, web robots (also named "crawlers," "web spiders," or just "bots") are hunting for content. Not all of these automatic harvesters act malevolently. Without bots, essential services on the Web would not work. Search engines like Google or Yahoo use web robots to keep their indices up-to-date. However, maintainers of websites sometimes want to keep at least some of their content prohibited from being crawled, for example, to keep their server traffic in check. This is what the *robots.txt* file is used for. This "Robots Exclusion Protocol" tells the robots which information on the site may be harvested.

The robots exclusion standard

The *robots.txt* emerged from a discussion on a mailing list and was initiated by Martijn Koster (1994). The idea was to specify which information may or may not be accessed by web robots in a text file stored in the root directory of a website (e.g., www.r-datacollection.com/robots.txt). The fact that *robots.txt* does not follow an official standard has led to inconsistencies and uncontrolled extensions of the grammar. There is a set of rules, however, that is followed by most *robots.txt* on the Web. Rules are listed bot by bot. A set of rules for the Googlebot robot could look as follows:

```
User-agent: Googlebot
Disallow: /images/
Disallow: /private/
```

This tells the Googlebot robot, specified in the `User-agent` field, not to crawl content from the subdirectories `/images/` and `/private/`. Recall from Section 5.2.1 that we can use the User-Agent field to be identifiable. Well-behaved web bots are supposed to look for

[18] See Mark Ward's article on business web scraping efforts at http://www.bbc.co.uk/news/technology-23988890.

their name in the list of User-Agents in the *robots.txt* and obey the rules. The `Disallow` field can contain partial or full URLs. Rules can be generalized with the asterisk (`*`).

```
User-agent: *
Disallow: /private/
```

This means that any robot that is not explicitly recorded is disallowed to crawl the `/private/` subdirectory. A general ban is formulated as

```
User-agent: *
Disallow: /
```

The single slash / encompasses the entire website. Several records are separated by one or more empty lines.

```
User-agent: Googlebot
Disallow: /images/

User-agent: Slurp
Disallow: /images/
```

A frequently used extension of this basic set of rules is the use of the `Allow` field. As the name already states, such fields list directories which are explicitly accepted for scraping. Combinations of `Allow` and `Disallow` rules enable webpage maintainers to exclude directories as a whole from crawling, but allow specific subdirectories or files within this directory to be crawled.

```
User-agent: *
Disallow: /images/
Allow: /images/public/
```

Another extension of the *robots.txt* standard is the `Crawl-delay` field which asks crawlers to pause between requests for a certain number of seconds. In the following *robots.txt*, Googlebot is allowed to scrape everything except one directory, while all other users may access everything but have to pause for 2 seconds between each request.[19]

```
User-agent: *
Crawl-delay: 2
User-Agent: Googlebot
Disallow: /search/
```

[19] The example is taken from the US Congress webpage: http://beta.congress.gov/

The robots `<meta>` tag

One problem of using *robots.txt* is that it can become quite voluminous for large webpages with multiple subdirectories and files. In addition, the way some crawlers work makes them ignorant to the centralized *robots.txt*. A disaggregated alternative to *robots.txt* is the robots `<meta>` tag which can be stored in the header of an HTML file.

```
<meta name="robots" content="noindex,nofollow" />
```

A well-behaved robot will refrain from indexing a page that contains this `<meta>` tag because of the `noindex` value in the `content` attribute and will not try to follow any link on this page because of the `nofollow` value in the `content` attribute.

An R parser for *robots.txt*

This book is not about web crawling, but focuses on retrieving content from specific sites with a specific purpose. But what if we still have to scrape information from several sites and do not want to manually inspect every single *robots.txt* file to program a well-behaved web scraper? For this purpose, we wrote a program that parses *robots.txt* by means of regular expressions and helps identify specific User-agents and corresponding rules of access. The program is displayed in Figure 9.9.

The `robotsCheck()` program reads the *robots.txt* which is specified in the first argument, `robotstxt`. We can specify the bot or User-agent with the second argument, `useragent`. Further, the function can return allowed and disallowed directories or files. This is specified with the `dirs` parameter. We do not discuss this program in greater detail here, but it can easily be extended so that a robot stops scraping pages that are stored in one of the disallowed directories.

We test the program on the *robots.txt* file of Facebook. First, we specify the link to the file.

```
R> facebook_robotstxt <- "http://www.facebook.com/robots.txt"
```

Next, we retrieve the list of directories that is prohibited from being crawled by any bot which is not otherwise listed. If we create our own bot, this is most likely the set of rules we have to obey.

```
R> robotsCheck(robotstxt = facebook_robotstxt, useragent = "*",
dirs = "disallowed")
This bot is blocked from the site.
```

Facebook generally prohibits crawling from its pages. Just to see how the program works, we make another call for a bot named “Yeti.”

```
R> robotsCheck(robotstxt = facebook_robotstxt, useragent = "Yeti",
dirs = "disallowed")
 [1] "/ajax/"             "/album.php"            "/autologin.php"
 [4] "/checkpoint/"       "/contact_importer/"    "/feeds/"
 [7] "/file_download.php" "/l.php"                "/p.php"
[10] "/photo.php"         "/photo_comments.php"   "/photo_search.php"
[13] "/photos.php"        "/sharer/"
```

Facebook disallows the “Yeti” bot to access a set of directories. It is important to say that *robots.txt* has little to do with a firewall against robots or any other protection mechanism. It does not prevent a website from being crawled at all. Rather, it is an advice from the website maintainer.

```
robotsCheck <- function(robotstxt = "", useragent = "*", dirs = "disallowed") {
# packages
require(stringr)
require(RCurl)
# read robots.txt
bots <- getURL(robotstxt, cainfo = system.file("CurlSSL", "cacert.pem", package = "RCurl"))
write(bots, file = "robots.txt")
bots <- readLines("robots.txt")
# detect if defined bot is on the list
useragent <- ifelse(useragent == "*", "\\*", useragent)
bot_line1 <- which(str_detect(bots, str_c("[Uu]ser-[Aa]gent:[ ]{0,}", useragent, "$"))) + 1
bot_listed <- ifelse(length(bot_line1)>0, TRUE, FALSE)
# identify all user-agents and user-agent after defined bot
ua_detect <- which(str_detect(bots, "[Uu]ser-[Aa]gent:[ ].+"))
uanext_line <- ua_detect[which(ua_detect == (bot_line1 - 1)) + 1]
# if bot is on the list, identify rules
bot_d_dir <- NULL
bot_a_dir <- NULL
bot_excluded <- 0
if (bot_listed) {
      bot_eline <- which(str_detect(bots, "^$"))
      bot_eline_end <- length(which(bot_eline - uanext_line < 0))
      bot_eline_end <- ifelse(bot_eline_end == 0, length(bots), bot_eline[bot_eline_end])
      botrules <- bots[bot_line1:bot_eline_end]
      # extract forbidden directories
      botrules_d <- botrules[str_detect(botrules, "[Dd]isallow")]
      bot_d_dir <- unlist(str_extract_all(botrules_d, "/.{0,}"))
      # extract allowed directories
      botrules_a <- botrules[str_detect(botrules, "^[Aa]llow")]
      bot_a_dir <- unlist(str_extract_all(botrules_a, "/.{0,}"))
      # bot totally excluded?
      bot_excluded <- str_detect(bot_d_dir, "^/$")
}
# return results
if (bot_excluded[1]) { message("This bot is blocked from the site.")}
if (dirs == "disallowed" & !bot_excluded[1]) { return(bot_d_dir) }
if (dirs == "allowed"  & !bot_excluded[1]) { return(bot_a_dir) }
}
```

Figure 9.9 R code for parsing *robots.txt* files

To the best of our knowledge, there is no law which explicitly states that *robots.txt* contents must not be disregarded. However, we strongly recommend that you have an eye on it every time you work with a new website, stay identifiable and in case of doubt contact the owner in advance.

If you want to learn more about web robots and how *robots.txt* works, the page http://www.robotstxt.org/ is a good start. It provides a more detailed explanation of the syntax and a useful collection of Frequently Asked Questions.

9.3.3 Be friendly!

Not everything that can be scraped should be scraped, and there are more and less polite ways of doing it. The programs you write should behave nicely, provide you with the data you need, and be efficient—in this order. We suggest that if you want to gather data from a website or service, especially when the amount of data is considerable, try to stick to our etiquette manual for web scraping. It is shown in Figure 9.10.

As soon as you have identified potentially useful data on the Web, you should look for an "official" way to gather the data. If you are lucky, the publisher provides ready-made files of the data which are free to download or offers an API. If an API is available, there is usually no reason to follow any of the other scraping strategies. APIs enable the provider to keep control over who retrieves which data, how much of it, and how often.

Friendly cooperation with APIs

As described in Section 9.2.2, accessing an API from within R usually requires one or more wrapper functions which pose requests to the API and process the output. If such wrappers already exist, all you have to do is to become familiar with the program and use it. Often, this requires the registration of an application (see Section 9.1.11). Be sure to document the purpose of your program. Many APIs restrict the user to a certain amount of API calls per day or similar limits. These limits should generally be obeyed.

Get into contact with the data providers

If there is no API, there might still be a more comfortable way of getting the data than scraping them. Depending on the type and structure of the data, it can be reasonable to assume that there is a database behind it. Virtually any data that you can access via HTTP forms is likely to be stored in some sort of database or at least in a prestructured XML. Why not ask proprietors of data first whether they might grant you access to the database or files? The larger the amount of data you are interested in, the more valuable it is for both providers and you to communicate your interests in advance. If you just want to download a few tables, however, bothering the website maintainer might be a little over the top.

Obey *robots.txt* and terms of use

Once you have decided that scraping the data directly from the page is the only feasible solution, you should consider the Robots Exclusion Protocol if there is any. The *robots.txt* is usually not meant to block individual requests to a site, but to prevent a webpage to be indexed by a search engine or other meta search applications. If you want to gather information from a page that documents disallowance of web robot activity in its *robots.txt*, you should reconsider your task. Do you plan to scrape data in a bot-like manner? Has your task the potential to do the web server any harm? In case of doubt, get into contact with the page administrator or take a look at the terms of use, if there are any. Ensure that your plans are with no ill intent, and stay identifiable with an adequate use of the identifying HTTP header fields.

Scraping dos and don'ts

If what you are planning is neither illegal nor has the potential to harm the provider in any way, there are still some scraping dos and don'ts you should consider with care.

As an example, we construct a small scraping program step-by-step, implementing all techniques from the bouquet of friendly web scraping. Say we want to keep track of the 250 most popular movies as rated by users of the Internet Movie Database (IMDb). The ranking is published at http://www.imdb.com/chart/top. Although the techniques implemented in this example are a bit over the top as we do not actually scrape large amounts of data, the procedure is the same for more voluminous tasks.

Suppose we have already worked through the checklist of questions of Figure 9.10 (as of March 2014, there is no IMDb API) and have decided that there is no alternative to scraping the content to work with the data. An inspection of IMDb's *robots.txt* reveals that robots are officially allowed to work in the */chart* subdirectory.

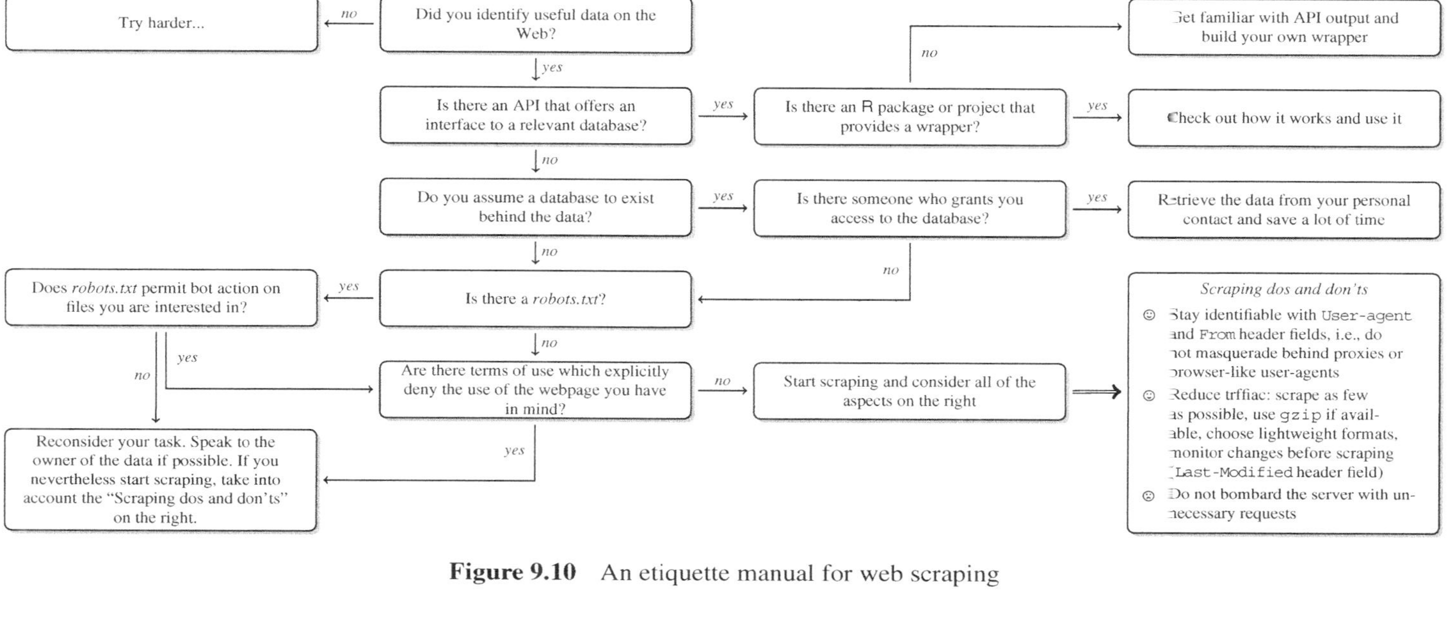

Figure 9.10 An etiquette manual for web scraping

The standard scraping approach using the RCurl package would be something like

```
R> library(RCurl)
R> library(XML)
R> url <- "http://www.imdb.com/chart/top"
R> top <- getURL(url)
R> parsed_top <- htmlParse(top, encoding = "UTF-8")
R> top_table <- readHTMLTable(parsed_top)[[1]]
R> head(top_table[1:10, 1:3])
                                             Rank & Title IMDb Rating
1                        1. The Shawshank Redemption (1994)       9.2
2                                   2. The Godfather (1972)       9.2
3                          3. The Godfather: Part II (1974)       9.0
4                                 4. The Dark Knight (2008)       8.9
5                                    5. Pulp Fiction (1994)       8.9
6                  6. The Good, the Bad and the Ugly (1966)       8.9
7                               7. Schindler's List (1993)       8.9
8                                    8. 12 Angry Men (1957)       8.9
9  9. The Lord of the Rings: The Return of the King (2003)       8.9
10                                   10. Fight Club (1999)       8.8
```

The first rule is to stay identifiable. We have learned in Chapter 5 how this can be done. When sending requests via HTTP, we can use the `User-agent` and `From` header fields. Therefore, we respecify the *GET* request as

```
R> getURL(url, useragent = str_c(R.version$platform, R.version$version.
string, sep = ", "), httpheader = c(from = "eddie@datacollection.com"))
```

The second rule is to reduce traffic. To do so, we should accept compressed files. One can specify which content codings to accept via the `Accept-Encoding` header field. If we leave this field unspecified, the server delivers files in its preferred format. Therefore, we do not have to specify the preferred compression style, which would probably be gzip, manually. The XML parser which is used in the XML package can deal with gzipped XML documents. We do not have to respecify the parsing command—the `xmlParse()` function automatically detects compression and uncompresses the file first.

Another trick to reduce traffic is applicable if we scrape the same resources multiple times. What we can do is to check whether the resource has changed before accessing and retrieving it. There are several ways to do so. First, we can monitor the `Last-Modified` response header field and make a conditional *GET* request, that is, access the resources only if the file has been modified since the last access. We can make the call conditional by delivering an `If-Modified-Since` or, depending on the mechanics of the function, `If-Unmodified-Since` request header field. In the IMDb example, this works as follows. First, we define a curl handle with the `debugGatherer()` function to be able to track our HTTP communication. Because we want to modify the HTTP header along the way, we store the standard headers for identifying ourselves in an extra object to use and redefine it.

```
R> info     <- debugGatherer()
R> httpheader <- list(from = "Eddie@r-datacollection.com", 'user-
agent' = str_c(R.version$version.string, ", ", R.version$platform))
R> handle <- getCurlHandle(debugfunc = info$update, verbose = TRUE)
```

We define a new function `getBest()` that helps extract the best movies from the IMDb page.

```
R> getBest <- function(doc) readHTMLTable(doc)[[1]][, 1:3]
```

Applying the function results in a data frame of the top 250 movies. To be able to analyze it in a later step, we store it on our local drive in an *.Rdata* file called *bestFilms.Rdata* if it does not exist already.

```
R> url <- "http://www.imdb.com/chart/top"
R> best_doc <- getURL(url)
R> best_vec <- getBest(best_doc)

R> if (!file.exists("bestFilms.Rdata")) {
    save(best_vec, file = "bestFilms.Rdata")
}
R> head(best_vec)
                              Rank & Title IMDb Rating
1        1. The Shawshank Redemption (1994)         9,2
2                   2. The Godfather (1972)         9,2
3          3. The Godfather: Part II (1974)         9,0
4                 4. The Dark Knight (2008)         8,9
5                    5. Pulp Fiction (1994)         8,9
6   6. The Good, the Bad and the Ugly (1966)         8,9
```

Now we want to update the file once in a while if and only if the IMDb page has been changed since the last time we updated the file. We do that by using the `If-Modified-Since` header field in the HTTP request.

```
R> httpheader$"If-Modified-Since" <- "Tue, 04 Mar 2014 10:00:00 GMT"
R> best_doc <- getURL(url, curl = handle, httpheader = httpheader)
```

It becomes a little bit more complicated if we want to use the time stamp of our *.Rdata* file's last update. For this we have to extract the date and supply it in the right format to the `If-Modified-Since` header field. As the extraction and transformation of the date into the format expected in HTTP request is cumbersome, we solve the problem once and put it into two functions: `httpDate()` and `file.date()`—see Figure 9.11. You can download the function from the book's webpage with

```
R> writeLines(str_replace_all(getURL("http://www.r-datacollection.
com/materials/http/HTTPdate.r"),"\r",""),"httpdate.r")
```

Let us source the functions into our session and extract the date of last modification for our best films data file with a call to `file.date()`.

```
R> source("http://www.r-datacollection.com/materials/http/HTTPdate.r")

R> (last_mod <- file.date("bestFilms.Rdata"))
[1] "2014-03-11 15:00:31 CET"
```

```
httpDate <- function(time="now", origin="1970-01-01", type="rfc1123"){
   if(time=="now") {
      tmp <- as.POSIXlt(Sys.time(), tz="GMT")
   }else{
      tmp <- as.POSIXlt(as.POSIXct(time, origin=origin), tz="GMT")
   }
   nday  <- c("Sun", "Mon" , "Tue" ,
              "Wed", "Thu" , "Fri" ,
              "Sat")[tmp$wday+1]
   month <- tmp$mon+1
   nmonth <- c("Jan" , "Feb" , "Mar" ,
             "Apr", "May" , "Jun" ,
             "Jul" , "Aug", "Sep" ,
             "Oct" , "Nov" , "Dec")[month]
   mday <- formatC(tmp$mday, width=2, flag="0")
   hour <- formatC(tmp$hour, width=2, flag="0")
   min  <- formatC(tmp$min , width=2, flag="0")
   sec  <- formatC(round(tmp$sec) , width=2, flag="0")
   if(type=="rfc1123"){
      return(paste0(nday, ", ",
                  mday," ", nmonth, " ", tmp$year+1900, " ",
                  hour, ":", min, ":", sec, " GMT") )
   }else{
     stop("Not implemented")
   }
}

file.date <- function(filename, timezone=Sys.timezone() ) {
   as.POSIXlt( min(unlist( file.info(filename)[4:6] )),
            origin = "1970-01-01",
            tz = timezone)
}

# usage:
# httpDate()
# httpDate( file.date("WorstFilms.Rdata") )
# httpDate("2001-01-02")
# httpDate("2001-01-02 18:00")
# httpDate("2001-01-02 18:00:01")
# httpDate(60*60*24*30.43827161*12*54+60*60*24*32)
# httpDate(-10*24*60*60,origin="2014-02-01")
```

Figure 9.11 Helper functions for handling HTTP If-Modified-Since header field

Now we can pass the date to the `If-Modified-Since` header field by making use of `httpDate()`.

```
R> httpheader$"If-Modified-Since" <- httpDate(last_mod)
R> best_doc <- getURL(url, curl = handle, httpheader = httpheader)
```

Via `getCurlInfo()` we can gather information on the last request and control the status code.

```
R> getCurlInfo(handle)$response.code
[1] 200
```

If the status code of the response equals *200*, we extract new information and update our data file. If the server responds with the status code 304 for "not modified" we leave it as is.

```
R> if (getCurlInfo(handle)$response.code == 200) {
     best_list <- getBest(best_doc)
     save(best_list, file = "bestFilms.Rdata")
}
```

Using the `If-Modified-Since` header is not without problems. First, it is not clear what the `Last-Modified` response header field actually means. We would expect the server to store the time the file was changed the last time. If the file contains dynamic content, however, the header field could also indicate the last modification of one of its component parts. In fact, in the example the IMDb website is always delivered with a current time stamp, so the file will always be downloaded—even if the ranking has not changed. We should therefore first monitor the updating frequency of the `Last-Modified` header field before adapting our scraper to it. Another problem can be that the server does not deliver a `Last-Modified` at all, even though HTTP/1.1 servers should provide it (see Fielding et al. 1999, Chapters 14.25, 14.28, and 14.29).

Another strategy is to retrieve only parts of a file. We can do this by specifying the `libcurl` option `range` which allows defining a byte range. If we know, for example, that the information we need is always stored at the very beginning of a file, like a title, we could truncate the document and specify our request function with `range = "1-100"` to only receive the first 100 bytes of the document. The drawbacks of this approach are that not all servers support this feature and we cut a document in two, making it not inaccessible with XPath.

In another scenario, we might want to download specific files from an index of files, but only those which we have not been downloaded so far. We implement a check if the file already exists on the local drive and start the download only if we have not already retrieved it. The following generic code snippet shows how to do this. Say we have generated a vector of HTML file names which are stored on a page like www.example.com with `filenames <- c("page1.html", "page2.html", page3.html)`. We can initiate a download of the files that have not yet been downloaded with:

```
R> for (i in 1:length(filenames)) {
     if (!file.exists(filenames[i])) {
         download.file(str_c(url, filenames[i]), destfile = filenames[i])
     }
}
```

The `file.exists()` function checks if the file already exists. If not, we download it. To know in advance how many files are new, we can compare the two sets of file names—the ones to be downloaded and the ones that are already stored in our folder—like this

```
R> existing_files <- list.files("directory_of_scraped_files")
R> online_files <- vector_of_online_files
R> new.files <- setdiff(online_files, existing_files)
```

The `list.files()` function lists the names of files stored in a given directory. The `setdiff()` function compares the content of two vectors and returns the asymmetric difference, that is, elements that are part of the first vector but not of the second. Note that these code snippets works properly only if we download websites that carry a unique identifier in the URL that remains constant over time, for example, a date, and if it is reasonable to assume that the content of these pages has not changed, while the set of pages has.

We also do not want to bother the server with multiple requests. This is partly because many requests per second can bring smaller servers to their knees, and partly because webmasters are sensitive to crawlers and might block us if our scraper behaves this way. With R it is straightforward to restrict our scraper. We simply suspend execution of the request for a time. In the following, a scraping function is programmed to process a stack of URLs and is executed only after a pause of one second, which is specified with the `Sys.sleep()` function.

```
R> for (i in 1:length(urls)) {
     scrape_function(urls[1])
     Sys.sleep(1)
}
```

There is no official rule how often a polite scraper should access a page. As a rule of thumb we try to make no more than one or two requests per second if `Crawl-delay` in the *robots.txt* does not dictate more modest request behavior.

Finally, writing a modest scraper is not only a question of efficiency but also of politeness. There is often no reason to scrape pages daily or repeat the same task over and over again. Although bandwidth costs have sunken over the years, server traffic still means real costs to website maintainers. Our last piece of advice for creating well-behaved web scrapers is therefore to make scrapers as efficient as possible. Practically, this means that if you have a choice between several formats, choose the lightweight one. If you have to scrape from an HTML page, it could prove useful to look for a "print version" or a "text only" version, which is often much lighter HTML than the fully designed page. This helps both you to extract content and the server who provides the resources. More generally, do not "overscrape" pages. Carefully select the resources you want to exploit, and leave the rest untouched. In addition, monitor your scraper regularly if you use it often. Webpage design can change quickly, rendering your scraping approach useless. A broken scraper may still consume bandwidth without any payoff.[20]

One final remark. We do not think that there is a reason to feel generally bad for scraping content from the Web. In all of the cases we present in this book this has nothing to do with stealing any private property or cheap copying of content. Ideally, processing scraped information comes with real added value.

9.4 Valuable sources of inspiration

Before starting to set up a scraping project, it is worthwhile to do some research on things others have done. This might help with specific problems, but the Internet is also full of more general inspirations for scraping applications and creative work with freely available data. In the following, we would like to point you to some resources and projects we find extraordinarily useful or inspiring.

---

[20]Much of this advice is inspired by the excellent "Walking Softly" introduction to web scraping with Perl by Hemenway and Calishain (2003).

CRAN Task View

The *CRAN Task View* on web technologies (http://cran.r-project.org/web/views/WebTechnologies.html) provides a very useful overview of what is possible with R in terms of accessing and parsing data from the Web. You will see that not all of the available packages are covered in this book, which is partly due to the fact that the community is currently very active in this field, and partly because we intentionally tried to focus on the most useful pieces of software. It might be a good exercise to set up an automated scraper that checks for updates of this site from time to time.

GitHub

GitHub is a hosting service for software projects or rather, users who publish their ongoing coding work (https://github.com/). It is not restricted to any programming language, so one can find many users who publish R code. Hadley Wickham and Winston Chang have provided the handy CRAN package devtools (Wickham and Chang 2013) which makes it easy to install R software that is not published on CRAN but on *GitHub* using the `install_github()` function.

rOpenSci

rOpenSci (http://ropensci.org/) is a fascinating project that aims at establishing convenient connections between R and existing science or science-related APIs. Their motto is nothing less than "Wrapping all science APIs." This implies a philosophy of "meta-sharing": The contributors to this project share and maintain software that helps accessing open science data. As we have shown in Section 9.1.10, maintenance of API access is indeed an important topic. The project's website provides R packages which serve as interfaces to several data repositories, full-texts of journals and altmetrics data. Some of the packages are also available on CRAN, some are stored on GitHub. To pick some examples, the rgbif package provides access to the Global Biodiversity Information Facility API which covers several thousand datasets on species and organisms (Chamberlain et al. 2013). The RMendeley package offers access to the personal Mendeley database (Boettiger and Temple Lang 2012). And with the rfishbase package it is possible to access the database from www.fishbase.org via R (Boettiger et al. 2014). Further, the site offers a potentially helpful overview of R packages that enable access to science APIs but that are not affiliated with *rOpenSci*—http://ropensci.org/related/index.html. It is well worth browsing this list to find R wrappers for APIs of popular sites such as Google Maps, the New York Times, the NHL Real Time Scoring System Database, and many more. All in all, the *rOpenSci* team works on an important goal for future scientific practice—the proliferation and accessibility of open data.

Omega Project

Large parts of what we can do with R and web scraping would likely not be possible without the work of the "Omega Project for Statistical Computing" at http://www.omegahat.org/. The project's core group is basically a Who is Who in R's core development team with Duncan Temple Lang being its most diligent contributor. With the creation of packages like RCurl and XML the project laid the foundation to R-Web communication. Today, the project makes available an impressive list of (not only) R-based software for interaction with web services and database systems. Not all of them are updated regularly or are of immediate use for standard web scraping tasks, but a look at the page is indispensable before any attempt to program a new interface to whatever web service. Chances are that it has been already done and published on this site. Many of the packages are also extensively discussed in an impressive new book by Nolan and Temple Lang (2014), which is well worth a read.

Summary

In this chapter, we demonstrated the practical use of the techniques from the book's first part—HTTP, HTML, regular expressions, and others—to retrieve information from webpages. Web scraping is more of a skill than a science. It is difficult to generalize web scraping practice, as every scenario is different. In the first part of this chapter, we picked some of the more common scenarios you might encounter when collecting data from the Web in an automated manner. If you felt overwhelmed from the vast amount of fundamental web technologies in the first part of the book, you might have been surprised how easy it is in many scenarios to gather data from the Web with R by relying on powerful network client interfaces like RCurl, convenient packages for string processing like stringr, and easy-to-implement parsing tools as provided by the XML package.

Regarding information extraction from web documents we sketched three broad strategies. Regular expression scraping, XPath scraping, and data collection with interfaces to web APIs. You will figure out for yourself which strategy serves your needs best in which scenarios as soon as you become more experienced in web scraping. Our description of the general procedure to automate data collection with each of the strategies may serve as a guideline. One intention of our discussion of advantages and disadvantages of each of the strategies was, however, to clarify that there is no single best web scraping strategy, and it pays of to be familiar with each of the presented techniques.

We dedicated the last section of this chapter to an important topic, the good practice of web scraping. Collecting data from websites is nothing inherently evil—successful business models are based on massive online data collection and processing. However, some formal and less formal rules we can and should obey exist. We have outlined an etiquette that gives some rules of behavior when scraping the Web.

Having worked through this chapter you have learned the most important tools to gather data from the Web with R. We discuss some more tricks of the trade in Chapter 11. If you deal with text data, information extraction can be a more sophisticated matter. We present some technical advice on how to handle text in R and to estimate latent classes in texts in Chapter 10.

Further reading

Many of the tutorials and how-to guides for web scraping with R which can be found online are rather case-specific and do not help much to decide which technique to use, how to behave nicely, and so on. With regard to the foundations of R tools to tap web resources, the recently published book by Nolan and Temple Lang (2014) offers great detail, especially regarding the use of RCurl and other packages which are not published on CRAN but serve specific, yet potentially important tasks in web scraping. They also provide a more extensive view on *REST*, SOAP, and XML-RPC. If you want to learn more about web services that rely on the *REST* technology on the theoretical side, have a look at Richardson et al. (2013). Cerami (2002) offers a more general picture of web services.

During the writing of this book, we found some books on practical web scraping inspiring, interesting, or simply fun to read, and do not want to withhold them from you. "Webbots, Spiders, and Screen Scrapers" by Schrenk (2012) is a fun-to-read introduction to scraping and web bot programming with PHP and Curl. The focus is clearly on the latter, so if you are interested in web bots and spiders, this book might be a good start. "Spidering Hacks" by Hemenway and Calishain (2003) is a comprehensive collection of applications and case studies on various scraping tasks. Their scraping workhorse is Perl, but the described hacks serve as good inspiration for programming R-based scrapers, too. Finally, "Baseball Hacks" by Adler (2006) is practically a large case study on scraping and data science mostly based on Perl (for the scraping part) and R (for data analysis). If you find the baseball scenario entertaining, Adler's hands-on book is a good companion on your way into data science.

Problems

1. What are important tools and strategies to build a scraper that behaves nicely on the Web?
2. What is an good extraction strategy for HTML lists on static HTML pages? Explain your choice.
3. Imagine you want to collect data on the occurrence of earthquakes on a weekly basis. Inform yourself about possible online data sources and develop a data collection strategy. Consider (1) an adequate scraping strategy, (2) a strategy for information extraction (if needed), and (3) friendly data collection behavior on the Web.
4. Reconsider the CSV file download function in Section 9.1.1. Replicate the download procedure with the data files for the primaries of the 2010 Gubernatorial Election.
5. Scraping data from Wikipedia, I: The Wikipedia article at http://en.wikipedia.org/wiki/List_of_cognitive_biases provides several lists of various types of cognitive biases. Extract the information stored in the table on social biases. Each of the entries in the table points to another, more detailed article on Wikipedia. Fetch the list of references from each of these articles and store them in an adequate R object.
6. Scraping data from Wikipedia, II: Go to http://en.wikipedia.org/wiki/List_of_MPs_elected_in_the_United_Kingdom_general_election,_1992 and extract the table containing the elected MPs int the United Kingdom general election of 1992. Which party has most *Sirs*?
7. Scraping data from Wikipedia, III: Take a look at http://en.wikipedia.org/wiki/List_of_national_capitals_of_countries_in_Europe_by_area and extract the geographic coordinates of each European country capital. In a second step, visualize the capitals on a map. The code from the example in chapter 1 might be of help.
8. Write your own *robots.txt* file providing the following rules: (a) no Google bot is allowed to scrape your web site, and (b) scraping your /private folder is generally not allowed.
9. Reconsider the R-based *robots.txt* parser on Figure 9.9. Use it as a start to construct a program that makes any of your scrapers follow the rules of the *robots.txt* on any site. The function has to fulfill the following tasks: (a) identification of the *robots.txt* on any given host if there is one, (b) check if a specific User-Agent is listed or not, (c) check if the path to be scraped is disallowed or not, and (d) adhere to the results of (a), (b), and (c). Consider scraping allowed if the *robots.txt* is missing.
10. Google Search allows the user to tune her request with a set of parameters. Make use of these parameters and set up a program that regularly informs you about new search results for your name.

11. Reconsider the Yahoo Weather Feed from Section 9.1.10.
   (a) Check out the wrapper function displayed in Figure 9.5 and rebuild it in R.
   (b) The API returns a weather code that has not been evaluated so far (see also the last column in the table on page 238). Read the API's documentation to figure out what the code stands for and implement the result in the feedback of the wrapper function.

12. The CityBikes API at http://api.citybik.es/ provides free access to a global bike sharing network. Choose a bike sharing service in a city of your choice and build an R interface to it. The interface should enable the user to get information about the list of stations and the number of available bikes at each of the stations. For a more advanced extension of this API, implement a feature such that the function automatically returns the station closest to a given geo-coordinate.

13. The New York Times provides a set of APIs at http://developer.nytimes.com/docs. In order to use them, you have to sign up for an API key. Construct an R interface to their best-sellers search API which can retrieve the current best-seller list and transform the incoming JSON data to an R data frame.

14. Let us take another look at the Federal Contributions Database.
   (a) Find out what happens when the window is not changed back from the pop-up window. Does the code still work?
   (b) Write a script building on the code outlined above that downloads all contributions to Republication candidates from 2007 to 2011.
   (c) Download all contributions from March 2011, but have the data returned in a plot. Try to extract the amount and party information from the plot.

15. Apply Rwebdriver to other example files introduced in this book:
   (a) *fortunes2.html*
   (b) *fortunes3.html*
   (c) *rQuotes.php*
   (d) *JavaScript.html*

10

Statistical text processing

Any quantitative research project that hopes to make use of statistical analyses needs to collect structured information. As we have demonstrated in countless examples up to this point, the Web is an invaluable source of structured data that is ready for analysis upon collection. Unfortunately, in terms of quantity such structured information is far outweighed by unstructured content. The Internet is predominantly a vast collection of more or less unclassified text.

Consequently, the advent of the widespread use of the Internet has seen a contemporaneous interest in *natural language processing*—the automated processing of human language. This is by no means coincidental. Never before have such massive amounts of machine-readable text been available. In order to access such data, numerous techniques have been devised to assign systematic meaning to unstructured text. This chapters seeks to elaborate several of the available techniques to make use of unclassified data.

In a first step, the next section presents a small running example that is used throughout the chapter. Subsequently, Section 10.2 elaborates how to perform large-scale text operations in R. Textual data can quickly become taxing on resources. While this is a more general concern when dealing with textual data, it is particularly relevant in R, which was not designed to deal with large-scale text analysis. We will introduce the tm package that allows the organization and preparation of text and also provides the infrastructure for the analytical packages that we will use throughout the remainder of the chapter (Feinerer 2008; Feinerer et al. 2008).

In terms of the techniques that are presented in order to make sense of unstructured text data, we start out by presenting supervised methods in Section 10.3. This broad class of techniques allows the categorization of text based on similarities to pre-classified text. Simply put, supervised methods allow users to label texts based on how much they resemble a hand-coded training set. The classic example in this area deals with the organization of text into topical categories. Say we have 1000 texts of varied content. Imagine further that half of the texts have been assigned a label of their topical emphasis. Using supervised methods we

---

Automated Data Collection with R: A Practical Guide to Web Scraping and Text Mining, First Edition.
Simon Munzert, Christian Rubba, Peter Meißner and Dominic Nyhuis.

can estimate the content of the unlabeled half.[1] Several supervised methods have been made available in R. This chapter introduces the RTextTools package which provides a wrapper to a number of the available packages. This allows a convenient access to several classifiers from within a single function call (Jurka et al. 2013).

A second approach to classifying text is presented in Section 10.4—unsupervised classifiers. In contrast to supervised learning algorithms that rely on similarities between pre-classified and unlabeled text, unsupervised classifiers estimate the categories along with the membership of texts in the different categories. The major advantage of techniques in this group is the possibility of circumventing the cumbersome hand-coding of training data. This advantage comes at the price of having to interpret the content of the estimated categories *a posteriori*.

As a word of caution we would like to point out that this chapter can only serve as a cursory introduction to the topics in question. We investigate some of the most important topics and packages that are available in R. It should be emphasized, however, that in many instances we cannot do full justice to the details of the topics that are being covered. You should be aware that if you care to deal with these types of models, there is a lot more out there that might serve your purposes better than what is being presented in this chapter. We provide some guidance for further readings in the last section of the chapter.

10.1 The running example: Classifying press releases of the British government

Before turning to the statistical processing of text, let us collect some sample text data that will serve as a running example throughout this chapter. For the running example, we want all the data to be labeled such that we have a benchmark for the accuracy of our classifiers. We have selected press releases from the UK government as our test case. The data can be accessed at https://www.gov.uk/government/announcements. Opening the website in a browser, you see several selection options at the left side of the screen. We want to restrict our analysis to press releases in all topics, from all departments, in all locations that were published before July 2010. At the time of writing this yields 747 results that conform to the request. The results page presents the title of the press release, the date of publication, an acronym signaling the publishing department, as well as the type of publication. For the statistical analysis in the subsequent chapters, we will consider the publishing agency as a marker of the press releases' content.

Notice how the URL of the page changes when you make the selections.

```
https://www.gov.uk/government/announcements?keywords=&announcem
ent_type_option=press-releases&topics[]=all&departments[]=all&
world_locations[]=all&from_date=&to_date=01%2F07%2F2010
```

[1] We are not technically restricted to statements on the overall topical content of texts. We can use the same techniques to estimate the content of particular text aspects, say sentences, as long as we are able to provide some pre-classified *training data*. The present chapter sticks to topical classification as the most common task in statistical text analysis. As a side note, learning algorithms are not limited to the analysis of text at all and are used in such diverse research fields as bio-informatics or speech and, more generally, pattern recognition.

You can clearly see how the selections we make become integrated into the URL. As the data are not too large to be stored locally, we will, in accordance with our rules of good practice in web scraping, start by downloading all 747 results onto our hard drive before collecting the text data in a tm corpus in a subsequent step. Check out the source code of the page. You will find the first results toward the end of the page. However, not all 747 results are contained in the source code. To collect them, we have to use the link that is contained at the bottom of the press releases. It reads

```
<a href="/government/announcements?announcement_type_option=press-
releases&amp;departments%5D%5D=all&amp;from_date=&amp;keywords=&amp;
page=2&amp;to_date=01%2F07%2F2010&amp;topics%5B%5D=all&amp;world_
locations%5B%5D=all">Next page <span>2 of 19</span></a>
```

Gathering press release hyperlinks

To assemble the links to all press releases, we collect the publication links in one page, select the link to the next page, and repeat the process until we have all the relevant links. This is achieved with the following short code snippet. First, we load the necessary scraping packages.

```
R> library(RCurl)
R> library(XML)
R> library(stringr)
```

We move on to download all the results. Notice that because the content is stored on an HTTPS server, we specify the location of our CA signatures (see Section 9.1.7 for details).

```
R> all_links <- character()
R> new_results <- 'government/announcements?keywords=&announcement_
type_option=press-releases&topics[]=all&departments[]=all&world_
locations[]=all&from_date=&to_date=01%2F07%2F2010'
R> signatures = system.file("CurlSSL", cainfo = "cacert.pem",
package = "RCurl")
R> while(length(new_results) > 0){
R>     new_results <- str_c("https://www.gov.uk/", new_results)
R>     results <- getURL(new_results, cainfo = signatures)
R>     results_tree <- htmlParse(results)
R>     all_links <- c(all_links, xpathSApply(results_tree,
R>                                           "//li[@id]//a",
R>                                           xmlGetAttr,
R>                                           "href"))
R>     new_results <- xpathSApply(results_tree,
R>                                "//nav[@id='show-more-documents']
R>                                //li[@class='next']//a",
R>                                xmlGetAttr,
R>                                "href")
R> }
```

We are left with a vector of length 747 but possibly some changes have been made since this book was published. Each entry contains the link to one press release. To be sure that your results are identical to ours, check the first item in your vector. It should read as follows

```
R> all_links[1]
[1] "/government/news/bianca-jagger-how-to-move-beyond-oil"
R> length(all_links)
[1] 747
```

Download procedure

To download all press releases, we iterate over our results vector.

```
R> for(i in 1:length(all_links)){
R>     url <- str_c("https://www.gov.uk", all_links[i])
R>     tmp <- getURL(url, cainfo = signatures)
R>     write(tmp, str_c("Press_Releases/", i, ".html"))
R> }
```

If everything was proceeded correctly, you should find the folder *Press_Releases* in your working directory which contains all press releases as HTML files.

```
R> length(list.files("Press_Releases"))
[1] 747
R> list.files("Press_Releases")[1:3]
[1] "1.html"   "10.html"   "100.html"
```

10.2 Processing textual data

The widespread application of statistical text analysis is a fairly recent phenomenon. It coincides with the almost universal storage of text in digital formats. Such massive amounts of machine-readable text created the need to come up with methods to automate the processing of content. A number of techniques in the tradition of performing statistical text analysis have been implemented in R. Concurrently, infrastructures had to be implemented in order to handle large collections of digital text. The current standard for statistical text analysis in R is the tm package. It provides facilities to manage text collections and to perform the most common data preparation operations prior to statistical text analysis.

10.2.1 Large-scale text operations—The tm package

Let us load all press releases that we have collected in the previous section into R and store them in a tm corpus.[2] Ordinarily, this could be accomplished by calling the relevant functions on the entire directory in which we stored the press releases. In this case, however, the press releases are still in the HTML format. Thus, before inputting them into a corpus, we want to strip out all the tags and text that is not specific to the press release.

Let us consider the first press release as an example. Open the press release in a browser of your choice. The press release starts with the words "Bianca Jagger, Chair of the Bianca Jagger Human Rights Foundation and a Council of Europe Goodwill Ambassador, has called for a "Copernican revolution" in moving beyond carbon to a decentralized, sustainable energy system." There is more layout information in the document. In a real research project, one might want to consider stripping out the additional noise. In addition to the text of the press

[2] A text corpus in linguistics simply refers to a structured collection of texts.

release we find the publishing organization and the date of publication toward the top of the page. We extract the first two bits of information and store them along with the press release as *meta information*. Let us investigate the source code of the press release. We find that the press release is stored after the tag <div class="block-4">. Thus, we get the release by calling

```
R> tmp <- readLines("Press_Releases/1.html")
R> tmp <- str_c(tmp, collapse = "")
R> tmp <- htmlParse(tmp)
R> release <- xpathSApply(tmp, "//div[@class='block-4']", xmlValue)
```

Extracting meta information

The extracted release is not evenly formatted since we discarded all the tags. However, as we will drop the sequence of the words later on, this is of no concern. Also, while we might like to drop several bits of text like (opens in new window), this should not influence our estimation procedures.[3] Before iterating over our entire corpus of results, we write two queries to extract the meta information. The information on the publishing organization is stored under <span class="organisation lead", the information on the publishing date under <dd class="change-notes">.

```
R> organisation <- xpathSApply(tmp, "//span[@class='organisation
lead']", xmlValue)
R> organisation
[1] "Foreign & Commonwealth Office"
R> publication <- xpathSApply(tmp, "//dd[@class='change-notes']",
xmlValue)
R> publication
[1] "Published  1 July 2010"
```

Creating a corpus

Now that we have all the necessary elements set up, we create a loop that performs the operations on all press releases and stores the resulting information in a corpus. Such a corpus is the central element for text operations in the tm package. It is created by calling the Corpus() function on the first press release we just assembled. The text release is wrapped in a VectorSource() function call. This specifies that the corpus is created from text which is stored in a character vector.[4]

```
R> library(tm)
R> release_corpus <- Corpus(VectorSource(release))
```

Adding meta information

The corpus can be accessed just like any ordinary list by specifying the name of the object (release_corpus) and adding the subscript of the element that we are interested in, enclosed by two square brackets. So far, we have only stored one element in our corpus that we can call using release_corpus[[1]]. To add the two pieces of meta information to the text, we use the meta() function. The variable specifies the document that we want

---

[3] Not discarding these technical pieces of text is identical to making the—not overly problematic—assumption that particular governmental departments do not systematically include features such as external links more often than others. If this were the case, then this could very well be picked up by the estimation procedures.

[4] Several alternatives have been implemented. We could, for example, create a text corpus from a directory (DirSource()) directly if we did not have to extract the press releases from the HTML files—or if we cared to store the entire source code in the text corpus.

Incidentally, using the Corpus() function creates a *volatile* corpus in the memory of R that is destroyed when the program is terminated. Alternatively, we could have created a *permanent* corpus that is stored in a database outside of R.

the meta information to be assigned to and the second variable specifies the tag name of the meta information, in our case we select `organisation` and `publication`. Note that we select the first organization for the meta information. Several press releases have more than one organizational affiliation. For convenience, we simply choose the first one. Again, this creates a little bit of imprecision in our data that should not throw off the classifiers terribly.

```
R> meta(release_corpus[[1]], "organisation") <- organisation[1]
R> meta(release_corpus[[1]], "publication") <- publication
R> meta(release_corpus[[1]])
Available meta data pairs are:
  Author       :
  DateTimeStamp: 2014-03-26 00:21:46
  Description  :
  Heading      :
  ID           : 1
  Language     : en
  Origin       :
User-defined local meta data pairs are:
$organisation
[1] "Foreign & Commonwealth Office"

$publication
[1] "Published  1 July 2010"
```

The meta information of any document can be accessed using the same function. Several meta information tags are predefined, such as `Author` and `Language`. Some are filled automatically upon creation of the entry. At the bottom of the meta information we see the two elements that we have created—the date of publication and the organization that has published the press release. In the next step, we perform the operations that we have introduced above for all the documents that we downloaded. We collect the text of the press release and the two pieces of meta information and add them our corpus using simple concatenation (`c()`). A potential problem of the automated document import is that the XPath queries may fail on press releases which have a different layout. Usually, this should not be the case. Nevertheless, if it did happen, our temporary corpus object `tmp_corpus` code would not be created and the loop would fail. We therefore specify a condition to conduct the corpus creation only if the `release` object exists, that is, has a length greater 0.[5]

```
R> n <- 1
R> for(i in 2:length(list.files("Press_Releases/"))){
R>     tmp <- readLines(str_c("Press_Releases/", i, ".html"))
R>     tmp <- str_c(tmp, collapse = "")
R>     tmp <- htmlParse(tmp)
R>     release <- xpathSApply(tmp,
R>                            "//div[@class='block-4']",
R>                            xmlValue)
R>     organisation <- xpathSApply(tmp,
R>                                 "//span[@class='organisation lead']",
R>                                 xmlValue)
```

[5]Such exceptions are typically the result of debugging our code when the functions fail.

```
R>     publication <- xpathSApply(tmp,
R>                                "//dd[@class='change-notes']",
R>                                xmlValue)
R>      if (length(release)!=0) {
R>             n <- n + 1
R>             tmp_corpus <- Corpus(VectorSource(release))
R>             release_corpus <- c(release_corpus, tmp_corpus)
R>             meta(release_corpus[[n]], "organisation") <-
               organisation[1]
R>             meta(release_corpus[[n]], "publication") <- publication
R>      }
R> }
```

A look at the full corpus reveals that all but one document have been added to the corpus object.

```
R> release_corpus
A corpus with 746 text documents
```

Collect meta information from the corpus

Recall that meta information is internally linked to the document. In many cases we are interested in a tabular form of the meta data to perform further analyses. Such a table can be collected using the `prescindMeta()` function. It allows selecting pieces of meta information from the individual documents to input them into a common `data.frame`.

```
R> meta_data <- prescindMeta(release_corpus, c("organisation",
"publication"))
R> head(meta_data)
  MetaID organisation  publication
1      0 Foreign .... Publishe....
2      0 Ministry.... Publishe....
3      0 Ministry.... Publishe....
4      0 Departme.... Publishe....
5      0 Departme.... Publishe....
6      0 Departme.... Publishe....
```

Let us inspect the meta data for a moment. As a simple summary statistic we call a count of the different publishing organizations. We find that the publishing behavior of the various governmental departments is fairly diverse. Assuming that the website of the UK government truly collects all the press releases from all governmental departments we find that while two departments have released over 100 announcements, others have published less than a dozen.

```
R> table(as.character(meta_data[, "organisation"]))

                                 Cabinet Office
                                             31
    Department for Business, Innovation & Skills
                                             65
  Department for Communities and Local Government
                                             22
           Department for Culture, Media & Sport
                                             12
```

```
                        Department for Education
                                               5
  Department for Environment, Food & Rural Affairs
                                              35
                        Department for Transport
                                              13
                   Department for Work & Pensions
                                              17
             Department of Energy & Climate Change
                                              20
                   Deputy Prime Minister's Office
                                               3
               Driver and Vehicle Licensing Agency
                                               4
                   Foreign & Commonwealth Office
                                             204
                                     HM Treasury
                                              14
                                     Home Office
                                               8
                             Ministry of Defence
                                             177
       Prime Minister's Office, 10 Downing Street
                                              62
                                 Scotland Office
                                              16
              Vehicle and Operator Services Agency
                                               4
                                    Wales Office
                                              34
```

Corpus filtering with `sFilter()`

As we will elaborate in greater detail in the upcoming sections, we need a certain level of coverage in each of the categories that we would like the classifiers to pick up. Thus, we discard all press releases from departments that have released 20 press statements or less. There are eight departments that have published more than 20 press releases for the period that is covered by the website up to July 2010. We select them to remain in the corpus. In addition to the rare categories, we exclude the cabinet office and the prime minister's office. These bodies are potentially more difficult to classify as they are not bound to a particular policy area. We perform the exclusion of documents using the `sFilter()` function. This function takes the corpus in question as the first argument and one or more value pairs of the form `"tag == 'value"'`. Recall that the pipe operator (|) is equivalent to `OR`.

```
R> release_corpus <- release_corpus[sFilter(release_corpus, "
organisation == 'Department for Business, Innovation & Skills' |
organisation == 'Department for Communities and Local Government' |
organisation == 'Department for Environment, Food & Rural Affairs' |
organisation == 'Foreign & Commonwealth Office' |
organisation == 'Ministry of Defence' |
organisation == 'Wales Office"')]
R> release_corpus
A corpus with 537 text documents
```

Excluding the sparsely populated categories as well as the umbrella offices, we are left with a corpus of 537 documents. As a side note, corpus filtering is more generally applicable in the tm package. For example, imagine we would like to extract all the documents that contain the term "Afghanistan." To do so, we apply the `tm_filter()` function which does a full text search and returns all the documents that contain the term.

Corpus filtering with `tm_filter()`

```
R> (afgh <- tm_filter(release_corpus,
                      FUN = function(x) any(str_detect(x, "Afghanistan"))))
A corpus with 131 text documents
```

We find that no fewer than 131 documents out of our sample contain the term.

10.2.2 Building a term-document matrix

Let us now turn our attention to preparing the text data for the statistical analyses. A great many applications in text classification take term-document matrices as input. Simply put, a term-document matrix is a way to arrange text in matrix form where the rows represent individual terms and columns contain the texts. The cells are filled with counts of how often a particular term appears in a given text. Hence, while all the information on which terms appear in a text is retained in this format, it is impossible to reconstruct the original text, as the term-document matrix does not contain any information on location. To make this idea a little clearer, consider a mock example of four sentences A, B, C, and D that read

A "Mary had a little lamb, little lamb"
B "whose fleece was white as snow"
C "and everywhere that Mary went, Mary went"
D "the lamb was sure to go"

These four sentences can be rearranged in a matrix format as depicted in Table 10.1. The majority of cells in the table are empty, which is a common case for term-document matrices.

The function in the tm package to turn a text corpus into a term-document matrix is `TermDocumentMatrix()`. Calling this on our corpus of press releases yields

```
R> tdm <- TermDocumentMatrix(release_corpus)
R> tdm
A term-document matrix (23350 terms, 537 documents)

Non-/sparse entries: 99917/12439033
Sparsity           : 99%
Maximal term length: 252
Weighting          : term frequency (tf)
```

Not surprisingly, the resulting matrix is extremely sparse, meaning that most cells have not a single entry (approximately 99%). In addition, upon closer inspection of the terms in the rows, we find that several are errors that can probably be traced back to unclean data sources. This concern is validated by looking at the figure of `Maximal term length` that takes on an improbably high value of 252.

Table 10.1 Example of a term-document matrix

	A	B	C	D
a	1	.	.	.
and	.	.	1	.
as	.	1	.	.
had	1	.	.	.
everywhere	.	.	1	.
fleece	.	1	.	.
go	.	.	.	1
lamb	2	.	.	1
little	2	.	.	.
Mary	1	.	2	.
to	.	.	.	1
that	.	.	1	.
the	.	.	.	1
snow	.	1	.	.
sure	.	.	.	1
was	.	1	.	1
went	.	.	2	.
white	.	1	.	.
whose	.	1	.	.

10.2.3 Data cleansing

10.2.3.1 Word removals

In order to take care of some of these errors, one typically runs several data preparation operations. Furthermore, the data preparation addresses some of the concerns that are leveled against (semi-)automated text classification which will be discussed in the next section. Several preparation operations have been made available in tm. For example, one might consider removing numbers and period characters from the texts without losing much information. This can either be done on the raw textual data or while setting up the term-document matrix. For convenience of exposition, we will run each of these functions on the original documents.

Removing numbers The main function we will be using in this section is `tm_map()`, which takes a function and runs it on the entire corpus. To remove numbers in our documents, we call

```
R> release_corpus <- tm_map(release_corpus, removeNumbers)
```

Removing punctuation characters We could use the `removePunctuation()` function to remove period characters. However, this function simply removes punctuation without inserting white spaces. In case of formatting errors of the text this might accidentally join two words. Thus, to be safe, we use the `str_replace_all()` function from the stringr package. The additional arguments to the function are simply added to the call to `tm_map()`.[6]

[6]The downside of this operation is that it takes out all punctuation indiscriminately. If one cares to be a little more elaborate, one might want to retain dashes within words, for example.

```
R> release_corpus <- tm_map(release_corpus, str_replace_all, pattern
= "[[:punct:]]", replacement = " ")
```

Another common operation is the removal of so-called stop words. Stop words are the most common words in a language that should appear quite frequently in all the texts. However, for the estimation of the topics they should not be very helpful as we would expect them to be evenly distributed across the different texts. Hence, the removal of stop words is rather an operation that is performed to increase computational performance and less in order to improve the estimation procedures. The list of English stop words that is implemented in tm contains more than a hundred terms at the time of writing.

Removing stop words

```
R> length(stopwords("en"))
[1] 174
R> stopwords("en")[1:10]
 [1] "i"          "me"         "my"         "myself"     "we"
 [6] "our"        "ours"       "ourselves"  "you"        "your"
```

Again, we remove these using the `tm_map()` function.

```
R> release_corpus <- tm_map(release_corpus, removeWords, words =
stopwords("en"))
```

Next, one typically converts all letters to lower case so that sentence beginnings would not be treated differently by the algorithms.

Removing upper cases

```
R> release_corpus <- tm_map(release_corpus, tolower)
```

10.2.3.2 Stemming

The following operation is potentially of greater importance than those that have been introduced so far. Many statistical analyses of text will perform a stemming of terms prior to the estimation. What this operation does is to reduce the terms in documents to their stem, thus combining words that have the same root. A number of stemming algorithms have been proposed and there are implementations for different languages available in R. Once more, we apply the relevant function from the tm package, `stemDocument()` via the `tm_map()` function.[7]

```
R> library(SnowballC)
R> release_corpus <- tm_map(release_corpus, stemDocument)
```

10.2.4 Sparsity and n-grams

Now that we have performed all the document preparation that we would like to include in our analysis, we can regenerate the term-document matrix. Note again that we did not have to perform the single operations on the original texts. We could just as easily have performed the operations concurrently with the generation of the term-document matrices. This is accomplished via the control parameters in the `TermDocumentMatrix()` function.

[7] Note that the stemming procedure requires the SnowballC package to be installed.

Note further that there are a number of common weighting operations available that are more elaborate than the mere term frequency. For simplicity of exposition, we will not discuss them in this chapter. Now let us see how the operations have changed the main parameters of our term-document matrix.

```
R> tdm <- TermDocumentMatrix(release_corpus)
R> tdm
A term-document matrix (9452 terms, 537 documents)

Non-/sparse entries: 74000/5001724
Sparsity           : 99%
Maximal term length: 34
Weighting          : term frequency (tf)
```

Sparse terms The list of terms has become a lot cleaner and we also observe a more realistic value for the `Maximal term length` parameter. One more operation that is commonly performed is the removal of sparse terms from a text corpus prior to running the classifiers. The primary reason for this operation is computational feasibility. Apart from that, the operation can also be viewed as a safeguard against formatting errors in the data. If a term appears extremely infrequently, it is possible that it contains an error. The downside of removing sparse terms is, however, that sparse terms might provide valuable insight into the classification which is stripped out. The following operation discards all terms that appear in 10 documents or less.

```
R> tdm <- removeSparseTerms(tdm, 1-(10/length(release_corpus)))
R> tdm
A term-document matrix (1546 terms, 537 documents)

Non-/sparse entries: 57252/772950
Sparsity           : 93%
Maximal term length: 22
Weighting          : term frequency (tf)
```

Bigrams A common concern that is voiced against the statistical analysis of text in the way that is proposed in the subsequent two sections is its utter disregard of structure and context. Furthermore, terms might have meaning associated to them that resides in several terms that follow one after another rather than in single terms. Moreover, concerns are often voiced that the methods have no way of dealing with negations. While there are diverse solutions to all of these problems, one possibility is to construct term-document matrices on bigrams. Bigrams are all two-word combinations in the text, that is, in the sentence "Mary had a little lamb," the bigrams are "Mary had," "had a," "a little," and "little lamb." Within the tm framework, a term-document matrix of bigrams can easily be constructed using the R interface to the *Weka* program using the RWeka package (Hornik et al. 2009; Witten and Frank 2005).

```
R> library(RWeka)
R> BigramTokenizer <- function(x){
R>     NGramTokenizer(x, Weka_control(min = 2, max = 2))}
R> tdm_bigram <- TermDocumentMatrix(release_corpus,
R>                                   control = list(
R>                                   tokenize =
R>                                   BigramTokenizer))
```

The disadvantages of a term-document matrix based on bigrams is the fact that the matrix becomes substantially larger and even more sparse.

```
R> tdm_bigram
A term-document matrix (87040 terms, 537 documents)

Non-/sparse entries: 116592/46623888
Sparsity           : 100%
Maximal term length: 39
Weighting          : term frequency (tf)
```

Especially the former point is relevant, as the computational task grows with the size of the matrix. In fact, depending on the specific task, the accuracy of classification using this operationalization does not increase dramatically. What is more, some of the aforementioned concerns are not too severe. Consider the negation problem. As long as negations are randomly distributed they should not greatly influence the classification task.

Before moving on, let us consider an interesting summary statistic of the resulting matrix. Using the `findAssocs()` function, we are able to capture associations between terms in the matrix. Specifically, the function calculates the correlation between a term and all other terms in the matrix.

```
R> findAssocs(tdm, "nuclear", .7)
        nuclear
weapon     0.93
disarma    0.91
treati     0.90
materi     0.80
```

In the above call we request the associations for the term "nuclear" where the correlation is 0.7 or higher. The output provides a matrix of all the terms for which this is true, along with the correlation value. We find that the stems "weapon,""disarma,""treati," and "materi" are most correlated with "nuclear" in the press releases that we collected.

10.3 Supervised learning techniques

In this and the following sections, we try to estimate the topical affiliation of the documents in the corpus. A first and important distinction we have to make in this regard is the one between latent and manifest characteristics of a document. Manifest characteristics describe aspects of a text that are clearly observable in the text itself. For example, whether or not a text contains numbers is typically not a quality up for debate. This is not the case for latent characteristics of a text. The topical emphasis of a text might be very well debatable. This distinction is important when thinking about the uncertainty that is part of our measurements. In text classification, we can distinguish between different forms of uncertainty and misclassification.

The first kind of uncertainty resides in the algorithms themselves and can be traced back to limited data availability and a number of simplifying assumptions one typically makes when using the algorithms—not least the assumption that the sequence of the words in the text has no effect on the topic it signals. This point becomes obvious when thinking about the way the data are structured that is underlying our analysis. The so-called bag-of-word

Simplifying assumptions

approaches hold that the mere presence or absence of a term is a strong indicator of a text's topical emphasis—regardless of its specific location. When creating a term-document matrix of the texts, we discard any sequence information and treat the texts as collections of words. Consider the following example. If you observe that a particular text contains the terms "Roe,""Wade,""Planned,"and "Parenthood"you have a decent chance of correctly guessing that the text in some way revolves around the issue of abortion. Moreover, many classifiers rely on the Naïve Bayes assumption. This suggests that observing one term in a text is independent from observing another term. This is to say that the presence of one term contributes independently to the probability that a text is written about a particular topic from all other terms.

Origins of misclassification

Apart from misclassifications based on these simplifying assumptions, there is a second, more fundamental aspect of uncertainty in text classification. This is related to the classification of latent traits in text. As the topical emphasis of a text is not a quantity that is directly observable, there can even be misclassification by human coders. This leads to two challenges in classifying latent traits. One, we are frequently faced with training data that was human-coded and thus might contain errors. Two, it is difficult for us to differentiate between the origins of a misclassification, that is, we cannot be certain whether a text is misclassified for technical or conceptual reasons.

Lack of benchmarks

Regardless of the origin, misclassification often poses a formidable problem for social scientists. Oftentimes, we would like to perform text classification and include the estimated categories in a subsequent analysis in order to explain external factors. This second step in a typical research program is frequently hampered by misclassification. In fact, in a real research situation we have no way of knowing the degree of misclassification. If we did have a benchmark, we would not need to perform text classification in the first place. What is worse, it cannot be assumed that classification errors are randomly distributed across the categories, which would pose a less dramatic problem. Instead, the classification errors might be systematically biased toward specific categories (Hopkins and King 2010).

The "supervised"in supervised methods

Keeping these shortcomings of the techniques in mind, we now turn to the technical aspects of supervised learners. The supervised in the term reflects the commonality of classifiers in this class that some pre-coded data are used to estimate membership of non-classified documents. The pre-coded data are called the training dataset. It is difficult to provide an estimate of the size of the needed pre-coded data, as the accuracy of classification depends among other things on the length of pre-coded documents and on how well the term usage in the documents is separable, that is, the more the language in the classes differs the easier the classification task. In general, however, the level of misclassification should decrease with the size of the available training data. In addition, it is important to guarantee a sufficient coverage of all categories in the training data. Recall that we discarded press releases from departments that published 20 pieces or less. Even if the overall training data are sizable—which, in our case, it is not—it is possible that one or several categories dominate the training data, thus providing little information on what the algorithm might expect in the less covered categories.

The advantage of setting a scheme

The major advantage of supervised classifiers is that they provide researchers with the opportunity to specify a classification scheme of their choosing. Keeping in mind that we are interested in a latent trait of the document, the topic, we could potentially be interested in a number of other latent categories of documents, say, their ideological or sentiment orientation. Supervised classifiers provide a simple solution to estimating different properties by supplying different training data for the estimation procedure. Before moving on to estimating the topical emphasis in our corpus, let us introduce three supervised classifiers.

10.3.1 Support vector machines

The first model we will estimate below is the so-called *support vector machine* (SVM). This model was selected as it is currently one of the most well-known and most commonly applied classifiers in supervised learning (D'Orazio et al. 2014). The SVM employs a spatial representation of the data. In our application, the term occurrences which we stored in the term-document matrices represent the spatial locations of our documents in high-dimensional spaces. Recall that we supplied the group memberships, that is, publishing agencies, of the documents in the training data. Using the SVMs, we try to fit vectors between the document features that best separate the documents into the various groups. Specifically, we select the vectors in a way that they maximize the space between the groups. After the estimation we can classify new documents by checking on which sides of the vectors the features of unlabeled documents come to lie and estimate the categorical membership accordingly. For a more detailed introduction to SVMs, see Boswell (2002).

10.3.2 Random Forest

The second model which will be applied is the *random forest* classifier. This classifier creates multiple decision trees and takes the most frequently predicted membership category of many decision trees as the classification that is most likely to be accurate. To understand the logic, let us consider a single tree first. A decision tree models the group membership of the object we care to classify based on various observed features. In the present case, we estimate the topical category of documents based on the observed terms in the document. A single decision tree consists of several layers that consecutively ask whether a particular feature is present or absent in a document. The decisions at the branches are based on the observed frequencies of presence and absence of features in the training dataset. In a classification of a new document we move down the tree and consider whether the trained features are present or absent to be able to predict the categorical membership of the document. The random forest classifier is an extension of the decision tree in that it generates multiple decision trees and makes predictions based on the most frequent prediction from the various decision trees.

10.3.3 Maximum entropy

The last classification algorithm we have selected is the *maximum entropy* classifier. We have selected this model as it might be familiar to readers who have some experience with advanced multivariate data analysis. The maximum entropy classifier is analogous to the multinomial logit model which is a generalization of the logit model. The logit model predicts the probability of belonging to one of two categories. The multinomial logit model generalizes this model to a situation where the dependent variable has more than two categories. In our classification task we try to estimate the membership in six different topical categories.

10.3.4 The RTextTools package

Several packages have been made available in R to perform supervised classification. For the present exposition we turn to the RTextTools package. This package provides a wrapper to several packages that have implemented one or several classifiers. At the time of writing, the package provides wrappers to nine different classification algorithms. Using a common framework, the RTextTools package allows a simple access to different classifiers without having to rearrange the data to the needs of the various packages, as well as a common framework for evaluating the model fit.

The most obvious advantage of applying several classifiers to the same dataset lies in the possibility that individual shortcomings of the classifiers cancel each other out. It is often most effective to choose the modal prediction of multiple classifiers as the category that most resembles the true state of the latent category of a text. For simplicity's sake, the present exposition will provide an introduction to three of the classifiers. Nevertheless, all of the algorithms perform an identical task in principle. In each case, the task of the classifiers is to assess the degree to which a text resembles the training dataset and to choose the best fitting label.

10.3.5 Application: Government press releases

Creating a Document-term matrix

Turning to the practical implementation, we first need to rearrange the data a little so that it conforms to the needs of the RTextTools package. First and foremost, the package takes a document-term matrix as input. So far, we generated a term-document matrix but tm can just as easily output document-term matrices. Appropriately enough the relevant function is called `DocumentTermMatrix()`. After generating the new matrix we discard terms that appear in ten documents or less. We assemble a vector of the labels that we collected from the press releases using the `prescindMeta()` function that we have introduced above.

```
R> dtm <- DocumentTermMatrix(release_corpus)
R> dtm <- removeSparseTerms(dtm, 1-(10/length(release_corpus)))
R> dtm
A document-term matrix (537 documents, 1546 terms)

Non-/sparse entries: 57252/772950
Sparsity           : 93%
Maximal term length: 22
Weighting          : term frequency (tf)

R> org_labels <- unlist(prescindMeta(release_corpus, "organisa-
tion")[,2])
R> org_labels[1:3]
[1] "Foreign & Commonwealth Office" "Ministry of Defence"
[3] "Ministry of Defence"
```

Finally, we create a container with all relevant information for use in the estimation procedures. This is done using the `create_container()` function from the RTextTools package. Apart from the document-term matrix and the labels we have generated we specify that the first 400 documents are training data while we want the documents 401–537 to be classified. We set the `virgin` attribute to `FALSE`, meaning that we have labels for all 537 documents.

```
R> library(RTextTools)
R> N <- length(org_labels)
R> container <- create_container(
        dtm,
        labels = org_labels,
```

```
        trainSize = 1:400,
        testSize = 401:N,
        virgin = FALSE
)
```

The generated `container` object is an S4 object of class `matrix_container`. It contains a set of objects that are used for the estimation procedures of the supervised learning methods:

```
R> slotNames(container)
[1] "training_matrix"       "classification_matrix" "training_codes"
[4] "testing_codes"         "column_names"          "virgin"
```

Estimation procedure

In a next step, we simply supply the information that we have stored in the `container` object to the models. This is done using the `train_model()` function.[8]

```
R> svm_model <- train_model(container, "SVM")
R> tree_model <- train_model(container, "TREE")
R> maxent_model <- train_model(container, "MAXENT")
```

Having set up the models, we want to use the model parameters to estimate the membership of the remaining 137 documents. Recall that we do have information on their membership which is stored in the container. This information is not used for estimating the membership of the remaining documents. Instead, the membership is estimated solely on the basis of the word vectors contained in the supplied matrix.

```
R> svm_out <- classify_model(container, svm_model)
R> tree_out <- classify_model(container, tree_model)
R> maxent_out <- classify_model(container, maxent_model)
```

Evaluation

Let us inspect the outcome for a moment. In all three models the output consists of a two-column data frame, where the first column represents the estimated labels and the second column provides an estimate of the probability of classification.

```
R> head(svm_out)
                      SVM_LABEL SVM_PROB
1 Foreign & Commonwealth Office   0.9854
2 Foreign & Commonwealth Office   0.8667
3 Foreign & Commonwealth Office   0.9900
4           Ministry of Defence   0.9878
5           Ministry of Defence   0.9842
6 Foreign & Commonwealth Office   0.5800
R> head(tree_out)
                     TREE_LABEL TREE_PROB
1 Foreign & Commonwealth Office    0.9848
2 Foreign & Commonwealth Office    0.9848
3 Foreign & Commonwealth Office    0.9615
4           Ministry of Defence    1.0000
5           Ministry of Defence    1.0000
6           Ministry of Defence    0.6667
```

[8]Note that we use the default settings for the three classifiers. Using the additional arguments in the `train_model()` function, we could change the default behavior.

```
R> head(maxent_out)
                 MAXENTROPY_LABEL MAXENTROPY_PROB
1 Foreign & Commonwealth Office          1.0000
2 Foreign & Commonwealth Office          0.9960
3 Foreign & Commonwealth Office          1.0000
4          Ministry of Defence           1.0000
5          Ministry of Defence           1.0000
6 Foreign & Commonwealth Office          0.5204
```

Since we know the correct labels, we can investigate how often the algorithms have misclassified the press releases. We construct a data frame containing the correct and the predicted labels.

```
R> labels_out <- data.frame(
        correct_label = org_labels[401:N],
        svm = as.character(svm_out[,1]),
        tree = as.character(tree_out[,1]),
        maxent = as.character(maxent_out[,1]),
        stringsAsFactors = F)

R> ## SVM performance
R> table(labels_out[,1] == labels_out[,2])

FALSE  TRUE
   20   117
R> prop.table(table(labels_out[,1] == labels_out[,2]))

FALSE  TRUE
0.146 0.854

R> ## Random forest performance
R> table(labels_out[,1] == labels_out[,3])

FALSE  TRUE
   37   100
R> prop.table(table(labels_out[,1] == labels_out[,3]))

 FALSE   TRUE
0.2701 0.7299

R> ## Maximum entropy performance
R> table(labels_out[,1] == labels_out[,4])

FALSE  TRUE
   18   119
R> prop.table(table(labels_out[,1] == labels_out[,4]))

 FALSE   TRUE
0.1314 0.8686
```

We observe that the maximum entropy classifier correctly classified 119 out of 137 or about 87% of the documents correctly. The SVM fared just a little worse and got 117 out of 137 or about 85% of the documents right. The worst classifier in this application is the random forest classifier, which correctly estimates the publishing organization in merely 100 or 73% of cases.

At the beginning of this section, we have elaborated factors that might be driving errors in topic classification. We suggested that above and beyond technical features of the models, there are conceptual aspects of topic classification that might be driving errors, that is, it might not always be self-evident which category a particular document belongs to. In the present application, there is an additional feature that could potentially increase the likelihood of topic misclassifications. We classified press releases of the British government. For convenience, we selected the publishing organization as a proxy for the document label. However, as governmental departments deal with lots of different issues, it is likely that the announcements cover a wide range of issues. Put differently, we might be able to boost the classification accuracy by including more training data so that we have a more complete image of the departmental tasks.

What is driving the results?

Having said that, we might in fact want to add that the classification outcome is remarkably accurate, given how little data we input into the classifier. Considering that some categories have a coverage in the training data of little more than 20 documents, it is extraordinary that we are able to get classification accuracy of roughly 80%. This puts the aforementioned question on its head and asks not what is driving the errors in our results but rather what is driving the classification accuracy. One common concern that is voiced against machine learning is the inability of the researcher to know precisely what is driving results. As we are not specifying variables like we are used to from classical regression analysis but are rather just throwing loads of data at the models, it is difficult to know what prompts the results. It is entirely possible that the algorithms are picking up something in the data that is not strictly related to topics at all. Imagine that each departmental press release is signed by a particular government official. If this were the case the algorithms might pick up the different names as the indicator that best separates the documents into the different categories.

In summary, the obvious advantage of supervised classifiers stems from their ability to apply a classification scheme of the researcher's choice. Conversely, the most obvious disadvantage stems from the need to either collect labels or to manually code large chunks of the data of interest that can serve as training data. In the next section, we introduce a way to circumvent this latter disadvantage by automatically estimating the topical categories from the data.

10.4 Unsupervised learning techniques

An alternative to supervised techniques is the use of unsupervised text classification. The main difference between the two lies in the fact that the latter does not require training data in order to perform text categorization. Instead, categories are estimated from the documents along with the membership in the categories. Especially for individual researchers without supporting staff, unsupervised classification might seem like an attractive option for large-scale text classification—while also conforming to the endeavor of this volume to *automate data collection*.

Limits

The downside of unsupervised classification lies in the inability of researchers to specify a categorization scheme. Thus, instead of having to manually input content information, the difficulty in unsupervised classification lies in the interpretation of results in a context-free analysis. Recall that we are estimating latent traits of texts. We established that texts express more than one latent category at a time. Consider as an example a research problem that investigates agenda-setting of media and politics. Say we would like to classify a text corpus of political statements and media reports. If we ran an unsupervised classification algorithm on the entire corpus, it is quite possible that it might pick up differences in tonality rather than in content. To put that in different terms, it might be that the unsupervised algorithms will take the ideologically charged rhetoric of political statements to be different from the more nuanced language that is used in political journalism. One possible solution for the problem would be to run the classifier on both classes of texts sequentially. Unfortunately, running a pure unsupervised algorithm on the two parts of the corpus creates yet another problem, as the categories in one run of the algorithm do not necessarily match up with the categories in a second run. In fact, this poses a more general problem in supervised classification when a researcher wants to match data thus classified to external data that is topically categorized, say, survey responses.

Depending on the specific research goal, it is quite possible that one finds these features of unsupervised classification an advantage of the technique rather than a disadvantage. For instance, the fact that unsupervised methods generate categories out of themselves might be interesting in research that is interested in the main lines of division in a text corpus. Conversely, unsupervised classification often expects the researchers to specify the number of categories that the corpus is to be grouped into. This requires some theoretically driven account of the documents' main lines of division.

10.4.1 Latent Dirichlet allocation and correlated topic models

The technique that we briefly explore in the remainder of this section is called the *Latent Dirichlet Allocation* (Blei et al. 2003). The model assumes that each document in a text corpus consists of a *mixture* of topics. The terms in a document are assigned a probability value of signaling a particular topic. Thus, the likelihood of a text belonging to particular categories is driven by the pattern of words it contains and the probability with which they are associated to particular topics. The number of categories that a corpus is to be split into is arbitrarily set and should be carefully selected to reflect the researcher's interest and prior beliefs.

A shortcoming of the latent Dirichlet model is the inability to include relationships between the various topics. This is to say that a document on topic A is not equally likely to be about topic B, C, or D. Some topics are more closely related than others and being able to include such relationships creates more realistic models of topical document content. To include this intuition into their model, Blei and Lafferty (2006) have proposed the correlated topic model which allows for a correlation of the relative prominence of topics in the documents.

10.4.2 Application: Government press releases

Shortening the corpus

Before turning to the more complex models of topical document content, we begin by investigating the similarity relationships between the documents using hierarchical clustering. In this technique, we cluster similar texts on the basis of their mutual distances. As before, this method also relies on the term occurrences. The *hierarchical* part in hierarchical clustering means that the most similar texts are joined in small clusters which are then joined with other texts to form larger clusters. Eventually all texts are joined if the distance criterion has been relaxed enough.

For simplicity, we select the first 20 texts of the categories "defence,""Wales,"and "environment, food & rural affairs"and store them in a shorter corpus.

```
R> short_corpus <- release_corpus[c(
        which(tm_index(
                        release_corpus,
                        FUN = sFilter,
                        s = "organisation == 'Ministry of Defence"'
                ))[1:20],
        which(tm_index(
                        release_corpus,
                        FUN = sFilter,
                        s = "organisation == 'Wales Office"'
                ))[1:20],
         which(tm_index(
                        release_corpus,
                        FUN = sFilter,
                        s = "organisation == 'Department for
                             Environment, Food & Rural Affairs"'
                ))[1:20]
)]

R> table(as.character(prescindMeta(short_corpus, "organisation")[,2]))

Department for Environment, Food & Rural Affairs
                                              20
                             Ministry of Defence
                                              20
                                    Wales Office
                                              20
```

We create a document-term matrix of the shortened corpus and discard sparse terms. We also set the names of the rows to the three categories.

```
R> short_dtm <- DocumentTermMatrix(short_corpus)
R> short_dtm <- removeSparseTerms(short_dtm, 1-(5/length(short_
corpus)))
R> rownames(short_dtm) <- c(rep("Defence", 20), rep("Wales", 20),
rep("Environment", 20))
```

The similarity measure in this application is the euclidean distance between the texts. To calculate this metric, we subtract the count for each term in document A from the count in document B, square the result, sum over the entire vector, and take the square root of the result. This is done using the `dist()` function. The resulting matrix is clustered using the `hclust()` function which clusters the resulting matrix by iteratively joining the two most similar clusters. The similarities can be visually inspected using a dendrogram where the clusters are increasingly joined from the bottom to the top. This is to say that the higher up the clusters are joined, the more dissimilar they are.

```
R> dist_dtm <- dist(short_dtm)
R> out <- hclust(dist_dtm, method = "ward")
R> plot(out)
```

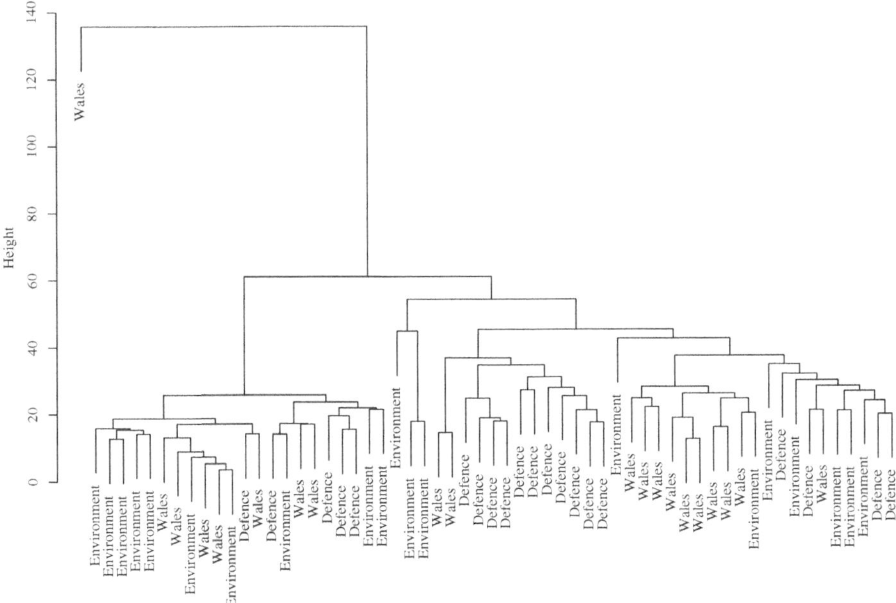

Figure 10.1 Output of hierarchical clustering of UK Government press releases

The resulting clusters roughly recover the topical emphasis of the various press releases (see Figure 10.1). Particularly toward the lower end of the graph we find that two press releases from the same governmental department are frequently joined. However, as we move up the dendrogram, the patterns become less clear. To a certain extent we find a cluster of the "environment"press releases at one end of the graph and particularly the "Wales" press releases are mostly joined. Conversely, the press releases pertaining to "defence" are dispersed across the various parts of the dendrogram.

Estimating LDA Let us now move on to a veritable unsupervised classification of the texts—the Latent Dirichlet Allocation. One implementation of the Latent Dirichlet model is provided in the topicmodels package. The relevant function is supplied in the `LDA()` function. As we know that our corpus consists of six "topics," we select the number of topics to be estimated as six. As before, the function takes the document-term matrix that we created in the previous section as input.

```
R> library(topicmodels)
R> lda_out <- LDA(dtm, 6)
```

After calculating the model, we can determine the posterior probabilities of a document's topics as well as the probabilities of the terms' topics using the function `posterior()`. We store the topics' posterior probabilities in the data frame `lda_topics` and investigate the mean probabilities assigned to the press releases of the government agencies. We set up a 6-by-6 matrix to store the mean topic probabilities by governmental body.

```
R> posterior_lda <- posterior(lda_out)
R> lda_topics <- data.frame(t(posterior_lda$topics))
R> ## Setting up matrix for mean probabilities
```

```
R> mean_topic_matrix <- matrix(
        NA,
        nrow = 6,
        ncol = 6,
        dimnames = list(
                names(table(org_labels)),
                str_c("Topic_", 1:6)
        )
)
R> ## Filling matrix
R> for(i in 1:6){
        mean_topic_matrix[i,] <- apply(lda_topics[, which(org_labels ==
rownames(mean_topic_matrix)[i])], 1, mean)
}
R> ## Outputting rounded matrix
R> round(mean_topic_matrix, 2)
                                                 Topic_1 Topic_2 Topic_3
Department for Business, Innovation & Skills        0.01    0.61    0.00
Department for Communities and Local Government     0.00    0.04    0.04
Department for Environment, Food & Rural Affairs    0.02    0.24    0.12
Foreign & Commonwealth Office                       0.01    0.07    0.05
Ministry of Defence                                 0.49    0.02    0.25
Wales Office                                        0.00    0.10    0.33
                                                 Topic_4 Topic_5 Topic_6
Department for Business, Innovation & Skills        0.02    0.02    0.33
Department for Communities and Local Government     0.02    0.08    0.82
Department for Environment, Food & Rural Affairs    0.06    0.07    0.49
Foreign & Commonwealth Office                       0.32    0.50    0.05
Ministry of Defence                                 0.13    0.05    0.06
Wales Office                                        0.04    0.13    0.39
```

We find that some topics tend to be strongly associated with the press releases from individual government agencies. For example, topic 2 is often highly associated with the Department for Business, Innovation & Skills, topic 5 has a high probability of occurring in announcements from the Foreign & Commonwealth Office. Topic 1 is most associated with the Ministry of Defence. We investigate the estimated probabilities more thoroughly when considering the correlated topic model.

Terms associated with topics

Another way to investigate the estimated topics is to consider the most likely terms for the topics and try to come up with a label that summarizes the terms. This is done using the function `terms()`.

```
R> terms(lda_out, 10)
      Topic 1   Topic 2   Topic 3     Topic 4   Topic 5     Topic 6
 [1,] "oper"    "busi"    "forc"      "nation"  "minist"    "will"
 [2,] "said"    "bis"     "defenc"    "british" "will"      "govern"
 [3,] "command" "will"    "royal"     "forc"    "foreign"   "local"
 [4,] "base"    "univers" "arm"       "peopl"   "secretari" "new"
 [5,] "royal"   "depart"  "servic"    "will"    "secur"     "work"
 [6,] "troop"   "educ"    "said"      "afghan"  "nuclear"   "busi"
 [7,] "forc"    "gov"     "day"       "secur"   "intern"    "can"
 [8,] "soldier" "skill"   "will"      "govern"  "govern"    "council"
 [9,] "marin"   "colleg"  "personnel" "travel"  "meet"      "make"
[10,] "will"    "innov"   "fox"       "can"     "state"     "communiti"
```

Particularly topics 1, 3, and 4 have a focus on aspects of the military, the terms in topic 5 tend to relate to foreign affairs, the emphasis in topic 6 is local government and topic 2 is related to business and education. This ordering nicely reflects the observations from the previous paragraph. Nevertheless, we also find that the dominance of press releases by the department of defence results in topics that classify various aspects of the defence announcements in multiple topics, thus lumping together the releases from other departments. This is to say that while there is some plausible overlap between the known labels and the estimated categories, this overlap is far from perfect.

Estimating CTM

Let us move on to estimating a correlated topic model to run a more realistic model of topic mixtures. Again, we select the number of topics to be six since there are six governmental organizations for which we include press releases.

```
R> ctm_out <- CTM(dtm, 6)

R> terms(ctm_out, 10)
      Topic 1       Topic 2      Topic 3   Topic 4     Topic 5  Topic 6
 [1,] "afghan"      "foreign"    "will"    "forc"      "govern" "will"
 [2,] "said"        "minist"     "busi"    "royal"     "will"   "new"
 [3,] "forc"        "will"       "local"   "arm"       "wale"   "work"
 [4,] "oper"        "secur"      "govern"  "command"   "peopl"  "project"
 [5,] "local"       "secretari"  "bis"     "defenc"    "can"    "provid"
 [6,] "afghanistan" "intern"     "council" "servic"    "work"   "plan"
 [7,] "secur"       "british"    "new"     "day"       "must"   "said"
 [8,] "base"        "meet"       "year"    "personnel" "right"  "system"
 [9,] "area"        "nation"     "depart"  "oper"      "said"   "use"
[10,] "patrol"      "nuclear"    "fund"    "air"       "make"   "build"
```

We now find two topics—1 and 4—to be clearly related to matters of defense.[9] Topic 2 is associated with foreign affairs, topic 3 with local government. The terms of topic 5 in the correlated topic model strongly suggest Welsh politics. A label for topic 6 is more difficult to make out.

Evaluation of posterior probabilities

We can plot the document-specific probabilities to belong to one of the three topics. To do so, we calculate the posterior probabilities of the topics and set up 2-by-3 panels to plot the sorted probabilities of the topics in the press releases. The result is displayed in Figure 10.2. Note that to save space we only displayed two of the estimated six topics. We invite you to run the models and plot all posterior probabilities yourself.

```
R> posterior_ctm <- posterior(ctm_out)
R> ctm_topics <- data.frame(t(posterior_ctm$topics))
R>
R> par(mfrow = c(2,3), cex.main = .8, pty = "s", mar = c(5, 5, 1, 1)
R> for(topic in 1:2){
R>      for(orga in names(table(org_labels))){
R>              tmp.data <- ctm_topics[topic, org_labels == orga]
R>              plot(
R>                      1:ncol(tmp.data),
R>                      sort(as.numeric(tmp.data)),
```

[9] Note that the numbers of the topics are arbitrary.

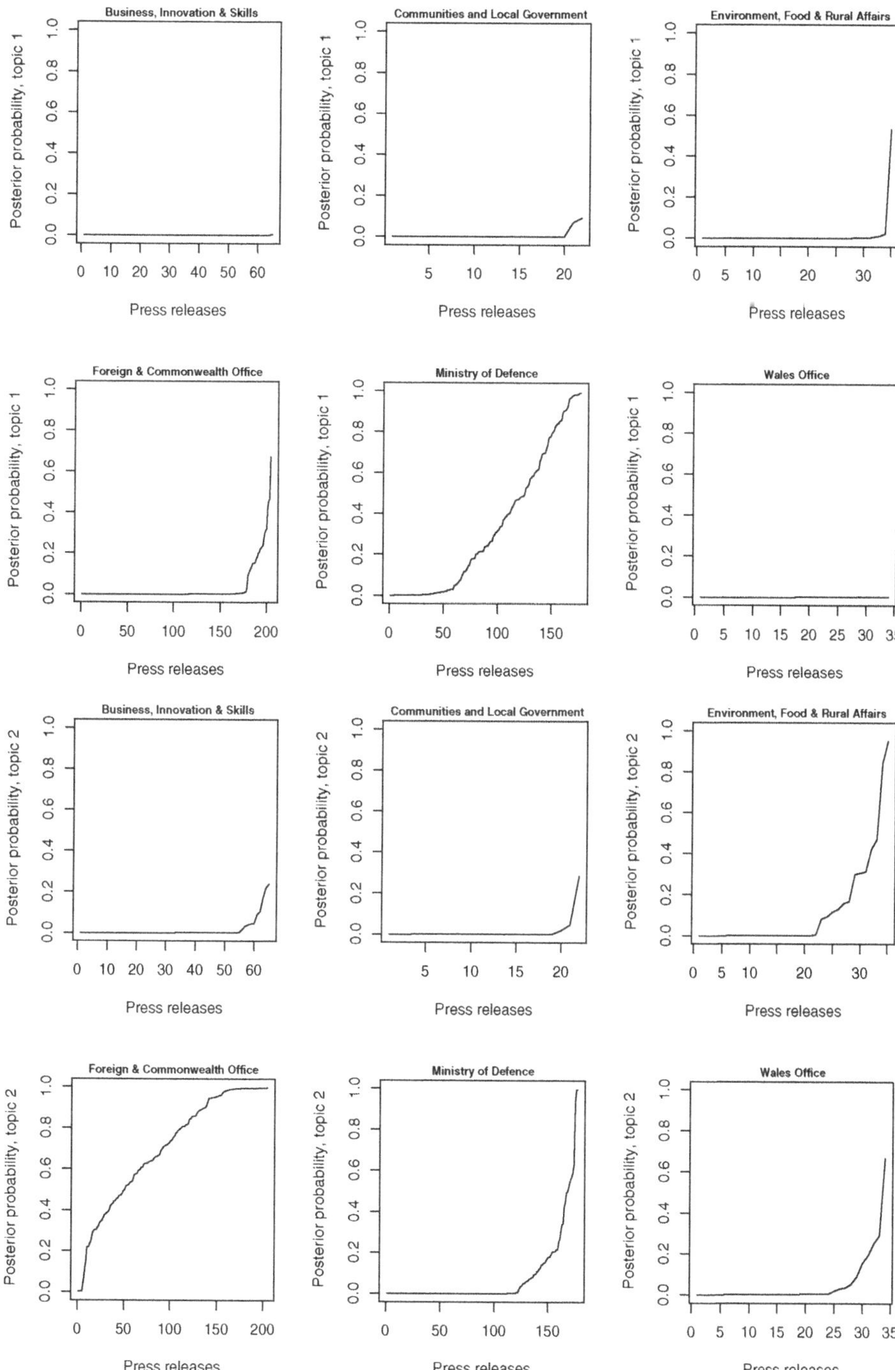

Figure 10.2 Output of Correlated Topic Model of UK Government press releases

```
R>                         type = "l",
R>                         ylim = c(0,1),
R>                         xlab = "Press releases",
R>                         ylab = str_c("Posterior probability, topic ",
topic),
R>                         main = str_replace(orga, "Department for", "")
R>                  )
R>       }
R> }
```

The figures are nicely aligned with expectations from looking at the terms most indicative of the various topics. The posterior probability of topic 1 is highest in press releases from the ministry of defense, whereas topic 2 has the highest probability in press releases from the foreign office. In summary, we are able to make out some plausible agreement between our labels and the estimated topical emphasis from the correlated topic model.

Summary

The chapter offered a brief introduction to statistical text processing. To make use of the vast data on the Web, we often have to post-process collected information. Particularly when confronted with textual data we need to assign systematic meaning to otherwise unstructured data. We provided an introduction to a framework for performing statistical text processing in R—the tm package—and two classes of techniques for making textual data applicable as data in research projects: supervised and unsupervised classifiers.

To summarize the techniques, the major advantage of supervised classification is the ability of the researcher to specify the categories for the classification algorithm. The downside of that benefit is that supervised classifiers typically require substantial amounts of training data and thus manual labor. Conversely, the major advantage of unsupervised classification lies in the ability of researchers to skip the coding of data by hand which comes at the price of having to interpret the estimation results ex post.

At the end, we would like to add that there is a vibrant research in the field of automated analysis of text, such that this chapter is potentially one of the first to contain somewhat dated information. For example, some headway has been made to allow researchers to specify the categories they are interested in without having to code a large chunk of the corpus for training data. This is accomplished using seed words. They allow the researcher to specify words that are most indicative of a particular category of interest (Gliozzo et al. 2009; Zagibalov and Carroll 2008).

Further reading

We introduced the most important features of the tm package in the first section of this chapter. However, we have not explored its full potential. If you care to learn more about the package check out the extensive introduction in Feinerer et al. (2008).

Natural language processing and the statistical analysis of text remain actively researched topics. Therefore, there are both numerous contributions to the topic as well as research papers with current developments in the field. For further insight into the topics that were introduced in this chapter take a look at Grimmer and Stewart (2013) for a brief but insightful introduction to some of the topics that were discussed in this chapter. For a more extensive treatment of the topics, see Manning et al. (2008).

A topic that is heavily researched in the area of automated text classification is the classification of the sentiment or opinion in a text. We will return to this topic in Chapter 17 where we try to classify the sentiment in product reviews on http://www.amazon.com. For an excellent introduction to the topic, take a look at Liu (2012).

11

Managing data projects

Deploying a successful data collection project requires more than knowledge of web technologies. The focus of this chapter is on R and operation system functionality that will be required for setting up and maintaining large-scale, automated data collection projects. Additionally, we discuss good practices to organize and write code that adds robustness and traceability in case of errors. In Section 11.1, we start by providing an overview of R functions for interacting with the local file system. In Section 11.2, we show methods for iterative code execution for downloading pages or extracting relevant information from multiple web documents. Section 11.3 provides a template for organizing extraction code and making it more robust to failed specification. We conclude the chapter with an overview of system tools that can executive R scripts automatically, which is a key requirement for building datasets from regularly updated Internet resources (Section 11.4).

11.1 Interacting with the file system

One type of R function that appears frequently in data projects is dedicated to working with files and folders on the local file system. Over the course of a data project, we are continuously interacting with the file system of our operating system. Web documents are stored locally, loaded into R, processed, and saved again after the post-processing or analysis. The file system has an important role in the data collection and analysis workflow and a firm command over the hard drive constitutes a valuable auxiliary skill. For the numerous virtues of a scripted approach, any interaction with the file management system should be performed in a programmable fashion. Luckily, R provides an extensive list of functions for interacting with the system and files located in it. Table 11.1 provides an overview of the basic file management functions which we rely upon in the case studies and in data projects more generally.

Automated Data Collection with R: A Practical Guide to Web Scraping and Text Mining, First Edition.
Simon Munzert, Christian Rubba, Peter Meißner and Dominic Nyhuis.

Table 11.1 Basic R functions for folder and file management

Function	Important arguments	Description
Functions for folder management		
`dir()`	`path`	Returns character vector of the names of files and directories in `path`
`dir.create()`	`path, recursive`	Creates new directory in `path` (only the last element). If `recursive=T` all elements on the path are created.
Functions for file management		
`file.path()`	`...`	Constructs a file path of character elements
`file.info()`	`path`	Returns character vector with information about a file in `path`
`file.exists()`	`path`	Returns logical value whether a file already exists in `path`
`file.access()`	`names, mode`	Tests files in `names` for existence (`mode=0`), execute permission (`mode=1`), writing permission (`mode=2`), read permission (`mode=4`). Returns integer with values 0 for success and −1 for failure
`file.rename()`	`from, to`	Renames a file in path `from` to a name in `to`
`file.remove()`	`path`	Deletes a file in `path` from the hard drive
`file.append()`	`file1, file2`	Appends contents in `file2` to `file1`
`file.copy()`	`from, to`	Creates a copy of a file in path `from` to path `to`
`basename()`	`path`	Returns the lowest level in a `path`
`dirname()`	`path`	Returns all but the lower level in a `path`
Functions for working with compressed files		
`zip()`	`zipfile, files`	Create a zip file in path `zipfile` of `files`
`unzip()`	`zipfile, files`	Extracts specific `files` (all when unspecified) from a zip file in path `zipfile`

Path arguments may usually be passed as complete or incomplete paths. In the latter case, paths are expanded to the working directory (`getwd()`). File paths may be passed in abbreviated form without the user's home directory. (`path.expand()` is used to replace a leading tilde by the user's home directory.)

11.2 Processing multiple documents/links

A frequently encountered task in web scraping is executing a piece of code repeatedly. In fact, using a programming language for data collection is most valuable as it allows the researcher to automate tasks that would otherwise have to be done in tedious and time-consuming manual processing of every file, URL, or document. To exemplify, consider the problem of downloading a bunch of HTML sites from a vector of URLs. Another job is the processing of multiple web documents, such as the pages from a news website where the task is extracting the text corpora, or the extraction of tabular information from economic indicators organized in XML files to create a single database.

This section illustrates that with only a little bit of overhead one can instruct R to repeatedly execute a function on a set of files and, thus, comfortably download countless pages or scan thousands of documents and reassemble the extracted information. We introduce two ways to accomplish this goal; the first one is through the use of standard R looping structures and the second one is through functionality from the plyr package.

11.2.1 Using *for*-loops

For illustrative purposes, we consider the set of 11 XML files that are located in the folder */stocks*.[1] The XML files contain stock information for four technology companies. Our interest is in extracting the daily closing values for the *Apple* stock over all years (2003–2013). We can divide this problem into two subtasks. First, we need to come up with an extraction code that loads the file, extracts, and recasts the target information into the desired format. The second task is executing the extraction code on all XML files. A straightforward approach is to wrap the extraction code in a *for*-loop. Loops are standard programming structures that help formulate an iterating statement over the set of documents from which information needs to be extracted.

A first step is to obtain the names of the files that we would like to process. To this end, we use the `dir()` function to produce a character vector with all the file names in the current directory. The file names are inserted into a new object called `all_files` and its content is printed to the screen.

```
R> all_files <- dir("stocks")
R> all_files
 [1] "stocks_2003.xml" "stocks_2004.xml" "stocks_2005.xml"
 [4] "stocks_2006.xml" "stocks_2007.xml" "stocks_2008.xml"
 [7] "stocks_2009.xml" "stocks_2010.xml" "stocks_2011.xml"
[10] "stocks_2012.xml" "stocks_2013.xml"
```

Next, we need to create a placeholder in which we can store the extracted stock information from each file. Although it might be necessary to obtain a data frame at the end of the process for analytical purposes, we set up a list as an intermediate data structure. Lists provide the flexibility to collect the information which we recast only afterwards. We create an empty list that we name `closing_stock` and which serves as a container for the yearly stock information from each file.

```
R> closing_stock <- list()
```

The core of the extraction routine consists of a `for`-loop over the number of elements in the `all_files` character vector. This structure allows iterating over each of the files and work on their contents individually.

```
R> for (i in 1:length(all_files)) {
    path <- str_c("stocks/", all_files[i])
    parsed_stock <- xmlParse(path)
    closing_stock[[i]] <- xpathSApply(parsed_stock, "//Apple", getStock)
}
```

[1] You can find the data on www.r-datacollection.com/materials.

First, we construct the path of each XML file and save the information in a new object called `path`. The information is needed for the next step, where we pass the path to the parsing function `xmlParse()`. This creates the internal representation of the file inside a new object called `parsed_stock`. Finally, we obtain the desired information from the parsed object by means of an XPath statement. Here, we pull the entire `Apple` node and do the post-processing in the extractor function, which we discuss below. The return value from `xpathSApply()` is stored at the *i*th position our previously defined list. The `get_stock()` extractor function is a custom function that works on the entire `Apple` node and returns the date and closing value for each day.

```
R> getStock <- function(x)  {
    date <- xmlValue(x[["date"]])
    value <- xmlValue(x[["close"]])
    c(date, value)
}
```

We go ahead and unlist the container list to process each information individually and put it into a more convenient data format. Here we go for a data frame and choose more appropriate column names.

```
R> closing_stock <- unlist(closing_stock)
R> closing_stock <- data.frame(matrix(closing_stock, ncol = 2, byrow = T))
R> colnames(closing_stock) <- c("date", "value")
```

Finally, we recast the value information into a numerical vector and the date information into a vector of class Date.

```
R> closing_stock$date <- as.Date(closing_stock$date, "%Y/%m/%d")
R> closing_stock$value <- as.numeric(as.character(closing_stock$value))
```

We are ready to create a visual representation of the extracted data. We use `plot()` to create a time-series of the stock values. The result is displayed in Figure 11.1.

```
R> plot(closing_stock$date, closing_stock$value, type = "l", main
 = "", ylab = "Closing stock", xlab = "Time")
```

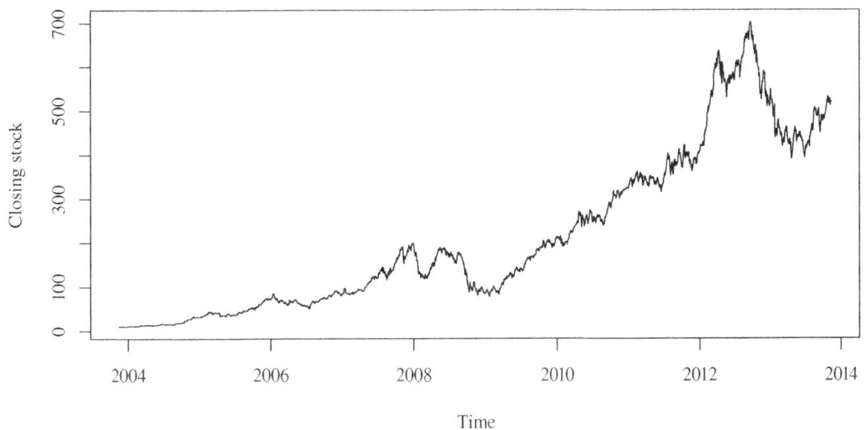

Figure 11.1 Time-series of Apple stock values, 2003–2013

11.2.2 Using *while*-loops and control structures

A second control statement that we can use for iterations is the `while()` expression. Instead of iterating over a fixed sequence, it will run an expression as long as a particular condition evaluates to `TRUE`. Consider the snippet below for an abstract usage of the expression.

```
R> a <- 0
R> while(a < 3){
        a <- a + 1
        print(a)
}
[1] 1
[1] 2
[1] 3
```

We set the a to 0 and while the a is lower than 3 it will continue looping. In each iteration we add 1 to a and print the value of a to the screen. Once the a has reached the critical value of 3, the loop will break.

Apart from setting a condition in the `while()` statement that evaluates to `FALSE` at some point, thus breaking the loop, we can also break a loop with an `if()` clause and a `break` command.

```
R> a <- 0
R> while(TRUE){
        a <- a + 1
        print(a)
        if(a >= 3){
             break
        }
}
[1] 1
[1] 2
[1] 3
```

In the above snippet, we set a condition in the `while()` statement that will always evaluate to `TRUE`, thus creating an infinite loop. Instead, in each iteration we test whether a is equal to or greater than 0. If that condition is `TRUE`, the `break` is encountered which forces R to break the current loop. Notice how we used the `if()` clause in the snippet.

In web scraping practice, the `while()` statement is handy to iterate over a set of documents where you do not know the total number of documents in advance. Consider the following scenario. You care to download a selection of HTML documents where the link to additional documents is embedded in the source code of the last inspected HTML document, say in a link to a `NEXT` document. If you do not happen to find a counter at the bottom of the page that contains information on the total number of pages, there is no way of specifying the number of pages you can expect. In such a case, you can apply the `while()` statement to check for the existence of a link before accessing the document.

```
R> # Load packages
R> library(XML)
R> library(stringr)
R>
R> # Mock URL
```

```
R> url <- "http://www.example.com"
R>
R> # XPath expression to look for additional pages
R> xpath_for_next_page <- "//a[@class='NextPage']"
R>
R> #Create index for pages
R> i <- 1
R>
R> # Collect mock URL and write to drive
R> current_document <- getURL(url)
R> write(tmp, str_c(i, ".html"))
R>
R> # Download additional pages while there are links to additional pages
R> while(length(xpathSApply(current_document, xpath_for_next_page,
xmlGetAttr, "href")) > 0){
R>      current_url <- xpathSApply(current_document, xpath_for_next_page,
xmlGetAttr, "href")
R>      current_document <- getURL(current_url)
R>      write(current_document, str_c(i, ".html"))
R>      i <- i + 1
```

11.2.3 Using the plyr package

The data structure which we typically wish to produce is tabular with variables populating the columns and each row presenting a case or unit of analysis. Producing tabular data structures from multiple web documents can be achieved easily using functionality from the plyr package (Wickham 2011) which allows performing an extraction routine more quickly on multiple documents. To illustrate, let us run through the previous example in the plyr framework. As the first step, we construct the paths to the XML files on the local hard drive.

```
R> files <- str_c("stocks/", all_files)
```

We create a function `getStock2()` that parses an XML file and extracts relevant information. This code is similar to the one we used before.

```
R> getStock2 <- function(file){
parsedStock <- xmlParse(file)
closing_stock <- xpathSApply(parsedStock,
                             "//Apple/date | //Apple/close",
                             xmlValue)
closing_stock <- as.data.frame(matrix(closing_stock,
                               ncol = 2,
                               byrow = TRUE))
}
```

The function returns an $n \times 2$ data frame with the first column holding information on the date and the second one on the closing stock. We are now set to evoke `ldply()` and initiate the extraction process.

```
R> library(plyr)
R> appleStocks <- ldply(files, getStock2)
```

For its input `ldply()` requires a **l**ist or a vector and it returns a **d**ataframe. `ldply()` executes `getStock2()` on every element in `files` and binds the results row-wise. We confirm that the procedure has worked correctly by printing the first five lines to the console.

```
R> head(appleStocks, 3)
          V1      V2
1 2013/11/13 520.634
2 2013/11/12  520.01
3 2013/11/11 519.048
```

If you are dealing with larger file stacks, plyr also provides the option `parallel` which, if set to `TRUE`, parallelizes the code execution which can speed up the process.

11.3 Organizing scraping procedures

Don't repeat yourself

When you begin scraping the Web regularly, you will find that numerous tasks come up over and over again. One of the central principles of good coding practice states that you should never repeat yourself. If you find yourself rewriting certain lines of code or copy-pasting elements of your code, then it is time to start thinking about organizing your code in a more efficient way. Problems arise when you need to trace all the places in your scripts where some particular functionality has been defined. The solution to this problem is to wrap your code in functions and store them in dedicated places. Not only does this guarantee that revisions happen in only one place, but it also greatly simplifies the maintenance of code.

Besides ensuring a better maintenance of code, writing functions also allows a generalization of functionality. This is a great improvement of your code when you want to apply a sequence of operations to lots of data, as is often the case in web scraping. In fact, by writing your code into functions you can frequently speed up the execution time of your R code dramatically by applying the function on a list or a vector via one of the apply functions from the plyr package as shown in the previous section. This section serves to elaborate how to modularize your code by using functions.

We demonstrate the use of functions with a scenario that we already discussed in Section 9.1.4. Imagine that we want to collect all links from a website. We have learned that the XML package provides the function `getHTMLLinks()` which makes link collection from HTML documents quite convenient. In fact, this function is a good example for a function which help tackle a frequently occurring task. Imagine that the function did not exist and we needed to build it.

We have learned in Chapter 2 that links are stored in `href` attributes of `<a>` elements. Our task is thus simply to collect the content of all nodes with this attribute. Let us begin by loading the necessary packages and specifying a URL that will serve as our running example.

```
R> library(RCurl)
R> library(XML)
R> url <- "http://www.buzzfeed.com"
```

We can perform the task for this single website by calling and parsing it via `htmlParse()` and collecting the relevant information via `xpathSApply()`.

```
R> parsed_page <- htmlParse(url)
R> links <- xpathSApply(parsed_page, "//a[@href]", xmlGetAttr, "href")

R> length(links)
[1] 945
```

Setting up functions

Now imagine that we care to apply these steps to several websites. To apply these three steps to other sites we wrap them into a single function we call `collectHref()`. This is done by storing the necessary steps in an object and calling the function `function()`. The argument in the function call represents the object that the function is supposed to run on, in this case the URL.

```
R> collectHref <- function(url){
        parsed_page <- htmlParse(url)
        links <- xpathSApply(parsed_page, "//a[@href]", xmlGetAttr, "href")
        return(links)
}
```

Now we can simply run the function on various sites to collect all the links. First we apply it to the URL we specified above and then we try out a second page.

```
R> buzzfeed <- collectHref("http://www.buzzfeed.com")

R> length(buzzfeed)
[1] 945

R> slate <- collectHref("http://www.slate.com")

R> length(slate)
[1] 475
```

Adding arguments

We are able to generalize functions by adding arguments to it. For example, we can add a variable to our function that will discard all links that do not explicitly begin with `http`. This could be done with a simple regular expression that detects whether a string begins in `http`, using the `str_detect()` function from the stringr package.

```
R> collectHref <- function(url, begins.http){
        if(!is.logical(begins.http)){
                stop("begins.http must be a logical value")
        }
        parsed_page <- htmlParse(url)
        links <- xpathSApply(parsed_page, "//a[@href]", xmlGetAttr, "href")
        if(begins.http == TRUE){
                links <- links[str_detect(links, "^http")]
        }
        return(links)
}
```

Notice that we also added a test to the function that checks whether `begins.http` is a logical value. If not, the function will throw an error (produced by `stop()`) and not return any results. Let us run the altered function on our example URL, and set `begins.http` to `TRUE`.

```
R> buzzfeed <- collectHref(url, begins.http = TRUE)
R> length(buzzfeed)
[1] 63
```

The vector of links has shrunk considerably. Now let us call the function on the base URL again, but change the `begins.http` variable to the wrong type.

```
R> testPage <- collectHref(url, begins.http = "TRUE")
Error: begins.http must be a logical value
```

We can add any number of arguments to the function. In order not to have to specify the value for each argument whenever we call the function, we can set predefined values for the arguments. For example, we can set `begins.http` to `TRUE` by default in the function definition.

```
R> collectHref <- function(url, begins.http = TRUE){
        if(!is.logical(begins.http)){
              stop("begins.http must be a logical value")
        }
        parsed_page <- htmlParse(url)
        links <- xpathSApply(parsed_page, "//a[@href]", xmlGetAttr, "href")
        if(begins.http == TRUE){
              links <- links[str_detect(links, "^http")]
        }
        return(links)
}
```

Thus, whenever we call the function, it will assume that we care to collect only those links that explicitly contain the sequence `http`.

Storing and calling functions

Once you start writing functions in R, you will find that grouping them into topical files is the most sensible way to collect functions for use in various projects. The advantage of generating a set of functions in modules ensures that you have to modify specific functions only in one location and that you do not have to create the same functionality over and over again with each project that you are beginning. Instead you can call the necessary module when you start a new project, almost like you would load a library that you download from CRAN.

A reasonable approach for storing such recurring functions is to create a dedicated folder where functions are stored in dedicated R script files. Whenever you want to draw on one of these functions, you can access them using the `source()` command. This automatically evaluates code from foreign R source files. Imagine we have stored our function from above in a file named *collectHref.r*. In order to run the command, we proceed as follows:

```
R> source("collectHref.r")
R> test_out <- collectHref("http://www.buzzfeed.com")
R> length(test_out)
[1] 63
```

Eventually you can also go one step further and create R packages yourself and upload them to CRAN or GitHub .

11.3.1 Implementation of progress feedback: Messages and progress bars

When performing a web scraping task, it can often be useful to receive a visual feedback on the progress that our program has made in order to get a sense of when your program will have finished. A very basic version of such a feedback would be a simple textual printout directly to the R console. We can accomplish this with the `cat()` function. To illustrate, consider the problem of downloading the stock XML files from the book homepage. The files are stored in the following path: http://www.r-datacollection.com/materials/workflow/stocks. Let us start by building a character vector for their URLs and save them in a new object called `links`.

```
R> baseurl <- "http://www.r-datacollection.com/materials/workflow/stocks"
R> links <- str_c(baseurl, "/stocks_", 2003:2013, ".xml")
```

Next, we set up a loop over the length of `links`. Inside the loop, we download the file, create a sensible name using `basename()` to return the source file name, and then write the XML code to the local hard drive.

Progress feedback with `cat()`

```
R> N <- length(links)
R> for(i in 1:N){
R>      stocks <- getURL(links[i])
R>      name <- basename(links[i])
R>      write(stocks, file = str_c("stocks/", name))
R>      cat(i, "of", N, "\n")
R> }
1 of 11
2 of 11
3 of 11
...
11 of 11
```

In the final line, we ask R to print the number of the document just downloaded to the console. We append the message with a \n so each new output is written to a new line.

We can enrich the information in the feedback, for example, by adding the name of the file that is currently being downloaded.

```
R> for(i in 1:N){
R>      stocks <- getURL(links[i])
R>      name <- basename(links[i])
R>      write(html, file = str_c("stocks/", name))
R>      cat(i, "of", N, "-", name, "\n")
R> }
1 of 11 - stocks_2003.xml
2 of 11 - stocks_2004.xml
3 of 11 - stocks_2005.xml
...
11 of 11 - stocks_2013.xml
```

In some cases, you might not want to get output on each individual case but only create summary information. One possibility for this is to shorten the output by providing information on, say, each tenth download. We add an `if()` statement to our code such that only those iterations are printed where the `i` divided by 10 does not result in a fraction.

```
R> for(i in 1:30)
        if(i %% 10 == 0){
                cat(i, "of", 30, "\n")
        }
}
10 of 30
20 of 30
30 of 30
```

Writing progress to a log file

Incidentally, you might want to store the progress information in an external file for later inspection to be able to trace potential errors. Possibly, this should consist of more extensive information than what is printed to your screen. For example, you can use the `write()` command to write the progress to a log file that is appended in each iteration. We begin by creating an empty file on our local hard drive.

```
R> write("", "download.txt")
```

We then append the information that is written to the screen to the external file. To make the information a little more useful for later inspection, we add information on the number of characters in the downloaded file. We also add dashes and a space to visually separate the various downloads.

```
R> N <- length(links)
R> for(i in 1:N){
R>      stocks <- getURL(links[i])
R>      name <- basename(links[i])
R>      write(html, file = str_c("stocks/", name))
R>      feedback <- str_c(i, "of", N, "-", name, "\n", sep = " ")
R>      cat(feedback)
R>      write(feedback, "download.txt", append = T)
R>      write(nchar(stocks), "download.txt", append = T)
R>      write("-----------\n", "download.txt", append = T)
R> }
```

Using built-in progress bars

In many instances, the best feedback is textual. Nevertheless, you can also create other types of feedback. For instance, you can easily create a simple progress bar for your function using the `txtProgressBar()` that is predefined in R. For our example we start by initializing a progress bar with the extreme values of 0 and N, that is 3. We set the style of the progress bar to 3, which generates a progress bar that displays the percentage of the task that is done at the right end of the bar.

```
R> progress_bar <- txtProgressBar(min = 0, max = N, style = 3)
```

Next, we download the documents once more with the shortest version of the code that was introduced previously. We add the command `setTxtProgressBar()` to our call which sets the value of the progress bar that we initialized above. The first argument specifies which progress bar we want to change the value of, the second argument sets the value, in this case the values 1, 2, and 3. We add a 1 second delay after each iteration using the `Sys.sleep()` function, so you can clearly see the development of the progress bar.

```
R> for(i in 1:N){
R>   stocks <- getURL(links[i])
R>   name <- basename(links[i])
R>   write(stocks, name)
R>   setTxtProgressBar(progress_bar, i)
R>   Sys.sleep(1)
R> }

|================================                    | 73%
```

Audio feedback

You can even create audio cues to signal that the execution of a piece of code is complete. For example, the escape sequence `\a` calls the alert bell.[2]

```
R> for(i in 1:N){
R>      tmp <- getURL(websites[i])
R>      write(tmp, str_c(str_replace(websites[i], "http://www\\.", ""), ".
html"))
R> }
R> cat("\a")
```

Imagine a *ping!* when reading `cat("\a")` in the last code snippet.

11.3.2 Error and exception handling

When you start to scrape the Web seriously, you will begin to stumble across exceptions. For example, websites might not be formatted consistently such that you will not find all the elements that you are looking for. It is sometimes difficult to build your functions sufficiently robust to be able to deal with all the exceptions. This section introduces some simple techniques that can help you overcome such problems. Let us consider as an example the same task that we have looked at in Section 11.3—downloading a list of websites. First, we expand the list with a mistyped URL.

```
R> wrong_pages <- c("http://www.bozzfeed.com", links)
```

The `try()` function

When we try to download the content of all of the sites to our hard drive using a simple loop over all the entries, we find that this operation fails as the function is unable to collect the first entry in our vector. The problem with errors is that they break the execution of the entire piece of code. Even though the remaining three entries could have been collected with the code snippet as we have previously shown, the single false entry stops the execution altogether. The simplest way to change this behavior is to wrap the `getURL()` expressions in a `try()` statement.

```
R> for(i in 1:N){
R>   url <- try(getURL(wrong_pages[i]))
R>   if(class(url) != "try-error"){
```

[2] Users have implemented more fun notification sounds in R. Be sure to check out the pingr package (see https://github.com/rasmusab/pingr).

```
R>      name <- basename(wrong_pages[i])
R>      write(url, name)
R>   }
R> }
```

The tryCatch() function

Notice that we added a statement to test the class of the `url` object. If the object is of class `try-error`, we do not write the content of the object to the hard drive. The disadvantage of wrapping code in `try()` statements is that you discard errors as inconsequential. This is a strong assumption, as something has gone wrong in your code and frequently it makes sense to consider more carefully what exception you encountered. R also offers the `tryCatch()` function which is a more flexible device for catching errors and defining actions to be performed as errors occur. For example, you could log the error to consider the systematics of the errors later on. First, we create a function that combines the two steps of our task in a single function. We also set up a log file to export errors and the relevant URL during the execution of the code.

```
R> collectHTML <- function(url){
R>   html <- getURL(url)
R>   write(html, basename(url))
R> }
R> write("", "error_log.txt")
```

We customize the error handling in the `tryCatch()` statement by making it print `Not available` and the name of the website that cannot be accessed.[3]

```
R> for (i in 1:N) {
    html <- tryCatch(collectHTML(site404[i]), error = function(err){
        errMess <- str_c("Not available - ", site404[i])
        write(str_c(errMess, "error_log.txt"))
    })
}
```

11.4 Executing R scripts on a regular basis

On many websites, smaller or larger parts of the contents are changed on a regular basis, which renders these resources dynamic. To exemplify, imagine a news site that publishes new articles every other hour or the press release repository of a non-governmental organization that adds new releases sporadically.

Implicitly, we assumed so far that scraping can be carried out in a one-time job. Yet, when dynamic web resources are concerned, it might be a key aspect of a data project to collect information over a longer period of time. While nothing prevents us from manually executing a script in regular intervals, this process is cumbersome and error-prone. This

[3]The added value of using the `tryCatch()` function compared to the `try()` statement in this case is fairly limited, as the error messages of the former are similarly informative and could easily be written to an external file. The added value of `tryCatch()` relative to `try()` stems from the fact that we can define customized action upon encounter of an error. The simple example only serves the purpose of exposition. For error handling with specification of alternative behavior see Section 5.4.7.

section discusses ways to free the data scientist from this responsibility by setting up a system task that initiates the scraping automatically and in the background. To this end, we employ tools that are built right into the architecture of all modern operating systems for scheduling the execution of programs. We provide an introduction to these tools and show how an R scraping script can be invoked in user-defined intervals.

We motivate this section with the problem of downloading information from http://www.r-datacollection.com/materials/workflow/rQuotes.php. Scraping this site is complicated by its very dynamic nature—the site changes every minute and displays a different R quote. We set ourselves to the task of downloading a day's worth of quotes. Clearly, a manual approach is out of the question for obvious reasons. We approach the problem by first assembling an R script that allows downloading and storing information from one instance of the site. The first line loads the stringr package and the second makes sure that we have a folder called *quotes* that serves as a container for the downloaded pages. The next three lines are overhead for the file names that include the date and time of the download. The last line conducts the download, using R's built-in `download.file()` function. We save the downloading routine under the name *getQuotes.R*.

```
R> library(stringr)
R> if (!file.exists("quotes")) dir.create("quotes")
R> time <- str_replace_all(as.character(Sys.time()), ":", "_")
R> fname <- str_c("quotes/rquote ", time, ".html")
R> url <- "http://www.r-datacollection.com/materials/workflow/rQuotes.php"
R> download.file(url = url, destfile = fname)
```

In the remainder of this section, we describe how to embed the R script with system utilities for regular execution in predefined intervals. We discuss solutions for Linux, Mac OS, and Windows.

11.4.1 Scheduling tasks on Mac OS and Linux

For users working on a UNIX-like operating system such as Mac OS or Linux, we propose using *Cron* for the creation and administration of time-based tasks. *Cron* is a preinstalled general-purpose system utility that allows setting up so-called jobs that are being run periodically or at designated times in the background of the system.

How *Cron* works

For the administration of tasks, *Cron* uses a simple text-based table structure called a crontab. A crontab includes information on the specific actions and the times when the actions should be executed. Notice that *Cron* will run the jobs regardless of whether the user is actually logged into the system or not. Although graphical interfaces exist to set up a task, it is convenient and quick to edit tasks using a text editor. To create a new task, open a system shell[4] and write.

```
crontab -e
```

[4]Depending or your system, the shell may be accessed differently. On Mac OS open 'Terminal,' on Ubuntu find Terminal or press CTRL+ALT+T.

Table 11.2 The five field *Cron* time format

Field	Description	Allowed values
MIN	Minute field	0–59
HOUR	Hour field	0–23 (0 = midnight)
DOM	Day of Month field	1–31
MON	Month field	1–12 or literals
DOW	Day of Week field	0–6 (0 = Sunday) or literals

Source: Adapted from http://www.thegeekstuff.com/2009/06/15-practical-crontab-examples/

This command opens the crontab specific to your logged in user in the default editor of your system. If you prefer a different text editor, prepend the command with the respective editor's name (e.g., *nano*, *emacs*, *gedit*). Conditional on the OS you use, the text file you are being shown can be empty or include some general comments on how this file can be edited. In any case, since crontab requires that each task has to appear on a separate line, go ahead and point the prompt to the last line of the file. The general layout of a crontab follows the pattern "[*time*] [*script*],"where the *script* component refers to a shell command and the *time* component describes the temporal pattern by which the script is executed.

Cron has its own time format to express chronological regularity. Essentially, this time format consists of five fields, separated by white space, that refer to the minute, hour, day, month, and weekday on which the task is to be executed. Take a look at Table 11.2 to learn about the allowed values for each of the five time fields. Notice, that any of the five fields may be left unspecified which in the *Cron* time format is indicated by the asterisk symbol `*`.

From this basic template, we can construct a wide range of temporal patterns for task execution. To illustrate their capability, take a look at the following three specifications.

`15 16 * * *`	executes the script everyday quarter past four
`15 16 * 1 *`	executes the script everyday quarter past four when the month is January
`15 16 * 1 0`	executes the script everyday quarter past four when the month is January and it's Sunday

In any of these five fields, one can produce an unconnected or connected series of time units by using "`,`" or "`-`" respectively.

`15 10-20 * * *`	executes the script quarter past every hour from 10 am to 8 pm
`15 10-20 * * 6,0`	executes the script quarter past every hour from 10 am to 8 pm on Saturdays and Sundays

In many circumstances, exact specification of a time is overly rigid for a given task. Instead, one can use the *Cron* time schema to express the intention of having a task executed in certain time intervals. The preferred way to do this is by using a "`*/n`"construct that specifies an interval of length *n* for the respective time unit. To illustrate, consider the following examples.

`*/15 * * * *`	executes the script every 15 minutes
`15 0 */2 * *`	executes the script 15 minutes past midnight on every second day

Executing tasks from the shell

The second piece of information in any *Cron* job is the shell command that has to be executed regularly. If you have never worked with the shell before, think of it as a command line based user-interface for accessing the operating system and installed programs (such as R). In order to set up a new task for the execution of *getQuotes.r* every minute, we append the following line to the crontab:

```
*/1 * * * * cd [DIRECTORY] && Rscript getQuotes.r
```

We first specify the chronological pattern "`*/1 * * * *`" for every-minute repeated execution. This is followed by the scripting part, where we first change the directory to the folder in which *getQuotes.r* is saved and then use the Rscript-executable on *getQuotes.r*. Rscript is a scripting front-end that should be used in cases when an R script is executed via the shell. Once you have saved the crontab, the task is active and should be executed in the background.

For the maintainability of *Cron*-induced R routines, it is helpful to retain an overview over the outputs that are generated from the script, such as warnings or errors. The UNIX shell allows to route the output of the R script to a log file by extending the *Cron* job as follows:

```
*/1 * * * * cd [DIRECTORY] && Rscript getQuotes.r >> log.txt 2>&1
```

11.4.2 Scheduling tasks on Windows platforms

On Windows platforms, the *Windows Task Scheduler* is the tool for scheduling tasks. To find the tool click *Start > All Programs > Accessories > System Tools > Scheduled Tasks*.

Working with the *Windows Task Scheduler*

To set up a new task, double-click on *Create Task*. From here, the procedure differs according to your version of Windows, but the presented options should be very similar. On Windows 7, we are presented with a window with five tabs—*General*, *Triggers*, *Actions*, *Conditions*, and *Settings*. Under *General* we can provide a name for the task. Here we put in *Testing R Batch Mode* for a descriptive title.

In the field *Triggers* we can add several triggers for starting the task—see Figure 11.2. There are schedule triggers which start the task every day, week, or month and also triggers that refer to events like the startup of the computer or when it is in idle mode, and many more. To execute *getQuotes.r* every minute for 24 hours, we select *On a schedule* as general trigger and define that it should be executed only once but repeated every *1 minutes* for *1 day*. Last but not least, we should make sure that the start date and time of our one-time scheduled task should be placed somewhere in the future when we will be done specifying the schedule.

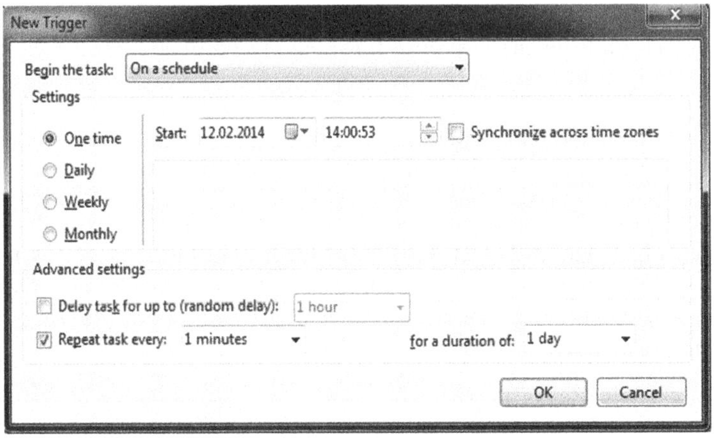

Figure 11.2 Trigger selection on Windows platform

After the trigger specification we still have to tell the program what to do if the task is triggered. The *Actions* tab is the right place to do that—see Figure 11.3. We choose *Start a program* for action and use the browse button to select the destination of *Rscript.exe*, which should be placed under, for example, C:\ProgramFiles\R\R-3.0.2\bin\x64\. Furthermore, we add *getQuotes.r* in the *Add arguments* field and type in the directory where the script is placed in the *Start in* field. If logging is needed we modify the procedure.

Program/script field: replace *Rscript.exe* by *R.exe*

Add arguments field: replace *getQuotes.r* by `CMD BATCH -vanilla getQuotes.r log.txt`

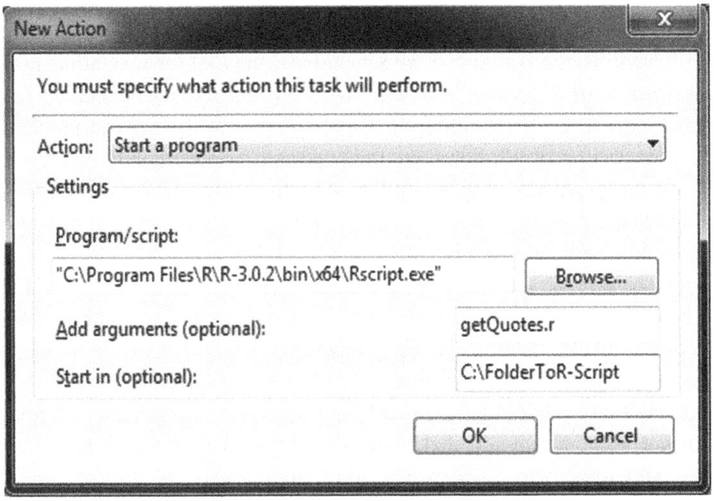

Figure 11.3 Action selection on Windows platform

While `CMD BATCH` tells R to run in batch mode, `-vanilla` ensures that no R profiles or saved workspaces are stored or restored that might interfere with the execution of the script. `log.txt` provides the name for the logfile. Now we can confirm our configuration and click on *Task Scheduler Library* in the left panel to get a list of all tasks available on our system.

Part Three

A BAG OF CASE STUDIES

Overview of all case studies

Case study	Description	Scraping and information extraction via...	Main packages	Important functions
Collaboration Networks in the U.S. Senate	Scraping of bill cosponsorship data from the US Senate at thomas.loc.gov, assessment of collaboration network structure	URL manipulation, regular expressions	RCurl, stringr, igraph	`getURL()`, `str_extract()`, `graph.edgelist()`, `get.adjacency()`
Parsing Information from Semi-Structured Documents	Scraping of climate data from Californian weather stations (ftp.wcc.nrcs.usda.gov), construction of a regex-based parser	FTP download, regular expressions and string manipulation tools	RCurl, stringr	`getURL()`, `str_extract()`, `str_replace()`
Predicting the 2014 Academy Awards using Twitter	Collection of tweets from Twitter API (dev.twitter.com/docs/api/streaming), frequency-based prediction of Oscar winners	Persistent connection to Streaming API via streamR, regular expressions	streamR, twitteR, lubridate, stringr, plyr	`filterStream()`, `parseTweets()`, `str_detect()`, `agrep()`
Mapping the Geographic Distribution of Names	Scraping phone book data from dastelefonbuch.de, extraction of zip codes and matching with geo-coordinates, creation of family name maps	HTML forms,XPath and regular expressions, R geographic functionality	RCurl, stringr, XML, maptools, maps, rgdal	`getForm()`, `htmlParse()`, `xpathSApply()`, `str_extract()`, `function()`
Gathering Data on Mobile Phones	Scraping of mobile phone product data from amazon.com, data storage in *SQLite* database	URL manipulation, XPath and regular expressions	RCurl, stringr, XML, RSQLite	`htmlParse()`, `xpathSApply()`, `str_extract()`, `dbGetQuery()`
Analyzing Sentiments of Product Reviews	Extension of *SQLite* database with customer reviews of mobile phones at amazon.com, dictionary and classification-based sentiment analysis	XPath, data preparation with tm functionality, sentiment dictionary, maximum entropy and SVM	RCurl, string, XML, RSQLite, tm, RTextTools, textcat	`dbReadTable()`, `dbGetQuery()`, `tm_map()`, `TermDocumentMa-trix()`, `classify_model()`

12

Collaboration networks in the US Senate

The inner workings of legislatures are inherently difficult to investigate. Political scientists have been interested in collaborations among parliamentarians as explanatory factors in legislative behavior for decades. Scholars have encountered difficulties, however, in collecting comprehensive data over time to investigate patterns of cooperation. The advent of large-scale, machine-readable databases on legislative behavior have opened up promising new research avenues in this regard. Among these, scholars have considered the possibility of treating bill cosponsorships as proxies for legislative cooperation in the United States. We follow this lead and investigate who cooperates with whom in the US Senate.

Every bill that is introduced to the US Senate is tied to one senator as its main sponsor, but other senators are free to cosponsor a bill in order to support the bill's content—a common practice in senatorial procedures. In fact, in many instances, a bill will have numerous cosponsors. Several authors have recently begun to truly appreciate the network-like structure in bill cosponsorships that is best analyzed using network-analytic methodology.[1] Using the rich and well accessible data source on bill cosigners provides researchers with an interesting insight into the black box of collaboration among senators. What is more, bill cosponsorships are moving targets. New proposals are constantly put on record. Being able to collect these data automatically provides researchers with a unique opportunity to consider structural changes in the networks as they are happening.

In this application, we generate the necessary data to replicate some of the analyses that have been put forward in recent years. For simplicity's sake, we only assemble data on bill cosponsorships for the US Senate in the 111th Congress, which was in session from 2009 to

[1]For recent contributions on the topic, see Bratton and Rouse (2011), Burkett (1997), Cho and Fowler (2010), Fowler (2006a), Fowler (2006b), and Zhang et al. (2008).

Automated Data Collection with R: A Practical Guide to Web Scraping and Text Mining, First Edition.
Simon Munzert, Christian Rubba, Peter Meißner and Dominic Nyhuis.

Table 12.1 Desired data structure for sponsorship matrix

	Senator A	Senator B	Senator C	...
S.1	Cosponsor	Sponsor	Cosponsor	...
S.2	.	.	.	...
S.3	.	Cosponsor	Sponsor	...
S.4	.	.	Sponsor	...
S.5	.	.	.	...
S.6	Cosponsor	.	Cosponsor	...
S.7	Sponsor	.	.	...
⋮	⋮	⋮	⋮	⋱

The table displays a mock example of the dataset we wish to generate. The rows list each bill, the columns list each senator. The cells display whether a senator was the main sponsor of a bill (`Sponsor`), has cosponsored a bill (`Cosponsor`) or did not sign a bill at all (`.`).

2010. Sections 12.1 and 12.2 provide the technical details on how the underlying data sources are generated. Again, our focus in this chapter is on data gathering; hence, we only analyze the data with simple metrics. Section 12.3 gives a brief overview on how the data can be employed—both descriptively and in a basic network application. Section 12.4 concludes the chapter.

12.1 Information on the bills

Our first task is to assemble a list of all sponsors and cosponsors on each bill. To keep matters simple, we will only gather data for the 111th Senate, which ran from 2009 to 2010. As we are more interested in the process of data gathering than in the actual application, there is more than enough material in one senatorial term. Should you wish to analyze the data for an actual application, it is fairly straightforward to adapt the script to encompass more legislative periods.

Our specific goal in this section is to construct a matrix that holds information on whether a senator has sponsored, cosponsored, or not participated at all in a given bill. A mock example of the data structure is presented in Table 12.1. Storing the data in this format provides the greatest flexibility for subsequent analyses. We could, for example, be interested in analyzing which senator was better able to collect cosponsors, or we might want to analyze which Senators were often cosponsors on the same piece of legislation to find collaboration clusters in the Senate. We can easily rearrange the proposed table using the facilities of R without having to reassemble all the data from scratch if we tailor the table to a particular application from the start. Furthermore, this data matrix even allows performing an ideal point estimation (Alemán et al. 2009; Desposato et al. 2011; Peress 2010) that we will, however, not tackle in this chapter.

Let us have a look at the database. Luckily, the bills of the US Congress are stored in a database that is relatively accessible at http://thomas.loc.gov.[2] The first step in our web

[2]Rather inadvertently, this case study is an example of rapid changes in the Web and their consequences for web scraping. The website of the Library of Congress at http://thomas.loc.gov/ will be retired by the end of 2014 and

scraping exercise is an inspection of the way the data are stored. In order to be able to track the scraping procedure,

1. Call http://thomas.loc.gov/home/thomas.php
2. Go to "`Try the Advanced Search`"
3. Click on "`Browse Bills & Resolutions`" right above it
4. Select "`111`" at the top of the page
5. On the resulting page click on "`Senate Bills`"

A scraping strategy

The resulting page holds the main information on the first 100 of 4059 bills proposed during the 111th Senate. Specifically, we see the title of the proposed bill, its sponsor, the number of cosponsors, and the latest major action for each item. Now click on `Cosponsors` of the first bill `S.1`. Apart from the previously mentioned elements, we additionally see a list of the bill's 17 cosponsors. This page holds all the information we are interested in for now which greatly facilitates our task. Check out the URL of the page—http://thomas.loc.gov/cgi-bin/bdquery/D?d111:1:./list/bss/d111SN.lst:@@@P. Despite its somewhat peculiar format the numerator of this piece of legislation, 1, is hidden right in the middle next to the senate term 111. To be sure, click on the `NEXT:COSPONSORS` button. Now the URL reads http://thomas.loc.gov/cgi-bin/bdquery/D?d111:2:./list/bss/d111SN.lst:@@@P:&summ2=m&. Disregarding the altered ending of the URL, we notice that the middle of the URL now reads 2 for the second bill in the 111th Senate.

As the attached ending is not a necessary prerequisite to get the information, we are looking for, but is rather added due to the referral from one site to the next, we can safely drop it. Choosing a random number, 42, we rewrite the original URL by hand to read http://thomas.loc.gov/cgi-bin/bdquery/D?d111:42:./list/bss/d111SN.lst:@@@P. Works like a charm. Now, in line with our rules of good practice in web scraping, we will download the web pages of all 4059 bills to our local hard drive and try to read it out in the second step.[3] We start our R session by loading some packages which we need for the rest of the exercise.

```
R> library(RCurl)
R> library(stringr)
R> library(XML)
R> library(igraph)
```

Data retrieval

The scraping function we set up comprises three simple steps—generating a unique URL for every bill, downloading the page, and finally writing the page as HTML file to the local

replaced by the new domain http://congress.gov/ (see http://beta.congress.gov/about). At the time of writing both http://thomas.loc.gov/ and http://beta.congress.gov/ were active. Changing websites frequently take us by surprise and changes in the page structure or even complete shutdowns are rarely communicated as transparently as in this case. On the upside, the case study demonstrates how data from abandoned sources can be used for analyses if they are stored appropriately.

[3] You can skip this step by downloading the files provided on the book's website.

folder *Bills_111*. We have also added a simple progress indicator to monitor the downloading process.

```
R> # Iterate over all 4059 pieces of legislation
R> for(i in 1:4059){
R> # Generate the unique URL for each piece of legislation
R>     url <- str_c("http://thomas.loc.gov/cgi-bin/bdquery/D?d111:",
R>         i, ":./list/bss/d111SN.lst:@@@P")
R> # Download the page
R>     bill_result <- getURL(url,
R>                           useragent = R.version$version.string,
R>                           httpheader = c(from = "i@datacollection.com"))
R> # Write the page to local hard drive
R>     write(bill_result, str_c("Bills_111/Bill_111_S", i, ".html"))
R> # Print progress of download
R>     cat(i, "\n")
R> }
```

Extracting sponsors and cosponsors

When you are finished downloading the data, inspect the source code of the first bill in a text editor of your choice. Notice that each senator—both sponsors and cosponsors—is provided with links which makes the task all the easier for us as we simply have to extract all the links in this specific format. Note the subtle difference in the link for the sponsor, Harry Reid,

```
/cgi-bin/bdquery/?\&amp;Db=d111\&amp;querybd=@FIELD(FLD003+@4
((@1(Sen+Reid++Harry))+00952))
```

and the—alphabetically speaking—first cosponsor, Mark Begich,

```
/cgi-bin/bdquery/?\&amp;Db=d111\&amp;querybd=@FIELD(FLD004+@4
((@1(Sen+Begich++Mark))+01898))
```

The former URL specifies that Harry Reid is in field 3 (`FLD003`) and Mark Begich in field 4 (`FLD004`). So, apparently, the Congress website internally differentiates between the sponsors and the cosponsors of a bill.

We can make use of this knowledge by writing two simple regular expressions to extract all the "field 3" links—there cannot be more than one in each site, as there is only one sponsor for each bill—and all the "field 4"links. To do so, we replace the senators' names in the form of `Sen+Reid++Harry` with a sequence of alphabetic, plus, and period characters—`[[:alpha:]+.]+?`.[4] Then, we precede all the characters with special meanings in regular expressions with two backslashes in order to have them interpreted literally.

```
R> sponsor_regex <- "FLD003\\+@4\\(\\(@1\\([[:alpha:]+.]+"
R> cosponsor_regex <- "FLD004\\+@4\\(\\(@1\\([[:alpha:]+.]+"
```

[4]Recall that we don't need to precede the + and . characters with backslashes, as they loose their special meaning inside a character class.

Now that we have our regular expressions set up, let us go for a test drive. We load the source code of the first senate bill into R and extract the link for the sponsor, as well as the links for the cosponsors.

```
R> html_source <- readLines("Bills_111/Bill_111_1.html")
R> sponsor <- str_extract(html_source, sponsor_regex)
R> (sponsor <- sponsor[!is.na(sponsor)])
[1] "FLD003+@4((@1(Sen+Reid++Harry"
R> cosponsors <- unlist(str_extract_all(html_source, cosponsor_regex))
R> cosponsors[1:3]
[1] "FLD004+@4((@1(Sen+Begich++Mark"   "FLD004+@4((@1(Sen+Bingaman++Jeff"
[3] "FLD004+@4((@1(Sen+Boxer++Barbara"
R> length(cosponsors)
[1] 17
```

Data cleansing

No problems here. Before moving on we write a small function that first extracts the senators' names in the parentheses, drops the parentheses, replaces the + signs with commas and spaces, and, finally, takes out the leading `Sen` for convenience.

```
R> cleanUp <- function(x){
    name <- str_extract(x, "[[:alpha:]+.]+$")
    name <- str_replace_all(name, fixed("++"), ", ")
    name <- str_replace_all(name, fixed("+"), " ")
    name <- str_trim(str_replace(name, "Sen", ""))
    return(name)
}
```

Applying the `cleanUp()` function to our previous results yields

```
R> cleanUp(sponsor)
[1] "Reid, Harry"
R> cleanUp(cosponsors)
 [1] "Begich, Mark"              "Bingaman, Jeff"
 [3] "Boxer, Barbara"            "Brown, Sherrod"
 [5] "Casey, Robert P., Jr."     "Clinton, Hillary Rodham"
 [7] "Durbin, Richard"           "Kennedy, Edward M."
 [9] "Kerry, John F."            "Klobuchar, Amy"
[11] "Lautenberg, Frank R."      "Levin, Carl"
[13] "Lieberman, Joseph I."      "McCaskill, Claire"
[15] "Menendez, Robert"          "Schumer, Charles E."
[17] "Stabenow, Debbie"
```

Exception and error handling

Perfect. Now we want to run this code on our entire corpus. Before doing so, we would like to add a couple of fail safes in order to ensure that the code actually extracts what we want. In order to do so, we apply some knowledge on what the results *should* look like. The first thing we know is that there can only be one single sponsor for each bill. Accordingly, we check whether our code returns either no sponsor or more than one sponsor.

The second fail safe is a little more tricky. A bill can have one, many, or no cosponsors at all. Luckily, each site tells us the number of cosponsors it lists. We will read out this information and compare this number to the number of cosponsors we find. Specifically, we look for the elements `COSPONSOR(S)` and `COSPONSOR(some_number)` in the source code. If neither of these strings are present, we know something might be wrong. We also know that if the number of cosponsors in these strings does not match our findings, we better double-check our results. We store these errors in a list for later inspection. We cannot store the results in the proposed format from the beginning of this section, as we do not have a list of all senators that have at one point (co-)sponsored a bill. Hence, we input our results into a list of its own for the time being. The procedure is plotted in Figure 12.1.

After assembling the list of sponsors and errors, we investigate the latter.

```
R> length(error_collection)
[1] 18
```

There are 18 errors in the `error_collection` list—all of them related to a discrepancy between the number of cosponsors recorded in the source code and the actual number collected by our code. A manual inspection of these cases reveals that all of them can be traced back to withdrawals of cosponsorship. We go back to them, load the source code again, count the number of withdrawals on a bill, and shorten the cosponsors list by the right amount—withdrawals are always last on the list.

```
R> for(i in 1:length(error_collection)){
    bill_number <- as.numeric(error_collection[[i]][1])
    html_source <- readLines(str_c("Bills_111/Bill_111_S", bill_number, ".
html"))

     count_withdrawn <- unlist(
     str_extract_all(
       html_source,
       "\\(withdrawn - [[:digit:]]{1,2}/[[:digit:]]{1,2}/[[:digit:]]{4}\\)"
       )
     )
    sponsor_list[[str_c("S.", bill_number)]]$cosponsors <-
      sponsor_list[[str_c("S.", bill_number)]]$cosponsors[1:(length(
sponsor_list[[str_c("S.", bill_number)]]$cosponsors) - length(
count_withdrawn))]
}
```

Now we have a complete list of all the senators that have either sponsored or cosponsored legislation in the 111th US Senate. We inspect the data by unlisting it, thus inputting it into a named character vector. Next, we deselect duplicates and print out the—alphabetically ordered—first five senators.

```
R> all_senators <- unlist(sponsor_list)
R> all_senators <- unique(all_senators)
R> all_senators <- sort(all_senators)
R> head(all_senators)
[1] "Akaka, Daniel K." "Alexander, Lamar" "Barrasso, John"
[4] "Baucus, Max"      "Bayh, Evan"       "Begich, Mark"
```

```
error_collection <- list()
sponsor_list <- list()
# Iterate over all 4059 pieces of legislation
for(i in 1:4059){
# Read the ith result
   html_source <- readLines(str_c("/Bills_111/Bill_111_S", i, ".html"))
# Extract and clean the sponsor
   sponsor <- unlist(str_extract_all(html_source, sponsor_regex))
   sponsor <- sponsor[!is.na(sponsor)]
   sponsor <- cleanUp(sponsor)
# Extract and clean the cosponsors
   cosponsors <- unlist(str_extract_all(html_source, cosponsor_regex))
   cosponsors <- cleanUp(cosponsors)
# Input the results into the sponsor list
   sponsor_list[[str_c("S.", i)]] <- list(sponsor = sponsor, cosponsors = cosponsors)
# Collect potential points of error / number of cosponsors
   fail_safe <- str_extract(html_source,
                  "COSPONSORS?\\(([[:digit:]]{1,3}|S)\\)")
   fail_safe <- fail_safe[!is.na(fail_safe)]
  # Error - no cosponsor string
   if(length(fail_safe) == 0){
      error_collection[[length(error_collection) + 1]] <- c(i, "String - COSPONSOR - not found")
   }
# Error - found more cosponsors than possible
  if(fail_safe == "COSPONSOR(S)"){
     if(length(cosponsors) > 0){
        error_collection[[length(error_collection) + 1]] <- c(i, "Found cosponsors where there should be none")
     }
  }else{
     right_number <- str_extract(fail_safe, "[[:digit:]]+")
     # Error - Found wrong number of cosponsors
     if(length(cosponsors) != right_number){
        error_collection[[length(error_collection) + 1]] <- c(i, "Did not find the right number of cosponsors")
     }
  }
# Error - Found no sponsors
  if(is.na(sponsor)){
     error_collection[[length(error_collection) + 1]] <- c(i, "No sponsors")
  }
# Error - Found too many sponsors
  if(length(sponsor) > 1){
     error_collection[[length(error_collection) + 1]] <- c(i, "More than one sponsor")
  }
}
```

Figure 12.1 R procedure to collect list of bill sponsors

Creating and filling the matrix

In the following step, we set up the matrix for the data as proposed in the beginning of the section. First, we create an empty matrix.

```
R> sponsor_matrix <- matrix(NA, nrow = 4059, ncol = length(all_senators))
R> colnames(sponsor_matrix) <- all_senators
R> rownames(sponsor_matrix) <- paste("S.", seq(1, 4059), sep ="")
```

Finally, we iterate over our sponsor list to fill the correct cells.

```
R> for(i in 1:length(sponsor_list)){
    sponsor_matrix[i, which(all_senators == sponsor_list[[i]]$sponsor)] <-
        "Sponsor"
    if(length(sponsor_list[[i]]$cosponsors) > 0){
        for(j in 1:length(sponsor_list[[i]]$cosponsors)){
            sponsor_matrix[i, which(all_senators == sponsor_list[[i]]
$cosponsors[j])] <- "Cosponsor"
        }
    }
}
R> sponsor_matrix[30:35,31:34]
     Cornyn, John Crapo, Mike DeMint, Jim Dodd, Christopher J.
S.30 NA           NA          NA          NA
S.31 NA           NA          NA          NA
S.32 NA           NA          NA          NA
S.33 NA           NA          NA          NA
S.34 "Cosponsor"  "Cosponsor" "Sponsor"   NA
S.35 "Cosponsor"  NA          NA          NA
```

12.2 Information on the senators

In this section, we want to collect some simple background information on the senators to use in our analysis. Specifically, we are interested in the party affiliation and the home state of the senators. We collect these data from the biographical archives of the Congress.[5] Let us check out the source code of the website http://bioguide.congress.gov/biosearch/biosearch.asp. It mainly consists of an HTML form that can be accessed using the `postForm()` command. To request an answer from the form, we have to specify values for the different options the form has. There are several types of input an HTML form can take—two out of which are used in this case (see Section 9.1.5). There are three free inputs and three selections we can make that come with a list of prespecified options. Let us take a look at the options first by collecting them from the source code of the website. Again, in line with our rules of good practice, we start by storing the source code on our local hard drive before accessing it.

```
R> url <- "http://bioguide.congress.gov/biosearch/biosearch.asp"
R> form_page <- getURL(url)
R> write(form_page, "form_page.html")
```

[5]Writing a script for a little over 100 senators is in some senses a bit excessive, as it probably takes longer to write a script to read out the website than to hand-code the data. However, doing so, we keep our analysis replicable and make it easily extensible.

Accessing the form with regular expressions yields

```
R> form_page <- str_c(readLines("form_page.html"), collapse = "")
R> destination <- str_extract(form_page, "<form.+?>")
R> cat(destination)
<form method="POST" action="http://bioguide.congress.gov/biosearch/
biosearch1.asp">

R> form <- str_extract(form_page, "<form.+?</form>")
R> cat(str_c(unlist(str_extract_all(form, "<INPUT.+?>")), collapse = "\n"))
<INPUT SIZE=30 NAME="lastname" VALUE="">
<INPUT SIZE=30 NAME="firstname" VALUE="">
<INPUT SIZE=4 NAME="congress" VALUE="">
<INPUT TYPE=submit VALUE="Search">
<INPUT TYPE=reset VALUE="Clear">

R> cat(str_c(unlist(str_extract_all(form, "<SELECT.+?>")), collapse = "\n"))
<SELECT NAME="position" SIZE=1>
<SELECT NAME="state" SIZE=1>
<SELECT NAME="party" SIZE=1>
```

Posting a form

We see the options `firstname`, `lastname`, and `congress` as the free fields and `position`, `state`, and `party` as the fields with given options. We are interested in a list of all the senators in the 111th Senate, hence we specify these two values and leave the other fields open. The URL destination is specified in the form tag. For this request, we use the RCurl package which provides the useful `postForm()`. Note that the form expects `application/x-www-form-urlencoded` encoded content, so we add the argument `style = 'POST'`.

```
R> senator_site <- postForm(uri =
R>     "http://bioguide.congress.gov/biosearch/biosearch1.asp",
R>         lastname = "",
R>         firstname = "",
R>         position = "Senator",
R>         state = "",
R>         party = "",
R>         congress = "111",
R>             style = 'POST'
R> )
R> write(senator_site, "senators.html")
```

Collecting senator data

The response to this call holds the information we are looking for. We collect the information using the `readHTMLTable()` function.

```
R> senator_site <- readLines("senators.html", encoding = "UTF-8")
R> senator_site <- str_c(senator_site, collapse = "")
R> senators <- readHTMLTable(senator_site, encoding="UTF-8")[[2]]
R> senators <- as.data.frame(sapply(senators, as.character),
stringsAsFactors = F)
R> names(senators)[names(senators)=="Birth-Death"] <- "BiDe"
R> head(senators, 3)
             Member Name  BiDe Position      Party State Congress(Year)
1 AKAKA, Daniel Kahikina 1924-  Senator   Democrat    HI 111(2009-2010)
```

```
2      ALEXANDER, Lamar 1940-  Senator Republican    TN 111(2009-2010)
3     BARRASSO, John A. 1952-  Senator Republican    WY 111(2009-2010)
```

Here is where things become a little messy. We would like to match the senators along with their background information that we have collected in this section and stored in the object `senators` to the data were collected in the previous section. Recall that we created an object `all_senators` where we stored the names of all the senators that have at one point either sponsored or cosponsored a piece of legislation.

```
R> senators$match_names <- senators[,1]
R> senators$match_names <- tolower(senators$match_names)
R> senators$match_names <- str_extract(senators$match_names, "[[:alpha:]]+")
R> all_senators_dat <- data.frame(all_senators)
R> all_senators_dat$match_names <- str_extract(all_senators_dat$all_senators,
"[[:alpha:]]+")
R> all_senators_dat$match_names <- tolower(all_senators_dat$match_names)
R> senators <- merge(all_senators_dat, senators, by = "match_names")
R> senators[,2] <- as.character(senators[,2])
R> senators[,3] <- as.character(senators[,3])
R> senators[,2] <- tolower(senators[,2])
R> senators[,3] <- tolower(senators[,3])
```

We match by last names but unfortunately, there are no less than eight senators in the 111th Senate of identical last names. We treat these duplicates by matching them by first name.

```
R> allDup <- function(x){
    duplicated(x) | duplicated(x, fromLast = TRUE)
}

R> dup_senators <- senators[allDup(senators[,1]),]
R> senators <- senators[rownames(senators) %in% rownames(dup_senators) == F,]
R> dup_senators[str_detect(dup_senators[,3], "\\("), 3] <- str_replace_all
(dup_senators[str_detect(dup_senators[,3], "\\("), 3], ", .+?\\(", ", ")
R> dup_senators[str_detect(dup_senators[,3], "\\("), 3] <- str_replace_all(
dup_senators[str_detect(dup_senators[,3], "$"), 3], "$", "")

R> for(i in nrow(dup_senators):1){
    if(str_detect(dup_senators[i, 2], str_extract(dup_senators[i, 3],
"[^,][[:alpha:] .]+?$")) == F){
            dup_senators <- dup_senators[-i,]
    }
}

R> senators <- rbind(senators, dup_senators)
R> senators$rownames <- as.numeric(rownames(senators))
R> senators <- senators[order(senators$rownames),]
R> dim(senators)
[1] 109   9
```

Finally, we replace the column names in the sponsor matrix with these shortened identifiers.

```
R> colnames(sponsor_matrix) <- senators$all_senators
```

Now that we have collected information on the bills and the Senators, we will briefly introduce how the data could be applied in a network analysis. If you simply care about data collection, but not about network analysis, you can skip the following section without much loss.

12.3 Analyzing the network structure

In order to analyze our data using network analysis techniques, we need to rearrange it to conform to a format that the network packages understand. Two common ways to arrange the data are an edge list or an adjacency list. In the former variant, we generate a two-column matrix where each edge between two nodes or vertices is represented by naming the two vertices an edge connects. In an adjacency list, on the other hand, we store the network data in a nodes-by-nodes matrix, setting a cell to the number of connections between two nodes. While an adjacency list would be computationally more efficient since our data have multiple edges, that is, any two Senators might have been cosponsors on numerous bills—we, nevertheless, create an edge list for coding convenience.

Identifying dyadic relationships

In the network analysis, we assume that there is an undirected relationship between each of the signatories of a particular bill, regardless of whether a senator is a sponsor or a cosponsor. For example, assume there is a bill with one sponsor and three cosponsors. What we would like to have is each possible dyadic relationship between these four actors (see Table 12.2).

There is a simple function available in R—`combn()`—which we will use to find all of these dyadic relationships. We create an empty edge list matrix with two columns and iterate over the matrix of sponsors and cosponsors from Section 12.1. In each iteration we take all

Table 12.2 Dyadic relationships between four hypothetical actors

Node 1	Node 2
Senator A	Senator B
Senator A	Senator C
Senator A	Senator D
Senator B	Senator C
Senator B	Senator D
Senator C	Senator D

The table displays an example of the resulting graph edge list. Specifically, it displays all six possible dyadic combinations with four input senators.

the non-empty elements from a row, find all possible combinations, and attach the resulting two-column matrix to our final matrix.

```
R> edgelist_sponsors <- matrix(NA, nrow = 0, ncol = 2)
R> for(i in 1:nrow(sponsor_matrix)){
R>     if(length(which(!is.na(sponsor_matrix[i,]))) > 1){
R>         edgelist_sponsors <- rbind(
R>             edgelist_sponsors,
R>             t(combn(colnames(sponsor_matrix)[which(!is.na
(sponsor_matrix[i,]))], 2))
R>         )
R>     }
R> }
R> dim(edgelist_sponsors)
```

Performing this operation yields a matrix with a little over 180,000 edges, that is, there are approximately 180,000 unique binary connections between the 109 senators in our dataset. Now we would like to convert these data into the format used in the igraph package which offers a range of tools and some decent plotting facilities.[6] Specifying that we are dealing with an undirected network, the command is

```
R> sponsor_network <- graph.edgelist(edgelist_sponsors,directed = F)
```

12.3.1 Descriptive statistics

Before moving on to some *real* network analysis, let us inspect the data we have gathered. Let us first look at who sponsors/cosponsors most/least. To do so, we simply create a two-row matrix where we collect the individual counts of being a sponsor and cosponsor for each senator.

```
R> result <- matrix(
    NA,
    ncol = ncol(sponsor_matrix),
    nrow = 2,
    dimnames = list(
        c("Sponsor", "Cosponsor"),
        colnames(sponsor_matrix)
    )
)
R> for(i in 1:ncol(sponsor_matrix)){
    result[1, i] <- sum(sponsor_matrix[, i] == "Cosponsor", na.rm = T)
    result[2, i] <- sum(sponsor_matrix[, i] == "Sponsor", na.rm = T)
}
R> result <- t(result)
```

Heavy sponsors Table 12.3 displays a subset of the results of this analysis. We see that Democrats have been the most active sponsors in the 111th Senate, although to be fair they have a slightly

[6]There are several good packages in R to perform network analysis. If you are interested, check out the network, statnet, and sna packages.

Table 12.3 The five top and bottom sponsors

Senator		Sponsor	Cosponsor
Brown, Sherrod	(D-OH)	377	107
Gillibrand, Kirsten E.	(D-NY)	357	74
Casey, Robert P., Jr.	(D-PA)	355	99
Schumer, Charles E.	(D-NY)	333	133
Kerry, John F.	(D-MA)	321	96
Coons, Christopher A.	(D-DE)	11	0
Goodwin, Carte Patrick	(D-WV)	5	1
Salazar, Ken	(D-CO)	4	6
Kirk, Mark Steven	(R-IL)	2	1
Manchin, Joe, III	(D-WV)	1	0

The tables displays the five senators which have sponsored most and least legislation.

better chance of being at the top of the table as our table holds 65 Democratic Senators compared to 43 Republicans and 2 independents.[7]

In the next descriptive statistic we care to find out which senators have the strongest binary connection with each other. The simplest way to do this is to convert our data to an adjacency matrix where the greatest dyadic relationships are summed in a vertex by vertex table. We get this table by making use of the export utility in the igraph package.

```
R> adj_sponsor <- get.adjacency(sponsor_network)
```

Naturally, the resulting matrix is symmetric, as we have no directed relationships. Therefore, we discard the lower triangle of the matrix before calculating the greatest binary relationships.

```
R> adj_sponsor[lower.tri(adj_sponsor)] <- 0
```

Finally, we extract the dyads with the strongest binary relationships. The results are displayed in Table 12.4.

```
R> s10 <- min(sort(as.matrix(adj_sponsor), decreasing = T)[1:10])
R> max_indices <- which(as.matrix(adj_sponsor) >= s10, arr.ind = T)
R> export_names <- matrix(NA, ncol = 2, nrow = 10)
R> for(i in 1:nrow(max_indices)){
R>     export_names[i, 1] <- rownames(adj_sponsor)[max_indices[i,1]]
R>     export_names[i, 2] <- colnames(adj_sponsor)[max_indices[i,2]]
R> }
```

It is fairly obvious that the most active sponsors and co-sponsors would rank high in this table as they have a greater probability to have a strong connection to any given other senator.

[7]To complicate matters, these figures overstate the simple probabilities of the Democratic Senators to be at the top of the table, as a number of Democrats have left the Senate during the 111th Congress. Notably, both Robert Byrd and Ted Kennedy died in office and Joe Biden, Hillary Clinton, and Ken Salazar resigned to work in the administration.

Table 12.4 The senators with the strongest binary connection

	Senator 1		Senator 2	
1	Brown, Sherrod	(D-OH)	Casey, Robert P., Jr.	(D-PA)
2	Brown, Sherrod	(D-OH)	Durbin, Richard	(D-IL)
3	Lautenberg, Frank R.	(D-NJ)	Menendez, Robert	(D-NJ)
4	Brown, Sherrod	(D-OH)	Schumer, Charles E.	(D-NY)
5	Durbin, Richard	(D-IL)	Schumer, Charles E.	(D-NY)
6	Kerry, John F.	(D-MA)	Schumer, Charles E.	(D-NY)
7	Menendez, Robert	(D-NJ)	Schumer, Charles E.	(D-NY)
8	Brown, Sherrod	(D-OH)	Stabenow, Debbie	(D-MI)
9	Casey, Robert P., Jr.	(D-PA)	Specter, Arlen	(D-PA)
10	Schumer, Charles E.	(D-NY)	Gillibrand, Kirsten E.	(D-NY)

12.3.2 Network analysis

Let us begin the analysis by visually inspecting the resulting network. As a first step we would like to simplify the network by turning multiple edges into unique edges and keeping multiples as weights. This is accomplished using the `simplify()` function from the igraph package.

```
R> E(sponsor_network)$weight <- 1
R> sponsor_network_weighted <- simplify(sponsor_network)
R> sponsor_network_weighted
R> head(E(sponsor_network_weighted)$weight)
```

Plotting the network After applying this simplification, our network still has more than 5000 unique edges—much more than can be visually inspected. Hence, for the purpose of plotting we only display those edges that conform to a cutoff point that we define as follows: Only display those edges that have an edge weight greater than the mean edge weight plus one standard deviation. This operation yields the graph in Figure 12.2.

```
R> plot_sponsor <- sponsor_network_weighted
R> plot_sponsor <- delete.edges(plot_sponsor, which(E(plot_sponsor)$weight <
  (mean(E(plot_sponsor)$weight) + sd(E(plot_sponsor)$weight))))
R> plot(plot_sponsor, edge.color = "lightgray", vertex.size = 0, ver-
tex.frame.color = NA, vertex.color = "white", vertex.label.color = "black")
```

We can clearly distinguish the two major parties in this graph as dense blocks. Interestingly, there a numerous senators which are completely disconnected to the graph after applying the thinning operation. If we go into a little more detail, there are a number of remarkable findings which confirm the intuition that cosponsorships are indeed a viable proxy for intra-parliamentary collaboration. Consider Olympia Snowe from Maine at the center of the graph. While still in office she was widely regarded as one of the most moderate Republicans in the Senate, which is nicely reflected in her being one of the only bridging nodes in the graph. In fact, this finding is even more remarkable if one considers that she has numerous strong connections to the Democratic party while her only strong connection to the Republican party

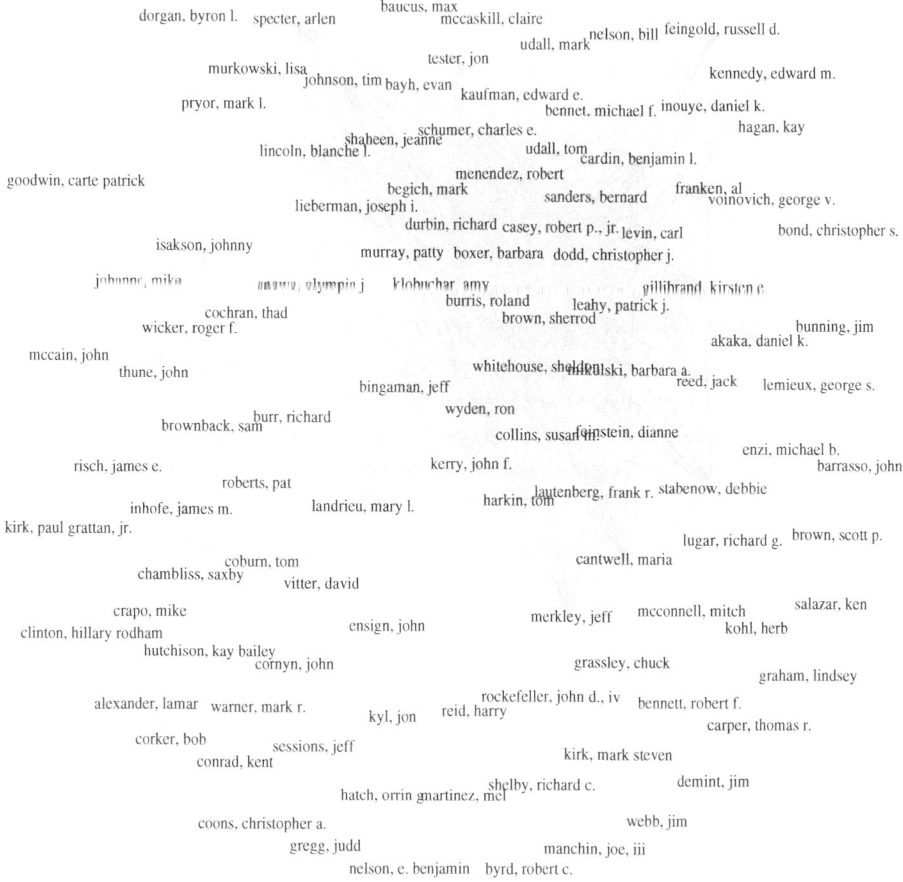

Figure 12.2 Cosponsorship network of senators

is Senator Richard Burr from North Carolina. Time and again, she was considered one of the likely candidates for a party switch which finds a clear visual expression in our analysis. By a similar token, consider Mary Landrieu from Louisiana. She is frequently labeled as one of the most conservative Democrats in the Democratic party and indeed she also takes up a central location in our graph.

Table 12.5 The five most central actors

Senator	Betweenness	
Goodwin, Carte Patrick	(D-WV)	2217
Salazar, Ken	(D-CO)	2058
Clinton, Hillary Rodham	(D-NY)	1062
Kirk, Paul Grattan, Jr.	(D-MA)	618
Coons, Christopher A.	(D-DE)	245

The tables displays the five most central senators, based on their betweenness scores.

Betweenness centrality

Consider now a true network metric—the betweenness centrality. This measure describes how central any given node is in the overall network, which is typically taken as an indicator of influence in a network. It is defined as the shortest path from all nodes to all other passing through a node. The higher the score, the more central the actor's position in the network. Table 12.5 provides an overview of the five most central actors, ranked by betweenness. We find that among the five most central actors there are no less than two who went on to serve as secretaries in the Obama Administration.

12.4 Conclusion

Scholars of parliamentary politics have recently begun employing large-scale data sources in order to come to terms with long-standing research questions. Among the issues that have come under scrutiny are patterns of intra-parliamentary collaboration. Using cosponsorships as proxies for cooperation, a number of scholars have investigated these manifested networks. This chapter has demonstrated how to assemble the necessary data to perform analyses of the like that have been proposed in the literature. We have shown that the data informing these analyses are vast. We were able to collect well over 100,000 unique dyadic relations in a single senatorial term. In terms of substance, we have not delved deeply into the data but, using very simple indicators, we were able to show that the data exhibit strong face validity. First, moderate members of either party have been shown to take up plausible center points in the network. Second, senators who are widely perceived as influential members of the body could indeed be shown to take up more central locations in the network.

As in many of the examples throughout this volume there are clear advantages of automatically collecting the data as proposed here. We have only assembled a single senatorial term, but the resulting dataset is immense. Never before have datasets of such size been in the reach of single researchers interested in a particular topic. What is more, not only is the data vast, it is also freely available to anyone who brings the right techniques to the table. It can quickly be updated so that results are informed by current events. And finally, using automatic data assembly one avoids the risk of coding errors in the data which are to be expected when hand-coding a dataset of this size. We encourage you to assemble the data yourselves, toy around with it and investigate the *ad hoc* claims in this exploratory chapter to present some new insights on patterns of parliamentary collaboration.

13

Parsing information from semistructured documents

We have learned how to handle and extract information from well-defined data structures like XML or JSON. There are standardized methods for translating these formats into R data structures. Content on the Web is highly heterogeneous, however. We are occasionally confronted with data which are structured but in a format for which no parser exists.

In this chapter, we demonstrate how to construct a parser that is able to transform pure character data into R data structures. As an example we identified climate data that are offered by the Natural Resources Conservation Service at the United States Department of Agriculture.[1] We focus on a set of text files that can be downloaded from an FTP server.[2] While the download procedure is simple, the files cannot be put into an R data structure directly. An excerpt from one of these files is shown in Figure 13.1. The displayed data are structured in a way which is human-readable but not (yet) understandable by a computer program. The main goal is to describe the structure in a way that a computer can handle them.

Over the course of the case study we make use of RCurl to list files on and retrieve them from FTP servers and draw on R's text manipulation capabilities to build a parser for the data files. Regular expressions are a crucial tool to solve this task.

---

[1]The example is inspired by a short code snippet in the RCurl manual which demonstrates how do download data from FTP servers (see http://cran.at.r-project.org/web/packages/RCurl/RCurl.pdf). The question is how to post-process semistructured data of this sort with R.

[2]The National Water and Climate Center also provides a *SOAP*-based web service (see http://www.wcc.nrcs.usda.gov/web_service/awdb_web_service_landing.htm). We ignore this tool for a moment and concentrate on the raw text files to demonstrate how to extract information from semistructured contexts.

Automated Data Collection with R: A Practical Guide to Web Scraping and Text Mining, First Edition.
Simon Munzert, Christian Rubba, Peter Meißner and Dominic Nyhuis.

13.1 Downloading data from the FTP server

First, we load RCurl and stringr. As we have learned, RCurl provides functionality to access data from FTP servers (see Section 9.1.2) and stringr offers consistent functions for string processing with R.

```
R> library(RCurl)
R> library(stringr)
```

A folder called *Data* is created to store the retrieved data files. The data we are looking for are stored on an FTP server and accessible at a single url which we store in `ftp`. Note that this is only a rather tiny subdirectory—the server provides tons of additional climate data.

```
R> dir.create("Data")
R> ftp <- "ftp://ftp.wcc.nrcs.usda.gov/data/climate/table/
temperature/history/california/"
```

The RCurl function `getURL()` with option `dirlistonly` set to `TRUE` asks the FTP server to return a list of files instead of downloading a file.

```
R> filelist <- getURL(ftp, dirlistonly = TRUE)
```

This is the returned list of files:

```
R> str_sub(filelist, 1, 119)
[1] "19103s_tavg.txt\r\n19103s_tmax.txt\r\n19103s_tmin.txt\r\n19105s_
tavg.txt\r\n19105s_tmax.txt\r\n19105s_tmin.txt\r\n19106s_tavg.txt\r\n"
```

In order to identify the file names, we split the text by carriage returns (`\r`) and new line characters (`\n`) and keep only those vector items that are not empty.

```
R> filelist <- unlist(str_split(filelist, "\r\n"))
R> filelist <- filelist[!filelist == ""]
R> filelist[1:3]
[1] "19103s_tavg.txt" "19103s_tmax.txt" "19103s_tmin.txt"
```

A comparison with the files at the FTP interface reveals that we have succeeded in identifying the file names. As we are not interested in minimum or maximum temperatures for now, we use `str_detect()` to only keep files containing `tavg` in their file name.

```
R> filesavg <- str_detect(filelist, "tavg")
R> filesavg <- filelist[filesavg]
R> filesavg[1:3]
[1] "19103s_tavg.txt" "19105s_tavg.txt" "19106s_tavg.txt"
```

To download the files we have to construct the full URLs that point to their location on the server. We concatenate the base URL and the created vector of file names and retrieve a vector of full URLs.

```
R> urlsavg <- str_c(ftp, filesavg)
R> length(urlsavg)
[1] 32
R> urlsavg[1]
```

```
[1] "ftp://ftp.wcc.nrcs.usda.gov/data/climate/table/temperature/
history/california/19l03s_tavg.txt"
```

Having built the URLs for the 32 files, we can now loop over each URL and save the text files to our local folder. We introduce a check if the file has previously been downloaded using the `file.exists()` function and stop for 1 second after each server request. The files themselves are downloaded with `download.file()` and stored in the *Data* folder.

```
R> for (i in seq_along(urlsavg)) {
     fname <- str_c("Data/", filesavg[i])
     if (!file.exists(fname)) {
         download.file(urlsavg[i], fname)
         Sys.sleep(1)
     }
}
```

A brief inspection of the local folder reveals that we succeeded in downloading all 32 files.

```
R> length(list.files("Data"))
[1] 32
R> list.files("Data")[1:3]
[1] "19l03s_tavg.txt" "19l05s_tavg.txt" "19l06s_tavg.txt"
```

13.2 Parsing semistructured text data

Now that we have downloaded all the files we want, we can have a look at their content. Let us reconsider Figure 13.1 which provides an example of the content of the files. Because they are quite long—more than 1,000 lines, we only present a small sample.

Each file provides daily temperature data for one station in California ranging from 1987 up to 2013. We see from the sample that for each year there is a separate section ending with `----------`. The first line tells us something about the source of the data (`/cdbs/ca/snot06`), followed by the year expressed as two digits (`88`) and the type of data that is presented (`Average Air Temperature`). Next is a line identifying the station at which the temperatures were measured (`Station : CA19L03S, HAGAN'S MEADOW`), followed by a line expressing the unit in which the measurements are stored (`Unit = degrees C`). **A look at the raw data**

After the header sections comes the actual data presented in a table, where columns indicate months and rows refer to days. If days do not exist within a month—like November 31—we find three dashes in the cell: `----`. Beneath the daily temperature we also find a section with monthly data that provides mean, maximum, and minimum temperatures for each month. If the temperature data tables would be the only information provided and the only information we were interested in, our task would be easy because R can handle tables written in fixed-width format: `read.fwf()` reads such data and transforms them automatically into data frames. The problem is that we do not want to loose the information from the header section because it tells us to which year and which station the temperatures belong to. **Why base R functions fail**

When we proceed, it is important to think about which information should be extracted and what the data should look like at the end. In the end a long table with daily temperatures and variables for the day, month, and year when the temperatures were measured as well as

```
/cdbs/ca/snot06  88  Average Air Temperature

Station : CA19L03S, HAGAN'S MEADOW
-------    Unit = degrees C

day    oct    nov    dec    jan    feb    mar    apr    may    [...]
---    ---    ---    ---    ---    ---    ---    ---    ---    [...]
  1     10      3     -0    -14     -9     -0     -1     -4    [...]
  2      9      2      0    -10    -10     -2     -1     -5    [...]
  3     10     -1      3     -3    -10     -1      3      1    [...]

[...]

 31      2    ---    -12     -4    ---     -3    ---     -0    [...]

mean     6     -0     -5     -3     -2     -0      2      4    [...]
max     11      6      5      3      2      6      7     11    [...]
min     -3     -6    -15    -14    -10    -12     -3     -5    [...]
----------
/cdbs/ca/snot06  89  Average Air Temperature

Station : CA19L03S, HAGAN'S MEADOW
-------    Unit = degrees C

day    oct    nov    dec    jan    feb    mar    apr    may    [...]

[...]
```

Figure 13.1 Excerpt from a text file on temperature data from Californian weather stations, accessible at ftp://ftp.wcc.nrcs.usda.gov/data/climate/table/temperature/history/california/

the station's id and its name should do. The resulting data structure should look like the one depicted in Table 13.1.

Import data

Because information is separated into sections, we should first split the text to turn them into separate vectors. To do this, we first read in all the text files via `readLines()` and input the resulting lines into a vector.

```
R> txt <- character()
R> for (i in 1:length(filesavg)) {
    txt <- c(txt, readLines(str_c("Data/", filesavg[i])))
}
```

In a next step, we collapse the whole vector into one single line, where the newline character (`\n`) marks the end of the original lines. We split that single line at each occurrence of `----------\n`, marking the end of a section.

```
R> txt <- str_c(txt, collapse = "\n")
R> txtparts <- unlist(str_split(txt, "----------\n"))
```

Table 13.1 Desired data structure after parsing

day	month	year	id	name
1	1	1982	XYZ001784	Deepwood
2	1	1982	XYZ001784	Deepwood
...	...	...	...	...
31	12	1984	XYZ001786	Highwood
1	1	1985	XYZ001786	Highwood
...	...	...	...	...
3	3	2003	XYZ001800	Northwood
4	3	2003	XYZ001800	Northwood

The resulting vector contains one section per line.

```
R> str_sub(txtparts[28:30], 1, 134)
[1] "\n***This data is provisional and subject to change.\n/cdbs/ca/snot06
84  Average Air Temperature\n\nStation : CA19L05S, BLUE LAKES\n----"
[2] "/cdbs/ca/snot06  85  Average Air Temperature\n\nStation : CA19L05S,
BLUE LAKES\n-------   Unit = degrees C\n\nday    oct    nov    dec    jan "
[3] "/cdbs/ca/snot06  86  Average Air Temperature\n\nStation : CA19L05S,
BLUE LAKES\n-------   Unit = degrees C\n\nday    oct    nov    dec    jan "
```

In a text editor, this would look as follows:

```
R> cat(str_sub(txtparts[28], 1, 604))

***This data is provisional and subject to change.
/cdbs/ca/snot06  84  Average Air Temperature

Station : CA19L05S, BLUE LAKES
-------   Unit = degrees C

day  oct  nov  dec  jan  feb  mar  apr  may  jun  jul  aug  sep
---  ---  ---  ---  ---  ---  ---  ---  ---  ---  ---  ---  ---
  1    1    2   -3   -4   -1   -2   -8   -1         12   12    8
  2    3    1   -2   -6   -4    0   -6   -2    7   14   12    9
  3    3    2   -3   -3   -5   -2   -4    0    6   16   11   11
  4    5    5   -6   -1   -4   -4   -1    3    6   17   11   12
  5    8    5  -11   -0   -4   -5   -0    1    2   17   12   13
```

Now we need to do some cleansing to get rid of the statement saying that the data are provisional and delete all lines of the vector that are empty.

```
R> txtparts <- str_replace(txtparts,"\n\\*\\*\\*This data is
provisional and subject to change.", "")
R> txtparts <- str_replace(txtparts,"^\n", "")
R> txtparts <- txtparts[txtparts!=""]
```

Having inserted each section into a separate line, we can now build functions for extracting information that can be applied to each line, as each line contains the same kind of information

Extracting information

structured in the same way. We start by extracting the year in which the temperature was measured. To do this, we build a regular expression that looks for a character sequence that starts with two digits, followed by two white spaces, followed by *Average Air Temperature*: `"[[:digit:]]{2}  Average Air Temperature"`. We then extract the digits from that substring and append the two digits in a third step to a four digit year.

```
R> year <- str_extract(txtparts, "[[:digit:]]{2}  Average Air Temperature")
R> year[1:4]
[1] "87  Average Air Temperature" "88  Average Air Temperature"
[3] "89  Average Air Temperature" "90  Average Air Temperature"
R> year <- str_extract(year, "[[:digit:]]{2}")
R> year <- ifelse(year < 20, str_c(20, year), str_c(19, year))
R> year <- as.numeric(year)
R> year[5:15]
 [1] 1991 1992 1993 1994 1995 1996 1997 1998 1999 2000 2001
```

We also gather the stations' names as well as the identification. For this we first extract the line where the station information is saved.

```
R> station <- str_extract(txtparts, "Station : .+?\n")
R> station[1:2]
[1] "Station : CA19L03S, HAGAN'S MEADOW\n"
[2] "Station : CA19L03S, HAGAN'S MEADOW\n"
```

We delete those parts that are of no interest to us—`Station :` and `\n` ...

```
R> station <- str_replace_all(station, "(Station : )|(\n)", "")
R> station[1:2]
[1] "CA19L03S, HAGAN'S MEADOW" "CA19L03S, HAGAN'S MEADOW"
```

...and split the remaining text into one part that captures the id and one that contains the name of the station.

```
R> station <- str_split(station, ", ")
R> station[1]
[[1]]
[1] "CA19L03S"        "HAGAN'S MEADOW"
```

The splitting of the text results in a list where each list item contains two strings. The first string of each list item is the id while the second captures the name. To extract the first and second string from each list item, we apply the `[` operator to each item.

```
R> id <- sapply(station, "[", 1)
R> name <- sapply(station, "[", 2)
R> id[1:3]
[1] "CA19L03S" "CA19L03S" "CA19L03S"

R> name[1:3]
[1] "HAGAN'S MEADOW" "HAGAN'S MEADOW" "HAGAN'S MEADOW"
```

Extracting temperatures Now we can turn our attention to extracting the daily temperatures. The temperatures form a table in fixed-width format that can be read and transformed by `read.fwf()`. In the fixed width format each entry of a column has the same width of characters and lines are separated by newline characters or carriage returns or a combination of both. What we have to do is to extract that part of each section that forms the fixed width table and apply `read.fwf()` to it.

Our first task is to extract the part that contains the temperature table. To do so, we use a regular expression that extracts `day` and everything after.

```
R> temperatures <- str_extract(txtparts, "day.*")
```

Further below, we will write the next steps into a function that we can apply to each of the temperature tables, but for now we go through the necessary steps using only one temperature table to develop all the intermediate steps.

As `read.fwf()` expects a filename as input, we first have to write our temperature table into a temporary file using the `tempfile()` function.

```
R> tf <- tempfile()
R> writeLines(temperatures[5], tf)
```

We can then use `read.fwf()` to read the content back in. The `width` option tells the function the column width in characters.

```
R> temptable <- read.fwf(tf, width=c(3, 7, rep(6, 11)), stringsAsFactors
= F)
R> temptable[c(1:5,32:38), 1:10]
     V1     V2    V3    V4    V5    V6    V7    V8    V9   V10
1   day    oct   nov   dec   jan   feb   mar   apr   may   jun
2   ---    ---   ---   ---   ---   ---   ---   ---   ---   ---
3     1     10     1    -3    -6    -2     0     2     2     7
4     2      9    -4    -7    -6     1    -3    -0    -4     6
5     3      8    -5    -5    -5     1    -3    -1    -2     6
32   30      5    -2   -13    -4   ---    -2     3     7     7
33   31      5   ---    -9    -3   ---     0   ---     7   ---
34 <NA>   <NA>  <NA>  <NA>  <NA>  <NA>  <NA>  <NA>  <NA>  <NA>
35  mea n    6    -1    -7    -4     0    -5    -1     2     6
36  max     10     7     5     1     3     1     6     8     7
37  min     -0   -10   -22    -9    -2   -10    -6    -4     6
38 <NA>   <NA>  <NA>  <NA>  <NA>  <NA>  <NA>  <NA>  <NA>  <NA>
```

There are several lines in the data that do not contain the data we need. Therefore, we only keep lines 3–33 and also discard the first column.

```
R> temptable <- temptable[3:33, -1]
```

In the next step, we transform the table into a vector. Using `as.numeric()` and `unlist()` all numbers will be transferred to type numeric, while all cells containing only white spaces or `---` are set to `NA`.

```
R> temptable <- as.numeric(unlist(temptable))
```

Reconstructing tables

Having discarded the table structure and kept only the temperatures, we now have to reconstruct the days and months belonging to the temperatures. Fortunately, `unlist()` always decomposes data frames in the same way. It starts with all rows of the first column and appends the values of the following columns one by one. As we know that in the temperature tables rows referred to days and columns to months, we can simply repeat the day sequence 1–31 twelve times to get the days right. Similarly, we have to repeat each month 31 times.

Note that the order of the months differs from the usual 1–12 because the tables start with October.

```
R> day <- rep(1:31, 12)
R> month <- rep(c(10:12, 1:9), each = 31)
```

Now we combine the information on the year of measurement and the weather station with the temperatures and get the data for 1 year.

```
R> temptable <- data.frame(avgtemp = temptable, day = day, month =
month, year = year[5], name = name[5], id = id[5])

R> head(temptable, 3)
  avgtemp day month year            name       id
1      10   1    10 1991 HAGAN'S MEADOW CA19L03S
2       9   2    10 1991 HAGAN'S MEADOW CA19L03S
3       8   3    10 1991 HAGAN'S MEADOW CA19L03S
```

Constructing a convenient parser function To get all the data, we have to repeat the procedure for all files. For convenience we have constructed a parsing function that takes a file name as argument and returns a ready-to-use data frame. The code is shown in Figure 13.2. Applying the function yields:

```
R> tempData1 <- parseTemp(str_c("Data/", filesavg[1]))

R> dim(tempData1)
[1] 9551    6
R> tempData1[500:502, ]
    avgtemp day month year       id           name
774       6  29    10 1989 CA19L03S HAGAN'S MEADOW
775       6  30    10 1989 CA19L03S HAGAN'S MEADOW
776       4  31    10 1989 CA19L03S HAGAN'S MEADOW
```

Parsing all files This looks like a successful parsing result. Furthermore, to conveniently parse all files at once, we can create a wrapper function that takes a vector of file names as argument and returns a combined data frame.

```
R> parseTemps <- function(filenames) {
    tmp <- lapply(filenames, parseTemp)
    tempData <- NULL
    for (i in seq_along(tmp)) tempData <- rbind(tempData, tmp[[i]])
    return(tempData)
}
```

Finally we apply the wrapper to all files in our folder.

```
R> tempData <- parseTemps(str_c("Data/", filesavg))

R> dim(tempData)
[1] 252463      6
```

```
parseTemp <- function(filename)
# get text
   txt <- paste( readLines(filename), collapse="\n")
# split text into year tables
   txtparts <- unlist(str_split(txt, "----------\n"))
# cleansing
   txtparts <- str_replace(txtparts,
   "\n\\*\\*\\*This data is provisional and subject to change.", "")
   txtparts <- str_replace(txtparts,"^\n","")
   txtparts <- txtparts[txtparts!=""]
# get the year
   year <- str_extract(txtparts,"[[:digit:]]{2}  Average Air Temperature")
   year <- str_extract(year,"[[:digit:]]{2}")
   year <- ifelse(year < 20, str_c(20,year), str_c(19,year))
   year <- as.numeric(year)
# get station and name
   station <- str_extract(txtparts, "Station : .+?\n")
   station     <- str_replace_all(station, "(Station : )|(\n)", "")
   station     <- str_split(station,", ")
   id          <- sapply(station, '[', 1)
   name        <- sapply(station, '[', 2)
# extract part of the sections that contains daily temperatures
   temperatures <- str_extract(txtparts, "day.*")
# prepare object to store temperature data
   tempData <- data.frame(avgtemp = NA, day = NA, month = NA,
                    year = NA, id = "", name = "")
# generate day and month patterns matching the order of temperatures
   day      <- rep(1:31, 12)
   month    <- rep( c(10:12,1:9), each=31 )
# helper function
   doTemp <- function(temperatures, year, name, id){
# write fixed width table into temporary file
    tf <- tempfile()
    writeLines(temperatures, tf)
# read in data and transform to data frame
    temptable <- read.fwf(tf, width = c(3,7,6,6,6,6,6,6,6,6,6,6,6),
                     stringsAsFactors = F)
# keep only those lines and rows entailing day-temperatures
    temptable <- temptable[3:33, -1]
# transform data frame of strings to vector of type numeric
    temptable <- suppressWarnings(as.numeric(unlist(temptable)))
# combine data
    temptable <- data.frame(avgtemp = temptable, day = day,
              month = month, year = year, name = name, id = id)
# add data to tempData
    tempData <<- rbind(tempData, temptable)
 }
 mapply(doTemp, temperatures, year, name, id)
 tempData <- tempData[!is.na(tempData$avgtemp),]
 return(tempData)
}
```

Figure 13.2 R-based parsing function for temperature text files

13.3 Visualizing station and temperature data

We conclude the study with some examples of what to do with the data. First it would be nice to know the location of the weather stations. We already know that they are in California, but want to be a little more specific. Browsing the FTP server we find a file that contains data on the stations—station names, their position expressed as latitudes and longitudes as well as their altitude. We download the file and read it in via `read.csv()` .

```
R> download.file("ftp://ftp.wcc.nrcs.usda.gov/states/ca/jchen/CA_
sites.dat", "Data_CA/CA_sites.dat")

R> stationData <- read.csv("Data_CA/CA_sites.dat", header = F, sep =
"|")[,-c(1,2,7:9)]
R> names(stationData) <- c("name","lat","lon","alt")

R> head(stationData,2)
        name lat   lon  alt
1   ADIN MTN 4115 12046 6200
2 BLUE LAKES 3836 11955 8000
```

With regards to the map which we are going to use, we have to rescale the coordinates. First, we multiply all longitudes by −1 to get general longitudes and divide all coordinates by 100. Altitudes are measured in foot, so we transform them to meters.

```
R> stationData$lon <- stationData$lon * -1
R> stationData[, c("lat", "lon")] <- stationData[, c("lat", "lon")]/100
R> stationData$alt <- stationData$alt/3.2808399
R> stationData <- stationData[order(stationData$lat), ]
R> head(stationData, 2)
                    name   lat    lon  alt
25 VIRGINIA LAKES RIDGE 38.05 -119.2 2804
14         LEAVITT LAKE 38.16 -119.4 2865
```

Downloading maps Now we plot the stations' locations on a map. In R, there are several packages suitable for plotting maps (see also Chapter 15). We choose RgoogleMaps which enables us to use services provided by Google and OpenStreetMap to download maps that we can use for plotting. We download map data from Open Street Maps using the `GetMap.OSM()` function. With this function we define a bounding box of coordinates and a scale factor. The map data are saved on disk in PNG format as *map.png* and in an R object called `map` for later use:

```
R> map <- GetMap.OSM(latR = c(37.5, 42), lonR = c(-125, -115), scale =
5000000, destfile = "map.png", GRAYSCALE = TRUE, NEWMAP = TRUE)
```

Mapping stations Now we can use `PlotOnStaticMap()` to print the weather stations' locations on the map we previously downloaded. The result is presented in Figure 13.3.

```
R> png("stationmap.png", width = dim(readPNG("map.png"))[2], height =
dim(readPNG("map.png"))[1])

R> PlotOnStaticMap(map, lat = stationData$lat, lon = stationData$lon,
cex = 2, pch = 19, col = rgb(0, 0, 0, 0.5), add = FALSE)
```

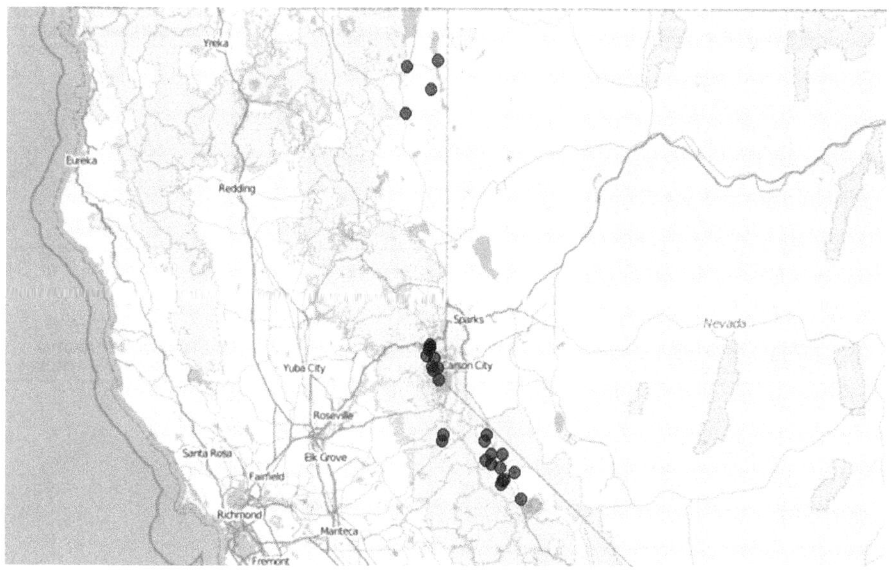

Figure 13.3 Weather station locations on an OpenStreetMaps map

Creating temperature curves

Finally, we visualize the temperature data. Let us look at the average temperatures per month for six out of 27 stations. First, we aggregate the temperatures per month and station using the `aggregate()` function.

```
R> monthlyTemp <- aggregate(x  = tempData$avgtemp, by = list(name =
tempData$name, month = tempData$month), FUN = mean)
```

The stations we choose are representative of all others—we select three stations which are placed north of the the mean latitude and three south of it. Furthermore, within each group stations should differ regarding their altitude and should roughly match one station of the other group. Looking through the candidates we find the following stations to be fitting and extract their coordinates and their altitude:

```
R> stationNames <- c("ADIN MTN", "INDEPENDENCE CAMP", "SQUAW VALLEY
G.C.", "SPRATT CREEK", "LEAVITT MEADOWS","POISON FLAT")

R> stationAlt <- stationData[match(stationNames, stationData$name), ]$alt
R> stationLat <- stationData[match(stationNames, stationData$name), ]$lat
R> stationLon <- stationData[match(stationNames, stationData$name), ]$lon
```

Then, we prepare a plotting function to use on all plots. The function first defines an object called `iffer` that serves to select only those monthly temperatures that belong to the station to be plotted. The overall average per station and month is plotted with adequate title and axis labels. We add a horizontal line to mark 0°C . To get an idea of the variation of temperature measurements over time, we add the actual temperature measurements in a last step as small gray dots.

```
R> plotTemps <- function(i){
R>      iffer <- monthlyTemp$name == stationNames[i]
```

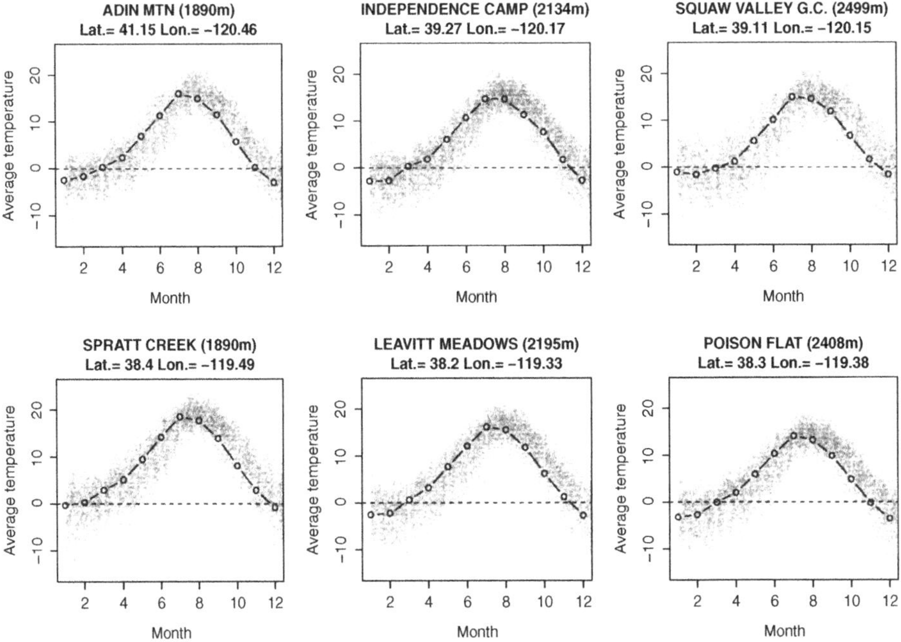

Figure 13.4 Overall monthly temperature means for selected weather stations. Lines present average monthly temperatures in degree Celsius for all years in the dataset. Small gray dots are daily temperatures for all years within the dataset.

```
R>      plot(monthlyTemp[iffer, c("month", "x")],
R>           type = "b", main = str_c(stationNames[i],
R>           "(",round(stationAlt[i]), "m)", "\n Lat.= ",
R>           stationLat[i], " Lon.= ", stationLon[i]),
R>           ylim = c(-15, 25), ylab = "average temperature")
R>      abline(h = 0,lty = 2)
R>      iffer2 <- tempData$name == stationNames[i]
R>      points(tempData$month[iffer2] + tempData$day[iffer2] *0.032,
R>             jitter(tempData$avgtemp[iffer2], 3),
R>             col = rgb(0.2, 0.2, 0.2, 0.1), pch = ".")
R>}
```

Having defined the plot function, we loop through the selection of stations.

```
R> par(mfrow = c(2, 3))
R> for (i in seq_along(stationNames)) plotTemps(i)
```

Figure 13.4 presents the average monthly temperatures. Little surprisingly, the higher the altitude of the station and the more north the station is located, the lower the average temperatures.

14

Predicting the 2014 Academy Awards using Twitter

Social media and the social network Twitter, in particular, have attracted the curiosity of scientists from various disciplines. The fact that millions of people regularly interact with the world by tweeting provides invaluable insight into people's feelings, attitudes, and behavior. An increasingly popular approach to make use of this vast amount of public communication is to generate forecasts of various types of events. Twitter data have been used as a prediction tool for elections (Tumasjan et al. 2011), spread of influenza (Broniatowski et al. 2013; Culotta 2010), movie sales (Asur and Huberman 2010), or the stock market (Bollen et al. 2011).

The idea behind these approaches is the "wisdom of the crowds" effect. The aggregated judgment of many people has been shown to frequently be more precise than the judgment of experts or even the smartest person in a group of forecasters (Hogarth 1978). In that sense, if it is possible to infer forecasts from people's tweets, one might expect a fairly accurate forecast of the outcome of an event.

In this case study, we attempt to predict the winners of the 2014 Academy Awards using the tweets in the days prior to the event. Specifically, we try to predict the results of three awards—best picture, best actress, and best actor. A similar effort to ours is proposed by Ghomi et al. (2013). In the next section, we elaborate the data collection by introducing the Twitter APIs and the specific setup we used to gather the tweets. Section 14.2 goes on to elaborate the data preparation and the forecasts.

Automated Data Collection with R: A Practical Guide to Web Scraping and Text Mining, First Edition.
Simon Munzert, Christian Rubba, Peter Meißner and Dominic Nyhuis.

Table 14.1 Overview of selected functions from the twitteR package

Function	Description	Example
`searchTwitter()`	Search for tweets that match a certain query; the query should be URL-encoded and special query operators can be used[1]	`searchTwitter("#superbowl")`
`getUser()`	Gather information about Twitter users with public profiles (or the API user)	`getUser("RDataCollection")`
`getTrends()`	Pull trending topics from a given location defined by a WOEID	`getTrends(2422673)`
`twListToDF()`	Convert list of *twitteR* class objects into data frame	`twListToDF(tweets)`

14.1 Twitter APIs: Overview

Before turning to the Twitter-based forecasts, we provide an overview of the basic features of Twitter's APIs.[2] The range of features is vast and we will only make use of a tiny part, so it is useful to get an intuition about the possibilities of Twitter's web services. Twitter offers various APIs for developers. They are documented at https://dev.twitter.com/docs. Using the APIs requires authentication via *OAuth* (see Section 9.1.11). In the following, we shortly discuss the *REST* API and the Streaming APIs.

14.1.1 The *REST* API

The *REST* API comprises a rich set of resources.[3] They offer access to the user's account, timeline, direct messages, friends, and followers. It is also possible to retrieve trending topics for a specific location (WOEID; see Section 9.1.10) or to collect tweets that match certain filter parameters, for example, keywords. Note, however, that there are restrictions regarding possibility to gather statuses retrospectively. There are also rate limits to bear in mind. As both limits are subject to changes, we refer to the documentation at https://dev.twitter.com/docs/rate-limiting/1.1 for details.

The twitteR package provides a wrapper for the *REST* API (Gentry 2013), thus we do not have to specify *GET* and *POST* requests ourselves to connect to Twitter's web service. The package provides functionality to convert incoming JSON data into common R data structures. We list a subset of the package's functions which we find most useful in Table 14.1. For a

---

[1] See https://dev.twitter.com/docs/using-search.

[2] We assume that you have a basic knowledge about how Twitter works. If not, check out the amusing introduction at http://www.momthisishowtwitterworks.com/

[3] For a detailed overview, see https://dev.twitter.com/docs/api/1.1

more detailed description of the package check out Jeff Gentry's helpful introduction at http://geoffjentry.hexdump.org/twitteR.pdf

14.1.2 The streaming APIs

Another set of Twitter APIs are subsumed under the label *Streaming APIs*. They allow *low latency* access to Twitter's global data stream, that is practically in real time.[4] In contrast to the *REST* APIs, the Streaming APIs require a persistent HTTP connection. As long as the connection is maintained, the application that taps the API streams data from one of the data flows.

Types of Streaming APIs

Several of these streams exist. First, *Public Streams* provide samples of the public data flow. Twitter offers about 1% of the full sample of Tweets to ordinary users of the API. The sample can be filtered by certain predicates, for example, by user IDs, keywords, or locations. For data mining purposes, this kind of stream might be one of the most interesting, as it provides tools to scour Twitter by many criteria. In this case study, we will tap this API to identify tweets that mention the 2014 Academy Awards by filtering a set of keywords. The second type of Streaming API provides access to *User Streams*. This API returns tweets from the user's timeline. Again, we can filter tweets according to keywords or types of messages, for example, only tweets from the user or tweets from her followings. Finally, the third type of Streaming API is *Site Streams* which provides real-time updates from users for certain services. This is basically not much different from *User Streams* but additionally indicates the recipient of a tweet.[5] At the time of writing, the *Site Streams* API is in a restricted beta status, so we refrain from going into more details.

Fortunately, we do not have to become experts with the inner workings of the streaming APIs, as the streamR provides a convenient wrapper to access them with R (Barberá 2013). Table 14.2 provides an overview of the most important functions that we have used to assemble the dataset that we draw on for the predictions in the second part of this chapter.

14.1.3 Collecting and preparing the data

To collect the sample of tweets that revolve around the 2014 Academy Awards, we set up a connection to the Streaming API. The connection was opened on February 28, 2014 and closed on March 2, 2014, the day the 86th Academy Awards ceremony took place at the Dolby Theatre in Hollywood.

We began by registering an application with Twitter to retrieve the necessary *OAuth* credentials which allow tapping the Twitter services. A connection to the Streaming API was established using the streamR interface. The command to initiate the collection was

```
R> filterStream("tweets_oscars.json", track = c("Oscars", "Oscars2014"),
timeout = 10800, oauth = twitCred)
```

We filtered the sample of tweets using `filterStream()` with the `track` option with the keywords "Oscars" and "Oscars2014", which matched any tweet that contained these terms in the form of hash tags or pure text. We split the process into streams of 3 hours each ($60 * 60 * 3 = 10,800$ for the `timeout` argument) to store the incoming tweets in

---

[4] See the Streaming APIs' documentation at https://dev.twitter.com/docs/api/streaming

[5] See also https://dev.twitter.com/docs/streaming-apis/streams/site

Table 14.2 Overview of selected functions from the streamR package

Function	Description	Example
`filterStream()`	Connection to the *Public Streams* API; allows to filter by keywords (`track` argument), users (`follow`), locations (`locations`), and language	`filterStream(file.name = "superbowl_tweets.json", track = "superbowl", oauth = twitter_sig)'`
`sampleStream()`	Connection to the *Public Streams* API; returns a small random sample of public tweets	`sampleStream(file.name = "tweets.json", timeout = 60, oauth = twitter_sig)'`
`userStream()`	Connection to the *User Streams* API; returns tweets from the user's timeline; allows to filter by message type, keywords, and location	`sampleStream(userStream = "mytweets.json", with = "user", oauth = twitter_sig)'`
`parseTweets()`	Parses the downloaded tweets, that is, returns the data in a data frame	`parseTweets("tweets.json")'`

manageable JSON files. All in all we collected around 10 GB of raw data, or approximately 2,000,000 tweets.

After the collection was complete, we parsed the single files using the `parseTweets()` function in order to turn the JSON files into an R data frame. We merge all files into a single data frame. Storing the table in the Rdata format reduced the memory consumption of the collected tweets to around 300 MB.

```
R> tweets <- parseTweets("tweets_oscars.json", simplify = TRUE)
```

14.2 Twitter-based forecast of the 2014 Academy Awards

14.2.1 Visualizing the data

Before turning to the analysis of the content of the tweets, let us visually inspect the volume of the data for a moment. Specifically, we want to create a figure of the number of tweets per hour in our search period from the end of February to the beginning of March, 2014.[6] The easiest thing to aggregate the frequency of tweets by hour is to convert the character vector in the dataset `created_at` to a true time variable of type `POSIXct`. We make use of the lubridate package which facilitates working with dates and times (Grolemund and Wickham 2011). We also set our locale to US English to be able to parse the English names of the months and

[6]The data are available at http://www.r-datacollection.com. We invite you to download the data and play around with it yourself. Maybe you are able to spot something that we failed to make out with our simple analysis.

week days. Chances are that you have to adapt the value in the `Sys.setlocale()` function to the needs of your machine.[7]

```
R> library(lubridate)
R> Sys.setlocale("LC_TIME", "en_US.UTF-8")
```

To parse the time stamp in the dataset, we use the function `as.POSIXct()` where we specify the variable, the timezone, and the format of the time stamp. Let us have a look at the first time stamp to get a sense of the format.

```
R> dat$created_at[1]
[1] "Fri Feb 28 10:11:14 +0000 2014"
```

We have to provide the information that is contained in the time stamp in abstract terms. In this case the stamp contains the weekday (`%a`), the month (`%b`), the day (`%d`), the time (`%H:%M:%S`), an offset for the timezone (`%z`), and the year (`%Y`). We abstract the various pieces of information with the percentage placeholders and let R parse the values.

```
R> dat$time <- as.POSIXct(dat$created_at, tz = "UTC", format = "%a
%b %d %H:%M:%S %z %Y")
```

Now that we have created a veritable time stamp where R is able to make sense of the information that is contained in the stamp, we can use the convenience functions from the lubridate package to round the time to the nearest hour. This is accomplished with the `round_date()` function where we specify the `unit` argument to be `hour`.

```
R> dat$round_hour <- round_date(dat$time, unit = "hour")
```

We aggregate the values in a table, convert it to a data frame and discard the last entry as we discontinued the collection around the time so it only contains censored information.

```
R> plot_time <- as.data.frame(table(dat$round_hour))
R> plot_time <- plot_time[-nrow(plot_time),]
```

Finally, we create a simple graph that displays the hourly tweets in the collection period from February 28 to March 2 (see Figure 14.1). We observe a sharp increase in the volume of tweets in the hours right before the beginning of the Academy Awards.

```
R> plot(plot_time[,2], type = "l", xaxt = "n", xlab = "Hour", ylab =
"Frequency")
R> axis(1, at = c(1, 20, 40, 60), labels = plot_time[c(1, 20, 40, 60),
1])
```

14.2.2 Mining tweets for predictions

In this part of the chapter, we use the stringr and the plyr packages. We begin by loading them.

```
R> library(stringr)
R> library(plyr)
```

[7] If you are operating on a Windows machine, the function has to be specified as `Sys.setlocale("LC_TIME", "English")`.

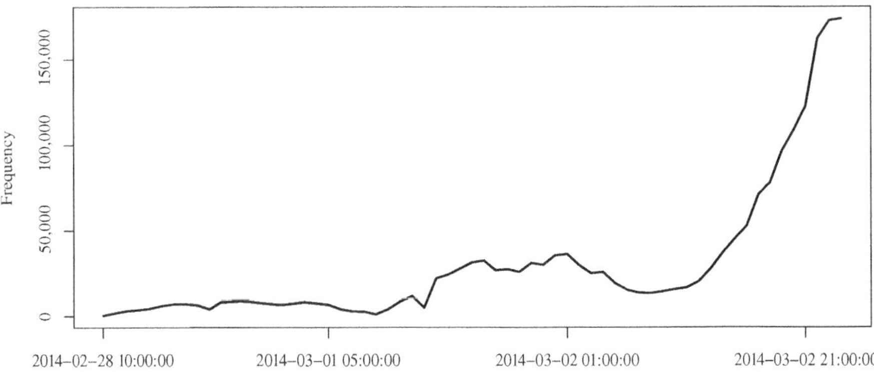

Figure 14.1 Tweets per hour on the 2014 Academy Awards

Let us inspect one line of the data frame to get a sense of what is available in the dataset:[8]

```
R> unlist(dat[1234,])

text
"RT @TheEllenShow: I'm very excited @Pharrell's performing his big
hit "Happy" at the #Oscars. Spolier alert: I'll be hiding in his hat."
retweet_count
"2383"
...
created_at
"Fri Feb 28 10:50:13 +0000 2014"
...
user_created_at
"Sun Jan 08 21:22:49 +0000 2012"
statuses_count
"475"
followers_count
"236"
favourites_count
"23"
...
friends_count
"132"
screen_name
"SophiaGracer007"
lotext
"rt @theellenshow: i'm very excited @pharrell's performing his big
hit "happy" at the #oscars. spolier alert: i'll be hiding in his hat."
time
"1393584613"
round_hour
"1393585200"
```

[8]We dropped some of the variables to save space.

You find that beside the actual text of the tweet there is a lot of the supplementary information, not least the time stamp that we relied upon in the previous section. The last three variables in the dataset are not created by twitter but were created by us. They contain the text of the tweet that was converted to lower case using the `tolower()` function, as well as the time (`time`) and the rounded time (`round_hour`).

Now, to look for references to the nominees for best actor, best actress, and best picture, we simply create three vectors of search terms. The search terms for the actors and actresses are simply the full name of the actor, in case of the films we created two regular expressions in the cases of "12 Years a Slave" and "The Wolf of Wall Street" as many users on Twitter might have used either variation of the titles. Notice that we have specified all the vectors as lower case as we intend to apply the search terms to the tweets in lower case.[9]

```
R> actor <- c(
        "matthew mcconaughey",
        "christian bale",
        "bruce dern",
        "leonardo dicaprio",
        "chiwetel ejiofor"
)

R> actress <- c(
        "cate blanchett",
        "amy adams",
        "sandra bullock",
        "judi dench",
        "meryl streep"
)

R> film <- c(
        "(12|twelve) years a slave",
        "american hustle",
        "captain phillips",
        "dallas buyers club",
        "gravity",
        "nebraska",
        "philomena",
        "(the )?wolf of wall street"
)
```

We go on to detect the search terms in the tweets by applying `str_detect()` to all tweets in lower case (`dat$lotext`) via a call to `lapply()`. The results are converted to a common data frame with `ldply()` and finally the column names are assigned meaningful names.

```
R> tmp_actor <- lapply(dat$lotext, str_detect, actor)
R> dat_actor <- ldply(tmp_actor)
R> colnames(dat_actor) <- c("mcconaughey", "bale", "dern", "dicaprio",
"ejiofor")
```

[9]We drop the movie "Her" as this creates a lot of noise and would require more elaborate methods than we use in the subsequent discussion.

```
R> tmp_actress <- lapply(dat$lotext, str_detect, actress)
R> dat_actress <- ldply(tmp_actress)
R> colnames(dat_actress) <- c("blanchett", "adams", "bullock", "dench",
"streep")

R> tmp_film <- lapply(dat$lotext, str_detect, film)
R> dat_film <- ldply(tmp_film)
R> colnames(dat_film) <- c("twelve_years", "american_hustle", "capt_
phillips", "dallas_buyers", "gravity", "nebraska", "philomena",
"wolf_wallstreet")
```

To inspect the results, we simply sum up the `TRUE` values. This is possible as the call to `sum()` evaluates the `TRUE` values as 1, `FALSE` entries as 0.

```
R> apply(dat_actor, 2, sum)

mcconaughey  bale  dern dicaprio  ejiofor
       6190  1255   912    23479     1531

R> apply(dat_actress, 2, sum)

blanchett  adams  bullock  dench  streep
     6790   5743     3272    765    3801

R> apply(dat_film, 2, sum)

twelve_years  american_hustle  capt_phillips  dallas_buyers
       11339             6122           2003           4560
gravity  nebraska  philomena  wolf_wallstreet
  22570      3602       2236             6741
```

We find that Leonardo DiCaprio was more heavily debated compared to the actual winner of the Oscar for best actor—Matthew McConaughey. In fact, there is a fairly wide gap between DiCaprio and McConaughey. Conversely, the frequencies with which the nominees for best actress were mentioned on Twitter are a little more evenly distributed. What is more, the eventual winner of the trophy—Cate Blanchett—was in fact the one who received most mentions overall. Finally, turning to the best picture we observe that it is not "12 Years a Slave" that was most frequently mentioned but rather "Gravity" which was mentioned roughly twice as often.

In case of the best actor and best actress, we decided to apply a sanity check. As some of the names are fairly difficult to spell, we might potentially bias our counts against those actors where this is the case. Accordingly, we performed an additional search that uses the `agrep()` function which performs approximate matching.[10] The results are summed up and unlisted to get numeric vectors of length five for both categories. Again, we assign meaningful names to the resulting vectors.

```
R> tmp_actor2 <- lapply(actor, agrep, dat$lotext)
R> length_actor <- unlist(lapply(tmp_actor2, length))
```

[10] For details on approximate matching, see Chapter 8.

```
R> names(length_actor) <- c("mcconaughey", "bale", "dern", "dicaprio",
"ejiofor")

R> tmp_actress2 <- lapply(actress, agrep, dat$lotext)
R> length_actress <- unlist(lapply(tmp_actress2, length))
R> names(length_actress) <- c("blanchett", "adams", "bullock", "dench",
"streep")

R> length_actor

mcconaughey  bale  dern  dicaprio  ejiofor
       8034  1663  3672     29643     1912

R> length_actress

blanchett  adams  bullock  dench  streep
    12556   6796     5464   1065    5250
```

The conclusions remain fairly stable, by and large. Leonardo DiCaprio was more heavily debated than Matthew McConaughey prior to the Academy Awards and the winner of best actress, Cate Blanchett, was most frequently mentioned after applying approximate matching.

14.3 Conclusion

Twitter is a rich playing ground for social scientists who are interested in the public debates on countless subjects. In this chapter, we have provided a short introduction to the various possibilities to collect data from Twitter and making it accessible for research. We have discussed the streamR and twitteR packages to connect to the two main access points for current and retrospective data collection.

In the specific application we have investigated whether the discussion on Twitter on the nominees for best actor and actress as well as best picture for the 2014 Academy Awards in the days prior to the awards reflects the eventual winners. As this book is more concerned with the data collection rather than the data analysis, the technique that was applied is almost banal. We invite you to download the data from the accompanying website to this book and play around with it yourself. Specifically, we invite you to repeat our analysis and apply a sentiment analysis (see Chapter 17) on the tweets to potentially improve the prediction accuracy.

15

Mapping the geographic distribution of names

The goal of this exercise is to collect data on the geographic distribution of surnames in Germany. Such maps are a popular visualization in genealogical and onomastic research, that is, research on names and their origins (Barratt 2008; Christian 2012; Osborn 2012). It has been shown that in spite of increased labor mobility in the last decades, surnames that were bound to a certain regional context continue to retain their geographic strongholds (Barrai et al. 2001; Fox and Lasker 1983; Yasuda et al. 1974). Apart from their scientific value, name maps have a more general appeal for those who are interested in the roots of their namesakes. Plus, they visualize the data in one of the most beautiful and insightful ways—geographic maps.

In this chapter, we briefly introduce the visualization of geographic data in R. This can be a difficult task, and if your data do not match the specifications of the data treated in this chapter, we recommend a look at Kahle and Wickham (2013) and Bivand et al. (2013b) for more advanced visualization tools of spatial data with R. In order to acquire the necessary data, we rely on the online directory of a German phone book provider (www.dastelefonbuch.de). As a showcase, we visualize the geographical distribution of a set of surnames in Germany. The goal is to write a program that can easily be fed with any surname to produce a surname map with a single function call. Further, the call should return a data frame that contains all of the scraped observations for further analysis.

The case study serves another purpose: It is not a storybook example of web scraping but shows some of the pitfalls that may occur in reality—and how to deal with them. The case study thus illustrates that textbook theory does not always match up with reality. Among the problems we have to tackle are (a) incomplete and unsystematic data, (b) data that belong

Automated Data Collection with R: A Practical Guide to Web Scraping and Text Mining, First Edition.
Simon Munzert, Christian Rubba, Peter Meißner and Dominic Nyhuis.

together but are dispersed in the HTML tree, (c) limited "hits per page" functionality, and (d) undocumented URL parameters.

15.1 Developing a data collection strategy

Before diving into the online phone book, we begin with some thoughts on the kind of information we want to collect and whether a phone book is an appropriate source for such information. The goal is to gain insight into the current distribution of surnames. The distribution is defined by the universe of surnames in the German population, that is, around 80 million people. We want to collect data for descriptive as well as for secondary analyses. The ideal source would provide a complete and up-to-date list of surnames of all inhabitants, linked with precise geographic identifiers. Such a list would raise severe privacy concerns.

Benefits of phone book data

By virtue of purpose, phone directories are open data sources. They provide information on names and residencies, so they are a candidate to approximate the true distributions of surnames. In terms of data quality, however, we have to ask ourselves: Are phone directories a reliable and valid source? There is good reason to believe they are: First, they are updated at least annually. Second, geographic identifiers like streets and zip codes are usually precise enough to assess people's locations within a circle of less than 20 km. The fact that phone books provide such accurate geographical identifiers is actually the crucial property of the data source in this exercise. It is difficult to come up with a freely available alternative.

Limitations of phone book data

On the downside, we have to be aware of the phone book's limitations. First, not everybody has a phone and not every phone is listed in the phone directory. This problem has aggravated with the proliferation of mobile phones. Second, phone books occasionally contain duplicates. Using zip codes as geographic identifiers adds some noise to the data, but this inaccuracy is negligible. After all, we are interested in the big picture, not in pinpointing names at the street level.

Regarding alternative data sources, there are several websites which provide ready-made distribution maps, often based on phone book entries as well.[1] However, these pages usually only offer aggregate statistics or remain vague about the source of the reported maps. The same is true for commercial software that is frequently offered on these sites. Therefore, we rely on online phone directories and produce our own maps.

Data collection

In order to achieve the goals, we pursue the following strategies:

1. Identify an online phone directory that provides the information we need.
2. Become familiar with the page structure and choose an extraction procedure.
3. Apply the procedure: retrieve data, extract information, cleanse data, and document unforeseen problems that occur during the coding
4. Visualize and analyze the data.
5. Generalize the scraping task.

---

[1] A nice overview of existing pages which offer name map services can be found at https://familysearch.org/learn/wiki/en/Surname_Distribution_Maps

Regarding our example, we have done some research on available online phone directories. There are basically two major providers in Germany, www.dastelefonbuch.de and www.dasoertliche.de. Comparing the number of hits for a sample set of names, the results are almost equivalent, so both providers seem to work with similar databases. The display of hits is different, however. www.dastelefonbuch.de allows accessing a maximum of 2000 hits per query and the number of hits per request can be adapted. Conversely, www.dasoertliche.de offers 10,000 hits at most that are are displayed in bundles of 20s. As we prefer to minimize the number of requests for reasons of efficiency and scraping etiquette, we decide to use www.dastelefonbuch.de as primary source of data for the exercise.

15.2 Website inspection

Inspecting the *robots.txt*

We start with a look at the *robots.txt* to check whether accessing the page's content via automated methods is accepted at all (see Section 9.3.3). We find that some bots are indeed *robota non grata* (e.g., the *Googlebot-Image* and the *trovitBot* bot; see Figure 15.1). For other undefined bots, some directories are disallowed, for example, `/scripts/` or `/styles/`. The root path is not prohibited, so we can direct small automated requests to the site with a

```
# robots.txt for http://www.dastelefonbuch.de/
# sc 20130402_1.56, Vorgaengerversion: sc 20130128
(...)

User-agent: Googlebot-Image
Disallow: /

User-agent: trovitBot
Disallow: /

User-agent: *
Disallow: /scripts/
Disallow: /styles/
Disallow: /katalog/scripts/
Disallow: /katalog/styles/
Disallow: /telefonbuch/scripts/
Disallow: /telefonbuch/styles/
(...)

# Sitemap files
Sitemap: http://www.dastelefonbuch.de/xml-sitemaps/
    telefonbuch_nachnamen_sitemap_index.xml
Sitemap: http://www.dastelefonbuch.de/xml-sitemaps/
    telefonbuch_behoerden_sitemap_index.xml
Sitemap: http://www.dastelefonbuch.de/xml-sitemaps/
    telefonbuch_branchen_sitemap_index.xml
(...)
```

Figure 15.1 Excerpt from the *robots.txt* file on www.dastelefonbuch.de

clear conscience. The bottom of the file reveals some interesting XML files. Accessing these links, we find large compressed XML files that apparently contain information on surnames in all cities. This is potentially a powerful data source, as it might lead to the universe of available surnames in the page's database. We do not make use of the data, however, as it is not immediately obvious how such a list could be used for our specific purpose.

Examining the page architecture

We continue with a closer inspection of the page's functionality and architecture. In the simple search mode, we can specify two parameters—whom to search for ("Wer/Was") and where ("Wo"). Let us start with a sample request. We search for entries with the surname "Feuerstein."[2] In the left column, the total number of hits are reported (837), 149 of which are businesses and 688 of which are private entries. We are only interested in private entries and have already selected this subsample of hits. The hits themselves are listed in the middle column of the page. Surname and, if available, first name is reported in an entry's first row, the address in the second. Some entries do not provide any address. In the rightmost column on the page, the hits are already displayed on a map. This is the information we are looking for, but it seems more convenient to scrape the data from the list of hits rather than from the JavaScript-based map.[3] We also observe that the URL has changed after passing the request to the server. In its complete form, it looks as follows:

```
http://www3.dastelefonbuch.de/?bi=76&kw=Feuerstein&cmd=search&seed=
1010762549&ort_ok=1&vert_ok=1&buab=622100&mergerid=A43F7DB343E7F461D
5506CA8A7DBB734&mdest=sec1.www1%2Csec2.www2%2Csec3.www3%2Csec4.www4
&recfrom=&ao1=1&ao2=0&sp=51&aktion=105
```

Evidently, passing the input form to the server has automatically added a set of parameters, which can be observed in the URL's query string, beginning after the `?` sign.[4] As we need to set these parameters with our program later on, we have to identify their meaning. Unfortunately, there is no documentation in the page's source code. Therefore, we try to detect their meaning manually by playing around with them and comparing the displayed outputs. We find that the `kw` parameter contains the keyword we are searching for. Note that URL encoding is required here, that is, we look for `M%FCller` instead of `Müller` and so on. `cmd=search` is the trigger for the search action, `ao1=1` means that only private entries are shown. Some of the parameters can be dropped without any changes in the displayed content. By manually specifying some of the search parameters, we identify another useful parameter: `reccount` defines the number of hits that are shown on the page. We know from search engine requests that this number is usually limited to around 10–50 hits for efficiency reasons. In this case, the options displayed in the browser are 20, 50, and 100 hits per page. However, we can manually specify the value in the URL and set it up to a maximum of 2000 hits. This is very useful, as one single request suffices to scrape all available results. In general, inspecting the URL before and after putting requests to the server often pays off in web scraping practice—and not only for an ad-hoc URL manipulation strategy as proposed in Section 9.1.3. In this case, we can circumvent the need to identify and scrape a large set of sites to download all hits. Having said that, we can now start constructing the web scraper.

[2]'Feuerstein' means 'Flint' or 'Firestone' in German and is, as we will see, a rather uncommon name. The name is quite well-known, as the German translation of the cartoon series 'The Flintstones' is 'Die Feuersteins'.

[3]We will have a closer look at the data behind the map at the end of this chapter.

[4]An inspection of the source code reveals that this is done with hidden input elements.

15.3 Data retrieval and information extraction

First, we load a couple of packages that are needed for the exercise. Beside the set of usual suspects RCurl, XML, and stringr, we load three additional packages which provide helpful functions for geographical work: maptools (Bivand and Lewin-Koh 2013), rgdal (Bivand et al. 2013a), maps (Brownrigg et al. 2013), and TeachingDemos (Snow 2013).

```
R> library(RCurl)
R> library(XML)
R> library(stringr)
R> library(maptools)
R> library(rgdal)
R> library(maps)
R> library(TeachingDemos)
```

The *GET* request We identified the parameters in the URL which tell the server to return a rendered HTML page that meets our requirements. In order to retrieve the results of a search request for the name "Feuerstein," we use `getForm()` and specify the URL parameters in the `.params` argument.

```
R> tb <- getForm("http://www.dastelefonbuch.de/",
R>                .params = c(kw = "Feuerstein",
R>                            cmd = "search",
R>                            ao1 = "1",
R>                            reccount = "2000"))
```

Note that we set the `reccount` parameter to the maximum value of 2000 to ensure that all hits that are retrievable with one request are actually captured. If the number of hits is greater, we just get the first 2000. We will discuss this shortcoming of our method further below. The returned content is stored in the object `tb` which we write to the file *phonebook_feuerstein.html* on our local drive.

```
R> dir.create("phonebook_feuerstein")
R> write(tb, file = "phonebook_feuerstein/phonebook_feuerstein.html")
```

We can now work with the offline data and do not have to bother the server again—the screen scraping part in the narrow sense of the word is finished. In order to be able to access the information in the document by exploiting the DOM, we parse it with `htmlParse()` and ensure that the original UTF-8 encoding is retained.

```
R> tb_parse <- htmlParse("phonebook_feuerstein/phonebook_feuerstein.html",
                         encoding = "UTF-8")
```

We can start extracting the entries. As a first benchmark, we want to extract the total number of results in order to check whether we are able to scrape all entries or only a subset. The number is stored in the left column as "`Privat (687).`" In order to retrieve this number from the HTML file, we start with an XPath query. We locate the relevant line in the HTML code—it is stored in an unordered list of anchors. We retrieve the anchor within that list that contains the text pattern "Privat."

```
R> xpath <- "//ul/li/a[contains(text(), 'Privat')]"
R> num_results <- xpathSApply(tb_parse, xpath, xmlValue)
R> num_results
[1] "\r\n              Privat (687)"
```

In the next step, we extract the sequence of digits within the string using a simple regular expression.

```
R> num_results <- as.numeric(str_extract(num_results, "[[:digit:]]+"))
R> num_results
[1] 687
```

As so often in web scraping, there is more than one way of doing it. We could replace the XPath/regex query with a pure regex approach, eventually leading to the same result.

We now come to the crucial part of the matter, the extraction of names and geographic information. In order to locate the information in the tree, we inspect some of the elements in the list of results. By using the "inspect element" or a similar option in our browser to identify the data in the HTML tree (see Section 6.3), we find that the name is contained in the attribute `title` of an element `<a>` which is child of a `<div>` tag of class `name`. This position in the tree can easily be generalized by means of an XPath expression. **Data extraction**

```
R> xpath <- "//div[@class='name']/a[@title]"
R> surnames <- xpathSApply(tb_parse, xpath, xmlValue)
R> surnames[1:3]
[1] "\r\n\t\t    \tBertsch-Feuerstein Lilli"
[2] "\r\n\t\t    \tBierig-Feuerstein Brigitte u. Feuerstein Norbert"
[3] "\r\n\t\t    \tBlatt Karl u. Feuerstein-Blatt Ursula"
```

Apart from redundant carriage return and line feed symbols which have to be removed in the data-cleansing step, this seems to have worked well. Extracting the zip codes for geographic localization is also simple. They are stored in the `<span>` elements with the attribute `itemprop="postal-code"`. Accordingly, we write

```
R> xpath <- "//span[@itemprop='postal-code']"
R> zipcodes <- xpathSApply(tb_parse, xpath, xmlValue)
R> zipcodes[1:3]
[1] " 64625" " 68549" " 68526"
```

When trying to match the names and the zip code vector, we realize that fetching both pieces of information separately was not a good idea. The vectors have different lengths.

```
R> length(surnames)
[1] 687
R> length(zipcodes)
[1] 642
```

A total of 45 zip codes seem to be missing. A closer look at the entries in the HTML file reveals that some entries lack an address and therefore a zip code. Unfortunately, the `<span>` element with the attribute `itemprop="postal-code"` is also missing in these cases. If we were only interested in the location of hits, we could drop the names and just extract the zip codes. To keep names and zip codes together for further analyses, however, we have to adapt the extraction function.

Making use of XPath axes

In Section 4.2.2 we have encountered a tool that is of great help for this problem—XPath axes. XPath axes help express the relations between nodes in a family tree analogy. This means that they can be used to condition a selection on attributes of related nodes. This is precisely what we need to extract names and zip codes that belong together. As names without zip codes are meaningless for locating observations on a map, we want to extract only those names for which a zip code is available. The necessary XPath expression is a bit more complicated.

```
R> xpath <- "//span[@itemprop='postal-code']/ancestor::div[@class='
popupMenu']/preceding-sibling::div[@class='name']"
R> names_vec <- xpathSApply(tb_parse, xpath, xmlValue)
```

Let us consider this call step by step from back to front. What we are looking for is a `<div>` object of class `name`. It is the `preceding-sibling` of a `<div>` object of class `popupMenu`. This `<div>` element is the ancestor of a `span` element with attribute `itemprop="postal-code"`. Applying this XPath query to the parsed document with `xpathSApply()` returns a vector of names which are linked to a zip code. By inverting the XPath expression, we extract the zip codes as well.

```
R> xpath <- "//div[@class='name']/following-sibling::div[@class='
popupMenu']//span[@itemprop='postal-code']"
R> zipcodes_vec <- xpathSApply(tb_parse, xpath, xmlValue)
```

We compare the lengths of both vectors and find that they are now of equal length.

```
R> length(names_vec)
[1] 642
R> length(zipcodes_vec)
[1] 642
```

In a last step, we remove the carriage returns (`\r`), line feeds (`\n`), horizontal tabs (`\t`), and empty spaces in the names vector, coerce the zip code vector to be numeric, and merge both variables in a data frame.

```
R> names_vec <- str_replace_all(names_vec, "(\\n|\\t|\\r| {2,})", "")
R> zipcodes_vec <- as.numeric(zipcodes_vec)
R> entries_df <- data.frame(plz = zipcodes_vec, name = names_vec)
R> head(entries_df)
    plz                                          name
1 64625                     Bertsch-Feuerstein Lilli
2 68549 Bierig-Feuerstein Brigitte u. Feuerstein Norbert
3 68526          Blatt Karl u. Feuerstein-Blatt Ursula
4 50733                                    Feuerstein
5 63165                                    Feuerstein
6 69207                                    Feuerstein
```

15.4 Mapping names

Regarding the scraping strategy outlined in the first section, we have just completed step 3 after having retrieved the data, extracted the information, and cleansed the data. The next step is to plot the scraped observations on a map. To do so, we have to (1) match geo-coordinates to the scraped zip codes and (2) add them to a map.

Geo-coding phone book entries

After some research on the Web, we find a dataset that links zip codes ("Postleitzahlen," PLZ) and geographic coordinates. It is part of the OpenGeoDB project (http://opengeodb.org/wiki/OpenGeoDB) and freely available. We save the file to our local drive and load it into R.

```
R> dir.create("geo_germany")
R> download.file("http://fa-technik.adfc.de/code/opengeodb/PLZ.tab",
destfile = "geo_germany/plz_de.txt")
```

```
R> plz_df <- read.delim("geo_germany/plz_de.txt", stringsAsFactors
= FALSE, encoding = "UTF-8")
R> plz_df[1:3, ]
  X.loc_id  plz   lon   lat     Ort
1     5078 1067 13.72 51.06 Dresden
2     5079 1069 13.74 51.04 Dresden
3     5080 1097 13.74 51.07 Dresden
```

We can easily merge the information to the entries_df data frame using the joint identifying variable plz.

```
R> places_geo <- merge(entries_df, plz_df, by = "plz", all.x = TRUE)
R> places_geo[1:3, ]
   plz                name X.loc_id   lon   lat        Ort
1 1159      Feuerstein Falk     5087 13.70 51.04    Dresden
2 1623    Feuerstein Regina     5122 13.30 51.17 Lommatzsch
3 2827 Feuerstein Wolfgang     5199 14.96 51.13    Görlitz
```

Retrieving shapefiles

In order to enrich the map with administrative boundaries, we rely on data from the Global Administrative Areas database (GADM; www.gadm.org). It offers geographic data for a multitude of countries in various file formats. The data's coordinate reference system is latitude/longitude and the WGS84 datum, which matches nicely with the coordinates from the zip code data frame.[5] We download the zip file containing shapefile data for Germany and unzip it in a subdirectory:

```
R> download.file("http://biogeo.ucdavis.edu/data/gadm2/shp/DEU_adm.zip",
destfile = "geo_germany/ger_shape.zip")
R> unzip("geo_germany/ger_shape.zip", exdir = "geo_germany")
R> dir("geo_germany")
 [1] "DEU_adm0.csv"  "DEU_adm0.dbf"  "DEU_adm0.prj"  "DEU_adm0.shp"
 [5] "DEU_adm0.shx"  "DEU_adm1.csv"  "DEU_adm1.dbf"  "DEU_adm1.prj"
 [9] "DEU_adm1.shp"  "DEU_adm1.shx"  "DEU_adm2.csv"  "DEU_adm2.dbf"
[13] "DEU_adm2.prj"  "DEU_adm2.shp"  "DEU_adm2.shx"  "DEU_adm3.csv"
[17] "DEU_adm3.dbf"  "DEU_adm3.prj"  "DEU_adm3.shp"  "DEU_adm3.shx"
[21] "ger_shape.zip" "plz_de.txt"    "read_me.pdf"
```

[5] If you want to learn more about geodetic systems that define different projections, you may want to check out http://en.wikipedia.org/wiki/Geodetic_datum and http://en.wikipedia.org/wiki/Map_projection

Working with shapefiles in R

The downloaded archive provides a set of files. A shapefile actually consists of at least three files: The *.shp* file contains geographic data, the *.dbf* file contains attribute data attached to geographic objects, and the *.shx* file contains an index for the geographic data. The *.prj* files in the folder are optional and contain information about the shapefile's projection format. Altogether, there are four shapefiles in the archive for different levels of administrative boundaries. Using the maptools package (Bivand and Lewin-Koh 2013), we import and process shapefile data in R. The `readShapePoly()` function converts the shapefile into an object of class `SpatialPolygonsDataFrame`. It contains both vector data for the administrative units (i.e., polygons) and substantive data linked to these polygons (therefore "`DataFrame`"). We import two shapefiles: the highest-level boundary, Germany's national border, and the second highest-level boundaries, the federal states. Additionally, we declare the data to be projected according to the coordinate reference system WGS84 with the `CRS()` function and the `proj4string` argument.

```
R> projection <- CRS("+proj=longlat +ellps=WGS84 +datum=WGS84")
R> map_germany <- readShapePoly(str_c(getwd(), "/geo_germany/DEU_adm0.shp"),
                                proj4string = projection)
R> map_germany_laender <- readShapePoly(str_c(getwd(),
                                        "/geo_germany/DEU_adm1.shp"),
                                        proj4string=projection)
```

Finally, we transform the coordinates of our entries to a `SpatialPoints` object that harmonizes with the map data.

```
R> coords <- SpatialPoints(cbind(places_geo$lon, places_geo$lat))
R> proj4string(coords) <- CRS("+proj=longlat +ellps=WGS84 +datum=WGS84")
```

In order to get a better intuition of where people are located, we add the location of Germany's biggest cities as well. The maps package (Brownrigg et al. 2013) is extraordinarily useful for this purpose, as it contains a list of all cities around the world, including their coordinates. We extract the German cities with a population greater than 450,000—an arbitrary value that results in a reasonable number of cities displayed—and add two more cities that are located in interesting areas.

```
R> data("world.cities")
R> cities_ger <- subset(world.cities,
                        country.etc == "Germany" &
                        (world.cities$pop > 450000 |
                        world.cities$name %in%
                        c("Mannheim", "Jena")))
R> coords_cities <- SpatialPoints(cbind(cities_ger$long,cities_ger$lat))
```

Generating the map

We compose the map sequentially by adding layer after layer. First, we plot the national border, then we add the federal states boundaries. The scraped locations of the "Feuersteins" are added with the `points()` function, as well as the cities' locations. Finally, we add the cities' labels.

```
R> plot(map_germany)
R> plot(map_germany_laender, add = T)
R> points(coords$coords.x1, coords$coords.x2, pch = 20)
R> points(coords_cities, col = "black", , bg = "grey", pch = 23)
R> text(cities_ger$long, cities_ger$lat, labels = cities_ger$name, pos = 4)
```

Figure 15.2 Geographic distribution of "Feuersteins"

The result is provided in Figure 15.2. The distribution of hits reveals some interesting facts. The largest cluster of Feuersteins lives in the southwestern part of Germany, in the area near Mannheim.

15.5 Automating the process

The benefit of speical-purpose scraping functions

Crafting maps from scraped surnames is an example of a task that is likely to be repeated over and over again, with only slight modifications. To round off the exercise, we develop a set of functions which generalize the scraping, parsing, and mapping from above and offer some useful options to adapt the process (see Section 11.3). In our case, the information for one name rarely changes over time. It is thus of less interest to repeat the task for one surname. Instead, we want to be able to quickly produce data and maps for any name.

We decide to split the procedure into three functions: a scraping function, a parsing and data cleansing function, and a mapping function. While on the one side this means that we have to call three functions to create a map, these functions are easier to debug and adapt.

```
namesScrape <- function(phonename, update.file = FALSE) {
## transform phonename
    phonename <- tolower(phonename)
## load libraries
    x <- c("stringr", "RCurl", "XML")
    lapply(x, require, character.only=T)
## create folder
    dir.create(str_c("phonebook_", phonename), showWarnings = FALSE)
    filename <- str_c("phonebook_", phonename, "/phonebook_", phonename, ".html")
    if (file.exists(filename) & update.file == FALSE) {
        message("Data already scraped; using data from ", file.info(filename)$mtime)
    } else {
## retrieve and save html
        tb <- getForm("http://www.dastelefonbuch.de/",
        .params = c(kw = phonename, cmd = "search", ao1 = "1", reccount = "2000"))
        write(tb, file = filename)
    }
}
```

Figure 15.3 Generalized R code to scrape entries from *www.dastelefonbuch.de*

The code in Figures 15.3, 15.4, and 15.5 displays the result of our efforts. It is the condensed version of the code snippets from above, enriched with some useful arguments for the function sets `namesScrape()`, `namesParse()`, and `namesPlot()`.

Usually, what distinguishes functions from ordinary code is that they (1) generalize a task and (2) offer flexibility in the form of arguments. It is always the choice of a function author which parameters to keep variable, that is, easily modifiable by the function user, and which parameters to fix. For our functions, we have implemented a set of arguments which is listed in Table 15.1.

Technical considerations

The choice of arguments is mainly focused on plotting the results. One could easily think of more options for the scraping process. We could allow more than one request at once, explicitly obey the *robots.txt*,[6] or define a User-agent header field. With regards to processing, we could have allowed specifying a directory where data and maps should be saved. For reasons of brevity, we refrain from such fine-tuning work. However, anybody should feel free to adapt and expand the function.

The functions explained

Let us consider the details of the code. In the scraping function `namesScrape()` (Figure 15.3), `phonename` is the crucial parameter. We use the `tolower()` function (see Section 8.1) to achieve a consistent naming of files. Data are stored as follows: Using a call to `dir.create()`, a directory is created where the HTML file and, if so desired, a PDF version of the graph are stored. Scraping is only performed if the file does not exist. This is checked with the `file.exists()` function or if the user explicitly requests that the file be updated (option `update.file == TRUE`). Otherwise, a message referring to the existing file is shown and the function loads the old data.

[6] In our example, it does not seem necessary to mind the *robots.txt*. We stay on one site and have already investigated the scraping policy.

```
namesParse <- function(phonename) {
      filename <- str_c("phonebook_", phonename, "/phonebook_", phonename,
      ".html")
## load libraries
      x <- c("stringr", "XML")
      lapply(x, require, character.only = TRUE)
## parse html
      tb_parse <- htmlParse(filename, encoding = "UTF-8")
## check number of hits
      xpath <- '//ul/li/a[contains(text(), "Privat")]'
      num_results <- xpathSApply(tb parse, xpath, xmlValue)
      num_results <- as.numeric(str_extract(num_results, '[[:digit:]]+'))
      if (num_results <= 2000) {
            message('Gross sample of ', num_results, ' entries retrieved.')
      }
      if (num_results > 2000) {
            message(num_results, ' hits. Warning: No more than 2,000 entries
             will be retrieved')
      }
## retrieve zipcodes and names
      xpath <- '//div[@class="name"]/following-sibling::div[@class="
      popupMenu"]//span[@itemprop="postal-code"]'
      zipcodes_vec <- xpathSApply(tb_parse, xpath, xmlValue)
      zipcodes_vec <- str_replace_all(zipcodes_vec, " ", "")
      xpath <- '//span[@itemprop="postal-code"]/ancestor::div[@class="
      popupMenu"]/preceding-sibling::div[@class="name"]'
      names_vec <- xpathSApply(tb_parse, xpath, xmlValue)
      names_vec <- str_replace_all(names_vec, "(\\n|\\t|\\r| {2,})", "")
## build data frame
      entries_df <- data.frame(plz = as.numeric(zipcodes_vec), name =
      names_vec)
## match coordinates to zipcodes
      plz_df <- read.delim("function_data/plz_de.txt", stringsAsFactors =
      FALSE, encoding = "UTF-8")
      geodf <- merge(entries_df, plz_df, by = "plz", all.x = TRUE)
      geodf <- geodf[!is.na(geodf$lon),]
## return data frame
      geodf <- geodf[,!names(geodf) %in% "X.loc_id"]
      return(geodf)
}
```

Figure 15.4 Generalized R code to parse entries from *www.dastelefonbuch.de*

In the parsing function `namesParse()` (Figure 15.4), the information extraction process remains the same as above, except that the number of results is reported. The function prints a warning if more than 2000 observations are found. This would mean that not the full sample of observations is captured. Further, first names are extracted from the names vector in a rather simplistic manner by removing the surname. The function returns the data frame which contains geographical and name information for further analysis and/or plotting.

Finally, the plotting function `namesPlot()` (Figure 15.5) uses the data frame and generates the map as outlined above. The function allows storing the plot locally as a PDF file. We also add the option `print.names` to print the first names of the observations.

```
namesPlot <- function(geodf, phonename, show.map = TRUE, save.pdf = TRUE,
                      minsize.cities = 450000, add.cities = "",
                      print.names = FALSE) {
## load libraries
      x <- c("stringr", "maptools", "rgdal", "maps")
      lapply(x, require, character.only = TRUE)
## prepare coordinates
      coords <- SpatialPoints(cbind(geodf$lon, geodf$lat))
      proj4string(coords) <- CRS("+proj=longlat +ellps=WGS84 +datum=WGS84")
## prepare map
      projection <- CRS("+proj=longlat +ellps=WGS84 +datum=WGS84")
      map_germany <- readShapePoly("function_data/DEU_adm0.shp",
                                    proj4string = projection)
      map_germany_laender <- readShapePoly("function_data/DEU_adm1.shp",
                                         proj4string = projection)
## add big cities (from maps package)
      data("world.cities")
      cities_ger <- subset(world.cities, country.etc == "Germany" &
                 (world.cities$pop > minsize.cities |
                 world.cities$name %in% add.cities))
      coords_cities <- SpatialPoints(cbind(cities_ger$long, cities_ger$lat))
## produce map
      i <- 0
      n <- 1
      while (i <= n) {
            if (save.pdf == TRUE & i < n) {
                  pdf(file = str_c("phonebook_", phonename, "/map-",
            phonename, ".pdf"), height = 10, width = 7.5,
            family = "URWTimes")
            }
            if (show.map == TRUE | save.pdf == TRUE) {
                  par(oma = c(0, 0, 0, 0))
                  par(mar = c(0, 0, 2, 0))
                  par(mfrow = c(1, 1))
                  plot(map_germany)
                  plot(map_germany_laender, add = TRUE)
                  title(main = str_c("People named ", toupper(phonename),
                  " in Germany"))
            if (print.names == FALSE) {
                  points(coords$coords.x1, coords$coords.x2,
              col = rgb(10, 10, 10, max = 255),
              bg = rgb(10, 10, 10, max = 255),
              pch = 20, cex = 1)
            } else {
                  text(coords$coords.x1, coords$coords.x2,
                      labels = str_replace_all(geodf$name,
                         ignore.case(phonename), ""), cex = .7)
            }
            points(coords_cities, col = "black", , bg = "grey", pch = 23)
            shadowtext(cities_ger$long,cities_ger$lat,
                    labels = cities_ger$name, pos = 4,
                           col = "black", bg = "white", cex = 1.2)
            }
            if (save.pdf == TRUE & i < n) {
                  dev.off()
            }
            if (show.map == FALSE) {
                  i <- i + 1
            }
            i <- i + 1
      }
}
```

Figure 15.5 Generalized R code to map entries from *www.dastelefonbuch.de*

Table 15.1 Parameters of phone book scraping functions explained

Argument	Description
`phonename`	Main argument for `namesScrape()` and `namesParse()`; defines the name for which entries should be retrieved
`geodf`	Main argument for `namesPlot`; specifies data.frame object which stores geographical information (object is usually returned by `namesParse()`)
`update.file`	Logical value indicating whether the data should be scraped again or if existing data should be used
`show.map`	Logical value indicating whether R should automatically print a map with the located observations
`save.pdf`	Logical value indicating whether R should save the map as pdf
`minsize.cities`	Numerical value setting the minimal size of cities to be included in the plot
`add.cities`	Character values defining names of further cities to be added to the plot
`print.names`	Logical value indicating whether people's names should be plotted

We test the functions with a set of specifications. First, we look at the distribution of people named "Gruber," displaying cities with more than 300,000 inhabitants.

```
R> namesScrape("Gruber")
R> gruber_df <- namesParse("Gruber", minsize.cities = 300000)
R> namesPlot(gruber_df, "Gruber", save.pdf = FALSE, show.map = FALSE)
```

Next, we scrape information for people named "Petersen." We have done this before and force the scraping function to update the file.

```
R> namesScrape("Petersen", update.file = TRUE)
R> petersen_df <- namesParse("Petersen")
9605 hits. Warning: No more than 2,000 entries will be retrieved
R> namesPlot(petersen_df, "Petersen", save.pdf = FALSE, show.map = FALSE)
```

Finally, we look at the distribution of the surname "Dimpfl." We ask the function to plot the surnames.

```
R> namesScrape("Dimpfl")
Data already scraped; using data from 2014-01-16 00:22:03
R> dimpfl_df <- namesParse("Dimpfl")
Gross sample of 109 entries retrieved.
R> namesPlot(dimpfl_df, "Dimpfl", save.pdf = FALSE, show.map = FALSE,
print.names = TRUE)
```

The output of all three calls is shown in Figure 15.6. We observe that both Gruber and Dimpfl are clustered in the southern part of Germany, whereas Petersens live predominantly in the very north. Note that for the Dimpfls we see first names instead of dots.

The JavaScript parts

Finally, we reconsider a technical concern of our scraping approach. Recall that in Section 15.2 we noted that the search on www.dastelefonbuch.de also returns a map where the findings

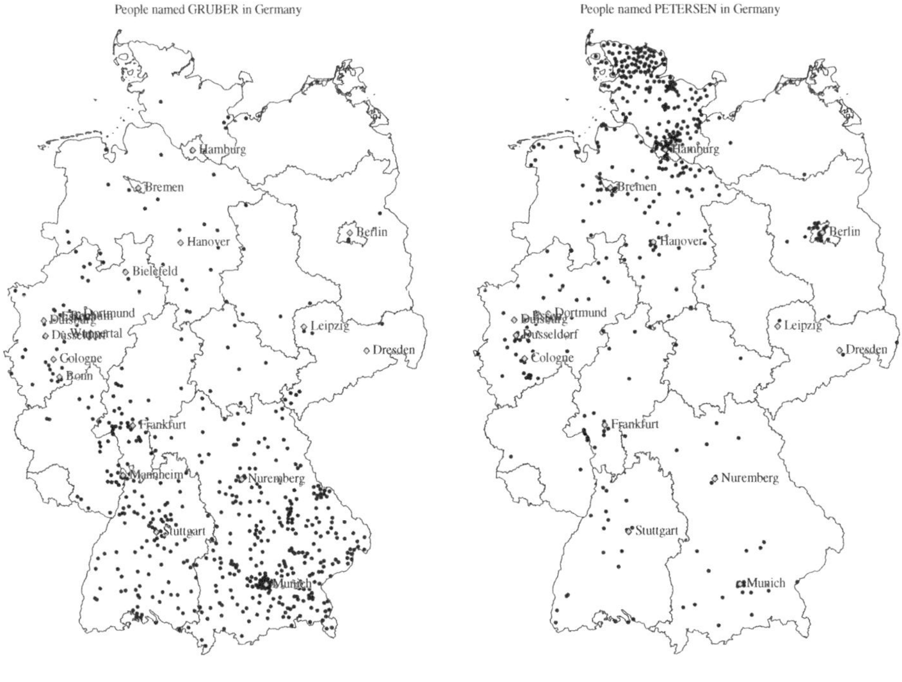

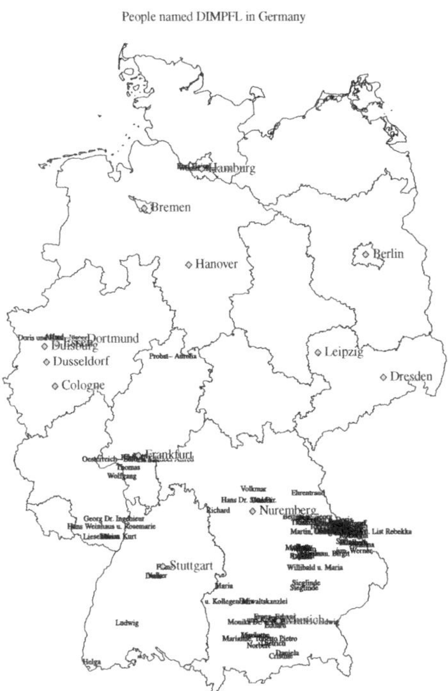

Figure 15.6 Results of three calls of the `namesPlot()` function

are located, which is essentially what we wanted to replicate. We argued that it seems easier to scrape the entries from the list instead of the JavaScript object. Indeed, the inspection of the source code of the page does not reveal any of the hits. But this is what we should expect knowing how dynamic webpages are constructed, that is, by means of AJAX methods (see Chapter 6). Therefore, we use the Web Developer Tools of our browser to identify the source of information which is plotted in the map (see Section 6.3). We find that the script initiates the following GET request:

```
http://maps.dastelefonbuch.de/DasTelefonbuch/search.html?queryType=
whatOnly&x=1324400.3811369245&y=6699724.7656052755&width=3033021.
2837500004&height=1110477.1474374998&city=&searchTerm=Feuerstein&
shapeName=tb/CA912598AEB53A4D1862D89ACA54C42E_2&minZoomLevel=4&
maxZoomLevel=18&mapPixelWidth=1240&mapPixelHeight=454&order=distance
&maxHits=200
```

The interesting aspect about this is that this request returns an XML file that contains essentially the same information that we scraped above along with coordinates that locate the hits on the map. One could therefore directly target this file in order to scrape the relevant information. Advantages would be that it is more likely that the XML file's structure remains more stable than the front-end page, making the scraper more robust to changes in the page layout. Second, one could probably skip the step where zip codes and coordinates are matched. However, some parameters in the related URL seem to further restrict the number of returned hits, that is, the zoom level and margins of the plotted area. Further, the structure of the XML document is largely identical with the relevant part of the HTML document we scraped above. This means that the information extraction step should not be expected to be easier with the XML document. Nevertheless, it is always worth looking behind the curtains of dynamically rendered content on webpages, as there may be scenarios in which relevant data can only be scraped this way.

Summary

The code presented in this chapter is only the first step toward a thorough analysis of the distribution of family names. There are several issues of data quality that should be considered when the data are used for scientific purposes. First, there is the limitation of 2000 hits. As the hits are sorted alphabetically, the truncation of the scraped sample is at least not entirely random. Further, the data may contain duplicates or "false positives." Even if one is not interested in detailed research on the data, there is plenty of room for improvement in the functions. The point representation of hits could be replaced by density maps to better visualize regions where names occur frequently.

More general take-away points of this study are the following. When dealing with dynamic content, it usually pays off to start with a closer look at the source code. One should first get a basic understanding of how parameters in a *GET* request work, what their limits are, and if there are other ways to retrieve content than to posit requests via the input field. Concerning the use of geo data, the lesson learned is that it is easy to enrich scraped data with geo information once a geographical identifier is available. Mapping such information in R is possible, although not always straightforward. Finally, splitting the necessary tasks into a set of specific functions can be useful and keeps the code manageable.

16

Gathering data on mobile phones

In this case study, we gather data on pricing, costumer rating, and sales ranks of a broad range of mobile phones sold on amazon.com, wondering about the price segments covered by leading producers of mobile phones. Amazon sells a broad range of products, allowing us to get comprehensive summary of the products from each of the big mobile phone producers.

The case study makes use of the packages RCurl, XML, and stringr and it features search page manipulation, link extraction, and page downloads using the RCurl curl handle. After reading the case study, you should be able to search information in source code and to apply XPath in real-life problems. Furthermore, within this case study a *SQLite* database is created to store data in a consistent way and make it reusable for the next case study.

16.1 Page exploration

16.1.1 Searching mobile phones of a specific brand

Amazon sells all kinds of products. Our first task is therefore to restrict the product search to certain categories and specific producers. Furthermore, we have to find a way to exclude accessories or used phones.

Searching in departments

Let us have a look at the Amazon website: www.amazon.com. Check out the search bar at the top of the page—see also Figure 16.1. In addition to typing in search keywords, we can select the department in which we want to search. Do the following:

1. Type *Apple* into the search bar and press enter.
2. Select *Cell Phones & Accessories* from the search filter and click *Go*.
3. Now click on *Unlocked Cell Phones* in the departments filter section on the left hand of the page.

Automated Data Collection with R: A Practical Guide to Web Scraping and Text Mining, First Edition.
Simon Munzert, Christian Rubba, Peter Meißner and Dominic Nyhuis.

Figure 16.1 Amazon's search form

4. Type in other producers of mobile phones and compare the resulting URLs—which parts of the URL change?
5. Try to eliminate parts of the query string in the address of your browser and watch what happens. Try to find those query strings which are necessary to replicate the search result and which can be left out.

The URL produced by searching for a specific producer in *Unlocked Cell Phones* in the browser looks like this:

http://www.amazon.com/s/ref=nb_sb_noss_1?url=node%3D2407749011&field-keywords=Apple&rh=n%3A2335752011%2Cn%3A7072561011%2Cn%3A2407749011%2Ck%3AApple

Trying to delete various parts of the URL we find that the following URL is sufficient to replicate the search results:

http://www.amazon.com/s/?url=node%3D2407749011&field-keywords=Apple

The `field-keywords` part of the query string changes the keywords that are searched for, while `url` restricts the search results to unlocked cell phones. We found a basic URL that allows us to perform searches in the department of unlocked mobile phones and that we can manipulate to get results for different keywords.

Brand restrictions

Browsing through the search results we find that often phones of other producers are found as well. A brand filter on the left-hand side of the page helps get rid of this noise. There are two strategies to get the brand-restricted search results: We can either find the rules according to which the link is generated and generate the link ourselves or start with a non-restricted search, extract the link for the restricted results, and later on use it to get filtered search results. We go for the second solution because it is easier to implement. To learn more about how to identify the link, we use the *inspect element* tool of our browser on the brand filter:

```
<a href="/s/ref=sr_nr_p_89_0?rh=n%3A2335752011%2Cn%3A7072561011%
    2Cn%3A2407749011%2Ck%3AApple%2Cp_89%3AApple&amp;keywords=Apple
    &amp;ie=UTF8&amp;qid=1389615535&amp;rnid=2528832011" class=" ">
  <img style="margin-right:4px; " height="12" width="12" border="
      0" align="top" alt="Apple" src="http://g-ecx.images-amazon.
      com/images/G/01/nav2/buttons/checkbox_unselected_enabled._
      V192545545_.jpg">
  <span class="refinementLink">Apple</span>
</a>
```

The link we are looking for is part of an <a> node. Unfortunately, the node has no specific class, but it has a <span> node as child with a very specific class called `refinementLink`. The content of the class is equal to the brand we want to restrict the search to—that should do. Translating this observation into XPath means that we are looking for a <span> node with class `refinementLink` for which the content of that node is equal to the keyword we are searching for. From this <span> node, we want to move one level up to the parent and select the parent's `href` attribute:

```
//span[@class="refinementLink" and text()="Apple"]/../@href
```

Sorting Now we have a way of restricting search results to specific producers, but the results are sorted in the default sorting order. Maybe sorting according to newness of the product is a better idea. After searching for a product on the Amazon page, we are presented with a drop-down list directly above the search results. It allows us to select one of several sorting criteria. Let us choose *Newest Arrivals* to have new products listed first. After selecting our preferred sorting, a new element is added to the URL—`&sort=date-desc-rank`. We can use it later on to construct an URL that produces sorted results.

Next page Last but not least, we want to download more than the 24 products listed on the first results page. To do so, we need to select the next page. A link called *Next Page* at the bottom of the page does the trick. Using the *inspect element* tool of our browser reveals that the link is marked by a distinctive class attribute—`pagnNext`:

```
<a title="Next Page" id="pagnNextLink" class="pagnNext" href="/
    gp/search/ref=sr_pg_2?rh=n%3A2335752011%2Cn%3A7072561011%2Cn%
    3A2407749011%2Ck%3AApple&amp;page=2&amp;sort=salesrank&amp;
    keywords=Apple&amp;ie=UTF8&amp;qid=1389618220">
 <span id="pagnNextString">Next Page</span>
 <span class="srSprite pagnNextArrow"></span>
</a>
```

We search for <a> nodes with a next page class and extract their `href` attribute. This is done using the following XPath expression:

```
//a[@class='pagnNext']/@href
```

Later on we will use the links gathered in this way to download subsequent search result pages.

The scraping strategy Now we have all the elements set up to run product searches for unlocked mobile phones of specific brands with a specific sorting. The following steps now have to be translated into R code:

1. Specify the basic search URL for unlocked mobile phones and download the file.
2. Search and extract the brand filtering link from the source code of the downloaded file.

3. Append the sorting parameter to the query string of the beforehand extracted link and download the page.
4. Search and extract the link to next page and download the next page. Repeat this step as needed.

Downloading search pages

First, we load the necessary packages. The stringr package serves as the all-purpose tool for extracting and manipulating text snippets, whereas XML and RCurl are the workhorses for the scraping tasks. RCurl enables us to download several files via one connection and XML is indispensable for HTML parsing and information extraction via XPath:

```
R> library(stringr)
R> library(XML)
R> library(RCurl)
```

Next we save the base URL for our searches and the first producer we want to search for in an object:

```
R> baseURL <- "http://www.amazon.com/s/ref=nb_sb_noss_2?url=node%3
D2407749011&field-keywords="
R> keyword <- "Apple"
```

Base URL and producer name are combined with a simple call to `str_c()` and the page is downloaded and saved in an object:

```
R> url <- str_c(baseURL, keyword)
R> firstSearchPage <- getURL(url)
```

To issue XPath queries, we parse the page with `htmlParse()` and save it in an object:

```
R> parsedFirstSearchPage <- htmlParse(firstSearchPage)
```

We specify the XPath expression to extract the link for the brand restricted search results by pasting the producer name into the XPath expression we outlined before:

```
R> xpath <- str_c('//span[@class="refinementLink" and text()="',
R>                keyword,
R>                '"]/../@href')
```

We use the XPath expression to extract the link and complete it with the base URL of the server:

```
R> restSearchPageLink <- xpathApply(parsedFirstSearchPage, xpath)
R> restSearchPageLink <- unlist(as.character(restSearchPageLink))
R> restSearchPageLink <- str_c("http://www.amazon.com", restSearchPageLink)
```

Finally, we add the desired sorting to the query string of the URL:

```
R> restSearchPageLink <- str_c(restSearchPageLink, "&sort=date-desc-rank")
```

… and download the page:

```
R> restrictedSearchPage <- getURL(restSearchPageLink)
```

This provides us with our first search results page for products restricted to a specific producer and the *Unlocked Cell Phones* product department.

Now we want to download further search results pages and store them in a list object. First, we create the list object and save the first search results page as its the first element. Next, the XPath expression that extracts the link for the next page is stored as well to make the code more readable. We create a loop for the first five search pages. In every iteration we extract the link for the next page and download and store the page in our list object:

```
R> SearchPages <- list()
R> SearchPages[[1]] <- restrictedSearchPage
R> xpath <- "//a[@class='pagnNext']/@href"
R> for (i in 2:5) {
    nextPageLink <- xpathApply(htmlParse(SearchPages[[i - 1]]), xpath)
    nextPageLink <- unlist(nextPageLink)
    nextPageLink <- str_c("http://www.amazon.com", nextPageLink)
    SearchPages[[i]] <- getURL(nextPageLink)
}
```

16.1.2 Extracting product information

In the previous section, we ran searches to collect our results. In this section, we gather the necessary data from the results.

Title and product page links

The first information to be extracted are the product titles of the search results pages as well as the links to the product pages. Using the *inspect element* tool, we find that links and titles are part of a heading of level three—an <h3> node. Searching the source code for other headings of level three reveals that they are only used for product titles and links to product pages:

```
<h3 class="newaps">
  <a href="http://www.amazon.com/Apple-iPhone-8GB-White-Sprint/
      dp/B0074SQUBY/ref=sr_1_1?s=wireless&amp;ie=UTF8&amp;qid=
      1389697991&amp;sr=1-1&amp;keywords=Apple">
   <span class="lrg bold">Apple iPhone 4 8GB (White) - Sprint
   </span>
  </a>
</h3>
```

We apply this information and construct two XPath expressions, `//h3/a/span` for titles and `//h3/a` for the links. As we have a whole list of search pages from which we want to extract data, we wrap the extraction procedure into a function and use `lapply()` to extract the information from all pages; first the titles:

```
R> extractTitle <- function(x) {
    unlist(xpathApply(htmlParse(x), "//h3/a/span", xmlValue))
}
R> titles <- unlist(lapply(SearchPages, extractTitle))
R> titles[1:3]
[1] "Apple iPhone 4 16GB (Black) - CDMA Verizon"
[2] "Apple iPhone 5s, Gold 16GB (Unlocked)"
[3] "Apple iPhone 4 16GB (Black) - AT&T"
```

then the links:

```
R> extractLink <- function(x) {
    unlist(xpathApply(htmlParse(x), "//h3/a", xmlAttrs))
}
R> links <- unlist(lapply(SearchPages, extractLink))
R> links[1:3]
[1] "http://www.amazon.com/Apple-iPhone-16GB-Black-Verizon/dp/
B004ZLV5UE/ref=sr_1_1/181-2441251-9365168?s=wireless&ie=UTF8&qid=
1391539292&sr=1-1&keywords=Apple"
[2] "http://www.amazon.com/Apple-iPhone-5s-Gold-Unlocked/dp/
B00F3J4E5U/ref=sr_1_2/181-2441251-9365168?s=wireless&ie=UTF8&qid=
1391539292&sr=1-2&keywords=Apple"
[3] "http://www.amazon.com/Apple-iPhone-16GB-Black-AT/dp/
B004ZLV5PE/ref=sr_1_3/181-2441251-9365168?s=wireless&ie=UTF8&qid=
1391539292&sr=1-3&keywords=Apple"
```

Retrieving product pages

For the retrieval of price, costumer rating, and sales rank, the search pages' structure is hard to exploit or simply does not provide the information we seek. Therefore, we first have to download the individual product pages and extract the information from there.

To avoid establishing new connections for all the downloads—which is time consuming—we create a handle that is reused for every call to `getURL()`. Furthermore, we want to give the server a break every 10 downloads, so we split our link vector into chunks of size 10 and loop over the list of chunks.[1] In every loop, we request 10 pages and append them to the list object we created for storage and move to the next chunk. Last but not least we parse all the pages and store them in another list object:

```
R> chunk <- function(x, n) split(x, ceiling(seq_along(x)/n))
R> Links <- chunk(links, 10)
R> curl <- getCurlHandle()
R> ProductPages <- list()
R> for (i in 1:length(Links)) {
    ProductPages <- c(ProductPages, getURL(Links[[i]]))
    Sys.sleep(2)
}
R> ParsedProductPages <- lapply(ProductPages, htmlParse)
```

[1] See the advice at http://stackoverflow.com/a/3321659/1144966 for several chunking solutions.

Extracting prices

Having gathered all product pages, we move on to extracting the product price. Often, several prices are displayed on a product page: list prices, prices for new items, prices for used or refurbished items, and prices for products that are similar to the one selected. Using the *inspect elements* tool on the price directly under the product title, we find that it is enclosed by a `<span>` node with id `actualPriceValue`. Translated to an XPath expression, it reads: `//span[@id="actualPriceValue"]`. One problem is that some items are not in stock anymore and the call to `xpathApply()` would return `NULL` for those items. To ensure that for these products we record a price of `NA` instead of `NULL` we check for the length of the `xpathApply()` result. If the length of the result is zero we replace it with `NA`. Below you find a source code snippet containing the price information we seek as well as the R code to extract the information:

```
<span id="actualPriceValue"><b class="priceLarge">$210.00</b></span>
```

```
R> extractPrice <- function(x) {
    x <- xpathApply(x, "//span[@id=\"actualPriceValue\"]", xmlValue)
    x <- unlist(x)
    x <- str_extract(x, "[[:digit:]]*\\.[[:digit:]]*")
    if (length(x) == 0)
        x <- NA
    return(as.numeric(x))
}
R> prices <- unlist(lapply(ParsedProductPages, extractPrice))
R> names(prices) <- NULL
R> prices[1:10]
 [1] 210.0 710.0 240.0 319.0 354.9 208.9 239.9 359.9 420.0 565.1
```

Extracting customer ratings

This seems to work. Extracting the average customer ratings—ranging from one star to five—works similar to the procedure we used for the prices. Directly under the product title you find a series of five stars that are filled according to the average costumer rating. This graphical representation is enclosed by a `<span>` node that contains the average rating in its title attribute. We extract the information with an XPath expression: `//span[contains (@title,' out of 5 stars')]]`, and a call to `xmlAttr()` within `xpathApply()`. The rating is then extracted from the title with a regular expression:

```
<span class="swSprite s_star_4_0 " title="3.6 out of 5 stars">
 <span>3.8 out of 5 stars</span>
</span>
```

```
R> extractStar <- function(x) {
    x <- xpathApply(x,"//span[contains(@title,' out of 5 stars')]",
xmlValue)
    if (length(x) == 0) {
        x <- NA
    } else {
```

```
        x <- x[[1]]
        x <- str_extract(x, "[[:digit:]]\\.?[[:digit:]]?")
    }
    return(as.numeric(x))
}
R> stars <- unlist(lapply(ParsedProductPages, extractStar))
R> names(stars) <- NULL
R> stars[1:10]
 [1] 3.6 3.5 3.7 3.2 3.3 3.7 3.8 3.8 3.5 4.0
```

Extracting sales ranks

Further down on the page we find a section called *Product Details*. In this section, further information like the Amazon Standard Identification Number (ASIN), the product model, and the sales rank on Amazon within the category of *Cell Phones & Accessories* are shown as separate items. Let us start with extracting the sales rank which is enclosed in a `<li>` node of id `SalesRank`. We extract the node with XPath and collect the rank with a regular expression that looks for digits after a hash tag character and a second one that deletes everything which is not a digit:

```
<li id="SalesRank">
 <b>Amazon Best Sellers Rank:</b> #423 in Cell Phones &
     Accessories (<a href="http://www.amazon.com/gp/bestsellers/
      wireless/ref=pd_dp_ts_cps_1">See Top 100 in Cell Phones &
      Accessories</a>)
</li>
```

```
R> extractRank <- function(x) {
    x <- unlist(xpathApply(x, "//li[@id='SalesRank']", xmlValue))
    x <- str_extract(x, "#.*?in")
    x <- str_replace_all(x, "[, in#]", "")
    if (length(x) == 0)
        x <- NA
    return(as.numeric(x))
}
R> ranks <- unlist(lapply(ParsedProductPages, extractRank))
R> names(ranks) <- NULL
R> ranks[1:10]
 [1]  423  502  542  617  789  885 1277 1380 1268 1567
```

Extracting the ASIN

Next, we extract the ASIN from the product page. This information will help us later on to get rid of duplicates and to identify products. The ASIN is found in a list item that is unfortunately not identified with an `id` attribute or a specific class:

```
<li><b>ASIN:</b> B00FBSOXGI</li>
```

Nevertheless, we can specify its position as XPath expression by searching for a `<b>` node that has a `<li>` node as parent and contains text of pattern `ASIN`. From this node, we move one level up the tree and select the text of the parent:

```
//li/b[contains(text(), 'ASIN')]/../text()
```

```
R> extractASIN <- function(x) {
    x <- xpathApply(x, "//li/b[contains(text(), 'ASIN')]/../text()",
xmlValue)
    x <- str_trim(unlist(x))
    if (length(x) == 0)
        x <- NA
    return(x)
}
R> asins <- unlist(lapply(ParsedProductPages, extractASIN))
R> names(asins) <- NULL
R> asins[1:5]
[1] "B004ZLV5UE" "B00F3J4E5U" "B004ZLV5PE" "B00598BY6W" "B005SSB0YO"
```

Extracting the product model

Finally, we extract the product model following the same strategy as before:

```
<li><b>Item model number:</b> MC637LL/A</li>
```

```
R> extractModel <- function(x) {
    xpath <- "//li/b[contains(text(), 'Item model number')]/../text()"
    x <- xpathApply(x, xpath, xmlValue)
    x <- str_trim(unlist(x))
    if (length(x) == 0)
        x <- NA
    return(x)
}
R> models <- unlist(lapply(ParsedProductPages, extractModel))
R> models[1:5]
[1] " A1349"     " 5s"         " MC608LL/A" " iPhone 4"   " MC924LL/A"
```

16.2 Scraping procedure

16.2.1 Retrieving data on several producers

Above we explored our *data source* step by step and developed solutions for various data collection and extraction problems. So far, we only used one producer as an example and have not gathered the data for others. To not have to repeat the whole code above for the other producers as well, we have to put its solutions into functions for convenient reuse. The functions can be loaded into our R-session via

```
R> source("amazonScraperFunctions.r")
```

After sourcing the functions, we set three global options: `forceDownload` is part of every download function and setting it to `TRUE` will cause the the functions to redownload all pages while setting it to `FALSE` will cause them to check whether or not the files to be downloaded exist already and should not be downloaded again. `KeyWords` is a vector of producer names that is also reused throughout the functions and defines for which producers mobile phone product details should be collected. The `n` parameter stores a single number that is used to determine how many search result pages should be gathered. With each search results page, we gain 24 further links to product pages:

```
R> forceDownload <- FALSE
R> KeyWords <- c("Apple", "BlackBerry", "HTC", "LG", "Motorola",
"Nokia", "Samsung")
R> n <- 5
```

After having set up our global options, we can use the sourced functions to collect search and product pages and extract the information we seek. The steps we take match those carved out in the exploration section before. We start with collecting search pages:

```
R> SearchPageList <- NULL
R> for (i in seq_along(KeyWords)) {
    message(KeyWords[i])
    SearchPageList <- c(SearchPageList, getSearchPages(KeyWords[i],
n, forceDownload))
}
```

… extract titles and product page links:

```
R> titles <- extractTitles(SearchPageList)
R> links <- extractLinks(SearchPageList)
```

… download product pages:

```
R> brands <- rep(KeyWords, each = n * 24)
R> productPages <- getProductPages(links, brands, forceDownload)
```

… and extract further data:

```
R> stars <- extractStars(productPages)
R> asins <- extractASINs(productPages)
R> models <- extractModels(productPages)
R> ranks <- extractRanks(productPages)
R> prices <- extractPrices(productPages)
```

16.2.2 Data cleansing

Although we have already done a lot of data cleansing along the way—trim leading and trailing spaces from strings, extract digits, and transform them to type numeric, there are still some tasks to do before we can begin to analyze our data. First of all, we recast the information as a data frame and then try to get rid of duplicated products as best as possible.

The first task is simple, as the information has already been saved in vectors of the same length with NAs where no information was collected. In addition to combining the information gathered so far, we add the names of the downloaded product pages and use their last change attribute (`file.info(fname)$ctime`) to store the time when the data were retrieved:

```
R> fnames <- str_c(brands, " ProductPage ", seq_along(brands), ".html")
R> phones <- data.frame(brands, prices, stars, ranks,
R>                      asins, models, titles, links,
R>                      fnames,
R>                      timestamp = file.info(
R>                                  str_c("dataFull/", fnames)
R>                                  )$ctime,
R>                      stringsAsFactors = FALSE)
```

Next, we only keep complete observations and exclude all observations with duplicated ASINs, as this is the easiest way to make sure that we have no redundant data:

```
R> phones <- phones[complete.cases(phones), ]
R> phones <- phones[!duplicated(phones$asins), ]
```

16.3 Graphical analysis

To get an overview of the distribution of prices, costumer ratings, and sales ranks, we build a figure containing several plots that show all three variables. We have seven producers and also want to include an *All* category. Therefore, we specify a plotting function once and reuse it to assemble a plot representing information in all three categories. The main idea is to use transparent markers that allow for different shades of gray, resulting in black regions, where products bulk together, and light or white regions, where products are sparse or non-existent. Because sales ranks are only of ordinal scale, we have a hard time visualizing them directly. For every plot, we take those five products that rank highest in sales and visualize them differently—white dots on dark background with horizontal and vertical lines extending to the borders of each plot.

The plot function accepts a data frame as input and consequently starts with extracting our three variables from it—allowing a data frame as input serves convenient reuse on subsets of the data without repeating the subset three times. Next, we do a dummy plot that has the right range for x and y but do not plot any data. After that we add a modified x-axis and guiding lines. Thereafter comes the plotting of data so that the guiding lines stay in the background. The reason for this procedure is that we want to add guidelines but do not want to overplot the actual data—hence, we do a dummy plot, plot the guidelines, and thereafter plot the actual data. As color of the points we choose black but with an alpha value of 0.2—`rgb(0,0,0,0.2)`. The `rgb()` function allows us to specify colors by combining red, green, and blue in different intensities. The alpha value which is the fourth parameter defines how opaque the resulting color is and therewith allows for transparent plotting of markers. Last but not least, we construct an index for the five lowest numbers in `Ranks`—the highest sales ranks—and plot vertical and horizontal lines at their coordinates as well as small white points to distinguish them from the other products.

```
R> plotResults <- function(X, title="") {
    Prices <- X$prices
    Stars  <- X$stars
    Ranks  <- X$ranks
    plot(Prices, Stars, pch = 20, cex=10, col = "white",
         ylim = c(1,5), xlim = c(0, 1000), main = title,
         cex.main = 2, cex.axis = 2, xaxt = "n")
    axis(1, at=c(0, 500, 1000), labels = c(0, 500, 1000), cex.axis=2)
# add guides
    abline(v=seq(0, 1000, 100), col = "grey")
    abline(h=seq(0, 5, 1), col = "grey")
# adding data
    points(Prices, Stars, col=rgb(0, 0, 0, 0.2), pch = 20, cex = 7)
# mark 5 highest values
    index <- order(Ranks)[1:5]
    abline(v = Prices[index], col="black")
    abline(h = Stars[index], col="black")
    points(Prices[index], Stars[index], col = rgb(1, 1,1,1), pch = 20)
}
```

The result of our efforts is displayed in Figure 16.2.

With regard to costumer satisfaction, it is most interesting that there are differences not in the level but in the range of costumer ratings. For example, for Apple products, costumers seem to be coherently satisfied, whereas for Motorola products the range is much higher, suggesting that quality and/or feature appealing does vary greatly in Motorola's product palette. Another result is that best sellers are usually in the segments of high costumer satisfaction except for Nokia, who manage to have one of their best selling models at medium costumer satisfaction levels.

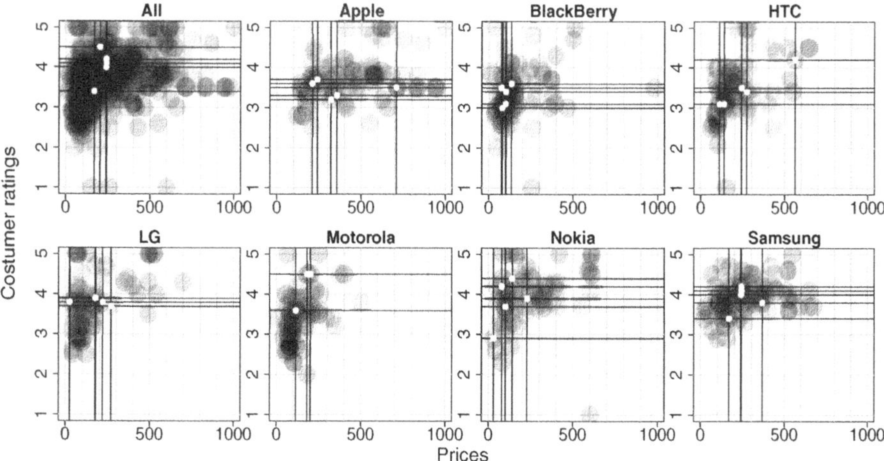

Figure 16.2 Prices, costumer rating, and best seller positioning of mobile phones. Black dots mark placement of individual products and white dots with horizontal and vertical lines mark the five best selling items per plot

16.4 Data storage

16.4.1 General considerations

At this stage, we might end the case study, having gathered all data needed and drawn our conclusions. Or we might think about future applications and further extensions. Maybe we want to track the development of prices and costumer ratings over time and repeat the data gathering process. Maybe we want to add further product pages or simply gather data for other producers as well. Our database grows larger and larger, gets more complex and someday we realize that we do not have a clue how all the *.Rdata* and HTML files fit together. Maybe we should have built for the future a database tailored to our needs?

In this section, we will build up an *SQLite* database that captures the data we have extracted so far and leaves room to add further information. These further information will be product reviews that are collected, stored, and analyzed in the next case study. At the end, we will have three functions that can be called as needed: one for creating the database and defining its structure, one for resetting everything and start anew, and one for storing gathered data within the database. Let us start with loading the necessary packages

```
R> library(RSQLite)
R> library(stringr)
```

Connecting to a database

... and establishing a connection to the database. Note that establishing a connection to a not existing database with RSQLite means that the package creates a new one with the name supplied in `dbConnect()`—here *amazonProductInfo.db*:

```
R> sqlite <- dbDriver("SQLite")
R> con <- dbConnect(sqlite, "amazonProductInfo.db")
```

Having established a connection to the database, thinking about the design of the database before storing everything in one table probably is a good idea to prevent having problems later on. We first have a look at our data again to recap what we have got:

```
R> names(phones)
 [1] "brands"    "prices"    "stars"     "ranks"     "asins"
 [6] "models"    "titles"    "links"     "fnames"    "timestamp"
R> phones[1:3, 1:7]
  brands prices stars ranks      asins     models
1  Apple    210   3.6   423 B004ZLV5UE      A1349
2  Apple    710   3.5   502 B00F3J4E5U         5s
3  Apple    240   3.7   542 B004ZLV5PE  MC608LL/A
                                   titles
1 Apple iPhone 4 16GB (Black) - CDMA Verizon
2      Apple iPhone 5s, Gold 16GB (Unlocked)
3         Apple iPhone 4 16GB (Black) - AT&T
```

Why databases are useful

So far our effort was on gathering data on phone models and all the data were stored in one table. Having all the data in one table most of the time is convenient when analyzing and plotting data within a statistics software, but needlessly complicates data management on the long run. Imagine that we download another set of product information. We could simply append those information to the already existing data frame. But over time model names and ASINs would pile up redundantly—already it takes more than 600 rows to store only seven producer names. Another fact to consider is the planned extension of the data collection. When we add reviews to our data, there are usually several reviews for one product inflating the data even more. If extending the collection further with other still unknown data, further problems in regard to redundancy and mapping may arise. To forestall these and similar problems, it is best to split the data into several tables—see Section 7.2.2 for a discussion of standard procedures to split data in databases.

16.4.2 Table definitions for storage

As our data are on phone models, we should start building a table that stores unique identifiers of phone models. The ASIN already provides such an identifier, so we build a table that only stores these strings and later on link all other data to that variable by using foreign keys. Another feature we might want to add is the `UNIQUE` clause which ensures that no duplicates enter the column, as it might happen that we gather new data on already existing phone models—so we try to add already existing ASINs into the database which results in an error—we use `ON CONFLICT IGNORE` to tell the database to do not issue an error but simply ignore the query if it violates the unique constraint. The `if(!dbExistsTable(...))` part also is thought to prevent errors—if the table exists already, the function does not send the query:

```
R> createPhones <- function(con){
     if(!dbExistsTable(con,"phones")){
     sql <- "CREATE TABLE phones (
                  id INTEGER NOT NULL PRIMARY KEY AUTOINCREMENT,
                  asin CHAR,
                  UNIQUE(asin) ON CONFLICT IGNORE);"
          dbGetQuery(con, sql)
     }else{
         message("table already exists")
     }
}
```

We set up similar functions `createProducers()`, `createModels()`, and `createLinks()` to define tables for producers, models, and links. They can be inspected in the supplementary materials to this chapter.

SQL query: items table

Having set up functions for defining tables for ASINs, producers, models, and links that ensure no redundant information is added to them, we now proceed with the table that should store product specific data. Within the table price, average costumer rating, rank in the selling list, title of the product page, the name of the downloaded file, and a time stamp should be saved. Adding a time stamp column to the table serves to allow for downloading information on the same phone model multiple times while allowing to discriminate between the time the information was received. To link the rows of this table to the other information, we furthermore add `id` columns for the phones, producers, models, and links tables. The `ON UPDATE CASCADE` part of the foreign key definition ensures that changes to the primary keys are passed through to the foreign keys. Also, we use a unique clause again to make sure no duplicated rows are included:

```
R> createItems <- function(con){
    if(!dbExistsTable(con,"items")){
        sql <- "CREATE TABLE items (
                id INTEGER NOT NULL PRIMARY KEY AUTOINCREMENT,
                price REAL,
                stars REAL,
                rank INTEGER,
                title TEXT,
                fname TEXT,
                time TEXT,
                phones_id      INTEGER NOT NULL REFERENCES phones(id)
                               ON UPDATE CASCADE,
                producers_id   INTEGER NOT NULL REFERENCES producers(id)
                               ON UPDATE CASCADE,
                models_id      INTEGER NOT NULL REFERENCES models(id)
                               ON UPDATE CASCADE,
                links_id       INTEGER NOT NULL REFERENCES links(id)
                               ON UPDATE CASCADE,
                UNIQUE(
                  price, stars, rank, time,
                  phones_id, producers_id, models_id, links_id
                ) ON CONFLICT IGNORE);"
        dbGetQuery(con, sql)
    }else{
        message("table already exists")
    }
}
```

… now we have built tables for all data gathered so far.

16.4.3 Table definitions for future storage

The next tables are thought to store review information that will be collected in the next case study. We start with a table for storing review information with columns for ASIN, the number of stars given by the reviewer, the number of people who found a review useful or not useful and the sum of both, the date the review was written, the title of the review, and of course the actual text:

```
R> createReviews <- function(con){
if(!dbExistsTable(con,"reviews")){
        sql <- "CREATE TABLE reviews (
                id INTEGER NOT NULL PRIMARY KEY AUTOINCREMENT,
                asin        TEXT,
                stars       INTEGER,
                helpfulyes  INTEGER,
                helpfulno   INTEGER,
                helpfulsum  INTEGER,
```

```
                date        TEXT,
                title       TEXT,
                text        TEXT,
                UNIQUE(asin, stars, date, title, text) ON CONFLICT IGNORE);"
        dbGetQuery(con, sql)
    }else{
        message("table already exists")
    }
}
```

An additional table stores meta information of all reviews on one model with columns for ASIN, the number of times one star was assigned to the product up to the number of times five stars were assigned:

```
R> createReviewsMeta <- function(con){
    if(!dbExistsTable(con,"reviewsMeta")){
        sql <- "CREATE TABLE reviewsMeta (
                id INTEGER NOT NULL PRIMARY KEY AUTOINCREMENT,
                asin        TEXT,
                one         INTEGER,
                two         INTEGER,
                three       INTEGER,
                four        INTEGER,
                five        INTEGER,
                UNIQUE(asin) ON CONFLICT REPLACE);"
        dbGetQuery(con, sql)
    }else{
        message("table already exists")
    }
}
```

16.4.4 View definitions for convenient data access

While the tables created are good for storing data on models and model reviews consistently and efficient, for retrieving data we probably would like to have something more convenient that automatically puts together the data needed for a specific purpose. Therefore, we create another set of virtual tables called *views* in database speak. The first view is designed for providing all information on items and therefore brings together information of the items, producers, models, as well as the phones table by making use of `JOIN`:

```
R> createViewItemData <- function(con){
    if(!dbExistsTable(con,"ItemData")){
        sql <- "CREATE VIEW ItemData AS
                SELECT items.id as itemid, price as itemprice,
                stars as itemstars, rank as itemrank,
                title as itemtitle, model, phones.asin as asin,
                producer from items
                JOIN producers on producers_id = producers.id
                JOIN models    on models_id    = models.id
                Join phones    on phones_id    = phones.id;"
```

```
        dbGetQuery(con, sql)
    }else{
        message("table already exists")
    }
}
```

The next view provides data on reviews:

```
R> createViewReviewData <- function(con){
    if(!dbExistsTable(con,"ReviewData")){
        sql <- "CREATE VIEW ReviewData AS
                SELECT phones.asin, reviews.id as reviewid,
                stars as reviewstars, one as allrev_onestar,
                two as allrev_twostar, three as allrev_threestar,
                four as allrev_fourstar, five as allrev_fivestar,
                helpfulyes, helpfulno, helpfulsum, date as reviewdate,
                title as reviewtitle, text as reviewtext
                FROM phones
                JOIN reviews on phones.asin=reviews.asin
                JOIN reviewsMeta on phones.asin=reviewsMeta.asin;"
        dbGetQuery(con, sql)
    }else{
        message("table already exists")
    }
}
```

Last but not least, we create a view that joins all data we have in one big table by joining together `ReviewData` and `ItemData`:

```
R> createViewAllData <- function(con){
    if(!dbExistsTable(con,"AllData")){
        sql <- "CREATE VIEW AllData AS
                SELECT * FROM ItemData
                JOIN ReviewData on ItemData.asin = ReviewData.asin"
        dbGetQuery(con, sql)
    }else{
        message("table already exists")
    }
}
```

Wrapper functions for table definition and deletion

Having created functions for defining tables on product data and review data as well as for creating views for convenient data retrieval, we can wrap all these functions up in one function called `defineDatabase()` and execute it:

```
R> defineDatabase <- function(con){
    createPhones(con)
    createProducers(con)
    createModels(con)
    createLinks(con)
    createItems(con)
    createReviews(con)
```

```
    createReviewsMeta(con)
    createViewItemData(con)
    createViewReviewData(con)
    createViewAllData(con)
}
```

To be able to reverse the process, we also define a function called `dropAll()` that asks the database which data tables and views exist and sends `DROP TABLE` and `DROP VIEW` statements, respectively, to the database to delete them. Note however that this function should be handled with care because calling it will result in loosing all data:

```
R> dropAll <- function(con){
    sql <- "select 'drop table ' || name || ';' from sqlite_master
    where type = 'table';"
    tmp <- grep("sqlite_sequence",unlist(dbGetQuery(con,sql)),
            value=T,invert=T)
    for(i in seq_along(tmp)) dbGetQuery(con,tmp[i])
    sql <- "select 'drop view ' || name || ';' from sqlite_master
    where type = 'view';"
    tmp <- grep("sqlite_sequence",unlist(dbGetQuery(con,sql)),
            value=T,invert=T)
    for(i in seq_along(tmp)) dbGetQuery(con,tmp[i])
}
```

16.4.5 Functions for storing data

So far we have build functions that define the structure of the database, but no data at all was added to the database. In the following, we will define functions that take our phones data (object `phones`) as argument and store bits of it in the right place. Later on we will put them all in a wrapper function that takes care of creating the database if necessary, defining all tables if necessary and adequately storing the data we pass to it.

Let us start with a function for storing ASINs. Although we could simply send all ASINs to the database and let it handle the rest—remember that the phones table was designed to ignore attempts to insert duplicated ASINs, it is faster to first ask which ASINs are stored within the database already and than only to add those that are missing. For each ASIN still missing in the database, we create a SQL statement for adding the new ASIN to the database and then send it:

```
R> addASINs <- function(x, con){
    message("adding phones ...")
    asinsInDB  <- unlist(dbReadTable(con,"phones")["asin"])
    asinsToAdd <- unique(x$asins[!(x$asins %in% asinsInDB)])
    for(i in seq_along(asinsToAdd)){
        sql <- str_c("INSERT INTO phones (asin) VALUES ('",
                     asinsToAdd[i], "') ;")
        dbGetQuery(con, sql)
    }
}
```

The functions for adding producers (`addProducers()`), models (`addModels()`), and links (`addLinks()`) follow the very same logic and are documented in the supplementary materials to this chapter.

The next function adds the remaining, product specific data to the database. First, we read in data from the phones, producers, models, and links tables to get up to date ids. Thereafter, we start cycling through all rows of `phones` extracting information from the price, stars, rank, title, fname, and time stamp variables. The next four lines match the ASIN of the current data row to those stored in the phones table; the current producer to those stored in producers; the current model to those stored in models and the current link to those stored in links for each retrieving the corresponding id. Then all these information are combined to an SQL statement that asks to add the data to the items table in the database. Last but not least the query is sent to the database:

```
R> addItems <- function(x, con){
    message("adding items ... ")
        # get fresh infos from db
        Phones      <-  dbReadTable(con, "phones")
        Producers   <-  dbReadTable(con, "producers")
        Models      <-  dbReadTable(con, "models")
        Links       <-  dbReadTable(con, "links")
    for(i in seq_along(x[,1])){
        priceDB      <- x$price[i]
        starsDB      <- x$stars[i]
        rankDB       <- x$rank[i]
        titleDB      <- str_replace(x$titles[i], "'", "''")
        fnameDB      <- x$fname[i]
        timeDB       <- x$timestamp[i]
        phonesDB <- Phones$id[Phones$asin %in% x$asin[i]]
        producersDB <- Producers$id[Producers$producer %in% x$brand[i]]
        modelsDB    <- Models$id[Models$model %in% x$model[i]]
        linksDB    <- Links$id[Links$link %in% x$link[i]]
        sql <- str_c(" INSERT INTO items
                        (price, stars, rank, title, fname, time,
                       phones_id, producers_id, models_id, links_id)
                       VALUES
                       ('",
                       str_c(  priceDB, starsDB, rankDB,
                               titleDB, fnameDB, timeDB,
                               phonesDB, producersDB, modelsDB, linksDB,
                               sep="', '"),
                    "'); ")
        dbGetQuery(con, sql)
    }
}
```

As announced, we finally define a wrapper function that establishes a connection to the database, defines the table structure if not already done before and adds the data and when finished closes the connection to the database again:

```
R> saveInDatabase <- function(x, DBname){
    sqlite <- dbDriver("SQLite")
    con    <- dbConnect(sqlite, DBname)
```

```
    defineDatabase(con)
    addASINs(x, con)
    addProducers(x, con)
    addModels(x, con)
    addLinks(x, con)
    addItems(x, con)
    dbDisconnect(con)
}
```

16.4.6 Data storage and inspection

Now we can write our data into the database:

```
R> saveInDatabase(phones, "amazonProductInfo.db")
```

… establish a connection to it:

```
R> sqlite <- dbDriver("SQLite")
R> con <- dbConnect(sqlite, "amazonProductInfo.db")
```

… and test if the data indeed has been saved correctly:

```
R> res <- dbReadTable(con, "phones")
R> dim(res)
[1] 623   2
R> res[1:3, ]
   id       asin
1 365 B0009FCAJA
2 390 B000CQVMYK
3 410 B000E95OAI
```

17

Analyzing sentiments of product reviews

17.1 Introduction

In the previous chapter, we have assembled several pieces of structured information on a collection of mobile phones from the *Amazon* website. We have studied how structural features of the phones, most importantly the cost of the phones, are related to consumer ratings. There is one important source of information on the phones we have disregarded so far—the textual consumer ratings. In this chapter, we investigate whether we can make use of the product reviews to estimate the consumer ratings. This might seem a fairly academic exercise, as we have access to more structured information on consumer ratings in the form of stars. Nevertheless, there are numerous circumstances where such structured information on consumer reviews is not available. If we can successfully recover consumer ratings from the mere texts, we have a powerful tool at our disposal to collect consumer sentiment in other applications.

In fact, while structured consumer ratings provide extremely useful feedback for producers, the information in textual reviews can be a lot more detailed. Consider the case of a product review for a mobile phone like we investigate in the present application. Besides reviewing the product itself, consumers make more detailed arguments on the specific product parts that they like or dislike and where they find fault with them. Researchers have made some effort to collect this more specific review (Meng 2012; Mukherjee and Bhattacharyya 2012). In this exercise, our goal is more humble. We investigate whether we are able to estimate the star that a reviewer has given to a product based on the textual review. To do so, we apply the text mining functionality that was introduced in Chapter 10.

We start out in the next section by collecting the reviews from the webpage. We download the files and store them in the previously created database. In the analytical part of the chapter, we first assess the possibility of using a dictionary-based approach to classify the reviews as

Automated Data Collection with R: A Practical Guide to Web Scraping and Text Mining, First Edition.
Simon Munzert, Christian Rubba, Peter Meißner and Dominic Nyhuis.

positive or negative. There are several English dictionaries where researchers have classified terms as signaling either positive or negative sentiment. We check whether the appearance of such signals in the reviews suffices to correctly classify the opinion of the review. In a final step, we use the text mining techniques to label the reviews based on the stars that reviewers have given. We train the algorithms based on half of the data, estimate the second half, and compare our estimates with the star reviews.

17.2 Collecting the data

As a first step we collect the additional data—the textual product reviews—from the *Amazon* website. We establish a connection to the database that we generated in the previous chapter. The database contains information on the mobile phones, the price and structural features, as well as the average number of stars that were assigned by the users. We download the individual reviews from the website, extract the textual reviews and the associated stars from the source code, and add the information to the database in a new table.

17.2.1 Downloading the files

Let us begin by loading the necessary packages for the operations in this section. For the scraping and extraction tasks, we need stringr, XML, and RCurl. We also load the RSQLite package to get the information in the database from the previous chapter and add the new information to the existing database.

```
R> library(stringr)
R> library(XML)
R> library(RCurl)
R> library(RSQLite)
```

We establish a connection to the database using the `dbDriver()` and `dbConnect()` functions:

Establishing a database connection

```
R> sqlite <- dbDriver("SQLite")
R> con <- dbConnect(sqlite, "amazonProductInfo.db")
```

Now we can get data from the database using `dbGetQuery()`. What we need are the phones' ASINs (Amazon Standard Identification Numbers) and the name of one of the phones' product pages. As the information is stored in different tables of the database, we make use of `JOIN` to merge them, where `id` from the phones table is matched with `phones_id` from the items table.

Tapping the database

```
R> sql <- "SELECT phones.asin, items.fname FROM phones
R>             JOIN items
R>             ON phones.id=phones_id;"
R> phonesData <- dbGetQuery(con,sql)
R> head(phonesData)
        asin                  fname
1 B004ZLV5UE Apple ProductPage 1.html
2 B00F3J4E5U Apple ProductPage 2.html
3 B004ZLV5PE Apple ProductPage 3.html
```

```
4 B00598BY6W Apple ProductPage 4.html
5 B005SSB0YO Apple ProductPage 5.html
6 B004ZLYBQ4 Apple ProductPage 6.html
```

We create the folder *dataReviews* via `dir.create()`, if it does not exist already, to store the downloaded review pages and change the working directory to that folder.

```
R> if(!file.exists("dataReviews")) dir.create("dataReviews")
R> setwd("dataReviews")
```

Parsing product pages The links to the review pages were part of the product pages we downloaded in the previous case study and were saved in *dataFull*. Therefore, we read in those files via `htmlParse()` to be able to extract the review page links.

```
R> productPageFiles <- str_c("../dataFull/", phonesData$fname)
R> productPages <- lapply(productPageFiles, htmlParse)
```

Extracting reviews We write a function that collects links to reviews from the phones' pages. This is done by looking for all `<a>` nodes that contain the text `customer review`. We generously discard minor errors, as there are lots more reviews than we can possibly hope to analyze in this application. Specifically, we discard results of length 0 and give them a value of `NA` and we do the same for links that create new reviews. We also discard the names of the resulting vector and return the results.

```
R> extractReviewLinks <- function(x){
R>     x <- xpathApply(x, "//a[contains(text(), 'customer review')]/@href",
R>                      as.character)[[1]]
R>     if(length(x) == 0) x <- NA
R>     if(str_detect(x, "create-review") & !is.na(x)) x <- NA
R>     names(x) <- NULL
R>     x
R> }
```

We apply our `extractReviewLinks()` function to all of the parsed phones' product pages and unlist the result to create a vector of links to the reviews.

```
R> reviewLinks <- unlist(lapply(productPages, extractReviewLinks))
```

To be able to manually inspect the pages where the review link is missing, we print the names of those product pages to our console. It turns out they are all products where no single review has been written.

```
R> noLink <- NULL
R> for(i in seq_along(reviewLinks)){
     if(is.na(reviewLinks[i])){
         noLink <- rbind(noLink, productPageFiles[i])
     }
}
R> noLink[1:3]
[1] "../dataFull/Apple ProductPage 81.html"
[2] "../dataFull/Apple ProductPage 99.html"
[3] "../dataFull/Apple ProductPage 102.html"
```

Finally, we add the host—`http://www.amazon.com`—to the links that we collected. We discard the host where it is already part of the link and add it to all the links, except in those cases where we set the entry to `NA`.

```
R> reviewLinks <- str_replace(reviewLinks, "http://www.amazon.com", "")
R> reviewLinks <- ifelse(is.na(reviewLinks), NA,
R>                       str_c("http://www.amazon.com", reviewLinks))
```

Now we are ready to download the first batch of review pages. We collect the pages by creating a file name that consists of the phones' ASIN and an index of `0001`. If the file does not already exist on the hard drive and the entry is not missing in the link vector we download the file, wrapping the function in a simple `try()` command. That way, if one download fails it will not stop running the rest of the loop. We add a random waiting period to our downloads to mimic human behavior and avoid being returned an error from amazon.com. We also add two status messages to provide information on the progress of the download. **Download**

```
R> N <- length(reviewLinks)
R> for(i in seq_along(reviewLinks)){
R> # file name
R>     fname <- str_c(phonesData[i, "asin"], "_0001.html")
R> # download
R>     if(!file.exists(fname) & !is.na(reviewLinks[i])){
R>         message("downloading")
R>         try(download.file(reviewLinks[i], fname))
R> # sleep
R>         sleep <- abs(rnorm(1)) + runif(1, 0, .25)
R>         message("I have done ", i, " of ", N,
R>                 " - gonna sleep ", round(sleep, 2),
R>                 " seconds.")
R>         Sys.sleep(sleep)
R>     }
R> # size of file info
R>     message(i, " size: ", file.info(fname)$size/1000, " KB")
R> }
```

Again, there is lots more information than we can possibly hope to analyze in this exercise, which is why we generously discard errors. We generate a vector of all downloads that we have collected so far—there should only be review sites that end in the pattern `001.html`—and remove pages with sizes of 0.

```
R> firstPages <- list.files(pattern = "001.html")
R> file.remove(firstPages[file.info(firstPages)$size == 0])
R> firstPages <- list.files(pattern = "001.html")
```

All remaining results are parsed and a list of all first review pages is created.

```
R> HTML <- lapply(firstPages, htmlParse)
```

In most cases, there is more than one review page for each mobile phone. For the sake of exposition, we download another four review pages, if available. To do so, we loop through the HTML object from the previous step. We extract the first link to the next review page by looking for an a node that contains the text Next and move one step down the tree to the associated href. While such a link is available and we have not reached the maximum number of review pages k—in our case five, we download another page. We generate a file name, download the link, and store it on our hard drive if it does not already exist. We also parse the downloaded file to look for another Next review page link. This operation is wrapped in a tryCatch() function, in case we fail to find a link.

```
R> for(i in seq_along(HTML)){
R> # extract link
R>     link <- xpathApply(
R>         HTML[[i]],
R>         "//a[contains(text(), 'Next')]/@href",
R>         as.character
R>     )[[1]]
R> # set k to 2
R>     k <- 2
R>     while(length(link) > 0 & k <= 5){
R>         # gen filename
R>         fname <- str_replace(
R>             firstPages[i],
R>             "[[:digit:]]{4}.html",
R>             str_c(
R>                 str_pad(k, 4, side = "left", pad = "0"),
R>                 ".html"
R>             )
R>         )
R>         message(i, ":", k, "... :", fname)
R> # download file
R>         if(!file.exists(fname) & length(link) > 0){
R>             download.file(link, fname, quiet = T)
R>             message(" download to file name: ", fname)
R>             Sys.sleep(abs(rnorm(1)) + runif(1, 0, .25))
R>         }
R>         htmlNext <- htmlParse(fname)
R> # extract link for next file
R>         link <- tryCatch(
R>             xpathApply(
R>                 htmlNext,
R>                 "//a[contains(text(), 'Next')]/@href",
R>                 as.character
R>             )[[1]],
R>             error = function(e){
R>                 message("xpath error")
R>                 NULL
R>             }
R>         )
R> # k + 1
R>         k <- k + 1
R>     }
R> }
```

Finally, we generate a vector of all the files in our *dataReviews* directory that contain the pattern `.html`. If all goes as planned, there should not be any file in the directory where this condition is false. We remove files of sizes smaller than 50,000 bytes, as there are presumably errors in these files.

```
R> tmp <- list.files(pattern = ".html")
R> file.remove(tmp[file.info(tmp)$size < 50000])
```

17.2.2 Information extraction

Having collected the review pages for the phones in our database, we now need to extract the textual reviews and the associated ratings from the pages and add them to the database.

Before extracting the data on individual reviews, we first extract some review meta information on all reviews made for a specific phone. The meta information contains the frequency of reviews giving a phone one up to five stars. The strategy for extracting the meta information is to use `readHTMLTable()` as the numbers are stored in a `table` node. To extract only the information we need—the number of reviews per star—we compose a little helper function—`getNumbers()`—that extracts one up to six digits. This function will be applied to each cell of the table when `readHTMLTable()` is called.

First, we define `getNumbers()` that extracts the value of a node and extracts digits from it.

```
R> getNumbers <- function(node){
R>      val <- xmlValue(node)
R>      x <- str_extract(val, "[[:digit:]]{1,6}")
R>      x
R> }
```

We create a vector of all the ASINs of those phones where we have access to customer reviews by listing all the HTML files in the review directory, discarding the indices and duplicate values.

```
R> FPAsins <- list.files(pattern="html$")
R> FPAsins <- unique(str_replace(FPAsins, "_.+", ""))
```

We create an empty data frame to store the meta information.

```
R> reviewsMeta <- data.frame(asin = FPAsins, one = NA, two = NA,
  three = NA, four = NA, five = NA, stringsAsFactors = F)
```

Then, we loop through all our first review pages stored in the list object `HTML`, extract all tables via `readHTMLTable()`, and apply `getNumbers()` to all its elements. From the resulting list of tables, we only keep the table called `productSummary` and from this only the third variable. The extracted numbers are written into the *i*th line of `reviewsMeta` for storage.

```
R> for(i in seq_along(HTML)){
R>      tmp <- as.numeric(
R>           readHTMLTable(
R>                HTML[[i]],
R>                elFun = getNumbers,
```

```
R>             stringsAsFactors = F
R>         )$productSummary$V3
R>     )
R>     print(tmp)
R>     reviewsMeta[i, c("one", "two", "three", "four", "five")] <- tmp[1:5]
R> }
```

We also compute the sum and the mean consumer rating per phone.

```
R> reviewsMeta$sum <- apply(reviewsMeta[, c("one", "two", "three",
R>                                          "four", "five")], 1, sum)
R> reviewsMeta$mean <- (reviewsMeta$one +
R>                         reviewsMeta$two * 2 +
R>                         reviewsMeta$three * 3 +
R>                         reviewsMeta$four * 4 +
R>                         reviewsMeta$five * 5
R>                         ) / reviewsMeta$sum
```

Having extracted the meta information, we now turn to the review specific information. What we would like to have in the resulting data frame are the ASIN, how many stars the reviewer gave the product, how many users found the review helpful and not helpful, the date the review was written, the title of the review, and the text of the review. To store the information, we first create an empty data frame.

```
R> reviews <- data.frame(asin = NA, stars = 0, helpfulyes = 0,
helpfulno = 0, helpfulsum = 0, date = "", title = "", text = "",
stringsAsFactors = F)
```

A purpose-built extraction function

The next block of code might seem a little complicated but it is really only a series of simple steps that is executed for all ASINs and all review pages belonging to the same ASIN. First of all, we use two loops for extracting the data. The outer loop with index `i` refers to the ASINs. The inner loop with index `k` refers to the one up to five review pages we collected for that product. The outer loop retrieves the file names of the review pages belonging to that product and stores them in `files`. It stores the ASIN for these review pages in `asin` and posts a progress message to the console.

In the inner loop, we first parse one file and store its representation in `html`. Next, we extract the value of all review nodes in a vector for later extraction of the consumer ratings and supplementary variables. All reviews are enclosed by a `div` node with `style='margin-left:0.5em;`. As this distinctive text pattern is easy to extract with a regular expression, we directly extract the value of the whole node instead of specifying a more elaborate XPath that would need further extraction via regular expressions anyways.

The information whether or not people found the review helpful is always given in the following form. *1 of 1 people found the following review helpful*. We make use of this pattern by extracting a string—as short as possible—that starts with one up to five digits and ends with *people*. We extract all sequences of digits from the substring and use these numbers to fill up the `helpful` variables—`helpfulyes`, `helpfulno`, and `helpfulsum`.

The consumer rating given to the product also follows a distinct pattern, for example, *5.0 out of 5 stars*. To collect this, we extract a substring starting with a digit dot digit and ending with *stars* and extract the first digit from the substring to get the rating.

The text of the reviews is extracted using XPath again as it has a distinct class—`reviewText`. We look for a `div` node with this class and specify that `xpathApply` should return the value of this node. Note, that both title and text of the reviews might contain single quotation marks that might later on interfere with the SQL statements. Therefore, we replace every single quotation mark by a sequence of two single quotation marks. Most SQL databases will recognize this as a way to escape single quotation marks and store only one single quotation mark.

The title and date are both located in a `span` node which is a child of a `div` node, which is a child of another `div` that encloses all review information. The `span`'s class is distinct in this subpath and while the title is set in bold a b node the date is enclosed by a `nobr` node. With two calls to `xpathApply()` we extract the value for each path.

As there are up to 10 reviews per page, all information—helpful variables, consumer rating, text, title, and date—result in vectors. These vectors are combined via `cbind()` into the matrix `tmp` and appended via `rbind()` to the prepared data frame `reviews`.

```
R> for(i in seq_along(FPAsins)){
R> # gather file names for ASIN
R>     files <- list.files(pattern = FPAsins[i])
R>     asin  <- FPAsins[i]
R>     message(i, " / ", length(FPAsins), " ... doing: ", asin)
R> # loop through files with same asin
R>     for(k in seq_along(files)){
R> # parsing one file
R>         html <- htmlParse(files[k])
R> # base path for each review : "//div[@style='margin-left:0.5em;']"
R>         reviewValue  <- unlist( xpathApply(
R>                                 html,
R>                                 "//div[@style='margin-left:0.5em;']",
R>                                 xmlValue))
R> # helpful
R>         helpful    <- str_extract(reviewValue,
R>                         "[[:digit:]]{1,5}.*?[[:digit:]]{1,5} people")
R>         helpful    <- str_extract_all(helpful,"[[:digit:]]{1,5}")
R>         helpfulyes <- as.numeric(unlist(lapply(helpful,'[',1)))
R>         helpfulno  <- as.numeric(unlist(lapply(helpful,'[',2)))
R>                                  - helpfulyes
R>         helpfulsum <- helpfulyes + helpfulno
R> # stars
R>         stars <- str_extract(reviewValue,
R>                         "[[:digit:]]\\.[[:digit:]] out of 5 stars")
R>         stars <- as.numeric(str_extract(stars, "[[:digit:]]"))
R> # text
R>         text <- unlist(xpathApply(
R>             html, "//div[@style='margin-left:0.5em;']
R>             /div[@class='reviewText']", xmlValue))
R>         text <- str_replace_all(text, "'", "''")
R> # title
R>         title <- unlist(xpathApply(
R>             html, "//div[@style='margin-left:0.5em;']
R>             /div/span[@style='vertical-align:middle;']/b",
R>             xmlValue))
R>         title <- str_replace_all(title, "'", "''")
R> # date
```

```
R>         date <- unlist(xpathApply(
R>             html, "//div[@style='margin-left:0.5em;']
R>             /div/span[@style='vertical-align:middle;']/nobr",
R>             xmlValue))
R> # putting it together
R>         tmp <- cbind(asin, stars, helpfulyes, helpfulno,
R>                   helpfulsum, date, title, text)
R>         reviews <- rbind(reviews, tmp)
R>         }
R> }
```

Finally, we keep only those lines of `reviews` where the first line is not `NA` to get rid of the dummy data we introduced to create the data frame in the first place.

```
R> reviews <- reviews[!is.na(reviews$asin),]
```

17.2.3 Database storage

Now that we have gathered all the data we need, it is time to store it in the database. There are two tables in the database that are set up to include the data: `reviewsMeta` for review data at the level of products and `reviews` for data at the level of individual reviews. For both tables, we construct SQL `INSERT` statements for each line of the data frame and loop through them to input the information into the database. The SQL statements for inserting data into the `reviewsMeta` table should have the following abstract form:

```
INSERT INTO reviewsMeta (col1, col2, col3)
VALUES ('val1', 'val2', 'val3');
```

To achieve this, we use two calls to `str_c()`. The inner call combines the values to be stored in a string, where each value is separated by `',  '`. These strings are then enclosed by the rest of the statement `INSERT INTO ... ('` and `');` to complete the statement.

```
R> SQL <- str_c(" INSERT INTO reviewsMeta
                (asin, one, two, three, four, five)
                VALUES
                ('",
                str_c(
                    reviewsMeta[, "asin"],
                    reviewsMeta[, "one"],
                    reviewsMeta[, "two"],
                    reviewsMeta[, "three"],
                    reviewsMeta[, "four"],
                    reviewsMeta[, "five"],
                     sep="', '")
                ,"'); ")
```

The first two entries in the resulting vector of statements look as follows

```
R> cat(SQL[1])
 INSERT INTO reviewsMeta
                 (asin, one, two, three, four, five)
                 VALUES
                 ('B0009FCAJA', '79', '74', '41', '35', '136');
R> cat(SQL[2])
 INSERT INTO reviewsMeta
                 (asin, one, two, three, four, five)
                 VALUES
                 ('B000AA7KZI', '45', '24', '12', '9', '13');
```

Now we can loop through the vector and send each statement via `dbGetQuery()` to the database.

```
R> for(i in seq_along(SQL)) dbGetQuery(con, SQL[i])
```

The process for storing the data of the individual reviews is similar to the one presented for `reviewsMeta`. First, we combine values and SQL statement snippets to form a vector of statements, and then we loop through them and use `dbGetQuery()` to send them to the database.

```
R> SQL <- str_c(" INSERT INTO reviews
                 (asin, stars, helpfulyes, helpfulno,
                   helpfulsum, date, title, text)
                 VALUES
                 ('",
                 str_c(
                     reviews[, "asin"],
                     reviews[, "stars"],
                     reviews[, "helpfulyes"],
                     reviews[, "helpfulno"],
                     reviews[, "helpfulsum"],
                     reviews[, "date"],
                     reviews[, "title"],
                     reviews[, "text"],
                     sep="', '")
                     ,"'); ")
```

Again, consider the first entry in the resulting vector of statements.

```
R> cat(SQL[1])
 INSERT INTO reviews
                 (asin, stars, helpfulyes, helpfulno,
                   helpfulsum, date, title, text)
                 VALUES
                 ('B0009FCAJA', '5', '4', '1', '5', 'June 20, 2007',
'One of the best in the market...', 'Have owned two in the past two
years and my daughter has another one.  Reliable, inexpensive,
practical, easy to use.  Tons of accesories and add-ons.  One of the
best, if not the best, Motorola has ever made.');
R> for(i in seq_along(SQL)) dbGetQuery(con,SQL[i])
```

17.3 Analyzing the data

Now that we have the reviews in a common database, we can go on to perform the sentiment scoring of the texts. After some data preparation in the next section, we make a first try by scoring the texts based on a sentiment dictionary. We go on to estimate the sentiment of the reviews using the structured information to assess whether we are able to train a classifier that recovers the sentiment of the texts that are not in the training corpus.

Connecting to the database Let us begin by setting up a connection to the database and listing all the available tables in the database.

```
R> sqlite <- dbDriver("SQLite")
R> con <- dbConnect(sqlite, "amazonProductInfo.db")
R> dbListTables(con)
 [1] "AllData"          "ItemData"         "ReviewData"
 [4] "items"            "links"            "models"
 [7] "phones"           "producers"        "reviews"
[10] "reviewsMeta"      "sqlite_sequence"
```

We read the `AllData` table to a `data.frame` and output the column names and the dimensions of the dataset. `AllData` is a view—a virtual table—combining information from several tables into one.

```
R> allData <- dbReadTable(con, "AllData")
R> names(allData)
 [1] "itemid"            "itemprice"          "itemstars"
 [4] "itemrank"          "itemtitle"          "model"
 [7] "asin"              "producer"           "asin.1"
[10] "reviewid"          "reviewstars"        "allrev_onestar"
[13] "allrev_twostar"    "allrev_threestar"   "allrev_fourstar"
[16] "allrev_fivestar"   "helpfulyes"         "helpfulno"
[19] "helpfulsum"        "reviewdate"         "reviewtitle"
[22] "reviewtext"
R> dim(allData)
[1] 4254   22
```

17.3.1 Data preparation

For data preparation, we rely on the tm package that was already introduced in Chapter 10. We also apply the textcat package to classify the language of the text and the RTextTools package to perform the text mining operations further below. vioplot provides a plotting function that is used in the next section.

```
R> library(tm)
R> library(textcat)
R> library(RTextTools)
R> library(vioplot)
```

Dropping non-english texts Before setting up the text corpus, we try to discard reviews that were not written in English. We do this by using the textcat package which categorizes the language of a text by considering the sequence of letters. Each language has a particular pattern of letter sequences. We can make use of this information by counting the sequences—so-called n-grams—in a text and comparing the empirical patterns to reference texts of known language.[1] The classification method is fairly accurate but some misclassifications are bound to happen. Due to the data abundance, we discard all texts that are estimated to not be written in English. We also discard reviews where the review text is missing.

```
R> allData$language <- textcat(allData$reviewtext)
R> dim(allData)
R> allData <- allData[allData$language == "english",]
R> allData <- allData[!is.na(allData$reviewtext),]
R> dim(allData)
[1] 3748   23
```

Next, we set up a corpus of all the textual reviews.

```
R> reviews <- Corpus(VectorSource(allData$reviewtext))
```

We also perform the preparation steps that were introduced in Chapter 10, that is, we remove numbers, punctuation, and stop words; convert the texts to lower case; and stem the terms.

```
R> reviews <- tm_map(reviews, removeNumbers)
R> reviews <- tm_map(reviews, str_replace_all, pattern =
"[[:punct:]]", replacement = " ")
R> reviews <- tm_map(reviews, removeWords, words = stopwords("en"))
R> reviews <- tm_map(reviews, tolower)
R> reviews <- tm_map(reviews, stemDocument, language = "english")
R> reviews
A corpus with 3748 text documents
```

17.3.2 Dictionary-based sentiment analysis

The simplest way to score the sentiment of a text is to count the positively and negatively charged terms in a document. Researchers have proposed numerous collections of terms expressing sentiment. In this application, we use the dictionary that is provided by Hu and Liu (2004) and Liu et al. (2005).[2] It consists of two lists of several thousand terms that reveal the sentiment orientation of a text. We load the lists and discard the irrelevant introductory lines.

```
R> pos <- readLines("opinion-lexicon-English/positive-words.txt")
R> pos <- pos[!str_detect(pos, "^;")]
R> pos <- pos[2:length(pos)]
R> neg <- readLines("opinion-lexicon-English/negative-words.txt")
R> neg <- neg[!str_detect(neg, "^;")]
R> neg <- neg[2:length(neg)]
```

---

[1]For an introduction to the topic, see Ramisch (2008). Generally speaking, non-English reviews should not deteriorate our estimates terribly, regardless of the specific technique that we apply. In case of the dictionary-based approach, non-English reviews should be assigned neutral values as barely any of the emotionally charged terms would appear in the texts. Conversely, statistical text mining techniques should fail to classify non-English texts but this should not have a strong effect on the overall classification accuracy of the English texts.

[2]The dataset is available at http://www.cs.uic.edu/~liub/FBS/opinion-lexicon-English.rar (last accessed February 15, 2014).

We stem the lists using the `stemDocument()` function and discard duplicates.

```
R> pos <- stemDocument(pos, language = "english")
R> pos <- pos[!duplicated(pos)]
R> neg <- stemDocument(neg, language = "english")
R> neg <- neg[!duplicated(neg)]
```

Let us have a brief look at a sample of positive and negative terms to check whether the dictionary contains plausible entries.

```
R> set.seed(123)
R> sample(pos, 10)
 [1] "exalt"        "sleek"        "gratitud"     "tidi"         "valiant"
 [6] "ardent"       "light-heart"  "top-notch"    "lyric"        "hottest"
R> sample(neg, 10)
 [1] "unview"          "impun"          "plea"           "martyrdom-seek"
 [5] "calam"           "tumultu"        "dissolut"       "avaric"
 [9] "flag"            "unsteadi"
```

The randomly drawn words seem to plausibly reflect positive and negative sentiment—although we hope that no reviewed phone is reviewed as suitable for martyrdom seekers. We go on to create a term-document matrix where the terms are listed in rows and the texts are listed in columns. In an ordinary term-document matrix, the frequency of the terms in the texts would be displayed in the cells. Instead, we count each term only once, regardless of the frequency with which it appears in the text. We thus argue that the simple presence or absence of the terms in the texts is a more robust summary indicator of the sentiment orientation of the texts. This is done by adding the `control` option `weighting` of the function `TermDocumentMatrix()` to `weightBin`. We also discard terms that appear in five reviews or less.

```
R> tdm.reviews.bin <- TermDocumentMatrix(reviews, control = list
  (weighting = weightBin))
R> tdm.reviews.bin <- removeSparseTerms(tdm.reviews.bin,
1-(5/length(reviews)))
R> tdm.reviews.bin
A term-document matrix (2212 terms, 3748 documents)

Non-/sparse entries: 121032/8169544
Sparsity           : 99%
Maximal term length: 12
Weighting          : binary (bin)
```

Computing sentiments To calculate the sentiment of the text, we shorten the matrices to contain only those terms with a known orientation—separated by positive and negative terms. We sum up the entries for each text to get a vector of frequencies of positive and negative terms in the texts. To summarize the overall sentiment of the text, we calculate the difference between positive and negative terms and discard differences of zero, that is, reviews that do not contain any charged terms or where the positive and negative terms cancel each other out.

```
R> pos.mat <- tdm.reviews.bin[rownames(tdm.reviews.bin) %in% pos, ]
R> neg.mat <- tdm.reviews.bin[rownames(tdm.reviews.bin) %in% neg, ]
R> pos.out <- apply(pos.mat, 2, sum)
```

```
R> neg.out <- apply(neg.mat, 2, sum)
R> senti.diff <- pos.out - neg.out
R> senti.diff[senti.diff == 0] <- NA
```

Let us inspect the results of the sentiment coding. First, we call some basic distributional properties.

```
R> summary(senti.diff)
   Min. 1st Qu.  Median    Mean 3rd Qu.    Max.    NA's
  -6.00    2.00    3.00    4.36    6.00   51.00     260
```

The mean review is positive (4.36 positive words on average), but the extremes are considerable, especially concerning the upper end of the distribution. The most positive text contains a net of 51 positive terms.[3] What this summary indicates is the obstacle of extreme variation in the length of the reviews.

```
R> range(nchar(allData$reviewtext))
[1]    76 23995
```

While the shortest review contains no more than 76 characters, the largest stemmed (!) review encompasses no fewer than 23,995. Students occasionally submit shorter term papers. Since we consider the differences between positive and negative reviews this should not be a dramatic problem. Nevertheless, we divide the sentiment difference by the number of characters in the review to get the estimates on a common metric. First, we set up a data frame with data that we want to plot and discard observations where the estimated sentiment is 0.

```
R> plot.dat <- data.frame(
     sentiment = senti.diff/nchar(allData$reviewtext),
     stars = allData$reviewstars)
R> plot.dat <- plot.dat[!is.na(plot.dat$sentiment),]
```

Visualizing sentiments

Using the `vioplot()` function from the vioplot package, we create a violin plot, a box plot-kernel density plot hybrid (Adler 2005; Hintze and Nelson 1998).

```
R> vioplot(
R> plot.dat$sentiment[plot.dat$stars == 1],
R> plot.dat$sentiment[plot.dat$stars == 2],
R> plot.dat$sentiment[plot.dat$stars == 3],
R> plot.dat$sentiment[plot.dat$stars == 4],
R> plot.dat$sentiment[plot.dat$stars == 5],
R> horizontal = T,
R> col = "grey")
R> axis(2, at = 3, labels = "Stars in review", line = 1, tick = FALSE)
R> axis(1, at = 0.01, labels = "Estimated sentiment by number of
characters", line = 1, tick = FALSE)
```

The result is plotted in Figure 17.1. We find that the order of estimated sentiment is in line with the structured reviews. The more stars a reviewer has given a product, the

[3]A closer inspection of the data reveals that the reviewer comments on a Google Nexus 4 phone—you be the judge whether the phone justifies such enthusiasm.

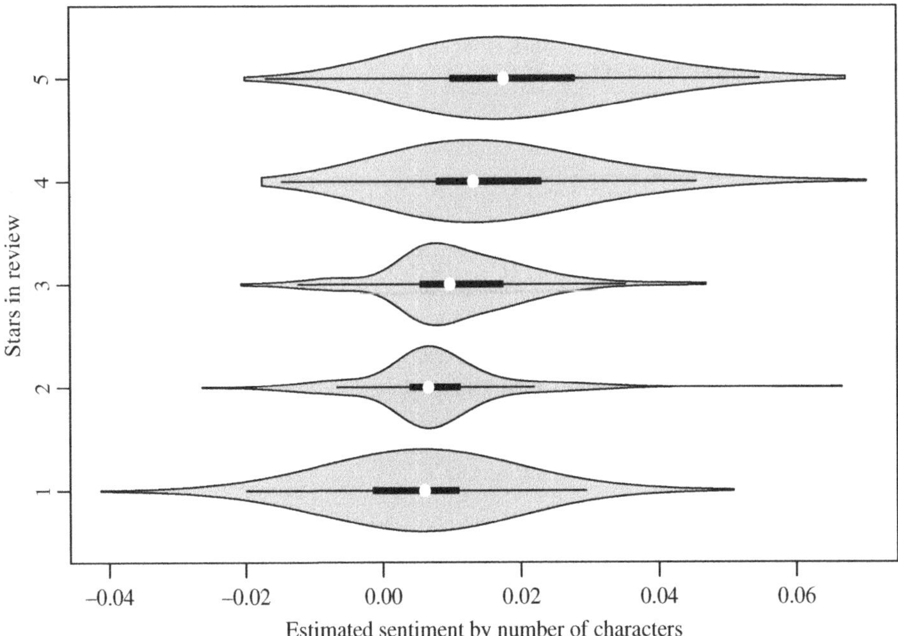

Figure 17.1 Violin plots of estimated sentiment versus product rating in Amazon reviews

better the sentiment that is expressed in the textual review and vice versa. However, there is also a considerable overlap of the five categories and even for one-star ratings we have an overall mean positive sentiment. Apparently, our estimates only roughly capture the expressed sentiment.

One alternative to estimating the sentiment of the review text is to consider the sentiment that is expressed in the headline. The advantage of this is that the headline often contains a summary statement of the review and is thus more easily accessible to a sentiment estimation. We create a corpus of the review titles and perform the same data preparation as before.

```
R> # Set up the corpus of titles
R> titles <- Corpus(VectorSource(allData$reviewtitle))
R> titles
R> # Perform data preparation
R> titles <- tm_map(titles, removeNumbers)
R> titles <- tm_map(titles, str_replace_all, pattern =
"[[:punct:]]", replacement = " ")
R> titles <- tm_map(titles, removeWords, words = stopwords("en"))
R> titles <- tm_map(titles, tolower)
R> titles <- tm_map(titles, stemDocument, language = "english")
R> # Set up term-document matrix
R> tdm.titles <- TermDocumentMatrix(titles)
R> tdm.titles <- removeSparseTerms(tdm.titles, 1-(5/length(titles)))
R> tdm.titles
```

```
R> # Calculate the sentiment
R> pos.mat.tit <- tdm.titles[rownames(tdm.titles) %in% pos, ]
R> neg.mat.tit <- tdm.titles[rownames(tdm.titles) %in% neg, ]
R> pos.out.tit <- apply(pos.mat.tit, 2, sum)
R> neg.out.tit <- apply(neg.mat.tit, 2, sum)
R> senti.diff.tit <- pos.out.tit - neg.out.tit
R> senti.diff.tit[senti.diff.tit == 0] <- NA
```

Since the sentiment difference has fewer than 10 distinct values in this case, we plot the estimates as points rather than as density distributions. For the same reason, we do not divide our results by the number of characters in the titles, as they are all of roughly the same length. A random jitter is added to the points before plotting. As there are only five categories in the structured reviews, we can better inspect our results visually if we add some noise to the points.

```
R> plot(jitter(senti.diff.tit), jitter(allData$reviewstars),
R>       col = rgb(0, 0, 0, 0.4),
R>      ylab = "Stars in Review",
R>      xlab = "Estimated sentiment"
R> )
R> abline(v = 0, lty = 3)
```

Again, we observe a rough overlap between the number of stars that were assigned by the reviewers and the estimated sentiment in the title (see Figure 17.2). Nevertheless, our

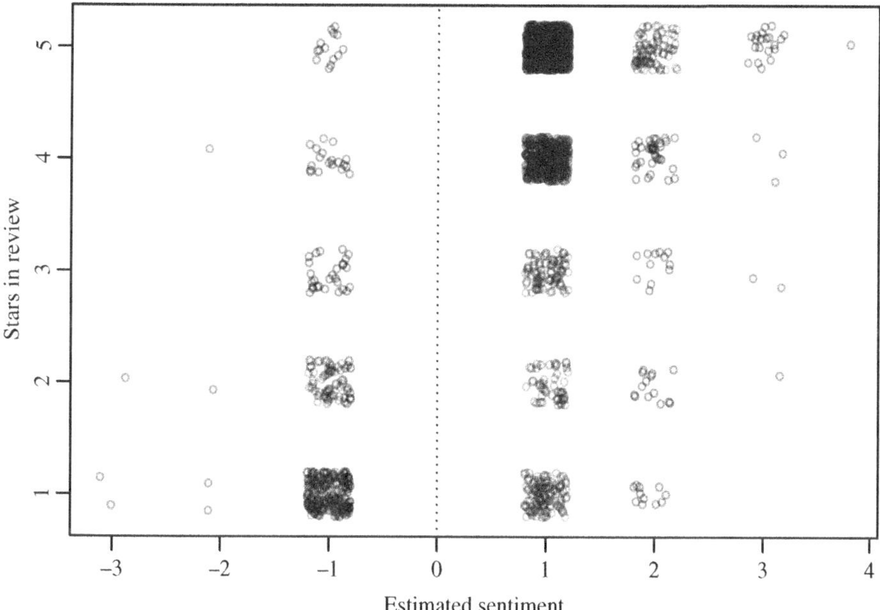

Figure 17.2 Estimated sentiment in Amazon review titles versus product rating. The data are jittered on both axes.

estimates are frequently somewhat off the mark. We therefore move on to an alternative text mining technique in the next section.

17.3.3 Mining the content of reviews

Chapter 10 discussed the possibilities of applying text mining to estimate the topical categories of text. This is done by assigning labels to a portion of a text corpus and estimating the labels for the unlabeled texts based on similarities in the word usages. There is no technical constraint on the type of label that we can try to estimate. This is to say that we do not necessarily have to estimate the topical emphasis of a text. We might as well estimate the sentiment that is expressed in a text as long as we have a labeled training set.

Document-term matrix

We set up a document-term matrix that is required by the RTextTools package. We remove the sparse terms and set up the container for the estimation. The first 2000 reviews are assigned to the training set and the remaining batch of roughly 2000 we use for testing the accuracy of the models.

```
R> dtm.reviews <- DocumentTermMatrix(reviews)
R> dtm.reviews <- removeSparseTerms(dtm.reviews, 1-(5/length(reviews)))
R> N <- length(reviews)
R> container <- create_container(
R>     dtm.reviews,
R>     labels = allData$reviewstars,
R>     trainSize = 1:2000,
R>     testSize = 2001:N,
R>     virgin = F
R> )
R> dtm.reviews
A document-term matrix (3748 documents, 2212 terms)

Non-/sparse entries: 121032/8169544
Sparsity           : 99%
Maximal term length: 12
Weighting          : term frequency (tf)
```

Maximum entropy and SVM

We train the maximum entropy and support vector models and classify the test set of reviews.

```
R> maxent.model <- train_model(container, "MAXENT")
R> svm.model <- train_model(container, "SVM")
R> maxent.out <- classify_model(container, maxent.model)
R> svm.out <- classify_model(container, svm.model)
```

Finally, we create a data frame of the results, along with the correct labels.

```
R> labels.out <- data.frame(
R>     correct.label = as.numeric(allData$reviewstars[2001:N]),
R>     maxent = as.numeric(maxent.out[,1]),
R>     svm = as.numeric(svm.out[,1])
R> )
```

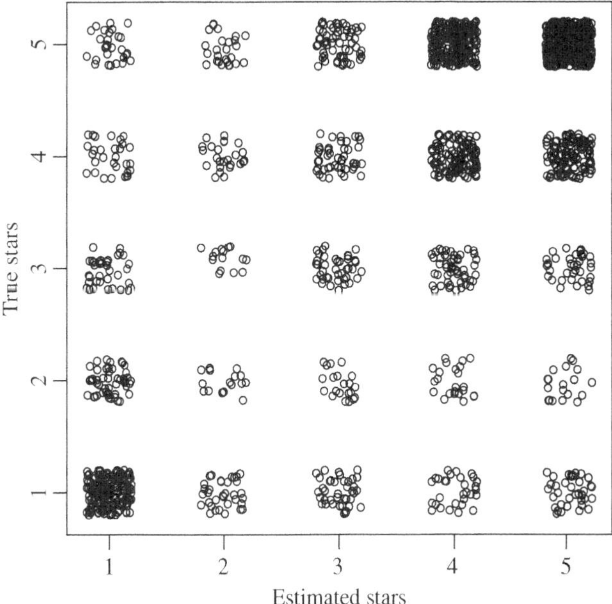

Figure 17.3 Maximum entropy classification results of Amazon reviews

As before, we plot the results as a point cloud and add a random jitter to the points for visibility.

```
R> plot(jitter(labels.out[,2]), jitter(labels.out[,1]),
R>      xlab = "Estimated stars",
R>      ylab = "True stars"
R> )
R> plot(jitter(labels.out[,3]), jitter(labels.out[,1]),
R>      xlab = "Estimated stars",
R>      ylab = "True stars"
R> )
```

The results are displayed in Figures 17.3 and 17.4—the data are jittered on both axes. Using either classifier we find that both procedures result in fairly accurate predictions of the number of stars in the review based on the textual review.

There are more classifiers implemented in the RTextTools package. Go ahead and try to estimate other models on the dataset. You simply have to adapt the `algorithm` parameter in the `train_model()` function.[4] You might also like to generate the modal estimate from multiple classifiers in order to further improve the accuracy of the sentiment classification of the textual reviews.

[4]On the available algorithms with RTextTools, see the documentation of the function using `?train_model`.

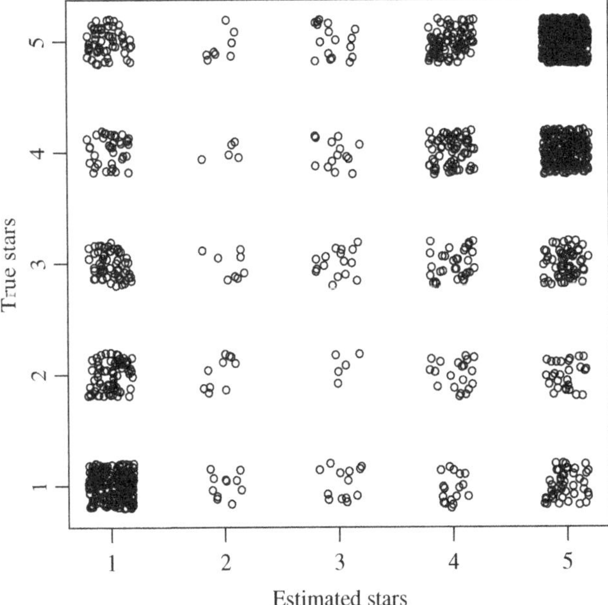

Figure 17.4 Support vector machine classification results of Amazon reviews

17.4 Conclusion

In this chapter, we have applied two techniques for scoring the sentiment that is expressed in texts. On the one hand, we have estimated the sentiment of product reviews based on the terms that are used in the reviews. On the other, we have shown that supervised text classification is not necessarily restricted to the topical category of texts. We can classify various aspects in texts, as long as there is a labeled training set.

The scoring of the texts is simplified in this instance, as product reviews refer to precisely one object—the product. This is to say that negative terms anywhere in the texts will most likely refer to the product that is being reviewed. Compare this to a journalistic text where multiple objects might be discussed in a way that it is not straightforward to estimate the object that a negative term refers to. Consequently, we cannot as easily make the implicit assumption of the analyses in this chapter that a term anywhere in the text refers to one particular object. Moreover, the sentiment in a product review is also simple to score as it is written to explicitly express a sentiment. Again, compare this to a journalistic text. While the text might in fact express a sentiment toward a topic or toward particular actors, the sentiment is ordinarily expressed in more subtle ways.

References

Adler D. 2005. *vioplot: Violin Plot*. R package version 0.2. http://wsopuppenkiste.wiso.uni-goettingen.de/ dadler

Adler J. 2006. *Baseball Hacks*. O'Reilly, Sebastopol, CA.

Adler J. 2009. *R in a Nutshell. A Desktop Quick Reference*. O'Reilly, Sebastopol, CA.

Alemán E, Calvo E, Jones MP, and Kaplan N. 2009. Comparing cosponsorship and roll-call ideal points. *Legislative Studies Quarterly* **34**(1), 87–116.

Asur S and Huberman BA. 2010. Predicting the future with social media. http://arxiv.org/abs/1003.5699v1 (Last accessed March 21, 2014).

Barberá P. 2013. *streamR: Access to Twitter Streaming API via R*. R package version 0.1. http://CRAN.R-project.org/package=streamR

Barberá P. 2014. *Rfacebook: Access to Facebook API via R*. R package version 0.3. http://CRAN.R-project.org/package=Rfacebook

Barrai I, Rodriguez-Larralde A, Marnolini E, Manni F, and Scapolini C. 2001. Isonymy structure of USA population. *American Journal of Physical Anthropology* **114**(2), 109–123.

Barratt N. 2008. *Who Do You Think You Are? Encyclopedia of Genealogy: The Definite Reference Guide to Tracing Your Family History*. HarperCollins, New York, NY.

Beaulieu A. 2009. *Learning SQL*. O'Reilly, Sebastopol, CA.

Berners-Lee T. 1989. Information management: A proposal. http://www.w3.org/History/1989/proposal.html (Last accessed February 26, 2014).

Berners-Lee T. 2000. *Weaving the Web: The Original Design and Ultimate Destiny of the World Wide Web by its Inventor*. HarperCollins, New York, NY.

Berners-Lee T, Fielding R, and Frystyk H. 1996. Hypertext transfer protocol—http/1.0. RFC 1945. http://tools.ietf.org/html/rfc1945 (Last accessed December 14, 2013).

Bhushan A. 1971. A file transfer protocol. RFC 114. http://tools.ietf.org/html/rfc114 (Last accessed December 16, 2013).

Bivand R and Lewin-Koh N. 2013. *maptools: Tools for Reading and Handling Spatial Objects*. R package version 0.8-27. http://CRAN.R-project.org/package=maptools

Bivand R, Keitt T, and Rowlingson B. 2013a. *rgdal: Bindings for the Geospatial Data Abstraction Library*. R package version 0.8-14. http://CRAN.R-project.org/package=rgdal

Automated Data Collection with R: A Practical Guide to Web Scraping and Text Mining, First Edition.
Simon Munzert, Christian Rubba, Peter Meißner and Dominic Nyhuis.

Bivand RS, Pebesma E, and Gómez-Rubio V. 2013b. *Applied Spatial Data Analysis with R* UseR! Series 2nd edn. Springer, Heidelberg/New York.

Blei DM and Lafferty JD. 2006. Correlated topic models. http://www.cs.cmu.edu/ lafferty/pub/ctm.pdf (Last accessed March 12, 2014).

Blei DM, Ng AY, and Jordan MI. 2003. Latent dirichlet allocation. *Journal of Machine Learning* **3**, 993–1022.

Boettiger C and Temple Lang D. 2012. *RMendeley: Interface to Mendeley API Methods*. R package version 0.1-2. http://CRAN.R-project.org/package=RMendeley

Boettiger C, Temple Lang D, and Wainwright PC. 2014. *rfishbase: R Interface to FishBASE*. R package version 0.2 2. http://CRAN.R-project.org/package=rfishbase

Bollen J, Mao H, and Zeng X. 2011. Twitter mood predicts the stock market. *Journal of Computer Science* **2**(1), 1–8.

Boswell D. 2002. Introduction to support vector machines. http://www.work.caltech.edu/boswell/IntroToSVM.pdf (Last accessed March 12, 2014).

Bratton K and Rouse SM. 2011. Networks in the legislative arena: How group dynamics affect cosponsorship. *Legislative Studies Quarterly* **36**(3), 423–460.

Broniatowski DA, Paul MJ, and Dredze M. 2013. National and local influenza surveillance through twitter: An analysis of the 2012-2013 influenza epidemic. *Plos One* **8**(12), doi:10.1371/journal.pone.0083672.

Brownrigg R, Minka TP, Becker RA, and Wilks AR. 2013. *maps: Draw Geographical Maps*. R package version 2.3-6. http://CRAN.R-project.org/package=maps

Burkett T. 1997. *Cosponsorship in the United States Senate: A Network Analysis of Senate Communication and Leadership, 1973-1990*. University of South Carolina, Columbia.

Castro E and Hyslop B. 2014. *HTML and CSS: Visual QuickStart Guide*. Peachpit Press.

Center for Responsive Politics. 2014. http://www.opensecrets.org/ (Last accessed March 1, 2014).

Cerami E. 2002. *Web Services Essentials*. O'Reilly, Sebastopol, CA.

Chamberlain S, Boettiger C, Ram K, Barve V, and Mcglinn D. 2013. *rgbif: Interface to the Global Biodiversity Information Facility API*. R package version 0.4.0.

Chamberlin DD and Boyce RF. 1974. *Sequel: A Structured English Query Language*. Proceedings of the 1974 ACM SIGFIDET Workshop on Data Description, Access and Control, May 1974, Ann Arbor, MI, pp. 249–264.

Chesney T. 2006. An empirical examination of Wikipedia's credibility. *First Monday* **11**(11), doi:10.5210/fm.v11i11.1413.

Cho WKT and Fowler JH. 2010. Legislative success in a small world: Social network analysis and the dynamics of congressional legislation. *Journal of Politics* **72**(1), 124–135.

Christian P. 2012. *The Genealogist's Internet: The Essential Guide to Researching Your Family History Online*. 5th revised edition. A & C Black Business Information and Development, London.

Clauson KA, Polen HH, Boulos MNK, and Dzenowagis JH. 2008. Scope, completeness, and accuracy of drug information in wikipedia. *The Annals of Pharmacotherapy* **42**(12), 1814–1821.

Codd EF. 1970. A relational model of data for large shared data banks. *Communications of the ACM* **13**(6), 377–387.

Conway J, Eddelbuettel D, Nishiyama T, Prayaga SK (during 2008), and Tiffin N. 2013. *RPostgreSQL: R Interface to the PostgreSQL Database System*. R package version 0.4.

Couture-Beil A. 2013. *rjson: JSON for R*. R package version 0.2.13. http://CRAN.R-project.org/package=rjson

Crawley MJ. 2012. *The R Book*. 2nd edn. John Wiley & Sons, Hoboken, NJ.

Crockford D. 2008. *JavaScript: The Good Parts*. O'Reilly, Sebastopol, CA.

Culotta A. 2010. Detecting influenza outbreaks by analyzing twitter messages. http://arxiv.org/pdf/1007.4748v1 (Last accessed September 03, 2014).

Dailey D. 2010. An SVG primer for today's browsers. http://www.w3.org/Graphics/SVG/IG/resources/svgprimer.html (Last accessed October 15, 2013).

Denis Mukhin DAJ and Luciani J. 2013. *ROracle: OCI based Oracle Database Interface for R*. 1.1-10.

Desposato SW, Kearney MC, and Crisp BF. 2011. Using cosponsorship to estimate ideal points. *Legislative Studies Quarterly* **36**(4), 531–565.

Dierks T and Allen C. 1999. The tls protocol version 1.0. RFC 2246. http://tools.ietf.org/html/rfc2246 (Last accessed December 12, 2013).

D'Orazio V, Landis S, Palmer G, and Schrodt P. 2011. Separating the wheat from the chaff: Applications of automated document classification using support vector machines. http://pan.oxfordjournals.org/content/early/2014/01/29/pan.mpt030.full. pdf+html (Last accessed March 12, 2014).

Döring H. 2013. The collective action of data collection: A data infrastructure on parties, elections and cabinets. *European Union Politics* **14**(1), 161–178.

Dreyer AJ and Stockton J. 2013. Internet 'data scraping': A primer for counseling clients. *New York Law Journal* July, 1–3.

Eisenberg JD. 2002. *SVG Essentials*. O'Reilly, Sebastopol, CA.

Essaid R. 2013a. Is web scraping illegal? Depends on what the meaning of the word is is. http://www.distilnetworks.com/is-web-scraping-illegal-depends-on-what-the-meaning-of-the-word-is-is/ (Last accessed January 26, 2014).

Essaid R. 2013b. Scraping just got a lot more dangerous. http://www.distilnetworks.com/scraping-just-got-a-lot-more-dangerous/ (Last accessed January 26, 2014).

Fall KR and Stevens WR. 2011. *TCP/IP Illustrated, Volume 1: The Protocols*. Addison-Wesley Professional, Indianapolis, IN.

Feinerer I. 2008. A text mining framework in R and its applications. Doctoral Thesis. Vienna University of Economics and Business Administration.

Feinerer I, Hornik K, and Meyer D. 2008. Text mining infrastructure in R. *Journal of Statistical Software* **25**(5), 1–54.

Ferguson N, Schneier B, and Kohno T. 2010. *Cryptography Engineering: Design Principles and Practical Applications*. John Wiley & Sons.

Fielding R, Gettys J, Mogul J, Frystyk H, Masinter L, Leach P, and Berners-Lee T. 1999. Hypertext transfer protocol – http/1.1. RFC 2616.

Fielding RT. 2000. Architectural styles and the design of network-based software architectures. Doctoral Thesis. University of California.

Flanagan D. 2011. *JavaScript: The Definitive Guide*. O'Reilly, Sebastopol, CA.

Forouzan BA. 2010. *TCP/IP Protocol Suite*. McGraw-Hill, Boston, MA.

Fowler JH. 2006a. Connecting the congress: A study of cosponsorship networks. *Political Analysis* **14**(4), 456–487.

Fowler JH. 2006b. Legislative cosponsorship networks in the us house and senate. *Social Networks* **28**(4), 454–465.

Fox WR and Lasker GW. 1983. The distribution of surname frequencies. *International Statistical Review* **51**, 81–87.

Franks J, Hallam-Baker P, Hostetler J, Lawrence S, Leach P, Luotonen A, and Stewart L. 1999. Http authentication: Basic and digest access authentication. RFC 2617. http://tools.ietf.org/html/rfc2617 (Last accessed December 14, 2013).

Freier A, Karlton P, and Kocher P. 2011. The secure sockets layer (ssl) protocol version 3.0. RFC 6101. http://tools.ietf.org/html/rfc6101 (Last accessed December 14, 2013).

Garfinkel S. 2002. *Web Security, Privacy and Commerce*. O'Reilly, Sebastopol, CA.

Gennick J. 2011. *SQL Pocket Guide.* 3rd edn. O'Reilly, Sebastopol, CA.

Gentry J. 2013. *twitteR: R Based Twitter Client.* R package version 1.1.7. http://CRAN.R-project.org/package=twitteR

Gentry J and Lang DT. 2013. *ROAuth: R Interface for OAuth*. R package version 0.9.3. http://CRAN.R-project.org/package=ROAuth

Ghomi AA, Shirzadi E, and Movassaghi A. 2013. Predicting the Academy Awards' result by analyzing tweets. *Global Journal of Science, Engineering and Technology*. **8**, 39–47.

Giles J. 2005. Internet encyclopae dias go head to head. *Nature* **438**, 900–901.

Gillespie P. 2012. Pronouncing sql: S-q-l or sequel? http://patorjk.com/blog/2012/01/26/pronouncing-sql-s-q-l-or-sequel/ (Last accessed August 11, 2014).

Gliozzo A, Strapparava C, and Dagan I. 2009. Improving text categorization bootstrapping via unsupervised learning. *ACM Transactions on Speech and Language Processing* **6**(1), 1–24.

Google. 2014. Chrome devtools. https://developers.google.com/chrome-developer-tools/ (Last accessed August 3, 2014).

Gourley D and Totty B. 2002. *HTTP. The Definitive Guide*. O'Reilly, Sebastopol, CA.

Grimmer J and Stewart BM. 2013. Text as data: The promise and pitfalls of automatic content analysis methods for political texts. *Political Analysis* **21**(3), 267–297.

Grolemund G and Wickham H. 2011. Dates and times made easy with lubridate. *Journal of Statistical Software* **40**(3), 1–25.

Hammer-Lahav E. 2010. The Oauth 1.0 protocol. RFC 5849. http://tools.ietf.org/html/rfc5849 (Last accessed February 25, 2014).

Hardt D. 2012. The Oauth 2.0 authorization framework. RFC 6749. http://tools.ietf.org/html/rfc6749 (Last accessed February 25, 2014).

Harold ER and Means WS. 2004. *XML in a Nuthsell: A Desktop Quick Reference.* 3rd edn. O'Reilly, Sebastopol, CA.

Harrington JL. 2009. *Relational Database Design and Implementation.* Morgan Kaufmann Series in Data Management Systems. 3rd edn. Elsevier, Amsterdam.

Hemenway K and Calishain T. 2003. *Spidering Hacks*. O'Reilly, Sebastopol, CA.

Hintze JL and Nelson RD. 1998. Violin plots: A box plot-density trace synergism. *The American Statistician* **52**(2), 181–184.

Hogarth RM. 1978. A note on aggregating opinions. *Organizational Behavior and Human Performance* **21**, 40–46.

Holdener III AT. 2008. *Ajax: The Definitive Guide*. O'Reilly, Sebastopol, CA.

Holzner S. 2003. *XPath Kick Start: Navigating XML with XPath 1.0 and 2.0*. Sams Publishing, Indianapolis, IN.

Hopkins D and King G. 2010. A method of automated nonparametric content analysis for social science. *American Journal of Political Science* **54**(1), 229–247.

Hornik K, Buchta C, and Zeileis A. 2009. Open-source machine learning: R meets weka. *Computational Statistics* **24**(2), 225–232.

Hu M and Liu B. 2004. *Mining and Summarizing Customer Reviews.* Proceedings of the ACM SIGKDD International Conference on Knowledge Discovery and Data Mining (KDD-2004), August 2004, Seattle, WA.

James DA and DebRoy S. 2013. *RMySQL: R Interface to the MySQL Database*. Version 0.9-3. http://biostat.mc.vanderbilt.edu/RMySQL (Last accessed August 29, 2013).

Jurka TP, Collingwood L, Boydstun AE, Grossman E, and Atteveldt WV. 2013. Rtexttools: A supervised learning package for text classification. *The R Journal* **5**(1), 6–12.

Kahle D and Wickham H. 2013. ggmap: Spatial visualization with ggplot2. *The R Journal* **5**(1), 144–161.

Kerr O. 2013. District court holds that intentionally circumventing ip address ban is 'access without authorization' under the cfaa http://www.volokh.com/2013/08/18/district-court-holds-that-intentionally-circumventing-ip-address-block-is-unauthorized-access-under-the-cfaa/ (Last accessed March 11, 2014).

Koster M. 1994. Important: Spiders, robots and web wanderers. http://inkdroid.org/tmp/www-talk/4113.html (Last accessed January 24, 2014).

Kriegel A and Trukhnov BM. 2008. *SQL Bible*. 2nd edn. John Wiley & Sons, Hoboken, NJ.

Leithner A, Maurer-Ertl W, Glehr M, Friesenbichler J, Leithner K, and Windhager R. 2010. Wikipedia and osteosarcoma: A trustworthy patients' information? *Journal of the American Medical Informatics Association* **17**(4), 373–374.

Liu B. 2012. *Sentiment Analysis and Opinion Mining*. Morgan and Claypool, San Rafael, CA.

Liu B, Hu M, and Cheng J. 2005. *Opinion Observer: Analyzing and Comparing Opinions on the Web*. Proceedings of the 14th International World Wide Web Conference (WWW-2005), May 2005, Chiba, Japan.

Liu C and Albitz P. 2006. *DNS and BIND*. O'Reilly, Sebastopol, CA.

Manning CD, Paghavan P, and Schütze H. 2008. *Introduction to Information Retrieval*. Cambridge University Press, Cambridge.

McJones P, Bamford R, Blasgen M, Chamberlin D, Cheng J, Daudenarde JJ, Finkelstein S, Gray J, Jolls B, Lindsay B, Lorie R, Mehl J, Miller R, Mohan C, Nauman J, Pong M, Price T, Putzolu F, Schkolnick M, Selinger B, Selinger P, Slutz D, Traiger I, Wade B, and Yost B. 1997. The 1995 SQL reunion: People, projects, and politics. http://www.scs.stanford.edu/~dbg/readings/SRC-1997-018.pdf (Last accessed October 30, 2013).

McSherry C and Opsahl K. 2013. AP. v. Meltwater: Disappointing ruling for news search. https://www.eff.org/deeplinks/2013/03/ap-v-meltwater-disappointing-ruling-news-search (Last accessed January 26, 2014).

Meng Y. 2012. Sentiment analysis: A study on product features. Dissertation. University of Nebraska, Lincoln.

Mukherjee S and Bhattacharyya P. 2012. Feature specific sentiment analysis for product reviews. In: *Computational Linguistics and Intelligent Text Processing*. Gelbukh A, ed. Springer, Berlin. pp. 475–487.

Murrell P. 2009. *Introduction to Data Technologies*. Chapman & Hall/CRC, Boca Raton, FL.

Mozilla Developer Network. 2013. XPath. https://developer.mozilla.org/en-US/docs/Web/XPath (Last accessed March 10, 2014).

Niederst Robbins J. 2013. *HTML5 Pocket Reference*. O'Reilly, Sebastopol, CA.

Nolan D and Temple Lang D. 2014. *XML and Web Technologies for Data Sciences with R*. Use R!. Springer, New York, NY.

O'Neil C and Schutt R. 2013. *Doing Data Science. Straight Talk from the Frontline*. O'Reilly, Sebastopol, CA.

Ooms J. 2013. A practical and consistent mapping between JSON data and R objects. http://cran.r-project.org/web/packages/jsonlite/vignettes/json-mapping.pdf (Last accessed February 2, 2014).

Ooms J and Temple Lang D. 2014. *jsonlite: A Smarter JSON Encoder/Decoder for R*. R package version 0.9.3. http://CRAN.R-project.org/package=jsonlite

Osborn H. 2012. *Genealogy: Essential Research Methods*. Robert Hale Ltd, London.

Paar C and Pelzl J. 2011. *Understanding Cryptography: A Textbook for Students and Practitioners*. Springer, New York, NY.

Pebesma EJ and Bivand RS. 2005. Classes and methods for spatial data in R. *R News* **5**(2), 9–13.

Peress M. 2010. Estimating proposal and status quo locations using voting and cosponsorship data. http://www.rochester.edu/College/faculty/mperess/Proposals_and_Status_Q uos.pdf (Last accessed October 8, 2012).

Postel J and Reynolds J. 1985. File transfer protocol (ftp). RFC 959. http://tools.ietf.org/html/rfc959 (Last accessed December 15, 2013).

Princeton University. 2010a. *About WordNet.*http://wordnet.princeton.edu (Last accessed February 27, 2014).

Princeton University. 2010b. *License and Commercial Use of WordNet.* http://wordnet.princeton .edu/wordnet/license/ (Last accessed February 27, 2014).

R Special Interest Group on Databases. 2013. *DBI: R Database Interface.* R package version 0.2-7. http://cran.r-project.org/web/packages/DBI/index.html (Last accessed August 13, 2014).

Ramisch C. 2008. N-gram models for language detection. http://www.inf.ufrgs.br/~ceramisch/ download_files/courses/Master_FRANCE/ENSIMAG_2008_2/Ingenierie_des_Langues_et_de_la_ Parole/Rapport.pdf (Last accessed March 22, 2014).

Ramon L and de Villa AR. 2013. Relenium. Selenium for R. http://lluisramon.github.io/relenium/ (Last accessed March 24, 2014).

Ray ET. 2003. *Learning XML.* 2nd edn. O'Reilly, Sebastopol, CA.

Reavley N, Mackinnon A, Morgan A, Alvarez-Jimenez M, Hetrick S, Killackey E, Nelson B, Purcell R, Yap M, and Jorm A. 2012. Quality of information sources about mental disorders: a comparison of Wikipedia with centrally controlled web and printed sources. *Psychological Medicine* **42**(8), 1753–1762.

Rector LH. 2008. Comparison of Wikipedia and other encyclopedias for accuracy, breadth, and depth in historical articles. *Reference Services Review* **36**(1), 7–22.

Richardson L, Amundsen M, and Ruby S. 2013. *RESTful Web APIs.* O'Reilly, Sebastopol, CA.

Ripley B and Lapsley M. 2013. *RODBC: ODBC Database Access.* Version 1.3-7, Lapsley participated from 1999 to 2002.

Selenium Project. 2014a. *Selenium Commands – Selenese.* Selenium Documentation. http://docs .seleniumhq.org (Last accessed March 24, 2014).

Selenium Project. 2014b. *Selenium Documentation.*http://docs.seleniumhq.org/docs/ (Last accessed March 24, 2014).

Schrenk M. 2012. *Webbots, Spiders, and Screen Scrapers. A Guide to Developing Internet Agents with PHP/Curl* , 2nd ed. No Starch Press, San Francisco, CA.

Snell J and Care D. 2013. Use of online data in the big data era: Legal issues raised by the use of web crawling and scraping tools for analytics purposes. http://about.bloomberglaw.com/ practitioner-contributions/legal-issues-raised-by-the-use-of-web-crawling-and-scraping-tools-for-analytics-purposes/ (Last accessed January 26, 2014).

Snow G. 2013. *TeachingDemos: Demonstrations for Teaching and Learning.* R package version 2.9. http://CRAN.R-project.org/package=TeachingDemos

Stenberg D. 2013. libcurl: The multiprotocol file transfer library. http://curl.haxx.se (Last accessed December 13, 2013).

Stepp M, Miller J, and Kirst V. 2012. *Web Programming Step by Step*, 2nd edn. Step by Step Publishing, http://www.stepbystepselfpublishing.net/

Teetor P. 2011. *R Cookbook.* O'Reilly, Sebastopol, CA.

Temple Lang D. 2012a. RCurl philosophy. http://www.omegahat.org/RCurl/philosophy.html (Last accessed December 13, 2013).

Temple Lang D. 2012b. *SSOAP: Client-Side SOAP Access for S.* R package version 0.9-1. http://www.omegahat.org/SSOAP, http://www.omegahat.org, http://www.omegahat.org/bugs

Temple Lang D. 2013a. *RCurl: General Network (HTTP/FTP/...) Client Interface for R.* R package version 1.95-4.1. http://CRAN.R-project.org/package=RCurl

Temple Lang D. 2013b. *RJSONIO: Serialize R Objects to JSON, JavaScript Object Notation.* R package version 1.0-3. http://CRAN.R-project.org/package=RJSONIO

Temple Lang D. 2013c. *XML: Tools for Parsing and Generating XML Within R and S-Plus.* R package version 3.95-0.2. http://CRAN.R-project.org/package=XML

Temple Lang D, Keles S, and Dudoit S. 2012. *RHTMLForms: Programmatically Create R Functions Corresponding to Web/HTML Forms.* R package version 0.6-0. http://www.omegahat.org/RHTMLForms

Tennison J. 2001. *XSLT and XPath on the Edge.* John Wiley & Sons, Hoboken, NJ.

Torgo L. 2010. *Data Mining with R: Learning with Case Studies.* Chapman & Hall/CRC, Boca Raton, FL.

Tumasjan A, Sprenger TO, Sandner PG, and Welpe IM. 2011. Election forecasts with twitter. How 140 characters reflect the political landscape. *Social Science Computer Review* **29**(4), 402–418.

United States District Court District of Massachusetts. 2013. USA v. Swartz. http://pacer.mad.uscourts.gov/dc/cgi-bin/recentops.pl?filename=gorton/pdf/swartz%20protective%20order%20mo.pdf (Last accessed January 26, 2014).

W3C. 1999. W3C. http://www.w3.org/TR/xpath/ (Last accessed December 2, 2013).

Warden P. 2010. How i got sued by Facebook. http://petewarden.com/2010/04/05/how-i-got-sued-by-facebook/ (Last accessed January 26, 2014).

Wickham H. 2010. Stringr: Modern, consistent string processing. *The R Journal* **2**(2), 38–40.

Wickham H. 2011. The split-apply-combine strategy for data analysis. *Journal of Statistical Software* **40**(1), 1–29.

Wickham H. 2012. *httr: Tools for Working with URLs and HTTP.* R package version 0.2. http://CRAN.R-project.org/package=httr

Wickham H and Chang W. 2013. *devtools: Tools to Make Developing R Code Easier.* R package version 1.4.1. http://CRAN.R-project.org/package=devtools

Wikipedia. 2014. Niccolò Machiavelli.

Witten IH and Frank E. 2005. *Data Mining: Practical Machine Learning Tools and Techniques*, 2nd ed. Morgan Kaufmann, San Francisco, CA.

Wong C. 2000. *HTTP Pocket Reference.* O'Reilly, Sebastopol, CA.

Yasuda N, Cavalli-Sforza L, Skolnick M, and Moroni A. 1974. The evolution of surnames: An analysis of their distribution and extinction. *Theoretical Population Biology* **5**(1), 123–142.

Zagibalov T and Carroll J. 2008. *Automatic Seed Word Selection for Unsupervised Sentimen Classification of Chinese Text.* Proceedings of the 22nd International Conference on Computational Linguistics, August 2008, Manchester, UK, pp. 1073–1080.

Zakas NC. 2010. *High Performance JavaScript.* O'Reilly, Sebastopol, CA.

Zhang Y, Friend AJ, Traud AL, Porter MA, Fowler JH, and Mucha PJ. 2008. Community structure in congressional cosponsorship networks. *Physica A* **387**(7), 1705–1712.

Zhao Y. 2012. *R and Data Mining. Examples and Case Studies.* Elsevier Academic Press, Waltham, MA.

Zumel N and Mount J. 2014. *Practical Data Science with R.* Manning, Greenwich, CT.

General index

Automated Data Collection with R: A Practical Guide to Web Scraping and Text Mining, First Edition.
Simon Munzert, Christian Rubba, Peter Meißner and Dominic Nyhuis.

Package index

Automated Data Collection with R: A Practical Guide to Web Scraping and Text Mining, First Edition.
Simon Munzert, Christian Rubba, Peter Meißner and Dominic Nyhuis.

Function index

Automated Data Collection with R: A Practical Guide to Web Scraping and Text Mining, First Edition.
Simon Munzert, Christian Rubba, Peter Meißner and Dominic Nyhuis.

Printed and bound by CPI Group (UK) Ltd, Croydon, CR0 4YY

27/10/2024

14580360-0001